A Reader in Health Policy and Man

A Reader in Health Policy and Management

Edited by Ann Mahon, Kieran Walshe and Naomi Chambers

Open University Press

Open University Press
McGraw-Hill Education
McGraw-Hill House
Shoppenhangers Road
Maidenhead
Berkshire
England
SL6 2QL

email: enquiries@openup.co.uk
world wide web: www.openup.co.uk

and Two Penn Plaza, New York, NY 10121—2289, USA

First published 2009

A catalogue record of this book is available from the British Library

ISBN-13: 978-0-33-523368-7 (pb)978-0-33-5233670 (hb)
ISBN-10: 0-33-523368-6 (pb) 0-33-523367-8 (hb)

Typeset by Kerrypress, Luton, Bedfordshire
Printed and bound in the UK by Bell and Bain Ltd, Glasgow

Fictitious names of companies, products, people, characters and/or data that may be used herein (in case studies or in examples) are not intended to represent any real individual, company, product or event.

Mixed Sources
Product group from well-managed forests and other controlled sources
www.fsc.org   Cert no. TT-COC-002769
© 1996 Forest Stewardship Council
FSC

The McGraw·Hill Companies

Contents

Publisher's acknowledgements

The editors and publisher wish to thank the following for permission to use copyright material:

Beveridge, W. (1942) *Social Insurance and Allied Services*. Cmnd 6404. London: HMSO [extracts from summary: pp 6–9 and 11–13].

Klein, R. (2006) *The New Politics of the NHS* (5th edn). Harlow: Longman [chapter 1: pp 1–5].

Starr, P. (1982) *The Social Transformation of American Medicine: The Rise of a Sovereign Profession and the Making of a Vast Industry*. New York: Basic Books [extracts from Chapter 5: pp 444–49].

Wanless, D. (2002) *Securing our Future: Taking a Long-term View*. HM Treasury, April 2002 [extracts from introduction: 1.1, 1.2, 1.5, 1.6, 1.8, 1.12, 1.13, 1.18; Chapter 6: 6.54–6.76 and Annex C: C.16–C.24].

Lipsky, M. (1971) *Street-level bureaucracy and the analysis of urban reform, Urban Affairs Review*, 6: 391–409, London: Sage Publications [extracts].

Klein, R. (1998) Why Britain is reorganizing its health service – yet again, *Health Affairs*, 17(4): 111–125 [extracts].

Harrison, S. and Wood, B. (1999) Designing health service organisation in the UK, 1968–1998: From Blueprint to Bright Idea and 'Manipulated Emergence', *Public Administration*, 77(4): 751–68 [extracts].

Bevan, R.G. and Robinson, R. (2005) The interplay between economic and political logics, *Journal of Health, Policy, Politics and Law*, 30(1) 2: 53–78 [extracts].

Culyer, A. and Wagstaff, A. (1993) Equity and equality in health and healthcare, *Journal of Health Economics*, 12: 431–57 [extract: pp 431–33, 445–48].

Ham, C. and Coulter, A. (2001) Explicit and implicit rationing: taking responsibility and avoiding blame for health care choices, *Journal of Health Services Research and Policy*, 6(3): 163–69 [extract: pp 163–66, 168].

Banta, D. (2003) The development of health technology assessment, *Health Policy*, 63: 121–32 [extract: pp 121–24, 128–30].

Williams, A. (1995) Economics, QALYs and medical ethics: a health economist's perspective, *Health Care Analysis*, 3: 221–26.

Diderichsen, F., Varde, E. and Whitehead, M. (1997) Resource allocation to health authorities: the quest for an equitable formula in Britain and Sweden, *British Medical Journal*, 315: 875–78.

Enthoven, A. (1985) *Reflections on the Management of the National Health Service: An American Looks at Incentives to Efficiency in Health Services Management in the UK*. London: Nuffield Provincial Hospitals Trust [extract].

Saltman, R.B. (1994) Patient choice and patient empowerment in northern European health systems: a conceptual framework, *International Journal of Health Services*, 24(2): 201–29 [extract].

Titmuss, R. (1970) The right to give, in R. Titmuss (ed.) *The Gift Relationship: From Human Blood to Social Policy*. London: Allen & Unwin [extract: Chapter 17, pp 305–14].

Davies, C. (2005) Links Between Governance, Incentives and Outcomes: A Review of the Literature. NCCSDO [extract].

Perri 6 (2003) Giving consumers of British public services more choice: what can be learned from recent history? *Journal of Social Policy*, 32: 239–70 [extracts].

Power, M. (2000) The audit society: second thoughts, *International Journal of Auditing*, 4: 111–19 [extract: pp 111–16, 117–18].

Hood, J. and Scott, C. (2000) Regulation of government: has it increased, is it increasing, should it be diminished? *Public Administration*, 78(2): 283–304 [extract: pp 283–87, 295–96, 301–02].

Shaw, C.D. (2001) External assessment of health care, *British Medical Journal*, 322: 851–54.

Walshe, K. and Shortell, S.M. (2003) Social regulation of healthcare organisations in the United States: developing a framework for evaluation, *Health Services Management Research*, 17: 79–99 [extract: pp 79–82, 85, 93–97].

Brennan, T.A. (1998) The role of regulation in quality improvement, *Milbank Quarterly*, 76(4): 709–31 [extract: pp 709–12, 725–28].

Bevan, G. and Hood, C. (2006) What is measured is what matters: targets and gaming in the English public healthcare system, *Public Administration*, 84(3): 517–38 [extract: pp 518–24, 533–36].

Donabedian, A. (1988) The quality of care: how can it be assessed? *Journal of the American Medical Association*, 260(12): 1743–748 [extract: pp 1743–44, 1745, 1745–17].

Berwick, D.M. (1989) Continuous improvement as an ideal in healthcare, *New England Journal of Medicine*, 320(21): 1424–425.

Berwick, D.M. (1996) A primer on leading the improvement of systems, *British Medical Journal*, 312: 619–23.

Leape, H. (1994). Error in medicine, *Journal of the American Medical Association*, 272: 1851–57 [extract: pp 1851–55].

Øvretveit, J. and Gustafson, D. (2002) Evaluation of quality improvement programmes, *Quality and Safety in Health Care*, 11: 270–75

Simon, H.A. (1997) *Administrative Behaviour* Rationality in Human Behaviour. New York: The Free Press [extracts: pp 87–9].

Garratt, B. (1997) *The Fish Rots from the Head*. London: HarperCollins [extracts: pp 31–51].

Griffiths, R. (1983) *Report of the NHS Management Enquiry*, London: HMSO [extracts].

Cornforth, C. (2003) *The Governance of Public and Non-profit Organisations*. London: Routledge [extracts: pp 6–11].

Pettigrew, A., Ferlie, E. and McKee, L. (1992) *Shaping Strategic Change*. London: Sage Publications [extracts: pp 275–87].

Peck, E., Perri 6, Gulliver, P., Towell, D. (2004) Why do we keep on meeting like this? The board as ritual in health and social care, *Health Services Management Research*, 17: 100–109 [extracts].

Cochrane, A. (1972) *Effectiveness and Efficiency: Random Reflections on Health Services*. London: Nuffield Provincial Hospitals Trust [chapter 4: pp 20–25].

Sackett, D.L. and Rosenberg, M.C (1995) On the need for evidence based medicine, *Journal of Public Health Medicine*, 17(3): 330–34.

Naylor, C.D. (1995) Grey zones of clinical practice: some limits to evidence based medicine, *Lancet*, 345: 840–42.

Walshe, K. and Rundall, T.G. (2001) Evidence based management: from theory to practice in healthcare, *Milbank Quarterly*, 79(3): 429–57 [extract: pp 429, 437–46, 451–53].

Rousseau, D.M. (2006) Is there such a thing as evidence based management? *Academy of Management Review*, 31(2): 256–69 [extract: pp 256, 258–60, 261–62, 267–68].

Chadwick, E. (1842) *Report from the Poor Law Commissioners on an inquiry into Sanitary Conditions of the Labouring Population of Great Britain*. London: Poor Law Commission [extracts: pp 421–25].

Tudor Hart, J. (1971) The Inverse Care Law, *The Lancet*, 27 February, 406–12 [extracts: pp 405–07, 409–10, 412].

Declaration of Alma Ata (1978) *International Conference on Primary Health Care*, Alma Ata, USSR, 6–12 September.

Black, D. (Chair) (1982) Report of a Research Working Group *Inequalities in Health*. London: Department of Health and Social Services [extracts: chapter 1, 41–43, 46–46, 49–50, chapter 2, 51–60, chapter 6 133–34].

Lalonde, M. (1974) *A New Perspective on the Health of Canadians*. Ottawa: Health Canada [extracts: pp 63–67].

Wanless, D. (2004) *Securing Good Health for the Whole Population*. London: HM Treasury [extracts from the summary: pp 3–9].

Tallis, R. (2004) Hippocratic Oaths. Atlantic Books [extracts from introduction: pp 1–3, 89–93].

Goffman, E. (1961) *Asylums: Essays on the Social Situation of Mental Patients and Other Inmates*. London: Penguin [extracts: pp 120–25, 134–38, 151–55].

Illich, I. (1977) Limits to medicine, in I. Illich, *Medical Nemesis: The Expropriation of Health*. London: Marion Boyars [extracts from part I, clinical iatrogenesis: pp 32–36, including footnotes].

Kennedy, I. (1983) *The Unmasking of Medicine*. London: Granada Publishing [extracts: chapter 2, page 25, 26–27, 28, 28–30, 31, 32, 32–33, 34, 37–38, 39, 40, 41].

Bunker, J. (1995) Medicine matters after all, *Journal of the Royal College of Physicians of London*, 29(2): 105–12 [reproduce].

Every effort has been made to trace the copyright holders but if any have been inadvertently overlooked the publisher will be pleased to make the necessary arrangement at the first opportunity.

Introduction
Ann Mahon, Kieran Walshe and Naomi Chambers

Policy context and the purpose of this reader

This reader aims to offer managers and leaders working in healthcare easy access to a selection of key readings that will help them to make sense of their day-to-day working experiences, and to see the 'bigger picture' of health system reform. Health care organizations are often complex, diverse and difficult to manage and there are many different types of manager, working in different ways, in different organizational settings and in different countries. Health system reform can be seen as a unifying concern for them all. They need to understand the factors shaping policy (policy drivers) and the many and varied responses to these (policy levers) (Mahon and Young, 2006). Those levers and drivers may be outside of the influence of most managers, but they must be in a strong position to *respond* to these drivers if they are to commission, provide and manage effective and timely healthcare. To respond to this challenge, managers have to combine practical experience of day-to-day management with a depth and a breadth of knowledge and understanding about the wider context of the health system in which they work. That is the purpose of this book.

Many of the recent reforms introduced in the public sector have been inspired by market-based approaches that in the past were simply not associated with, nor deemed to be relevant to, healthcare. This has changed and management theories, concepts and practices developed in the business world have now extended into the 'business' of healthcare. As a consequence, we have witnessed a move away from models associated with public administration towards those associated with the worlds of business and private enterprise. The global term for this trend is 'new public management'. It is outside the scope of this introduction and indeed this reader to offer an in-depth overview and critique of the new public management debate. This has been offered by others working closely in this field (Hood, 1995; Ferlie et al., 1997; Ferlie, Lynn and Pollitt (eds), 2005). However, a framework setting out key policy drivers and policy levers will be introduced to provide a conceptual framework that sets the scene for the readings included in this book. First, it is helpful to explain how this reader has been compiled.

The purpose of the reader

As directors of various postgraduate programmes in health policy, management and leadership, we have observed a number of trends of interest and concern in recent years. As is apparent in the different disciplinary bases of our selected readings, the field of health policy and management draws on a range of disciplines including *inter alia* economics, political science, sociology, social psychology, business and management and philosophy. This diversity, combined with the proliferation of published material in the field, means that managers get over-whelmed, cannot see the wood for the trees and simply 'don't know where to start' when it comes to searching the literature. As well as the proliferation of published material, the ever increasing use of the Internet with electronic databases and journals have contributed to the growth in the literature. They have also changed the way we search and gather sources. Papers can be searched, accessed and printed within a matter of minutes and at any time of day or night, providing immediate access for busy managers and clinicians and facilitating the combination of challenging working lives with part-time study. However, this has also meant fewer trips to the library, fewer hand searches of journals and perhaps fewer serendipitous moments of discovery while trawling through the archives.

Furthermore, why seek out original sources of material when writers of health policy and management text books provide us with adequate summaries of primary sources? The short answer is that they often do not. Original ideas can get diluted and distorted over time and summaries often fail to capture the context they were written in.

Programmes in health management, policy and leadership tend to be applied programmes that encourage the application of concepts and theories, often at the level Robert Merton referred to as 'theories of the middle range' (Merton, 1968). By this he meant theories that were not distant, abstract or grand ideas but rather concepts and frameworks that can be accessed and used to elucidate, elaborate and explore the challenges that managers face in their day-to-day jobs. We see this reader as providing access to a number of papers developing or testing out middle-range theories in order to shed new light on contemporary problems.

Finally, as policy initiatives come and go, young leaders can often believe that policies are breaking into brand new ground and sparking debates that have not previously been on the agenda. The readings selected for this reader provide ample evidence to support the notion of 'path dependency' in health policy and management – a theme explored more fully in Part 2 of this reader.

So, the reader has been compiled in response to these observations and concerns. We hope this provides managers and others who – for whatever purpose wish to explore topics in greater depth – a place to start their journey. We hope it gives a thirst for tracing readings back to primary sources and the energy and enthusiasm for making that extra effort to seek out classic papers in their full and original glory. We hope it provides managers and leaders with illustrations of how papers, some of which were first published many years ago, continue to have relevance as we enter the second decade of the twenty-first century.

Before introducing the structure of the reader and the readings selected, the policy context is set out by looking at the factors that are driving reforms and the various ways that governments are responding.

Healthcare reforms – drivers and levers

The impetus for reforms across many developed and developing countries have emerged from sociological, technological, economic and political developments that have accelerated in recent decades. The drivers for reform in public services in general and health policy and management in particular, are well rehearsed (e.g. Baggott, 2007; OECD, 2005; Dubois et al., 2006; Walshe and Smith, 2006). The main driver for reform has, without doubt, been governments' concerns with increasing costs and efforts to contain them. Other factors relating to rising public expectations, changing demographics, technological developments and globalization are also important. These drivers, with some examples, are summarized in Table I1.1.

The OECD review '*Modernising Government: The Way Forward*' was carried out to provide a greater depth of understanding of how governments have responded to these various pressures for reform with a concern to help policy makers and managers prepare for future challenges. They identify six management reform policy levers as follows:

- open government;
- enhancing public sector performance;
- modernizing accountability and control;
- reallocation and restructuring;
- the use of market-type mechanisms;
- modernizing public employment.

These levers, with some examples of related policy options, are summarized in Table I1.2.

Table I1.1 Policy drivers

Consumerism – A general rise in expectations and a reduction in confidence and trust in professions and institutions

- Increasingly well-educated, informed and critical citizens expect high-quality services, streamlined administrative procedures and to have their views and knowledge taken into account in public decision making (OECD, 2005)
- Increased population mobility and a preparedness to travel as a consequence of cheaper air travel (Baggott, 2007)
- The users or consumers of health care are no longer 'passive patients' accessing and utilizing care in deference to health professionals. Patients have high expectations of the services they access, they are less deferential and more demanding (Coulter, 2003)

Socio-economic and demographic changes – Changes in age distribution and ethnicity

- Ageing population and associated changes in the patterns of illness (Baggott, 2007)
- Population displacement due to war (Baggott, 2007)
- Economic migration including health workers (Young et al., 2008)
- Failure to reduce inequalities in health/increasing inequalities within and between nations (Baggott, 2007)
- Epidemiological transition (Mahon, 2006)

Technological advances

- More advanced systems in accounting and auditing (OECD, 2005)
- Technological advances: biomedical science, genetics, pharmacology, computing, e-Health, telemedicine, genetics internet, email (McDonald and Walley, 2006; Donaldson, 2007)

Costs – An increasing concern about increasing costs, cost-effectiveness and productivity

- Increasing demands on public expenditure, calls for higher-quality services and in some countries an increasing unwillingness to pay higher taxes (OECD, 2005)
- Costs and concerns with efficiency, effectiveness and productivity. Increasing costs and concerns with productivity (OECD, 2005)
- Issues of costs and cost-effectiveness relate to choices about what governments choose to invest their resources in (OECD, 2005)

Globalization/internationalization

- Internationalization of the health policy process – the role of international bodies such as the WHO and the World Bank in policy making (Baggott, 2007)
- Increasing role of the European Union in shaping domestic health policies (Dubois, McKee and Nolte, 2006)
- Threat of war and terrorism (Donaldson, 2007)

Table I1.2 Policy levers (summarized from OECD, 2005)

Policy levers	Summary of the key features
Open government	Countries are moving from a situation where governments decided what information to make public to a greater willingness to make information available unless there is a defined public interest in it being withheld. Often citizens have a legal right to information. For example 90 per cent of OECD countries have a Freedom of Information Act and an Ombudsman office. The three main characteristics of open government are: • transparency – that its actions and the individuals responsible for those actions will be exposed to public scrutiny and challenge; • accessibility – that its services and information on its activities will be readily accessible to citizens; • responsiveness – that it will be responsive to new ideas, demands and needs.
Enhancing public sector performance	To enhance performance countries have adopted a range of approaches to management including budgeting, personnel and institutional structures. Examples of institutional change include the creation of executive agencies and the privatization or outsourcing of the provision of public services. This lever of reform seeks to move the focus of activity such as budgeting away from inputs and towards results. The quantity of performance information is continuously increasing although problems are encountered with the quality and the application of the information. Performance information is important for governments in assessing and improving policies: • in managerial analysis, direction and control of public services; • in budgetary analysis; • in Parliamentary oversight of the executive; • for public accountability – the general duty on governments to disclose and take responsibility for their decisions.
Modernizing accountability and control	There has been a move from ex ante to ex post control and the development of stronger processes of internal control. This means a trend from a system where transactions were approved prior to commitment from a controller outside of the spending ministry (ex ante) to one where internal management makes many financial and non-financial resource allocation decisions that are externally checked after the event (ex post). This has resulted in more external audits and new and more complicated auditing and accounting regimes being put in place. As control becomes increasingly ex post, accountability becomes more important.
Concern with costs and demand leading to reallocation and restructuring	Fiscal constraints combined with increasing demands have led to the need for a range of structures tailored to specific requirements. In the past two decades many countries have restructured public services in a variety of ways which include: • devolution of authority and functions from central to local government; • reorganization of functions driven by the globalization of public concerns such as trade, environment and anti-terrorism; • governments have been withdrawing from/selling off their interests in activities that could be conducted by private entities without direct involvement by the State; • moving away from being a direct provider of services towards creating market structures increases the regulatory role of the State; • whole of government reform reorganization; • devolution, privatisation, contracting out.
The use of market-type mechanisms to provide government services	Market-type mechanisms are a broad concept 'encompassing all arrangements where at least one significant characteristic of markets is present' (OECD, 2005, p. 131). In service provision these characteristics include outsourcing, contracting out, public–private partnerships and user charges. Significant management challenges exist in moving to a market-type mechanism model, especially in separating the role of government as purchaser and provider of services, where traditionally governments have performed both roles.
Organizing and motivating public servants: modernizing public employment	A variety of initiatives have attempted to reduce public employment and increase managerial flexibility through decentralization of human resource management, accountability and pay. As a result of these changes many assumptions about the way public service works – such as jobs for life and generous pension packages – are no longer true.

The structure of this reader

The fifty selected readings have been organized in ten parts. It is not anticipated that anyone reading this book will read it cover to cover and in sequence, and it has not been designed to be read in that way. Instead, we expect it to be used as a resource to provide instant access to classic readings in specific areas of policy and management and to address some of our concerns that such readings should be available to as wide an audience as possible, whether as a layperson with an interest in health policy and management, a manager or clinician pursuing topics of personal interest or for professional development on short courses or postgraduate programmes. With this in mind, a similar format for each part has been adopted so that the readings selected for each part are preceded by a short introduction with some background and scene-setting to the general topic, an introduction to the selected readings and a summary of the key messages, references and further reading.

Part 1 includes papers with different perspectives on *the role of the state in healthcare*. The shift from bureaucratic and paternalistic models of healthcare towards more market-oriented systems of healthcare has meant an evolving rather than diminishing role for the state. This part of the reader includes selections that set out or critique the impact of the state on health policy from the period preceding the introduction of welfare in England up to the present day.

Part 2 focuses on the *policy-making process*. Healthcare managers need to understand how policy is developed and implemented in order to understand their role and contribution, but also as a touchstone for personal priority setting in their day-to-day work. This part of the reader therefore focuses on classic texts in relation to policy development and implementation.

The *allocation and distribution of resources* is the focus of part 3 that explores the way in which healthcare funding is organized and the readings focus on the implications of funding mechanisms for issues of equity, effectiveness and efficiency in health systems and also how systems of funding have shaped both the nature and the behaviour of healthcare organizations and health services.

Governments throughout the world are increasingly attracted by the use of market mechanisms and choice in health and public sector reforms to drive up efficiency and quality. Part 4, *Markets and choice in healthcare,* identifies some key readings that have influenced the marketization of healthcare and the increasing emphasis on choice.

The readings selected for part 5, *Accountability and regulation,* consider the changing relationship between society and healthcare and how organizations and the professionals working in them are held to account with a growth in formal and external systems of monitoring.

Recent years have witnessed increasing interest throughout the developed world in the quality of health services, and in systems to measure, assure and improve quality in healthcare. The selections in part 6, *Quality and safety,* consider developments and responses to this trend with a focus on the development of clinical governance, total quality management in healthcare and patient safety.

With the emergence of the 'new public management' era, the language used to describe the administration of health services changed dramatically in the 1980s. In part 7, *General management and governance,* the selections cover the origins of general management in the NHS, new responsibilities for managing strategic change and the nature and performance of Boards.

The rise over the 1990s of the 'evidence-based medicine' movement has influenced not just health but also those in other sectors such as education, social care, criminal justice and housing. Part 8, *Evidence-based health policy and management,* focuses primarily on the use of evidence by decision makers to shape health policy and the organization and delivery of health services.

Adopting a broader and more positive definition of health shifts our attention away from health services that are provided to treat illness and disease and towards the wider socio-economic and political contexts where health, illness and disease are defined, experienced and determined. Part 9 thus focuses on *The social context of health* locating healthcare in its wider context as one of many factors contributing to the health of a population.

Part 10 considers aspects of the *Cultural critiques of formalized healthcare systems.* The 1970s witnessed the growth of these 'cultural critiques' of medicine as well as other established institutions and professions in society. The debate is brought up to date with more recent readings seeking to address the balance.

A note on the selections

Space does not permit inclusion of all the relevant themes and readings that could be covered in this reader, although some may be conspicuous by their absence (such as leadership, patient and public involvement, healthcare commissioning, and so on.) The final ten themes and fifty readings that have been agreed upon emerged from discussions reflecting the editors' understanding of contemporary policy drivers and levers and their respective areas of interest. They also reflect some of the constraints imposed on us as a result of seeking copyright permissions. Nevertheless, we believe that these ten themes cover some of the key policy drivers and levers set out earlier in this introduction. They also cover topics that reflect the multidisciplinary content of many postgraduate programmes in the field of health policy and management.

This book and its companion: 'Healthcare management'

The idea for this book emerged in part from the work we and many colleagues did in writing and editing a comprehensive text on healthcare management, designed for use in management development and postgraduate programmes (Walshe and Smith, 2006). That book ended up with 28 chapters (and over 500 pages), and there are many connections – implicit or explicit – between its content and the content of this reader. We have not tried to follow the same thematic structure in this reader as we used in the text on healthcare management, in part because the primary focus of the former was on managing healthcare organizations, while this book tends to tackle the wider context of health systems and health policy. However, we anticipate that many people will want to use them alongside each other, and for those readers, the connections will, we think, be readily apparent. For example, anyone grappling with the complexities of healthcare financing might want to read Chapter 3 in the textbook in which Suzanne Robinson offers a clear and structured typology and explanation of how health system funding is organized, alongside part 3 of this reader, which explores the question of how resources are allocated and distributed, with contributions from Alan Williams, Antony Culyer, Chris Ham, Angela Coulter and others.

However, our main hope is that for many managers, this book and its companion text will be not the end of their reading, but the beginning. If we have stimulated you to want to know more, to follow up the suggested readings and references at the end of each part or chapter, and to use our work as your stepping-off point into a wider literature, then we will be more than pleased.

Ann Mahon, Kieran Walshe and Naomi Chambers
Manchester, March 2009

References

Baggott, R. (2007) *Understanding Health Policy*. Bristol: The Policy Press and the Social Policy Association.

Coulter, A. (2003) An unacknowledged workforce: patients as partners in health-care, in C. Davies (ed.) *The Future Health Workforce*. Basingstoke: Palgrave Macmillan: Chapter 2.

Donaldson, L. (2007) *On the State of the Public Health: 2006 Annual Report of the Chief Medical Officer*. London: Department of Health.

Dubois, C.-A., McKee, M. and Nolte, E. (2006) *Human Resources for Health in Europe*. Maidenhead: Open University Press.

Ferlie et al. (1997) *The New Public Management in Action*. Oxford: Oxford University Press.

Ferlie, Lynn and Pollitt (eds) (2005) *The Oxford Handbook of Public Management*. Oxford: Oxford University Press.

Hood, C. (1995) Contemporary public management: a new global paradigm? *Public Policy and Administration*, 10(2): 104–17.

Mahon, A. and Young, R. (2006) Health care managers as a critical component of the health care workforce, in C.-A. Dubois, M. McKee and E. Nolte (eds) *Human Resources for Health in Europe*. Maidenhead: Open University Press.

Mahon, A. (2006) The wider context of health, in K. Walshe and J. Smith *Healthcare Management*. Maidenhead: Open University Press.

McDonald, R. and Walley, T. (2006) Managing healthcare technologies and innovation, in K. Walshe and J. Smith *Healthcare Management*. Maidenhead: Open University Press.

Merton, R.K. (1968) *Social Theory and Social Structure*. New Jersey: The Free Press.

OECD (2005) *Modernising Government – The Way Forward*. Paris: OECD.

Walshe, K. and Smith, J. (eds) (2006) *Healthcare Management*. Maidenhead: Open University Press.

PART 1

The role of the state in healthcare

Introduced by Ann Mahon

Healthcare demands ever increasing resources and as Moran observes 'health care looms large in the modern welfare state and states loom large in modern health care systems' (Moran, 2002: 139). At one level this may seem to be an outdated and somewhat counter-intuitive observation since, as discussed in the introduction, a recurring theme in health policy and management is the shift from bureaucratic, centralized, state-dominated models of healthcare towards more market-oriented systems. Does not the introduction of market principles necessarily mean that the role of the state in healthcare diminishes? While for some the trend towards marketization equates with a diminishing role for the state and a rolling-back of its frontiers, for others this shift inevitably changes its role but its role nevertheless remains central. Indeed the 'steer more, row less' role of the state in an environment receptive to market mechanisms may not only incur extra transaction and administrative costs, but may also require more sophisticated approaches to regulation (a topic covered in more detail in Part 5) which, in turn, require the restructuring of state bureaucracies and the reallocation of roles and responsibilities (Saltman, 2002; OECD, 2005). States are also interested in health systems as major economic players employing large numbers of people in a wide range of different roles. In the NHS in England, for example, the NHS employs a remarkable 1.3 million people out of a population of 49.1 million (Dixon, 2006). Thus, whatever system of health care predominates in a nation, the state plays a central role in determining coverage, the nature and extent of benefits, the systems of funding (including user charges), the allocation and distribution of resources and the structure and organization of services.

National systems are often described on the basis of how their funding is generated, rather than how resources are allocated (which is the focus of Part 3). These include private health insurance, taxation (which may be direct or indirect, general or hypothecated and national or local), social health insurance and charges and co-payments. In practice, most countries' systems operate through a mixed system of funding, which usually includes some element of taxation

(Robinson, 2006). The funding bases of health systems are often located on a continuum with state-dominated systems at one end of the spectrum, typified by the UK NHS predominantly funded through general taxation and market-dominated systems at the other extreme, characterized by a heavy reliance on private insurance as the source of funding and typified by the US system. This can be misleading as closer scrutiny of OECD figures for 2006 reveal a substantial state role for both the USA and the UK. Looking first at total expenditure on health as a percentage of gross domestic product (GDP), the USA spends a staggering 15.3 per cent of its GDP on healthcare, compared with the UK's 8.4 per cent. Total spending per capita shows a similar pattern with the USA spending US$6714 per capita compared to the UK's US$2760. However, almost a half of this massive allocation of US resources comes from the state so that 45.8 per cent of the total expenditure on health in the USA came from the public purse with the corresponding figure for the UK being 87.3 per cent (OECD, 2008). These figures disguise appalling patterns of inequalities in both health status and in access to health services across different social and ethnic groups, particularly for the USA where access to healthcare for the majority is dependent on employment-linked insurance and where up to a fifth of the population are not insured. Nevertheless, they illustrate the significant investment that states make, even in the most apparently *laissez-faire* of health systems like the USA. This fundamental role of the state is captured by Saltman in the following quote:

> A fundamental characteristic of contemporary health policy is the centrality of the state to the design and management of an effective healthcare system. This core characteristic holds true for tax-funded, social insurance-funded and private-insurance funded health systems alike. It also holds true for developing as well as developed countries, and across countries with broadly different demographic characteristics and widely varying geographic locations.
>
> (Saltman, 2002: 1677)

Managers of health services should therefore be familiar with how the state determines policy, defines the content of policy, implements policy and then responds to the consequences – both unintended and intended. As noted above, states may be a substantial financer of health care, through taxation or through other benefits but they may also be providers of care, alongside private or voluntary providers and a regulator of the organizations that commission and provide care. What the centrality of the role of the state also highlights is the political nature of health, played out most visibly through media coverage of 'public interest' health stories, particularly at election times, such as the 'Jennifer's ear' news story that dominated the English press during the 1992 general election campaign and highlighting the impact of the close proximity between politics and politicians with the NHS often referred to as 'a political football' (Black, 1992). As health care becomes increasingly complex, a number of commentators have questioned not just the appropriateness but also its ability to be 'managed' by such political processes and there are increasing calls for an independent NHS (Edwards, 2007). However, it is not just national politics that determines and influences health systems – medical politics and the power and influence of other key players within systems – like insurance and the pharmaceutical industries – all operate to maximize their interests. States do not therefore start with a 'blank slate' on which to design their optimum system of health care and systems are politically derived introducing and implementing what is feasible and acceptable to key players at a particular point in history.

Turning to the readings selected under the theme of the role of the state. William Beveridge (1942) essentially published the blueprint for the welfare state in England, designed to attack what he called the five giants of want, disease, ignorance, squalor and idleness. Various Acts of Parliament were subsequently passed covering education, social security and health. The attack on disease culminated in the creation of the NHS, with the implementation of the 1946 NHS Act in 1948. Beveridge's report is therefore of significance for its place in history. But this selection also demonstrates the value of returning to original sources to capture both the tone and content of proposals at particular points in history and also the extent to which original aims were implementable. Beveridge sets out three guiding principles. First, that any proposals for the future should not be restricted by consideration of 'sectional interests' (somewhat ironic given Rudolf Klein's subsequent analysis of events (Klein, 2006)). Second, his proposal was for social insurance (and not general taxation) as one part of a comprehensive policy of social progress and, third, that social security must be achieved by cooperation between the state and individual – Beveridge believed that the state should not stifle incentive, opportunity or responsibility and should leave room for individual responsibility to flourish – a sentiment echoed in another government publication some 60 years later (Wanless, 2002). For pragmatic rather than political reasons national taxes (favoured by Bevan) rather than local taxes or social insurance became and remain the predominant source of funding for the NHS (Lowe, 2008). The desirability of a tax-funded system has of course been open to continuous debates and reviews, all of which, including the most recent, have defended the status quo and continued to follow the path set in the 1940s. The focus instead has shifted more towards performance and how money is spent rather than how the NHS is funded.

Rudolf Klein's now classic text provides a unique analysis of the politics of the creation of the NHS, which he presents as dramatic but evolutionary. Klein emphasizes the political dynamics of the creation of the NHS and brings to centre stage the main groups of actors that shaped it. While enmeshed within the politics and ideological debates, Klein demonstrates yet again that pragmatism won the day and the emerging consensus produced an 'irrational' system in the name of the rationalist paternalists who, according to Klein, were less concerned with social injustice than in sorting out the mess that preceded nationalization. Paul Starr (1982) introduces us to a new set of actors in a different setting and yet facing now familiar concerns with controlling healthcare expenditure. This concerns both state and insurance companies, while physicians, protective of their clinical and economic autonomy, opposed increased public control. For Starr the irony here is that medical opposition to public programmes did not cease progressive rationalization by the private sector bringing with it accusations of the deprofessionalization and proletarianization of medicine.

The final reading includes extracts from a document that reports on the findings from the first ever long-term assessment of the resources required to fund the health service in England, Chaired by Derek Wanless (Wanless, 2002) and published some 60 years after Beveridge. Wanless departed from, or at least elaborated on, his brief in at least two significant ways. First, he recognized that although the brief related to healthcare, health and social care are inextricably linked to health and so should be considered together. Second, he notes that the brief for his review did not include looking at how healthcare resources are financed. However, he argued that such a review was necessary because of the potential relationship between how a health care system is funded and the subsequent demand and indeed costs of the total resources required. While his conclusion supported the status quo, it also opened the door for a greater role for out-of-pocket payments. Performance, he warns, is a prerequisite for continued public support for a public funded service.

Summary

- National healthcare systems are often described on the basis of how they are resourced. This may be through private insurance, social insurance, taxation or charges and co-payments. In practice, most systems operate with a combination of these different sources of funding and systems are often located on a continuum with state-dominated systems at one end of the spectrum (characterized by the English NHS) and market-dominated systems at the other end (characterized by the US system).
- The state has a central role in the design, management and regulation of healthcare irrespective of how the system is funded. Even in the archetypal market system of healthcare, nearly a half of resources are derived from state sources.
- The increasing marketization of healthcare and an increase in the plurality of providers, changes, rather than diminishes, the role of the state.
- Healthcare systems are political products emerging from the complex interactions between stakeholders.
- The selections in this part of the reader cover a 60-year period beginning with Beveridge's blueprint for welfare followed by Klein's eagle-eye analysis of the politics of the creation of the NHS. From a US perspective, Paul Starr's contribution introduces new actors, not least the health insurance industry and finally the 2002 Wanless report provides a contemporary review of the long-term implications for funding the NHS.

References and further reading

Black, N. (1992) Jennifer's ear: airing the issues, *Quality in Health Care*, 1: 213–14.

Dixon, J. (2006) The politics of healthcare and the health policy process: implications for healthcare management, in K. Walshe and J. Smith (eds) *Healthcare Management*. Maidenhead: Open University Press.

Edwards, B. (2007) *An independent NHS: A Review of the Options*. London: The Nuffield Trust.

Lowe, R. Financing healthcare in Britain since 1939 (www.historyandpolicy.org/ papers: accessed 2008).

Moran, M. (2000) Understanding the welfare state: the case of health care, *British Journal of Politics and International Relations*, 2(2): 135–60.

OECD (2005) Modernising Government: The Way Forward. Paris: OECD.

OECD (2008) Health Data 2008 – Version June 2008 (*www.oecd.org/*).

Robinson, S. (2006) Financing healthcare: funding systems and healthcare costs, in K. Walshe and J. Smith (eds) *Healthcare Management*. Maidenhead: Open University Press.

Saltman, R.B. (2002) Regulating incentives: the past and present role of the state in healthcare systems, *Social Science and Medicine*, 54: 1677–84.

The readings

Beveridge, W. (1942) *Social Insurance and Allied Services*. Cmnd 6404. London: HMSO.

Klein, R. (2006) *The New Politics of the NHS* (5th edn). Harlow: Longman.

Starr, P. (1982) *The Social Transformation of American Medicine: The Rise of a Sovereign Profession and the Making of a Vast Industry*. New York: Basic Books.

Wanless, D. (2002) *Securing our Future: Taking a Long-term View*. London: HM Treasury.

1

Social insurance and allied services
William Beveridge

Extracts from Beveridge W (1942) Social insurance and Allied Services.
Cmnd 6404. London, HMSO.

Three Guiding Principles of Recommendations

6.   In proceeding from this first comprehensive survey of social insurance to the
next task—of making recommendations—three guiding principles may be laid
down at the outset.

7.   The first principle is that any proposals for the future, while they should
use to the full the experience gathered in the past, should not be restricted by
consideration of sectional interests established in the obtaining of that experience.
Now, when the war is abolishing landmarks of every kind, is the opportunity for
using experience in a clear field. A revolutionary moment in the world's history is a
time for revolutions, not for patching.

8.   The second principle is that organisation of social insurance should be
treated as one part only of a comprehensive policy of social progress. Social
insurance fully developed may provide income security; it is an attack upon Want.
But Want is one only of five giants on the road of reconstruction and in some ways
the easiest to attack. The others are Disease, Ignorance, Squalor and Idleness.

9.   The third principle is that social security must be achieved by co-operation
between the state and the individual. The state should offer security for service and
contribution. The state in organising security should not stifle incentive, opportunity, responsibility; in establishing a national minimum, it should leave room and
encouragement for voluntary action by each individual to provide more than that
minimum for himself and his family.

The Way to Freedom from Want

11.   The work of the Inter-departmental Committee began with a review of
existing schemes of social insurance and allied services. The Plan for Social
Security, with which that work ends, starts from a diagnosis of want—of the
circumstances in which, in the years just preceding the present war, families and
individuals in Britain might lack the means of healthy subsistence. During those

years impartial scientific authorities made social surveys of the conditions of life in a number of principal towns in Britain, including London, Liverpool, Sheffield, Plymouth, Southampton, York and Bristol. They determined the proportions of the people in each town whose means were below the standard assumed to be necessary for subsistence, and they analysed the extent and causes of that deficiency. From each of these social surveys the same broad result emerges. Of all the want shown by the surveys, from three-quarters to five-sixths, according to the precise standard chosen for want, was due to interruption or loss of earning power. Practically the whole of the remaining one-quarter to one-sixth was due to failure to relate income during earning to the size of the family. These surveys were made before the introduction of supplementary pensions had reduced the amount of poverty amongst old persons. But this does not affect the main conclusion to be drawn from these surveys: abolition of want requires a double re-distribution of income, through social insurance and by family needs.

12.   Abolition of want requires, first, improvement of state insurance, that is to say provision against interruption and loss of earning power. All the principal causes of interruption or loss of earnings are now the subject of schemes of social insurance. If, in spite of these schemes, so many persons unemployed or sick or old or widowed are found to be without adequate income for subsistence according to the standards adopted in the social surveys, this means that the benefits amount to less than subsistence by those standards or do not last as long as the need, and that the assistance which supplements insurance is either insufficient in amount or available only on terms which make men unwilling to have recourse to it. None of the insurance benefits provided before the war were in fact designed with reference to the standards of the social surveys. Though unemployment benefit was not altogether out of relation to those standards, sickness and disablement benefit, old age pensions and widows' pensions were far below them, while workmen's compensation was below subsistence level for anyone who had family responsibilities or whose earnings in work were less than twice the amount needed for subsistence. To prevent interruption or destruction of earning power from leading to want, it is necessary to improve the present schemes of social insurance in three directions: by extension of scope to cover persons now excluded, by extension of purposes to cover risks now excluded, and by raising the rates of benefit.

13.   Abolition of want requires, second, adjustment of incomes, in periods of earning as well as in interruption of earning, to family needs, that is to say, in one form or another it requires allowances for children. Without such allowances as part of benefit or added to it, to make provision for large families, no social insurance against interruption of earnings can be adequate. But, if children's allowances are given only when earnings are interrupted and are not given during earning also, two evils are unavoidable. First, a substantial measure of acute want will remain among the lower paid workers as the accompaniment of large families. Second, in all such cases, income will be greater during unemployment or other interruptions of work than during work.

2

The new politics of the NHS
Rudolf Klein

Extracts from Klein R (2006) The New Politics of the NHS (5th edn).
Harlow, Longman.

> If many simultaneous and variously directed forces act on a given body, the
> direction of its motion cannot coincide with any of those forces, but will always
> be a mean – what in mechanics is represented by the diagonal of a parallelo-
> gram of forces. If in the descriptions given by historians ... we find their wars
> and battles carried out in accordance with previously formed plans, the only
> conclusion to be drawn is that those descriptions are false.

Leo Tolstoy, War and Peace

Britain's National Health Service (NHS) came into existence on 5 July 1948. It
was the first health system in any Western society to offer free medical care to the
entire population. It was, furthermore, the first comprehensive system to be based
not on the insurance principle, with entitlement following contributions, but on
the national provision of services available to everyone. It thus offered free and
universal entitlement to state-provided medical care. At the time of its creation it
was a unique example of the collectivist provision of health care in a market
society. It was destined to remain so for almost two decades after its birth when
Sweden, a country usually considered as a pioneer in the provision of welfare,
caught up. Indeed, it could be held up as 'the greatest Socialist achievement of the
Labour Government', to quote Michael Foot, the biographer of Aneurin Bevan
who, as Minister of Health in that Government, was the architect of the NHS.[1]

The transformation of an inadequate, partial and muddled patchwork of
health care provision into a neat administrative structure was dramatic, even
though the legislative transformation was built on the evolutionary developments
of the previous decades. At a legislative stroke, 1,000 hospitals owned and run by a
large variety of voluntary bodies and 540 hospitals operated by local authorities
were nationalised. At the same time, the benefits of free general practitioner care,
hitherto limited to the 21 million people covered by the insurance scheme
originally set up by Lloyd George in 1911, were extended to the entire population.
From then on, everyone was entitled, as of right, to free care – whether provided
by a general practitioner or by a hospital doctor – financed by the state. At the

summit of the administrative structure there was the Minister of Health. Under the terms of the 1946 Act setting up the NHS, the Minister was charged with the duty 'to promote the establishment in England and Wales of a comprehensive health service designed to secure improvement in the physical and mental health of the people of England and Wales and the prevention, diagnosis and treatment of illness, and for that purpose to provide or secure the effective provision of services'. The services so provided, the Act further laid down, 'shall be free of charge'.

How did this transformation come about? It is not the aim of this chapter to provide a history of the creation of the NHS: other sources are available, giving a detailed blow by blow account of what happened in the years leading up to 1948.[2] The intention, rather, is to analyse the political dynamics of the creation: to identify the main groups of actors in the arena of health care politics and to delineate the world of ideas in which the plans for a national health service evolved. In doing so, it is necessary to explore the complex interplay between the ineluctable pressure on politicians and administrators to do something about the practical problems forced on to their agenda by the clamouring inadequacies of health care in Britain, as it had evolved over the previous century up to 1939, and their resolution of the policy puzzles involved in accommodating competing values and insistent pressure groups. It was the historical legacy which made it inevitable that *a* national health service would emerge by the end of the Second World War. It was the ideological and practical resolution of the policy puzzles which determined the precise shape taken by the NHS as it actually emerged in 1948.

The emerging consensus

First, let us examine the nature of the consensus that had emerged by 1939: the movement of ideas which made it seem inevitable that some kind of national health service would eventually evolve – dictated, as it were, by the logic of circumstances, rather than by the ideology of politicians or the demands of pressure groups. Basically, this consensus embodied agreement on two linked assumptions. These were that the provision for health care in Britain, as it had grown up over the decades, was both inadequate and irrational.

Health care, it was agreed, was inadequate in terms both of coverage and of quality. Lloyd George's 1911 legislation had provided insurance coverage only for general practitioner services. In turn this coverage was limited to manual workers, excluding even their families. Hospital care was provided by municipal and voluntary institutions on the basis of charging those who could afford to pay and giving free care to those who could not. Even though the bewildering mixture of state insurance, private insurance and the availability of free care in the last resort meant that everyone had access to some form of medical treatment, the quality varied widely. The general practitioner, operating usually on the small shopkeeper principle of running his own practice single-handed and relying mainly on the income from the capitation fees of his insured patients, was isolated from the mainstream of medicine. 'It is disturbing to find large numbers of general practitioners being taught at great trouble and expense to use modern diagnostic equipment, to know the available resources of medicine and to exercise judgement as between patient and specialist', the 1937 Political and Economic Planning (PEP) survey of health care in Britain commented,[3] 'only to be launched out into a system which too often will not permit them to do their job properly'. In the case of the hospital sector, the quality of specialist care varied greatly; indeed there was no officially agreed definition of who should be considered a specialist – the title of consultant being attached to specific posts, mostly in the prestigious teaching hospitals, rather than being a generally accepted description of doctors with special skills recognised according to explicit criteria. In many of the smaller voluntary hospitals, especially, it was general practitioners who carried out both medical and surgical procedures, with no check on their qualifications or competence for the job.

The system, it was further agreed, was irrational. Specialists gravitated to those parts of the country where the population was prosperous enough to pay for private care, since hospital consultancies were honorary and they were thus dependent on income from private practice. By definition, the most prosperous parts of the country were not necessarily those which generated most need for medical care. Voluntary and municipal hospitals competed with, and against, each other. The distribution of beds across the country was determined by historical hazard, not the logic of the distribution of illness: Birmingham, for example, had 5.7 beds per 1,000 population, while Liverpool had 8.6. Hospitals shuffled off responsibility for patients to each other: the voluntary hospitals regularly dumping chronic cases onto the municipal sector. Municipal hospitals could, and indeed did, refuse admission to patients coming from outside their local authority area. A further article of faith in the emerging consensus was, therefore, the need to co-ordinate the various systems – voluntary and municipal – that had emerged, and to introduce some rationality into the distribution of resources.

The consensus had another ingredient. There was widespread acceptance of the fact that the voluntary hospital system was no longer viable financially. By the mid 1930s traditional forms of fund-raising from the public – the appeal to altruistic charitable instincts – were not yielding anything like enough to support their activities: only 31 per cent of the income of London teaching hospitals and 20 per cent of the income of the provincial teaching hospitals came from this source. More important was income from charges to patients, financed – on a 50: 50 basis – either out of their own income or out of contributory insurance schemes. The bankruptcy of the voluntary sector was staved off by the Second World War, when these hospitals drew large-scale benefits from the Government's scheme of paying for stand-by beds for war casualties. But it was clear that, in the long term, their dependence on public finance was both irremediable and likely to increase.[4] Equally, it had long since become clear that the original purpose of the most prestigious of the voluntary hospitals – to provide free care for the poor- – could not be fully carried out, since financial pressures were forcing them to rely on attracting precisely those patients who could afford to pay. The price of survival was, to an extent, the repudiation of the inspiration which had led to their creation in the first place.

Not surprisingly, therefore, the years between the two world wars – between 1918 and 1939 – were marked by the publication of a series of reports from a variety of sources, all sharing the same general perspective. In 1920 the Minister of Health's Consultative Council on Medical and Allied Services (the Dawson report) enunciated the principle that 'the best means of maintaining health and curing disease should be made available to all citizens' – a principle to be later echoed by Aneurin Bevan when he introduced the 1946 legislation – and elaborating this principle in a detailed scheme of organising health care; a hierarchy of institutions starting from the Primary Health Centre and culminating in the Teaching Hospital.[5] In 1926 the Royal Commission on National Health Insurance came to the conclusion, although it baulked at spelling it out in its immediate recommendations, that 'the ultimate solution will lie, we think, in the direction of divorcing the medical service entirely from the insurance system and recognising it along with all other public health activities as a service to be supported from the general public funds'.[6] In 1930 the British Medical Association (BMA) came out in favour of extending the insurance principle to the dependents of the working population and supported a co-ordinated reorganisation of the hospital system, while in 1933 the Socialist Medical Association added its radical treble to the conservative bass drum of the BMA and published its plan for a comprehensive, free and salaried medical service, to be managed by local government but with a regional planning tier.[7]

There are a number of strands within this consensus which need disentangling. In the first place, the consensus speaks with the accents of what might be called rationalist paternalists, both medical and administrative. This is the voice not so much of those outraged by social injustice as of those intolerant of muddle, inefficiency and incompetence: a tradition going back to the days of Edwin Chadwick, via the Webbs. It is further, the voice of practical men of affairs, trying to find solutions to immediate problems. In the second place, the consensus reflects a view of health care which was rooted in British experience, though not unique to it: an intellectual bias which helps to explain why the institutional solution devised in the post-war era was unique to Britain.

The second point requires elaboration. When, confronted by the muddle of health care, men started thinking about possible solutions, they had before them two models – either of which could have been developed into a fully-fledged national system. The first model was that of Lloyd George's insurance scheme for general practice: an import from Bismarck's Germany. In theory, there was no reason why such a model could not have been elaborated into a comprehensive national insurance scheme: the road followed by nearly all other Western societies in the post-war period, and advocated by the BMA not only in the 1930s but also subsequently. The other model, however, was that of the public health services, developed and based on local authority provision in Britain in the nineteenth century: a model based on seeing health as a public good rather than as an individual right. While the first model emphasised the right of individuals to medical care – a right to be based, admittedly, on purchasing the appropriate insurance entitlements – the second model emphasised the obligation of public authorities to make provision for the health of the community at large. While the first model was consistent with individualistic medical values – given that the whole professional ethos was to see medical care in terms of a transaction between the individual patient and the individual doctor – the second model was consistent with a collectivist approach to the provision of health care. Indeed throughout it is important to keep in mind the distinction between medical care in the strict sense (that is, care and intervention provided by doctors with the aim of curing illness) and health care in the larger sense (that is, all those forms of care and intervention which influence the health of members of the community).

Thus the whole logic of the Dawson report was based on the proposition that 'preventive and curative medicine cannot be separated on any sound principle. They must likewise be both brought within the sphere of the general practitioner, whose duties should embrace the work of both communal as well as individual medicine'. Nor was this just a matter of intellectual tradition. Local government was already in the business of providing health care, ranging from curative medicine in its hospitals to chronic care for the elderly and mentally ill in its institutions, from the provision of maternity clinics to looking after the health of schoolchildren. Organisational bias thus reinforced intellectual bias in the sense that the services provided by local government would have to be incorporated into any national scheme that might emerge. To have adopted an insurance-based scheme would therefore have meant actively repudiating the service-based legacy of the past.

Given this convergence of views on the necessity of devising some form of national health service, as distinct from some form of national health insurance, it is tempting to interpret the eventual emergence of the 1948 NHS in a deterministic fashion: to see it as the child not of Labour ideology, not as a Socialist triumph, but as the inevitable outcome of attempts to deal with a specific situation in the light of an intellectual consensus, both about what was desirable and about what was possible. Equally, given this convergence, it would seem redundant to search for explanations in Britain's wartime experience, whether administrative or emotional. The acceptance of the need for a national health service long predates, as we have seen, the wartime administrative experience of running the emergency medical service: an experience which, at best, can have generated confidence that it was actually possible to run a complex web of hospitals and services. Similarly, this acceptance long predates the wartime commitment to a collectivist solution of welfare problems: a commitment epitomised in the 1942 Beveridge report which assumed, without elaborating in detail, the creation of a 'comprehensive national health service'.

Accepting a general notion is, of course, one thing. Devising and implementing a specific plan is, however, a very different matter. The consensus may have provided a foundation. It did not provide a blueprint: when it came to detail, the various proposals put forward during the inter-war period had all come up with somewhat different schemes. To examine the evolution of plans from the outbreak of war in 1939 to the enactment of the 1946 legislation for setting up the National Health Service is to identify a whole series of clashes not only between interest groups but also between competing values. If everyone was agreed about the end of policy in a general sort of way, there was little by way of consensus about means – and much awareness of the fact that the means chosen might, in turn, affect the end. It was a conflict of a peculiar sort: conflict contained, and limited, by an overarching consensus – a constraint which forced compromise and caution on all the protagonists. Indeed, as we shall find, the theme of conflict within consensus is one which runs through the entire history of the NHS.

Notes

1   Michael Foot, *Aneurin Bevan*, vol. 2, Davis-Poynter: London, 1973.
2   In many ways the best account remains Harry Eckstein, *The English Health Service*, Harvard UP: Cambridge, Mass. 1958. At the time of writing, the government documents were not accessible and the book is perhaps biased by the sources that were available: Eckstein's exclusive emphasis on the central role of the medical profession reflects the fact that the main sources available were the published accounts of negotiations in the medical press. Another account based on published sources is AJ Willocks, *The Creation of the National Health Service*, Routledge & Kegan Paul: London 1967. The first book to be based on the documents now available in the Public Records Office is John E Pater, *The Making of the National Health Service*, King Edward's Hospital Fund for London: London 1981. Pater himself was a civil servant at the Ministry during the period in question, and his book therefore is a most authoritative (if extraordinarily discreet and self-effacing) account.
3   Political and Economic Planning, *Report on the British Health Services*, PEP: London 1937.
4   Brian Abel-Smith, *The Hospitals in England and Wales, 1800–1948*, Harvard UP: Cambridge, Mass. 1964.
5   Ministry of Health, *Interim Report on the Future Provision of Medical and Allied Services*, HMSO: London 1920, Cmnd. 693.
6   Royal Commission on National Health Insurance, *Report*, HMSO: London 1926, Cmnd. 2596.
7   British Medical Association, *A General Medical Service for the Nation*, BMA: London 1930; Socialist Medical Association, *A Socialized Medical Service*. SMA: London 1933.

3

The social transformation of American medicine: the rise of a sovereign profession and the making of a vast industry
Paul Starr

Extracts from Starr P (1982) The Social Transformation of American Medicine: The Rise of a Sovereign Profession and the Making of a Vast Industry. New York, Basic Books.

Doctors, corporations, and the state

The great illusion of physicians and the hospital industry in the 1970s was that liberal government was causing their troubles. The real threat to their autonomy lay in the demands they were placing upon private health insurance as well as public programs. Private insurers and employers want medical expenditures to be controlled. And though business has become more wary of planning and regulation, it wants medicine put under constraint of some kind.

In the early 1980s, spokesmen for business are calling for control over costs by the private sector. Though this approach has ideological affinities with the competitive model in health policy, the two are not exactly the same. The chief instance of private-sector regulation is the business coalition. In 1974 the Business Roundtable, whose members consist of the chief executive officers (CEOs) of the largest corporations in the United states, created a new organization called the Washington Business Group on Health. The initial purpose was to defeat national health insurance, but the group increasingly became involved in other medical policy issues, particularly cost containment. Local business coalitions to encourage containment of medical costs have been the next step. By early 1982 about eighty such coalitions were in process of formation around the United States. Their agenda includes such issues as utilization review and review of capital spending by medical institutions, not altogether different from the concerns of the PSROs and HSAs that the Reagan administration was intent on dismantling. The attack on regulation may not presage its disappearance but rather a transfer of functions from federally-sponsored organizations to business-sponsored organizations and the states. It is not difficult to imagine a situation in which some corporations (i.e., employers) lean on other corporations (i.e., insurers, HMOs, hospital chains), which, in turn, lean on the professionals to control costs. However, some critics object the employers won't lean hard enough because their stake is too small.[1]

The emergence of corporate enterprise in health services is part of two broad currents in the political economy of contemporary societies. The older of these two movements is the steady expansion of the corporation into sectors of the economy traditionally occupied by self-employed small businessmen or family enterprises. In this respect, the growth of corporate medical care is similar to the growth of corporate agriculture. The second and more recent movement is the transfer of public services to the administrative control or ownership of private corporations—the reprivatization of the public household.

As I've already indicated, liberal and conservative policies, in opposite ways, have both promoted corporate health care. Medicare and Medicaid stimulated the huge growth in proprietary nursing homes and hospitals and later the rise of dialysis clinics, home care businesses, and emergicenters. Cutbacks in financing have encouraged the same developments. This shift was not inevitable. The legal rule against the corporate practice of medicine might conceivably have been steadfastly enforced by the courts. The early liberal programs might have emphasized neighborhood health centers instead of Medicaid and more generally have fostered public facilities instead of public financing for private health care. The great irony is that the opposition of the doctors and hospitals to public control of public programs set in motion entrepreneurial forces that may end up depriving both private doctors and local voluntary hospitals of their traditional autonomy.

The profession was long able to resist corporate competition and corporate control by virtue of its collective organization, authority, and strategic position in mediating the relation of patients to hospitals, pharmaceutical companies, and use of third-party payment. Today, physicians still hold authority and strategic position, but these have eroded. Specialization has diminished the scope of relations between doctors and patients. Although patients who have established satisfactory relationships with private physicians are less likely to enroll in HMOs, HMOs have been developing more rapidly than before partly because ties between doctors and patients are so much weaker. (The rise in malpractice suits against private physicians has the same cause.) Employers and the government have become critical intermediaries in the system because of their financial role, and they are using their power to reorient the system.

In addition, the profession is no longer steadfastly opposed to the growth of corporate medicine. Physicians' commitment to solo practice has been eroding; younger medical school graduates express a preference for practicing in groups. The longer period of residency training may cultivate more group-oriented attitudes. Young doctors may be more interested in freedom *from* the job than freedom *in* the job, and organizations that provide more regular hours can screen out the invasions of private life that come with independent professional practice.

The AMA is no longer as devoted to solo practice either. "We are not opposed to the corporate practice of medicine," says Dr. Sammons of the AMA. "There is no way that we could be," he adds, pointing out that a high proportion of the

AMA's members are now involved in corporate practice. According to AMA data, some 26 percent of physicians have contractual relationships with hospitals; three out of five of these doctors are on salary.[2] About half the physicians in private practice have set up professional corporations to take advantage of special tax-sheltering provisions.[3] Many physicians in private practice receive part of their income through independent practice associations, HMOs, and for-profit hospitals and other health care companies. The growth of corporate medicine has simply gone too far for the AMA to oppose it outright. Dr. Sammons explains that the AMA would oppose any interference by organizations in medical decisions, but says that he is satisfied that none of the forms of corporate practice currently threaten professional autonomy.[4] However, at the local level, medical societies often still vigorously oppose HMOs and other forms of integrated control.[5]

Doctors are not likely, as some sociologists have suggested, to become "proletarianized" by corporate medicine. "Proletarianized" suggests a total loss of control over the conditions of work as well as a severe reduction in compensation. Such a radical change is not in prospect. Corporations will require the active cooperation of physicians. Profit-making hospitals require doctors to generate admissions and revenues; prepaid health plans, while having the opposite incentives, still require doctors' cooperation to control hospital admissions and overall costs. Because of their dependence on physicians, the corporations will be generous in granting rewards, including more autonomy than they give to most other workers. The new generation of women physicians may find the new corporate organizations willing to allow more part-time and intermittent work than is possible in solo practice.

Nonetheless, compared with individual practice, corporate work will necessarily entail a profound loss of autonomy. Doctors will no longer have as much control over such basic issues as when they retire. There will be more regulation of the pace and routines of work. And the corporation is likely to require some standard of performance, whether measured in revenues generated or patients treated per hour. To stimulate admissions, Humana offers physicians office space at a discount in buildings next to its hospitals and even guarantees first-year incomes of $60,000. It then keeps track of the revenues each doctor generates. "They let you know if you're not keeping up to expectations," says one young physician. Humana's president is frank about what happens if they fail to produce: "I'm damn sure I'm not going to renegotiate their office leases. They can practice elsewhere."[6]

Under corporate management, there is also likely to be close scrutiny of mistakes, if only because of corporate liability for malpractice. An enthusiastic management consultant writes that "individual incompetence and sloppy clinical performance will be less tolerated there than in freestanding large voluntary hospitals ... The large conglomerate can purchase and/or develop sophisticated quality-of-care control programs managed by statisticians. Working at corporate headquarters, the statisticians will not be concerned about individual physicians' reactions. Their reports, however, will supply individual hospitals with results about physicians who are not measuring up ... Senior management at the corporate level will constantly be mindful that the corporation's reputation comes first ... "[7] This, of course, may be management fantasy, but unlike PSROs, which this control system resembles, it cannot be denounced as government regulation.

New distinctions will need to be made among owning, managing, employed, and independent physicians. The rise of corporate medicine will restratify the profession. A key question will be the control over the appointment of managing physicians. If the managers are accountable to doctors organized in medical groups, the profession may be able to achieve some collective autonomy within the framework of the corporation (as they do in Kaiser). Another key issue will be the boundary between medical and business decisions; when both medical and economic considerations are relevant, which will prevail and who will decide? Much will depend on the external forces driving the organization. Thus far, conflict has been muted by affluence. A regime of medical austerity will test the limits of professional autonomy in the corporate system.

One reason that there will be a loss of autonomy is that the organizations in which physicians work are themselves likely to become *heteronomous*—that is, the locus of control will be outside the immediate organization. Professional autonomy has been protected by the institutional autonomy of hospitals. In the multihospital systems, centralized planning, budgeting, and personnel decisions will deprive physicians of much of the influence they are accustomed to exercise over institutional policy.

Perhaps the most subtle loss of autonomy for the profession will take place because of increasing corporate influence over the rules and standards of medical work. Corporate management is already thinking about the different techniques for modifying the behavior of physicians, getting them to accept management's outlook and integrate it into their everyday work. That way they do not need to be supervised and do not sense any loss of control. Sociologists have long talked about the "professional socialization" that takes place in medical school as students acquire the values and attitudes of mature physicians. Now they will have to study "corporate socialization" as young doctors learn to do things the way the plan or the company has them done.[8]

The rise of a corporate ethos in medical care is already one of the most significant consequences of the changing structure of medical care. It permeates voluntary hospitals, government agencies, and academic thought as well as profit-making medical care organizations. Those who talked about "health care planning" in the 1970s now talk about "health care marketing." Everywhere one sees the growth of a kind of marketing mentality in health care. And, indeed, business school graduates are displacing graduates of public health schools, hospital administrators, and even doctors in the top echelons of medical care organizations. The organizational culture of medicine used to be dominated by the ideals of professionalism and voluntarism, which softened the underlying acquisitive activity. The restraint exercised by those ideals now grows weaker. The "health center" of one era is the "profit center" of the next.

No less important than its effect on the culture of medical care institutions is the likely political impact of the growth of corporate enterprise. As an interest group, the new health care conglomerates will obviously be a powerful force. In one case—the renal dialysis clinics—the influence of one corporation prevented Congress from adopting legislation that would have cut federal health care costs, which is to say corporate profits. The profit-making hospitals clearly benefit from the structure of private health insurance and can be counted on to oppose any national health program that might threaten to end private reimbursement. The corporate health services industry will also represent a powerful new force resisting public accountability and participation.

A corporate sector in health care is also likely to aggravate inequalities in access to health care. Profit-making enterprises are not interested in treating those who cannot pay. The voluntary hospital may not treat the poor the same as the rich, but they do treat them and often treat them well. A system in which corporate enterprises play a larger part is likely to be more segmented and more stratified. With cutbacks in public financing coming at the same time, the two-class system in medical care is likely to become only more conspicuous.

This turn of events is the fruit of a history of accommodating professional and institutional interests, failing to exercise public control over public programs, then adopting piecemeal regulation to control the inflationary consequences, and, as a final resort, cutting back programs and turning them back to the private sector. The failure to rationalize medical services under public control meant that sooner or later they would be rationalized under private control. Instead of public regulation, there will be private regulation, and instead of public planning, there will be corporate planning. Instead of public financing for prepaid plans that might be managed by the subscribers' chosen representatives, there will be corporate financing for private plans controlled by conglomerates whose interests will be determined by the rate of return on investments. That is the future toward which American medicine now seems to be headed.

But a trend is not necessarily fate. Images of the future are usually only caricatures of the present. Perhaps this picture of the future of medical care will also prove to be a caricature. Whether it does depends on choices that Americans have still to make.

Notes

1   Paul W. Earle, "Business Coalitions – A New Approach to Health Care Cost Containment." (American Medical Association, January 1982); for two reports on business views, see John Iglehart, "Health Care and American Business," *New England Journal of Medicine* 306 (January 14, 1982), 120–24, and idem, "Drawing the Lines for the Debate on Competition," *New England Journal of Medicine* 305 (July 30, 1981), 291–96. For a skeptical view that business is not really that much interested in health costs, see Harvey M. Sapolsky, "Corporate Attitudes toward Health Care Costs," *Milbank Memorial Fund Quarterly* 59 (Fall 1981), 561–85.
2   American Medical Association, *SMS Report* [Sociomedical Monitoring System] (February 1982), 1.

3   Goldsmith, *Can Hospitals Survive?*, 33–34.
4   Interview, January 15, 1982.
5   Clark Havighurst, "Professional Restraints on Innovation in Health Care Financing," *Duke Law Journal* (May 1978), 303–87.
6   Kinkhead, "Humana's Hard-Sell Hospitals," 76.
7   Johnson, "Health Care 2000 A.D.," 49–50.
8   Freidson distinguishes between physicians' "technical" autonomy in defining the "content" of their work and their social and economic autonomy in controlling the organization or "terms" of work. Eliot Freidson, *Profession of Medicine* (New York: Dodd, Mead, 1970), 373. This distinction may become increasingly untenable as corporate organizations make the technical standards an object of modification.

4

Securing our future: taking a long-term view
Derek Wanless

Extracts from Wanless D (2002) Securing our Future: Taking a Long-term View. HM Treasury, April 2002.

Introduction

1.1   The Acts of Parliament which founded the National Health Service (NHS) set out a vision of: "a comprehensive health service designed to secure improvement in the physical and mental health of the people ... and the prevention, diagnosis and treatment of illness".[1] In the half century since, the NHS has established itself as the public service most valued by the people of the UK.

1.2   To meet its original vision in future, and to justify the value which people attach to it, the health service requires radical reform.

1.5....In March 2001, the Chancellor of the Exchequer commissioned this Review to examine future health trends and the resources required over the next two decades to close the gaps in performance and to deliver the NHS Plan and the vision of the original Acts.

1.6   This is the first time in the history of the NHS that the Government has commissioned such a long-term assessment of the resources required to fund the health service. Making a long-term projection of this kind is, of course, fraught with uncertainty, but there are good reasons for attempting it.

1.7   Many decisions about resources need to be made for the long term; for example, the number of people to be trained, the skills they will require, the types of buildings likely to be needed and the information and communication technologies upon which the efficient operation of the system will depend. The whole system, including prevention, diagnosis and treatment, rehabilitation and long-term care must be seen from the perspective of the individual patient, with appropriate structures in place to produce sensible incentives and to direct resources efficiently.

1.8   It is hoped that this Review will help to contribute towards greater stability in the funding and delivery of health care over the next 20 years. While total health spending has risen on average by 3.9 per cent a year in real terms over the past 40 years, annual changes in real terms have varied substantially – from reductions, to an increase of over 10 per cent. Such instability in funding acts as a serious barrier to long-term planning. Taking a long-term view should also provide the opportunity for more effective management of the health service. Good management requires clarity about the long-term, strategic direction of the service coupled with flexibility to respond decisively and appropriately to changes as they occur.

1.12   The Review has considered the resource requirements for a publicly funded, comprehensive and high quality health service. Although the Terms of Reference relate to health care, it is clear that social care is inextricably linked to health care. They must be considered together. The Review has therefore attempted to identify and draw out some of the key relationships between the two and, as a first step, sets out illustrative projections of resource requirements for social care for adults (especially older people) based on the present position adjusted for changes in the population and in the level of ill health. However, with the time and resources available, it has not been possible to develop social care projections in the same amount of detail as the projections for health care. Further work is required as part of a "whole systems" approach to analysing and modelling health and social care.

1.13   Public funds are used to commission services not only from the NHS and local authorities but also from private and voluntary organisations. The Review has made no judgement about the relative merits of different forms of public and private delivery; the resource estimates make no assumption about the public/private mix in the delivery of services in 20 years' time.

Financing of care

6.54   The Review was established to estimate the resources needed to deliver a high quality health service over the next two decades. Its remit was not to look at how those resources should be financed. Nevertheless, it has been important to examine whether the way health care is financed might itself be a driver of the total resources required.

6.55   Chapter 4 of the Interim Report considered this issue and concluded that the current method by which health care is financed through general taxation is both fair and efficient and that "a continuation of a system of funding broadly similar to that at present is not, in itself, anticipated to be a factor leading to additional resource pressures over the next 20 years". The Interim Report took the view that "it is therefore appropriate to conduct the Review on the basis of a continuation of the current system for funding UK health care".

6.56   The Interim Report identified four main mechanisms for financing health care:

- **general taxation**: general taxation revenues, incorporating both direct and indirect tax receipts, collected by government;
- **social insurance:** earnings-related employee contributions and/or employer payroll taxes;
- **out-of-pocket payments:** payments made directly by patients for the use of particular health services in either the public or private sector; and

- **private insurance:** private medical insurance taken out by individuals or by employers on their behalf.

6.57 Most countries use a combination of these to finance their health care systems, although the balance differs between countries. The UK and Sweden have the highest share of public funding: in both, under a fifth of total health spending is privately financed, compared to between a quarter and a third in the other comparator countries considered in Chapter 5 of the Interim Report.

6.58 Drawing on evidence from these comparator countries, the Interim Report considered the four financing mechanisms against three objectives: efficiency, equity and choice. A summary is provided in paragraphs C.15 to C.24 of Annex C.

Consultation views

6.59 The consultation responses generally supported the Interim Report's conclusions about the efficiency and equity of general taxation financing and that the current mechanism of funding health care in the UK is unlikely itself to be a driver of cost. Strong support for a continuation of the current financing system was received from some respondents. The King's Fund recently stated that "on the grounds of equity and efficiency of collection, the existing financing arrangements – predominantly through general taxation – are currently the best way of paying for health care[2]". UNISON "supported the broad conclusions of the Review, i.e. that the NHS ... should continue as a tax funded service." However, a few responses questioned the Interim Report's conclusions.

6.60 Some claimed a causal link between financing health care predominantly through general taxation and the historic under-investment in the health service. For example, the Association of British Insurers said that "the UK's publicly financed health care system has been associated with a significant cumulative under-investment in resources, infrastructure and poor service provision". While there has undoubtedly been significant under-investment in the NHS in the past as a result of the failure of successive governments to commit sufficient resources to the health service, the Review does not believe that this is an inevitable feature of tax-financed systems. For example Sweden, which has a predominantly tax funded system, is not generally considered to have suffered from such a problem. Levels of health care spending vary significantly across countries irrespective of the particular financing system used.

6.61 It was suggested that the UK's method of financing health care hides the real cost of health care, so impacting adversely on patient responsibility and engagement. The funding of health care from general taxation does obscure its cost, but it is not evident that a greater exposure of patients to the costs involved would necessarily lead them to take more responsibility for their own care. People covered by social and private insurance systems are more directly aware of the amount they are paying but there is no evidence that this constrains demand. In systems such as France where patients face direct charges they often take out additional insurance to cover these costs. The Review accepts that it is important that the public should be better informed about the cost of delivering health care.

6.62   It was also suggested that, in private or social insurance schemes, where people choose regularly whether to stay with their existing insurer or move to another, they could exert more influence over what is provided, could show their willingness to pay more for better services and could help exert discipline on total spending. The Review accepts that these are possible benefits although it appears not to have been the recent trend in many countries. For example, benefits packages tend to be the same or very similar across social insurance funds and, as noted in the Interim Report, cost containment has been a growing issue in many countries. The governments of France and Germany have been trying to limit the growth in social insurance contributions.

6.63   It has also been suggested that the UK's method of financing restricts patient choice and limits the responsiveness of the service. The major private medical insurers and some research groups made this point strongly in consultation. The Review believes it is entirely appropriate that under a publicly-funded system choices about what clinical services are and are not provided should be made centrally and transparently on the basis of best available evidence. In England and Wales, this is the developing role of NICE.

6.64   But in any insurance system there will be rules laid down about what is and what is not covered. Private providers are free to make their own decisions, and provide choice about what is covered. In terms of non-clinical services, the Review recognises that people will increasingly demand greater choice and responsiveness, and that financing greater choice in this area through general taxation may be neither acceptable nor equitable. As discussed below, introducing charges for certain additional non-clinical services would be one way of expanding the degree of choice.

6.65   It should also be noted that in the UK in the past, and at present, the opportunity for introducing greater choice has been restricted by a lack of capacity in the system. If such capacity constraints can be alleviated in the period ahead, this will open up the possibility of introducing greater choice across the service. The Government has made clear its intention to do so and it is certainly necessary. The Review accepts that it will require patients expressing their views to ensure this happens efficiently and in an appropriately responsive way.

6.66   The points presented above are all important, although some appear to relate more to the particular experience of the UK in the past than to inevitable consequences of the health care financing mechanism. The Review has carefully analysed the views which were put to it in meetings and in written submissions. It has considered the administrative burden of any changes at a time when the NHS is under such pressure for change. It is clear that there are deeply held beliefs about the extent to which private financing should exist in health care and that other countries, notably Canada, are engaged in similar debates over the best way of funding health care. However, the Review still does not believe that there is an alternative financing method to that currently in place in the UK which would deliver a given level and quality of health care either at lower cost to the economy or in a more equitable way. The issue is the sustainability of the individual components of the financing mechanism, and that needs to be addressed in the context of long-term estimates of the resource requirements.

6.67   The projected resource requirements for the health service over the next two decades set out in the previous chapter are very high and, should subsequent reviews confirm projections of similar magnitude, they will clearly present significant financing challenges. As expectations and quality standards rise, there will also be significant challenges in defining both clinical need and what level of patient choice can and should be accommodated through public funding.

Out-of-pocket payments

6.68   Out-of-pocket payments could play a role in meeting this challenge, both in terms of generating extra income for the service and in terms of providing extra choice for patients.

6.69   What role such payments should play in the future is not a matter for this Review, but for the government of the day. As noted in the Interim Report, decisions on the balance of financing should, on a continuing basis, be addressed in the context of the macroeconomic background against which the Chancellor considers the implications of the estimates of future resource requirements for the Government's wider economic and fiscal strategy and, in particular, considers the capacity of the UK's general taxation base.

6.70   Whatever role they do play, however, such charges should only be considered in cases where the principle that access to health care should be based on clinical need and not ability to pay can be assured. With this in mind, two factors are particularly important in considering the possible role of such payments: the scope of charges and the exemptions applied for those who cannot afford to pay.

6.71   Charges already exist in the UK for a limited number of clinical services (mainly prescriptions, dental treatments and sight tests, glasses and contact lenses) and non-clinical services (for example, single maternity rooms, televisions, telephones and car parking).

6.72   The Review remains of the view that it would be inappropriate to extend out-of-pocket payments to clinical services such as visits to a GP or a specialist. As discussed in the Interim Report, such charges are inequitable unless accompanied by adequate exemptions and risk increasing inequalities in access to care. A few responses advocated such charges but NACAB's work on patient charges argued strongly against them.[3] While they could yield substantial revenues, they would also involve additional administrative costs.

6.73   The impact on equity of out-of-pocket payments for items, such as prescriptions, depends on how effective a safety net is in place to exempt all of those who cannot afford such payments.

6.74   Currently 50 per cent of the population of England is exempt from prescription charges, including the young, the elderly, the unemployed and those on low incomes. As a result, 85 per cent of prescription items dispensed by community pharmacists and appliance contractors in England in 2000 were free to patients. Yet in consultation, NACAB pointed to research commissioned from MORI showing that of those liable to pay, 1 in 20 had failed to get all of a prescription dispensed and a further 1 in 50 had failed to get part dispensed, because of the cost. On the other hand, some of those who are exempt could easily afford to pay and are unlikely to be deterred by the level of charges, especially as they are capped by prepayment certificate arrangements.

6.75   Recognising the political sensitivities and the limited amount of money which might be raised, this may not be a priority for attention. However, the present structure of exemptions for prescription charges is not logical, nor rooted in the principles of the NHS. If related issues are being considered in future, it is recommended that the opportunity should be taken to think through the rationale for the exemption policy.

6.76   The Review believes that there is an argument for extending out-of-pocket payments for non-clinical services and recommends that they should be kept under review. Such services are likely to become more important as demand for greater patient choice increases and it may prove difficult to justify the public financing of such services. For example, payments could be considered for the provision of IT facilities in patients' rooms. This would offer a way of allowing patients to experience a greater choice in non-clinical services while at the same time enabling the health service to preserve its resources for clinical services. Better information technology will help to ensure that increased administrative costs do not use up the incremental income.

Annex C

Financing health care

C.16   This Review has been commissioned to estimate the resources required to run the NHS in 20 years' time. It is not set up to examine the way in which those resources are financed. My Terms of Reference specify that I should examine the resources required for a *publicly funded, comprehensive and high quality* health service and I am asked to identify the key factors that will determine the resources required. I have therefore needed to consider whether the method of funding the health service is itself a factor determining the resources required.

C.17   Health spending in most major countries is predominantly publicly financed – the US being the main exception. In the UK, 83 per cent of health spending is publicly funded. This is high by international standards – the EU average is 75 per cent.[4] Although a higher proportion of health spending is publicly funded in the UK, publicly-funded health spending accounts for a smaller share of GDP than in any of the seven European and Commonwealth countries considered as the most important comparators for this Review.[5]

C.18   Public funding of health care can come from two sources: general taxation and social insurance. Private funding comes mainly from medical insurance and out-of-pocket payments by patients. Work by the OECD (Organisation for Economic Development and Co-operation) suggests that a greater share of public financing of health care is associated with better population health outcomes for a given level of expenditure. In terms of its impact on the economy, the evidence suggests that, in general: *"private health spending has no advantages over public health spending. The most obvious consequence of shifting from public to private spending is to shift the burden from the relatively rich to the relatively poor"*.[6]

C.19   There are relatively high levels of dissatisfaction with health systems in many developed countries, whatever the funding system and overall level of resources devoted to health. The UK system of financing appears to be relatively efficient and equitable. It delivers strong cost control and prioritisation and minimises economic distortions and disincentives. A further key advantage of the UK's funding system is its fairness, providing maximum separation between an individual's financial contributions and their use of health care.

C.20   The main disadvantage of a predominantly social insurance based model is that the revenue base is more concentrated, falling on employment to a greater extent than in countries with a higher proportion of general taxation funding. As a result, many countries such as France with a tradition of social insurance have been shifting the balance in their funding towards general taxation.

C.21   Private funding mechanisms tend to be inequitable, regressive (those with greater health needs pay the most), have weak incentives for cost control, high administration costs and can deter appropriate use.

C.22   My conclusion is that there is no evidence that any alternative financing method to the UK's would deliver a given quality of health care at a lower cost to the economy. Indeed other systems seem likely to prove more costly. Nor do alternative balances of funding appear to offer scope to increase equity.

C.23   The main weakness of public financing of health care (whether through general taxation or social insurance) is that it provides limited scope for expression of individual preferences and choice. Where there is a clinical need for a particular service, a process is needed to decide whether the service will be available through the NHS or not. Such a process must be acceptable to the public. The National Institute for Clinical Excellence (NICE) and NSFs provide the main building blocks for this process. On equity grounds, I do not think it right that some individuals should be able to access clinically necessary services through the NHS by paying when others whose need is at least as great could not simply because they could not afford to pay.

C.24   However, as patient expectations increase, the UK will need to consider whether to provide a mechanism to allow patients to express their preferences for greater choice in non-clinical services. There are currently limited charges for non-clinical services such as single maternity rooms and car parking. The NHS Plan announced the Government's intention to negotiate contracts with private companies to install bedside TVs and phones with modest charges for the service. It may not be considered appropriate for public money to be used to offer patients greater choice of non-clinical services when these resources could be used for better treatment and clinical care for all. Such patient charges for non-clinical services may offer a way to extend choice for these services without diverting NHS resources away from clinical care. These are matters for consideration, if thought necessary, after this Review, or subsequent reviews, have reported on the likely total resources required in the long term.

C.25 The key conclusion for my Review is that the current method by which health care is financed through general taxation is both a fair and efficient one. I believe that a continuation of a system of funding broadly similar to that at present is not, in itself, a factor which will lead to additional resource pressures over the next two decades.

Notes

1 National Health Service Act (England and Wales) 1946, National Health Service Act (Scotland) 1947, Health Services (Northern Ireland) Act 1948.
2 King's Fund (2002), The future of the NHS: a framework for debate, discussion paper, January 2002.
3 National Association of Citizens Advice Bureaux (NACAB) (2001), Unhealthy charges: CAB evidence on the impact of health charges, July 2001.
4 1998 unweighted average.
5 France, Germany, the Netherlands, Sweden, Australia, Canada and New Zealand.
6 Normand C (1998), Ten popular health economic fallacies, Journal of Public Health Medicine 20: 129–132.

PART 2

The policy-making process
Introduced by Naomi Chambers

Senior health care managers are constantly seeking clarity about how and why policy is developed. There is always a powerful need to sense-make at a local level; to be able to tell the story convincingly to staff, patients and above all to themselves. Managers are further concerned with how policy should be implemented, in order to understand their role and contribution, and as a touchstone for personal priority setting in their day-to-day work. In terms of clear answers, the policy process literature appears largely at first a chimera, although there are some beguiling models and theories that do help to make sense of what appears to be a messy picture; indeed, described by Kingdon (1995) as the 'primeval soup' of problems, policies and politics.

This part focuses on four classic texts in relation to health policy development and implementation to illuminate the topic and to clarify the potential role of managers as policy entrepreneurs rather than policy victims (Roberts and King, 1991). One of the four texts has been drawn from a wider canvas rather than from the health-related field, to underline the perspective that there are lessons to be drawn for health care from the broader public policy arena. The texts have also been selected on the basis of their durability, either because the ideas that they introduced have already entered the lexicon, or because in our judgement they will do.

To set the scene however, it is helpful to begin by referring to Lindblom's classic text. The memorably entitled article 'The science of "Muddling through" ' (1959) elegantly puts the case that policy formulation and execution are intertwined rather than separate, and sets the scene for later elucidations of his argument for 'successive limited comparisons' , 'partisan mutual adjustment' and 'bureaucratic intelligence'. His argument is that attempts to formalize rational policy formulation have emphasized an idealized and comprehensive approach (the rational-comprehensive or root method) whereas the alternative (the successive limited comparisons or branch method) has heretofore been relatively neglected. Lindblom provides the theoretical explanation for managers as policy actors as they go about the iterative business of putting new policies into practice, in a way that has echoes of Mintzberg's (1973) critique of the realities of managerial life some time later.

Dilys Hill (1978), meanwhile, provides a helpful analysis of the concept of political ambiguity that elucidates how policy is made and implemented when the decision-making process is, as it usually is, based on compromise. Hill describes how ambiguity allows the political system to take the strain when there are divergent values about a public issue, how national and local structures pulling in different directions can produce policy ambiguity, and how ambiguity in implementation can have both beneficial and harmful results when there is a groundswell of societal disagreement concerning public welfare area. Continuing with the theme of continuous and iterative production of policy, and far from the popularized notion of civil servants as either conspirators, bureaucrats or wise counsellors as popularized by *Yes, Minister*,[1] Michael Hill (2005) offers a measured and nuanced analysis of the role of civil servants; an area that can puzzle and confuse even very senior health managers. Rather than holding with the traditional dichotomy of 'politics' (the agenda-setting processes of the politicians) and 'administration' (the arrangements for implementation handled by the civil servants), Hill argues that the latter belong at the very centre of the policy community, and thus shape, interpret, translate and reinvent policy.

Turning to the four selected readings, Michael Lipsky's (1971) particular contribution lies in his analysis of the process of implementation and recreation of policy at the grassroots, in his notion of 'street-level bureaucrats', which has now entered the canon. Lipsky starts with the premise that there are two opposite belief systems in place when policy is implemented at street level: public service workers believe they are doing a good job but the recipients of their services disagree and transfer that belief in their judgement of the whole bureaucracies in which they work. Lipsky argues that perceived inadequacy of resources, threats and challenges to authority and contradictory or ambiguous job expectations all contribute to worker stress and, as a defence mechanism kicks in, the combination leads workers to routinize, simplify, distort and reinterpret their role, thereby reinventing government policy at street level. Lipsky's prescriptions lie both in greater decentralization and neighbourhood control and in the recruitment of new cadres of graduates with intellectual acumen, staying power and a public service orientation to reinvigorate the street-level workforce. This has resonances with the 'problem of middle management' (Sergeant, 2003) and the aspirations of, for example, the UK NHS graduate training schemes in challenging 'the way we do things round here', although the jury must be out as to the enduring impact of such graduate schemes, given the apparent entrenchment of street-level bureaucracy in healthcare organizations.

Turning now to the politics of health, Rudolph Klein's oeuvre over a quarter of a century, focusing largely on an analysis of the UK health policy context, is one of the most compelling and illuminating, drawing as it does on the author's journalistic roots. His article in 1998 heralding the new (and New) Labour government's health policy priorities also succinctly sets the historical context, summarized as a centralized service based on the principle of parsimony, giving the medical profession a stronger hold on policy than in countries with more diverse and devolved systems of health care. The author is generally remarkably prescient about enduring UK health policy paradoxes and challenges a decade later across the themes of decentralization, incentives for performance improvement and challenges to medical autonomy, although not altogether accurate in his prediction about Labour's repudiation of the market by 2008 (at least in England). This paper outlines the influence of US health policy and how its central tenets of competition, markets and managed care come up against very different domestic politics that results in the emergence of new language – or as Klein puts it – new ways of thinking about health care in the UK.

Stephen Harrison and Bruce Wood (1999), in their critique of reorganizations over a period of 30 years, have identified subtle changes in health service reorganization policy, moving away from the early days of prescriptive blueprints spelling out the detail of the desired landscape (e.g. in 'The Grey Book'[2]) to what they term 'bright ideas', which are then translated by local incentivized policy actors into specific new arrangements in a process that they term 'manipulated emergence'. The concept can be applied beyond reorganization into other areas of health policy; for example, in relation to care closer to home, configuration of acute care, and so on. The question remains whether this is a cyclical process; that is, whether there will be a return to the prescriptive emphasis or whether, as part of Whitehall 'letting go' of the NHS, manipulated emergence will endure as a favoured health government policy tool. Talbot's (2005) thesis would favour the former: the paradox of human nature played out in policy terms would indicate that those policy makers who are keen to 'spell it out in full in advance' will again come to the fore in due course. Indeed, there are already examples of different styles coexisting: for example, the blueprint for reducing unplanned hospital admissions among over 65s (precise numbers of community matrons and job descriptions were issued by the Department of Health in 2006) as opposed to the uneven playing out of practice-based commissioning policy (in contrast with fundholding rules) from 2005 onwards with probably rather weakly incentivized local policy actors.

The final reading offers a painstaking economic analysis of the development of the NHS since 1948. Gwyn Bevan and Ray Robinson (2005) show how the theory of path dependency has continuously acted upon health policy development and implementation to slow it down and dilute it. Path dependency essentially is about the power of history, previous decisions, existing institutions and country-specific structural forces to constrain really new policy ideas and to prevent them from being implemented (Wilsford, 1994). The authors argue that the three economic logics in healthcare of controlling total costs, the equitable distribution of hospital and community services and efficiency are undermined by the political framework of a state hierarchical system and one in which GPs and hospital doctors, in a long-term collegial relationship, determine demand and supply. Occasionally, forces come together, as they did in the early 1990s, to force policy into a new trajectory, with the introduction of the internal market, money following the patient and the purchaser-provider split. The longer-term result, despite Labour's apparent ideological protests while in opposition, was an incremental readjustment and dilution following their coming into power, with the anticipated impacts of productivity and cost control remaining a mirage.

What 'space' can health managers occupy in terms of health policy development and implementation in the light of the theories and arguments developed in these selected readings? What prospects are there for them to be policy entrepreneurs? The literature on policy implementation (e.g. Hogwood and Gunn, 1984) indicates that there are a number of circumstances in which managers can stumble in the gaps between policy formation and implementation. Three main areas of insight are particularly relevant. First, the recognition that the policy process is likely to be iterative, ambiguous, compromised and emergent (Lindblom, 1959; Hill, 1978; Harrison and Wood, 1999) provides a steer for the sense-making contribution and the management of expectations at local level. Second, an understanding of the part played by street-level bureaucrats (Lipsky, 1971) should lead to more of a focus on the values, beliefs, behaviours and actions of front-line staff in checking out the realpolitik of policy implementation. Finally, a more strategic reading of the shape and durability of particular policy initiatives is enabled by reference to theories about manipulated emergence and path dependency.

Summary

- Many writers have described the messiness and iterative nature of the policy process.
- The influence of US health policy on the English health system is significant and long term but initiatives have been diluted because of the different paths taken by the two countries.
- Health managers may have a particular role to play in policy implementation and are better placed if they have insights with regard to the part played by front-line staff, the power of path dependency and the management of policy ambiguity.

Notes

1 *Yes Minister* is a popular 1980s' satirical British situation comedy set in Whitehall (and rumoured to have been Margaret Thatcher's favourite TV programme).
2 The Grey Book is the colloquial term for the administrator's handbook that characterized the bureaucracy of the NHS during the 1970s. It contained highly structured and detailed descriptions of policies, structures and lines of accountability.

References and further reading

Hill, D. (1978) Political ambiguity and policy: the case of welfare, *Social and Economic Administration*, 12(2): 89–119.

Hill, M. (2005) Civil servants and policy formulation, in M. Hill (ed.) *The Public Policy Process*. London: Pearson Education Limited.

Hogwood, B. and Gunn, L. (1984) *Policy Analysis for the Real World*. Oxford: Oxford University Press.

Kingdon, J.W. (1995) *Agendas, Alternatives and Public Policies*. New York: Addison, Wesley, Longman.

Lindblom, C.E. (1959) The science of 'muddling through', *Public Administration Review*, 19(2): 19–88.

Mintzberg, H. (1973) *The Nature of Managerial Work*. New York: Harper & Row.

Roberts, N. and King, P. (1991) Policy entrepreneurs: their activity structure and function in the policy process, *Journal of Public Administration Research and Theory*, 1(2): 147–75.

Sergeant, H. (2003) *Managing not to Manage*. London. Centre for Policy Studies.

Talbot, C. (2005) *The Paradoxical Primate*. Exeter, UK: Imprint Academic.

Wilsford, D. (1994) Path dependency, or why history makes it difficult but not impossible to reform health care systems in a big way, *Journal of Public Policy*, 14: 251–83.

The readings

Lipsky, M. (1971) Street-level bureaucracy and the analysis of urban reform, *Urban Affairs Review*, 6: 391–409.

Klein, R. (1998) Why Britain is reorganizing its health service – yet again, *Health Affairs*, 17(4): 111–25.

Harrison, S. and Wood, B. (1999) Designing health service organisation in the UK, 1968–1998: from blueprint to bright idea and 'manipulated emergence'. *Public Administration*, 77(4): 751–68.

Bevan, R.G. and Robinson, R. (2005) The interplay between economic and political logics: path dependency in healthcare in England, *Journal of Health Policy, Politics and Law*, 30(1,2): 53–78.

5

Street-level bureaucracy and the analysis of urban reform
Michael Lipsky

Extracts from Lipsky M (1971) Street-level bureaucracy and the analysis of urban reform, Urban Affairs Review, 6: 391–409.

In American cities today, policemen, teachers, and welfare workers are under siege. Their critics variously charge them with being insensitive, unprepared to work with ghetto residents, incompetent, resistant to change, and racist. These accusations, directed toward individuals, are transferred to the bureaucracies in which they work.

Street-level bureaucracy

Men and women in these bureaucratic roles deny the validity of these criticisms. They insist that they are free of racism, and that they perform with professional competence under very difficult conditions. They argue that current procedures are well designed and that it is only the lack of resources and of public support and understanding which prevents successful performance of their jobs. Hence bureaucrats stress the need for higher budgets, better equipment, and higher salaries to help them do even better what they are now doing well, under the circumstances.

How are these diametrically opposed views to be reconciled? Do both sides project positions for advantage alone, or is it possible that both views may be valid from the perspective of the policy contestants? Paradoxically, is it possible that critics of urban bureaucracy may correctly allege bias and ineffectiveness of service, at the same time that urban bureaucrats may correctly defend themselves as unbiased in motivation and objectively responsible to bureaucratic necessities?

What is particularly ominous about this confrontation is that these "street-level bureaucrats," as I call them, "represent" American government to its citizens. They are the people citizens encounter when they seek help from, or are controlled by, the American political system. While, in a sense, the Federal Reserve Board has a greater impact on the lives of the poor than, say, individual welfare workers (because of the Board's influence on inflation and employment trends), it nonetheless remains that citizens *perceive* these public employees as most influential in shaping their lives. As ambassadors of government to the American people, and as ambassadors with particularly significant impacts upon the lives of the poor and of relatively powerless minorities, how capable are these urban bureaucrats in providing high levels of service and responding objectively to individual grievances and needs?

It is one conclusion of this paper that both perspectives have some validity. Their simultaneous validity, reflecting differences in perspective and resulting from the responses of street-level bureaucrats to problems encountered in their jobs, focuses attention on one aspect of the institutional racism with which the Kerner Commission charged American society.

In analyzing the contemporary crisis in bureaucracy, and the conflicting claims of urban bureaucrats and their nonvoluntary clients, I will focus on those urban bureaucrats whose impact on citizens' lives is both frequent and significant. Hence the concentration on street-level bureaucrats–those government workers who directly interact with citizens in the regular course of their jobs; whose work within the bureaucratic structure permits them wide latitude in job performance; and whose impact on the lives of citizens is extensive. Thus, the analysis would include the patrolman on the beat, the classroom teacher, and the welfare investigator. It would be less relevant to the public school principal, who deals primarily with subordinates rather than with pupils, or to the traffic cop, whose latitude in job performance is relatively restricted.

Further, I want to concentrate on ways in which street-level bureaucrats respond to conditions of stress imposed by their work environment, where such stress is relatively severe. Analytically, three kinds of stress may be readily observed in urban bureaucracies today.

(1) *Inadequate resources.* Street-level bureaucracies are widely thought to lack sufficient organizational resources to accomplish their jobs. Classrooms are over-crowded. Large welfare caseloads prevent investigators from providing all but cursory service. The lower courts are so overburdened that judges may spend their days adjourning but never trying cases. Police forces are perpetually understaffed, particularly as perceptions of crime and demands for civic order increase (Silver, 1967).

Insufficiency of organizational resources increases the pressures on street-level bureaucrats to make quick decisions about clients and process cases with inadequate information and too little time to dispose of problems on their merits. While this may be said about bureaucratic decision-making in general, it is particularly salient to problems of street-level bureaucracy because of the importance of individual bureaucratic outcomes to citizens subject to the influence of urban institutions. The stakes are often high–both to citizen and to bureaucrat.

(2) *Threat and challenge to authority.* The conditions under which street-level bureaucrats work often include distinct physical and psychological threats. Policemen are constantly alert to danger, as are other street-level bureaucrats who function in neighborhoods which are alien to them, are generally considered dangerous, or are characterized by high crime rates. Curiously, it may make little

difference whether or not the probabilities of encountering harm are actually high, so long as people think that their jobs are risky.

Even if actual physical harm is somewhat remote, street-level bureaucrats experience threat by their inability to control the work-related encounter. Teachers especially fear the results of loss of classroom discipline or their ability to manage a classroom. Policemen have been widely observed to ensure the deference of a suspect by anticipatory invocation of authority.

(3) *Contradictory or ambiguous job expectations.* Confronted with resource inadequacies and threats which increase the salience of work-related results, street-level bureaucrats often find their difficulties exacerbated by uncertainties concerning expectations of performance. Briefly, role expectations may be framed by peers, by bureaucratic reference groups, or by public expectations in general (Sarbin and Allen, 1968). Consider the rookie patrolman who, in addition to responding to his own conceptions of the police role, must accommodate the demands placed upon him by

(i) fellow officers in the station house, who teach him how to get along and try to "correct" the teachings of his police academy instructors;
(ii) his immediate superiors, who may strive for efficiency at the expense of current practices;
(iii) police executives, who communicate expectations contradictory to stationhouse mores; and
(iv) the general public, which in American cities today is likely to be divided along both class and racial lines in its expectations of police practices and behavior.

One way street-level bureaucrats may resolve job-related problems without internal conflict is to drift to a position consistent with dominant role expectations. This resolution is denied bureaucrats working under conflicting role expectations.

Controversy over schools, police behavior, or welfare practices exacerbate these stress conditions, since they place in the spotlight of public scrutiny behavior which might otherwise remain in the shadows. These stresses result in the development of psychological and behavioral reactions which seem to widen the already existing differences between street-level bureaucrats and spokesmen for the nonvoluntary clienteles.

In their need to routinize and simplify in order to process work assignments, teachers, policemen, and welfare workers may be viewed as bureaucrats. Significantly, however, the workload of street-level bureaucrats consists of *people,* who in turn are reactive to the bureaucratic process. Street-level bureaucrats, confronted with inadequate resources, threat and challenge to authority, and contradictory or ambiguous role expectations, must develop mechanisms for reducing job-related stresses. It is suggested here that these mechanisms, with their considerable impact on clients' futures, deserve increasing attention from students of urban affairs.

Public policy reform in street-level bureaucracies

Although much more could be said about the stresses placed on street-level bureaucrats, the remainder of this paper will focus on the implications for public policy and for public perceptions of urban bureaucracy, of an analysis of the ways street-level bureaucrats react to problems related to specified work conditions. Where does this kind of analysis lead?

First, it may help bridge the gap between, on the one hand, allegations that street-level bureaucrats are racist and, on the other hand, insistence by individuals working in these bureaucracies that they are free from racism. Development of perceptual simplifications and subtle redefinitions of the population to be served–both group psychological phenomena–may be undetected by bureaucracies and clientele groups. These phenomena will significantly affect both the perception of the bureaucrats and the reactions of clienteles to the bureaucracies. Perceptual modes which assist bureaucrats in processing work and which, though not developed to achieve discriminatory goals, result in descriminatory bias may be considered a manifestation of institutional as opposed to individual racism. So there must be a distinction between institutional routinized procedures which result in bias and personal prejudice.

Second, we may see the development of human relations councils, citizen review boards, special equal opportunity units, and other "community relations" bureaus for what they are. They may provide citizens with increased marginal access to the system, but, equally important, they inhibit institutional change by permitting street-level bureaucrats to persist in behavioral patterns because special units to handle "human relations problems" have been created. These institutional developments do not fundamentally affect general bureaucratic performance. Instead, they insulate bureaucracies from having to confront behavioral factors affecting what appears to be racist work performance. These observations particularly obtain when, as is often the case, these units lack the power to impose on the bureaucracy decisions favorable to aggrieved citizens.

Third, tracking systems, vocational schools with basically custodial functions, and other institutionalized mechanisms for predicting capacities should be recognized as also serving to ease the bureaucratic burden at the expense of equal treatment and opportunity.

Fourth, the inherent limitation of "human relations" (sensitivity training, T-group training) training for street-level bureaucrats should be recognized as inadequate to the fundamental behavioral needs of street-level bureaucrats. Basic bureaucratic attitudes toward clients appear to be a function of workers' background and of socialization on the job. Training designed to improve relationships with black communities must be directed toward helping bureaucrats improve performance, not toward classroom lessons on equality which are soon forgotten (McNamara, 1967). The psychological forces which lead to the kinds of biased simplifications and discriminatory behavior mentioned earlier, appear sufficiently powerful to suggest skepticism over the potential for changing behavior patterns through human relations training efforts.

Fifth, just as training should be encouraged which relates to job performance needs, incentives should be developed which reward successful performance-utilizing indicators of clientele assistance. While performance standards can be trivialized, avoided, or distorted through selective use statistics, their potential utility has hardly been explored.

Sixth, this analysis is more generally supportive of proposals for radical decentralization and neighborhood control. Advocacy of neighborhood control has recently revolved around five kinds of possible rewards resulting from a change in present organizational arrangements. It has been variously held that neighborhood control would

(1) increase loyalty to the political system by providing relatively powerless groups with access to governmental influence;
(2) increase citizens' sense of well-being as a result of greater participation;
(3) provide greater administrative efficiency for overly extended administrative systems;
(4) increase the political responsibility and accountability of bureaucracies currently remote from popular influence; and
(5) improve bureaucratic performance by altering the assumptions under which services are dispensed (Altshuler, 1970; Kotler, 1969).

The analysis of street-level bureaucracy presented here has been supportive of that strand of neighborhood control advocacy which focuses on the creation of standards by which to judge improved bureaucratic performance. Specifically, it has been proposed, among other things, that the performance of policemen, teachers, and other street-level bureaucrats is significantly affected by the availability of personal resources in the job situation, the sense of threat which is experienced, the ambiguity of role expectations, and the diversity of potential clientele groups. Most community control proposals are addressed to these considerations.

This analysis is further supportive of proposals for radical decentralization to the extent that minority group employment under community control would be increased through changes in recruitment methods and greater attraction (for some) of civic employment. Increasing minority group employment in these street-level bureaucratic roles is not suggested here for the symbolism of minority group inclusion or for the sake of increasing minority groups opportunities (although these reasons are entirely justified). Rather, this analysis suggests that such people will be less likely to structure task performance simplifications in stereotypic ways.

These comments are made in full recognition that they are supportive of structural and institutional changes of considerable magnitude. If the analysis developed here is at all persuasive, then it may be said that the bureaucratic crises I have described are built into the very structure of organizational bureaucratic life. Only structural alterations, made in response to a comprehensive analysis of the bureaucratic crisis, may be expected to be effective.

Conclusion

Let me conclude and summarize by indicating why the current situation, and this analysis, point to a continuing crisis in city politics. It is not only that bureaucracy-client antagonisms will continue to deepen or that black separatism will continue to place stress on street-level bureaucracies which they are poorly equipped to accommodate. In addition to these factors, we face a continuing crisis because certain modes of bureaucratic behavior effectively act to shield the bureaucracies from the nature of their own shortcomings.

Street-level bureaucrats, perceiving their clients as fully responsible for their actions–as do some policemen, mental hospital workers, and welfare workers–may thereby absolve themselves from contributing to the perpetuation of problems. Police attribution of riots to the riff-raff of the ghetto provides just one illustration of this tendency (see Rossi et al., 1968: 110–113).

On the other hand, attributing clients' performance to cultural or societal factors beyond the scope of human intervention also works to absolve bureaucrats from responsibility for clients' futures (Rossi et al., 1968: 136). While there may be some validity to both modes of perception, the truth (as it often does) lies somewhere in between. Meanwhile both modes of perception function to trivialize the bureaucrat-client interaction, at the expense of responsibility.

Changing role expectations provides another mechanism which may shield street-level bureaucrats from recognizing the impact of their actions. This may take at least two forms. Bureaucrats may try to influence public expectations of their jobs, so as to convince the public of their good intentions under difficult conditions. Or they may seek role redefinition in such a way as to permit job performance according to role expectations *in some limited way*. The teacher who explains that "I can't teach them all, so I will try to teach the bright ones," is attempting to foster an image of fulfilling role expectations in a limited way. While this may be one way to utilize scarce resources and deserves some sympathy, it should be recognized that such tendencies deflect pressures *away* from providing for more adequate *routine* treatment of clients.

But perhaps most significantly, it is difficult for street-level bureaucrats to acknowledge the impact of their behavior toward clients because their very ability to function in bureaucratic roles depends upon routines, simplifications, and other psychological mechanisms to reduce stress. Under such circumstances, attacks upon the substance or content of these reactions to job stress may be interpreted as criticisms of the basic requirements of job performance. As such, the criticisms are interpreted as ignorant or inaccurate.

Even if street-level bureaucrats are prepared to accept the substance of criticisms, they are likely to view them as utopian in view of the difficulties of the job. They may respond by affirming the justice of criticism in theory, but reject the criticism as inapplicable in the real world. Because they (and we) cannot imagine a world in which bureaucratic simplifications do not take place, they reject the criticism entirely.

This inability to recognize or deal with substantive criticism is reinforced by the fact that street-level bureaucrats find the validity of their simplifications and routines confirmed by selective perception of the evidence. Not only do the self-fulfilling prophecies mentioned earlier confirm these operations, but street-level bureaucrats also affirm their judgments because they depend upon the routines that offer a measure of security and because they are unfamiliar with alternative procedures which might free them to act differently. That street-level bureaucrats are in some sense shielded from awareness of the impact to their job-related behavior ensures that the crisis between street-level bureaucrats and their clients will continue; even while administrators in these bureaucracies loudly proclaim the initiation of various programs to improve community relations, reduce tensions among clientele groups, and provide token measures of representation for clientele groups on lower-level policy-making boards.

The shelter from criticism may contribute to conservative tendencies in street-level bureaucracies, widely commented upon in studies of bureaucracy generally. For our purposes they may help to explain the recourse of community groups to proposals for radical change, and the recognition that only relatively radical alternatives are likely to break the circle of on-the-job socialization, job stress, and reaction formation.

An illustration of relatively drastic changes may be available in the recent recruitment of idealistic college students into the police and teaching professions.[1] These individuals are not only better educated, but are presumed to approach their new jobs with attitudes toward ghetto clients quite different from those of other recruits. What higher salaries, better working conditions, and professionalization were unable to accomplish is being achieved on a modest level by the selective service system, the war in Vietnam, and the unavailability of alternative outlets for constructive participation in reforming American society. Higher salaries (which go mostly to the kinds of people who would have become policemen and teachers anyway) have not previously resulted in recruitment of significantly more sensitive or skillful people in these bureaucracies, although this has been the (somewhat self-serving) recommendation for bureaucratic improvement for many years. On the contrary, the recruitment of college students whose career expectations in the past did not include this kind of public service orientation may accomplish the task of introducing people with the desired backgrounds to street-level bureaucratic work independent (or even in spite) of increased salaries, professionalization, seniority benefits, and the like.

It is obviously too early to evaluate these developments. The new breed of street-level bureaucrat has yet to be tested in on-the-job effectiveness, ability to withstand peer group pressures and resentments, or staying power. But their example does illustrate the importance of changing basic aspects of the bureaucratic systems fundamentally, instead of at the margin. If the arguments made here are at all persuasive, then those who would analyze the service performance of street-level bureaucracies should concentrate attention on components of the work profile. Those components discussed here–resource inadequacy, physical and psychological threat, ambiguity of role expectations, and the ways in which policemen, teachers, and other street-level bureaucrats react to problems stemming from these job-related difficulties–appear to deserve particular attention.

Notes

1   See, for example, the *New York Times* of February 13, 1970.

References and further reading

Altshuler, A. (1970) Community Control: The Black Demand for Participation in American Cities. New York: Western.

Becker, H. (1957) "Social class and teacher-pupil relationships," in B. Mercer and E. Carr (eds.) Education and the Social Order. New York: Holt, Rinehart.

Bordua, D. [ed.] (1967) The Police: Six Sociological Essays. New York: John Wiley.

Clark, K. (1965) Dark Ghetto. New York: Harper & Row.

Downs, A. (1967) Inside Bureaucracy. Boston: Little, Brown.

Gittell, M. and A. G. Hevesi [eds.] (1969) The Politics of Urban Education. New York: Praeger.

Glazer, N. (1969) "For white and black community control is the issue." New York Times Magazine (April 27).

Goffman, E. (1969) Asylums. Chicago: Aldine.

Kotler, M. (1969) Neighborhood Government. Indianapolis: Bobbs-Merrill.

Lazarus, R. (1966) Psychological Stress and the Coping Process. New York: McGraw-Hill.

Lipsky, M. (1969a) "Is a hard rain gonna fall: issues of planning and administration in the urban world of the 1970's." Prepared for delivery at the Annual Meetings of the American Society of Public Administration, Miami Beach, May 21.

—. (1969b) "Toward a theory of street-level bureaucracy." Prepared for delivery at the Annual Meetings of the American Political Science Association, New York, September 20.

McNamara, J. (1967) "Uncertainties in police work: the relevance of police recruits' background and training," in D. Bordua (ed.) The Police: Six Sociological Essays. New York: John Wiley.

Niederhoffer, A. (1967) Behind the Blue Shield. New York: Doubleday.

ROGERS, D. (1968) 110 Livingston Street. New York: Random House.

Rosenthal, R. and L. Jacobson (1968) Pygmalion in the Classroom. New York: Holt, Rinehart & Winston.

Rossi, P. et al. (1968) "Between white and black, the faces of American institutions in the ghetto." Supplemental Studies for the National Advisory Commission on Civil Disorders. Washington, D.C.

Sarbin, T. and V. Allen (1968) "Role theory," in G. Lindzey and E. Aronson (eds.) The Handbook of Social Psychology. Reading, Mass.: Addison-Wesley.

Silver, A. (1967) "The demand for order in civil society," in D. Bordua (ed.) The Police: Six Sociological Essays. New York: John Wiley.

Skolnick, J. (1967) Justice Without Trial. New York: John Wiley.

Walker, D. (1968) Rights in Conflict. New York: Bantam.

Waskow, A. (1969) "Community control of the police." Transaction (December).

Wilson, J. Q. (1968) Varieties of Police Behavior. Cambridge, Mass.: Harvard Univ. Press.

6

Why Britain is reorganizing its National Health Service – yet again

Rudolf Klein

Extracts from Klein R (1998) Why Britain is reorganizing its National Health Service – yet again Health Affairs 17(4) 111–25.

Britain's National Health Service (NHS) has succeeded in combining universal coverage and rigorous cost control—two aims that have persistently eluded American policymakers. Britain spends only a little more than half the proportion of its national income on health care than the United States spends while guaranteeing access to the entire British population. Yet Prime Minister Tony Blair's Labour government is celebrating the fiftieth anniversary of the NHS by introducing yet another reorganization, the fifth shake-up in the past twenty-five years in the way the NHS is run. The government's plans for reorganization, set out in a White Paper, have been presented as a reaffirmation of the fundamental values of the NHS.[1] But they underline, as did the 1991 reforms of Prime Minister Thatcher's administration, the tensions in the system—the fact that the NHS, in common with all health care systems, faces competing and, in practice, conflicting objectives.[2] Although the NHS has indeed managed to provide comprehensive care at a remarkably low cost and achieved a large degree of equity in access to care, it is perceived to have failed in meeting rising demands, ensuring uniformly high quality care, and responding to consumers' preferences.[3] If rationing by exclusion is the hallmark of the U.S. system, rationing by professionally defined need is the distinguishing characteristic of the NHS; that is, if the forty million uninsured Americans are a symbol of the U.S. system's shortcomings, the more than one million Britons on waiting lists are the symbol of the NHS's shortcomings.

Successive governments' obsession with tinkering with the structure of the NHS can be seen as an attempt to devise a formula that will reconcile the various competing aims of policy. In making this attempt, Conservative and Labour administrations have, as we shall see, followed different strategies. But despite the inflated political rhetoric of clashing assertions, there has been consensus about the central architectural feature of the NHS: It remains, as it was constituted in 1948, a predominantly tax funded service in which access is a right of residence and copayments are marginal both in their scope and in the contribution they make to the budget. For Labour this is an article of faith, deriving from its pride in setting up the NHS in the first place, the one achievement of the postwar Labour government that still commands overwhelming public support. For Conservatives the consensus marks the acceptance that alternative systems of funding—considered but rejected in the review that generated the 1991 reforms—would be less effective in containing costs.[4]

The NHS internal market, as originally conceived, was something of a hybrid: a market within a publicly financed service. However, this quasi or mimic market (as it was variously labeled) was conceived as having one key characteristic: competition among providers for purchasers. Competition was to provide the dynamic of the new system, creating the incentives to achieve greater efficiency and responsiveness. However, competition was—to exaggerate only a little—conspicuous by its absence. By 1996 one commentator concluded that "quietly in the night, competition in British health care has slipped away, its passing unremarked and little noticed by those who brought it into being."[5]

Why competition failed

There are many reasons why the internal market failed to live up to the expectations of its sponsors. There was the asymmetry in the information available to purchasers and providers, favoring the latter, compounded by the inadequate quality of many of the information systems. There was the lack of expertise and skill among purchasers: Looking at the British scene from an American perspective, one commentator concluded, "There is no serious purchaser in the NHS."[6] There was the heavy reliance by health authorities on block contracts (that is, buying specified levels of activity).[7] One result of this was that money did not, as anticipated, necessarily follow patients; once the specified level of activity had been achieved, providers had no incentive to treat more patients. The pre-1991 pattern of many hospitals' stopping operations near the end of the financial year persisted.

But the two main reasons for failure of the internal market spring from the very nature of the NHS. First, the fact that the NHS is funded out of general taxation means that the secretary of state for health is accountable to Parliament for everything that happens in the service. As the creator of the NHS, Aneurin Bevan, put it, "When a bedpan is dropped on a hospital floor, its noise should resound in the Palace of Westminster."[8] Everything that happens in the NHS is therefore likely to be politicized. Decisions cannot be left to the market, since ministers will be left with the consequences. Far from leading to the devolution of decision making—the ultimate logic of a market system—the Conservative reforms led to increasing centralization. From the start, ministers insisted that the internal market should not cause disruption. For example, when market competition threatened the viability of some London hospitals, given their high costs, the government intervened to set up a committee to plan services in the capital.[9] In short, competition was hobbled by central regulation and direction; the logic of market competition and the logic of NHS politics pulled in opposite directions.

Second, the importation of U.S. notions of competition into Britain meant transplanting ideas born in an environment of plenty into an environment of scarcity. The anarchy of the U.S. health care system has tended to produce surpluses of both doctors and beds. The rigorous financial discipline of the NHS has led to tight control over the number of both. This is not to claim that central planning has succeeded in avoiding all duplication of facilities—closing down hospitals is not easy given the politicization of decision making in the NHS—but simply to assert that there is less scope for competition to slice out fat in the United Kingdom than in the United States. Further still, competition as a concept is alien to the NHS culture, and in repudiating it, Labour is going, for better or worse, with the grain of the service's history.

Overall assessment

The 1991 reforms, then, did transform the institutional landscape of the NHS and, perhaps even more important, change ways of thinking about health care in the United Kingdom. But did they achieve Conservatives' hopes? Did they, by improving efficiency and responsiveness, allow the NHS to move closer to achieving all of its competing and conflicting policy objectives? The available evidence, based on research studies rather than a systematic evaluation, is incomplete and inconclusive.[10] It does not yield a clear answer, except on one point: Transaction costs certainly increased.

A central paradox

Nothing in Labour's White Paper in 1997 has changed the central paradox of the NHS: a centralized service based on the principle of parsimony gives the medical profession a stronger hold on public policy than it has in countries with more diverse and devolved systems of health care. There is, in effect, an implicit concordat between the state and the profession. On the one hand, successive governments over the past fifty years have allowed the profession an extraordinary degree of autonomy in the way in which it uses public resources. On the other hand, the profession has accepted responsibility for rationing resources. Political decisions about resource allocation have been translated into clinical decisions about whom to treat and how, thus shielding politicians from the consequences of their budgetary policies.[11] To the extent that governments start infringing on medical autonomy, the profession may be tempted to renege on its side of the concordat by giving visibility to rationing decisions and putting responsibility for them onto politicians. Indeed, there were signs of this happening under the Conservative government. If improved performance went hand in hand with increasing public dissatisfaction, as already noted, it was in part because the medical profession was determined to lay the blame for any shortcomings on the doorstep of ministers.

Labour therefore is engaged in an extraordinarily delicate balancing act. If the NHS is to deliver the hoped-for improvements in quality and effectiveness, there will have to be changes in the way doctors practice. But if changes are seen to be introduced by central government diktat, government will alienate the profession. The gamble therefore is that Labour will succeed where its predecessors have failed—in persuading the medical profession to trade collective autonomy for individual autonomy. In short, will the threat of ever-greater government control persuade the medical profession to exercise more collective control over its members as the lesser evil?

Cautious optimism

There may be reason for cautious optimism on this point. The reason is, once again, that Labour is building on a legacy from the Conservatives. One of the hallmarks of the Thatcher government was precisely that it challenged the power of the trade unions and the professions. In a sense, the medical profession was given warning that it no longer had a veto on public policy and that more rigorous self-regulation was the only alternative to greater managerial control. The relatively enthusiastic reception given to Labour's White Paper may be an indication that the message has been received and understood by the profession's leaders, although whether the same is true for the rank and file is another matter.

But Labour's strategy also carries a risk: that the emphasis on strengthening the grip of the center on the NHS will lead to an even greater degree of centralization of blame. If all goes according to plan, ministers will receive the credit. But if the rhetoric of collaboration and cooperation is not translated into practice, ministers will take the blame. One must therefore doubt whether the 1997 White Paper will be the last attempt to reform the structure of the NHS. If the political costs of maintaining the existing structure—where the price of containing expenditure is the centralization of political blame—start to become too high, ministers may start reflecting on what makes the NHS unique. This is not that it is a universal, tax-financed service, but rather that it is a health care system funded and operated by central government.

Notes

1   Secretary of State for Health, *The New NHS: Modem Dependable* (London: Her Majesty's Stationery Office, Command 3807, 1997).
2   A. Weale, "The Search for Accountability," in *Cost and Choice in Health Care*, ed. A. Weale (London: King's Fund, 1988).
3   M.A. Powell, *Evaluating the National Health Service* (Buckingham: Open University Press, 1997).
4   R. Klein, *The New Politics of the National Health Service*, 3d ed. (London: Longman, 1995).

5   C. Ham, "Contestability: A Middle Path for Health Care," *British Medical Journal* (13 January 1996): 70–71.

6   D.W. Light, "Is NHS Purchasing Serious? An American Perspective," *British Medical Journal* (17 January 1998): 217–220.

7   M. Goddard, R. Mannion, and B. Ferguson, *Contracting in the UK NHS: Purpose, Process, and Policy*. Discussion Paper 156 (York: Centre for Health Economics, University of York, 1997).

8   Quoted in P. Nairne, "Parliamentary Accountability and Control," in *Working with People*, ed. R.J. Maxwell and V. Morrison (London: King's Fund, 1983).

9   J.H. James, *Transforming the NHS: The View from Inside* (Bath: Centre for the Analysis of Social Policy, University of Bath, 1994).

10 J. Le Grand et al., *Models of Purchasing and Commissioning Review of the Research Evidence* (forthcoming). I am grateful to the authors for allowing me to draw on this—the first comprehensive review of the available research evidence—before publication.

11 R. Klein, P. Day, and S. Redmayne, *Managing Scarcity: Priority Setting and Rationing in the National Health Service* (Buckingham: Open University Press, 1996).

7

Designing health service organization in the UK, 1968 to 1998: from blueprint to bright idea and 'manipulated emergence'
Stephen Harrison and Bruce Wood

Extracts from Harrison S and Wood B (1999) Designing health service organisation in the UK, 1968 to 1998: from blueprint to bright idea and 'manipulated emergence' Public Administration 77(4) 751–68.

Introduction

Critiques, on both normative and empirical grounds, of those aspects of rational 'top-down' policy models that entail a sharp distinction between policy and action/implementation go back a long way (Lindblom 1959; Barrett and Fudge 1981) and, despite many criticisms (Etzioni 1967; Hill 1997) have been carried through into modern models of policy analysis such as those of Hogwood and Gunn (1984) and Parsons (1995). The approach to policy analysis espoused by these latter authors is eclectic, containing a number of stages which can be represented as more or less logical, but in respect of which no claims to sequential occurrence or overall rationality are made; the all-too-obvious possibility of errors, iterations and implementation failures is fully recognized. But these are the comments of *analysts*: until recently at least policy practitioners themselves have continued to be insistent on the maintenance of the policy/action distinction (Stewart 1996), perhaps partly because the rationale of many of their job roles is built upon it.

We characterize the change in health service reorganization policy as occurring on two related but analytically distinct dimensions. First, as our title suggests, there has been a shift away from the presentation of a blueprint as the intended endpoint of reorganization, and its replacement by the 'bright idea': a rather unspecific vision of how to proceed. Second, the role and timing of advice and consultation has changed from a situation where expert advice significantly shaped the content of the blueprint to one in which the expert contribution lay in the translation by incentivized local actors of the bright idea into specific organizational arrangements which accord with the philosophy behind the original idea; we term this 'manipulated emergence'.

In order to illustrate this claim of a change in the mode of policy making, we discuss four specific moments of NHS reorganization, the first three of which manifest a progressive dissolution of the policy/action dichotomy. The first is the April 1974 reorganization, literally conducted according to a blueprint which had been carefully developed over a period of several years. The second is the series of health service reforms of the 1980s associated with the late Sir Roy Griffiths: the introduction of 'general management' and of community care. Both took forms which were not intended by those who commissioned them, and can be seen as examples of 'policy-making on the hoof', that is something of an accidental dissolution of the dichotomy. The third is the reorganization along the lines of the 'purchaser/provider split' introduced in 1991 following the Conservative white paper *Working for Patients* (Secretaries of State for Health 1989). This latter document was brief and vague, the very antithesis of a blueprint, and gave rise to an emergent new organizational form; 1974 was the integrated outcome of a proactive process whilst 1991 was the fragmented product of policy making on the hoof. Between these two extremes occurred what with hindsight can be seen as a transitional period characterized by the *accidental* dissolution of the policy/action distinction. The fourth moment of reorganization is that proposed in the recent Labour white paper *The New NHS: Modern, Dependable* (Secretary of State for Health 1997); at the time of writing (July 1998), the consequences of this have not fully unfolded but there are clear signs of both continuity with, and departure from the trend that we have identified and we therefore examine how far these latest changes might represent the beginning of a reversal.

The 1974 reorganization

The details of the new organization were conveyed to the NHS in a document which became known as the 'Grey Book' (DHSS 1972b), a detailed and densely packed 174 page organizational prescription of structures, and institutional, managerial and professional roles and relationships, including elaborate consultative mechanisms and formal powers of veto. It is difficult to convey the character of this volume in a few sentences, but to describe it as a 'blueprint' is not an exaggeration. Successive chapters discuss organization in general and of particular skill groups, and management and planning processes. The document contains sixteen detailed diagrams of different segments of DHSS and NHS organization, specifying functions and relationships between statutory bodies, and managerial and professional relationships within and between them; a key element of this was the system of 'consensus decision making' which was to operate within the various multi-disciplinary top management teams (Harrison 1982). An appendix contains 27 detailed role specifications, together with definitions of key terms such as 'manager', 'accountable', 'monitor' and 'co-ordinate'. The blueprint was uniformly implemented throughout the service on 1 April 1974, at the same time as corresponding changes to the structure of local government.

The character of the Grey Book was to some extent the reflection of a specific approach to organization, developed in the Health Services Organization Research

Unit at Brunel University (Rowbottom *et al.* 1973). This approach seems to have been built on the assumption that most organizational problems were, at root, problems of misunderstanding of role; consequently, its prescriptions very much emphasized clarity of definition of roles and relationships. But the Grey Book's approach was also consonant with contemporary received wisdom which stressed planning, integration of social policy and the various health and social services. For whatever reason however, the history and outcome of the 1974 reorganization of the NHS manifests a clear policy/action distinction; there was a long period of careful planning and design of the new policy, which transcended changes of government and was then adopted almost in its entirety by the government of the day, and implemented nationally and uniformly.

From 1974 to 1989: the accidental death of the blueprint

It is important to note that during this period, the dissolution seems to have occurred accidentally rather than as the article of policy which it later became. We illustrate this in terms of two important NHS organizational reforms of the 1980s, the introduction of 'general management' and of community care, both associated with the late Sir Roy Griffiths, and both taking forms which were not intended by those who commissioned them.

In the case of general management, Harrison (1994) has shown the series of accidents that occurred. The government attempted in 1982 to commission an inquiry into NHS 'manpower'. The person offered its chair declined the offer. Ministers and officials did not have an immediate substitute in mind and sought advice from a number of industrial *confidants*; Griffiths, then Managing Director of the Sainsbury supermarket chain, who had no previous contact with government, was proposed and was subsequently offered the role. Griffiths declined, on the ground that if there were problems with the size of the workforce, that was only a symptom of a deeper problem, one of management; he would accept the chair only if the terms of reference were changed to focus upon NHS *management*. The government conceded this. The eventual policy recommendations were radical and included the abolition of the system of consensus team decision making and its replacement with individual general managers/chief executives. But the recommendations were also vague; the 'Griffiths I' report (NHS Management Inquiry 1983) took the form of a 24 page, double spaced typescript letter from Griffiths to the secretary of state and contained only the sketchiest account of the functions of various new institutions. Thus the roles of the new general managers and the shape of local organizational structures were left to emerge.

In the subsequent case of community care, Wistow and Harrison (1998) have shown how Griffiths, with one success and some NHS experience under his belt and now known to policy makers, was asked in 1986 to examine what was recognized to be an intractable problem of community care. A central government which had clearly demonstrated its hostility to local government and its powers and had already moved to abolish the GLC and metropolitan county authorities (Stoker 1988) could hardly be expected to anticipate that Griffiths would recommend the allocation of the lead role in community care to local authorities and that the financial resources to support this should be transferred from the central Social Security budget to local authority coffers (Griffiths 1988). Yet that is what happened. Despite various attempts to sabotage the recommendation, including the official publication of the report on the eve of a statutory holiday, while Griffiths himself was recovering from coronary artery surgery, some fifteen months later the Prime Minister was eventually convinced that there was no logical alternative. Nevertheless, there was a further two years before implementation in 1993 during which other important details of Griffiths' recommendations, such as the role of 'care managers', were left to emerge.

The 1991 reorganization

The 1991 introduction of the quasi-market was very different from that of the 1974 reorganization in four respects. One was a characteristic shared by the policy accidents described above; the process of initial design of the reforms was shorter and more closed. The remaining three, however, seem to signal a move towards a new style of policy making: a deliberate eschewing of blueprints in favour of the promulgation, in vague terms, of a core set of ideas combined with an invitation to relevant actors (which they could not easily refuse) to constitute the formal institutions which would embody these ideas. The key differences were as follows.

First, the White Paper *Working for Patients* (Department of Health *et al.* 1989), though some 102 pages long, devoted substantial space to Scotland, Wales and Northern Ireland and had a generously spaced and repetitive text containing only the barest account of the purchaser/provider split, the role of health authority purchasers, NHS trusts (providers) and general practice (GP) fundholders. Second, and presumably as a result, even by the formal implementation date of April 1991 aspects of the reorganization fundamental to the purchaser/provider split, not least the contracting process, had not been thought through, in some cases with disastrous results for individual institutions (Harrison *et al.* 1994). Third, the implementation arrangements were not uniform, but rather centred upon a process of annual waves of volunteers for (as the case may be) trust or fundholding status. The criteria for admission of volunteers to the new status were developed 'on the hoof' in parallel with the application process.

Indeed, there were incentives for managers and senior professionals not only to acquiesce in the innovations, but to volunteer to participate in their development, hence our description of the process as 'manipulated emergence'. Early adopters of trust or fundholding status stood themselves to gain, to contribute to the plausibility of the project's success, and to diffuse the perception that this was the direction which others would either be compelled to follow, or would suffer deprivation for not following (Lee-Potter 1997).

Thus, in terms of implementation, the 'bright idea' approach to NHS reorganization under the Conservative governments of 1987 to 1997 can be seen as highly successful. The absence of a blueprint allowed unannounced policy adjustment to emerge when deemed necessary.

Post-1997 labour policy for NHS organization: bright idea or blueprint?

The initial proposals of a further reorganization appeared in a White Paper *The New NHS: Modern, Dependable* (Secretary of State for Health 1997) which, despite 86 pages and several diagrams is actually quite insubstantial. Considerable repetition of central ideas is accompanied by only the sketchiest details of key institutions and processes.

Three of the four key elements of the 'bright idea' approach practised by the Conservative administration in respect of the 1991 reorganization clearly apply to Labour policy; the white paper was developed in a secret process; it gave only bare details of policy content (though certain of these were fleshed out in the later consulation document) and it provided for the subsequent development of 'policy on the hoof'. However, it did largely abandon the fourth element, that is the strategy of implementation by volunteers, underpinned by material incentives. Unlike GP fundholding (which is to be abolished), membership of a Primary Care Group will be compulsory for all GPs, and there will be strict rules about the geographical coverage of such groups.

Whatever the outcome, incentivized volunteering, arguably a key feature of the success of implementation after 1991, is not at present such a prominent feature of policy as before. The future of 'policy making on the hoof' in respect of NHS reorganization is unclear.

'Manipulated emergence': understanding the new approach

We have shown that a new approach to health policy making in respect of NHS organization arose between about 1983 and 1991 and has largely been retained by the new Labour government. This approach may be characterized as a deliberate attenuation of the policy/action dichotomy formerly regarded by policy practitioners as an essential feature of their task; the outcome of the new approach is that policy is emergent, yet seems to have an overall strategic direction shaped by prevailing government ideology and propelled by incentives for the relevant actors to volunteer to participate. We have labelled this new approach *manipulated emergence*. It is important to note that this is not the same as the decentralization to local managers of the choice of how to implement predetermined objectives. One way of seeking to understand this shift is through the changing context of assumptions in the UK about government, policy and organization. We emphasize that, despite superficial appearances arising from the chronology, these cannot clearly be attributed to party politics. For the 1960s and early 1970s, these assumptions, which are somewhat interrelated, can be briefly characterized as follows.

First, there was a strong belief in the role of *science and technology*, loosely defined. Second, there was a belief in *expertise*, one manifestation of which was what could be termed technocratic politics, that is a belief that policy and administration could and should be separated (Self 1972), with the latter being left to non-elected officials. Third, there was a set of related assumptions about both the value and feasibility of *planning* at all levels as a means of determining the future.

Three strands of literature seem useful in characterizing the organizational and management prescriptions which predominantly flowed from acceptance of the above set of beliefs and assumptions. First, there was an approach to policy, involving a clear policy/action dichotomy, which is highly consonant with the kind of rational model of decision making posited by Simon (1957). Second, there was an acceptance of a large part of the Fordist notion that there is a single 'best way' of production: mass production by a large integrated organization (Hoggett 1990). The third strand centres on the acceptance of bureaucracy, with clear hierarchies and clear procedures, as the appropriate form of organization, with concepts such as 'span of control' and 'line/staff management' current in the vocabulary.

The context of prevailing assumptions described above had greatly changed by the 1980s; the new situation can be characterized in terms of the following four interrelated components. First, faith in science and technology (at least in social situations) had been somewhat overtaken by the recognition that fast-moving events tended to render carefully thought-out policies obsolete; something of a *preference for 'gut feeling'* developed in its place. Sir Roy Griffiths was opposed on principle to pilot studies on the ground that they served merely to obstruct or delay implementation (Wistow and Harrison 1998). Second, a *suspicion of experts* had developed and there was something of a resurgence of politics, especially when informed by strong ideological conviction. As a consequence, professionals were no longer immune from scrutiny and public sector managers were expected to work under tighter political control. At the same time, the growth of 'anti-politics', that is negative public beliefs about politics and politicians encouraged the strategy of what Klein (1983, p. 140) has termed 'blame diffusion': the appropriation of credit by politicians for perceived policy successes, accompanied by the attribution of blame for failures to those to whom implementation has been delegated. Third, faith in planning and bureaucracy as the means of social co-ordination was increasingly replaced by a *preference for interactive, especially market approaches*. No doubt this was partly ideological, stemming from Conservative beliefs about the virtues of markets and the perceptions of professions as cartels, but it was also a result of manifest planning 'disasters' (Hall 1980; see also Hood 1976). And, fourth, beneath all these was *anti-statism*, a complex of assumptions about why the state could not solve social and economic problems, theorized by such New Right authors as Bacon and Eltis (1976) and Niskanen (1971).

The usual polar opposites to rational theory which occur in the policy-making literature do not do justice to manipulated emergence. The latter cannot be described as either incremental politics (since it resulted in radical change) or incremental analysis (since it did not consist simply of heuristic responses to current problems) (Lindblom 1979), though the interim period of 'policy accidents' can perhaps be seen as having led to 'policy learning' (Hall and Taylor 1996). Nor does manipulated emergence accord with the kind of irrationalist approaches typified by 'garbage can' theory (Cohen *et al.* 1972), since it clearly involves deliberate strategic choice.

Concluding remarks

We have shown that over the period of some three decades, from about 1968 to 1998, government policy making related to NHS organization progressively changed away from the production of a blueprint of what was to be implemented and towards the promulgation of a 'bright idea' which local actors were given incentives to develop in accordance with government philosophy. We have termed this partial dissolution by policy makers themselves of the policy/action distinction 'manipulated emergence'. We have related this development to broader changes in prevailing assumptions about the nature of government in the UK, and have raised the question of whether new Labour policy for NHS organization marks continuity or a departure from this, suggesting that it embraces almost all of the key characteristics.

References and further reading

Audit Commission. 1996. *What the doctor ordered: a study of GP fundholders in England and Wales*. London: HMSO.

Bacon, R.W. and W.A. Eltis. 1976. *Britain's economic problem: too few producers*. London: Macmillan.

Barrett, S. and C. Fudge. 1981. *Policy and action*. London: Methuen.

Burch, M. and B. Wood. 1983. *Public policy in Britain*. Oxford: Martin Robertson.

Child, J. 1984. *Organization: a guide to problems and practice*. London: Harper and Row.

Cohen, M.D., J.G. March and J.P. Olsen. 1972. 'A garbage can model of organizational choice', *Administrative Science Quarterly* 72, 1, 1–25.

Committee on the Functions of the District General Hospital. 1969. *Report*. London: HMSO.

Committee on the Management of Local Government. 1967. *Report*. (Maud) London: HMSO.

Day, P. (ed.). 1992. *Managing change: implementing primary health care policy*. Bath: University of Bath Centre for the Analysis of Social Policy.

Department of the Environment. 1972. *The new local authorities: management and structure*. (Bains) London: HMSO.

Department of Health. 1989. *Self-governing hospitals: an initial guide*. London: HMSO.

DHSS. 1970. *The future structure of the National Health Service*. (The Crossman Green Paper) London: HMSO.

—. 1972a. *National Health Service reorganisation: England*. Cmnd 5505. London: HMSO.

—. 1972b. *Management arrangements for the reorganised National Health Service*. London: HMSO.

DHSS and Welsh Office. 1979. *Patients first: consultative paper on the structure and management of the National Health Service in England and Wales*. London: HMSO.

Donnison, D. 1982. *The politics of poverty*. Oxford: Martin Robertson.

Etzioni, A. 1967. 'Mixed scanning: a third approach to decision making', *Public Administration Review* 27, 4, 385–92.

Friend, J.K. and W.N. Jessop. 1969. *Local government and strategic choice: an operational research approach to the process of public planning*. London: Tavistock.

Glennerster, H. 1981. 'From containment to conflict: social planning in the seventies', *Journal of Social Policy* 10, 1, 31–51.

Glennerster, H., M. Matsaganiz, P. Owens and S. Hancock. 1994. *Implementing GP fundholding: wild card or winning hand?* Buckingham: Open University Press.

Griffiths, R. 1988. *Community care: agenda for action*. London: HMSO.

Hall, P. 1980. *Great planning disasters*. London: Weidenfeld and Nicolson.

Hall, P.A. and R.C.R. Taylor. 1996. 'Political science and the three new institutionalisms', *Political Studies* XLIV, 5, 936–57.

Harrison, S. 1982. 'Consensus decision making in the National Health Service: a review', *Journal of Management Studies* 19, 2, 377–94.

—. 1991. 'Working the markets: purchaser/provider separation in English health care', *International Journal of Health Services* 21, 4, 625–35.

—. 1988. *Managing the National Health Service: shifting the frontier?* London: Chapman and Hall.

—. 1994. *Managing the National Health Service in the 1980s: policymaking on the hoof?* Aldershot: Avebury.

—. 1998. 'Clinical autonomy and UK health policy: past, present and future' in M. Exworthy and S. Halford (eds.), *Professionals and managers in the public sector: conflict, compromise and collaboration*. Buckingham: Open University Press.

Harrison, S. and N. Choudhry. 1996. 'General Practice in the UK National Health Service: evidence to date', *Journal of Public Health Policy* 17, 3, 331–46.

Harrison, S., D.J. Hunter, G. Marnoch and C. Pollitt. 1992. *Just managing: power and culture in the National Health Service*. London: Macmillan.

Harrison, S. and C. Pollitt. 1994. *Controlling health professionals*. Buckingham: Open University Press.

Harrison, S., N. Small and M.R. Baker. 1994. 'The wrong kind of chaos? The early days of a National Health Service hospital trust', *Public Money and Management* 14, 1, 39–46.

Hill, M. 1997. 'Implementation theory: yesterday's issue?' *Policy and Politics* 25, 4, 375–85.

Hirst, P. and J. Zeitlin. 1992. 'Flexible specialisation versus post-Fordism: theory, evidence and policy implications' in M. Storper and A.J. Scott (eds.), *Pathways to industrialisation and regional development*. London: Routledge.

Hoggett, P. 1990. *Modernisation, political strategy and the welfare state: an organisational perspective*. Bristol: University of Bristol School for Advanced Urban Studies.

—. 1996. 'New modes of control in the public service', *Public Administration* 74, 1, 9–32.

Hogwood, B.W. and L.A. Gunn. 1984. *Policy/analysis for the real world*. Oxford: Oxford University Press.

Hood, C. 1976. *The limits of administration*. London: Wiley.

Jaques, E. (ed.). 1978. *Health services: their nature and organisation and the role of patients, doctors and the health professions*. London: Heinemann.

Jessop, B. 1992. 'Fordism and post-Fordism: a critical reformulation' in M. Storper and A.J. Scott (eds.), *Pathways to industrialisation and regional development*. London: Routledge.

Joint Working Party on the Organization of Medical Work in Hospitals. 1967. (Chairman Sir George Godber) *First report*. London: HMSO.

Klein, R.E. 1983. *The politics of the National Health Service*. London: Longman.

—. 1995. *The new politics of the National Health Service*. London: Longman.

—. 1998. 'Why Britain is reorganizing its National Health Service—yet again', *Health Affairs* 17, 4, 111–25.

Lee-Potter, J. 1997. *A damn bad business: the NHS deformed*. London: Gollancz.

Le Grand, J. 1990. *Quasi-markets and social policy*. Bristol: University of Bristol School for Advanced Urban Studies.

Levitt, R. 1979. *The reorganized National Health Service*. 2nd edn. London: Croom Helm.

Levitt, R. and A. Wall. 1984. *The reorganized National Health Service*. 3rd edn. London: Croom Helm.

—. 1992. *The reorganized National Health Service*. 4th edn. London: Chapman and Hall.

Levitt, R., A. Wall and J. Appleby. 1995. *The reorganized National Health Service*. 5th edn. London: Chapman and Hall.

Lindblom, C.E. 1959. 'The science of muddling through', *Public Administration Review* 19, 3, 79–88.

—. 1979. 'Still muddling, not yet through', *Public Administration Review* 39, 6, 517–26.

Lukes, S. 1974. *Power: a radical view*. London: Macmillan.

Marks, L. and D.J. Hunter. 1998. *The development of primary care groups: policy into practice*. London: NHS Confederation.

Maynard, A.K. 1998. 'Curbing private enterprise', *Health Service Journal*, 12 March, p. 21.

Mays, N., N. Goodwin, G. Bevan and S. Wyke. 1997. *Total purchasing: a profile of national pilots*. London: King's Fund.

Ministry of Health. 1962. *A hospital plan for England and Wales*. Cmnd 1604. London: HMSO.

—. 1968. *National Health Service: the administrative structure of the medical and related Services in England and Wales*. London: HMSO.

Ministry of Health and Scottish Home and Health Department. 1966. *Report of the Committee on Senior Nursing Staff Structure*. London: HMSO.

Mintzberg, H. 1979. *The structuring of organizations*. Englewood Cliffs, NJ: Prentice Hall.

NHS Management Inquiry. 1983. *Report*. London: DHSS.

Niskanen, W.A. 1971. *Bureaucracy and representative government*. Chicago: Aldine-Atherton.

Osborne, D. and T. Gaebler. 1992. *Reinventing government: how the entrepreneurial spirit is transforming the public sector.* New York: Addison Wesley.

Painter, J. 1995. 'Regulation theory, post-Fordism and urban politics' in D. Judge, G. Stoker and H. Wolman (eds.), *Theories of urban politics.* New York: Sage.

Parsons, W. 1995. *Public policy: an introduction to the theory and practice of policy analysis.* Aldershot: Edward Elgar.

Paton, C.R. 1992. *Competition and planning in the NHS: the danger of unplanned markets.* London: Chapman and Hall.

Peck, E. 1991. 'Power in the National Health Service: a case study of a unit considering NHS Trust status', *Health Services Management Research* 4, 2, 120–30.

Peters, T.J. and R.H. Waterman. 1982. *In search of excellence: lessons from America's best-run companies.* New York: Harper and Row.

Pollitt, C.J. 1993. *Managerialism and the public services.* Oxford: Blackwell.

Pollitt, C.J. and S. Harrison. (eds.). 1994. *The handbook of public services management.* Oxford: Blackwell.

Rowbottom, R., J. Balle, S. Cang, M. Dixon, E. Jaques, T. Packwood and H. Tolliday. 1973. *Hospital organization.* London: Heinemann.

Royal Commission on the National Health Service. 1979. *Report.* Cmnd 7615. London: HMSO.

Secretaries of State for Health, Wales and Scotland. 1989. *Working for patients.* Cm 555. London: HMSO.

Secretary of State for Health. 1997. *The new NHS: modern, dependable.* London: HMSO.

—. 1998. *A first class service: quality in the new NHS.* London: Department of Health.

Self, P. 1972. *Administrative theories and politics.* London: Allen and Unwin.

Simon, H.A. 1957. *Administrative behaviour.* New York: Macmillan.

Spiers, M. 1975. *Techniques and public administration: a contextual evaluation.* London: Fontana.

Stewart, J.D. 1996. 'A dogma of our times: the separation of policy making and implementation', *Public Money and Management* 16, 3, 33–40.

Stoker, G. 1988. *The politics of local government.* London: Macmillan.

Stoker, G. and K. Mossberger. 1995. 'The post-Fordist local state: the dynamics of its development' in J.D. Stewart and G. Stoker (eds.), *Local government in the 1990s.* London: Macmillan.

Watkin, B. 1975. *Documents on health and social services: 1834 to the present day.* London: Methuen.

—. 1978. *The National Health Service: the first phase—1948–1974 and after.* London: Allen and Unwin.

Wistow, G. and S. Harrison. 1998. 'Rationality and rhetoric: the contribution to social care policymaking of Sir Roy Griffiths 1986–1991', *Public Administration* 76, 4, 649–68.

Wood, B. 1976. *The process of local government reform 1966–74.* London: Allen and Unwin.

8

The interplay between economic and political logics: path dependency in health care in England

Gwyn Bevan and Ray Robinson

Extracts from Bevan G and Robinson R (2005) The interplay between economic and political logics, path dependency in health care in England, Journal of Health, Policy, Politics and Law 30(1) 2: 53–78.

David Wilsford (1994), using the ideas of Paul David (1985), argues that path dependency explains why health care policies that are actually in place in any country are typically suboptimal. This is because the inertia from the history of previous decisions and existing institutions dominated by structural forces mean that policy movements are typically incremental, and strong conjunctural forces are required to move from an existing path onto a new trajectory. We use the ideas of path dependency to see whether they help us understand why policies as implemented in the National Health Service (NHS) in England were and are suboptimal in terms of achieving the control of total costs, the equitable distribution of supply, and efficiency in delivery. We recognize that each of these desiderata may conflict and is, like Lukes's argument about the power of ideas, well described as being "essentially contested"—that is, intrinsically open to dispute (Lukes 1974: 9). Cost control follows from decisions on the total budget, and economics cannot decide what the United Kingdom ought to spend on health care, and defining, and hence measuring, equity and efficiency are problematic.

Robert Evans and others, in analyzing the natural experiment offered by Canada, with universal coverage free at the point of delivery, and the United States, with partial coverage and high user charges, have shown how Canada's policies, adopted on grounds of equity of access, were better able to contain the total costs of health care (Evans 1987; Evans, Barer, and Hertzman 1991; Evans et al. 1989). These and other studies (Evans 2003) emphasize that the explanation for this economic paradox is political and that once this is grasped, cost control is in essence a remarkably simple process. All that is required is to design a payment system in which all expenditures flow through one budget and then place that budget in the hands of government with the political authority and motivation to limit its growth. The downside is that this makes government open to allegations of underfunding, as in the financial crisis in the UK NHS that confronted the Thatcher government in the winter of 1987–1988 (Webster 1998: 183–186; Timmins 1996: 453–458).

The Thatcher review explored and rejected pluralism in finance and then sought policies to generate incentives for efficiency in the NHS (Webster 1998: 183–186; Timmins 1996: 453–458). The outcome was the policies of the government's White Paper *Working for Patients* (UK Department of Health 1989a). This transformed the NHS from a hierarchical organization to an internal market in which public and private providers could compete—a model followed, and then rethought, in Sweden (Saltman 1998) and New Zealand (Gould 2000; Devlin, Maynard, and Mays 2001). The UK internal market was a mix of continuity and radical change. The NHS continued to be financed through taxation (based on ability to pay), free at the point of access (in principle available according to need), with resources allocated within the NHS using capitation formulas (to promote geographical equity). The radical change was to create purchasers—districts and general practitioners (GPs) who opted to be fundholders—that were separate from providers. The objectives of this change, as promulgated in *Working for Patients*, were that purchasers funded equitably would seek efficiency by meeting patients' needs and choosing between competing providers on the basis of cost and quality (Robinson and Le Grand 1994). This is an interesting combination of socialism and capitalism: indeed, one young adviser to the prime ministerial review team is reported to have described this combination as what Aneurin Bevan, in creating the NHS in 1948, would have introduced if only he had had the imagination.

Wilsford (1994) used the ideas of path dependency to understand the formulation of the radical policies of the internal market in the United Kingdom. He argues that this was due to a rare confluence of factors: a majority government in its third successive term with the authority and will to enact policy changes intended to change the mix of instruments and the balance of influence. His comparison with Germany, France, and the United States led him to conclude that the structures of the British system give strategically placed actors, through hierarchy and centralization, a more leveraged hand against history. This means that these actors are more successful at prosecuting big reform and better able to direct systems along more optimal policy paths and, as conditions render the status quo less desirable, establish new paths that significantly deviate from the status quo.

Carolyn Tuohy (1999a) echoes Wilsford's analysis of the conjunctural forces that enabled the policies of the internal market to be formulated in the United Kingdom. But she uses Maurice Shock's graphic language to distinguish this blitzkrieg from the much more difficult exercise of policy implementation—akin to being an army of occupation (Shock 1994). Her comparison with Canada and the United States comes to quite a different conclusion from Wilsford's, albeit one that powerfully illustrates path dependency, and explains why the model of the internal market as implemented by two successive conservative governments turned out to be only a pallid version of the core ideas originally promulgated. She argues that the logic of the NHS is that of a state-hierarchical system with two key structural elements that inevitably tempered market-oriented reforms based on contracts between purchasers and providers. First, at the micro-level, as decisions on individual patients continued to be made by GPs and hospital doctors, contracts had to be designed to accommodate, rather than challenge, these collegial relationships. Second, ministers remained accountable when purchasers sought to use the internal market to shift contracts that threatened to destabilize whole hospitals or even the closure of hospital departments. This is in sharp contrast to the United States, where private investors have driven rapid and volatile change.

Tuohy (1999a, 1999b) considered the Labour Party's response to the policies of the internal market to be a move from apocalyptic and vitriolic denunciation of the internal market when in opposition to, when in government, adapting this pallid model. But, in response to another financial crisis in the NHS, the Blair government is now committed to increasing substantially the level of NHS funding and to reintroducing a provider market (U.K. Department of Health 2002a). Tuohy's analysis raises troubling questions about these policy commitments. How can the United Kingdom build on a system that contains costs and promotes equity to deliver efficiency? Can the U.K. government deliver efficiency only through the austerity of a budgetary squeeze and not when it increases NHS resources? Will it be unable to implement lessons from America on ways to improve efficiency, which include both the models of finance by capitation through health maintenance organizations (HMOs) and case-based prospective payment of hospitals by diagnosis-related groups (DRGs) (Enthoven 1985; Maynard, Marinker, and Gray 1986; Bardsley, Coles, and Jenkins 1987; Havighurst et al. 1988; Enthoven 1990; Weiner and Ferris 1990; Robinson and Steiner 1998; Enthoven 1999; Feachem, Sekhri, and White 2002; U.K. Department of Health 2002b; Ham et al. 2003)?

To examine path dependency in the NHS, we outline what we see as the economic implications of market failure in health care for policies that aim to optimize performance in terms of cost control, equity, and efficiency. We then consider how and why the policy paths actually taken were at variance with what economic analysis would suggest over four periods marked by significant structural change: the creation of the NHS, the 1974 reorganization, the 1991 internal market, and finally the policies of the Labour government since 1997. We begin with a brief outline of these different eras in the funding of the NHS and conclude with some observations on economic and political logics and path dependency. This article is essentially about the NHS in England. Prior to 1997, policies that applied in England set the model for other countries in the United Kingdom; since then there have been important differences following devolution. Scott Greer (2004) has characterized these differences as follows: England has focused on regulation and markets, whereas Scotland has opted for professionalism, Wales for localism, and Northern Ireland for permissive managerialism.

Conclusions

We began by asking whether the ideas of path dependency help us understand why policies as formulated and implemented in the NHS in England were and are suboptimal in terms of achieving cost control, equity, and efficiency. To achieve these three desiderata, economic logic suggests allocating a cash-limited budget by capitation to purchasers that employ GPs to manage demand, regulating their performance, and letting them decide whether to contract with or manage local providers. Economic analysis can also identify whether policies in place offer the requisite mix to achieve these three desiderata. The NHS in England, as Tuohy (1999a. 1999b) has argued, has its own political logic of a state-hierarchical system in which GPs and hospital doctors determine demand and supply. This means that the government can use its position and authority as a single payer to secure cost control and equity, but also that ministers are accountable for policies that entail reductions in local services. This logic drives path dependency, which explains why NHS policies for hospitals began by incremental budgeting, sought equity by leveling up, and implemented the internal market to avoid destabilizing hospitals: contracts became a new way of incremental budgeting, and efficiency was sought by an index that preserved, rather than challenged, relative (in)efficiencies. Path dependency also illuminates how the seeds of the 1987–1988 crisis were sown forty years earlier, when the political logic that shaped the creation of the NHS put it on a policy path of an organization that was committed to equity but privileged teaching hospitals, and illustrates why the manifest policy response to that crisis, the internal market, was not used to resolve the problem. Path dependency also suggests that although current policies aim to promote equity and efficiency—by introducing a case-based payment for providers within finance by capitation of purchasers—the way these policies will be implemented is unlikely to achieve either goal.

Finally, our account brings out the latent and dynamic force of path dependency. It is, of course, natural to focus on the actors engaged in conjunctural events, the blitzkrieg of policy formulation, and the new policies that emerge. But, as Lukes (1974) emphasized, the subtleties of power require us to look beyond interests explicitly represented. Path dependency emphasizes how policies that have continued will have renewed force and reflect powerful interests. In contrast, as Machiavelli warned, those seeking to implement the new policies are subject to many difficulties, which are well described as akin to those of an army of occupation.

References

Abel-Smith, B. 1964. *The Hospitals, 1800–1948: A Study in Social Administration in England and Wales.* London: Heinemann.

Abel-Smith, B., and R. M. Titmuss. 1956. *The Cost of the National Health Service in England and Wales.* Cambridge: Cambridge University Press.

Appleby, J., and V. Little. 1993. Health and Efficiency. *Health Services Journal* 103: 20–22.

Arrow, K. J. 1963. Uncertainty and the Welfare Economics of Medical Care. *American Economic Review* 53: 941–973.

Ashby, W. R. 1956. *An Introduction to Cybernetics.* London: Methuen.

Bardsley, M., J. Coles, and L. Jenkins, eds. 1987. *DRGs and Health Care: The Management of Case-Mix.* London: King Edwards Fund.

Baxter, K., M. Bachmann, and G. Bevan. 2000. Primary Care Groups: Trade-Offs in Managing Budgets and Risk. *Public Money and Management* 20: 53–62.

Baxter, K., H. Stoddart, and G. Bevan. 2001. Evidence-Based Medicine: Conflict between Rigour and Reality? *Primary Health Care Research and Development* 2: 7–24.

Beech, R., G. Bevan, and N. Mays. 1990. Spatial Equity in the NHS: The Death and Rebirth of RAWP. In *Health Care UK*, ed. A. Harrison, 44–61. Newbury: Policy Journals.

Bevan, G. 1984. Organising the Finance of Hospitals by Simulated Markets. *Fiscal Studies* 5: 44–63.

—. 1987. Financing the Additional Service Costs of Teaching English Medical Students by the Service Increment for Teaching (SIFT): An Exposition and Critique. *Financial Accountability and Management* 3: 147–160.

—. 1989a. Financing UK Hospital and Community Health Services. *Oxford Review of Economic Policy* 5: 124–135.

—. 1989b. Reforming UK Health Care: Internal Markets or Emergent Planning? *Fiscal Studies* 10: 53–71.

Bevan, G., and J. Brazier. 1987. Reviewing RAWP—Financial Incentives of Subregional RAWP. *British Medical Journal* 295: 836–838.

Bevan, G., H. A. Copeman, J. Perrin, and R. Rosser. 1980. *Health Care: Priorities and Management.* London: Croom Helm.

Bevan, G., K. F. Sisson, and P. Way. 1981. Cash Limits and Public Sector Pay Bargaining. *Public Administration* 59: 379–398.

Bloor, K., and A. Maynard. 1993. *Expenditure on the NHS during and after the Thatcher Years: Its Growth and Utilisation.* York: Centre for Health Economics, University of York.

Bloor, K., A. Maynard, and A. Street. 2000. The Cornerstone of Labour's "New NHS": Reforming Primary Care. In *Reforming Markets in Health Care*, ed. P. C. Smith, 18–45. Buckingham: Open University Press.

Boyle, S., and A. Harrison. 2000. PFI in Health: The Story So Far. In *A Healthy Partnership: The Future of Public-Private Partnerships in the Health Service,* ed. G. Kelly and P. Robinson. London: Institute for Public Policy Research.

Clarke, R. 1978. *Public Expenditure Management and Control.* London: Macmillan.

Coase, R. H. 1991. *The Nature of the Firm.* In *The Nature of the Firm,* ed. O. E. Williamson and S. G. Winter, 20–25. Oxford: Oxford University Press. Originally published 1937 in *Economica* 4: 386–405.

Craig, M. 1987. Estimating Resources Required to Train Medical Students and Provide Services: A Survey of English Teaching Authorities. *Financial Accountability and Management* 3: 135–146.

Croxson, B. 1999. *Organisational Costs in the New NHS*. London: Office for Health Economics.

David, P. A. 1985. Clio and the Economics of QWERTY. *American Economic Review* 75: 332–337.

Dawson, D. 1995. *Regulating Competition in the NHS*. Discussion Paper 131. York: Centre for Health Economics, University of York.

Dawson, D., and M. Goddard. 2000. Longer-Term Agreements for Health Care Services: What Will They Achieve? In *Reforming Markets in Health Care*, ed. P. C. Smith, 67–93. Buckingham: Open University Press.

Day, P., and R. Klein. 1991. Britain's Health Care Experiment. *Health Affairs* 10: 39–59.

Devlin, N., A. Maynard, and N. Mays. 2001. New Zealand's New Health Sector Reforms: Back to the Future? *British Medical Journal* 322: 1171–1174.

Dredge, B. 2003. Spell It Out. *Health Service Journal*, October 30, 35.

Ellwood, S. 1996. Pricing Service in the UK National Health Service. *Financial Accountability and Management* 12: 281–301.

Enthoven, A. 1985. *Reflections on the Management of the NHS*. London: Nuffield Provincial Hospitals Trust.

—. 1990. What Can Europeans Learn from Americans? In *Health Care Systems in Transition*, 57–71. Paris: Organisation for Economic Co-operation and Development.

—. 1999. *In Pursuit of an Improving National Health Service*. London: Nuffield Trust.

European Observatory. 1999. *Health Care Systems in Transition: United Kingdom*. Copenhagen: World Health Organization.

Evans, R. G. 1987. Public Health Insurance: The Collective Purchase of Individual Care. *Health Policy* 7: 115–134.

—. 2003. *Political Wolves and Economic Sheep: The Sustainability of Public Health Insurance in Canada*. CHSPR 03:16W. Vancouver: Centre for Health Services and Policy Research, University of British Columbia.

Evans, R. G., M. L. Barer, and C. Hertzman. 1991. The Twenty-Year Experiment: Accounting for, Explaining, and Evaluating Health Care Cost Containment in Canada and the United States. *American Review of Public Health* 12: 481–518.

Evans, R. G., J. Lomas, M. L. Barer, R. J. Labelle, C. Fooks, G. L. Stoddart, G. M. Anderson, D. Feeney, A. Gafni, G. W. Torrance, and W. G. Tholl. 1989. Controlling Health Expenditures—The Canadian Reality. *New England Journal of Medicine* 320: 571–577.

Feachem, R. G., A. N. K. Sekhri, and K. L. White. 2002. Getting More for Their Dollar: A Comparison of the NHS with California's Kaiser Permanente. *British Medical Journal* 324: 135–143.

Foot, M. 1975. *Aneurin Bevan, 1945–60*. St Albans: Paladin.

Forsyth, G. 1975. *Doctors and State Medicine*. London: Pitman.

Glennerster, H., M. Matsaganis, P. Owens, and S. Hancock. 1994. *Implementing GP Fundholding*. Buckingham: Open University Press.

Goddard, M., R. Mannion, and P. C. Smith. 2000. The Performance Framework: Taking Account of Economic Behaviour. In *Reforming Markets in Health Care*, ed. P. C. Smith. Buckingham: Open University Press.

Gould, R. D. C. 2000. Big Bang and the Policy Prescription: Health Care Meets the Market in New Zealand. *Journal of Health Politics, Policy and Law* 25: 815–844.

Greer, S. L. 2004. *Four Way Bet: How Devolution Has Led to Four Different Models for the NHS.* London: Constitution Unit, School of Public Policy, University College London.

Ham, C. 1996. Contestability: A Middle Path for Health Care. *British Medical Journal* 312: 70–71.

—. 2000. *The Politics of NHS Reform, 1988–97.* London: King's Fund.

Ham, C., N. York, S. Sutch, and R. Shaw. 2003. Hospital Bed Utilisation in the NHS, Kaiser Permanente, and the US Medicare Programme: Analysis of Routine Data. *British Medical Journal* 327: 1257.

Hart, J. T. 1971. The Inverse Care Law. *Lancet* 1: 405–412.

Havighurst, C. C., R. B. Helms, C. Bladen, and M. V. Pauly. 1988. *American Health Care. What Are the Lessons for Britain?* London: Institute for Economic Affairs.

Health Services Journal. 2004. *DoH Confirms Rescue Fund.* April 8, 4, News and Opinion.

Heclo, H., and A. Wildavsky. 1981. *The Private Government of Public Money.* 2nd ed. London: Macmillan.

Hollinghurst, S., G. Bevan, and C. Bowie. 2000. Estimating the "Avoidable" Burden of Disease by Disability Adjusted Life Years (DALYs). *Health Care Management Science* 3: 9–21.

Honigsbaum, F. 1979. *The Division in British Medicine.* London: Kogan Page.

Joskow, P. L. 1991. Asset Specificity and the Structure of Vertical Relationships: Empirical Evidence. In *The Nature of the Firm*, ed. O. E. Williamson and S. G. Winter, 117–137. Oxford: Oxford University Press.

Klein, R. E. 1983. *The Politics of the National Health Service.* London: Longman.

—. 1985. Why Britain's Conservatives Support a Socialist Health Care System. *Health Affairs* 4: 41–58.

—. 1995. *The New Politics of the National Health Service.* 3rd ed. London: Longman.

—. 1998. Why Britain Is Reorganizing Its National Health Service—Yet Again. *Health Affairs* 17: 111–125.

Le Grand, J., N. Mays, and M. Mulligan. 1998. *Learning from the NHS Internal Market.* London: King's Fund.

Levitt, R. 1976. *The Reorganised National Health Service.* London: Croom Helm.

Levitt, R., and A. Wall. 1984. *The Reorganised National Health Service.* 3rd ed. London: Croom Helm.

Light, D. 2000. Sociological Perspectives on Competition in Health Care. *Journal of Health Politics, Policy and Law* 25: 969–974.

Lukes, S. 1974. *Power: A Radical View.* London: Macmillan.

MacKenzie, W J. M. 1963. The Plowden Report: A Translation. *Guardian,* May 25. Republished in *Policy-Making in Britain* (1969), ed. R. Rose, 273–282. London: Macmillan.

Maddox, G. L. 1999. General Practitioner Fundholding in the British National Health Service Reform, 1991–1997: GP Accounts of the Dynamics of Change. *Journal of Health Politics, Policy and Law* 24: 815–834.

Majone, G. 1996. The Rise of Statutory Regulation in Europe. In *Regulating Europe,* ed. G. Majone, 47–60. London: Routledge.

Maynard, A., M. Marinker, and D. P. Gray. 1986. The Doctor, the Patient, and Their Contract: III. Alternative Contracts: Are They Viable? *British Medical Journal* 292: 1505–1510.

Mays, N., and G. Bevan. 1987. *Resource Allocation in the Health Service.* London: Bedford Square Press.

Mays, N., S. Wyke, G. Malbon, and N. Goodwin, eds. 2001. *The Purchasing of Health Care by Primary Care Organisations: An Evaluation and Guide to Future Policy.* Buckingham: Open University Press.

McGuire, A., J. Henderson, and G. Mooney. 1987. *The Economics of Health Care.* London: Routledge and Kegan Paul.

Miles, A., J. R. Hampton, and B. Hurwitz, eds. 2000. *NICE, CHI, and the NHS Reforms.* London: Aesculapius Medical Press.

Milgrom, P., and J. Roberts. 1992. *Economics, Organization, and Management.* London: Prentice-Hall.

Propper, C. 1995. Agency and Incentives in the NHS Internal Market. *Social Science and Medicine* 40: 1683–1690.

Raftery, J., R. Robinson, J.-A. Mulligan, and S. Forrest. 1996. Contracting in the NHS Quasi-market. *Health Economics* 5: 353–362.

Rivett, G. 1986. *The Development of the London Hospital System.* London: King's Fund.

—. 1998. *From Cradle to the Grave: Fifty Years of the NHS.* London: King's Fund.

Robinson, R. 2002. NHS Foundation Trusts. *British Medical Journal* 325: 506–507.

Robinson, R., and J. Le Grand, eds. 1994. *Evaluating the NHS Reforms.* London: King's Fund.

Robinson, R., and J. Le Grand. 1995. Contracting and the Purchaser-Provider Split. In *Implementing Planned Markets in Health Care: Balancing Social and Economic Responsibility,* ed. R. B. Saltman and C. van Otters. Buckingham: Open University Press.

Robinson, R., and A. Steiner. 1998. *Managed Health Care.* Buckingham: Open University Press.

Saltman, R. B. 1998. Health Reform in Sweden: The Road beyond Cost Containment. In *Markets and Health Care,* ed. W. Ranade, 164–178. Harlow: Longman.

Saltman, R. B., R. Busse, and E. Mossialos, eds. 2002. *Regulating Entrepreneurial Behaviour in European Health Care Systems.* Buckingham: Open University Press.

Shock, M. 1994. Medicine at the Centre of the Nation's Affairs. *British Medical Journal* 309: 1730–1733.

Smee, C. 2000. United Kingdom. *Journal of Health Politics, Policy and Law* 25: 945–951.

Smith, P. 2004a. The Scandal That Persuaded Ministers to "Let Go" of the NHS. *Health Service Journal*, April 1, 12–13.

—. 2004b. Foundations Will Not Take Over the Whole World. *Health Service Journal*, April 1, 3.

Stevens, A., and J. Raftery, eds. 1994. *Health Care Needs Assessment: The Epidemiologically Based Needs Assessment Reviews.* Oxford: Radcliffe Medical Press.

Sussex, J. 2001. *The Economics of the Private Finance Initiative in the NHS.* London: Office of Health Economics.

Timmins, N. 1996. *The Five Giants.* London: Fontana.

Tuohy, C. 1999a. Dynamics of a Changing Health Sphere: The United States, Britain, and Canada. *Health Affairs* 18: 114–134.

—. 1999b. *Accidental Logics: The Dynamics of Change in the Health Care Arena in the United States, Britain, and Canada.* New York: Oxford University Press.

—. 2003. Agency, Contract, and Governance: Shifting Shapes of Accountability in the Health Care Arena. *Journal of Health Politics, Policy and Law* 28: 195–215.

United Kingdom Audit Commission. 1996. *What the Doctor Ordered: A Study of GP Fundholders in England and Wales.* London: HMSO.

United Kingdom Commission for Health Improvement. 2003a. *NHS Performance Ratings: Acute Trusts, Specialist Trusts, Ambulance Trusts 2002/03.* London: Stationery Office.

—. 2003b. *NHS Performance Ratings: Primary Care Trusts, Mental Health Trusts, Learning Disability Trusts 2002/03.* London: Stationery Office.

United Kingdom Department of Health. 1989a. *Working for Patients.* CM 555. London: HMSO.

—. 1989b. *Practice Budgets for General Medical Practitioners: Working for Patients.* Working Paper 3. London: HMSO.

—. 1992. *Report of the Inquiry into London's Health Service, Medical Education, and Research* [the Tomlinson Report]. London: HMSO.

—. 1994. *The Operation of the NHS Internal Market.* NHS Executive. London: Department of Health.

—. 1997. *The New NHS: Modern, Dependable.* Cm 3807. London: Stationery Office.

—. 2000. *The NHS Plan.* Cm 4818-I. London: Stationery Office.

—. 2001. *Learning from Bristol—Report of the Public Inquiry into Children's Heart Surgery at the Bristol Royal Infirmary* [the Kennedy Report]. Cm 5207(1). London: Stationery Office.

—. 2002a. *Delivering the NHS Plan.* Cm 5503. London: Stationery Office.

—. 2002b. *Reforming NHS Financial Flows: Introducing Payment by Results.* London: Department of Health.

—. 2002c. *The Shipman Inquiry, First Report: Death Disguised* (Chair, Dame Janet Smith). www.the-shipman-inquiry.org.uk.

—. 2003. *Choice of Hospitals: Guidance for PCTs, NHS Trusts, and SHAs on Offering Patients Choice of Where They Are Treated.* London: Department of Health.

United Kingdom Department of Health and Social Security. 1969. *Report of the Committee of Inquiry into Allegations of Ill Treatment of Patients and Other Irregularities at the Ely Hospital, Cardiff.* Cmnd 3975. London: HMSO.

—. 1971. *Report of the Farleigh Hospital Committee of Inquiry.* Cmnd 4557. London: HMSO.

—. 1972a. *Management Arrangements for the Reorganised Health Service.* London: HMSO.

—. 1972b. *Report of the Committee of Inquiry into Wittingham Hospital.* Cmnd 4861. London: HMSO.

—. 1976. *Sharing Resources for Health in England: Report of the Resource Allocation Working Party* [the RAWP Report]. London: HMSO.

—. 1978. *Report of the Committee of Inquiry into Normansfield Hospital.* Cmnd 7357. London: HMSO.

—. 1979. *Patients First.* London: HMSO.

United Kingdom HM Treasury. 1961. *Control of Public Expenditure* [the Plowden Report]. Cmnd 1432. London: HMSO.

United Kingdom Ministry of Health. 1956. *Report of the Committee of Inquiry into the Cost of the National Health Service* [the Guillebaud Report]. Cmnd 9663. London: HMSO.

—. 1962. *A Hospital Plan for England and Wales.* Cmnd 1604. London: HMSO.

United Kingdom Parliament. 1942. *Social Insurance and Allied Services* [the Beveridge Report]. Cmnd 6404. London: HMSO.

—. 1988. *Fifth Report: The Future of the National Health Service.* HC 613. Social Services Committee. London: HMSO.

—. 1994. *General Practitioner Fundholding in England.* HC 51. National Audit Office. London: HMSO.

—. 1995. *Contracting for Acute Care in England.* HC 261. National Audit Office. London: HMSO.

—. 2003. *Fifth Report on Target? Government by Measurement.* HC 62–I. Public Administration Select Committee. London: Stationery Office.

Vickers, J., and G. Yarrow. 1993. *Privatization—An Economic Analysis.* London: MIT Press.

Walshe, K. 2003. *Regulating Health Care.* Maidenhead: Open University Press.

Webster, C. 1988. *The Health Services since the War. Volume 1. Problems of the National Health Service before 1957.* London: HMSO.

—. 1991. *Aneurin Bevan on the National Health Service.* Oxford: Wellcome Unit for the History of Medicine.

—. 1996. *The Health Services since the War. Volume 2. Government and Health Care. The British National Health Service, 1958–79.* London: HMSO.

—. 1998. *The National Health Service—A Political History.* Oxford: Oxford University Press.

—. 2002. *The National Health Service—A Political History.* 2nd ed. Oxford: Oxford University Press.

Weiner, J. P., and D. M. Ferris. 1990. *GP Budget Holding in the UK: Lessons from America.* London: King's Fund Institute.

Williamson, O. E. 1975. *Markets and Hierarchies.* New York: Free Press.

—. 1985. *The Economic Institutions of Capitalism: Firms, Markets, and Relational Contracting.* New York: Free Press.

Wilsford, D. 1994. Path Dependency, or Why History Makes It Difficult But Not Impossible to Reform Health Care Systems in a Big Way. *Journal of Public Policy* 14: 251–283.

Wyke, S., N. Mays, G. Bevan, N. Goodwin, G. Malbon, H. McLeod, and A. Street. 2003. Should General Practitioners Purchase Health Care? The Total Purchasing Experiment in Britain. *Health Policy* 65: 243–259.

PART 3

The allocation and distribution of resources

Introduced by Kieran Walshe

Every country's health care system faces two basic but difficult questions: how to raise money to pay for health services, and how to spend it. This part brings together a number of seminal contributions from the last two decades that address the policy challenges and complexities of the latter question – how resources for health care are or should be allocated and distributed. It is a question on which health economists (like Alan Williams and Anthony Culyer, whose work is included in the selections for this part) have often seemed to dominate debate, though as contributors like medical sociologists (Angela Coulter), political scientists (Chris Ham) and others have regularly noted, decisions about resources are not simply technical matters to be dealt with technocratically, to a set of economic rules designed to maximize some notion of utility. They are often fundamentally moral or philosophical matters, which turn on values and ideas like individual liberty and freedom of choice, social solidarity, the nature of community obligations and rights, and notions of equity or equality in health and healthcare. Concepts like 'the rule of rescue' – whether life-saving treatments, even when they are not particularly cost-effective, should have priority over other demands for resources; and the 'fair innings' – whether we should accord greater importance to the healthcare needs of the young and middle-aged than to the elderly, on the basis that each person is entitled to the opportunity of a certain lifespan – involve intensely difficult moral choices and value judgements that can spark heated debates. As such, what might sometimes seem a dry subject- – whether the health benefits, measured in quality adjusted life years, of treatment A are greater than those of treatment B – becomes at times a matter of life and death, and the stuff of newspaper headlines and TV documentaries.

The allocation of resources involves decisions about both *who* will receive funding for health services and *what* will be funded. While these two sets of decisions cannot be simply separated, it is helpful to consider them separately because they involve different sorts of choice, as the diagram below illustrates.

What treatments get funded? / **Who** gets treated?	Non-selective	Selective
Non-selective	Access to health services is open to all, regardless of who they are and what services they need. Might be seen as the 'Ideal' of a universal tax-funded health service, but in practice all health systems ration or limit access explicitly or implicitly	Access depends on who you are. For example, are you insured? Do you live in a town with good health services? Does your education and class affect your ability to seek and use services?
Selective	Access depends on what you need. For example, your insurance may only cover hospital services but not primary care or pharmaceuticals. Experimental treatments may not be included. Cosmetic procedures and treatments of known low effectiveness may be excluded	Access depends both on what you need and who you are. For example, access to infertility services may be rationed on the basis of age and medical history, while access to joint replacement surgery may be limited according to pain, mobility and capacity to benefit

Choices about who gets treated turn on how health care systems control or organize access for individuals or groups of people. For example, in a system based on private or employer-paid insurance, some people will be uninsured and their access to health services will obviously be limited (unless they are able to pay for themselves from their own pocket). They are likely to suffer greater morbidity and mortality because they do not have access to needed health services. But in a tax-funded health care system, decisions about how to allocate those tax resources may also shape or constrain access for people. If, for historical reasons, the money goes to long-established hospitals and health systems in big cities, then suburban and rural areas are likely to be underserved. Because doctors in primary care tend to go to work in affluent areas, if the money simply follows the doctors, then more economically and socially deprived areas will suffer the double injustice of getting less than their fair share of health care resources. If tax-funded budgets are capped, then once the cash runs out, access will be rationed through some sort of waiting list for treatment.

In contrast, choices about what treatments get funded turn on the way health care systems assess the value or benefit of different sorts of treatment. At its simplest, this may involve working out whether treatment A or treatment B works better for a given disease or condition. But even here, two important complications soon emerge. First, we often find that treatment A is more effective but more expensive than treatment B – so a judgement has to be made about whether the improvement in effectiveness is worth the cost. Second, we sometimes do not have two or more possible treatments – just the options of treatment A or leaving the patient untreated and allowing the disease to progress. This often leads to great pressure to 'do something' for the patient on the basis that a treatment of limited effectiveness is better than no treatment at all. However, the really difficult challenge of making choices about which treatments to fund comes when we have to compare different treatments for different patients with different conditions. Should we fund dialysis and renal transplantation services for elderly people with kidney failure, or put money into joint replacement surgery for other elderly people, or fund infertility treatment for young and middle-aged people who want to start a family, or invest in neonatal intensive care to save the lives of very premature babies? Can we make fair or meaningful comparisons in such cases, or should we even try to do so?

In some of the readings for this part, the two issues of whose health care needs should we meet and what treatments should we fund are inevitably and inextricably intertwined, but the first two papers are mainly concerned with the first question. The first reading is an extract from a thoughtful and reflective paper on equity and equality in health by Anthony Culyer and Adam Wagstaff (1993). They explore the way in which we talk and write about equity and equality – does it mean spending the same on every person, or spending proportionate to each person's health needs, or giving people equal opportunity to access healthcare, or aiming to give each person equal health benefits (in terms of their morbidity and mortality). Culyer and Wagstaff point out that these different 'equity principles' conflict, and they argue that the tenets of moral philosophy demand an approach based on equity in health, though they concede that its implementation is not straightforward. This is followed by a much less theoretically inclined and more policy-oriented paper by Finn Diderichsen, Eva Varde and Margaret Whitehead (1997) about resource allocation to health authorities. They describe how in a number of countries with tax-funded health care systems (they focus on the UK and Sweden) decisions need to be made about how to allocate resources to health care funders and providers. They outline the long history (three decades or more in the UK) of efforts to move away from patterns of resource allocation based simply on historical precedent, which served to reinforce long-standing inequalities between cities, towns and rural areas and between affluent and less affluent areas. In their place, governments put funding formulae that tried to take account of health needs and the health consequences of wider social and economic deprivation, and to redistribute resources accordingly. They outline how this approach was used in Sweden, and then highlight the political and methodo-logical challenges involved in measuring need, taking appropriate account of deprivation, and implementing changes when they involve taking money away from some parts of the healthcare system. In both countries, this kind of resource reallocation has had to be done slowly and incrementally, and has been easier at times of overall resource growth.

Then to the second question – how to make decisions about what treatments to fund. Alan Williams (1995) was a pioneering British health economist and a leading advocate of the quality adjusted life year (QALY) – invented as a currency to allow us to make comparisons between treatments on the basis of the health benefit they provide. He offers a robust defence both of the technical construction of QALYs and the moral and ethical case for making such comparisons and collective judgements, in a world where we cannot, he argues, fund all healthcare for everyone. From a much more practical perspective, David Banta (2003) describes the international growth of the health technology assessment industry, with the rise of government agencies like NICE (the National Institute for Health and Clinical Excellence) in England, established to assess new and existing health technologies, often using tools like QALYs, and to make recommendations on which treatments should be funded. He highlights many of the political and organizational challenges that arise when policy makers try to put the theories of priority setting into practice, but also makes a good argument that such systems for health technology assessment are here to stay.

The final paper examines the complex and difficult business of priority setting or rationing. Chris Ham and Angela Coulter (2001) explore the process of priority setting in practice, arguing that while the gap between what medicine can do and what society can afford has created a growing need to ration health care, our ability to make these difficult and complex decisions has lagged behind. They suggest the politics of rationing favours an implicit and incremental approach or 'muddling through', an approach discussed more fully in Part 2 of this reader. This is hard to sustain in the face of public demands for transparency, the prospects of judicial review, and pressure from stakeholders including pharmaceutical companies and powerful patient groups.

The further reading and references list contains a wide range of additional materials on the topic of allocating resources for healthcare, including an excellent edited volume of international contributions from Chris Ham and Glenn Roberts.

Summary

- Allocating resources for health services involves two related and difficult sets of questions – who will receive funding, and what services will be funded? These are complex and value-driven questions – not simply a matter of arithmetic or economics.
- Decisions about who will receive funding usually focus on ideas of equity or equality, but determining 'fairness' is difficult and depends in part on how much you hold individuals responsible for their own health and allow them to make their own decisions about health care (as they do, by and large, on education, social care and other services).
- Decisions about what services to fund are often focused on ideas of effectiveness or efficiency – what treatments work best, and how expensive they are. There have been great advances in health technology

assessment that enable us to make complex quantitative evaluations of the cost-effectiveness of treatments.
- All countries ration healthcare one way or another, and there are advantages and disadvantages to being tough and explicit about rationing decisions, or leaving latitude and scope for variation and clinical judgement.

References and further reading

Birch, S. and Gafni, A. (2004) The 'NICE' approach to technology assessment: an economics perspective, *Health Care Management Science*, 7(1): 35–31.

Braveman, P. (2006) Health disparities and health equity: concepts and measurement, *Annual Review of Public Health*, 27: 167–94.

Churchill, L.P. (1987) *Rationing Health Care in America: Perceptions and Principles of Justice*. Paris: University of Notre Dame Press.

Ham, C. and Roberts, G. (eds) (2003) *Reasonable Rationing: International Experience of Priority Setting in Health Care*. Maidenhead: Open University Press.

Macinko, J. and Starfield, B. (2002) Annotated bibliography on equity in health 1980–2001, *International Journal for Equity in Health*, 1(1): 1–20 published online: doi: 10.1186/1475-9276-1-1.

Maynard, A. (1999) Rationing health care: an exploration, *Health Policy*, 49(1): 5–11.

Mullen, P.M. (1998) Rational rationing? *Health Services Management Research*, 11(2): 113–23.

Ubel, P.A. (2000) *Pricing Life: Why it's Time for Health Care Rationing*. Cambridge, MA: The MIT Press.

Williams, A. (1988) Priority setting in public and private healthcare, *Journal of Health Economics*, 7: 173–83.

The readings

Culyer, A. and Wagstaff, A. (1993) Equity and equality in health and healthcare, *Journal of Health Economics*, 12: 431–57.

Diderichsen, F., Varde, E. and Whitehead, M. (1997) Resource allocation to health authorities: the quest for an equitable formula in Britain and Sweden, *British Medical Journal*, 315: 875–78.

Williams, A. (1995) Economics, QALYs and medical ethics: a health economist's perspective, *Health Care Analysis*, 3: 221–26.

Banta, D. (2003) The development of health technology assessment, *Health Policy*, 63: 121–32.

Ham, C. and Coulter, A. (2001) Explicit and implicit rationing: taking responsibility and avoiding blame for health care choices, *Journal of Health Services Research and Policy*, 6(3): 163–69.

9

Equity and equality in health and healthcare
Anthony Culyer and Adam Wagstaff

Extracts from Culyer A, Wagstaff A (1993). Equity and equality in health and healthcare. Journal of Health Economics, 12: 431–57.

Introduction

Equity is widely acknowledged to be an important policy objective in the health care field. Despite the relatively high profile accorded to equity by policy-makers, and despite the relatively large academic literature on equity in health care, there appears to be considerable confusion over what is meant by equity in this context. This led McLachlan and Maynard (1982) to remark somewhat cynically that '... equity, like beauty, is in the mind of the beholder ...' (p. 520). Our purpose in this paper is to try to clarify some of the confusion surrounding the term 'equity'.

Mooney and Le Grand have identified several definitions of equity in the context of health care provision, of which we explore four. The first is 'equality of expenditure per capita'. This definition, which underlies the regional budget allocation formulae used in some countries, is open to the obvious objection that it makes no allowance for 'need'. So, the second definition to be explored is 'distribution according to need'. Exploration of this definition, which is to be found in several policy documents and is frequently encountered in the academic literature, is severely hampered by the absence of agreement as to the meaning of 'need'. The third definition of equity which we explore is 'equality of access'. This definition is more common in policy documents than any other definition but, as will become apparent, there is at least as much confusion – if not more – about the meaning of the term 'access' as there is about 'need'. The fourth definition of equity we explore is 'equality of health' – a definition which underlies the Black Report [Black (1980); Townsend and Davidson (1982)] and which has produced an enormous empirical literature.

The claim that health care ought to be distributed according to 'need' is frequently encountered in both the academic literature and policy documents. The principle comes in two versions: a horizontal version (persons in equal need should be treated the same) and a vertical version (persons with greater needs should be treated more favourably than those with lesser needs). In what follows we adopt the Aristotelian version of the latter and require that persons in unequal need be treated *in proportion* to the inequality in need. Non-proportionality in respect of vertical equity may be assumed without damage to the arguments which follow. Horizontal and vertical equity by reference to need as a relevant respect are thus similar to horizontal and vertical equity in respect of, for example, desert.

The notion that access to health care ought to be the same for everyone is also a popular distributive principle in the context of health care as it is, of course, in certain other areas of social policy. Occasionally [cf. e.g. Mooney (1986)] this principle is coupled with the notion of need, the idea being that access ought to be the same for those in equal need but different for persons with different needs. In this case, therefore, the horizontal – vertical distinction arises as before.

Which equity principle should dominate?

That the equity principles will, in general, tend to conflict with one another raises the question: is there any compelling reason for selecting one in preference to the others? It is not, of course, the first time this question has been asked and before we indicate which is our preferred principle and why, it is worth going through the conclusions reached by previous writers.

Mooney's equality of access

Mooney (1983) comes out firmly against equality of utilization and equality of health, arguing that 'equality of utilization is ... too elitist. I cannot accept the notion of compulsory health care ... Equality of health is simply too expensive in terms of the other good things in life' (p. 122). Instead, Mooney favours 'equality of marginal met need', but indicates that if this 'cannot be made a practical alternative', he would opt for 'a mix of equal inputs for equal need and equal access for equal need, the mix to be determined empirically by examining the trade-off between access and health' (p. 120).

Several points seem worth making. First, we have argued that equality of marginal met need is better interpreted as an efficiency principle rather than as an equity principle. Second, we find the argument that equality of health is an unacceptable equity principle because it is too expensive rather odd. Attaining – or at least getting as close as possible to – equality of health may well entail a substantially lower per capita health status than would otherwise be the case. But that is not an argument for rejecting equality of health as an equity principle. One should not surely allow efficiency considerations to determine which equity principle is to be favoured over others, since this makes a nonsense of the notion that equity exists as a separate principle from efficiency. Third, it is unclear why equality of utilization entails an unacceptable degree of compulsion whilst equal utilization for equal need does not. The latter surely entails just as much compulsion as the former; it is just that need determines the appropriate amount of utilization in the latter but not in the former. Fourth, it is far from clear just how the proposed mix between equal access for equal need and equal inputs for equal need is to be worked out, or indeed *why* this solution is to be preferred.

More recently, in this Journal, Mooney [Mooney et al. (1991, 1992)] has come out firmly in favour of equality of access, interpreted in terms of utilization costs. One argument is that 'equality of access' is what policy-makers understand by equity. As we have indicated elsewhere [Culyer et al. (1992a, 1992b)], this argument is unconvincing. Many policy documents contain references not only to the principle of equality of access but also to the principles of distribution according to need and equality of health [cf. e.g. Le Grand (1982)]. Moreover, there is no evidence that policy-makers always share the interpretation by Mooney et al. of access as the costs incurred in receiving health care. Policies which profess to be based on the notion of equalizing access are very frequently directed at equalizing *expenditures* (often adjusted for need).

Another argument proffered by Mooney et al. is that, unlike other equity principles, equality of access does not imply a departure from Paretian welfare economics, since it respects consumer preferences. This argument is also unconvincing since it takes for granted that the value judgements underlying Paretian welfare economics ought also to be those which govern one's choice of equity principle – a premise which is at odds with the revealed preferences of policy-makers in the context of health care [cf. Williams (1976)]. That the principles of equal treatment for equal need and equality of health are inconsistent with such value judgements may, therefore, actually be a point in their favour, since they are at least candidates for what might supersede the Paretian value judgements. By the same token, that equality of access is consistent with such judgements would seem to be a point against it.

Le Grand's equality of choice sets

Le Grand (1987, 1991) rejects all the principles of equity considered in the previous sections. He rejects distribution according to need on the grounds that it fails to accord sufficient status to desert (some individuals may, by their actions – say, robbing a bank – reduce their entitlement to health care, whilst others by honourable actions – going to the rescue of a policeman under fire from the robber – increase their entitlements) and to preferences (risk averse individuals may prefer not to opt for a risky operation). He also rejects equality of access, in part because the 'equality of prices' interpretation fails to take into account that people have some control over the costs they face (people may choose to live in a remote rural area) and in part because the Olsen–Rodgers definition appears to lead inexorably towards equalizing access to *all* commodities and hence fails to face the fact that people are concerned about access to commodities such as health care but not about access to commodities such as skiing holidays. Finally, Le Grand also rejects equality of health on the grounds that it accords insufficient status to preferences (is it fair to attach as much importance to restoring the health of a smoker as it is to restoring the health of a non-smoker?).

Le Grand's favoured conception of equity is equality of choice sets. He argues that providing individuals are making choices under equal constraints, inequalities in health are not inequitable. Thus if two well-informed and otherwise identical individuals have different health statuses simply because one smokes and the other does not, the health disparity is to be deemed to be equitable. Interestingly, however, Le Grand argues that it would be *inequitable* for such differences in health-related behaviour to have *any* bearing on the way people are treated by the health care system.[1] Rather it is in the *finance* of health care that such health-related behaviour ought to be taken into account. He suggests that it would be inequitable for smokers who fall ill to be charged the full cost of their treatment, since whether or not they fall ill depends not only on whether they smoke but also on chance. Rather *all* smokers should pay an annual premium to cover the *expected* costs of treatment. Having paid this, they should then receive the same treatment (or access to treatment) as non-smokers.

There are several problems with this argument. It is surely inconsistent to claim, on the one hand, that it is equitable for health differences to exist where they are the result of different choices made from the same choice set and, on the other, that people who damage their health through their own actions nonetheless have the same rights to health care as those who look after their health. One cannot, in other words, consistently maintain that it is equitable *both* that smokers have a lower health status than non-smokers *and* that they have the same rights as non-smokers to receiving treatment to restore their health when they fall ill. If the health differences between smokers and non-smokers *are* equitable, then treatment to restore the health of smokers must surely be *inequitable*!

The problem seems to lie in the claim that it is equitable that people making different choices end up with different health statuses. If it is unfair that the health care costs associated with smoking are borne only by those smokers who fall ill, then it is surely also unfair that the distress and disability associated with smoking-related diseases be borne only by those smokers who fall ill. Just as it is fair for all smokers to pay the expected costs associated with their consumption, so too ought it to be considered fair that all smokers bear the distress and disability associated with smoking-related diseases. But since it is impractical and unethical to harm people's health deliberately (in this case the health of those smokers who do not contract any smoking-related illness), this cannot happen. The fairest option therefore would be to give smokers the same entitlements to health care as non-smokers. This provides a rationale for Le Grand's suggestion that smokers should not be treated differently by the health care system, but since it implies that smokers who fall ill will be treated, it follows both that some equity principles are required to determine the distribution of health care expenditures and that any health differences between smokers and non-smokers that are attributable to the fact that members of one group smoke while members of the other do not must be inequitable.

An alternative view

It seems to us that in order to answer the question 'which equity principle is to be preferred?', one has to answer a logically prior question, namely 'why should health care be a concern for equity purposes in the first place?'. What is it, in other words, that accounts for the facts that (i) equity considerations seem to feature prominently in discussions about the distribution of some commodities but not others (a phenomenon labelled by Tobin (1970) as 'specific egalitarianism') and (ii) health care is one of these commodities?

Le Grand's (1991) answer to this is that people demand health care because they fall ill and that, since whether or not they fall ill is not within their control, the demand for health care is qualitatively different from the demand for, say, televisions and other commodities where equity considerations do not feature prominently if at all. It is for this reason, contends Le Grand, that the term 'need' is applied to health care but not to televisions. This argument seems weak. There is, of course, a large stochastic component to the demand for health care. But an individual's health – and hence his demand for health care – is also affected by his behaviour. Once this is accepted, it becomes hard to use this line of argument to draw a meaningful distinction between health care and other commodities whose demand is also subject to uncertainty. An individual's demand for automobile spares, for example, is highly stochastic, but is also influenced by the way the individual drives and how carefully he looks after his vehicle.

A more plausible answer to the question 'what is special about commodities like health care?' is to be found, we believe, in much of the moral philosophy literature. There it is argued that entities such as 'good health' are necessary for an individual to 'flourish' as a human being.[2] Insofar as health care is necessary to 'good health', this provides a strong ethical justification for being concerned with the distribution of health care and not with the distribution of, say, automobile spares, and for using the word 'need' in the context of health care and not in the context of, say, skiing holidays.

But this raises the question: what is a fair distribution of health? It appears to be accepted in the moral philosophy literature that a position other than one in which everyone has the same opportunity to 'flourish' would be hard to defend. Insofar as health is a necessary condition for 'flourishing', it follows that a just distribution of health is an equal distribution. This also appears to follow from our remarks above concerning Le Grand's notion of equity as equality of constraints. If it is accepted that differences in health-related behaviour cannot, after all, provide a justification for differences in health, and if it is accepted that differences that are *not* attributable to different choices are unjustifiable, it would indeed appear to follow that *all* inequalities in health must be inequitable.

It follows from this that an equitable distribution of health care is simply one which gives rise to an equal distribution of health. Of course, this will almost certainly have to be qualified by a side condition that greater equality cannot be achieved by reducing the health of some as a deliberate act of policy. Moreover, to say that the fairness of a distribution of health care cannot be assessed without reference to the resultant distribution of health does not imply that *all* aspects of health care will equally the object of equitable concern. Ineffective health care cannot be of any equitable concern at all, save insofar as resources wasted in its provision are denied to uses that might promote equity. Nor, we conjecture, are some of the complementary services provided by hospitals, such as private, or semi-private rooms (save in special cases), better than two-star hotel services in hospital, or bed-side office services. It may be perfectly satisfactory for these to be allocated according to willingness-to-pay, either directly or via insurance packages whose benefits include such services and up-grades. But these provisos aside, equity in health care implies distributing health care so as to equalize health.

Our argument clearly implies a rejection of the principle of equalizing health care expenditures. It also implies a rejection of the principle of distribution according to need, since irrespective of how one interprets 'need', equality of health will not be attained if persons in equal need are treated the same and persons in unequal need are treated in proportion to the relevant inequalities. Furthermore, our argument implies a rejection of the principle of equality of access to health care, since irrespective of how one interprets access, and irrespective of whether equality of access is applied only to those in equal 'need' (however this is interpreted), application of the principle of equality of access to health care will not yield an equal distribution of health.

This does not imply, of course, that the concepts of 'need' and 'access' are irrelevant to resource allocation decisions in health care. The administration of health care which does not have a positive marginal product – and hence is not 'needed' – seems hard to defend on either efficiency or equity grounds. The notion of 'need' thus picks out which resources are to be distributed. What it does not do is indicate the appropriate distribution of these resources. Access to health care also has a part to play, since policy-makers are unlikely to want to coerce people into consuming health care against their wishes. What policy-makers *can* do is alter the size and shape of the individuals' feasible sets (and hence alter their 'access') in the hope that they will consume the appropriate type and amount of health care. But this will not entail giving everyone the same access, irrespective of how access is defined, or even giving, say, everyone with the same capacity to benefit the same access. Rather it will involve manipulating feasible sets in such a way that the post-treatment distribution of health will be as close to being equal as is feasible. There is, however, one sense in which 'equality of access' would appear to be a necessary condition for getting as close as possible to an equal distribution of health, namely equality of access to diagnosis. But it ought to be more than merely equal. It should also be cheap. The allocation of effective treatments so as to promote greater equality of health can, after all, only be done if output functions have been determined first.

The objective of health equality cannot be an absolute ethical imperative for there may be other conditions to meet with which it may conflict if individuals are to 'flourish' and to flourish more equally. One way of tempering the apparent severity of the objective is to invent a social welfare function (SWF) embodying inequality-of-health aversion [cf. Wagstaff (1991)]. Another would be to adopt specific weights in a SWF that accorded the health of some a higher priority than that of others (say, on grounds of desert). It may, moreover, be that the claim of equal liberty is more conducive to an equitable distribution of 'flourishing' than is an equal distribution of health and which would provide both a warrant for discretionary choices of treatment[3] and for refusing even highly effective treatments (such as the right of Jehovah's Witnesses to decline potentially life-saving blood transfusions). Despite these qualifications, however, (which would apply, *mutatis mutandis,* to the other equitable principles for determining the interpersonal allocation of health care), we consider that equity as 'equality of health' has substantial advantages over the other principles in this paper. Moreover, it is grounded in a more general and fundamental egalitarian objective (viz. equal 'flourishing').

Enduring gross inequalities in lifetime health and their systematic association with other dimensions of deprivation are a notable feature of wealthy societies, even those with a long-standing political rhetoric of equality. The removal of such gross inequalities is not in self-evident conflict with liberty or other primary goods, and may indeed serve to promote equal liberty for all and a more effective enjoyment of other primary goods. Allocation in proportion to need (equal allocation for equal need; proportionately greater allocation for greater need) may actually serve to widen these gross inequalities in health – a possibility that highlights the most apparent deficiency of allocation principles built on need: that they lack a plausible equitable distributive purpose. The pursuit of equality of health provides an answer to the question 'which needs ought to be met?', which the other principles signally fail to do. What, after all, is ethically compelling about an allocation of resources that matches resources to sickness, or capacity to benefit, or marginal capacity to benefit, or that ensures equal access? If they have any ethical attraction at all, they have it only insofar as they promote efficiency in maximizing health. But even if these principles do promote efficiency in this sense (and it is far from self-evident that they do), to be efficient is not the same thing as to be equitable. And if it is ethically important to maximize health, may it not also be important to ensure its equitable distribution too?

Conclusions

We have demonstrated that previous analyses of interpersonal equity in the distribution of health care are subject to serious objections. Moreover, they are, in general, mutually incompatible. We have attempted to develop an analysis that is free from these objections. The mutual incompatibility of previous analyses (and of our's with each of them) forces one to choose. The ultimate criterion that we propose for evaluating the equity of distributions of health care is (conditional) equality of health, which is, in turn, a necessary condition for (conditional) equality of 'flourishing'. In this (consequentialist) sense, the 'demand' for equity in health care is a 'derived demand' from the equality of health and acquires its especially compelling nature – in contrast with some other forms of consumption – from the compelling character of health and 'flourishing'. Equality of health is conditional upon a respect for personal preferences (or, in medical ethics, the principle of 'autonomy') and upon a prohibition on reductions in current health (flow or stock interpretation).

All equity claims seem to derive from egalitarian claims. Even libertarian claims for the equity of inequalities of holdings and portfolios of personal characteristics are typically based on a claim of equal liberties for each. Within the sphere of health, we have argued that equality of health is a preferable equity goal to other contenders, such as equality of marginal products or equal expenditures for equal needs. Similarly, in considering vertical equity, we have argued that resource allocation in proportion to differential needs (of whatever type) is likely to lead to inequity in the distribution of health.

The analysis leaves unsettled a number of questions which remain for further investigation. One of these is the way in which health equality may be traded off against other desiderata (there is a similar agendum for other research programmes in health-related distributional questions, such as the trade-off between such desiderata and the fair meeting of need according to other criteria of fairness). Another concerns the interpersonal comparison of health for individuals of different ages (which is particularly important when health is interpreted as a stock). Another concerns intergenerational issues and the manner in which poor health may be transmitted from one generation to another by, for example, poor quality parenting. A further area of enquiry generalizes the latter issue by asking about the non-medical determinants of health and ill-health, the non-medical determinants of 'flourishing' and would seek to develop a more general theory of the equitable distribution of every (relevant) thing.

References and further reading

Aday, L.A. and R. Andersen, 1975, Access to medical care (Health Administration Press, Ann Arbor).

Barry, B., 1965, Political argument (Routledge and Kegan Paul, London).

Barry, B., 1991, Political argument (Harvester Wheatsheaf, Hemel Hempstead).

Black, D., 1980, Inequalities in health (HMSO, London).

Braybrooke, D., 1987, Meeting needs (Princeton University Press, Princeton, NJ).

Collins, E. and R. Klein, 1980, Equity and the NHS: self-reported morbidity, access and primary care, British Medical Journal 281, 1111–1115.

Culyer, A.J. 1976, Need and the National Health Service (Martin Robertson, Oxford).

Culyer, A.J. 1978, Need, values and health status measurement, in: A.J. Culyer and K.G. Wright, eds, Economic aspects of health services (Martin Robertson, London).

Culyer, A.J. 1989, The normative economics of health care finance and provision, Oxford Review of Economic Policy 5, 34–58.

Culyer, A.J., E. van Doorslaer and A. Wagstaff, 1992a, Comment: Utilisation as a measure of equity, Journal of Health Economics 11, 93–98.

Culyer, A.J., E. van Doorslaer and A. Wagstaff, 1992b, Access, utilisation and equity: A further comment, Journal of Health Economics 11, 207–210.

Daniels, N., 1985, Just health care (Cambridge University Press, Cambridge).

Davis, K., 1993, Equity and health care policy: The American experience, in: E. van Doorslaer, A. Wagstaff and F. Rutten, eds, Equity in the finance and delivery of health care: An international perspective (OUP, Oxford).

Gillon, R., 1986, Philosophical medical ethics (Wiley, Chichester).

Gilson, L., 1988, Government health care charges: Is equity being abandoned?, Publication Number 15 (Evaluation and Planning Centre for Health Care, London School of Hygiene and Tropical Medicine).

Le Grand, J., 1978, The distribution of public expenditures: The case of health care, Economica 45, 125–45.

Le Grand, J., 1982, The strategy of equality: Redistribution and the social services (Allen and Unwin, London).

Le Grand, J., 1984, Equity as an economic objective, Journal of Applied Philosophy 1, 39–51.

Le Grand, J., 1987, Equity, health and health care, Social Justice Research 1, 257–274.

Le Grand, J., 1991, Equity and choice (Harper Collins, London).

Lockwood, M., 1988, Quality of life and resource allocation, in: M. Bell and S. Mendus, eds, Philosophy and medical welfare (Cambridge University Press, Cambridge).

McCloskey, H.J., 1976, Human needs, rights and political values, American Philosophical Quarterly 13, 1–11.

McLachlan, G. and A. Maynard, 1982, The public/private mix in health care: The emerging lessons, in: G. McLachlan and A. Maynard, eds, The public/private mix in health care: the relevance and effects of change (Nuffield Provincial Hospitals Trust, London).

Miller, D., 1976, Social justice (Clarendon Press, Oxford).

Mooney, G., 1983, Equity in health care: Confronting the confusion, Effective Health Care 1, 179–185.

Mooney, G., 1986, Economics, medicine and health care (Wheatsheaf, Brighton).

Mooney, G., J. Hall, C. Donaldson and K. Gerard, 1991, Utilisation as a measure of equity: Weighing heat?, Journal of Health Economics 10, 475–480.

Mooney, G., J. Hall, C. Donaldson and K. Gerard, 1992, Reweighing heat: Response to Culyer, van Doorslaer and Wagstaff, Journal of Health Economics 11, 199–205.

Nordenfeldt, L., 1984, On the circle of health, in: L. Nordenfeldt and B.I.B. Lindahl, eds, Health, disease and causal explanations in medicine (Reidal, Dordrecht).

O'Donnell, O. and C. Propper, 1991, Equity and the distribution of UK National Health Service resources, Journal of Health Economics 10, 1–20.

Olsen, E.O. and D.L. Rodgers, 1991, The welfare economics of equal access, Journal of Public Economics 45, 91–106.

Puffer, F., 1986, Access to primary care: A comparison of the US and UK, Journal of Social Policy 15, 293–313.

Salkever, D.S., 1975, Economic class and differential access to health care: Comparisons among health care systems, International Journal of Health Services 5, 373–395.

Steele, R., 1981, Marginal met need and geographical equity in health care, Scottish Journal of Political Economy 28, 186–195.

Thatcher, M., 1989, Foreword to Working for patients: The health service, caring for the 1990s (HMSO, London).

Tobin, J., 1970, On limiting the domain of inequality, Journal of Law and Economics 13, 263–278.

Townsend, P. and N. Davidson, 1982, Inequalities in health: the Black report (Penguin, Harmondsworth).

Van Doorslaer, E., A. Wagstaff and F. Rutten, eds, 1993, Equity in the finance and delivery of health care: An international perspective (OUP, Oxford).

Wagstaff, A., 1991, QALYs and the equity-efficiency trade-off, Journal of Health Economics 10, 21–41.

Wagstaff, A., E. van Doorslaer and P. Paci, 1991, On the measurement of horizontal equity in the delivery of health care, Journal of Health Economics 10, 169–205.

Weale, A. 1978, Equality and social policy (Routledge and Kegan Paul, London).

Wiggins, D., 1984, Claims of need, in: T. Honerich, ed., Morality and objectivity (Routledge and Keegan Paul, London).

Wiggins, D., 1987, Need, values, truth (Basil Black well, Oxford).

Williams, A., 1974, Need as a demand concept (with special reference to health), in: A.J. Culyer, ed., Economic policies and social goals (Martin Robertson, London).

Williams, A., 1976, Cost-benefit analysis in public health and medical care: Comments on a thesis written by Bengt Jönsson, Report 1976:28 (Department of Economics, University of Lund).

Williams, A., 1978, Need: An economic exegesis, in: A.J. Culyer and K.G. Wright, eds., Economic aspects of health services (Martin Robertson, London).

Williams, A., 1986, The cost-benefit approach to the evaluation of intensive care units, in: D. Reis Miranda and A. Langehr, eds., The ICU: A cost-benefit analysis (Elsevier, Amsterdam).

Williams, B., 1962, The idea of equality, in: P. Laslett and W.G. Runciman, eds., Philosophy, politics and society (Basil Blackwell, Oxford).

Williams, B., 1973, Utilitarianism: For and against (Cambridge University Press, Cambridge).

Notes

1   This argument appears, in fact, only in the 1987 version of Le Grand's article.
2   Cf. e.g. Braybrooke (1987), Daniels (1985), Gillon (1985), Lockwood (1988), Miller (1976), Wiggins (1987).
3   The effectiveness of most treatments is so uncertain, so frequently contingent upon individual circumstances, and so bound up with individual attitudes to

risk and uncertainty, that the scope for personal discretion, even within a health care system that is tightly constrained by insurers or governments to offer only 'effective' health care, is extremely broad. There is a danger in straining out the gnat of offending personal liberty that one swallows the camel of enduring and outrageous inequalities of health.

10

Resource allocation to health authorities: the quest for an equitable formula in Britain and Sweden
Finn Diderichsen, Eva Varde and Margaret Whitehead

Extracts from Diderichsen F, Varde E and Whitehead M (1997) Resource allocation to health authorities: the quest for an equitable formula in Britain and Sweden. British Medical Journal 315: 875–878.

In recent years countries with very different healthcare systems have been showing increasing interest in resource allocation policies based on weighted capitation. In countries whose healthcare systems have competing health insurers the main concern has been to construct capitation formulas that prevent favourable risk selection or "cherrypicking". Reforms to the American Medicare programme and Dutch healthcare proposals have stimulated renewed efforts to find a way of overcoming this problem.[1] [2] [3] [4]

Countries with national health services, such as the United Kingdom and Sweden, have also experienced far-reaching reforms of health care, with important implications for equity in access to care.[5] [6] Risk selection should be less of a problem, at least with health authority purchasing, as the population is assigned to a purchaser based on area of residence. The new role of local purchaser, however, calls for more exact methods to allocate "purchasing power," because local areas will show stronger variation in relative need than regions and counties.

We outline British experiences in attempting to devise an equitable formula then present the new model that we have developed in Sweden for Stockholm County Council. We discuss what lessons these experiences hold for other countries facing a similar challenge.

British developments

In Britain serious attempts to devise more equitable mechanisms for resource allocation for the NHS date back to the 1970s, when it became clear that funding to the regions based on historical activity had perpetuated the inequalities in funding that existed before the NHS. Since then, development work has gone through three distinct phases.[7]

In the first phase the formula created by the Resource Allocation Working Party was developed for distributing resources from central government to regions. It used mortality in each area as an indicator of healthcare need.[8] The formula was in use from 1977–90 and gradually managed to redistribute resources from the metropolitan regions to the poorer regions in the north.[9]

In the second phase the argument that the measurement of need should be based on empirical data led to a new formula for weighted capitation, applied from 1991 to 1995.[10] This empirical approach was severely criticised on methodological grounds and because it seemed inequitable.[11] [12] [13] [14] [15] [16]

Clearly, the Department of Health needed a more sophisticated model for allocating funds directly to local districts now that they were purchasers. It commissioned health economists at York University to develop a more sensitive, empirically based model, to be incorporated into a third allocation formula from April 1995 onwards.

The York model is based on an ecological study of small areas to identify the determinants of use of hospital services.[17] [18] The need variables identified include both health and socioeconomic factors (Table 10.1). In addition, statistical models were developed to distinguish several confounding influences on the use of services, such as the supply of hospital beds and general practitioners. The effect of applying the formula in full at the district level would be to redistribute funds towards poorer, inner city areas.[18] The Department of Health decided, however, that the full York model would apply to only 76% of funding and the new arrangements would be introduced only gradually over several years. Other adjustments for "market forces" were also added. In effect, these adjustments watered down the full potential of the York model to allocate resources equitably. As about 70% (£23bn a year) of NHS funding is distributed through these formulas, even slight adjustments can make a big difference to local allocations.

Is a demographic profile of the population adequate for determining health need and therefore resource allocation?

Table 10.1 Need variables used in the current British formula for resource allocation (York model)[18]

Need variables	General and acute model	Psychiatric model
Standardised limiting long standing illness ratio <75	✔	
Standardised mortality ratio <75	✔	✔
Proportion of economically active people who are unemployed	✔	
Proportion of people of pensionable age living alone	✔*	✔*
Proportion of dependents in single carer households	✔	
Proportion of persons in single parent households		✔
Proportion of dependants in no carer households		✔
Proportion of adult population permanently sick		✔
Proportion of population born in New Commonwealth		✔

*These variables are included in both models but with different coefficients.

Table 10.2 Matrix (abridged version) used in Stockholm for resource allocation to hospital care showing cost (Kr per inhabitant) spent by health authorities in Stockholm County Council, 1994

Age of inhabitant (years)	Acute and non-acute medical and surgical care		Psychiatric care	
	Owner occupied home	Rented home	Owner occupied home	Rented home
0 to <1	7200*		0	0
1–24	1900	2100	400	600
25–64 cohabiting:				
Higher non-manual	3100	3600	400	800
Lower/intermediate non-manual	3700	4300	600	900
Manual	4000	4400	900	1300
Not employed	5300	6400	1400	2400
25–64 living alone:				
Higher non-manual	3600	3900	900	1600
Lower/intermediate non-manual	3600	4200	1000	2400
Manual	3900	4600	1400	3800
Not employed	5100	6400	4900	12 700
65–84 years:				
Cohabiting	13 500	16 500	500	1000
Living alone	15 400	18 200	1100	2100
≥85 years:				
Cohabiting	27 600	29 800	300	1000
Living alone	24 200	29 400	500	1000

*Split between both categories of housing.

New approach in Sweden

Like Britain, Sweden has a national health service, publicly funded and provided. Of the total healthcare budget of Kr82bn (£8bn), 82% comes from regional income taxes raised by the 26 county councils responsible for administering health care.

This regional funding has until recently been distributed directly to public hospitals and primary care centres on the basis of historical activity, adjusted for inflation. This has changed in the past four years in counties that have introduced an internal market. In particular, Stockholm has been at the forefront of the introduction of a purchaser-provider split, and associated developments in resource allocation have consequently gone further than in the other counties.

Stockholm County Council serves a population of 1.7 million with a healthcare budget of £1,6bn. Most (90%) of the county budget is distributed to nine health authorities, each covering populations of between 50 000 and 300 000.

Basis of model

The contrasting features of the Swedish and British approaches are listed in the box. Individual level analysis was chosen not only because of the practical availability of data but also because of the problems inherent in ecological analysis.[19] [20]

Distinctive features of resource allocation in Sweden and Britain

Sweden (Stockholm model)

- Need for health care is measured by demographic and socioeconomic variables rather than mortality or other health status indicators.
- Analysis is based on individual level data rather than at a small area (ecological) level.
- Actual, rather than estimated, relative costs of health care used.

Britain (York model[17] [18])

- Need is measured by mortality, self reported morbidity, and various socioeconomic variables.
- Analysis based on an ecological study of small areas to identify the determinants of impatient services.
- The estimates are adjusted for the confounding influences of supply on geographic variations in use.
- Estimated costs of health care are used.

Finding a direct indicator of health status for measuring healthcare need that could be linked to individual use of health care and cost data proved difficult. The model therefore uses various socioeconomic indicators as proxies for healthcare need, over and above that created by the demographic profile of the population. The choice was based on evidence showing that use of hospital services in Sweden was proportional to the relative need of major socioeconomic groups.[21] [22] Higher use by more socially disadvantaged groups is assumed to translate into higher costs of care, for which health authorities need to be funded.

Psychiatric services, however, were used at a low level by non-Nordic immigrants, perhaps not reflecting all their needs.[22] Immigrant status was therefore excluded from the analysis. A different model was devised for primary care (not reported here).

Statistical analysis

The analysis makes use of the personal identification number, which everyone in Sweden has and which can link healthcare records with census and other socioeconomic databases. Since a new system of payment was introduced in 1994, actual costs of care billed to purchasers have also been available for each individual in the population. The analysis has four main stages.

Stage 1—We created two new databases each year, linking the records on healthcare use and related costs to data on age, sex, socioeconomic group, education, cohabitation and marital status, country of birth, and housing conditions. One database covered a 30% random sample of the country's population, containing their socioeconomic characteristics and any health care they had used. The other database included all people with inpatient care and their background variables.

Stage 2—We then tested different models (with multivariate Poisson regression of outpatient and inpatient episodes) to select the demographic and socioeconomic variables that had the greatest effect on use, controlling for other variables. The variables selected by this process for the final model were (*a*) age in 10 classes; (*b*) socioeconomic groups in four groups based on occupation and employment (education for pensioners); (*c*) cohabitation and marital status in four classes; and (*d*) housing in five classes, according to tenure and size. Sex was not included in the final model. The effect of including sex made a negligible difference to the distribution of resources as the distribution of men and women did not differ between districts.

Stage 3—A matrix was constructed in which each cell represented a unique combination of the selected variables. In each cell, weights were calculated equal to average costs per inhabitant. Separate weights were calculated for acute medical and surgical care, non-acute care, and psychiatric care. Because actual costs were not available for psychiatry, the costs for this specialty were estimated on the basis of number of bed days and outpatient visits. Table 10.2 shows an abridged version of the matrix.

Stage 4—A corresponding matrix with the number of inhabitants in each of the nine health authority areas was then constructed, and each individual was ascribed a weight based on their social and demographic characteristics. These weighted individuals were then summarised for each area and the budget calculated as a proportion of the total sum for the whole county council (Table 10.3).

Table 10.3 Per capita weighting for the nine health authorities in Stockholm County Council, according to Stockholm model, 1995–7

Health authority	Per capita weights		
	Interim model, 1995	1996	1997
Norrtälje	98.5	96.4	100.6
North east	96.7	96.6	97.9
North west	91.4	94.5	94.2
Central Stockholm	127.7	120.3	119.2
West Stockholm	99.1	100.3	98.6
South Stockholm	122.7	116.3	117.4
South west	97.6	99.5	98.1
South east	83.4	85.9	86.2
Södertälje	93.0	96.0	95.7
Whole Stockholm county	100*	100*	100*

*100=Kr9166 per inhabitant in 1995; Kr9082 per inhabitant in 1996; Kr8979 per inhabitant in 1997.

Implementation

The model has been applied gradually in calculating health authority budgets in Stockholm County Council since 1992. Before 1996, costs were estimated from the number of admissions and bed days, whereas the 1996 budget was based on actual costs for the purchasers.

Overall, the model has allocated more resources for the care of people living in more disadvantaged socioeconomic circumstances (Table 10.2). The resulting ranking of authorities in Table 10.3, based on these costs, follows the known differentials in health, demographic, and socioeconomic factors in the county.[23]

The interim model used in 1995, based on estimated costs, allocated a large share of the budget to areas containing a high proportion of elderly people and people living alone. As the year unfolded, it became apparent that the interim model might have overcompensated for the costs of providing health services for elderly people. In fact, central Stockholm, with the highest proportion of elderly people, could not spend all its allocated budget, whereas the suburban areas with young families ran up budget deficits. When actual costs became available for the 1996 model, it was found that each bed day was cheaper for elderly than for younger age groups. In 1996 therefore the share of the budget was reduced for central and south Stockholm and increased for suburban areas (a shift of 1.4% of the budget) (Table 10.3). Politically, this was seen as too great a shift to be achieved in one year. The county council therefore gave extra funds in the 1996 allocation to the authority hardest hit by the redistribution.

Insights from these developments

What are the lessons from these British and Swedish experiences? In both countries the principle has been firmly established that healthcare resources should be distributed in proportion to the relative needs of local populations. It is a step forward that serious attempts are being made to translate this principle into practice, but the quest for improvements continues.

Making best use of available data

The experiences illustrate two different ways of going about the task, largely determined by the need to make the best use of whatever data are routinely available in each country. This has led to an analysis based on area of residence (ecological analysis) in Britain and an approach based on data from individuals in Sweden. Several commentators have concluded that individual level analysis is the better option, to reduce the problems of confounding and misclassification.[24] [25] The Swedish approach has made the most of the opportunity offered by newly available individual data, though this was the only practicable option for Sweden because the small numbers obtained from area based data would have made the resulting statistical models unstable. It did, however, restrict the choice of indicators of need. For example, no suitable health indicators were available that could be linked to the other individual level data.

The York model has to rely on data for small areas, not directly linked to individuals, which brings added problems of interpretation. On the other hand, with care it can include additional local data on mortality and morbidity, increasing its sensitivity to geographical variations that are not simply the sum of individual variations in the basic sociodemographic characteristics.

Proxies for need

Both the British and Swedish approaches are based on the assumption that the different needs for health care of the various sections of the population are matched by their differential use of services. But in practice the use of services is influenced not only by legitimate need but also by supply and many other socioeconomic factors, so the match is not perfect. Given the circumstances, informed judgments have to be made on the most practical solutions. The Swedish decision, for example, to leave out an indicator of "ethnic group" from the final analysis was based on the evidence that non-Nordic immigrants have higher psychiatric morbidity but a relatively low rate of use of psychiatric services.

Incorporating a factor based on use by ethnic group would have led to fewer resources being allocated to health authorities with large immigrant populations.

Taking deprivation into account

Both approaches consider it essential to take social and material deprivation into account. They have both selected employment factors and living alone as important indicators of increased need for healthcare resources. Sweden has added indicators of poorer housing, and Britain has added households containing singlehanded carers (including single parents) as well as direct health indicators.

Two new relevant findings emerge from the Swedish data on differential costs of care. Firstly, the analysis of actual costs for care of different groups provides a direct demonstration of the higher costs incurred by more disadvantaged groups in the population and the need for extra resources in areas where the proportion of people from these groups is greatest. Secondly, the comparison of estimated costs in 1995 with actual costs in 1996 revealed the scale of the bias introduced when only estimated costs are used. A similar problem with estimated age-cost weights was encountered in the British formula introduced in 1991, when it was applied to populations at district level.[16]

Political reality

Both experiences illustrate the highly political nature of resource allocation. The Swedish model ran into some difficulties when quite large shifts had to be achieved in the switch from the interim model in 1995 to the full model in 1996, particularly as the overall funding per inhabitant was falling over the same period. Although full implementation was agreed for 1996, a one-off compensation, as mentioned above, was given to the authority that stood to lose the most. Agreement on full implementation for 1997 was politically easier, as the shifts in funding were not as great.

In 1995 the York model was not implemented in full in Britain because of the government's nervousness over the size and direction of the implied shifts in resources, generally from suburban towards poorer areas. Identifying two separate models (Table 10.1) allowed room for subsequent manoeuvre. There are even suggestions now that the market forces factor, introduced into the British formula by the Department of Health, is seriously undermining the model's attempt to allocate resources according to need.[26]

This illustrates the need to ask continually whether the policy as implemented is achieving its original objectives of equitable resource allocation.

Effects of cost containment

Finally, both approaches illustrate the complications of trying to devise and implement an equitable formula in a time of cost containment, when any redistribution of resources is much more painful. Some commentators suggest that the strain imposed by the prolonged underfunding of the British NHS in the 1980s was a key factor in the decision to overhaul the original formula created in the late 1970s.[13] The drastic cuts that have had to take place in Sweden in the 1990s with the economic recession mean that the effects of resource allocation are not easy to disentangle from the effects of cutbacks.

Yet it is at just such times that efforts need to intensify. The joint effects of cutbacks and market-style reforms could be especially damaging to access to healthcare for the sections of the population in greatest need, as in a more competitive environment resources tend to flow to more prosperous areas and groups. It is important that the quest for equitable methods of resource allocation continues and is taken up by the growing number of other countries facing a similar challenge.

Summary

- The United Kingdom and Sweden face similar problems in how to achieve a fair allocation of resources within a purchaser-provider system.
- In contrast with the British formula, the new Swedish approach is based on individual level data and uses demographic and socioeconomic variables as proxy measures of healthcare need.
- The Swedish model incorporates actual, rather than estimated, costs of care.
- The resulting model allocates proportionately more resources to populations with poorer health and socioeconomic characteristics.
- Both the Swedish and British approaches illustrate the practical problems and the highly political nature of resource allocation.
- These experiences hold important lessons—not least for the growing number of other countries with a similar quest.

Notes

1   Newhouse J, Manning W, Keeler E, Sloss E. Adusting capitation rates using objective health measures and prior utilisation. *Health Care Financing Review* 1989;10:41–54. [Medline]

2   Brown RS, Hill JW. The effects of Medicare risk HMOs on Medicare costs and service utilization. In: Luft HS, ed. *HMOs and the elderly*. Ann Arbor, MI: Health Administration Press, 1994.

3   Van Vliet RCJA, Van den Ven WPMM. Towards a capitation formula for competing health insurers. An empirical analysis. *Soc Sci Med* 1992;34:1035–48.

4   Van Vliet RCJA, Van den Ven WPMM. Capitation payments based on prior hospitalizations. *Health Economics* 1993;2:177–88.

5 Whitehead M. Who cares about equity in the NHS? *BMJ* 1994; 308:1284–7.
6 Diderichsen F. Market reforms in health care and sustainability of the welfare state. *Health Policy* 1995;32:141–53.
7 Mays N. Geographical resource allocation in the English national health service 1971–94: the tension between normative and empirical approaches. *Int J Epidemiol* 1995;24:96–102.
8 Department of Health and Social Security. *Sharing resources for health in England: report of the resource allocation working party.* London: HMSO, 1976.
9 Holland W. The RAWP review: pious hopes. *Lancet* 1986;ii:1087–90.
10 NHS Management Board. *Review of the resource allocation working party formula.* London: Department of Health and Social Security, 1988.
11 Judge K, Mays N. Allocating resources for health and social care in England. *BMJ* 1994;308:1363–6.
12 Mays N. NHS resource allocation after the 1989 white paper: a critique of the research for the RAWP review. *Community Med* 1989;11:173–86.
13 Sheldon T, Carr-Hill R. Resource allocation by regression in the NHS: a critique of the RAWP review. *J R Stat Soc A* 1992;155:403–20.
14 Sheldon T, Davey Smith G, Bevan G. Weighting in the dark: resource allocation in the new NHS. *BMJ* 1993;306:835–9.
15 Royston G, Hurst J, Lister E, Stewart P. Modelling the use of health services by populations of small areas to inform the allocation of central resources to larger regions. *Socioeconomic Planning Science* 1992;26:169–80.
16 Raftery J. Capitation funding: population, age, and mortality adjustments for regional and district health authorities in England. *BMJ* 1993;307:1121–4.
17 Carr-Hill R, Sheldon T, Smith P, Martin S, Peacock S, Hardman G. Allocating resources to health authorities: development of methods for small area analysis and use of inpatient services. *BMJ* 1994;309:1046–9.
18 Smith P, Sheldon T, Carr-Hill R, Martin S, Peacock S, Hardman G. Allocating resources to health authorities: results and policy implications of small area analysis of use of inpatient services. *BMJ* 1994;309:1050–4.
19 Diderichsen F, Spetz C-L. *Need based planning in health care.* Stockholm: National Board of Health Care and Social Welfare, 1987. (In Swedish.)
20 Morgenstern H. Uses of ecological analysis in epidemiological research. *Am J Public Health* 1982;72:1336–44.
21 Health policy targets and need based planning. *Health care in the 1990s.* Stockholm: Allmänna Förlaget, 1984:40–1. (In Swedish.)
22 Haglund B. *Equity in care.* Stockholm: National Board of Health and Welfare (Socialstyrelsen), 1994:3. (In Swedish.)
23 Diderichsen F, ed. *Public health report 1994.* Stockholm: Stockholm County Council, 1995. (In Swedish.)
24 Benzeval M, Judge K. The determinants of hospital utilisation: implications for resource allocation in England. *Health Economics* 1994;3:105–16.
25 Carr-Hill R, Rice N, Roland M. Socioeconomic determinants of rates of consultation in general practice based on fourth national morbidity survey of general practices. *BMJ* 1996;312:1008–13.

26 Hacking J. Capitation funding: is it worth the weight? *Health Service Journal* 1996;18 Jan:26–7.

11

Economics, QALYs and medical ethics: a health economist's perspective
Alan Williams

Extracts from Williams A (1995) Economics, QALYs and medical ethics: a health economist's perspective. Health Care Analysis 3: 221–226.

Introduction

This paper explores how medical practice ought to be conducted, in the face of scarcity, if our objective is to maximise the benefits of health. After explaining briefly what the cost-per-QALY criterion means, a series of ethical objections to it are considered one by one. The objectors fall into four groups:

a. those who reject *all* collective priority-setting as unethical;
b. those who accept the need for collective priority-setting, but believe it is contrary to medical ethics;
c. those who accept the need for collective priority-setting, and do *not* believe that it is contrary to medical ethics, but reject the role of QALYs in it;
d. those who accept the need for collective priority-setting in principle, but are unwilling to specify how it should be done in practice.

The purpose of this discussion paper is to give each group a hard time!

Economics is about scarcity. Quality Adjusted Life Years (QALYs) are about the benefits of health care. *Medical ethics* are about the way in which medical practice ought to be conducted. This paper is therefore about how medical practice ought to be conducted, in the face of scarcity, if our objective is to maximise the benefits of health care.

Commonsense tells us that in the face of scarcity we should use our limited resources in such a way that they do as much good as possible. In health care, 'doing good' means improving people's life expectancy and the quality of their lives. Since people value *both* of these fundamental attributes of life, we need a measure of outcome which incorporates both, and which reflects the fact that most people are willing to sacrifice some quality of life in order to gain some additional life expectancy, and vice versa. This is precisely the role of the Quality Adjusted

Life Year. If some health care activity would give someone an extra year of healthy life expectancy, then that would be counted as one QALY. But if the best we can do is provide someone with an additional year in a rather poor state of health, that would count as less than one QALY, and would be lower the worse the health state is. Thus the QALY is to be contrasted with measures such as 'survival rates', commonly used as the sole success criteria in clinical trials, which implicitly assume that only life expectancy is of any concern to people. The essence of the QALY concept is that effects on life expectancy and effects on quality of life are brought together in a single measure, and the bulk of the empirical work involved in making the concept operational is concerned with eliciting the values that people attach to different health states, and the extent to which they regard them as better or worse than being dead. For the purpose of priority-setting in health care, being dead is regarded as of zero value. A QALY measure can in principle embrace any health-related quality-of-life characteristic that is important to people. The particular measure with which I am most familiar (the Euroqol measure) covers mobility, self-care, usual activities, pain-discomfort, and anxiety/depression. Note that 'usual activities' are whatever the individual's usual activities are, and are not restricted to work activities. So although developed primarily by economists, the QALY is not a measure of people's economic worth, but a measure of whatever aspects of life they themselves value.

In the presence of scarcity, resources devoted to the health care of one person will be denied some other person who might have benefited from them. Clinicians are quite used to this phenomenon with respect to the allocation of their own time, and of any other resources that they control as practice managers. They are trained to discriminate between those who will benefit greatly from treatment and those who won't, and by this means 'clinical priorities' are established, which are based on some broad assessment of risks, benefits and costs. The role of costs here is crucial, because they represent sacrifices made by other potential patients who did not get treated. Thus the economists' argument that medical practice should concentrate on those treatments that are known to be cost-effective, is designed to ensure that the benefits gained by the treatments that are actually provided should be greater than the benefits sacrificed by those who were denied treatment. That is what 'doing as much good as possible with our limited resources' means.

Objections

I am constantly amazed at how controversial these commonsense propositions seem to be. Priority-setting is inevitably painful, and its consequences are bound to be unfortunate for someone or other. It is therefore understandable that many people cling, with childlike naivety, to the romantic illusion that if only more resources were devoted to health care they can escape from the process altogether. But when more resources are made available, we still have to decide which are the highest priority uses to which they should be put, so this is really no escape route at all.

The more interesting and substantial objections come from those who accept the fact of scarcity, and are willing to face up to its implications, but reject the approach I have outlined. They fall into four groups:

1. those who reject *all* collective priority-setting as unethical;
2. those who accept the need for collective priority-setting but believe that it is contrary to medical ethics;
3. those who accept the need for collective priority-setting, and do not believe that it is contrary to medical ethics, but reject the role of QALYs in it;
4. those who accept the need for collective priority-setting in principle, but are unwilling to specify how it should be done in practice.

By 'collective priority-setting' I mean priority-setting intended to guide the use of public resources devoted to health care. I will summarise the key points at issue for each group in turn.

Is all collective priority-setting unethical?

Those who reject all collective priority-setting as unethical typically assert that it is immoral for one person to sit in judgement on the worth of other people's lives, which is what collective priority-setting requires us to do. However, since they accept the fact of scarcity, they acknowledge that some people must be denied the benefits of health care, but they want that done in a manner which is free of any interpersonal judgements of relative worth. They believe that this can be done by recourse to a lottery. The trouble with this supposed solution is that lotteries do not fall like manna from heaven, but have to be devised and run by people, who have to determine who shall be eligible, when, and under what conditions, for each and every treatment that is on offer. So recourse to a lottery simply brings us back to the very same priority-setting issues that it was supposed to avoid. They simply appear in a different context, i.e. determining who is eligible to enter the lottery, and with what probability they may win each prize.

Instead of seeking to avoid the making of interpersonal judgements of life's value, it seems more fruitful to seek as much detachment as possible when making them. An entirely different sort of lottery could have an important role to play in that process. What I have in mind is the thought experiment involved in approaching collective priority-setting from behind the 'veil of ignorance'. We have to imagine ourselves outside the society of which we are members, and then choose that set of rules for collective priority-setting which would be most likely to achieve the distribution of health benefits that we think best for our society. Then, and only then, will we be assigned, *by lottery*, an actual place in that society. We may find ourselves favoured by our rules, or we may be one of the unfortunate people who are disadvantaged by them, but we would have achieved a set of rules which we would have to accept as fair. The question which I would ask the reader to consider is whether, under these conditions, *you* would choose a set of rules which would maximise the health of the community as a whole, as measured in QALY terms, and, if not, why not?

Is collective priority-setting contrary to medical ethics?

My second group of objectors are those who accept the need for collective priority-setting, but believe that it is contrary to medical ethics. In the extreme, such people believe that it is the doctor's duty to do everything possible for the patient in front of him or her, no matter what the costs. But in a resource-constrained system 'cost' means 'sacrifice' (in this case the value of benefits foregone by the person who did not get treated). Thus 'no matter what the costs' means 'no matter what the sacrifices borne by others'. This does not sound to me like a very ethical position to be in. Indeed, people who behave regardless of the costs of their actions are usually described as 'fanatical', not as 'ethical'. Moreover, if medical ethics include an injunction to deal justly with patients, then there *has to be* some weighing of the benefits to one person against the sacrifices of another. So I think that this supposed ethical conflict between the economists' argument that costs (i.e. sacrifices) must be taken into account *in every treatment decision*, and the precepts of medical ethics, is non-existent, because medical ethics does *not* require everything possible to be done for one patient no matter what the consequences for any of the others.

Why might QALYs be unethical?

My third group consists of those who accept the need for collective priority-setting, and do not believe that it is contrary to medical ethics, but cannot accept the QALY approach to it. There seem to be four distinct ethical issues raised here. First, whose values should count? Second, how should we move from individual values to group values? Third, should we not be concerned with the distribution of the benefits of health care across different people, as well as with the total amount of such benefits? Fourth, are there other benefits from health care which QALYs do not pick up. I will tackle each of these in turn.

Whose values should count?

Whose values should count? As a health economist it is really not for me to say. Nor, as a health economist, do I have to say, because the QALY concept is extremely accommodating in this respect. In principle it can accept anybody's views about what is important in health-related quality of life, and anybody's views about the trade-off between length and quality of life. In practice, the early empirical work was based on professional judgements (mostly those of doctors). More recent work has been based on the views of patients and of the general public, and my own work has concentrated on the latter, because I am anxious to find out whether the values of the practitioners, their patients, and the general public coincide. What the QALY concept does, quite properly, is bring this question to the fore, and points up the difficulties that are likely to arise if the priorities of a particular group of patients differ from those of their doctors or of the wider society of which they are part. In principle, since every treatment decision entails benefits to some and disbenefits to others, in a democratic society the views of *all* affected parties should count. Since the sacrifices involved in treating particular groups of patients will be widely spread and difficult to identify with any precision, this points inexorably to the general public as the most appropriate reference group. Some people have advocated using the values of a particular reference group as the collective view (e.g. the views of the most disadvantaged, or of people with particular moral, legal or political authority). At a personal level I feel distinctly uncomfortable about such proposals, preferring a simple populist stance. But, as I said earlier, adoption of the QALY approach does not require you to adopt this particular stance, although I must confess that it is one that I personally find very compelling.

Individual values or group values?

How should we move from individual values to group values? Once again, as a health economist, who am I to say? Once again, I don't have to say, because there is nothing in the QALY approach which requires aggregation to be accomplished in any particular way. But collective priority-setting does require a collective view, so *some* method of aggregation has to be adopted, and whatever method is used, it will have strong ethical implications. The simplest method is to postulate that everybody's views count equally, and a simple average is then taken to represent the collective view. A somewhat more complicated position is involved in taking the median view as the collective view. The median view is the one that would command a simple majority in a voting system. With a skewed distribution of values (which is what is commonly found) it gives less weight to extreme views than would the taking of a simple average. But whichever position is taken on this issue, the QALY approach has the great advantage that it is not possible to hide what you have done, so it is quite easy for others to tease out the ethical implication and help ensure that you are held accountable!

Is the distribution of QALYs important?

The next set of objections to the QALY approach concentrates on whether simple maximisation of health (with all its utilitarian overtones) is really an adequate representation of social objectives in the health care field, or whether we are not also concerned with how the benefits of health care are distributed with the population. My theme here is the same as before ... there is nothing in the QALY approach which requires QALYs to be used only in a maximising context, although it was QALY *maximisation* that I asked you to think about earlier as a collective prioritising rule. The use of QALYs in more complex rules is perfectly possible, and almost certainly needed if collective priority-setting is to reflect the views of the general public. The simplest and commonest use of QALY calculations at present is based on the assumption that a year of healthy life expectancy is to be regarded as of equal value to everybody. Note that this does not say that it is of equal value to everybody, because that is unknowable. What it says is that if that social judgement is appropriate, then what follows from it will be appropriate. If it is not, then what follows will be irrelevant. A strong egalitarian case could be made for that assumption, since it implies that it does not matter at all who the beneficiary is. Like Justice, it is Blind. There is no discrimination on grounds of race, sex, occupation, family circumstances, wealth or influence. In this respect it follows precisely the assumptions underlying the use of the more conventional outcome measures used in clinical trials, which just count the number of people with the specified outcomes characteristic. But following hallowed tradition may not carry much weight if a sizeable majority of the general public would prefer some discrimination between potential beneficiaries according to their personal characteristics or circumstances. For instance, there is ample evidence that most people (including the elderly) would give extra weight to benefits accruing to young people over the same benefits accruing to old people. There is a similarly widespread view that people with young children should have some priority over their childless contemporaries. It is quite possible to build these differential weightings into QALY calculations, the implication being that instead of maximising *unweighted* QALYs, we would need to weigh them according to the relative priority assigned to the particular characteristics of the beneficiary. There are some especially interesting issues concerning the preferential treatment of the poor. The general principle, which is widely assented to, is that access to health care should not depend on people's wealth. This implies that it should not depend on people's *lack* of wealth either! So discrimination in favour of the poor seems inconsistent. But if it is desired to use the health care system as a way of compensating people for other deprivations they suffer, then again, QALYs can be weighted accordingly.

Are there benefits other than health improvements?

Last in this group of objectors are those who assert that there are other benefits from health care than improvements in health. There obviously are. For instance, the provision of health care generates a livelihood for millions of people. Moreover, some people get satisfaction from health care in ways which do not show up as improved health. But the question is, how relevant are these other benefits for priority-setting in health care? To the extent that health improvements are the dominant consideration, then QALYs, in some form or other, must be the dominant concept, on the benefit side, in collective priority-setting. If the improvement of health plays only a subsidiary role, then QALYs will play only a subsidiary role. There seems little more to be said, except possibly to challenge those who reject QALYs to say what they believe the main benefits of health care are, if they are not improvements in the length and quality of people's lives.

Fine in theory – but unacceptable in practice?

This brings me to my final set of people, those who accept the need for collective priority-setting in principle, but are unwilling to specify how it should be done in practice. At a personal level they have my sympathy, because of all the difficulties I have outlined. But at a professional level I feel somewhat aggrieved by their behaviour, because a typical stance is to point out all the difficulties involved with some particular approach, and then to sit on the fence waiting for the next candidate to come by, and then do the same again. This would be fine if the implied ideal method were available to us, or if we could suspend all health care decision-making until it were. But there is no perfect system on offer, and we can't wait. As with a well-conducted clinical trial, the new has to be compared systematically, according to preselected criteria, with what already exists. This is what needs to happen in the field of priority-setting. If the same criteria as are used to criticise the QALY approach were used **in an even-handed way** to criticise current practice, or any feasible alternative to it, how would these *other* methods make out?

So let me end with my favourite Maurice Chevalier story. When he was getting quite old he was asked by a reporter how he viewed the ageing process. 'Well' he said 'there is quite a lot I don't like about it, but it's not so bad when you consider the alternative!'

Perhaps the same is true of the QALY approach to collective priority-setting in health care. If so, we should beware of rejecting potential improvements simply because they fall short of perfection!

12

The development of health technology assessment
David Banta

Extracts from Banta D (2003) The development of health technology assessment. Health Policy 63: 121–32.

Introduction

Health technology assessment (HTA) was first conceptualised in about 1976.[1] During the last decade, the field has grown remarkably, especially in Western Europe, and it gains visibility and support everyday. At the same time, important related evaluation activities, such as the Cochrane Collaboration (CC) and the evidence-based medicine (EBM) movement, have also developed.

This paper attempts to answer three questions:

1) Why has the evaluation of health interventions grown so rapidly?
2) Whose interests are driving this development?
3) What can be expected from HTA in the future?

An important point to keep in mind is that the context of HTA is crucial. The health system of any country reflects its history, its culture, and many values and preferences. The same applies to HTA, which is part of that health system. Therefore, any global conclusions concerning HTA can only be partial and tentative, and may risk excessive dependence on partial evidence, anecdote and stereotype.

Furthermore, those working in HTA are not academics. They are not involved in comparative analysis of what they do and why. Nor are they under any pressure to develop conceptual clarity. Instead, they are involved in the demanding, everyday business of trying to help policy-makers solve difficult problems. Therefore, even good descriptions of HTA activities are hard to find. As to answering why a particular country has chosen a particular model for its programme and a particular model of HTA, such information is just not available in a formal and analytical sense.

A historical perspective on health technology

Despite the long history of health technology, effective therapies were rare until recently. In 1980, Beeson compared treatments recommended in a 1927 textbook of medicine to those recommended in 1975. He rates the value of 60% of the remedies in 1927 as harmful, dubious, or merely symptomatic, while only 3% provided fully effective treatment or prevention.[2] By 1975, effective regimens increased sevenfold and dubious ones decreased by two-thirds.

Technology can be simply defined as: "... the systematic application of scientific or other organised knowledge to practical tasks".[3] This definition, in its breadth, emphasises the pervasiveness of technology. Health care technology may be defined as "The drugs, devices, and medical and surgical procedures used in healthcare, and the organisational and supportive systems within which such care is provided".[4] Thus, a cardiac monitor is a technology. At the same time, an intensive care unit—one of its component parts being the monitor—is itself also a technology.

Scientific evaluation is largely a development of very recent times. Throughout recorded history, physician assessment has had an important role in the selection of therapy. Most studies, however, utilised personal and anecdotal information.[5] The singlemost important problem with this early research was lack of a control or comparison group to assure that the observed effect was in fact due to the intervention.

It was not until Bradford Hill formulated the principles of the randomised controlled clinical trial (RCT) in the mid-1930s that scientific assessment began to be accepted. The first randomised, controlled, double blind study was directed by Hill and tested a vaccine for pertussis (whooping cough). Hill also collaborated with Daniels in developing a randomised clinical trial of streptomycin in tuberculosis, published in 1948.[5] By 2002, hundreds of thousands of RCTs have been carried out. Cost-benefit and cost-effectiveness analyses (CEA) is a development of the 20th century; the growth in the number of CEAs in health care began in the mid-1960s.[6] In recent years, a great effort has gone into developing more standardised and valid methods of economic appraisal.[7]

A landmark in the development of the field of HTA was the 1972 publication of Archie Cochrane's book *Effectiveness and Efficiency*.[8] He proposed a thoroughgoing reform of health care evidence generation: "Its [the RCT's] importance cannot be exaggerated. It opened up a new world of evaluation and control which will, I think, be the key to a rational health service"([8], p. 11). Cochrane noted that "the increase in input since the start of the NHS has not been matched by any marked increase in output in the 'cure' section" ([8], p. 67). He advocated a "marked increase in knowledge through applied medical research", referring particularly to randomised controlled trials to determine the efficacy (benefits) of interventions ([8], p. 78). With rare prescience, he suggested that the then Department of Health and Human Services "might organise applied medical research to meet the need of assessing medical research priorities and assuring that appropriate research was carried out" ([8], p. 79). The United Kingdom actually did set up such a programme in 1990.[9] Cochrane recognised that an increase in applied medical research would result in a probable decrease in clinical and administrative freedom ([8], p. 81).

Development of HTA

The term HTA was first used in the United States Congress in about 1967, and the U.S. Congressional Office of Technology Assessment (OTA) was established in 1972. The general definition of technology assessment used was: "a comprehensive form of policy research that examines the short- and long-term social consequences of the application or use of technology" ([1], p. 45). In the health field, OTA recognised that assessment would emphasise "efficacy", since the goal of health care is to improve health. The impact of health technology depends on its pervasiveness; it touches virtually everyone's life. Nonetheless, an important motivation for development of the field was the rising expenditures for health care. Therefore, costs and cost-effectiveness analysis have also been an important part of HTA, gaining increasing attention.[10]

Simultaneous with the beginnings of the OTA in the U.S., Swedish researchers began to evaluate selected health care technologies. The pressures were similar: high expenditures for health care, the visibility of new technologies, and the necessity to begin to rationalise health care technology.[11] As the ideas of technology assessment gradually spread to other countries, formal technology assessment activities started.[12] During the 1990s almost all Member States of the European Union (EU) developed national and regional public HTA agencies and programmes.

Much of what the OTA did in its early years was transferred readily to other industrialised countries, especially in Europe. Assessments were done in similar style, focusing on effectiveness and cost-effectiveness. Policy analysis, however, has not been as central a part of technology assessment in Europe. In part this is because policy analysis in the broader sense is not as developed in Europe as it is in the United States. Nevertheless, technology assessments done in Europe have tended to pay more attention to broader social implications, especially issues such as ethics and threats to solidarity.

In the United States, technology assessment has not been effectively established within the national government. The Congress established a national programme, the National Centre for Health Care Technology (NCHCT) in 1978,[13] but it was abolished in 1981 as the result of budget cuts. The OTA was itself abolished in 1997 because of cuts in the Congress' own budget.

With time, HTA began to operationalise its original definition of technology as "applied knowledge". The term "medical technology" was more-or-less dropped, to be replaced by "health care technology". Within the last few years, the term "health technology" has been more favoured. This change goes hand-in-hand with the change in focus of HTA.

The CT scanner was OTA's first target for HTA. Other early assessments dealt with coronary artery bypass surgery, radical mastectomy, and other common and expensive surgical procedures. Assessments of intensive care units and diagnostic equipment and tests were also undertaken. Over time, other areas of health care have become the subject of assessments in HTA programmes. Nursing care, mental health care, physiotherapy, and the doctor–patient relationship have been the subject of assessments in recent years. The focus of HTA has shifted away from technology to focus more often on health needs in what is sometimes termed "needs-based technology assessment".[14] Again, the term health technology has been increasingly operationalised. For example, assessments of strategies to help people quit smoking, including the use of tax policies or regulations concerning smoking in public places, have been carried out. The scope of HTA today is enormous, potentially covering all determinants of health.

Beginning in 1987 in Sweden, formal public HTA programmes associated with ministries of health developed in Western Europe, and in many other countries of the world.

Discussion

It seems obvious to say that HTA has developed and grown up in a time of heightened concern for rising health care expenditures, associated in part with rapid technological change. These expenditures and their apparently obvious link to new technologies helped lead to a search for the "culprit".[15] The culprit seems to be technology, associated with the ageing of the population and increased population demands. At the same time, clinicians and researchers have produced growing evidence of poor quality of care, use of ineffective and untested technology, and overuse and inappropriate use of technology.[11] This has led to calls for "value for money" in health care.

In effect, concerns about expenditures have drawn attention to technology, its benefits and harms. Clinicians and clinical epidemiologists have laboured to produce evidence of this poor quality when it occurs; and policy-makers have, in general, been sensitive to this evidence. However, despite considerable media attention to these problems, the general public in most countries has not yet been drawn into a public debate, nor into the search for solutions.

Despite early concerns about social and ethical issues surrounding the development and diffusion of health technologies, these have been relatively invisible in the growing field of HTA. In effect, the field has been driven since its early days by policy-makers' concerns about expenditures (costs). With time, quality concerns have become increasingly prominent. Clinicians, especially those dedicated to EBM, have advocated a new form of practice, which would address quality directly. Managers and administrators have generally not yet actively embraced HTA.

The future of HTA

The future is not easy to predict. One thing is clear, however. The linkage of HTA and formal policy-making has its limits. Formal policies provide a structure for administrative and clinical decisions, but they leave a great deal of freedom to make decisions, especially with physicians. For this reason there is increasing attention given to the dissemination and implementation of HTA.[16] In essence, this means actions at the operational level of clinical medicine.[17] There is also increasing discussion of the importance of involving the lay public in these matters.

As Cochrane observed more than 20 years ago, the development of better and better information to guide decisions seems to imply a decrement in professional and managerial freedom.[8] This judgement seems correct. As better and better evidence for benefits and cost-effectiveness becomes available, it seems unlikely that practice not in accord with the evidence will be tolerated by consumers and policy-makers. Coverage decisions are already made more and more frequently based on HTA. Still, implementing HTA results into clinical practice remains a formidable challenge.

International co-ordination and co-operation is not yet well-developed, but it seems to offer large advantages in the future. The main reason for this is the sheer magnitude of the task. Thousands of health technologies need to be assessed. Many of these have never been assessed and remain unproven. Others are efficacious for some indications but are over-used. The task of identifying candidates for assessment, synthesising the evidence, and, where necessary, carrying out prospective research such as RCTs, is the work of many years.

Notes

1   Office of Technology Assessment. Development of medical technology: opportunities for assessment. Washington DC: U.S. Government Printing Office, 1976.

2   Beeson KPB. Changes in medical therapy during the past half century. Medicine 1980;59:79–99.

3   Galbraith J. The new industrial state. New York: The New American Library, Inc, 1977:31.

4   Office of Technology Assessment. Assessing the efficacy and safety of medical technologies. Washington DC: U.S. Government Printing Office, 1978.

5   Bloom BS. Controlled studies in measuring the efficacy of medical care: a historical perspective. International Journal of Technology Assessment in Health Care 1986;2:299–310.

6   Elixhauser A, Luce B, Taylor W, Reblando J. Health care cost-benefit and cost-effectiveness analysis from 1979 to 1990: a bibliography. Paper delivered to Academy for Health Services Research and Health Policy Annual Meeting (AHSR), 1992.

7   Davies L, Coyle D, Drummond M. Current status of economic appraisal of health technology in the European Community: report of a network. Social Science and Medicine 1994;38:1601–7.

8   Cochrane A. Effectiveness and efficiency. Abingdon: Burgess & Son, 1972:11.

9   Peckham M. Research and development for the National Health Service. Lancet 1991;33:367–71.

10 Office of Technology Assessment. The implications of cost-effectiveness analysis of medical technology. Washington DC: U.S. Government Printing Office, 1980.

11 Banta H David, Bryan Luce. Health care technology and its assessment, an international perspective. Oxford: Oxford University Press, 1993:223–36.

12 Banta, H. David, Gelband, Hellen, Jonsson, Egon, Battista, Renaldo. Health care technology and its assessment in eight countries, Health Policy 1994;30(1–3) (special issue).

13 Perry S. The brief life of the National Centre for Health Care Technology. New England Journal of Medicine 1982;307:1095–100.

14 Feeny D, Guyatt G, Tugwell P. Health care technology: effectiveness, efficiency and public policy. Montreal: The Institute for Research on Public Policy, 1986:41.

15 Altman S, Blendon R, editors. Medical technology: the culprit behind health care costs? Washington DC: U.S. Department of Health, Education, and Welfare (DHEW Publication No. PHS 79-3216), 1979.

16 Battista R, Banta HD, Jonsson E, et al. Lessons from the eight countries. In: Banta HD, Gelband H, Battista R, Jonsson E, editors. Health care technology and its assessment in eight countries. Washington DC: U.S. Government Printing Office, 1995:335–54.

17 Granados A, Jonsson E, Banta HD. EUR-ASSESS project subgroup report on dissemination and impact. International Journal of Technology Assessment in Health Care 1997;13:220–86.

13

Explicit and implicit rationing: taking responsibility and avoiding blame for health care choices
Chris Ham and Angela Coulter

Extracts from Ham C and Coulter A (2001) Explicit and implicit rationing: taking responsibility and avoiding blame for health care choices. Journal of Health Services Research and Policy 6(3): 163–69.

Introduction

In an era of ever-increasing medical possibilities, publicly financed health care systems face the challenge of determining what services should be covered for the insured population. This challenge, usually referred to as health care rationing or priority-setting – terms we shall use interchangeably – has led governments in a number of countries to take a more systematic approach to the determination of service coverage than has usually been the case in the past. Specifically, policy-makers in these countries have encouraged explicit debate about priority-setting, starting in the second half of the 1980s and continuing into the 1990s. In so doing, they have built on efforts to strengthen health technology assessment and to determine coverage of pharmaceuticals in order to address priority-setting in the round.

One of the earliest examples was the US state of Oregon, whose work to draw up a list of priorities for Medicaid as a way of expanding population coverage has been widely studied and reported.[1] The experience of Oregon finds echoes in countries as diverse as Denmark, Finland, Norway, Sweden, the Netherlands, New Zealand, Israel and now the UK as policy-makers seek to square the circle of increasing demands and limited resources.[2] In all of these systems, work has been undertaken to develop more explicit approaches to rationing at a macro level in recognition that diffusing blame and muddling through may no longer be sufficient. In parallel, there have been efforts to strengthen decision-making at the meso and micro levels in recognition that responsibility for rationing is located at many different points. This work can be seen as an attempt by policy-makers to supplement political bargaining over the allocation of health care resources with efforts to puzzle more intelligently about priority-setting. This paper summarises the results of these efforts and assesses the implications for those charged with making rationing decisions.

Rationing all around the world

Experience in systems that have sought to be more systematic in their approach to determining what services should be covered for the insured population demonstrates the menu of possibilities available to health policy-makers in setting priorities at a macro level. Despite the attention given in health policy debates to the development of a basic benefits package or a set of core services, only in Oregon's Medicaid programme has the priority-setting dilemma been addressed mainly by excluding certain categories of treatments from funding. In Oregon this was done by drawing up a list of condition–treatment pairs and ranking these in order of priority.

When it was implemented in 1994, the Oregon Health Plan funded 565 out of 696 treatments, the main exclusions being treatments for minor medical conditions or those for which evidence of effectiveness was lacking. In taking this approach, policy-makers in Oregon were seeking to increase population coverage by limiting service coverage, although even the original Oregon Plan included some services that had previously been outside Medicaid, such as dental care. Subsequent revisions have tended to increase the scope of service coverage to the extent that most treatments are now covered.[3] An example is cochlear implants, which were added to the list of funded services when new evidence on the benefits offered by implants became available.

Oregon aside, those responsible for rationing have adopted an approach centred on the development of national frameworks to guide priority-setting rather than on defined lists of treatments or services to be covered. The Netherlands and New Zealand exemplify this approach. In the Netherlands, politicians have shied away from the exclusion of services from funding after flirting with this strategy. One of the reasons for their reluctance to go down the road of exclusions was criticism from groups opposed to the removal of services from funding. An example was the proposal to exclude funding of contraceptive pills from coverage in the Netherlands, a proposal that was withdrawn after opposition from women's groups and family planning organisations. Similarly, in New Zealand, the government-appointed Core Services Committee declined to draw up a list of services to be publicly funded, even though it was charged with this task. The view of the Committee was that priority-setting was best approached not by limiting service coverage but by determining how services could be targeted on those patients most likely to benefit. In both the Netherlands and New Zealand, effort has focused on the development of evidence-based guidelines intended to ensure that services are provided appropriately.

Research into explicit rationing at a macro level demonstrates that there are no simple or technical solutions that can resolve the dilemmas facing decision-makers. As Oregon discovered, techniques drawn from economics designed to compare the costs and outcomes of health technologies are not sufficiently developed to provide a reliable basis for decision-making.[4] This was starkly illustrated by the ranking of tooth-capping above appendicectomy in the original Oregon list. Anomalous results of this kind show the difficulties of applying economic analysis in practice and also reveal gaps in the availability of information on costs and benefits.

Yet, even if information were more complete, the results of economic analysis would still have to be interpreted by policy-makers in the process of determining priorities, given that the aim of health policy is not simply to maximise health gain for the resources available. As an example, the pursuit of equity may result in resources being allocated to services for which the cost of achieving a certain quantum of benefit is greater than for alternatives. Trade-offs of this kind are made all the time in health policy and indicate the potential incompatibility of efficiency and equity objectives.

Those responsible for priority-setting therefore have to confront the need to make decisions in conditions of incomplete information and likely conflicts between objectives. While one response has been to seek to fill the gaps in information and to refine the tools to support decision-making – for example, through an investment in health technology assessment and evidence-based medicine – another approach has been to widen the debate beyond the experts (whether physicians or economists) to include other stakeholders. An important motivation in this context is that choices in health care involve making judgements about the relative priority to be attached to different objectives and services. It follows that these choices need to be informed by an understanding of community preferences if they are to gain acceptance among those affected.

Public involvement in rationing

It was for this reason that decision-makers in Oregon, for example, sought to strengthen their approach by drawing on public consultation and evidence of community values in determining priorities for Medicaid. Other systems have also endeavoured to engage the public in debate about rationing and a wide range of methods have been used for this purpose. In part, this has been stimulated by a concern to inform the public about the inevitability of rationing, and in part it has been designed to use the public's views to inform decision-making.

The need to make trade-offs in health care rationing has also led to an interest in clarifying the values that should guide decision-making. In some systems, such as in the Netherlands, Oregon and Sweden, values have been defined explicitly, whereas in others they have emerged implicitly. The work done on values has been used to aid the process of rationing by identifying criteria for making choices and in some cases for ordering priorities. A distinctive feature of the Swedish approach is the attempt to rank values, the highest priority being attached to respect for human dignity, followed by solidarity or equity and then by efficiency.[5] The experience of Sweden reinforces our earlier observation on the potential conflict between objectives.

With few exceptions, the articulation of values has remained a high-level activity and little effort has been put into the use of values in decision-making or in day-to-day clinical practice. As a consequence, there is often a gap between the proposals put forward by government committees and expert groups in relation to rationing and what happens at the meso and micro levels. This is most apparent in the case of countries like Norway and Sweden where the emphasis has been placed on the promulgation of ethical frameworks at a macro level to guide decision-making. The impact of such frameworks, based on the identification of core values rather than core services, is difficult to determine precisely because they are expressed in general terms and their effects have not been fully evaluated.

Set against this, explicit rationing may result in more resources being allocated to the health care budget if the approaches adopted are sufficiently specific to expose areas of underfunding and unmet need. This was one of the effects of the Oregon Health Plan in that the legislature voted more resources for Medicaid to enable the cut-off point for funding to be lowered when the effects of maintaining previous funding levels became transparent. Similarly, in New Zealand, the government provided extra funds to reduce waiting lists for surgery when it was possible to identify patients who would benefit from treatment but were not receiving it because of financial constraints. Experience in Israel reinforces this point, with the government there increasing the health care budget to enable new and relatively expensive drugs for cancer care to be included in the benefits package following publicity demonstrating the denial of treatment to patients (including children) in need.[6]

The politics of rationing

One clear conclusion from experience so far is the sheer messiness of health care decision-making and the inherently political nature of priority-setting. The allocation of scarce resources between competing demands is both an economic challenge and a political puzzle. Giving higher priority to one service means giving low priority to another when budgets are fixed, and the evidence indicates that this is likely to stimulate lobbying among those groups affected. One of the reasons political leaders have been reluctant to engage in explicit rationing at a macro level in the past is that in determining priorities they are also accepting responsibility for what may be unpopular choices. This helps to explain why politicians in most countries have declined to ration by excluding treatments or services from funding even though priority-setting has become more explicit.

In these circumstances, there is a tendency for policy-makers to seek to avoid blame either by ducking tough choices or by devolving responsibility to others. Rationing by guidelines rather than exclusions is one manifestation of this in that it leaves ultimate responsibility for deciding who should get access to health care resources to agencies such as sickness funds and health authorities at the meso level and to physicians at the micro level. The tendency of political leaders to avoid blame for rationing is consistent with research into the motivations of politicians.[7] It is also congruent with the findings of research into comparative social policy demonstrating that retrenchment strategies are more likely to take the form of relatively incremental and invisible initiatives than direct cut-backs.[8]

Partly because of this, but also because of the obstacles to developing more systematic approaches, some writers argue that muddling through is a virtue rather than a sin and that whatever its weaknesses is to be preferred to the fruitless quest for a technical 'fix'. In other words, disillusion with the results of systematic attempts to setting priorities is used to justify the status quo ante and to caution against the pursuit of more 'rational' solutions. This is the contention of, among others, Mechanic, who argues that implicit decision-making offers greater flexibility in circumstances in which judgements about treatments are surrounded by uncertainty and the needs of patients are diverse.[9] Mechanic acknowledges that explicit approaches have a part to play at the macro and meso levels, but even so he maintains that these approaches are liable to political manipulation and are not sufficiently responsive to change. Mechanic's view is endorsed by Hunter, who contends that 'muddling through elegantly' is the most that can be expected and who is even more sceptical than Mechanic about the desirability of explicitness.[10]

A related argument is advanced by Klein, who is sympathetic to the case for muddling through but places greater emphasis on the need to strengthen the institutional basis of decision-making. Writing as a policy analyst, Klein sees priority-setting as 'inescapably a political process' in which debate and discussion between different interests are inevitable.[11] It follows from this that the challenge is to devise mechanisms for addressing the intractable questions involved, while being cautious about the likelihood of finding answers. Klein is here echoing Holm's analysis of experience in the Nordic countries which points to the increasing interest in transparent and accountable decision-making processes at a macro level rather than the pursuit of technical solutions.[12]

As Holm shows, policy-makers in these countries have turned their attention to ways of strengthening decision-making processes to generate legitimacy for rationing as the limits of technical approaches have been exposed. Specifically, expert committees in both Denmark and Norway have made proposals for widening the debate about priority-setting and involving a range of stakeholders. The importance of transparent and accountable decision-making processes is reinforced by Daniels and Sabin's analysis of limit-setting decisions in managed care organisations. On the basis of their analysis, Daniels and Sabin set out four conditions that have to be met to demonstrate 'accountability for reasonableness':[13]

1   *Publicity condition*: decisions regarding coverage for new technologies (and other limit-setting decisions) and their rationales must be publicly accessible.
2   *Relevance condition*: these rationales must rest on evidence, reasons and principles that all fair-minded parties (managers, clinicians, patients, and consumers in general) can agree are relevant to deciding how to meet the diverse needs of a covered population under necessary resource constraints.
3   *Appeals condition*: there is a mechanism for challenge and dispute resolution regarding limit-setting decisions, including the opportunity for revising decisions in the light of further evidence or arguments.
4   *Enforcement condition*: there is either voluntary or public regulation of the process to ensure that the first three conditions are met.

The relevance of these conditions has been demonstrated in studies of priority-setting decisions in the UK as well as the USA, suggesting that the characteristics of defensible decision-making apply regardless of differences in the funding and provision of health care. This was clearly illustrated by the case of Child B, in which an English health authority that declined to fund further intensive treatment for a girl with end-stage leukaemia found itself vulnerable because of weaknesses in the decision-making process.[14] The common thread in both North American and European experience is the need to show that the way in which priorities are set is fair and reasonable even if agreement on the outcome is not possible. A similar motivation can be detected in New Zealand where the work of the Core Services Committee (since renamed the National Health Committee) has given particular emphasis to raising public awareness of priority-setting in health care and bringing choices out into the open.[15] Having made this point, those involved in this work recognise that much remains to be done to promote public involvement in and understanding of priority-setting. In other words, just as techniques drawn from economics and other disciplines are still in the process of development, so too methods of public participation and stakeholder debate need to be refined.

A new synthesis?

To articulate these arguments is to illustrate that approaches to priority-setting do not simply involve a choice between muddling through implicitly or pursuing systematic and explicit alternatives. Our reading of the international evidence is that these and related dichotomies fail to capture the complexity of rationing in practice. Put another way, the policy learning that has occurred in the decade or so since political leaders in Oregon and elsewhere grasped the nettle of explicit priority-setting has highlighted not only the absence of technical solutions but also the need to join together approaches that have often been presented as alternatives.[16]

The argument can be taken a stage further by invoking the debate between Klein and Williams that formed the centrepiece of the second international conference on priorities in health care.[17] Writing as an economist, Williams challenged Klein's contention (see above) that strengthening the institutional basis of rationing was the issue that needed most urgent attention. Rather, Williams maintained that effective priority-setting required clarity about objectives, information about costs and outcomes, and the ability to measure performance. In other words, Williams reasserted the case for technical solutions. For his part, Klein responded that the key task was less to refine the technical basis of decision-making than to construct a process that enabled a proper discussion to occur given that questions of rationing 'cannot be resolved by an appeal to science'.

Our view is that the debate between Williams and Klein is a defining example of the false antitheses that have been so much in evidence in discussions in this field, even accepting that their respective positions may have been artificially polarised for the purpose of debate. The choice available to policy-makers is not between more information and stronger institutions; rather it is how the work of institutions can be enhanced through the provision of better information and other mechanisms. Expressed in the language used earlier in this paper, the challenge is to improve both technical approaches *and* decision-making processes to enable the judgements that lie behind rationing to be as soundly based as possible. In relation to techniques, this means developing further the work of economists and others to inform decisions on priorities. And in relation to decision-making processes, it entails developing institutions capable of using these techniques and also of involving the public and other stakeholders in debating priorities and making choices.

To make this point is to suggest that strengthening information and institutions also involves transcending another dichotomy – namely, that concerning the role of experts and lay people in rationing. The challenge here is to find ways of enhancing the contribution of the public in its many different guises alongside that of experts. International experience testifies to the efforts that have been made to consult the public and to promote democratic deliberation in health care through the use of surveys, focus groups, consensus conferences and other methods. In parallel, the advice of experts has been drawn on through membership of government commit-tees set up to advise on priority-setting and use of the findings of evaluative research. A new synthesis requires that the input of both experts and lay people is seen as legitimate and relevant to decision-making on priorities and that continu-ing efforts are made to find the most appropriate mechanisms for securing this input. This has recently been recognised in the UK with the proposal to set up a citizens' council to advise the national agency charged with advising government on priority-setting.

Similar considerations apply to the debate about the comparative advantages of explicit and implicit decision-making. As experience shows, the choice between explicit and implicit rationing hinges on how political leaders deal with controver-sial choices when they arise. In the case of Israel, for example, an explicit approach to the determination of additions to the services that should be covered was combined with the imposition of limits on an implicit basis. Confirming our reading of international experience, analysts of this approach have concluded that 'The Israeli case suggests that explicit and implicit approaches to rationing and priority-setting are not exclusive alternatives but rather complementary tools which support each other'.[6]

Much the same applies in the UK, which is belatedly following the example of the other countries reviewed here through the establishment of the other countries reviewed here through the establishment of the National Institute for Clinical Excellence (NICE) to advise politicians on priority-setting. The modus operandi of NICE follows (unconsciously) the precepts of Daniels and Sabin with a commitment to transparency and accountability in decision-making on the funding of new technologies. This explicit approach goes hand in hand with a continuation of implicit decision-making in many other aspects of rationing within the National Health Service (NHS), including the decisions that physicians make on the implementation of NICE guidelines and advice. Explicit rationing at a macro level is in this way combined with implicit rationing at a micro level. And at the meso level, health authorities have adopted both explicit and implicit approaches in discharging their responsibilities.[18–20]

The other element of the new synthesis is the use of exclusions as well as guidelines in addressing the priority-setting dilemma. We have emphasised the political obstacles to rationing by exclusion but, in addition, it has to be acknowledged that there are other reasons for avoiding this approach to priority-setting. The weight of evidence suggests that there are few treatments that are wholly good or entirely bad and the challenge for decision-makers is to ensure that services are funded and provided to those patients who stand to benefit. This was expressed clearly by the chairman of the New Zealand Core Services Committee:

> The approach we decided to take was one that has flexibility to take account of an individual's circumstances when deciding if a service or treatment should be publicly funded. For example ... instead of a decision that says hormone replacement therapy (HRT) is either core or non-core ... the committee has decided that in certain circumstances HRT will be a core service and in others it won't be. The committee has recommended that HRT be a core service where there is clinical and research-based agreement that it constitutes an appropriate and effective treatment.[21]

It is this that provides the rationale for the development of guidelines designed to target services and resources to achieve the most health gain for the population served. In reality, guidelines can be used alongside exclusions, as in the approach taken in the Netherlands, which combines the exclusion of a limited number of services – examples being cosmetic surgery, adult dental care and homeopathic medicines – with the use of guidelines for the majority of services in a manner that is also finding favour elsewhere. Another example is the UK, where the exclusion of new drugs such as Relenza from NHS funding is occurring at the margins, with the main emphasis being placed on the use of guidelines intended to ensure that those services that are funded are used appropriately and effectively. Indeed, in the UK, NICE has since reversed its original decision on Relenza and the drug can now be prescribed within defined guidelines. A further example is Oregon, where the inclusion of services on the list of funded treatments is accompanied by the use of guidelines to ensure that these services are provided appropriately. It might be added that setting priorities through guidelines preserves the degree of discretion in the treatment of individual patients that, for Mechanic, provides the basis for implicit rationing in health care.[9]

Having made this point, it is important to recognise the force of Norheim's argument that guidelines themselves need to be developed through fair and open procedures. That is, the increasing reliance on guidelines in rationing requires the same rigour in relation to how guidelines are determined as decisions on whether or not to exclude services entirely from funding. Only in this way, Norheim argues, will it be possible to demonstrate that guidelines are acceptable and the decisions on which they are based defensible.[22]

Conclusion

In conclusion, it is not necessary to subscribe to a view of policy-making as red in tooth and claw to recognise the way in which debates about priority-setting illustrate the quest for power and influence in the health sector. This is evident in the role of pressure groups in lobbying for additional resources for their priorities and the strategies used by political leaders to evade responsibility for unpopular choices. One of the conundrums in this context is the willingness of politicians to be brave (or foolish, depending on your point of view) in some systems, but not in others, by encouraging explicit rationing at the macro level. The point here, to reiterate our earlier argument, is that explicitness tends to enhance accountability by making transparent the location of decisions and runs counter to the blame avoidance strategies that often motivate politicians.

Having made this point, there is evidence of learning in the policy process, exemplified by the retreat from purely technical solutions and the efforts made to involve the public in debates on rationing. There is also an increasing focus – in what Holm describes as the second phase of priority-setting[23] – on the process of determining priorities. The interest in decision-making processes is at once a response to the shortcomings of technical solutions and an attempt to earn legitimacy for what will often be difficult choices. Furthermore, by widening the circle of participants in decision-making and demonstrating that the way in which decisions are made is rigorous and fair, those responsible for rationing are, consciously or unconsciously, striving to achieve accountability for reasonableness in the rationing process.

There is also evidence of learning in the partial retreat from explicitness in some countries. The renewed (in some cases, continuing) focus on the meso and micro levels of rationing can be interpreted as a return to blame avoidance as decision-makers respond to the costs of being explicit about priorities at the macro level by shifting (or maintaining) the emphasis and responsibility to agencies such as sickness funds and health authorities and to physicians. If this interpretation is correct, then the recent interest in explicit rationing may be a temporary aberration in a much longer history of muddling through and evading responsibility. In other words, the political costs of explicitness may outweigh the benefits and this could result in a return to previous decision-making processes.

The force of this observation is underlined by experience in those countries such as the USA that (with limited exceptions like Oregon) have chosen not to ration explicitly. As the US experience suggests, there remain fundamental political obstacles to adopting a different approach, not least because:

> The American way of rationing is to decentralize (in political terms hide) the choices; the result is rationing through an accumulation of narrow public policies, private decisions and luck.[24]

This is because, in the USA, 'attempts to ration health care explicitly are political dynamite'. Nevertheless, decisions about limits to coverage and whether to fund new technologies have to be taken. In the USA, these decisions fall to public agencies, insurers and managed care organisations. Whether they like it or not, these agencies are involved in rationing.[25,26]

In both the USA and elsewhere, the release of the rationing genie from the bottle has had the effect of initiating a debate that will be difficult to halt. At a time when there is increasing public awareness of the possibilities created by medical advances and the denial of access to treatment, the challenge is not how to avoid discussion of rationing at the macro level but rather how to develop an informed democratic consensus model in which through broad mechanisms of public deliberation there is debate about how limited health care resources can be distributed. The rationale for encouraging democratic deliberation is that choices in health care involve moral issues that should be neither hidden nor fudged.[27] If those responsible for rationing continue to obfuscate and fail to confront the dilemmas directly, then public confidence in the legitimacy of decisions and those charged with making them will be further undermined. In this sense, the case for a systematic approach is at root an argument to maintain, and in some cases restore, faith in the political system and to strengthen democratic practices. It is also an argument for finding a way of increasing the resources available for health care in the light of evidence that explicitness makes it more difficult for policy-makers to evade responsibility for difficult choices.

Notes

1 Strosberg M, Wiener J, Baker R, Fein I, eds. Rationing America's medical care: the Oregon plan and beyond. Washington: The Brookings Institution, 1992

2 Coulter A, Ham C, eds. The global challenge of health care rationing. Buckingham: Open University Press, 2000

3 Jacobs L, Marmor T, Oberlander J. The Oregon health plan and the political paradox of rationing: what advocates and critics have claimed and what Oregon did. Journal of Health Politics, Policy and Law 1999; 24: 161–180

4 Hadorn D. Setting health care priorities in Oregon. Cost effectiveness meets the rule of rescue. Journal of the American Medical Association 1991; 265: 2218–2225

5 Swedish Parliamentary Priorities Commission. Priorities in health care: ethics, economy, implementation. Stockholm: Ministry of Health and Social Affairs, 1995

6 Chinitz D, Shalev C, Galai N, Israeli A. Israel's basic basket of health services: the importance of being explicitly implicit. BMJ 1998; 317: 1005–1007

7 Weaver K. The politics of blame avoidance. Journal of Public Policy 1986; 6: 371–398

8 Pierson P. Dismantling the welfare state. Cambridge: Cambridge University Press, 1994

9 Mechanic D. Muddling through elegantly. Health Affairs 1997; 16: 83–92

10 Hunter D. Rationing dilemmas in healthcare. Birmingham: National Association of Health Authorities and Trusts, 1993

11 Klein R. Puzzling out priorities. BMJ 1998; 317: 959–960
12 Holm S. Goodbye to the simple solutions. BMJ 1998; 317: 1000–1002
13 Daniels N, Sabin J. The ethics of accountability in managed care reform. Health Affairs 1998; 17: 50–64
14 Ham C, Pickard S. Tragic choices in health care: the story of child B. London: King's Fund, 1998
15 Edgar W. Rationing health care in New Zealand – how the public has a say. In: Coulter A, Ham C, eds. The global challenge of health care rationing. Buckingham: Open University Press, 2000
16 Martin D, Singer P. Priority setting and health technology assessment: beyond evidence-based medicine and cost-effectiveness analysis. In: Coulter A, Ham C, eds. The global challenge of health care rationing. Buckingham: Open University Press, 2000
17 Klein R, Williams A. Setting priorities: what is holding us back – inadequate information or inadequate institutions? In: Coulter A, Ham C, eds. The global challenge of health care rationing. Buckingham: Open University Press, 2000
18 Hope T, Hicks N, Reynolds DJM, Crisp R, Griffiths S. Rationing and the health authority. BMJ 1998; 317: 1067–1069
19 Ham C. Priority setting in the NHS: reports from six districts. BMJ 1993; 307:435–438
20 Klein R, Day P, Redmayne S. Managing scarcity. Buckingham: Open University Press, 1996
21 Jones L. The core debator. Wellington: National Advisory Committee on Core Health and Disability Services, 1993
22 Norheim OF. Healthcare rationing – are additional criteria needed for assessing evidence based clinical practice guidelines? BMJ 1999; 319: 1426–1429
23 Holm S. Goodbye to the simple solutions. BMJ 1998; 317: 1000–1002
24 Morone JA. The bias of American politics: rationing health care in a weak state. University of Pennsylvania Law Review 1992; 140: 1923–1938
25 Rodwin MA. Promoting accountable managed health care: the potential role for consumer voice. School of Public and Environmental Affairs, Indiana University, 2000 (www.consumerfed.org/hmoreport.pdf)
26 Daniels N. Accountability for reasonableness. BMJ 2000; 321: 1300–1301
27 Fleck LM. Just health care rationing: a democratic decision making approach. University of Pennsylvania Law Review 1992; 140: 1597–1636

PART 4

Markets and choice in health care
Introduced by Naomi Chambers

As noted in the introductory chapter to this reader, governments throughout the world (OECD, 2005) have been attracted by the use of markets and choice in health and public sector reforms in order to drive up efficiency, quality and responsiveness. This part identifies those key texts that have influenced both the marketization of health care and the increasing emphasis on choice.

The evidence base for this policy direction is not clear. The USA, for example, is an extreme example of the use of markets both in financing and provision of health care and demonstrates both the best features (clinical outcomes and resource utilization) and the worst (population coverage) of this policy, described vividly by Walshe (2001).

Certain writers have provided the rationale for the use of markets. Above all, Enthoven's analysis of the principles of managed competition in relation to health care has been particularly influential (Enthoven, 1993). Enthoven writes from a US health system perspective, with its strong cultural preferences for limited government, pluralism and individual choice, and in which, for the majority of the population, the employer provides health insurance as part of the remuneration package. Managed competition is defined as a purchasing strategy to obtain maximum value for money for employers and consumers. The price competition that it focuses on is the annual premium for comprehensive health care services, not the price for individual services. Crucial to the concept of managed competition is also the role of the 'sponsor', which is the employer, or representative of the employer (but could also be a state government in the case of Medicaid and Medicare programmes for the poor and elderly) who establishes rules of equity, selects plans and manages the enrolment process, and creates price elasticity (reduced prices with increased demand). To underline the influence of Enthoven, it could be argued that successive health system reforms in many other countries; for example, the UK, the Netherlands and New Zealand have been predicated largely on the virtues of the principles of managed competition but further influenced by a communitarian or solidarity ethos that is largely absent in the US cultural tradition.

Julian Le Grand offers an interesting argument around the need to take account of human motivation and behaviour in the development of quasi-markets and the growth of legal welfare (legislation about minimum wage, working hours, etc.) in social policy. The quasi-market has been seen as a response to the wastefulness, inefficiency and unresponsiveness of post-war welfare institutions financed and operated by the state. Le Grand argues however that the increasing preoccupation of policy makers with viewing, respectively, the providers (particularly the professionals) as no longer 'knights' (public spirited altruists), and recipients of welfare as no longer 'pawns' (passive and grateful), but both sets as 'knaves' (in one way or another self-interested) is essentially flawed as the reality is much more complex and not yet well understood. Clumsily constructed policies can 'crowd out' altruism and turn knights into knaves and what is required instead is robust policies that do not depend on any simplistic view of human behaviour (Le Grand, 1997).

One of the operating tools of the quasi-market in health care has been the discipline of commissioning, which also incorporates the activities of purchasing, contracting and procurement. Evidence for the impact in terms of efficiency and effectiveness is mixed, although there are signs that as far as responsiveness is concerned, at least in terms of access, some gains have been made (Ham, 2008). Asymmetry with regard to power and influence with provider organizations and lack of integrated clinical governance and clinical engagement structures appear to continue to hamper efforts of commissioners, at least in the UK (Light and Dixon, 2004; Woodin, 2006).

When Alain Enthoven first turned his gaze to the UK NHS in 1985, he coined the term 'the internal market', which has been a cornerstone of (at least) English health policy ever since, and out of which the commissioning discipline was developed. His reflections, from an academic public policy perspective, and as someone with no NHS background but a sophisticated grasp of the US health system, go nicely hand in hand with the Griffiths Management Inquiry report, produced by a prominent UK businessman, also without NHS experience, which was published two years earlier and is examined in some detail, with original extracts, in Part 7 of this reader. Enthoven talks compellingly of the 'gridlock' of forces that make change difficult to come about, mirroring Griffiths' metaphor of the NHS as a directionless and floating 'mobile'. In addition to the notion of the internal market, Enthoven's prescription includes the need for demonstration projects (pilots), the necessity of understanding costs of services and the construction of a competing health maintenance organisation (HMO) model of care. Over 20 years later, the NHS has made considerable progress with regard to costing and pricing, but still underuses the discipline of piloting to assess the appropriateness of policy interventions. The HMO model continues to be scrutinized. Presciently, and in remarkably similar terms to Griffiths, he talks of the need for medical leadership to be strengthened.

The lack of an evidence base for the greater use of markets in health care has already been touched on. Celia Davies, Paul Anand, Lidia Artigas et al. (2005) take the three forms of governance of markets, hierarchies and networks, and, using the governance-incentives-outcomes (GIO) model, explore differences between them in relation to incentives and with regard to outcomes. The thrust is a rich and dense multidisciplinary literature review covering the domains of economics, psychology, organizational studies, political science and socio-legal studies. They provide a useful framework that link four main modes of governance and types of incentive, and alert us to the dangers of building individualized incentives into organizational design. The authors arrive at four main conclusions of particular relevance to health care managers. First, in an echo of Le Grand's note of caution on this point, an expanded, more rounded and more critical framework of thinking around incentives is required. Second, a clearer focus on the impact of management practice rather than organizational form on outcomes is timely. Third, issues of co-governance and multi-level governance are highlighted in an era when partnership and whole system working is coming to the fore. Finally, the study develops the notion of 'democratic anchorage' as an approach to assessing performance that goes beyond measurement as the meeting of central government dictated targets.

The final text relating to the place of markets in health care is a powerful antidote to its allure. Richard Titmuss (1970) in the Gift Relationship makes a conceptual connection from the procurement of human blood to social policy in a plea for a non-market system based on altruism. He does this through a study of the private market in blood in the USA and concludes that, in economic terms, it is inferior in terms of efficiency as it is highly wasteful of blood, it is administratively inefficient, costs five to fifteen times as much as the voluntary system in the UK, and finally it is inferior in quality with higher risks of contamination. In ethical terms, he argues that it results in redistribution of blood from the poor to the rich. But his central point is that the buying and selling of blood (and, by extension, the marketization of care) represses the expression of altruism and the possibility of providing this lifegiving gift to 'the universal stranger'.

Debate about markets and choice seemingly go hand in hand. Titmuss argues that the true nature of choice in the social policy field is not made apparent by those who argue for the market approach to medical care, as choice cannot be considered independently from its social context (Titmuss, 1970: 312). Richard Saltman (1994) cogently lays out the terrain with regard to choice within publicly operated health systems. First, he provides a typology of patient empowerment that appears to correspond closely to Arnstein's frequently cited ladder of citizen participation (Arnstein, 1969). The central point here is the degree of individual leverage over specific service delivery decisions. Second, he goes further by distinguishing two world views about patient choice: one is of 'economic man' or patient as consumer (or object) in a business-driven model and the other is of 'political man' or patient as user (or subject) in a democratically driven analysis. The former focuses on patient satisfaction indicators, about which he is scathing, in a fashion that would now be deemed by some as dated, but provides a timely reminder of the limitations of the patient satisfaction perspective. He provides a critique of the primary and secondary factors that impact on the ability and desire of patients to exercise choice. Finally, he argues for the long-term political benefits of an educated empowered population, which go beyond the specifics of service delivery and are a reminder of Wanless' 'fully engaged scenario' (Wanless, 2002).

Perri 6 (2003) asks what can be learned from recent history in an analysis of the experience of providing more choice across nine fields of UK public services. He establishes that there is little consistency in the level of achievement of goals that appear to have been achieved across the nine fields and identifies a number of unintended consequences including distributional and efficiency problems exacerbated by issues related to political risk. The former set of problems were highlighted by Titmuss (1970). In contrast, however, Perri 6 argues that despite the technical challenges and conflicts of values presented by choice policies, incremental increases in satisfaction and efficiency can be achieved as long as clear goals are set and policies are adequately funded '... to bear the costs of conscientious choice' (Perri 6, 2003: 265). His main caveat is that the 'policy inheritance' (an echo of the path dependency argument rehearsed in Part 2 of this reader) may define the range of organizational capabilities of the service that is required to provide choice.

Summary

- Use of markets in health care has an enduring appeal despite a lack of evidence about its effectiveness as a policy tool.
- 'Managed competition' is seen as a means of bridging the apparent economic advantages of a market with ensuring desired social policy goals.
- A number of writers are appealing for a more nuanced understanding of the complexity of human motivations when constructing a market model of health care.
- The construction and implementation of patient choice is not straightforward nor is it well understood but may be worth while in terms of engagement and empowerment of patients, and building political legitimacy and responsiveness of services.

References and further reading

Arnstein, S. (1969) *A ladder of citizen participation, Journal of the American Planning Association,* 35(4): 216–24.

Enthoven, A. (1993) The history and principles of managed competition, *Health Affairs* 12 (Supplement 1): 24–48.

Ham, C. (2008) Competition and integration in the English National Health Service, *British Medical Journal,* 336: 805–07.

Le Grand, J. (1997) Knights, knaves or pawns? Human behaviour and social policy, *Journal of Social Policy,* 26 (02): 149–69.

Light, D. and Dixon, M. (2004) Making the NHS more like Kaiser Permanente, *British Medical Journal,* 328: 763–65.

OECD (2005) *Modernising Government: The Way Forward.* Paris: OECD.

Walshe, K. (2001) 'Don't try this at home': health policy lessons for the NHS from the United States, *Economic Affairs,* 21(4): 28–32.

Wanless, D. (2002) *Securing our Future: Taking a Long-term View.* London: HM Treasury.

Woodin, J. (2006) Healthcare commissioning and contracting, in K. Walshe and J. Smith (eds) *Healthcare Management.* Maidenhead: Open University Press.

The readings

Enthoven, A. (1985) *Reflections on the Management of the National Health Service: An American Looks at Incentives to Efficiency in Health Services Management in the UK.* London: Nuffield Provincial Hospitals Trust.

Davies, C., Anand, P., Artigas, L. et al. (2005) *Links Between Governance, Incentives and Outcomes: A Review of the Literature.* NCCSDO.

Titmuss, R. (1970) The right to give, in *The Gift Relationship: From Human Blood to Social Policy.* London: Allen & Unwin.

Saltman, R. B. (1994) Patient choice and patient empowerment in northern European health systems: a conceptual framework, *International Journal of Health Services,* 24(2): 201–29.

Perri 6 (2003) Giving consumers of British public services more choice: what can be learned from recent history? *Journal of Social Policy,* 32: 239–70.

14

Reflections on the management of the National Health Service: an American looks at incentives to efficiency in health services management in the UK
Alain Enthoven

Extracts from Enthoven A (1985) Reflections on the Management of the National Health Service: An American Looks at Incentives to Efficiency in Health Services Management in the UK. London: Nuffield Provincial Hospitals Trust.

Summary

This essay is meant to be a sympathetic review of some problems of organization and management in the National Health Service (NHS), with particular focus on incentives for efficiency and innovation.

The NHS enjoys widespread support in Britain, and it produces a great deal of care for the money spent. But given the tight limits under which it must operate, the NHS will find it increasingly difficult to meet the demands placed upon it. The NHS will need to find ways to produce even more value for money if it is to make effective new medical technology available to all who can benefit from it at the standards enjoyed in other industrialized democracies.

The NHS is caught in a 'gridlock' of forces that make change exceedingly difficult to bring about. Public policy should seek to create an environment for the NHS that is hospitable to quality-improving and efficiency-improving change. Opportunities for constructive change should be nurtured, not politicized or otherwise abused.

The NHS runs on the ability and dedication of the many people who work in it. But its structure contains no serious incentives to guide the NHS in the direction of better quality care and service at reduced cost. In fact, the structure of the NHS contains perverse incentives.

The Griffiths NHS Management Inquiry recommended establishment of a Health Services Supervisory Board to set policy and a full-time Management Board to supervise implementation and control performance. It also recommended that General Managers (GMs) be identified at Authority and Unit levels. Both seem to me to be very sensible ideas. But if the structure and incentives in the NHS are not changed more fundamentally, these changes are likely to be little more than cosmetic.

A decree requiring all Authorities to implement GMs is an unlikely way to bring about real change. The idea of GMs would have had a greater likelihood of success if it had first been developed and tested in a few interested pilot Districts. National uniformity should not be a requirement in such organizational matters.

Competitive tendering from commercial contractors for catering, cleaning, and laundry services could yield significant financial savings. Competitive tendering can be the entering wedge for a great deal of management improvement.

Again, a circular directing all Districts to submit programmes is not the best way to go about implementing this good idea. Better to begin with a dozen pilot Districts whose managements are enthusiastic about the idea, develop and test it with the benefit of expert advice, then push it to the maximum in the pilot districts, and display the benefits for all to see.

NHS purchasing of acute care services from the private sector now appears to be a matter of 'targets of opportunity'. The NHS doesn't know its own costs so it isn't able to recognize a good deal when it sees one. Cost finding systems ought to be developed. The NHS ought to be willing to buy acute care services from the private sector when it can get them at a lower price than the internal cost of providing the services. The NHS could become more of a discerning purchaser of services from competing private suppliers and thereby realize some of the benefits of efficiency and innovation that competition in the private sector offers.

The NHS could benefit from making much greater use of demonstration projects. As described to me, the 'clinical budgeting' experiments are too narrow in scope and not likely to change things significantly. We do many demonstration projects in the United States, and we learn a great deal from them.

Regional and District Medical Officers are drawn from community medicine. They are not trained for management and their background is not the best for persons expected to give leadership to the consultants. Medical leadership might be strengthened by giving postgraduate management training to selected consultants and by finding ways to make careers in top-level management attractive to them.

Despite the efforts to implement the recommendations of the Resource Allocation Working Party (RAWP), many inequalities of access and spending persist. Moves toward equalization are inhibited by the difficulty of closing facilities in the better-served areas. RAWP has been interpreted in a way that implicitly equates spending in a District, with spending for services for the people in a District. As a consequence, the only way to equalize the latter is to attempt to equalize the former. But that is hard to do because of all the difficulties in shutting down hospitals. I suggest dropping the implicit assumption that people must get all their services in their own District, equalizing the need-adjusted per capita spending on the people in each District by appropriating the funds to the District Health Authority (DHA), and letting Districts buy services from other Districts as needed. Among other things, this might let the London Teaching Hospitals compete for referrals from other Districts rather than face being ground down by the relentless application of the RAWP formula.

This line of thinking could lead to an 'Internal Market Model' for the NHS. Each District would receive a RAWP-based per capita revenue and capital allowance. It would continue to be responsible to provide and pay for comprehensive care for its own resident population, but not for care for other people without current compensation at negotiated prices. Each District would resemble a nationalized company. It would buy and sell services from and to other Districts and trade with the private sector. In such a scheme, District managers would be freed to use all their resources most efficiently. Some perverse incentives would be eliminated. But the main defect in this model is a lack of powerful incentives for NHS personnel to serve patients as efficiently as possible.

The dominant system of health care organization and finance in the USA is still solo practice, fee-for-service payment to doctors, fee-for-service or cost-reimbursement for hospitals, and insured patients with a cost-unconscious free choice of doctor. This system is the most important contributor to the rapid rate of increase in spending on health services that has now reached crisis proportions.

The main alternative to this system of organization and finance are HMOs whose enrolled membership reached nearly 17 million Americans by the end of 1984, up 22 per cent from a year earlier. A HMO accepts responsibility for providing comprehensive health care services to a voluntarily enrolled population for a fixed periodic 'capitation' payment set in advance. Comparative studies show that HMOs cut cost roughly 25 per cent compared to fee-for-service. Even if Britain were never to adopt the HMO idea, I believe the HMO experience offers useful insights and examples for the NHS.

For example, when it is in the doctors' interest, they can do effective audit and control of quality and economy of care. Economic interest can even motivate doctors to expel poor performers from their group. In competition, doctors impose on themselves controls they would never dream of accepting if the government tried to impose them. Thus, 'clinical freedom' is giving way to effective control of quality and cost-effectiveness.

I do not sense any serious demand for radical change in the structure of the NHS. However, if British policy-makers were to seriously wish to examine a radically different scheme for health care, I would recommend the competing HMO model as the most promising candidate.

15

Links between governance, incentives and outcomes
Celia Davies, Paul Anand, Lidia Artigas et al.

Extracts from Davies, Anand P Artigas et al (2005) Links Between Governance, Incentives and Outcomes: A Review of the Literature. Lnodon: NCCSDO.

Section 4 Governance: policy analysis, public management and political-science perspectives

The last 15 years have seen a transformation in the state, accompanied by changes in the scope, organisation and significance of public-sector organisations. We have witnessed not only the arrival of different techniques of management and the disappearance of monopoly providers, but experimentation with new forms of governmental control and the emergence of new kinds of agency engaged in regulatory activity. Longstanding and monolithic public bureaucracies in health, as in other areas of the public sector, have become discredited. The value not just of hierarchies, but of markets and networks, has become part of a discussion of NPM that has attracted attention among scholars and practitioners nationally and internationally. At the same time, in a field that is growing rapidly, governance as a concept has moved to centre stage and served to expand thinking from structures of government to more complex processes of governing.

4.1 Governance regimes and incentive effects

It was always clear that the move to markets and managerialism in health, education and other areas of public policy on the part of successive neo-liberal governments in the UK and elsewhere from the 1980s onwards had a significance that went beyond technique to the reconfiguring and re-imagining of public services, the public sector and the role of the state itself. The much-cited articles by Hood (1991) in the UK, Aucoin (1990) in Canada and the earlier full-length monograph of Ostrom (1973) in the USA (cited in Toonen, 1998) are among works that began to demarcate and assess the changes which together have come to be known as NPM. They include a strong emphasis on efficiency savings, meeting performance targets, private-sector-style freedom to manage, regulation, and restructurings to introduce quasi-markets and to create more autonomous agencies.

Governance helps to capture these shifts, reinforcing the sense of an historical break. Despite repeated attempts to clarify sets of meanings (Rhodes, 1997; Stoker, 1998), the concept remains both contested and confused (Newman, 2001; Pierre and Peters, 2000; Daly, 2003). Nonetheless, it serves an important function in going beyond the straightforward notion that only governments govern. It recognises a capacity for getting things done which is not captured in any simple way by the power of government to command, encouraging analysts to study political mobilisation across diverse networks and to probe beneath the surface of the formal relations of co-ordination and rule (Stoker, 1998).

4.2 Markets, hierarchies and networks – typologies

Shifts between markets, networks and hierarchies as modes of co-ordination are frequently alluded to in these discussions of regime change. Arguments positing a move from bureaucracy to markets and thence to networks abound and are a source of much debate (for example, see Blatter, 2003).

Newman sets out not three but four different models of governance. The *hierarchical model* is oriented towards predictability, control and accountability and corresponds to a now much-criticised 'command and control' form, high on probity, yet castigated for inflexibility, slowness and reluctance to change. The *rational goal model* reflects a focus on shorter time lines and attempts to maximise outputs. Here, government exerts power through managerial means – attempting to create direct incentives to deliver on its goals and targets in a context where local managers are held accountable through contractual or quasi-contractual means. The *open systems model* is oriented towards networks, where power is dispersed and relationships adapt constantly to meet changed demands. It draws from a substantial body of recent work in systems theory to depict a form that is 'fluid, fast and highly responsive' and 'accountability is low but sustainability is high' (Newman, 2001: 35). Government steers but does not control in a direct way; self-organisation predominates. Finally, the *self-governance model* is oriented inwards, focusing on peer accountability among a company of equals and on fostering relationships of interdependence and reciprocity. Newman uses it to characterise government moves to build sustainable communities, drawing in local citizens. She also uses it to depict self-regulation of the professions (Newman, 2001: 86ff). Figure 15.1 represents a further development of this, focusing on incentives.

Newman avoids neat narratives of directional change and stresses the complex overlay of these types on each other. Hierarchical governance remains crucial in securing appropriate forms of accountability, while the idea of self-governance is seeing something of a renaissance, albeit in rather different forms from the older and now somewhat discredited idea of the self-governing profession. Self-governance also, is perhaps emerging in a rather different guise in the increased

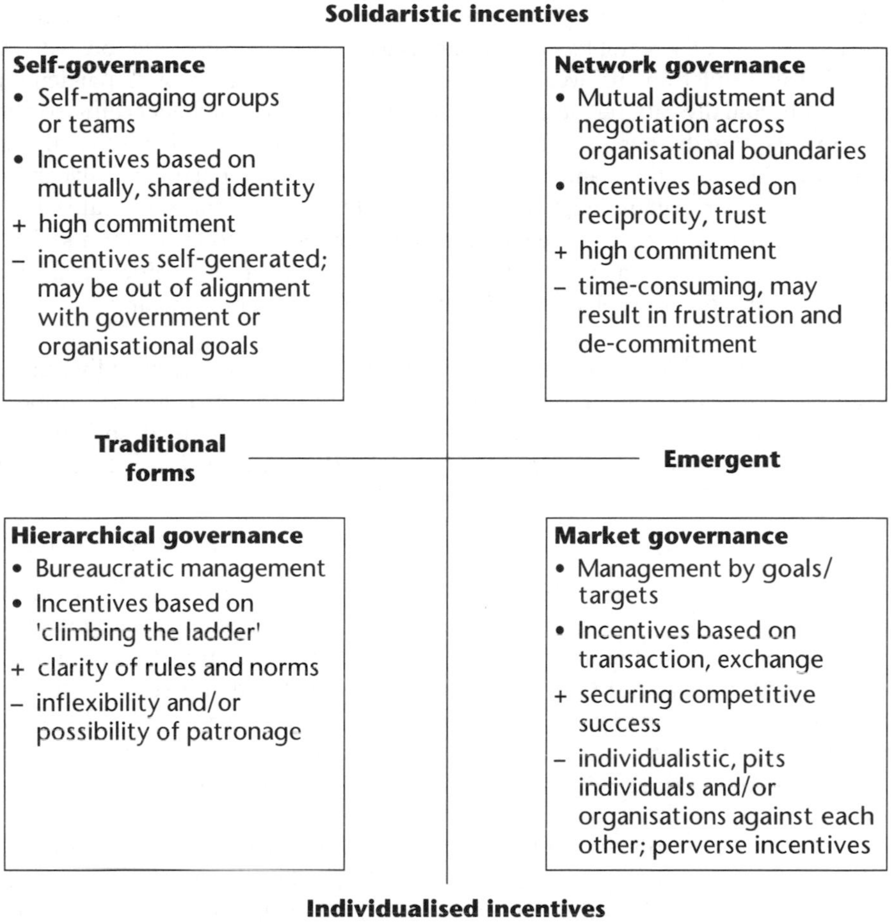

Solidaristic incentives

Self-governance
- Self-managing groups or teams
- Incentives based on mutually, shared identity
+ high commitment
− incentives self-generated; may be out of alignment with government or organisational goals

Network governance
- Mutual adjustment and negotiation across organisational boundaries
- Incentives based on reciprocity, trust
+ high commitment
− time-consuming, may result in frustration and de-commitment

Traditional forms ───────────────── **Emergent**

Hierarchical governance
- Bureaucratic management
- Incentives based on 'climbing the ladder'
+ clarity of rules and norms
− inflexibility and/or possibility of patronage

Market governance
- Management by goals/ targets
- Incentives based on transaction, exchange
+ securing competitive success
− individualistic, pits individuals and/or organisations against each other; perverse incentives

Individualised incentives

Figure 15.1 Modes of governance and incentives

significance of ideas of delegation to self-governing trusts or even to community-based or self-help organisations. While such organisations may be in market- or network-based relationships with each other and may be held to account through hierarchical modes of governance, delegation endows them with considerable autonomy coupled with new forms of responsibility for delivering outcomes in line with government priorities. Arguments for the co-existence of markets, hierarchies and networks have been advanced in the health context, both in the longer term (Powell, 2003) and in the context of more recent NHS developments (Exworthy *et al.*, 1999).

6 and Peck (2004) offer a somewhat different way of mapping institutional forms. Drawing from classic sociological theorising on the nature of social integration advanced by Durkheim, they highlight four forms of solidarity with associated clusters of institutionalised interests and preferences. There is the familiar *hierarchy*, highly regulated and structured by rules, where actors are well

integrated and pursue status within the system. There is the *enclave*, internally egalitarian but weakly regulated and sometimes in hostile confrontation with the outside. Weak regulation and weak integration yield *individualism* with participants pursuing individually rational strategies and becoming stratified according to their success in this. Finally there is 'the social world of the isolate', which is 'hardly able to sustain collective action' and where bonds to others are particularly weak and sparse. While this typology maps less readily on to forms of formal organisational arrangement than does that of Newman, the authors go on to tease out a series of propositions about the dynamics of these forms, suggesting that initial reinforcing factors for each type are replaced by disintegrative ones. They explain:

> gradually more hierarchy undermines trust and clarity, more individualism leads to mistrust and even corruption, more enclave leads to sectarian paranoia, and more isolation erodes collective action. Political and management reform projects ... can readily set such dynamics in train. In this way, what is in the first instance functional becomes dysfunctional.

> 6 and Peck (2004: 88)

This is a crucial point that highlights the dangers of reform projects producing what Bovens *et al.* (2001) term 'governance failure' by intensifying the reliance on a preferred model. The possibility that 'the functional becomes dysfunctional' is also particularly important in the context of this section in that it suggests that any fixed notion of a best practice in terms of governance arrangements may produce efficiencies and improved outcomes in the short term, but may militate against an organisation's or service's capacity to innovate or to address new problems or issues.

How stable are mixed modes of governance? Newman argues that the co-existence of competing governance forms within a single service or organisation is likely to produce tensions that have to be resolved on the ground by practitioners, and traces some of the stresses, strains and sometimes de-motivational effects that result. 6 and Peck talk a dynamic of change and also suggest the existence of 'hybrids' as a more settled combination. They argue that:

> the greatest chance of stability ... arises from certain kinds of four-way settlement, which articulate all four solidarities in ways that each provides some services to the others. These four-way settlements are sometimes called 'clumsy institutions' (Thompson, 1997) because they accept high transaction costs for the robustness that comes from requisite variety.

> 6 and Peck (2004: 89)

4.5 Governance and performance

In the last 5 years there has been a growing emphasis on studying the links between governance and performance. The papers from an international colloquium bringing together leading experts on governance and performance that took place around the start of this study point to the complexity of such a project. While rarely mentioning incentives in a direct way, these papers (along with others in the database) do identify a number of ways in which the incentive effects of different governance forms can be understood.

One theme problematises the outcomes to which incentives should be directed (Baggott, 1997). Much of the literature, it has been pointed out, 'takes the side of elected government' (Considine and Lewis, 1999), running the risk of being in effect only about compliance (Schofield and Sausman, 2004). Skelcher and Mauther (2004) importantly broaden the idea of performance to encompass a notion of 'democratic anchorage', arguing that it is this that provides the means of linking organisational activity and performance to collectively determined goals. A second theme turns to outcomes in the context of networked governance. Based on studies across Organization for Economic Cooperation and Development (OECD) countries, Considine (2004: 10) notes the potentially innovative capacity of partnerships. He embeds this, however, in a rich theoretical analysis and critique of networked governance, arguing *inter alia* that partnerships must help service-sector professionals and their counterparts 'to "imagine" a different form of community enterprise' (Considine, 2004: 10).

This raises questions of context and of intervening variables that might mediate the links between governance and outcomes. Ingraham (2004), in a 6-year comparison of 'high-capacity' and 'low-capacity' cities in the US, offers two important conclusions. First, management matters; the ability to provide leadership stood out (Taylor, 2000; Meier and O'Toole, 2003). Second, external structural and political constraints exerted a significant influence on overall performance across both low- and high-capacity cities. The importance of political constraints was a strong theme in Pollitt's (2004) review of the application of a model of governance, shared across a number of European countries, that separates agencies from ministries, gives enhanced managerial freedoms and at the same time performance-manages them (see also Pollitt and Talbot, 2004). His analysis suggests that there is little evidence that this model is implemented in a straightforward way or leads to significant performance improvements and he concludes that:

> reformers should direct their attention to a more fine grained analysis of the nature of each task, of its likely political salience, and of what can realistically be done about the motivation and skills of the staff concerned ... effective reforms need to take more account of the specifics of tasks, politics and people.
>
> Pollitt (2004: 17)

If the chain of cause and effect from governance through incentives to outcomes is problematic in these ways, dynamics *over time* may also need to be the focus for research. We have already noted the warning that the development of more complex regulatory roles by states has created a more complicated set of institutional incentives that, in turn, generates further regulatory activity (Saltman,

2002). Drawing on their model discussed earlier, 6 *et al.* (2004) have now compared defence procurement and health care in terms of patterns of inter-organisational relations, institutional constraints and incentive effects. Their collo-quium paper concludes that:

> the governance strategies adopted have not invariably been successful not least because of a tendency to reinforce hierarchical network forms to a degree that may not always be appropriate and which may then produce unintended effects, including the recrudescence of other forms.
>
> 6 *et al.* (2004: 10)

Also relevant to performance and equally challenging of a simple model of determination of outcomes is the recently renewed interest in the theme of policy implementation. Classic work by Lipsky (1980) gives attention to dilemmas of discretion faced by the frontline welfare bureaucrat in a hierarchy and links with a well-known stream of work in public policy analysis highlighting weaknesses in a 'perfect implementation' model (Hogwood and Gunn, 1984). More direct study of the local 'decision space' for officials (Bossert, 1998) has been proposed recently, and Considine and Lewis (1999) give a strongly empirically based demonstration of variations in interpretations of new governance regimes at ground level. Martin (2000) examines the transitions involved in implementing 'best value' in local government. A recent symposium collects together and reviews papers on this theme (Schofield and Sausman, 2004). These editors indicate that a return to 'Lipskean discretion' in contexts beyond hierarchy is now an important item for the research agenda and suggest that implementation in collaborative forms of governance may be more unpredictable than in the hierarchical settings studied by Lipsky.

Bringing frontline professionals into this frame is important. The complex ways in which professionals in the probation field assimilate and also transform policy has been explored (Newman and Nutley, 2003). The work of Sheaff *et al.* (2004a), examining the effects of (network-based) clinical governance on the self-governance regime of GPs is relevant here. A Foucauldian perspective enables these authors to highlight new forms of discipline and regulation that accompany the apparent freedoms of network governance, while also suggesting ways in which compliance was achieved through appeals to the legitimacy of clinical governance as consistent with the self image of clinicians. Both papers can be viewed as examples of a shift to the more constructivist post-structural perspectives offering ways of understanding incentives as socially constructed and focusing on the meanings which actors bring to their encounters and how these meanings are linked to broader cultural and social processes. Study after study in the organisa-tional and HRM literature has highlighted the critical importance of such factors in shaping outcomes.

4.6 Conclusions

Political science provides a wealth of scholarship on national and international scales, exploring changes in the scope and reach of the state as it shapes and reshapes understandings of its task of providing or regulating the provision of public services. In doing so, it offers both important contextual understandings of the changes with which health-care-delivery organisations must grapple and warnings about overly simple modelling of the incentive effects of governance forms. How then, does this material look when set against the questions of the commissioning brief?

What are the different incentive effects of markets, hierarchies and networks respectively on organisations and individuals who plan, manage and deliver health and social care? The typology devised by Newman offers a distinction between individualised incentives in markets and hierarchies and solidaristic/relational incentives in different kinds of networks organisation. There is an important degree of convergence here with the work of Hill and Lynn, working at the level of interagency collaboration. Such typologies identify, at a broad and societal level, coherent forms of governance, showing how these can be derived from a positioning on axes relating for example to centralised control, stability and change or integration. The logical types that emerge are capable of generating a series of testable propositions about incentive effects, although it has not been the focus of work in this field to take this route. However, authors draw attention to the reality of mixed and hybrid forms where different governance forms may be overlaid on each other and produce complex effects. This work also identifies added complexities in that an outcome in one context may not be the same as an outcome in another; and an outcome at time *a* may not be the same outcome at time *b*.

How do the different incentives of different forms of governance affect organisational performance and how can these questions be researched? Political science has done more than other disciplines to put the concept of governance on the map, recognising the multiplicity of actors and agencies involved in getting things done and seeking to capture historical shifts and to make societal comparisons. It offers critiques of market-oriented governance that can be cast in terms of negative incentives. Current work says less about hierarchy, giving attention instead to network governance. There are moves to name new forms – co-governance, multilevel governance and regulatory governance being some of these. Much of this work seeks to delineate new forms rather than to test hypotheses about their impact. An emerging area, however, does address performance effects. Key points here include the importance of expanding notions of performance to encompass democratic performance and innovative capacity, the crucial need to explore both contextual and intervening variables which are capable of constraining performance, and the likely instability of chains of cause and effect over time. The rather small amount of work at present concerned with frontline professionals and the mindsets they bring when faced with policy levers with inbuilt assumptions about incentives suggests that there is scope here for more study.

Do different forms of governance produce different incentive effects on users of health and social care and/or their carers? Much political-science scholarship takes for granted a critique of both hierarchy and markets from the point of view of the service user of public services. It focuses attention on new forms of networked governance that have the potential to include service users, carers and members of the public in various ways. Within this way of thinking, analysts tend to focus not so much on incentive effects of governance forms but on leadership styles and practices that are capable of sustaining participation of service users and carers with a view to creating shared forms of governance and joint decision-making. Coming at this issue from a different tradition of scholarship, post-structuralist theory emphasises how discourse constructs the user as passive in relation to bureaucratic governance and as active, discerning and capable of choice in relation to markets. Work on cultural governance questions the adequacy of both of these formulations. Incorporation of this thinking into mainstream research is still at an early stage.

What are the implications of the foregoing issues for the organisation of health and social care services in England? This section offers several messages. First, it insists on the importance of studying governance in a holistic way, paying attention to ways in which the state itself is being reshaped through the rise, for example, of regulatory agencies and the shift away from direct service provision. Second, it warns of the potential loss of public values in the reorganisations that have occurred. Thirdly, it firmly puts non-economic and non-individual incentives into the frame, asking questions about performance in terms of legitimacy, 'democratic anchorage', solidarity, integration and inclusion – implicitly offering the message that building individualised incentives into organisational design runs the risk of damaging social integration and dismantling notions of the public good.

6.2 Re-examining markets, hierarchies and networks

How useful is the model of markets, hierarchies and networks for describing key variations in governance form and for predicting outcomes? The idea of a sharp contrast between hierarchies and markets and their portrayal as alternative ways of organising activity has been a leading idea in the social sciences for many years, and this literature review has demonstrated the continuing importance of research and scholarship on markets, networks and hierarchies (and variants of these) across many of the disciplines represented in the report. A cynic, however, might be tempted to conclude that *markets have been over-modified* (that is, that the form has been so hedged about by qualifications that the 'quasi' in the quasi-markets argument is in danger of eclipsing the 'market'; see Exworthy *et al.*, 1999: 17); that *hierarchies have been abandoned* (in face perhaps of a common wisdom that discredits bureaucracy as costly, inflexible and lacking in innovative capacity) and that the concept of *networks has been overextended*.

Our proposals here are both to *descend a level of analysis* in order to carry out more fine-grained work on the specificities of organisational forms and combinations of forms, and to *ascend a level of analysis* to attend to the complex relationships that are captured in the concept not so much of networks *per se*, but certainly in discussions of networked governance.

Taking descent first: blanket assessments of market reforms in the public sector remain unconvincing and points to a mixed bag of results. Encouraging research which now focuses on some of the more specific institutional practices that are encompassed by the notion of market and building a better understanding of the way that these work in practice in the private sector may now be more productive. Contracting is a case in point. The literature that we have assessed suggests that it would be timely to bring together work reviewed in economics, the theorising on relational contracting and a stream of small-scale empirical studies present in our database but not 'owned' by any particular disciplinary and theoretical perspective, with a view to devising new comparative research. Such research, focusing both on the construction and the day-to-day operation of contracts in a series of different industries and sectors, should advance real-world understanding and result in some clearer pointers on how to devise and operate contracts that are more capable of delivering the health-sector outcomes that are required. The related area of supply-chain management may offer another example for comparative study, as might a study of the thinking that underpins different decisions about decentralisation and divisional structures in large companies.

There is now also a detectable call for a return to studying the operation of bureaucracy. From political science, Bevir and Rhodes (2003a) argue that notwithstanding markets, hierarchy is still a major way of delivering services; from sociology too, there are indications that a return to a consideration of the value of bureaucracy is relevant (Du Gay, 1999, 2004; Kirkpatrick, 1999). Our review thus suggests that it is now timely to revisit the classic positive outcomes of bureaucracy – its reliability, probity and formal accountability with an empirical study – and to ask whether modern bureaucratic forms can deliver these. Such a proposal perhaps links with the widespread calls we have noted for more study on the ground of the way that markets, hierarchies combine. It is time to recognise that markets, hierarchies and networks are merely building blocks and to 'meet complexity with complexity' (Bang, 2004: 160). New analytical schemes for classifying organisational forms are overdue (see Lowndes and Skelcher, 1998; Thynne, 2003). There are signs also that a closer look at ways of organising and integrating professionals is going to happen soon, as the discussion, for example, of P2 structures and managed professional businesses indicated. Revisiting professional organisation thus suggests a way forward. We did not find that the concept of hybrids at present, however, serves to advance understanding much further.

6.3 Outcomes and the determinants of outcomes

Finally, underpinning the whole of this literature review has been the GIO model – the notion that forms of governance (in the shape of markets, hierarchies and networks) give rise to incentives and hence affect organisational outcomes. What conclusions can now be drawn? Each of the sections, in their different ways, has addressed aspects of the GIO model and most, in one way or another, have taken issue with it. Psychology illuminates the space between incentives and outcomes, helping to uncover something of the mechanisms by which incentives may work (or why they may not), and to explain some of the complexity of apparent effects.

In this sense, it can be said to contribute to part but not all of the GIO chain. At the same time, both psychology and HRM offer a more challenging message, namely that a key variable or set of variables affecting performance/outcome in organisations is not 'governance', however defined, but managerial practice. Considerable evidence is amassed to suggest that management, including HRM practices, and leadership styles, together also with cultural factors, act as key intervening variables and that it would be wrong to concentrate on structural variables of governance alone. We have already seen unease about the concept of incentives that is expressed strongly in work from the political-science/policy-studies field. The messages of a series of very recent studies on governance and performance summarised in that section concern: the multiplicity of outcomes that need to be considered; the importance (again) of variables that intervene between structure and outcome; the possibility of a changing dynamic over time that is not captured easily by the statistical approaches usually employed in quantitative studies; and the place of the discretion in implementation at the frontline of service delivery. There is a plea too for research concentrating more on the meanings that actors bring to their encounters in organisations and the different narratives they construct. In the opinion, indeed, of at least one reviewer, the interpretive turn in political science will set the agenda for the next decade (Hay, 2004). There are parallels perhaps with the re-emergence of interest in 'sense-making' in organisational sociology (Weick, 1995) and with recent influential work on the power of narrative as a technique in the study of organisations (Czarniawska, 1997).

References

6, P. and Peck, E. 2004. New Labour's Modernization in the Public Sector: a neo-Durkheimian approach and the case of mental health services. *Public Administration* 82: 83–108

6, P., Peck, E. and Goodwin, N. 2004. Governance and management in networks: comparing structures and fields. ESRC/EPSRC Advanced Institute for Management Research Colloquium on Governance and Performance: Organizational Status, Management Capacity and Public Service Performance, University of Birmingham, 15–16 March 2004

Aucoin, P. 1990. Administrative reform in public management: paradigms, principles, paradoxes, and pendulums. *Governance* 3: 115–37

Baggott, R. 1997. Evaluating Health Care Reform: The case of the NHS internal market. *Public Administration* 75: 283–306

Bevir, M. and Rhodes, R. 2003a. Searching for civil society: changing patterns of governance in Britain. *Public Administration* 81: 41–62

Blatter, J. 2003. Beyond hierarchies and networks: institutional logics and change in transboundary spaces. *Governance* 16: 503–26

Bossert, T. 1998. Analyzing the decentralization of health systems in developing countries: decision space, innovation and performance. *Social Science & Medicine* 47: 1513–27

Bovens, M., t'Hart, P. and Peters, B.G. 2001. *Success and Failure in Public Governance: A comparative analysis.* Cheltenham: Edward Elgar

Considine, M. 2004. Choosing one's history wisely: network governance and the question of institutional performance. In *Governance and Performance: How do modes of governance affect public service performance?* Birmingham: University of Birmingham

Considine, M. and Lewis, J.M. 1999. Governance at ground level: the frontline bureaucrat in the age of markets and networks. *Public Administration Review* 59: 467–80

Czarniawska, B. 1997. *Narrating the Organization.* London: University of Chicago Press

Daly, M. 2003. Governance and social policy. *Journal of Social Policy* 32: 113–28

Du Gay, P. 1999. *In Praise of Bureaucracy: Weber, organization ethics.* London: Sage

Du Gay, P. 2004. Against 'Enterprise' (but not against 'enterprise', for that would make no sense). *Organization* 11: 37–57

Exworthy, M., Powell, M. and Mohan, J. 1999. The NHS: quasi-market, quasi-hierarchy and quasi-network? *Public Money and Management* 14: 15–22

Hay, C. 2004. The return to interpretivism in public administration [book review]. *Public Administration,* 82(2): 525–7

Hill, C. and Lynn, L. 2003. Producing Human Services: why do agencies collaborate? *Public Management Review* 5: 63–81

Hogwood, B. and Gunn, L. 1984. *Policy Analysis for the Real World.* Oxford: Oxford University Press

Hood, C. 1991. A public management for all seasons? *Public Administration* 69: 3–19

Ingraham, P.W. 2004. *Management Systems and Performance in Local Governments.* ESRC/EPSRC Advanced Institute for Management Research Colloquium on Governance and Performance: Organizational Status, Management Capacity and Public Service Performance. Birmingham: University of Birmingham

Kirkpatrick, I. 1999. The worst of both worlds? Public services without markets or bureaucracy. *Public Money & Management* 19: 7–14

Lipsky, M. 1980. *Street-Level Bureaucracy: Dilemmas of the individual in public services.* New York: Russell Sage Foundation

Martin, S. 2000. Implementing 'best value': local public services in transition. *Public Administration* 78: 209–27

Meier, K.J. and O'Toole, L.J. 2003. Public management and educational performance: the impact of managerial networking. *Public Management and Educational Performance* 63: 689–99

Newman, J. 2001. *Modernising Governance: New Labour, policy and society.* London: Sage

Newman, J. and Nutley, S. 2003. Transforming the probation service: 'what works', organisational change and professional identity. *Policy & Politics* 31: 547–63

Pierre, J. and Peters, B.G. 2000. *Governance, Politics and the State.* London: Macmillan

Pollitt, C. 2004. Strategic Steering and Performance Management: agencies beautiful form or weak variable? *International Colloquium Governance and Performance*. Birmingham: University of Birmingham

Pollitt, C. and Talbot, C. (eds) 2004. *Unbundled Government: A critical analysis of the global trend to agencies, quangos and contractualisation*. London: Routledge

Powell, M. 2003. Quasi-markets in British Health Policy: a longue durée perspective. *Social Policy and Administration* 37: 725–41

Rhodes, R. 1997. *Understanding Governance*. Buckingham: Open University Press

Saltman, R.B. 2002. Regulating incentives: the past and the present role of the state in health care systems. *Social Science and Medicine* 54: 1677–84

Schofield, J. and Sausman, C. 2004. Symposium on Implementing Public Policy: learning from theory and practice – Introduction. *Public Administration* 82: 235–48

Sheaff, R., Marshall, M., Rogers, A., Roland, M., Sibbald, B. and Pickard, S. 2004a. Governmentality by Network in English Primary Healthcare. *Social Policy and Administration* 38: 89–103

Skelcher, C. and Mathur, N. 2004. Governance arrangements and public service performance: reviewing and reformulating the research agenda. *International Colloquium on Governance and Performance*. Birmingham: University of Birmingham

Stoker, G. 1998. Governance as theory: five propositions. *International Social Science Journal* 50: 17–28

Taylor, M. 2000. Communities in the lead: power, organisational capacity and social capital. *Urban Studies* 37: 1019–35

Thynne, I. 2003. Making sense of organisations in public management: a back-to-basics approach. *Public Organization Review* 3

Toonen, T.A.J. 1998. Networks, management and institutions: public administration as 'normal science'. *Public Administration* 76: 229–52

16

The gift relationship: from human blood to social policy
Richard Titmuss

Extracts from Titmuss R (1970) The gift relationship: From human blood to social policy. London: Allen & Unwin.

> We need not wait for the Moralist's verdict before calling one kind of action good and another bad.
>
> Lan Freed

Practically all the voluntary donors whose answers we set down in their own words employed a moral vocabulary to explain their reasons for giving blood. Their view of the external world and their conception of man's biological need for social relations could not be expressed in morally neutral terms. They acknowledged that they could not and should not live entirely as they may have liked if they had paid regard solely to their own immediate gratifications. To the philosopher's question 'What kind of actions ought we to perform?' they replied, in effect, 'Those which will cause more good to exist in the universe than there would otherwise be if we did not so act'.

For most of them, the universe was not limited and confined to the family, the kinship, or to a defined social, ethnic or occupational group or class; it was the universal stranger. Unlike some of the 'tied', 'credit' and 'deposit' systems depicted in earlier chapters, there was no prescribed and specified discrimination in the destination of the gift. One of the principles of the National Blood Transfusion Service and the National Health Service is to provide services on the basis of common human needs; there must be no allocation of resources which could create a sense of separateness between people. It is the explicit or implicit institutionalisation of separateness, whether categorised in terms of income, class, race, colour or religion, rather than the recognition of the similarities between people and their needs, which causes much of the world's suffering. By not doing something – by not giving donors a 'right' to prescribe the group characteristics of recipients – the Service thus presumes an unspoken shared belief in the universality of need. This case study of blood donor systems demonstrates the extent to which the policy values of the Service are held in common by the individual voluntary donor in Britain.

It also shows that detailed, concrete programs of political change – undramatic and untheatrical as they may often appear to be – can facilitate the expression of man's moral sense. Thus, it serves as an illustration of how social policy, in one of its potential roles, can help to actualise the social and moral potentialities of all citizens.

None of the donors' answers was purely altruistic. They could not be, for no donor type can be depicted in terms of complete, disinterested, spontaneous altruism. There must be some sense of obligation, approval and interest; some feeling of 'inclusion' in society; some awareness of need and the purposes of the gift. What was seen by these donors as a good for strangers in the here-and-now could be (they said or implied) a good for themselves – indeterminately one day. But it was not a good which they positively desired for themselves either immediately or ultimately.

In certain undesired circumstances in the future – situations in which death or disability might be postponable – then the performance by a stranger of a similar action would constitute for them or their families a desired good. But they had no assurance of such action nor any guarantee of the continued existence of the National Health Service. Unlike gift-exchange in traditional societies, there is in the free gift of blood to unnamed strangers no contract of custom, no legal bond, no functional determinism, no situations of discriminatory power, domination, constraint or compulsion, no sense of shame or guilt, no gratitude imperative and no need for the penitence of a Chrysostom.

In not asking for or expecting any payment of money, these donors signified their belief in the willingness of other men to act altruistically in the future, and to join together to make a gift freely available should they have a need for it. By expressing confidence in the behaviour of future unknown strangers, they were thus denying the Hobbesian thesis that men are devoid of any distinctively moral sense.

As individuals they were, it may be said, taking part in the creation of a greater good transcending the good of self-love. To 'love' themselves, they recognised the need to 'love' strangers. By contrast, one of the functions of atomistic private market systems is to 'free' men from any sense of obligation to or for other men regardless of the consequences to others who cannot reciprocate, and to release some men (who are eligible to give) from a sense of inclusion in society at the cost of excluding other men (who are not eligible to give).

Those donors to the National Blood Transfusion Service we have described in much detail were free not to give. They could have behaved differently; that is to say, they need not have acted as they did. Their decisions were not determined by structure or by function or controlled by ineluctable historical forces. They were not compelled, coerced, bribed or paid to give. To coerce a man is to deprive him of freedom. Yet, as this study has shown comparatively, private market systems in the United States and other countries not only deprive men of their freedom to choose to give or not to give but, by so doing, escalate other coercive forces in the social system which lead to the denial of other freedoms (and maybe life itself) to other men who biologically are in no position to choose – the young and the old, the sick, the excluded and the inept as well as the sellers of blood.

As freedoms are lost in the blood marketplace, truth is an accompanying victim. In studying different blood donation, clinical laboratory and medical care systems we were led to ask, in earlier chapters, what particular conditions and arrangements permit and encourage maximum truthfulness on the part of donors – the maximum now demanded by medical science? To what extent can honesty be maximised? Is a society's need for honesty in one critical area of life compatible with incentives towards dishonesty in others? We were led to these questions not simply because of a belief in the will to know what is true as a value in itself but because of its crucial role today in the application of scientific medicine.

The paid seller of blood is confronted and, moreover, usually knows that he is confronted, with a personal conflict of interests. To tell the truth about himself, his way of life and his relationships may limit his freedom to sell his blood in the market. Because he desires money and is not seeking in this particular act to affirm a sense of belonging, he thinks primarily of his own freedom; he separates his freedom from other people's freedoms. It may be of course that he will not be placed, or may not fully realise that he has been placed in such situations of conflicting interests. If so, it can only be because medicine in the person of the doctor has failed to fulfil its scientific basis; it is not seeking to know what is true. In this, as in increasingly large areas of medical care today, the rationality of applying scientific knowledge now imposes on medicine new obligations to make explicit (where they are concealed), and to eliminate, situations of conflicting interests. These obligations are logical consequences of the transformation of folk medicine into scientific medicine. They raise in scientific forms the question of 'truth maximisation'. The social costs of untruthfulness are now clear and they fall randomly on rich and poor alike. The dishonesty of donors can result in the death of strangers.

The unethical consequences of not seeking to know what is true in one sector of medical care spreads corrosively into other sectors and begins to envelop broader areas of social life and non-market institutions; some evidence of the growth of unethical practices affecting prisons, homes for retarded children, hospitals and clinical laboratories was provided in earlier chapters. It seems that more people have less protection against new forms of exploitation as market considerations and the conformities of market behaviour invade the territory of social policy.

It is because we reject both the notion of historical inevitability in the making of social policy and the fetish of the final solution that we have ended this study with some discussion of the individual's right and freedom to give. We have tried to argue in relation to this particular area of human conduct that certain instruments and institutions of policy have a potential role to play in sustaining and extending personal freedoms. These have positive and negative aspects; both have to be exercised politically and have to be continually facilitated if they are to survive.

In a positive sense, we believe that policy and processes should enable men to be free to choose to give to unnamed strangers. They should not be coerced or constrained by the market. In the interests of the freedom of all men they should not, however, be free to sell their blood or decide on the specific destination of the gift. The choice between these claims – between different kinds of freedom – has to be a social policy decision; in other words, it is a moral and political decision for society as a whole.

There are other aspects of freedom raised in this study which are, or can be, the concern of social policy. Viewed negatively or positively, they relate to the freedom of men not to be exploited in situations of ignorance, uncertainty, unpredictability and captivity; not to be excluded by market forces from society and from giving relationships, and not to be forced in all circumstances – and particularly the circumstances described in this study – to choose always their own freedom at the expense of other people's freedom.

There is more than one answer and there should be more than one choice in responding to the cry, 'Why should I not live as I like?'. The private market in blood, in profit-making hospitals, operating theatres, laboratories and in other sectors of social life limits the answers and narrows the choices for all men – whatever freedoms it may bestow, for a time, on some men to live as they like. It is the responsibility of the state, acting sometimes through the processes we have called 'social policy', to reduce or eliminate or control the forces of market coercions which place men in situations in which they have less freedom or little freedom to make moral choices and to behave altruistically if they so will.

The notion of social rights – a product of the twentieth century – should thus embrace the 'right to give' in non-material as well as material ways. 'Gift relationships', as we have described them, have to be seen in their totality and not just as moral elements in blood distribution systems; in modern societies, they signify the notion of 'fellowship' which Tawney, in much that he wrote, conceived of as a matter of right relationships which are institutionally based. Voluntary blood donor systems, analysed in this book, represent one practical and concrete demonstration of fellowship relationships institutionally based in Britain in the National Health Service and the National Blood Transfusion Service. It is one example of how such relationships between free and equal individuals may be facilitated and encouraged by certain instruments of social policy. If it is accepted that man has a social and a biological need to help, then to deny him opportunities to express this need is to deny him the freedom to enter into gift relationships.

From our study of the private market in blood in the United States, we have concluded that the commercialisation of blood and donor relationships represses the expression of altruism, erodes the sense of community, lowers scientific standards, limits both personal and professional freedoms, sanctions the making of profits in hospitals and clinical laboratories, legalises hostility between doctor and patient, subjects critical areas of medicine to the laws of the marketplace, places immense social costs on those least able to bear them – the poor, the sick and the inept – increases the danger of unethical behaviour in various sectors of medical science and practice, and results in situations in which proportionately more and more blood is supplied by the poor, the unskilled, the unemployed, Negroes and other low income groups and categories of exploited human populations of high blood yielders. Redistribution in terms of blood and blood products from the poor to the rich appears to be one of the dominant effects of the American blood-banking systems.

Moreover, on four testable non-ethical criteria, the commercialised blood market is bad. In terms of economic efficiency, it is highly wasteful of blood; shortages, chronic and acute, characterise the demand and supply position and make illusory the concept of equilibrium. It is administratively inefficient and results in more bureaucratisation and much greater administrative, accounting and computing overheads. In terms of price per unit of blood to the patient (or consumer), it is a system which is five to fifteen times more costly than the voluntary system in Britain. And, finally, in terms of quality, commercial markets are much more likely to distribute contaminated blood; the risks for the patient of disease and death are substantially greater. Freedom from disability is inseparable from altruism.

17

Patient choice and patient empowerment in northern European health systems: a conceptual framework
Richard Saltman

Extracts from Saltman RB (1994) Patient choice and patient empowerment in northern European health systems: a conceptual framework, International Journal of Health Services. 24(2): 201–29.

The issue of patient choice has become an important touchstone of health care reform across Northern Europe. The proper role for patients as against physicians and other professional providers, on the one hand, and health sector administrators and managers, on the other, is under increasing scrutiny with publicly operated health systems in Britain and the Nordic countries. In a similar if converse pattern, the existing degree of patient choice and/or influence over both logistical and clinical issues has come under growing cost-related questions in liberal, social-insurance-based systems of continental Europe such as those of The Netherlands, France, and Germany.

The introduction of greater patient choice can be very much a two-edged sword, cutting both for and against the ability of a health system to achieve sound policy objectives. Like most market-derived reforms, the balance of positive to negative consequences in the introduction of choice reflects the organizational and institutional context within which patients make their decisions. Indeed, the outcome of the same act—for instance, selecting one's primary care physician—can have opposite effects upon the overall performance of a health system. Choosing one's primary care physician can have positive policy-related results if, by selecting from among a number of general practitioner (GP) or GP-led primary care teams, a patient feels a stronger commitment to what shifts from "the" to "his or her" doctor, and thus greater comprehensiveness and continuity of preventive as well as curative health services are possible. This type of bond between patient and primary care provider also can result in lower health care costs, because of both more knowledgeable diagnosis and patient management as well as higher levels of patient compliance.

Alternatively, increased patient choice can result in exactly the opposite policy-related outcome. If, as in some continental countries and, most egregiously, in the United States, patients can choose a narrowly trained specialist or subspecialist as his or her primary care physician in a fee-for-service payment environment, the outcome is likely to be expensive, technically driven, curative rather than less expensive, socially driven, preventive-directed services. In this latter instance, the combination of patients hopping around from specialist to specialist in search of coordinated care, with physicians earning a fee-for-service payment for each extra diagnostic test or therapeutic effort, is likely to produce high costs, low continuity, and less favorable rates of patient compliance.

In sum, the question of choice needs to be analyzed as a question not only of the patient role but of the structural context within which the patient exercises that role. The same act can have different outcomes for health policy, and thus lead to different recommendations, contingent upon the general characteristics of the health system within which choice is adopted. As a consequence, patient choice cannot stand alone as an isolated policy objective. By itself, choice would result in the dismantling of major health, social, and financial advantages that have been built up within publicly operated health systems over a number of decades. If accompanied by major changes in system structure such as the privatization of publicly operated facilities, the introduction of voucher systems for private sector services, and a reduction in direct administrative controls without a requisite increase in regulative and evaluatory mechanisms, the introduction of choice can have very different—and very deleterious—consequences. Thus, the central policy challenge regarding choice is to understand it as a mechanism capable of improving the performance of *current* publicly operated health systems, within *existing* publicly accountable parameters that define present arrangements. It is within this specific policy framework that this study is presented.

Conceptualizing patient empowerment

The notion of empowering patients has taken on considerable currency within the last several years. It is not uncommon to hear managers and planners in the United Kingdom claim that the central motivation behind one or another structural change in the delivery system is to "better empower" their patients. This language will likely become a feature of Nordic health care debates as well: in Sweden, the conclusion of the National Commission on Power and Citizenship that citizens felt "least powerful" in the health sector[1] suggests that this type of discussion is already underway.

The phrase "empowerment" is one that takes on different meanings for different groups. What managers in the United Kingdom have in mind is not at all related to what patient advocates understand by the term. Moreover, the notion of empowerment reflects a variety of connected components, ranging from choice of individual provider to influence over treatment modalities, from control over budgetary allocations to elections for health-related politicians. Like much of the current search toward a new paradigm in Northern European health systems, there is as yet little agreement as to what the proper meaning of this term should incorporate.

Drawing on varying opinions being voiced in current debates, Figure 17.1 presents a rudimentary typology of patient empowerment. Starting with patient advice and appeals, it moves from the least to the most empowered priorities for the individual patient. This continuum is characterized by the change from moral suasion (the ability only to ask to be heard) through formal political control (the ability to select key health-related officials) to countervailing power (the ability to control one's own organizational destiny). This is of course a composite overview, in which certain finer distinctions have been overlooked: for example, that citizens select insurance packages and elect political officials, while patients choose physicians and hospitals. Some analysts also might disagree about the relative placement of different activities: there is a tendency for elected officials and planners to overstate the value of elected officials and collective choice, thereby conflating formal or content democracy with direct or process democracy.[2]

The central point, however, is the degree of individual leverage over specific service delivery decisions. Ultimately, as the hierarchical arrangement of alternatives suggests, it is budgetary authority and resource allocation that are the only practical surrogates for organizational power. To become empowered, therefore, patients have to wrest substantial control over these two financial mechanisms away from managers as well as from physicians.

The typology set out in Figure 17.1 attempts to classify the concrete degrees of authority that can be considered to create "empowered patients." Among various distinctions established within it, two analytically important dichotomies bear mention. One is the distinction between logistical and clinical treatment forms of choice. (For an example of the intellectual confusion created by conflating these two strategies, see note 3, which insists that evidence indicating patients know little about clinical conditions leads to the conclusion that patients are incapable of choosing a GP.) Logistical in this context refers to issues of scheduling, timing, physician responsiveness, and convenience; clinical treatment refers to selection among alternative indicated medical, surgical, rehabilitative, or long-term custodial options. The second dichotomy is that between content and process forms of democratic authority.[2] As noted above, content democracy is a measure of formal political control over decisions in a particular subject area—for example, through general election of a national government and representative assembly. Process democracy refers to the direct participation of citizens in decisions about a subject area—both collectively through local boards and/or individually through personal decisions. Modifying Hirshman's[4] notions about organizational behavior, the concept of process democracy moves beyond formal electoral authority to create both "voice" (forums for verbal participation) and "choice" (options to select alternative approaches). Saltman and von Otter[2] have argued that "choice" should include not just the option to withdraw from the public arena and "go private," but also "lateral entry" within present public institutions—that is, withdrawing only from one particular public provider not from the entire publicly operated system. In Figure 17.2, content democracy refers to patient choice among both logistical and clinical alternatives, but both available *within* existing publicly operated health systems.

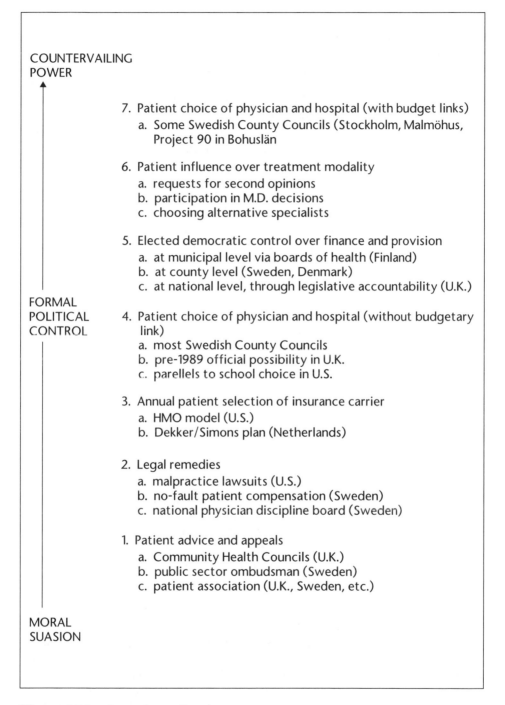

COUNTERVAILING
POWER

↑

FORMAL
POLITICAL
CONTROL

MORAL
SUASION

7. Patient choice of physician and hospital (with budget links)
   a. Some Swedish County Councils (Stockholm, Malmöhus, Project 90 in Bohuslän

6. Patient influence over treatment modality
   a. requests for second opinions
   b. participation in M.D. decisions
   c. choosing alternative specialists

5. Elected democratic control over finance and provision
   a. at municipal level via boards of health (Finland)
   b. at county level (Sweden, Denmark)
   c. at national level, through legislative accountability (U.K.)

4. Patient choice of physician and hospital (without budgetary link)
   a. most Swedish County Councils
   b. pre-1989 official possibility in U.K.
   c. parellels to school choice in U.S.

3. Annual patient selection of insurance carrier
   a. HMO model (U.S.)
   b. Dekker/Simons plan (Netherlands)

2. Legal remedies
   a. malpractice lawsuits (U.S.)
   b. no-fault patient compensation (Sweden)
   c. national physician discipline board (Sweden)

1. Patient advice and appeals
   a. Community Health Councils (U.K.)
   b. public sector ombudsman (Sweden)
   c. patient association (U.K., Sweden, etc.)

Figure 17.1   A typology of patient empowerment

Beyond viewing patient choice in terms of logistical versus clinical and content democracy versus process democracy terms, one can also see it in commercial versus democratic and thus economic versus political categories (Figure 17.2). Taking this perspective, patient choice has increasingly been viewed in the United Kingdom as the introduction of a commercial or "business" model into the prior catchment-based planning structure. In this approach, health services are implicitly understood to become commodities in a market within which patients exercise "consumer-sovereignty" in their selection of one over another "product," with patient decisions based on essentially the same criteria as those used to select any other consumer durable in a competitive marketplace: that is, price, quality, the availability of after-purchase servicing, and the like. This commercial or business approach applies in practice what neoclassical economists discuss in theory: notions about "rational economic man" making individual decisions based on sufficient information and time. This perspective typically is associated with conservative political parties, and is often utilized to justify the introduction of vouchers for purchase of services from either public or private providers (about which more will be said below).

- logistical vs. clinical
- content democracy vs. process democracy
- commercial vs. democratic
- economic vs. political
- individualist vs. communitarian

Figure 17.2 Alternative forms of patient choice

The conceptual alternative is to view patient choice as an exercise in democratic rather than commercial rights. In this second perspective, patient choice becomes a mechanism whereby individuals can exercise more influence over what happens to them inside a publicly operated health system, and thus more control over the conditions within which they live—a central tenet of democratic theory in general. In this understanding, choice of hospital and physician (like that of school or day-care center) gives individuals the ability to influence the provision of important residence-tied services in much the same way that citizens in advanced industrial societies have at least some degree of influence if not control over political activity (through elections), economic activity (through labor union membership and (codetermination), and also social insurance (through registration, payout options, and so forth). Patient choice becomes a political characteristic in which patients through their participation help legitimate the underlying authority and appropriateness of the service delivery system. This democratic political view of patient choice logically should be associated with progressive political parties, which in other areas of society traditionally have supported individual participation and local control.

A further dichotomy regarding choice, and an interesting concomitant of the economic versus political argument, might be termed the possessive individualist versus the social communitarian view of patient choice. These distinctions are derived from an ongoing academic debate in the United Kingdom about the need to revive the necessary characteristics for what has been termed "civic republicanism."[5] In this context, patient choice can be seen as part of a general movement not just toward empowered patients but rather a broader notion of "citizenship." Drawing on the ancient Greek tradition of the polis, civic republicanism would understand choice as a duty not a right, as based in motivation and education not passive consumption, and as requiring "doing" rather than "getting" or "taking." In effect, citizens in this model contribute to the social whole by their acts—hence the classification social communitarian—rather than simply taking from it as a part of "possessive individualism."[6] One valuable insight into choice from this analytic perspective is that appropriate exercise of patient choice, like that of political citizenship generally, is not natural at all but rather the gradual outcome of learning and education. In effect, competent patients like sagacious citizens are made not born. In taking the distinctions between economic and political notions to this level, one can argue that patient choice, seen as a component of civil republicanism, can become part of the philosophical antidote to possessive individualism rather than its synonym. In concrete political terms, rather than adding yet another instrument to the 1980s armamentarium that eliminates social responsibility over increasing areas of human activity, patient choice—properly construed and introduced in a correctly constructed environment—could become a mechanism to educate citizens into greater participation in society and responsibility for their fellows. This would be a considerably different outcome from the current state of patient powerlessness as described in some of the Swedish Commission on Power and Citizenship studies.[1]

A third set of conceptual frameworks reflect the distinction between *patient satisfaction* and *patient empowerment* (Figure 17.3). Stated starkly, the extensive paraphernalia that managers have begun to develop in the United Kingdom and elsewhere to address the patient as a consumer—service guides, marketing surveys, advertisement campaigns, patient advocacy schemes, and patient satisfaction surveys—reflect a fundamentally different understanding of the role of the patient than does direct decision-making about appropriate providers made by the patient as user. To draw on a 19th century philosophical metaphor, the patient as consumer remains the compliant *object* of the service delivery system, in contrast to the patient as decision-making user who thereby becomes the active *subject* of the service system.[2]

These distinctions reflect an assessment that managerial decision-making authority is neither challenged by nor shared with patients when the patient is viewed as a consumer. On the contrary, managers seize upon various marketing vehicles in an effort primarily directed toward increasing the market share of their own institutions. Winkler has characterized this process of managerial manipulation along the following three-part continuum: (*a*) customer relations: polite attentiveness in the attitudes of receptionists, telephone operators, etc.;(*b*) neutralization:

including a token consumer representative on various provider committees; and (c) marginalization: emphasizing patient satisfaction within the existing resource-allocating infrastructure. Even self-advocacy, whether by formal advisory groups such as community health councils in the United Kingdom, by organized patient groups or by officially appointed "patient representatives" (such as the Swedish ombudsman), fails to break out of this manipulative context. In the final analysis, advocacy is premised on the "good will" of the manager, and as such involves the exercise, to refer to the earlier conceptual continuum (Figure 17.1), of *moral suasion* rather than anything approximating *countervailing power*. As recent history in the United Kingdom, Sweden, and Finland has demonstrated, even recourse to the ultimate advocacy tactic—utilizing the media to print unfavorable stories about managerial abuses—can be dismissed by managers and planners as unrepresentative and no more than "waving the bloody shirt."

- consumer vs. user
- object vs. subject
- marketing vs. decision-making
- patient satisfaction surveys vs. patient choice
- managerial paternalism vs. managerial responsiveness

Figure 17.3   Patient satisfaction versus patient empowerment

What emerges from this conceptual analysis is a complicated two-part picture. First, the notion of patient empowerment can be viewed as a continuum, in which substantially varying degrees of patient involvement in the workings of the health system are referred to as "empowerment" by one or another participant in the current health care debate. Second, there are the substantially less nuanced set of dichotomies that distinguish what can be broadly characterized as two distinct *Weltanshauungen* or world-views about patient choice. One view is that of "economic man" in a consumer-characterized business-driven model; the other is "political man" in a user-characterized democratically driven analysis. While these two world-views of patient choice partially overlap with the continuum framework, they represent the two basic nuts-and-bolts alternatives that could be deemed the "true" form of patient choice. During the 1980s, the view of the patient as the economic consumer received a wide and substantive airing in many international forums. In contrast, the notion of patients as political or democratic users has only begun to be explored within the context of publicly operated health systems.[2]

Achieving patient empowerment

The process of empowering patients within publicly operated health systems is far from a *tabula rasa* situation. In bits and pieces, patients already have considerable empirical experience with the exercise of influence (or even occasionally control)

over logistical and/or clinical aspects of the health care they receive. Moreover, past experience has clarified the objectives that an effective patient-empowering system should seek to accomplish, and the types of institutional innovations that greater empowerment would require.

Modifying factors

In thinking about patient choice and the process of empowering patients, one limiting factor is the degree of patient willingness to utilize choice options when offered. While this restriction is the obvious concomitant of any new form of freedom—that people who receive it may not be either prepared for or interested in utilizing it—thus far there has been little relevant research about factors that influence patient willingness and/or ability to make choices about the use of specific health services.

Conceptually, four major categories of modifying factors can be identified. As indicated in Figure 17.4, they fall into primary and secondary categories of influence.

I.   Primary Influences
        Structure of health care services
        Structure of financing
        Type of care (acute vs. elective)
        Number of accepted treatment options
II. Secondary Influences
    A.   Social Influences
        Education
        Occupation
        Social class
        Social networks
        Religious affiliation or ethnic status
    B.   Psychological Influences
        Mental attitude
        Childhood experiences and habits
    C.   Demographic Influences
        Rural vs. urban
        Majority vs. minority (ethnic or racial group)
        Age
        Sex

Figure 17.4   Factors that modify patient decision-making

Primary factors clearly reflect the types of systemic opportunities and/or obstacles discussed above. Whether patients have a structural alternative, for example, in terms of service provider or institutions, and whether that alternative is financed on an equal basis to other forms of care, has a fundamental impact on the ability of patients to exercise choice. Also in this category are the clinical characteristics of the care involved: acute care, particularly trauma care, is very limited in terms of the latitude for patient choice that is available for elective, rehabilitative, or chronic care. Similarly, if a particular condition is viewed by most clinicians as having only one acceptable treatment modality, patient choice becomes limited to a single yes-or-no decision.

The more helpful portion of Figure 17.4, however, falls in the area of secondary influences. They include the elements of an individual's makeup and/or situation that help explain how different types of patients can be expected to respond to opportunities regarding influence or choice regarding health care services. As Figure 17.4 indicates, these secondary influences can be separated into three sub-groups: social influences, psychological influences, and demographic influences.

Patients' preferences

In reviewing the evidence that supports the notion of patient choice as a viable goal, perhaps the most important aspect is that patients *prefer* to have choice. How much choice, at what level, and to what degree may well be secondary to the simple desire of patients to be empowered in the process itself. In logical terms, one only needs two good alternatives in order to become empowered. Moreover, as the marketing strategies of large retail businesses suggest, a small shift of 1 or 2 percent of patronage can make a substantial impact on a supplier's overall financial situation. Thus, only a few patients need exercise choice for the impact to have a salutary influence on provider expectations in a way that benefits all patients whether they intend to change provider or not.

Moreover, patients prefer to make good choices. Outcomes-related research in the United States indicates that patients choose to go more often to hospitals that had better-than-expected outcomes and/or a medical school affiliation.[7] Thus, even when systematic information about outcomes is not available, patients who have the ability to choose their provider appear to select a higher-quality institution.

An important observation is that modern medical procedures often involve personal life-style as much as expert scientific criteria.[8] The prostatectomy, mastectomy, and childbirth examples all involve what are personal preferences regarding treatment alternatives and/or how one wishes to lead ones' life. As a consequence, patients are increasingly insistent that they as well as their physicians be involved in making elective treatment decisions.

One should further note that it is the *perception* of a choice that can be equally as important as the *reality* of it.[8] If a patient feels he or she had a hand in selecting the site and provider, or an influence in deciding the treatment modality, the patient not only is likely to be more satisfied with the outcome but also—an important clinical issue—may well be more compliant with the treatment and pharmacological schedules established by the physician. This is not an argument for fraudulent marketing on the image of choice alone, but rather a recognition that the perception of choice itself is valuable.

Objectives of effective patient influence

Having surveyed the current evidence for patients' interest in and ability to make decisions related to their care, and then reviewed the key factors that appear to modify and/or delimit that interest and ability, it is possible to draw together what the objectives or goals of empowering patients might be. What precisely could be achieved by empowering patients? What contribution to the structure of health services and of the overall welfare state could a well-designed program of patient choice make?

The objectives of patient empowerment include a wide range of changes in the structure, character, and outcome of health-related activities (Figure 17.5). At the most concrete level, patient empowerment should result in a practical improvement in the patient's situation within the service delivery system. Improvement should take place with regard to logistical matters—for example, shorter queues, increased on-time appointments by physicians, and greater responsiveness to patient desires for information and education—as well as clinical decision-making matters—direct participation where appropriate in decisions about elective, rehabilitative, and/or chronic treatment patterns.

A necessary concomitant of these direct service delivery outcomes is increased patient influence over budgetary allocations. In most aspects of publicly operated health systems, budgets are distributed on a command-and-control basis according to incremental criteria. For patients to enjoy enhanced logistical and clinical influence, however, their decisions must be directly tied to the short-term budgetary mechanism—patient choice must be the steering mechanism.[9] Thus, a key objective of enhanced patient influence is a restructured budgetary framework in publicly operated health systems, such that patients not providers or managers make the central allocative decision. Of course, this reformed budgetary framework in no way requires that exclusively fee-for-service medicine be introduced, nor that global budgetary ceilings cease to be set by politically accountable authorities. Experience from the United States with exploding health care costs, overinvestment in expensive medical facilities, and overtreatment of many clinical conditions makes clear the debilitating consequences of allowing pure fee-for-service reimbursement to predominate at either the GP or hospital level. What is necessary, however, is to enable patient choice to replace much of the present top-down command-and-control allocative mechanism for distributing health care resources within the established financial ceilings.

- Reduction of logistical obstacles (queues, etc.)
- Influence over clinical treatment decisions
- Influence over budgetary allocations
- Improvement in clinical quality
- Direct participation in residence-tied services ("process democracy")
- Direct political accountability of providers
- Legitimation of health system decision-making
- Civic republicanism and public duty
- Education for choice and self-autonomy

Figure 17.5 Objectives of patient empowerment

Parallel to improved outcomes in clinical and logistical arenas is an improvement in the quality of care. Generally speaking, the quality of clinical care per se is high in publicly operated health systems. One area of potential quality improvement that does exist concerns consistency of outcomes—ensuring that patients in smaller and/or more rural institutions receive the same standard of clinical care and as a result have similar levels of outcomes after treatment. Additional improvements are important in developing arrangements in areas such as continuity of care (between hospital, primary care, and social and home care services) and responsiveness of professional personnel to patient preferences and concerns. In all these matters, heightened patient involvement in the choice of provider, and in the concomitant allocation of budgets, can have a salutary impact. While patients obviously are not qualified to pass judgment on technical aspects of health services, they are entirely capable of making astute assessments about many outcomes, as well as about the process involved in achieving them. Further, on issues connected with selecting treatment options for rehabilitative or chronic conditions, custodial care for the elderly, and also elective clinical procedures amenable to patient involvement through such devices as interactive video discs, the central patient pressure is likely to focus on the quality of the services available, and the likelihood of as successful an outcome as possible. This emphasis by empowered patients on quality contrasts notably with the probable primary emphasis of managers in a contract-based reform system upon issues of cost.[10]

Continuing through the objectives of patient empowerment (Figure 17.5), the remaining five outcomes focus on issues of politics and education. With regard to politics, empowered patients can be expected to have an impact on at least four areas. First, enhanced patient choice and influence involves direct participation by patients in one of the key residence-tied services they receive in modern society (education and child care are two other important services to residential communities). This outcome reflects a broader argument about the need for the welfare state to move beyond formal to process forms of democratic control.[11] If citizens can have at least some direct input into the political, economic, and social insurance dimensions of their lives, then the logic of democratic theory suggests that citizens also should have similar levels of direct input into key welfare state services that are tied to the communities in which they live—such as health care and education. Patient choice of provider and site as well as influence over treatment decisions, when tied to budgetary allocations, increases the direct participation of the citizenry in the process of governing what is ostensibly *their* health system.

A second political factor concerns accountability of providers. In the prior command-and-control model, physicians and nurses were accountable not to patients but to the elected authorities that administered the health care system whether at the national (United Kingdom), regional (Sweden, Denmark), or municipal (Finland) level. Once patient choice is put in place—and backed up with a budgetary mechanism—then providers also become directly accountable to the patients they serve. This is not to argue that physicians will suddenly become subservient to patients any more than they have been to politicians and administrators. Indeed, the potential for "provider capture" will continue as before. However, empowered patients reflect a shift in at least some authority from politicians to individual citizens, and as such have the opportunity to redress the decision-making balance in a positive manner.

A third political outcome from patient empowerment concerns the overall legitimacy of the service delivery system. An important long-term factor in citizen willingness to pay for publicly operated health systems is their sense that the overall goals and structure of the health system are politically appropriate and broadly acceptable to the population as a whole. Legitimacy enables a health system to impose changes and/or sacrifice on various components—on patients and providers in particular—in order to achieve benefits for the good of the system overall. If citizens feel that they have a direct participatory role in the decisions made within the health system, particularly as they affect the specific care they receive, they are more likely to regard the entire sector as politically legitimate and thereby worthy of their long-term support.

Fourth and last, patient empowerment can, as noted above, take the form of enhancing citizen duty and "civic republicanism." Properly construed and constructed, patient choice can overcome the centrifugal tendencies of possessive individualism by leading citizens to recognize that their participation and decisions can construct a new public "commons," within which choice enhances rather than reduces the options available to their peers. Thus, seen as a duty rather than a personal indulgence, patient empowerment can add a new participatory democratic dimension to the political reconstruction of post-industrial society.

These four outcomes from patient empowerment—direct participation, political accountability, system legitimation, and civic republicanism—together indicate the potentially powerful political consequences that patient choice can generate. Well beyond its impact on the specifics of service delivery (i.e., logistical, clinical, and quality of care activities), patient choice has a strongly political dimension that should be borne in mind by both advocates and detractors.

The final outcome from a properly defined program of patient empowerment involves citizen education. In many respects, this category reflects the translation of the other outcomes listed in Figure 17.5 from patient choice into a learning process: that is, learning to choose a provider, learning to participate politically, etc. Nonetheless, the educational component of the benefits of a patient choice program is considerable, and in a certain sense deeper and more potentially long lasting. Indeed, to return to the theme of civic republicanism, it is difficult to overestimate the importance of an educated citizenry, capable of participating in the political decision-making process, for the maintenance and continuation of a strong and stable democratic system of government.

Notes

1   Petersson, O., et al. *Medborgarnas Makt.* Carlsson's bokförlag, Helsingborg, 1989.

2   Saltman, R. B., and von Otter, C. Voice, choice, and the question of civil democracy in the Swedish welfare state. *Econ. Ind. Democracy* 10: 195–209, 1989.

3   Charny, M., Klein, R., and Tipping, G. K. Britain's new market model of General Practice: Do consumers know enough to make it work? *Health Policy* 14: 243–252, 1990.

4   Hirshman, A. O. *Voice, Exit and Loyalty.* Harvard University Press, Cambridge, Mass., 1970.

5   Oldfield, A. *Citizenship and Community: Civic Republicanism and the Modern World.* Routledge, London, 1990.

6   MacPherson, C. B. *The Political Theory of Possessive Individualism: Hobbes to Locke.* Clarendon Press, Cambridge, England, 1962.

7   Luft, H., Granick, D. W., and Mark, D. H. Does quality influence choice of hospital? *JAMA* 263(27): 2899–2906, 1990.

8   von Otter, C. Personal communication, 1991.

9   von Otter, C., and Saltman, R. B. *Valfrihet som stymedal.* Arbetslivscentrum, Stockholm, 1990.

10 Saltman, R., and von Otter, C. Public competition versus mixed markets: An analytical comparison. *Health Policy* 11: 43–55, 1989.

11 Saltman, R. B., and von Otter, C. *Planned Markets and Public Competition: Strategic Reform in Northern European Health Systems.* Open University Press, Buckingham, England, 1992.

18

Giving consumers of British public services more choice: what can be learned from recent history?
Perri 6

Extracts from Perri 6 (2003) Giving consumers of British public services more choice: what can be learned from recent history? Journal of Social Policy 32: 239–70.

If there is to be a significant extension of individual consumer choice schemes in public services, it will be important that their design reflects learning from the experience of choice in the last decade or more. There is a need for comparative analysis of that experience between different fields of public service. For, while many factors that explain the consequences of introducing or extending individual choice may be specific to particular services, comparative analysis is the most effective method for distinguishing those service-specific factors from ones that are more generic. Moreover, policy debate about choice is often conducted by reference to general claims about its benefits, difficulties or unwanted conse-quences, or to hypothesised inferences from one field to another, for the evaluation of which comparative analysis is well suited. Comparison should also illuminate the range of possible designs for choice schemes, and may suggest important clues about the reasons for their being selected, and, we might hope, at least some hypotheses for further exploration about the relationship between goals, designs and consequences.

This article offers a preliminary and provisional comparison based on a review of literature on the experience of individual consumer choice since the late 1980s in nine fields of British public services, examining what can be said about the extent to which the likely goals were achieved, and of other problems encountered.

The social policy literature is bulging with very diverse taxonomies and discussions of problems with consumer choice programmes. In order to introduce some order into the discussion, some forcing of material into a taxonomy and perhaps even some arbitrariness in selecting priority problems is unavoidable. In focusing on the three categories of problems, Table 18.1 attempts to mitigate these problems by taking categories from the literature wherever possible, and by selecting problems on each of what appear to be the three main areas. These are problems of distributional process and outcome (coded D), problems of efficiency (coded E) (one problem at least has had to be given both codes: no doubt there is a case that others could be too), and problems of political risk (coded P) by which is meant the possibility that politicians and professionals may be subject to embarrassment and criticism in the media or from interest groups for allowing some consumers to rely on public funds when they choose certain services that may be deemed by others to be 'bad', 'frivolous', 'inappropriate' or 'ineffective' choices.

Table 18.1 summarises the findings of the review of the literature on these problems.

On the evidence of the literature reviewed here, there is remarkable variation between the nine fields in the UK, in what has been attempted, in what has been achieved, and in the incidence of the problems encountered.

Table 18.1 Unintended problems with consumer choice programmes in the UK

Field of choice/problem type	School choice	Nursery vouchers	Higher education	Choice of GP	Choice of consultant	Choice of treatment	Direct payments	Community care	Social rented housing
D: Zero-sum polarisation	Potentially quite severe; may be limited by regulation; prior polarisation was in any case severe	Not tried for long enough to tell	Slight	Not severe	Not severe	Not severe	No	May be a small problem in some parts of residential care	Some evidence
D: Segregationist consumer choice within publicly financed sector	Significant, severe in some areas esp. SE England, but always true	Not tried for long enough to tell	Significant, but not severe; may be partly compensated by regulation of teaching quality	May be some	Unlikely	Not relevant	Not relevant	May be some in residential care	Some evidence: too early to tell re Choice-based lettings schemes
D: Uncompensated cream-skimming by suppliers	Significant problem in some areas	May have been important	Not a severe problem; may have been worse re Oxford and Cambridge prior to 1988	Probably limited	Limited	May be relevant	Not relevant	May be significant	Some evidence for RSLs, and some LAs against homeless
D: Inadequate differential voucher compensation for individual disadvantage	May be significant	May have been important	Probably limited prior to 1998 introduction of tuition fee loans	Even less significant even than under internal market	Not important	Probably limited	May be important, but too early to tell	Significant in respect of some disabilities	Not relevant

Field of choice/problem type	School choice	Nursery vouchers	Higher education	Choice of GP	Choice of consultant	Choice of treatment	Direct payments	Community care	Social rented housing
D/E: Producers choose consumers	Severe, at top of market	Significant	Important phenomenon, but not considered a problem, or at least partially compensated	Limited risk	May be significant	Not relevant	Significant problem due to discretionary nature of eligibility for scheme	May be significant	May become more significant as RLs replace local authorities
E: Lack of market entry	Severe problem	No: schools entered rapidly	Small problem, offset by strong capability of existing universities to expand in response to demand expansion	Problems, but not arising from consumer choice	Problems, but not arising from consumer choice	Not relevant	Not important in most areas: in future, there may be labour shortages for certain helper roles	Significant problem in domiciliary care in some areas	Entry by RSIs is mainly response to administrative measures, not consumer choice
E: Lack of exit: consumers locked into failing suppliers	Significant, despite administrative 'special measures'	Not tried for long enough to tell	Relatively small problem	Not known	Possibly important	No	No	May be a problem in some areas	Significant problem
E: High transaction costs for consumers, producers, financing agency	Significant problem for more conscientious choosers	Significant problem for suppliers	Moderately high for consumers and suppliers	Part of wider problem of administrative burden on suppliers	Not important	Not relevant	Too early to tell: at present, seems containable	Some evidence of burden for some suppliers	Significant costs for LA suppliers in administering points schemes
E: Weak incentives for consumers to shop around for more economical option	No	No	No	Observed, but may not be important	May be significant	May be significant		Significant problem in residential care	Significant problem

Field of choice/ problem type	School choice	Nursery vouchers	Higher education	Choice of GP	Choice of consultant	Choice of treatment	Direct payments	Community care	Social rented housing
P: Political risks from financing choices unpopular with others	Only at the margin for some stigmatised faith schools, surviving 'progressive', schools, etc	No	At the margin for some courses	No	No	At the margin, mainly for IVF, some elective cosmetic procedures	Some evidence re alternative therapies	Only important in occasional scandal	No
Sources	Gewirtz et al., 1995; Glatter and Woods, 1994; Woods et al., 1998; Gorard, 1997; Noden, 2000; 2000a,b; Gorard and Fitz, 1998a,b; Goard and Taylor, 2002; Taylor, 2001; Kendall and Holloway, 2001; Walford, 1996; Levačić, 1994; Whitty et al., 1998; David et al., 1994; Flatley et al., 2001; Adnett and Davies, 2000; Bradley et al., 1999	Education and employment committee, 1997; Sparkes and West, 1998	Ahier, 2000; Watson and Bowden, 1999; Dolton et al., 1997; Johnes, 1997; Hesketh, 1999; Middleton, 2000; Parry, 1999; Power, 1999; 2000; Power, 2000	Charny et al., 1990; Shackley and Ryan, 1994; Fotaki, 1998; Goodwin, 1998; Glennerster et al., 1994	Mahon et al., 1993; Jones et al., 1993	Mahon et al., 1993; Jones et al., 1993	Maglajlic et al., 2000; Clark and Spafford, 2001; Glendinning et al., 2000a,b	Knapp et al., 2001; Wistow et al., 1994; 1996; Wigley et al., 1998; Bland, 1999; Ware et al., forthcoming	DETR, 2001; DTLR, 2001; Clapham and Kintrea, 1986; Pawson and Kearns, 1998

Few would oppose increased choice for consumers of public services on general principle. However, designing policies to support greater individual choice presents government with both technical challenges and with conflicts of values. If they are willing to settle upon clear goals – a big 'if' in any policy process – then they must choose between the available goals, and be willing to accept that all the good things do not go together. The review suggests that goals of maintaining and incrementally raising satisfaction, and some improvement in efficiency can be achieved, but those of responsiveness and experiment are more difficult and more expensive to achieve. The tighter the fiscal constraints and rationing, the more difficult it is to achieve these goals.

Moreover, if policy makers are concerned about equitable distributional outcomes, and want to avoid some of the problems of adverse selection, zero-sum polarisation and segregation on the basis of ascribed characteristics, then they must be prepared to spend large sums, for none of the design solutions to these problems are cheap. Adequate differential weighting of vouchers, expansion of total market size, compensation for incentives to cream-skim, and transaction cost absorption are all expensive. That there are hard choices to be made between combating social exclusion and fiscal rectitude is hardly news, but at a time when New Labour ministers are proclaiming loudly that they can achieve both, perhaps a reminder is timely.

Moreover, any initiative to extend consumer choice must take account of the lessons of the last fifteen years, and in particular of the experience of implementing the reforms of the third Thatcher administration. These represent the policy inheritance (Rose and Davies, 1994), and that inheritance, whilst by no means immutable, also defines the range of existing organisational capabilities in each of these services. New or extended programmes of consumer choice would require new capabilities among voucher-issuers and producers, even if they can be designed in ways that do not assume any change in the patterns of consumer preferences and willingness to bear the costs of conscientious choice.

Reference and further reading

Adnett, N. and Davies, P. (2000), 'Competition and curriculum diversity in local schooling markets: theory and evidence', *Journal of Education Policy*, 15(2): 157–67.

Ahier, J. (2000), 'Financing higher education by loans and fees: theorising and researching the private effects of a public policy', *Journal of Education Policy*, 15(6): 683–700.

Archer, L. and Hutchings, M. (2000), '"Bettering yourself": discourses of risk, cost and benefit in ethnically diverse, young working class non-participants' constructions of higher education', *British Journal of Sociology of Education*, 21(4): 555–74.

Argys, L., Rees, D. and Brewer, D. (1996), 'Detracking America's schools: equity and zero cost?', *Journal of Policy Analysis and Management*, 15(4): 623–64.

Ball, S. J., Davies, J., David, M. and Reay, D. (2002), '"Classification" and "judgement": social class and "cognitive structures" in choice of higher education', *British Journal of Sociology of Education*, 23(1): 51–72.

Bearse, P., Glomm, G. and Ravikumar, B. (2000), 'On the political economy of means-tested education vouchers', *European Economic Review*, 44: 904–15.

Beisäcker, A. E. (1988), 'Aging and the desire for information and input in medical decisions: patient consumerism in medical encounters', *The Gerontologist*, 28(3): 330–5.

Blair, T. (2001), Prime Minister's speech on public service reform, available at http://www.number10.gov.uk/news.asp?NewsId=2765&SectionId=32.

Bland, R. (1999), 'Independence, privacy and risk: two contrasting approaches to residential care for older people'. *Ageing and Society*, 19(5): 539–60.

Bowles, S. and Gintis, H. (1996), 'Efficient redistribution: new rules for markets, states and communities', *Politics and Society*, 24(4): 307–42.

Bradley, S., Johnes, G. and Millington, J. (1999), 'School choice, competition and the efficiency of secondary schools in England', Working paper, EC3/99, Centre for Research in the Economics of Education Discussion Paper, Department of Economics, Lancaster University, Lancaster.

Brighouse, H. (2000), *School Choice and Social Justice*, Oxford: Oxford University Press.

Carvel, J. (2002), 'Milburn retreats on care home standards', *The Guardian*, 20 August, p. 5, available at http://politics.guardian.co.uk/publicservices/story/0,11032,777610,00.html.

Charny, M., Klein, R. E., Lewis, P. A. and Tipping, G. K. (1990), 'Britain's new market model of general practice: do consumers know enough to make it work?', *Health Policy*, 14(4): 243–52.

Chubb, J. and Moe, T. (1990), *Politics, Markets and America's Schools*, Washington, DC: Brookings Institute.

Clapham, D. and Kintrea, K. (1986), 'Rationing, choice and constraint: the allocation of public housing in Glasgow', *Journal of Social Policy*, 15(1): 51–67.

Clark, H. and Spafford, J. (2001), *Piloting Choice and Control for Older People: An Evaluation*, York: Policy Press and Joseph Rowntree Foundation.

Darkins, A. (1996), 'Shared decision making in health care systems', unpublished paper, cited in O. Morgan (1998), *Who Cares? The Great British Health Debate*, Oxford: Radcliffe Press, p. 76, n.15.

David, M., West, A. and Ribbens, J. (1994), *Mother's Intuition? Choosing Secondary Schools*, London: Palmer Press.

Davis, A., Ellis, K. and Rummery, K. (1997), *Access to Assessment: Perspectives of Practitioners, Disabled People and Carers*, Bristol: Policy Press.

Department of the Environment, Transport and the Regions (2000), 'Quality and choice: a decent home for all', The Housing Green Paper, Department of the Environment, Transport and the Regions, London.

Department of Health (1999), 'National service framework for mental health', Department of Health, London.

Department of Health (2002), 'Expanded services and increased choices for older people: investment and reform for older people's social services', Department of Health, London, July, available at http://tap.ukwebhost.(eds.)com/doh/Intpress.nsf/page/2002–0324? Open Document.

Department for Transport, Local Government and the Regions (2001), 'Choice based lettings', Newsletter issue No 1, Department for Transport, Local Government and the Regions, London, available at http://www.housing.dtlr.gov.uk/information/cbaselet/newsletter.htm.

Dolton, P. J., Greenaway, D. and Vignoles, A. (1997), '"Whither higher education?" an economic perspective for the Dearing Committee of Inquiry', *The Economic Journal*, 107: 710–26.

Doty, P., Kasper, J. and Litvak, S. (1996), 'Consumer-directed models of personal care: lessons from Medicaid', *Milbank Quarterly*, 74(3): 377–409.

Dowding, K. (1992), 'Choice: its increase and its value', *British Journal of Political Science*, 22: 301–14.

Education and Employment Committee (1997), The operation of the nursery education voucher scheme', 12 March, 3rd report, session 1996–97, House of Commons papers, vol. 25.

Fiske, E. B. and Ladd, H. F. (2000), *When Schools Compete: A Cautionary Tale*, Washington, DC: Brookings Institution.

Flatley, J., Connolly, H., Higgins, V., Williams, J., Coldron, J., Stephenson, K., Logie, A. and Smith, N. (2001), 'Parents' experiences of the process of choosing a secondary school', Research report 278, Department for Education and Skills, London.

Fotaki, M. (1998), 'The impact of market oriented reforms on patient choice and information: a case study of cataract surgery in outer London and Stockholm', *Social Science and Medicine*, 48(10): 1415–32.

Gewirtz, S., Ball, S. J. and Bowe, R. (1995), *Markets, Choice and Equity in Education*, Buckingham: Open University Press.

Gibson, A. and Asthana, S. (1999), 'What's in a number?', *Research Papers in Education*, 15: 133–54.

Glatter, R. and Woods, P. (1994), 'The impact of competition and choice on parents and schools', in W. Bartlett, C. Propper, D. Wilson and J. Le Grand (eds.), *Quasi-Markets in the Welfare State*, Bristol: SAUS Press, pp. 56–77.

Glendinning, C., Halliwell, S., Jacobs, S., Rummery, K. and Tyrer, J. (2000a), 'Bridging the gap: using Direct Payments to purchase integrated care', *Health and Social Care in the Community*, 8(3): 192–200.

Glendinning, C., Halliwell, S., Jacobs, S., Rummery, K. and Tyrer, J. (2000b), 'New kinds of care, new kinds of relationships: how purchasing services affects relationships in giving and receiving personal assistance', *Health and Social Care in the Community*, 8(3): 201–11.

Glennerster, H. (1992), *Paying for Welfare: The 1990s*, Hemel Hempstead: Harvester Wheatsheaf.

Glennerster, H. (1993), 'The economics of education: changing fortunes', in N. Barr and D. Whynes (eds.), *Current Issues in the Economics of Welfare*, Basingstoke: Macmillan, pp. 176–99.

Glennerster, H. (1998), 'Education: reaping the harvest?', in H. Glennerster and J. Hills (eds.), *The State of Welfare: The Economics of Social Spending*, 2nd edn, Oxford: Oxford University Press, pp. 27–74.

Glennerster, H., Matsaganis, M. and Owens, P. with Hancock, S. (1994), *Implementing GP Fundholding*, Buckingham: Open University Press.

Goodwin, N. (1998), 'GP fundholding', in J. Le Grand, N. Mays and J.-A. Mulligan (eds.), *Learning from the NHS Internal Market: A Review of the Evidence*, London: King's Fund, pp. 43–68.

Gorard, S. (1997), *School Choice in an Established Market*, Aldershot: Ashgate.

Gorard, S. (2000a), 'One of us cannot be wrong: the paradox of achievement gaps', *British Journal of Sociology of Education*, 21(3): 391–400.

Gorard, S. (2000b), 'Questioning the crisis account: a review of evidence for increasing polarisation in schools', *Educational Research*, 42(3): 309–21.

Gorard, S. and Fitz, J. (1998a), 'The more things change ... the missing impact of marketisation?', *British Journal of Sociology of Education*, 19(3): 365–76.

Gorard, S. and Fitz, J. (1998b), '"Under starters" orders: the established market, the Cardiff study and the Smithfield project', *International Studies in Sociology of Education*, 8: 299–314.

Gorard, S. and Taylor, C. (2002), 'Market forces and standards in education: a preliminary consideration', *British Journal of Sociology of Education*, 23(1): 6–18.

Gordon, L. (1996), 'School choice and the quasi-market in New Zealand', in G. Walford (ed.), *School Choice and the Quasi-Market Oxford, Studies in Comparative Education*, vol. 6 (1), Wallingford: Triangle Books, pp. 129–42.

Hardy, B., Young, R. and Wistow, G. (1999a), 'Dimensions of choice in the assessment and care management process: the views of older people, carers and care managers', *Health and Social Care in the Community*, 7(6): 483–91.

Hardy, B., Forder, J., Kendall, J., Knapp, M. R. J. and Wistow, G. (1999b), 'Provider relationships with local authority purchasers', Nuffield Institute for Health, University of Leeds, Leeds.

Hasler, F., Campbell, J. and Zarb, G. (1999), 'Direct routes to independence: a guide to local authority implementation and management of direct payments', National Centre for Independent Living and Policy Studies Institute, London.

Hassel, B. C. (1999), *The Charter School Challenge: Avoiding the Pitfalls, Fulfilling the Promise*, Washington, DC: Brookings Institution.

Henig, J. R. (1994), *Rethinking School Choice: Limits of the Market Metaphor*, Princeton, NJ: Princeton University Press.

Hesketh, A. J. (1999), 'Towards an economic sociology of the student financial experience of higher education', *Journal of Educational Policy*, 14(4): 385–410.

Horvath, A. O. and Symonds, B. D. (1991), 'Relation between working alliance and outcome in psychotherapy: a meta-analysis', *Journal of Consulting and Clinical Psychology*, 38: 139–49.

Hoxby, C. (2001), 'School choice and school productivity, or could school choice be a tide that lifts all boats?', paper presented at the National Bureau for Economic Research conference on The economics of school choice, Islamorada, Florida, 22–24 February.

Inglehart, J. K. (1995), 'Medicaid and managed care', *New England Journal of Medicine*, 332: 1727–31.

Johnes, G. (1997), 'Cost and industrial structure in contemporary British higher education', *The Economic Journal*, 107: 727–37.

Jones, D., Lester, C. and West, R. (1993), 'Monitoring changes in health services for older people', in R. Robinson and J. Le Grand (eds.), *Evaluating the NHS Reforms*, Buckinghamshire Hermitage Policy Journals, pp. 130–54.

Kendall, I. and Holloway, D. (2001), 'Education policy', in S. P. Savage and R. Atkinson (eds.), *Public Policy under Blair*, Basingstoke: Palgrave, pp. 154–73.

Klein, R. E. (1995), *The New Politics of the NHS*, 3rd edn, Harlow: Longman.

Klein, R. E. and Millar, J. (1995), 'Do-it-yourself social policy: searching for a new paradigm?', *Social Policy and Administration*, 29(4): 303–16.

Knapp, M., Hardy, B. and Forder, J. (2001), 'Commissioning for quality: ten years of social care markets in England', *Journal of Social Policy*, 30(2): 283–306.

Ladd, H. F. and Fiske, E. B. (2001), 'The uneven playing field of school choice: evidence from New Zealand', *Journal of Policy Analysis and Management*, 20(1): 43–64.

Le Grand, J. (1989), 'Markets, welfare and equality', in J. Le Grand and S. Estrin (eds.), *Market Socialism*, Oxford: Oxford University Press.

Le Grand, J., Mays, N. and Mulligan, J.-A. (eds.) (1998), *Learning from the NHS Internal Market: A Review of the Evidence*, London: King's Fund.

Levačić, R. (1994), 'Evaluating the performance of quasi-markets in education', in W. Bartlett, C. Propper, D. Wilson and J. Le Grand (eds.), *Quasi-Markets in the Welfare State*, Bristol: SAUS Press, pp. 35–55.

Maglajlic, R., Brandon, D. and Given, D. (2000), 'Making Direct Payments a choice: a report on research findings', *Disability and Society*, 15(1): 99–113.

Mahon, A., Wilkin, A. and Whitehouse, C. (1993), 'Choice of hospital for elective surgery referral: GPs' and patients' views', in R. Robinson and J. Le Grand (eds.), *Evaluating the NHS Reforms*, Buckinghamshire: Hermitage Policy Journals, pp. 108–29.

Matsaganis, M. and Glennerster, H. (1994), 'Cream skimming and fundholding', in W. Bartlett, C. Propper, D. Wilson and J. Le Grand (eds.), *Quasi-Markets in the Welfare State*, Bristol: SAUS Press, pp. 245–67.

Merrett, S. (1979), *State Housing in Britain*, London: Routledge & Kegan Paul.

Middleton, C. (2000), 'Models of state and market in the "modernisation" of higher education', *British Journal of Sociology of Education*, 21(4): 537–54.

Milburn, A. (2002), 'Redefining the National Health Service', Speech by Rt Hon Alan Milburn MP, Secretary of State for Health, to the New Health Network, London, 15 January 2002.

Moe, T. (ed.) (1995), *Private Vouchers*, Stanford, CA: Hoover Institution Press.

Morgan, O. (1998), *Who Cares? The Great British Health Debate*, Oxford: Radcliffe Press.

Mulligan, J.-A. (1998), 'Health authority purchasing', in J. Le Grand, N. Mays, and J.-A. Mulligan (eds.), *Learning from the NHS Internal Market: A Review of the Evidence*, London: King's Fund, pp. 20–42.

Noden, P. (2000), 'Rediscovering the impact of marketisation: dimensions of social segregation in England's secondary schools, 1994–99', *British Journal of Sociology of Education*, 21(3): 371–90.

Office of Public Services Reform (2002), 'Reforming our public services: principles into practice', Office of Public Services Reform, Cabinet Office, London.

Parry, G. (1999), 'Education research and policy making in higher education: the case of Dearing', *Journal of Education Policy*, 14(3): 225–41.

Pawson, H. and Kearns, A. (1998), 'Difficult to let housing association stock in England: property, management and context', *Housing Studies*, 13(3): 391–414.

Power, S. (2000), 'Educational pathways into the middle class(es)', *British Journal of Sociology of Education*, 21(2): 133–46.

Redmayne, S. (1995), 'Reshaping the NHS: strategies, priorities and resource allocation', NAHAT Research Paper 13, National Association of Health Authorities and Trusts, Birmingham.

Robinson, R. and Le Grand, J. (eds.) (1993), *Evaluating the NHS Reforms*, Buckinghamshire: Hermitage Policy Journals.

Rose, R. and Davies, P. (1994), *Inheritance in Public Policy: Change without Choice in Britain*, New Haven: Yale University Press.

Roth, A. and Fonay, P. (1996), *What Works for Whom?*, New York: Guilford Press.

Safran, J. D. and Muran, J. C. (1996), 'The resolution of ruptures in the therapeutic alliance', *Journal of Consulting and Clinical Psychology*, 64: 447–58.

Secretary of State for Health (2002), 'Delivering the NHS plan: next steps on investment, next steps on reform', Cm 5503, Stationery Office, London.

Segal, L. (1998), 'The important of patient empowerment in health system reform', *Health Policy*, 44(1): 31–44.

Shackley, P. and Ryan, M. (1994), 'What is the role of the consumer in health care?', *Journal of Social Policy*, 23(4): 517–41.

Social Services Inspectorate (2002), 'Modern Social Services: A Commitment to Reform', London.

Sparkes, J. and West, A. (1998), 'An evaluation of the English Nursery Voucher Scheme, 1996–1997', *Education Economics*, 6(2): 171–84.

Syme, S. L. (1996), 'To prevent disease: the need for a new approach', in D. Blane, E. Brunner and D. Wilkinson (1996), *Health and Social Organisation: Towards a Health Policy for the Twenty First Century*, London: Routledge, pp. 21–31.

Taylor, C. (2001), 'Hierarchies and "local" markets: the geography of the "lived" marketplace in secondary education provision', *Journal of Education Policy*, 16(3): 197–214.

Tudor Hart, J. (1971), 'The inverse care law', *The Lancet*, 1: 405–12.

Walford, G. (1996), 'School choice and the quasi-market in England and Wales', in G. Walford (ed.), *School Choice and the Quasi-Market, Oxford Studies in Comparative Education*, 6(1), Wallingdon: Triangle Books, pp. 49–62.

Ware, T., Matosevic, T., Hardy, B., Knapp, M., Kendall, J. and Forder, J. (forthcoming), 'Commissioning services for older people: the view from care managers, users and carers', *Ageing and Society.*

Waslander, S. and Thrupp, M. (1995), 'Choice, competition and segregation: an empirical analysis of a New Zealand secondary school market', *Journal of Education Policy*, 10(1): 1–26.

Watson, D. and Bowden, R. (1999), 'Why did they do it? The Conservatives and mass higher education, 1979–1997', *Journal of Education Policy*, 14(3): 243–56.

West, A., Noden, P., Edge, A., David, M. and Davies, J. (1998), 'Choices and expectations at primary and secondary stages in the state and private sectors', *Educational Studies*, 24(1): 45–60.

Whitty, G., Power, S. and Halpin, D. (1998), *Devolution and Choice in Education: The State, the School and the Market*, Buckingham: Open University.

Wigley, V., Fisk, M., Gisby, B. and Preston-Shoot, M. (1998), 'Older people in care homes: consumer perspectives', Liverpool John Moores University, Liverpool.

Wilton, P. and Smith, R. D. (1998), 'Primary care reform: a three country comparison of "budget holding"', *Health Policy*, 44(2): 149–66.

Wistow, G., Knapp, M., Hardy, B. and Allen, C. (1994), *Social Care in a Mixed Economy*, Buckingham: Open University Press.

Wistow, G., Knapp, M., Hardy, B., Forder, J., Kendall, J. and Manning, R. (1996), *Social Care Markets: Progress and Prospects*, Buckingham: Open University Press.

Woods, P. A., Bagley, C. and Clatter, R. (1998), *School Choice and Competition: Markets in the Public Interest*, London: Routledge.

Zimmer, R. W. and Toma, E. F. (2000), 'Peer effects in private and public schools across countries', *Journal of Policy Analysis and Management*, 19(1): 75–92.

6, P. (1998), 'Ownership and the new politics of the public interest services', *Political Quarterly*, 69(4): 404–14.

PART 5

Accountability and regulation
Introduced by Kieran Walshe

We live in the age of accountability – what Michael Power memorably termed 'the audit society' (Power, 1999). Teachers, doctors, social workers, lawyers, managers, architects and accountants – all have found themselves and the organizations they work in subject to ever greater external scrutiny, as the willingness of the public to trust professionals and the organizations they work in to do a good job has been replaced by an increasing demand that they demonstrate or prove how well they are doing. This part explores the relatively recent growth of regulation and other forms of external accountability in the health care sector.

It is worth beginning with some theory, by way of background. In conventional economics, the need for regulation is often somewhat reluctantly acknowledged and seen as an unfortunate consequence of 'market failure' that should be avoided if at all possible (Ogus, 1994). In other words, economists would generally prefer to see systems managed by the idealized discipline of the marketplace, rather than overseen by regulators or subject to intervention and control from government agencies. In a market, they argue, poor performance by a provider leads to consumers going elsewhere, and that provider must improve or go out of business. Scarcity of a product results in the price going up, and that leads to increased production until a price is found at which supply and demand are in balance. Competitive pressures act continually to drive providers to innovate and improve in order to keep pace with others and to secure competitive advantage. That is all very well, but the practical reality is that perfect markets are rarer than economists would like them to be, and that many markets exhibit one or more signs of market failure.

There are five commonly acknowledged causes of market failure: the existence of natural monopoly or monopsony (where there is only one supplier or purchaser of something and so no effective competition); information asymmetry (typically when purchasers lack information about the goods or services they are buying or know less than producers do, and so they cannot make informed purchasing decisions); so-called moral hazard (where a good is paid for by one person or group and consumed by someone else so the consumer has no economic incentives to constrain or limit use); public goods (where what is being produced is effectively for a whole community and so cannot really be purchased by individuals just for themselves); or externalities (where the production and supply of something has effects or consequences for others, apart from the purchaser or consumer alone). All of them apply, to varying degrees, to the health care industry and this helps to explain why there are very few countries in which markets and competition play significant roles in health care provision, and why government intervention and regulation are commonplace. Moreover, healthcare systems are laden with non-economic goals, which cannot be secured through the market alone. There are often distributional justice concerns like fairness and equity, and social goals like promoting social solidarity, and protecting vulnerable groups like the old, the young, socially excluded groups, immigrants and those unfortunate enough to have serious or chronic illnesses. These legitimate and important goals are another reason why governments choose to intervene in the health care system, and why they often play substantial roles in healthcare financing and provision, as discussed in Part 1.

In the past, governments often secured their control of the health care system through ownership – the state both raised the funds (whether through taxation or compulsory insurance schemes) and spent it (through hospitals and clinics for which government owned the assets, employed the staff and controlled their operation). Paradoxically, in such state-operated health care systems, health care professionals often had considerable clinical freedom and performance was often not actively measured or managed. However, in health care and in other public services, there has been an increasing shift over the last two decades away from government-run health care systems and towards systems in which funding and provision are in the hands of a variety of more independent and autonomous entities, and government is at arm's length from the health care system (Preker and Harding, 2003). In place of direct control through ownership, governments have increasingly turned to systems of regulation to govern health care systems and to provide them with mechanisms to achieve their policy goals. Moreover, changing societal notions of accountability have led to a growth in performance measurement and management, designed to assure us that health care providers are offering high-quality, effective health care.

But how should governments regulate health care systems, or how should performance be measured? What needs to be regulated, and what are the structures, systems and processes that government needs to put in place? What makes for effective (or ineffective) regulation and how do governments ensure that they are not simply replacing market failure with some form of regulatory failure? How should performance targets, incentives or measures be set, and what effects do they have on providers' behaviour and performance?

This part presents a series of readings that explore the widespread growth in public services performance measurement and regulation over the last 20 years, and offers a number of theoretical and conceptual frameworks for understanding, analysing and critiquing regulatory and other approaches to improving perform-ance.

It starts with a contribution from Michael Power (2000), who originated the term 'audit society' to describe the growth of all forms of formal oversight and accountability in his seminal book of the same name (Power, 1999). Here, he reviews the central arguments of that book, writes thoughtfully and reflectively about the way in which the ideas he pioneered have been taken up and used by others, and sets out the case for further empirical research to understand the effects of the audit explosion. He outlines the capacity for audit to be either a force for improvement and a foundation for intelligent and sensitive oversight, or an increasingly ritualized, formulaic and bureaucratic exercise undertaken for symbolic reasons. Audit can be used to rebuild trust in institutions or to replace it.

Then Christopher Hood, Oliver James and Colin Scott 2000) present a cogent and comprehensive analysis of the growth of public services regulation in the UK, and its causes and consequences. They argue that despite the deregulatory rhetoric of government, there has been a continuing growth in the scale and scope of regulation in government, driven in part by the reduction or removal of other control mechanisms. They analyse the nature of those regulatory regimes, and point in particular to growing concerns about regulatory burden and the emergence of ideas like responsive regulation and enforced self-regulation as important developments in regulatory policy.

There is a long and important history of external assessment in the health care sector, which Charles Shaw (2001) describes in his paper, ranging from voluntary and fairly informal programmes of medical peer review, to more formalized and mandated systems of accreditation. He notes the growth or proliferation of such schema across the health care systems of many or most developed nations, and documents a shift towards more formal, explicit and mandatory forms of assessment. While Shaw's paper approaches the topic from a UK perspective, Troyen Brennan (1998) provides a complementary account oriented primarily towards the USA, which has probably the most closely regulated health care system in the world. He considers the evolution of systems for regulating doctors, hospitals and health insurers, before turning to explore the extent to which regulation has contributed to improving quality, or could do so if regulatory systems and policies more closely reflected our understanding of the science of quality improvement in organizations. After Shaw and Brennan's more descriptive contributions, we move to Kieran Walshe and Stephen Shortell's (2004) paper that offers a framework for understanding and analysing systems of social regulation, based on fieldwork undertaken mainly in the USA, and which tentatively sets out a number of principles for effective regulation.

Finally, this part moves from focusing on regulation to tackling the systems for performance measurement, with a paper from Gwyn Bevan and Christopher Hood, (2006), which elegantly explores another aspect of Power's audit explosion – the growth of targets, performance measures and league tables and their effects on health care organizations. They conclude that while there is evidence that target setting drives performance improvement, the widespread and pervasive nature of gaming and perverse incentives creates serious concerns about its wider benefits, though there are ways in which such problems can be ameliorated or minimized.

Summary

- Public trust in health professionals has been replaced by an increasing expectation that they demonstrate how well they are doing. As a consequence, professionals such as teachers, doctors, accountants and others are subject to greater scrutiny and this has resulted in the growth of regulation and other forms of external accountability.
- In conventional economics the need for regulation is seen as a consequence of 'market failure' and hence something to be avoided. In reality perfect markets rarely exist and many markets exhibit various signs of market failure that are applicable to the health care industry.
- Health care systems are also characterized by the existence of non-economic goals so that concerns over fairness and equity, protecting the vulnerable and promoting social cohesion are legitimate goals for government intervention in health care.
- The reading selected in this part explores some key questions in relation to the regulation of health care and offers some theoretical and conceptual frameworks for understanding and analysing regulation and other approaches to improving performance.

References and further reading

Ayres, I. and Braithwaite, J. (1992) *Responsive Regulation: Transcending the Deregulation Debate*. Oxford: Oxford University Press.

Brennan, T.A. and Berwick, D.M. (1996) *New rules: Regulation, Markets and the Quality of American Health Care*. San Francisco, CA: Jossey-Bass.

Hood, C., Scott, C., James, O. et al. (1999) *Regulation Inside Government*. Oxford: Oxford University Press.

Ogus, A. (1994) *Regulation: Legal Form and Economic Theory*. Oxford: Clarendon Press.

O'Neill, O. (2002) *A Question of Trust*. Cambridge: Cambridge University Press.

Power, M. (1999) *The Audit Society: Rituals of Verification*. Oxford: Oxford University Press.

Preker, A.S. and Harding, A. (2003) *Innovations in Healthcare Delivery: The Corporatization of Public Hospitals*. Washington, DC: World Bank.

Walshe, K. (2003) *Regulating Healthcare: A Prescription for Improvement?* Maidenhead: Open University Press.

The readings

Power, M. (2000) The audit society: second thoughts. *International Journal of Audit*, 4: 111–19.

Hood, C., James, O. and Scott, C. (2000) Regulation of government: has it increased, is it increasing, should it be diminished? *Public Administration*, 78(2): 283–304.

Shaw, C.D. (2001) External assessment of health care. *British Medical Journal*, 322: 851–54.

Brennan, T.A. (1998) The role of regulation in quality improvement, *Milbank Quarterly*, 76(4): 709–31.

Walshe, K. and Shortell, S.M. (2003) Social regulation of healthcare organisations in the United States: developing a framework for evaluation, *Health Services Management Research*, 17: 79–99.

Bevan, G. and Hood, C. (2006) What is measured is what matters: targets and gaming in the English public healthcare system, *Public Administration*, 84(3): 517–38.

19

The audit society – second thoughts[1]
Michael Power

Extracts from Power M (2000) The audit society: second thoughts, International Journal of Auditing 4: 111–19.

Summary

This essay reviews the central arguments of *The Audit Society* (Power, 1999) and re-considers the causes and consequences of the audit explosion. In the UK during the 1980s there was a systemic growth of auditing activity which needed to be explained. The causes of this audit explosion can be found in three areas: the rise of the 'new public management; increased demands for accountability and transparency; the rise of quality assurance models of organisational control. It is argued that these hypothesized causes require further empirical support and that more research is needed, particularly to demonstrate that the audit explosion is not simply a UK phenomenon. The consequences of the audit explosion are also considered and the role of auditable performance measures in shaping individual and organizational activity is discussed. Again, it is concluded that greater empirical analysis is required. The essay then addresses the criticism that the book does not define auditing sufficiently clearly. It is argued that the vagueness of the word 'audit' was an important condition of possibility for the audit explosion. Finally, the prospects for reconstructing audit to avoid dysfunctional side effects are considered.

Introduction

Financial auditing is an *inferential* practice which seeks to draw conclusions from a limited inspection of documents, such as budgets and written representations, in addition to reliance on oral testimony and direct observation. There is an established tradition of investigating this inference process experimentally within the frame of cognitive science, although very little, if any, of this kind of auditing research is done in the United Kingdom. In contrast to this experimental tradition, a smaller body of work has focused on the *social* and *institutional* support for the elements of this inference process. Indeed, it is argued that the appropriate organizing model for understanding auditing is not that of the isolated act of practitioner judgement, but that of collectively negotiated settlements (Power, 1995). From this point of view, the very possibility of individual judgement is the product of many other factors, including training in institutionally accepted practices of evidence collection, such as statistical sampling (Power, 1992; Carpenter and Dirsmith, 1993).

This modest sociological project was given a new context and a dramatic shift of focus as auditing broadly understood began to play a prominent social and economic role during the mid to late 1980s. For example, the word 'audit' began to be used with increasing frequency by politicians, regulators and consultants in many different fields: health and safety, medicine, education, intellectual property, environmental management as well as the more established corporate financial auditing area (Power, 1994). During some ICAEW funded research on the border territory between environmental and financial auditing (Power, 1997) I had a hunch that something systematic was going on, something that could not be captured or explained only by reference to financial auditing. This required a fresh view of financial auditing as just one possibility in an evolving assembly of techniques and procedures. From this point of view, it made sense to explore the connections and resemblances between financial auditing and other forms of assessment, evaluation and inspection. In short, it was necessary to look beyond the 'silo' of financial auditing studies at monitoring, checking and reporting in their most general sense.

The label for the hunch that something systematic was going on over and above financial auditing was the 'audit society'. The concept was invented, like many ideas before it, in the LSE staff bar sometime in 1994; it was a kind of marker, a logical space for future work, rather than a well-defined concept with a clear point of reference. The German sociologist Max Weber once wrote that: 'an ingenious error is more fruitful for science than stupid accuracy' (Quoted in Collins, 1992). It is for others to judge whether, for all their flaws, the arguments supporting the idea of the audit society are a useful error (see the critiques by Bowerman et al., 2000; Humphrey and Owen, 2000). It is clear that the ideas of the 'audit society' and of the 'audit explosion' (Power, 1994) require a great deal more conceptual and empirical work.

To understand the audit society it is not sufficient, although undoubtedly useful, simply to quantify the amount of auditing going on. It is also important to understand the growth and circulation of an idea of audit, a growth in which accountants have been powerful agents in selling their auditing capabilities but which cannot solely be explained in this way. A practice like financial auditing is not simply a collection of routines for collecting and evaluating evidence. It is also very importantly an idea or model circulating in the institutional environment, an idea whose fortunes practitioners themselves cannot control, hence the 'expectations gap' for financial auditing. This means that auditing is not merely done in a technical sense, it is also used and appealed to, blamed, praised, regulated, reformed, written about and debated. The idea of audit and what it can or might deliver expresses the *aspirational* dimensions of the practice(s), dimensions which are not always closely linked to actual operational capacity. In short, the further one is from the detail, the easier it is to talk of what auditing might, can and must do. Naturally, some of this talk takes place in the profession itself, but it is not only an internal affair.

Value for Money (VFM) auditing is a good example of the thesis; it was a powerful idea for public sector reform long before it approached anything like a consistent and coherent practice at the operational level. Indeed, the nuts and bolts of VFM auditing continue to be hotly debated (e.g. whether effectiveness auditing extends to evaluation type work) and the concept itself circulates freely despite considerable operational variety (Pollitt et al., 1999). So the audit explosion was not only the explosion of concrete practices, it was also and necessarily the growth and intensification of an idea about audit in a number of different spheres. But why?

Causes

Although it is undoubtedly a simplification, three more or less discrete causes or pressures gave rise to the audit explosion in the UK in the late 1980s:

1. The cluster of ideas which constitute the 'New Public Management' (Hood, 1991) increased demands for financial and VFM auditing. The 1980s were characterised by financial constraint and a commitment to organizational and financial reform in public sector institutions. In this setting auditing and inspecting practices became highly valued and important tools of change. In different ways the National Audit Office and the Audit Commission became prominent forces in government, playing an evolving and complex constitutional role. In the late 1990s these pressures for change in the UK have not abated: for example, the Audit Commission will establish a 'best value' inspectorate (Thatcher, 1999) and in health care standards of clinical practice will be enforced by the Commission for Health Improvement (CHI). While the word 'audit' may have decreased in importance, the demand for monitoring has not. A fresh explosion may even be predicted on the back of 'best value' demands.

2. The audit explosion was also driven by closely related political demands on behalf of citizens, taxpayers, patients, pupils and others for greater accountability and transparency of service providing organizations. These demands in the name of accountability were not only confined to the public sector; they have also surfaced in the private sector, most notably in the developments in corporate governance. Indeed, private sector corporate governance thinking now provides a template for the organisation of public sector control (London Stock Exchange, 1998). As accountability and governance issues span the traditional public-private divide, financial auditing has been drawn into, and affected greatly by, these pressures. It is still unclear how many of the proposals in the much discussed 'Audit Agenda' (APB, 1994), which was an exploration of the *idea* of financial auditing, will work out and the field is being pushed in many new directions in the name of accountability and assurance (AICPA). For example, internal auditing is acquiring a new prominence, particularly as a result of recent guidance in the UK

on internal control (APB, 1998; ICAEW, 1999; Power, 1999) and organizations like the National Health Service are investing in risk management practices.

3. The third related cluster of pressures for an audit explosion have come about from the rise of quality assurance practices and related transformations in regulatory style. The origins of these pressures are complex and diverse, but a simple and plausible story can be told with two parts.

The first part of the story concerns the emergence of quality assurance from an industrial production context to become a universal schema (e.g. ISO 9000). This all purpose structure is represented in Figure 19.1.

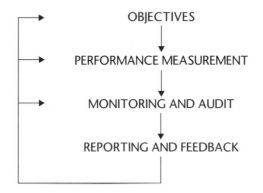

Figure 19.1 A general model of self-auditing and control

Quality assurance programmes require that organizations and their sub-units establish objectives, design performance measures to reflect those objectives, monitor actual performance and then feed the results of this monitoring back for management attention. Quality auditing works both as the specific monitoring and reporting part of the system and also, importantly, as the verification of the system structure as a whole i.e. the integrity of the entire loop of self-observation which this procedural structure represents. This epitomizes 'control of control' (Power, 1999, p.66).

The second part of the explanation is a parallel transformation in regulatory style, which is moving away from a command and control mode of operation. The intention is to regulate target organizations indirectly 'from below'. Audit in its various forms becomes an important possible solution to the problem of regulatory compliance, it defines a space in which regulatory compliance can be negotiated and constructed (Hutter, 1997). Regulatory systems rely increasingly upon 'control of control' i.e. the audit of self-control arrangements which are increasingly characterized in terms of risk management. The audit of these internal controls or self-checking arrangements is a growing industry, an internal control 'explosion' (Maijoor, 2000) which borrows its structure from the quality assurance model in Figure 19.1. Perhaps nowhere is it more apparent than in the financial services industry where regulation is explicitly designed to rely on internal and external checking functions (Goodhart et al., 1998). Whether regulators are relying on in-house risk management models for derivatives, or systems for teaching quality

(Gray and Berry, 2000), the general model in Figure 19.1 is the same. Delegation and internalization of control are coupled to audit processes which seek to reconcile local learning and improvement mechanisms to demands for performance and regulatory compliance.

These then are three overlapping pressures for increased auditing, evaluation and monitoring activity. But does this story make too little of accountants and of Thatcherism in the 1980s? Certainly the large accounting firms have been influential agents of change, and the position and role of accountants within economic and political life in the UK as compared to other countries has undoubtedly been a decisive factor in shaping the rise of auditing in this context. However, that this is an incomplete picture is suggested by the fact that financial audit, following the Eighth Directive, is itself subject to the same style of auditing, through the operations of the Joint Monitoring Unit (JMU), as many hospitals, schools and other organizations. One can hardly talk of a conspiracy, a rational one at least, when the conspirators are subject to the very same changes they are imposing on everyone else. It is interesting that many small UK accounting practitioners have complained about the 'audit' of their auditing practices in exactly the same terms that have been levelled against quality and medical auditing i.e. it is too bureaucratic and too focused on form and process.

That *The Audit Society* is not simply about the consequences of 'Thatcherism' is clear from the intensification of the 'culture' of checking under 'New Labour' in the UK. The welfare state is increasingly being displaced by the 'regulatory' state, and instruments of audit and inspection are becoming more central to the operational base of government. However, it remains to be seen how well this argument travels to other countries and systems. The analysis was intended to be generic, and one can hypothesize that an audit explosion would follow the diffusion of the new public management. Further comparative research is needed to test this view.

Consequences

It has been suggested that society is experimenting on itself (Beck, 1992). Certainly, there has been little planning or testing of new auditing practices. Auditing has been introduced as an agency of organizational change without a measured consideration of benefits and possible dysfunctional effects. Although some assessment in terms of compliance costs has been introduced, audit and related ideas of monitoring continue to be understood uncritically; they can be rapidly disseminated without developing an understanding of what may be at stake. In this respect it is plausible to suggest that the audit explosion is fundamentally an ideologically driven system for disciplining and controlling doctors, teachers, university lecturers and so on, and not an instrument of genuine accountability.

To analyse the consequences of auditing it is necessary to focus on the development of what is audited i.e. the performance measures and other forms of accounting which provide an auditable front stage for an organization (see Figure

19.1). There is a developed research literature which draws attention to the role of accounting innovations, particularly in management accounting, in constructing organisational life (Miller 1994). This is not just a matter of what has been called 'creative accounting' i.e. the games that exist to circumvent the intentions behind rules and regulations. Rather, accounting practices, and performance measurement systems more generally, create and support a window on organizational life, one which is often demanded by outside agencies, and which makes various kinds of internal and external intervention possible.

The hunch behind *The Audit Society* is that the design of accounting reports, and of the performance measures by which organizations can be judged, is greatly influenced by the imperative of 'making them auditable', and that this has much to do with agendas for control of these organizations. It follows that many audit processes are not neutral acts of verification but actively shape the design and interpretation of 'auditable performance'. Audit agencies, such as the UK Audit Commission, are active in shaping performance measures which enable audit and inspection. Indeed, Bowerman et al. (2000) argue that it is audit which is really a by-product of a more fundamental performance measurement explosion. They have evidence that many performance indicators are produced but are not audited, and that there is more of an audit 'mess' than a coherent 'audit society'. However, just because a performance measure is not in fact audited does not mean that it was not designed with potential auditability in mind. In the end the argument is an empirical one.

Empirical work also needs to focus on the growing population of 'auditees', ie on the individuals who have experienced an intensification of checking and evaluation of what they do. We are beginning to see how different games of 'creative compliance' are being played around the audit process, games which both frustrate official intentions and which also lead to dysfunctional behaviour. Auditing can create new interests at the expense of others.

The audit explosion refers to the rise of this systems structure and its role in supporting regulation and managerial control. However, Figure 19.1 and the system loop are only a blueprint. There is an extensive literature which questions whether organizations do or could ever function according to the formal self-transparency and vigilance required of Figure 19.1 and its real world instantiations (such as ISO 9000 and its variants) (see Strathern, 1997). The formal management control system functions primarily to make a certain style of auditing possible; it buffers the auditor from an increasingly complex evidence base, is cheaper than extensive attention to actual organizational process, and permits the audit to provide more or less comforting signals to regulators and politicians.

In *The Audit Society* I argue that institutionalized pressures exist for audit and inspection systems to produce comfort and reassurance, rather than critique. If this is true and auditing systems are primarily about reaffirming order, then it will be interesting to see how auditable outcome based performance measurement progresses in the face of system decay, especially given political rhetorics of zero tolerance for poor performance. We can expect to see acute problems for anxious managers who, much like their former Soviet counterparts, will need considerable creativity to manage auditable performance favourably in the face of objective decline. New pressure points, in the form of control agents and audit departments, will be created at great cost to manage these contradictory forces.

Teaching and medicine are in a similar position; newly established systems of auditing may have damaged local cultures of first order practice. Certain activities, which are valued locally, are not represented by official systems or are lost in some general concept of 'goodwill'. Official auditable indicators, in the form of, say, exam results and waiting times, have strange effects on the incentive structure of individuals in organizations.[2] If auditing processes get decoupled from core organizational activities, these effects may be minimal and the audit process becomes an expensive but harmless ritual, which is important for external legitimacy. Where performance measures and systems developed for audit do eventually force changes in organizational habits, these effects need to be systematically documented and fed back into the design process. In short, there is a need for more research on the effects of making agents in organizations accountable in terms of auditable measures of performance.

The audit society reflects the growing influence of auditors themselves as they move into areas of wider influence and service provision. In particular, auditors are de facto major interpreters of political mandates; accountability is concretely realized in the audit process. While there is considerable discussion about the constitutional position of the NAO and Audit Commission (White and Hollingsworth, 1999) ideals of policy neutrality contrast with operational realities where jurisdictions are blurred and where the distinction between audit and policy is unclear. The UK Audit Commission has come to be an explicit agent of change by promoting the systems which make auditing possible (Henkel, 1991; Thatcher, 1999).

Organizations must be changed internally to be audited, and in many cases this may be desirable. It is not denied that it may be a good thing to require teachers to think seriously about their objectives (Gray and Berry, 2000) or to make the private world of hospital consultants more transparent. Nor does the idea of the audit society assume a homogenous process of transformation across all fields. The key issue is to draw attention to the fact that audits do not operate neutrally and have effects on the auditee. The audit explosion has been insensitive to whether these intended changes have been successful, and what unintended changes may have resulted. But to say all this is to leave much of the empirical work to be done in exploring the consequences of the growth of auditing and views of these consequences will undoubtedly differ, as the essays in this volume demonstrate.

Critique

Because the concept of the audit society was invented in advance of detailed empirical work, there remain many unresolved issues and problems. Two will be addressed below.

1. It has been argued that the use of the word 'audit' is not significant. Auditing practices are varied, and evaluation and inspection are different again (Bowerman et al., 2000; Humphrey and Owen, 2000). A great deal of time and effort has been invested in defining and distinguishing meanings of audit, especially in emergent areas such as environmental and clinical auditing. There are also ongoing discussions about the nature of VFM auditing and the difference between performance or effectiveness auditing and financial auditing (Pollitt et al., 1999). Add to this discussions about evaluations and assessments which do not have a verifiable assertion, claimed as one of defining characteristics of audit, as their object and it begins to seem as if the 'audit society' concept has no clear reference point.

It is difficult to deny the reality of this diversity, especially when this is reflected in text books and official accounts. Despite a reasonable attempt (Power, 1999, chapter 6), the relation between auditing, evaluation and inspection remains far from clear. However, two points must be made. First, despite all these attempts at definition and distinction, the vague idea of audit has been an important reference point in policy; this vagueness can be *observed* and analysed. From this point of view, *The Audit Society* is as interested in understanding the power of the word 'audit' as it is in defining it. The idea of audit (and auditors) consists of general and highly idealized elements, and is appealed to and used in a wide variety of policy contexts. The rise of auditing is also as much about the cultural and economic authority granted to people who call themselves auditors as it is about what *exactly* these people do. Indeed, we know that the people we call auditors (and inspectors) actually do many different things.

To call something an 'audit' places it within a field of social and economic relations which would be different if it was called an 'assessment' or 'evaluation'. Labelling activities as audits makes it possible for them to acquire the idealized characteristics of audit over time. For example, the label 'clinical auditing' was used to rename idiosyncratic research activity. Once this collection of ad hoc practices came to be called 'auditing', it also became possible for it to acquire a new public accountability role. In short, against critics of *The Audit Society*, the argument is that vagueness is an essential part of the phenomenon. Once practices can be appropriated by the discourse of audit they can begin to acquire similarities and shared operational templates. In the audit society definitions of auditing are dependent variables.

2. A second unresolved problem is the relation between auditing, organizational democracy and transparency. Being made to be accountable, being required to account and having this account audited, are not the same as being made more transparent or publicly accessible (Bowerman et al., 2000). One might argue that some audit processes discharge a certain style of accountability precisely to *avoid* transparency. In other words, that an audit is done can be more important than what is done and to whom any report is made; being audited *per se* is a badge of legitimacy. Indeed, what seems to be important is less the disclosure to stakeholders promised by the rhetorics of accountability, which lit the fuse for the audit explosion, and more the private discipline of information gathering and control which the audit process imposes.

A related puzzle or paradox of the audit society concerns the nature and periodicity of audit and inspection reports and the extent to which such reports support deliberative processes. Where audit reports are not designed to continue stakeholder dialogue then it is necessary to trust the auditors and their independence becomes an important benchmark of trust. Quality kitemarks and financial audit reports are like this. They are intended simply to indicate the quality of systems, products or services. In contrast National Audit Office VFM audit reports are in narrative form. And social audits, which seem messy and diverse, may worry much less about independent audit reporting and more about stakeholder involvement (Cotton et al., 2000). Here the hypothesis is intriguing: greater stakeholder involvement in auditing, of whatever kind, may alleviate anxieties about auditor independence and may support less standardized reporting.

In *The Audit Explosion* I suggested that the audit society is a less trusting society. However, it was pointed out that audit may in certain circumstances be essential to restore trust between parties and to support institutions, such as capital markets (Hatherly, 1995). This needs further investigation since many teachers and doctors claim that evaluation processes have achieved precisely the opposite by eroding informal goodwill and by making individuals develop new incentives around crude performance measures. There is some work on these effects and more is needed, but it is unlikely that issues of trust in the audit society are as self-evident as *The Audit Society* suggests.

Research is also needed to address and evaluate the implications of new auditing and inspection institutions for the audit society thesis. For example, the National Institute for Clinical Excellence (NICE) will set clinical standards and the Commission for Health Improvement (CHI) will enforce them and oversee local clinical auditing activity. A super regulator for OFTEL, OFSTED and other regulators has been proposed. Where do these processes of 'control of control' end? I have suggested that the audit society threatens an infinite regress to the nth auditor as further layers of regulatory influence are created. But such a theoretical regress must in practice stop somewhere, and further work is needed to document and explain the patterns of 'control of control' in different fields.

Conclusion: reconstructing audit

The primary critical intention of *The Audit Society* remains relevant despite its weaknesses as an empirical set of arguments; the book is simply a plea for greater understanding of the consequences of checking and monitoring for industries, organizations and individuals. Some forms of audit and inspection need to be radically redesigned with greater sensitivity to their consequences and without slavish adherence to performance measures which serve the audit process and little else. But there is no general critical argument here, and each area needs to be looked at on its own merits. The prospects of a light, self directed audit process, which harnesses productive learning and self-help to regulatory compliance, is an attractive ideal. Defensive auditing is the antithesis of this ideal.

The audit implosion thesis is consistent with a more 'responsive' regulatory philosophy (Ayres and Braithwaite 1992) and there is a potential both for the worst excesses of the audit society to be realized and for something more relevant, effective and sensitive to be created. As audit processes are re-designed to reflect risk management ideals, the distinction between audit and consulting becomes increasingly blurred (Jeppeson, 1998), and this may not be to the taste of regulators like the SEC. But a form of anticipatory and integrated risk management, overseen by the auditor/risk specialist may represent the best opportunity to align public policy and corporate objectives. The motif of 'control of control' is likely to remain relevant and useful in characterizing a regulatory system with a greater accent on internal self-inspection. This is especially evident from recent developments in financial services regulation (Goodhart et al., 1998).

Finally, the 'audit society' can be understood as a label for a loss of confidence in the central steering institutions of society, particularly politics. So it may be that a loss of faith in intellectual, political and economic leadership has led to the creation of industries of checking which satisfy a demand for signals of order. In the UK auditing and inspection will be set to work in the name of 'best value' and 'joined-up' government, but we may be forced to understand auditing as part of a general language of decline which attempts to bridge the widening gulf between plans and achievements. One might even see auditing as an elaborate form of confession and periodic purification of organizational order. The interpretations can become ever more exotic but the critical point is clear: a great deal of audit activity has had little to do with efficiency, and few large companies believe the stories of value added that financial auditors promote. The audit explosion is not simply a functional response to complexity and to increasing risk in different areas of society. And yet equally there is a need for more sensitive and more efficient technologies of checking and assurance because of the manufactured dangers that we now face.

Notes

1   This paper was originally presented at the Seventh National Auditing Conference, Cranfield School of Management, Cranfield University, March 21–2 1997 and at the ESRC/CIMA New Public Sector workshop, London School of Economics and Political Science, April 28–9, 1997.

2   In the private sector it might be assumed that auditable performance measures are fully integrated into the core of corporate life. However, here there have also been extensive discussions about the limitations of financial indicators and there is currently much interest in the reporting of non-financial information (ICAEW, 1999). Experimentation in the UK with the Operating and Financial Review is an attempt to pluralize corporate reporting, but the doubtful auditability of qualitative information is regarded as a serious constraint on developments.

References and further reading

AICPA *Assurance Services: New opportunities for CPAs*, http://www.aicpa.org/assurance.

Auditing Practices Board (1998) *Providing Assurance on Internal Control*, London: Auditing Practices Board.

Auditing Practices Board (1994) *The Audit Agenda*, London: Auditing Practices Board.

Ayres, I. and Braithwaite, J. (1992) *Responsive Regulation: Transcending the Deregulation Debate*, Oxford: Oxford University Press.

Beck, U. (1992) *The Risk Society*, London: Sage.

Bowerman, M., Raby, H. and Humphrey, C. (2000) In Search of the Audit Society: Some Evidence from Health Care, Police and Schools. *International Journal of Auditing* 4(1), pp. 71–100.

Carpenter, B. and Dirsmith, M. (1993) Sampling and the Abstraction of Knowledge in the Auditing Profession: An Extended Institutional Theory Perspective. *Accounting, Organizations and Society* 18(1), pp. 41–63.

Collins, R. (1992) Weber's lost Theory of Capitalism: A Systematization. In Granovetter, M. and Swedburg, R. (eds) *The Sociology of Economic Life*, Boulder, Co: Westview Press, pp. 85–110.

Cotton, P., Fraser, I. and Hill, W.Y. (2000) The Social Audit Agenda – Primary Health Care in a Stakeholder Society. *International Journal of Auditing* 4(1), pp. 3–28.

Goodhart, C, Hartmann, P., Llewellyn, D., Rojas-Suarez, L. and Weisbrod, D. (1998) *Financial Regulation: Why, How and Whither Now?* London: Routledge.

Gray, I. and Berry, A. (2000) Some Things in Moderation: A Case Study of Internal Audit. *International Journal of Auditing* 4(1), pp. 51–69.

Hatherly, D. (1995) Review of 'The Audit Explosion'. *Accounting and Business Research* 24(96): 350–351.

Henkel, M. (1991) *Government, Evaluation and Change*, London: Jessica Kingsley.

Hood, C. (1991) A Public Management for All Seasons. *Public Administration* 69(1), pp. 3–19.

Humphrey, C. and Owen, D. (2000) Debating the 'Power' of Audit. *International Journal of Auditing* 4(1), pp. 29–50.

Hutter, B. (1997) *Compliance: Regulation and Environment*, Oxford: Clarendon Press.

ICAEW (1999) *Internal Control: Guidance for Directors of Listed Companies Incorporated in the United Kingdom*, London: Institute of Chartered Accountants in England and Wales.

ICAS (1993) *Auditing into the Twenty First Century*, Institute of Chartered Accountants in Scotland.

Jeppesen, K.K. (1998) Reinventing Auditing, Redefining Consulting and Independence. *European Accounting Review* 7(3), pp. 517–539.

London Stock Exchange (1998) *The Combined Code*, London: LSE.

Maijoor, S. (2000) The Internal Control Explosion. *International Journal of Auditing* 4(1), pp. 101–109.

McInnes, W. (1993) *Auditing into the Twenty First Century*, Edinburgh: Institute of Charterted Accountants in Scotland.

Miller, P. (1994) Accounting as Social and Institutional Practice: An Introduction. In Hopwood, A. and Miller, P. (eds) *Accounting as Social and Institutional Practice*. Cambridge: Cambridge University Press, pp. 1–39.

Pollitt, C., Girre, X., Lonsdale, J., Mul, R., Summa, H. and Waerness, M. (1999) *Performance or Compliance? Performance Audit and Public Management in Five Countries*, Oxford: Oxford University Press.

Power, M. (1992) From Common Sense to Expertise: Reflections on the Pre-History of Audit Sampling. *Accounting, Organizations and Society* **17**(1), pp. 37–62.

Power, M. (1994) *The Audit Explosion*, London: DEMOS.

Power, M. (1995) Auditing, Expertise and the Sociology of Technique. *Critical Perspectives on Accounting* **6**, pp. 317–339.

Power, M. (1997) Expertise and the Construction of Relevance: Accountants and Environmental Audit. *Accounting, Organizations and Society* **22**(2), pp. 123–146.

Power, M. (1999) *The Audit Society: Rituals of Verification*, Oxford: Oxford University Press.

Power, M. (2000) *The Audit Implosion: Regulating Risk from the Inside*, London: ICAEW.

Selim, G. and McNamee, D. (1999a) Risk Management and Internal Auditing: What are the Essential Building Blocks for a Successful Paradigm Change? *International Journal of Auditing* **3**(2), pp. 147–155.

Selim, G. and McNamee, D. (1999b) The Risk Management and Internal Auditing Relationship: Developing and Validating a Model. *International Journal of Auditing* **3**(3), pp. 159–174.

Strathern, M. (1997) 'Improved Ratings': Audit in the British University System. *European Review* **5**, pp. 305–21.

Thatcher, M. (1999) Riding Audit's Big Bang. *Public Finance* March, pp. 18–21.

Various (1999) Knowledge for What? The Intellectual Consequences of the Research Assessment Exercise. *History of the Human Sciences* **12**(4), pp. 111–146.

White, F. and Hollingsworth, K. (1999) *Audit, Accountability and Government*, Oxford: Clarendon Press.

20

Regulation of government: has it increased, is it increasing, should it be diminished?
Christopher Hood, Oliver James and Colin Scott

Extracts from Hood C, James O and Scott C (2000) Regulation of government: has it increased, is it increasing, should it be diminished? Public Administration 78(2): 283–304.

This article looks at regulation of UK government, focusing on the secondary overseers of public bodies beyond the courts and the legislature, the two classic primary regulators of government in constitutional theory. First, it examines the growth of such regulation from the mid-1970s to 1997 – an era of largely Conservative rule witnessing the rise both of the so-called 'New Public Management' and the claimed development of an 'Audit Society' (Power 1997). This first section briefly summarizes findings to 1997 from our earlier research on regulation of government (see Hood *et al.* 1999). In the rest of the article we apply the same framework to examining changes in regulation of UK government under the Blair New Labour government up to the publication of its *Modernising Government* White Paper of 1999 (Cabinet Office 1999). The aim is to characterize and assess the Blair government's plans, practice and philosophy for regulation of government and in particular to evaluate the precepts for regulation of the public sector embodied in *Modernising Government*.

Our argument is that the two decades to the mid-1990s were an era of dramatic but largely unacknowledged growth in regulation of government while public service staff declined. This growth was not even and the style was not uniform across the public sector. But regulation of government seems to have become more formal, complex and specialized in many of its domains despite – or perhaps because of – the ostensible 'New Public Management' drive to 'let managers manage' in the public services. In some ways the Blair New Labour government continued the pattern by announcing plans to extend regulation of government by adding new regulators (notably for 'OFSTED-izing' the NHS) to the Conservative-created ones. But in contrast to the unacknowledged and unrationalized style of regulatory growth of the earlier era, a distinct philosophy of such regulation began to emerge, partly expressed in the 1999 *Modernising Government* White Paper. That philosophy embraced a first, albeit tentative, recognition of the compliance cost problem associated with public-sector regulation and a doctrine of 'enforced self-regulation' involving aspirations to combine the iron fist of Draconian central intervention with the velvet glove of self-regulation. In our assessment of the public-sector regulatory philosophy associated with *Modernising Government*, we argue that the strength of this approach is that it embodies a basic design that could limit regulatory compliance costs in those circumstances where wholesale abandonment of public-sector regulation is neither possible nor desirable. Its corresponding weaknesses include a half-hearted and limited development of the regulatory-design logic and untested assumptions about the politics of regulatory escalation.

As noted earlier, we are concerned here with the secondary regulation of government beyond the direct activity of the primary regulators (parliaments and law courts). Such secondary regulation (roughly though not exactly analogous with regulation of business firms) involves oversight of bureaucracies by other public agencies operating at arm's-length from the direct line of command, the overseers being endowed with some sort of official authority over their charges (cf. Light 1993, pp. 16–17; Harden 1995, p. 302). This secondary regulation is a form of steering or control system that involves a combination of information-gathering, standard-setting and attempts at behaviour modification, but its particular institutional manifestation as regulation broadly comprises three elements (see Hood *et al.* 1999, pp. 8ff), all of which must be present:

1   one public bureaucracy in the role of an overseer aiming to shape the activities of another;
2   an organizational separation between the 'regulating' bureaucracy and the 'regulatee', with the regulator outside the direct line of command (this feature distinguishes intra-organizational controls from arm's-length oversight by another organization);
3   some official 'mandate' for the regulator organization to scrutinize the behaviour of the 'regulatee' and seek to change it.

No one of these elements (discussed at more length in Hood *et al.* 1999) is sufficient on its own to distinguish secondary regulation of government from other processes (like direct line-of-command control, advice or lobbying). It is only when the three elements come together that the arm's-length, authority-based features characteristic of regulation are produced, and that secondary regulation (by bureaucracies) is distinguished from primary control by legislatures and law courts.

On that three-part definition, numerous different families of secondary regulators of government can be distinguished. For instance, some are agents of legislatures (like parliamentary auditors), some are international overseers established by treaty, some are quasi-independent from both legislature and executive government (like probity overseers), some are executive-government organizations created to oversee 'doer' organizations at arm's-length, and some are regulators of both public and private sector organizations (like data protection and safety-at-work agencies). Methods vary too, including audit, inspection, adjudication, authorization and certification. Like regulation of business, regulation of government involves a range of diverse organizations employing different instruments but sharing the three characteristics outlined above.

Has it increased? Regulation of government to 1997

The scale of secondary regulation of UK government on the multi-criterion definition given above cannot be estimated with precision. Dependent on precisely what organizations we count as located within the public sector, our estimate of the number of national-level 'regulator' organizations overseeing public-sector bodies in the mid-1990s ran from about 135 to over 200. Our estimate of the staff size of such regulator organizations ran from almost 14,000 to almost 20,000 and our estimate of the direct annual running costs from about £750m at the low end to about £1bn at the top end (see Hood *et al.* 1998 and 1999, pp. 21–8).

To the direct staff and operational costs of regulator organizations must be added the compliance costs of such regulation – what it costs regulatees to meet the requirements of those who regulate them. Compliance cost data are not routinely collected across government as a whole, and we could only estimate them on the basis of limited data (ibid). Defining compliance costs in the narrowest possible way (excluding other costs and looking only at what it costs regulatees to interact with their regulator, including provision of information requested, consulting the regulator, setting up and acting as guides on visits and inspections), we concluded that the compliance costs of regulation in UK government at the very minimum matched the £750m to £1bn of direct spending on regulatory bureaucracies in the mid-1990s.

Moreover, there is evidence of considerable growth in regulation of government as defined above over the two decades to the mid-1990s. Over a time when UK government substantially downsized in public service staff numbers, secondary regulation of government seems to have 'upsized' markedly, in numbers of organizations, direct spending and staffing. When we examined numbers of regulators in 1976 and 1995 in different parts of the public sector, we concluded that the number of 'regulator' organizations overseeing government had risen by over a fifth during those two decades. Spending appeared to have grown more than the body count of organizations. Over two decades to the mid-1990s overall spending (in constant prices) on regulation of government seemed to have more than doubled, with particularly vigorous growth in ombudspeople and funder-regulators (see Hood *et al.* 1998; Hood *et al.* 1999, pp. 28–33).

For employment, we estimated that the total staffing of regulators of UK government grew by about 90 per cent between 1976 and 1995, and that too is a conservative figure. This dramatic staff growth contrasts sharply with what happened to staffing in the public sector as a whole, with a fall of more than 30 per cent in total civil servants and over 20 per cent in local authority staff (Cabinet Office 1995, p. 47; DOE 1996, p. 57).

In general, therefore, the answer to the first part of the question in the title of this article would seem to be a resounding 'yes'. Secondary regulation of government outside the law courts and legislature grew substantially over the twenty years to the mid-1990s. This finding links to Hoggett's (1996) observation that the public management revolution produced increasing formality of controls and Power's (1997) claim that there was an explosion of formal audit associated with declining trust in professional self-regulation. Whether or not Majone (1994) and others are correct in identifying growth of a 'regulatory state' in society at large, there certainly seems to have been increasing regulation *of* the state. But there was no official policy of increasing regulation of UK government over the twenty years to 1997, no official recognition of the overall pattern and no official discussion of how regulatory growth fitted with the received managerial rhetoric of 'letting managers manage' in public services. Regulation of government grew in an *ad hoc* and unrationalized way and there was no equivalent to the official concern with compliance costs imposed by government regulation of business.

Is it increasing?

The brief summary of our earlier work indicates that the Blair government inherited a legacy of growth in numbers and cost of arm's-length regulators of the public sector, but no coherent doctrine about the design of such regulation. Examination of the Blair government's plans and activities from its election in 1997 to the publication of *Modernising Government* in 1999 indicates at least three main features. The first is continuation and even acceleration of the previous pattern of long-term growth in arm's-length regulation of government. The second is a continuing difference in the style of regulation applied to core Whitehall departments from that applied to local government and other parts of the public sector. The third is aspiration to move public-sector regulation in the direction of 'enforced self-regulation'.

Regulation of government apparently continued to grow in the early years of New Labour. But there were some indications of a change in style, at least in official doctrine. *Modernising Government* and the institutional design ideas on which it built marked a departure from previous practice over public-sector regulation in at least three ways.

One was the first tentative acknowledgement that excessive regulation and regulatory compliance costs could be a problem for the public sector as well as business firms. *Modernising Government* announced the extension of the deregulation provisions (Part 1) of the Deregulation and Contracting Act 1994 to the public-sector (Cabinet Office 1999, p. 38). This proposal was less dramatic than might at first appear, since few of the burdensome regulatory requirements placed on public-sector actors derive from legislation (and, as will be shown in the next section, the deregulatory commitment appeared likely to have very limited overall impact). But it was at least a notable shift in rhetorical tone from a previous pattern of blithe disregard for the costs and burdens of public-sector regulation coupled with official concern about compliance costs and egregious burdens of regulation for business.

A second was more official concern with consistency of practice and linkages among different regulators. *Modernising Government* (ibid, p. 23) expressed concern about the effect of audit and inspection processes in 'hindering cross-cutting work' and proposed more co-ordination of inspection functions, with the development of a common set of inspection principles (ibid, p. 43). This theme was linked to an emphasis on co-ordination that ran through the White Paper, and was reflected in developments like the creation of a Public Audit forum and proposals for a new Best Value inspectorate forum (ibid, p. 37). It suggests some reaction against the *ad hoc* pattern of public-sector regulatory growth over the previous twenty years, with no common practice and even deliberate proliferation of regulators pursuing different and conflicting agendas (as in the early days of the Audit Commission). How far the measures proposed were likely to achieve the co-ordination desired, however, will be discussed in the next section.

A third was official embrace of 'enforced self-regulation' for large parts of public-sector regulation. As noted earlier, Labour inherited a trend towards greater formality in regulation of many public bodies (especially of local government and the outer reaches of the public sector as seen from Whitehall), in the sense of less involvement of regulatees in regulatory decision making and more formal sanctioning rather than persuasion (see Hood *et al.* 1999, pp. 194–7). By contrast, *Modernising Government* (Cabinet Office 1999, pp. 30–1) stated a doctrine of intervening 'in inverse proportion to success' and striking 'an appropriate balance between intervening where services are failing and giving successful organizations the freedom to manage' (skating delicately over the fundamental tension that may be implied in those two goals). The same aspiration to 'enforced self-regulation' (developing a trend towards more formal and external regulation for public-sector regulatees seen as poor performers whereas good performers are rewarded with lighter oversight regimes) appeared in plans and designs announced by the Blair government in several domains of public-sector regulation.

Enforced self-regulation consists of external enforcement of rules written by regulated bodies and internal enforcement of externally set rules. Different types of regulation are arranged in the form of a pyramid, with self-regulation at the bottom, more interventionist styles of regulation in the middle and the most interventionist types at the apex. Ayres and Braithwaite (1992, p. 116) elaborate this approach, arguing that in many conditions it is an improvement on both pure 'self-regulation' and externally set and enforced regulations. Perhaps it is not surprising that such a 'third way' model should appeal to New Labour policy makers.

But – as with so many successful rhetorical strategies – whether this design for both more and less regulation could be reflected in actual outcomes is problematic and remains to be seen. How conflictual the model turns out to be depends on how many public-sector regulatees are picked up as unsatisfactory by overseers and pushed up to the higher levels of the enforcement pyramid. And here there is a fundamental dilemma in regulatory strategy. To keep conflict to a manageable level, the logic of enforcement pyramids suggests killing only an occasional public-service admiral to encourage the others. That applies to school closures under the OFSTED regime since 1992, in spite of recurrent tough-talking rhetoric from successive governments about 'zero tolerance' of failure (cf. Hood *et al.* 1999, pp. 1544–5). But if failure and chronic under-performance in public services provision is really as widespread as some of the 'standards' rhetoric suggests (cf. Blair 1998, pp. 11 and 20), the logic would imply the execution of whole admiralties, overloading the capacity of the centre. The compliance climate could alter if central-local relations worsen, and high-level intervention against too many authorities could turn what is intended to be an 'enforcement pyramid', with most regulatees at the base, into a costly, litigious enforcement 'cube'.

Should it be diminished?

If secondary regulation of UK government seems to have grown markedly over the two decades to 1997 and to have continued in the early years of New Labour, is there a case for reducing it? Those who complain about the burden of an 'audit explosion' certainly think so. They see the advance in regulation of government, with its growing direct and compliance costs, as over-ripe for a robust application of the sort of cost-benefit scrutiny used for the appraisal of business regulation over the past fifteen years. For those who accept Power's (1997) thesis about an 'audit explosion', more regulation of government might be expected to consume extra public resources in unnecessary 'rituals of verification' (ibid) without removing deep-seated policy and administrative failings and possibly weakening collegial systems of self-regulation inside the public sector.

Our interview programme (involving some 80 public-sector regulators and regulatees) predictably indicated that regulatees outside central government departments were more inclined to endorse some form of Power's 'audit explosion' thesis than regulators and central departmental officials. But the implication that formal regulation of government needed to be radically reduced was contested by several senior civil servants, who argued that such regulation had developed precisely because older, less formal systems of control had weakened in many parts of the public sector. They pointed to trends such as a relative move away from traditional career-service and jobs-for-life employment patterns in the public sector (with more lateral entry into senior positions) undermining the traditional internal conditions and incentives that supported mutuality-based controls in the public sector. A Permanent Secretary drew an explicit parallel with the more formal regulation applied to financial services as participation widened beyond a traditional elite whose unwritten rules were foreign to a new breed of entrants. Some of the regulators related the growth of regulation to a broader change in the social habitat of public services, with more litigious and less compliant consumers (cf. Wood 1999) and less deference to public-service professionals. Even if there had been no internal degeneration of mutuality-based collegial systems of control, such external changes could be expected to prompt more challenges to cosy collegiality. Given that it is unfeasible (and for many, undesirable) to turn the clock back on such developments, it might be argued that it would be dangerous to return formal regulation of government to the level of the 1950s and 1960s. Indeed, for bodies like the World Bank (1999, p. 7, §3.12), explicit and properly enforced formal regulation of government is a key element in achieving transparency and accountability.

Modernising Government, and the various Blair government initiatives it described and embraced, implied that regulation of government should both be
diminished and expanded. The 'enforced self-regulation' doctrine, as discussed
earlier, involves the deployment of heavier regulatory tackle against the incompetent or recalcitrant, while lightening the regulatory yoke over good performers.
Some of the cultural and political conditions that appear to be needed for the
success of such a policy have already been discussed. Along with the enforced
self-regulation doctrine, *Modernising Government* implied that the quality of public-
sector regulation was more important than its quantity, and proposed a mixture of
mutuality among regulators and regulation of the regulators to improve the quality.
That represented a more coherent approach to designing regulation of government
than anything that had been produced in the previous two decades.

Conclusion

Regulation of UK government seems to have grown substantially during the 'New
Public Management' era (of bureaucratic downsizing and changing styles of public
service delivery) that preceded the Blair Labour government. Along with apparently deregulatory 'let managers manage' rhetoric went a marked (but largely
unremarked) increase in the resources, staffing and organizational numbers of
arm's-length regulators of the public sector. The UK's New Public Management
era cannot be adequately understood without reference to this growth of public-
sector regulation. (Light's (1993, p. 17) study of the Inspectors-General in the US
federal government also points to the contrast between Congressional and presidential efforts to reduce regulatory compliance costs on business and 'willingness
to impose an ever-increasing level of regulatory and reporting requirements on
executive agencies and their employees'.) Were the growth rates of the recent past
to be maintained, the new century would see rapid further expansion of public
service regulators relative to the 'doers' – a feature not usually included in visionary
statements about what public management will or should be like in the new
millennium.

   Regulation in government continues to increase. Growth in regulator organizations and the direct and indirect resource costs of regulation were a marked
feature of the plans and activities of the Blair Labour government up to the
publication of *Modernising Government* in 1999. But, as suggested earlier, the story
of public-sector regulation under the first two years of that government was not
simply one of continuing expansion but also of the emergence of a doctrine of
public-sector regulation explicitly embracing the idea of more 'reflexive' regulation
or 'enforced self-regulation'.

   Careful thought about the organization and administrative strategy of public-
sector regulation certainly seems to be needed, since it is hard to see how such
regulation could be returned to the level of thirty or forty years ago. A more
fragmented public service structure with more lateral entry is likely to be hard to
govern through traditional informal, mutuality-based approaches to bureaucratic
control, particularly when coupled with broader social developments augmenting

legal formalism, transparency and declining public trust in middle-class profession-als. But (whatever novelty it may represent in other aspects of public management: it has been examined here solely from a regulatory perspective), *Modernising Government* represented only a modest break with traditional approaches to public-sector regulation. It did not grapple seriously with the compliance cost issue, beyond vaguely acknowledging the existence of the problem. Its enthusiasm for administrative and policy fora did not apparently extend to promoting more general exchanges across the regulatory 'families' and its enthusiasm for competi-tion as one of five principles for improving public services did not appear to extend to the regulators of those services. It would be easy to conclude that the traditional pattern, in which regulators of government neither fully compete nor fully collaborate, follow no general or consistent principles, and are not exposed to the disciplines they impose on their charges, is set to continue.

The key doctrinal change over public-sector regulation in *Modernising Government* (articulating a pattern developing particularly in local authority regulation and partly built into pre-existing practice by some public-sector regulators) is the enunciation of 'enforced self-regulation' as a general recipe. Some likely limitations of that approach have been suggested earlier, including capacity limits to putting hard cases 'in the clinic' and political processes tripping the enforcement escalator. But unless a twenty-first century future in which more and more regulators oversee each public service 'doer' is acceptable, some slackening in the pace of growth of secondary regulation of UK government will need to take place. 'Enforced self-regulation' in principle offers a way both to increase and diminish regulation of government, reducing high-level bureaucratic routine while increasing overall regulatory hitting power. It remains to be seen how far that approach lives up to its promise.

References and further reading

Audit Commission. 1999a. *From principles to practice: a consultation document.* London: Audit Commission.

—. 1999b. *Best assured: the role of the Audit Commission in best value.* London: Audit Commission (http://www.audit-commission.gov.uk/).

Ayres, I. and J. Braithwaite. 1992. *Responsive regulation.* Oxford: Oxford University Press.

Benefit Fraud Inspectorate. 1998. *Annual report 1998.* London: HMSO.

Black, D. 1976. *The behaviour of law.* New York: Academic Press.

Blair, T. 1998. *Leading the way: a new vision for local government.* London: Institute for Public Policy Research.

Blau, P.M. 1955. *The dynamics of bureaucracy.* Chicago: Chicago University Press.

Breyer, S.G. 1993. *Breaking the vicious circle.* Cambridge, MA: Harvard University Press.

Cabinet Office. 1995. *Civil service statistics 1995.* London: HMSO.

—. 1998a. *Written statement on the Cabinet Office Review* (http://www.open.gov.uk/co/review.htm.)

—. 1998b. *Service first: the new charter programme.* London: HMSO.

—. 1999. *Modernising government*. Cm 4310. London: HMSO.

Cabinet Office and Treasury. 1996. *Spending public money: government and audit issues*. Cm 3179. London: HMSO.

Civil Service Department. 1980. *The integration of HM Treasury and the Civil Service Department*. Working Paper 2. London: HMSO.

Daintith, T. and A. Page. 1999. *The executive in the constitution*. Oxford: Oxford University Press.

Department for Education and Employment. 1997. *The Government's legislative proposals: a summary*. http://www.dfee.gov.uk/raising/summary.htm

Department of the Environment. 1996. *Report of the Financial Management and Policy Review of the Commission for Local Administration in England: Stage Two*. London: DOE.

Department of the Environment, Transport and the Regions. 1998. *Modern local government: in touch with the people*. http://www.local-regions/detr.gov.uk/lgwp.

Department of Health. 1998a. *The new NHS*. Cm 3807. London: HMSO.

—. 1998b. *A first class service: quality in the NHS*. London: HMSO.

—. 1998c. *Modernising social services*. Cm 4169. London: HMSO.

Harden, I. 1995. 'Regulating government', *Political Quarterly* 66, 4, 299–306.

Hoggett, P. 1996. 'New modes of control in the public service', *Public Administration* 74, 9–32.

Hogwood, B.W, D. Judge and M. McVicar. 1998. 'Too much of a good thing? The pathology of accountability.' Paper presented at the Political Studies Association Annual Conference, University of Keele 7–9 April 1998.

Hood, C. 1998. *The art of the state*. Oxford: Clarendon.

Hood, C., O. James, G.W. Jones, C. Scott and A. Travers. 1998. 'Regulation inside government: where new public management meets the audit explosion', *Public Money and Management* 18, 2, 61–8.

Hood, C., C. Scott, O. James, G.W. Jones and A. Travers. 1999. *Regulation inside government*. Oxford: Oxford University Press.

Hutter, B.M. 1997. *Compliance*. Oxford: Clarendon.

Light, P. 1993. *Monitoring government*. Washington, DC: The Brookings Institution.

Majone, G. 1994. 'The rise of the regulatory state in Europe', *West European Politics* 17, 3, 77–101.

McCahery, J., B. Bratton, S. Picciotto and C. Scott (eds.). 1996. *International regulatory competition and coordination*. Oxford: Oxford University Press.

Niskanen, W. 1971. *Bureaucracy and representative government*. Chicago: Aldine Atherton.

Office for National Statistics. 1995. *Annual employment survey 1995*. London: ONS.

—. 1996. *Annual employment survey: Results for Great Britain*. London: ONS.

OECD. 1997. *Regulatory reform*. (2 vols.). Paris: OECD.

Power, M. 1997. *The audit society*. Oxford: Oxford University Press.

Rose-Ackerman, S. 1978. *Corruption*. New York: Academic Press.

Treasury. 1996. *Public expenditure: statistical analyses 1996–97*. Cm 3201. London: HMSO.

Vincent-Jones, P. 1998. 'Responsive law and governance in public services provision: a future for the local contracting state', *Modern Law Review* 61, 362–81.

Walshe, K. 1999. 'Improvement through inspection? The development of the New Commission for Health Improvement in England and Wales', *Quality in Health Care* 18, 3, 191–6.

Wood, B. 1999. *Patient power?* Buckingham: Open University Press.

World Bank. 1999. *Civil service reform: a review of World Bank assistance*. Report No. 19599, Operations Evaluation Department, Washington, DC, World Bank.

21

External assessment of health care
Charles Shaw

Extracts from Shaw, CD (2001) External assessment of healthcare. British Medical Journal, 322: 851–54.

A rash of external inspection is affecting the delivery of health care around the world. Governments, consumers, professions, managers, and insurers are hurrying to set up new schemes to ensure public accountability, transparency, self regulation, quality improvement, or value for money. But what do we know of such schemes' evidence base, the validity of their standards, the reliability of their assessments, or their ability to bring improvements for patients, staff, or the general population?

In short, not much. The standards, measurements, and results of management systems have not been, and largely cannot be, subjected to the same rigorous scrutiny and meta-analysis as clinical practice. No one has published a controlled trial, and there are too many confounding variables to prove that inspection causes better clinical outcomes, although there is evidence that organisations increase their compliance with standards if these are made explicit. But experience and consensus are gradually being codified into guidelines to make external quality systems as coherent, consistent, and effective as they could be (Box 21.1). Much of this consensus is ignored by those who develop and operate new programmes.

Box 21.1   Characteristics of effective external
assessment programmes

Give clear framework of values–To describe elements of quality, and their weighting, such as the enablers and results defined by the European Foundation for Quality Management

Publish validated standards–To provide an objective basis for assessment

Focus on patients–To reflect horizontal clinical pathways rather than vertical management units

Include clinical processes and results–To reflect perceptions of patients, staff, and public

Encourage self assessment–To give time and tools to internalise assessment and development

---

Train the assessors–To promote reliable assessments and reports

Measure systematically–To describe and weight compliance with standards objectively

Provide incentives–To give leverage for improvement and response to recommendations

Communicate with other programmes–To promote consistency and reciprocity and to reduce duplication and burden of inspection

Quantify improvement over time–To demonstrate effectiveness of programme

Give public access to standards, assessment processes, and results–To be transparent and publicly accountable

In Britain there has been no consistent central strategy to support or coordinate existing external assessment programmes. The NHS has introduced new statutory bodies and triggered more formal programmes of visiting and assessment. Each brings a burden of inspection and requires resources for development, but responsibility for ensuring the integration, consistency, and value of such programmes has not been defined.

This article describes the growth of external assessment and the issues it raises around the world, particularly in Britain.

Common approaches

Many countries have voluntary and statutory mechanisms for periodic external assessment of healthcare organisations against defined standards, and some have been systematically compared.[1-3] They are all meant to assure or improve some elements of quality, but they are usually run by different organisations without national coordination to make them consistent, mutually supportive, economical, and effective. Broadly, these mechanisms include variants on five approaches (Box 21.2).

The International Organization for Standardization provides standards against which organisations or functions may be certificated by accredited auditors. These have been applied in health care, specifically to radiology and laboratory systems, and more generally to quality systems in clinical departments.[4]

The Baldrige criteria have evolved into national and international assessment programmes such as the Australian Business Excellence Model (www.aqc.org.au/) and the European Foundation for Quality Management (www.efqm.org/).[5]

Box 21.2 Common models of external assessment in health care

International Organization for Standardization (www.iso.ch/)

Origin and focus–European manufacturing industry 1946; quality systems (often within individual department or function)

Standards–ISO 9000 series (quality systems); also specific for radiology and laboratory systems

Products–Certification

Malcolm Baldrige "excellence" model (www.asq.org/abtquality/awards/baldrige.html)
Origin and focus–US industry 1987; management systems and results
Standards–European and national variants published with criteria
Products–Self assessment, national awards

Peer review
Origin and focus–Health care; specialty based professional training, clinical practice, and organisation
Standards–Variable detail, limited access
Products–Accreditation (of specialty training)

Accreditation
Origin and focus–US health care 1919; service organisation, performance
Standards–Published with criteria such as acute care, long term care, primary care, networks
Products–Accreditation (of organisation or service)

Inspection
Origin and focus–National or regional statutes; competence, safety
Standards–Published regulations such as for fire safety, radiation exposure, hygiene
Products–Registration, licensing

Peer review is based on collegiate, usually single discipline, programmes to assess and give formal accreditation to training programmes but is now also extended to clinical services.[6]

Accreditation relies on independent voluntary programmes developed from a focus on training into multidisplinary assessments of healthcare functions, organisations, and networks. These have spread from Western countries into Latin America,[7] Africa,[8] and South East Asia[9][10] during the 1990s. Mandatory programmes have recently been adopted in France,[11] Italy,[12] and Scotland.[13]

Registration and licensing are statutory programmes to ensure that staff or provider organisations achieve minimum standards of competence. There are also inspectorates for specific functions to ensure public health and safety.

National requirements

Several countries have recently received recommendations on their ability to ensure high standards in health care nationally. The general conclusions on the role of external agencies have been remarkably similar.

The US president's advisory commission on consumer protection and quality in health care recommended in 1998 that public and private programmes of external review should make their standards, survey protocols, decision criteria, and results available to the public at "little or no cost."[14] The organisations themselves should work towards a common set of standards, coordinate their activities to avoid conflict and duplication, and commit themselves to a national quality forum. This forum aims to devise a national strategy for measuring and reporting healthcare quality and in 1999 began to standardise performance measures for the nation's 5000 acute general hospitals.[15]

In 1999 the US inspector general of the Department of Health reviewed the external quality oversight of hospitals that participate in Medicare.[16] She concluded that voluntary "collegiate" accreditation by the Joint Commission on Accreditation of Healthcare Organisations and "regulatory" Medicare certification by state agencies had considerable strengths (Box 21.3) but also major deficiencies. She recommended that both systems should harmonise their methods, disclose more details of hospital performance on the internet, and be held more fully accountable at federal level for their performance in reviewing hospitals.

An Australian taskforce recommended in 1996 that the government should formally acknowledge independent assessment programmes that met defined criteria and should enable them to disseminate information about their processes and findings to the public.[17] Two years later an expert advisory group recommended "that accreditation or certification of healthcare organisations be strongly encouraged with incentives, or indeed made mandatory, but choice of accreditation/certification/award approaches be allowed."[18]

In Scotland the Carter report on acute services recommended a single mandatory system of accreditation for hospitals and primary care.[19] This should be patient centred, clinically focused, and complementary to internal quality improvement, and its explicit, measurable standards and reports should be in the public domain. This recommendation led to the Clinical Standards Board for Scotland.

International solutions

Countries have good reasons to be able to show that healthcare standards are not only consistent within their own territory but also that they are comparable with those of their neighbours, suppliers, and competitors. Several recent European and international initiatives are making traditional assessment methods more accessible, convergent, and relevant to health care.

Box 21.3   Features of collegiate and regulatory systems for assessing health care

Collegiate

- Focus on education, self development; improved performance, and reducing risk
- General review of internal systems
- Based on optimum standards, professional accountability, and cooperative relationships

Regulatory

- Timely response to complaints and adverse events
- In depth probe of conditions and activities
- Based on minimum standards, investigation, enforcement, and public accountability

International Organization for Standardization–The ISO 9000 series of standards were designed for manufacturing industries and have been criticised for using language that is difficult to interpret in terms of health services. The 2000 version will be more readily applied, and US and European initiatives are under way to develop ISO guidelines specific to health care.

European Foundation for Quality Management–The original "business excellence" model has given way to "excellence" in the 1999 version and has shifted emphasis from "enabling processes" to results of concern to patients, staff, and society.

Accreditation–The international arm of the US Joint Commissions on Accreditation of Healthcare Organisations has developed a set of multinational accreditation standards.[20] In addition the International Society for Quality in Health Care has developed ("ALPHA") standards and criteria (available from the society's website www.isqua.org.au) against which an accreditation programme may apply to have its standards and process assessed and internationally accredited.[21] These also offer a template for standardisation and self assessment to any external assessment programme.

Programmes in Britain

The royal commission on the NHS recommended in 1979 that a special health authority be set up as a development agency and guardian of standards.[22] In the early 1980s several monitoring agencies were suggested or piloted,[23] but, despite favourable response from national professional bodies to leaked proposals, no such national agency featured in the government's white paper of 1989 *Working for Patients*.[24]

In the absence of any governmental lead, several small peer review and (some large) accreditation programmes emerged as external voluntary mechanism for organisational development. There are now over 35 such programmes with a wealth of standards and trained assessors but little integration, consistency, or reciprocity between them. Their number could be doubled if each royal college, faculty, and professional association were to establish independent accreditation programmes as a collegiate approach to clinical governance. NHS institutions also have their share of visits from clinical training programmes, inspectors (such as for fire regulations, environmental health, etc), and other watchdogs that have begun to publish standards (such as the NHS Information Authority Information Management Centre for data quality and NHS Controls Assurance for risk management and controls assurance).

The Clinical Standards Board for Scotland and the National Institute for Clinical Excellence (NICE), and Commission for Health Improvement (CHI) for England and Wales have been established to improve standards in the NHS. After years of policy vacuum, an early common task must be to tidy up: they must synthesise the experience of Britain and other countries;[25] provide public access to their own valid standards, reliable assessments, and fair judgments; and, above all, avoid duplication and inconsistency in defining and measuring standards. In short, they should be open to assessment against international criteria and lead the way to consistency and reciprocity within and between systems for improving patient services, clinical training, and public accountability.

Britain could borrow from the US and Australian recommendations for partnership between state and independent programmes for external assessment and define the terms of collaboration. Independent and statutory programmes could be jointly assessed and harnessed according to general criteria drawn from UK policy and experience overseas and from the more specific ALPHA standards.

We need to catalogue, harmonise, and orchestrate organisational standards and their assessment, not only in the NHS but also in the independent and social care sectors. The National Institute for Clinical Excellence has a clear responsibility for defining clinical standards in England and Wales. The Commission for Health Improvement is concerned with the organisation and delivery of clinical governance and national service frameworks, but it has no mandate to define or orchestrate organisational standards (even for its own reviews), and it is specifically excluded from the independent sector. In Scotland the Clinical Standards Board integrates some key features of these two bodies, particularly the task of defining and measuring standards, both clinical and organisational. With yet broader vision, the Scottish Executive has adopted a charter that sets out principles for public and professional inspectorates whose role includes evaluation of cases in the public interest, including health, education, and social work services (www.scotland.gov.uk). This offers a starting point for coherence and learning within and between sectors, and an example for the rest of Britain.

The UK Accreditation Forum (www.caspe.co.uk) was set up in 1998 to support accreditation and peer review programmes, and the Academy of Medical Royal Colleges (www.aomrc.org.uk/) is working towards more coherent procedures for hospital visiting for recognition of training. Neither body has the resources or the authority to standardise standards or to regulate the regulators across the country.

What we need is a formal means to pool current experience, to drive convergence, and to help new programmes to be efficient, complementary, and effective–a resource centre to do for organisational and management standards what NICE, the Cochrane Centre, and the Scottish Intercollegiate Guidelines Network are doing for clinical practice. Its task should be to ensure that organisational standards, assessments, and general results are in the public domain; that the legitimate interests of the public, professions, providers, and funding bodies are balanced and supported; that lessons from successes and failures are systematically embedded in common core standards for assessment; that assessment methods and reporting are consistent in time, place, and service; and that expenditure on the development and operation of external assessment programmes is demonstrably justified by improvements in patient care.

Conclusions

Schemes for inspection, registration, revalidation, and review are proliferating with little national coordination or regard for the evidence of what has worked or not worked for health care in Britain or overseas. This leads to uncertainty among service providers about which standards to adopt, inefficiency in developing new inspection and development programmes, duplication and inconsistency of external assessments, and an excessive burden on the services under scrutiny. The collegial and statutory mechanisms need a public-private partnership, perhaps similar to the National Quality Forum in the United States, to bring clarity, consistency, and transparency to external assessment in Britain.

Summary points

External assessment and inspection of health services are becoming more common worldwide, using a combination of models – ISO certification, business excellence, peer review, accreditation, and statutory inspection

There is common concern that voluntary and statutory programmes need to be integrated to ensure valid standards, consistent assessments, transparency, and public accountability

International consensus on the effective organisation and methods of external assessment is growing, but hard evidence of clinical benefit is lacking

The United Kingdom has many independent and statutory programmes but no effective mechanism for coordinating their activity, standards, and methods according to this consensus

The NHS must be willing to support a public-private coalition to bring realism, clarity, consistency, efficiency, and transparency to external assessment

---

Notes

1   Klazinga N. Re-engineering trust: adoption and adaptation of four external quality assurance models in Western European health care systems. *Int J Quality Health Care* 2000;12:183–9.

2 Australian Business Excellence Framework Healthcare Advisory Group. *A comparison of quality programmes*. St Leonards, NSW: Australian Quality Council, 1999.

3 Donahue KT, van Ostenberg P. Joint Commission International accreditation: relationship to four models of evaluation. *Int J Quality Health Care* 2000;12:243–6.

4 Sweeney J, Heaton C. Interpretations and variations of ISO 9000 in acute health care. *Int J Quality Health Care* 2000;12:203–9.

5 Nabitz U, Klazinga N, Walburg J. The EFQM excellence model: European and Dutch experience with the EFQM approach in health care. *Int J Quality Health Care* 2000;12:191–201.

6 Van Weert C. Developments in professional quality assurance towards quality improvement. *Int J Quality Health Care* 2000;12:239–42.

7 Arce H. Accreditation: the Argentine experience in the Latin American region. *Int J Quality Health Care* 1999:11; 425–8.

8 Whittaker S, Burns D, Doyle V, Fenney Lynam P. Introducing quality assurance to health service delivery—some approaches from South Africa, Ghana and Kenya. *Int J Quality Health Care* 1998;10:263–7.

9 Huang P, Hsu YE, Kai-Yuan T, Hsueh Y-S. Can European external peer review techniques be introduced and adopted into Taiwan's hospital accreditation system? *Int J Quality Health Care* 2000;12:251–4.

10 Ito H, Iwasaki S, Nakano Y, Imanaka Y, Kawakita H, Gunji A. Direction of quality improvement activities of health care organizations in Japan. *Int J Quality Health Care* 1998;10:361–3.

11 Agence Nationale d'Accréditation et d'Evaluation en Santé. *Décret en Conseil d'Etat no 97–311 du 7 Avril*. Paris: ANAES, 1997 (Journal Officiel (82)8) (www.anaes.fr/ANAES/anaesparametrage.nsf/HomePage?readform).

12 *Decree of 14 January 1997*. Rome: Gazetta Ufficiale della Repubblica Italiana, 1997.

13 Steele DR. Promoting public confidence in the NHS: the role of the Clinical Standards Board for Scotland. *Health Bull* Jan 2000 (www.scotland.gov.uk/library2/doc09/hbj0–05.asp).

14 President's Advisory Commission on Consumer Protection and Quality in the Health Care Industry. *Quality first: better health care for all Americans*. Washington DC: US Department of Health and Human Services, 1998 (www.hcqualitycommission.gov/final/chap09.html).

15 Kizer KW. The National Quality Forum enters the game. *Int J Quality Health Care* 2000;12:85–7.

16 Brown JG. *The external review of hospital quality: a call far greater accountability*. Boston, MA: Office of Inspector General, Department of Health and Human Services, 1999 (OEI-01-97-00050; 7/99) (www.dhhs.gov/progorg/oei/reportindex.html).

17 Taskforce on Quality in Australian Health Care. *The final report of the Taskforce on Quality in Australian Health Care*. Canberra: Australian Department of Health and Aged Care, 1996 (www.health.gov.au/pubs/hlthcare/toc.htm).

18 National Expert Advisory Group on Safety and Quality in Australian Health Care. Interim report April 1998. Canberra: Australian Department of Health and Aged Care, 1998 (www.health.gov.au/about/cmo/report.doc).
19 Scottish Office. Quality assurance and accreditation. In: *Acute services review report*. Edinburgh: Scottish Office Publications, 1998 (www.scotland.gov.uk/library/documents5/acute-06.htm#1).
20 *Joint Commission International accreditation standards for hospitals*. Chicago: Joint Commission International, 2000 (www.jcrinc.com/internat.htm).
21 Heidemann EG. The ALPHA program. *Int J Quality Health Care* 1999;11:275–7.
22 Royal Commission on the National Health Service. *Report of the Royal Commission on the National Health Service*. London: HMSO, 1979 (Cmnd 7615).
23 Shaw CD. Monitoring and standards in the NHS. *BMJ* 1982;284:217–8.
24 Department of Health. *Working for patients. White paper*. London: HMSO, 1989.
25 Oldham J. An inspectorate for the health service? *BMJ* 1997;315:896–7.

22

The role of regulation in quality improvement
Troyen Brennan

Extracts from Brennan TA (1998) The role of regulation in quality improvement, Milbank Quarterly 76(4): 709–31.

The quality of health care is not heavily regulated. Except for clinical laboratories and nursing homes, few areas of health care are governed by rules, statutes, or laws. Instead, the industry has been allowed to self-regulate, which means that the rules regarding quality in health care are largely self-imposed. Perhaps in no other industry has the privilege of profession been so dominant.

Over the course of the last 25 years, the field of health services research has bloomed, as have new methods for measuring the quality of health care. Before 1970, quality existed simply in the eyes of the beholder. Since then, however, various tools have been devised to measure health status, satisfaction, and a series of outcomes.

For the past ten years, health care has struggled to integrate industrial methods of quality improvement. Known in health care as "continuous quality improvement," these industrial models emphasize self-motivation to improve in cycles. Only in the last five years have the two streams of health services research and continuous quality improvement come together (Brennan and Berwick 1996; Gosfield 1997).

Now that we are developing methods to assess quality and to integrate the newly emerging data into improvement of health care, we might expect regulation to become more effective. In order to judge whether regulation has evolved, it is critical to find the answers to three questions:

1. Is there measurable evidence that regulation is working to improve the quality of health care?
2. Are regulators aware of the tools developed by quality researchers, and are they integrating them into their oversight activities?

After answering these two questions, we can then address the final one:

3. Is there a way to combine continuous quality improvement and modern methods of quality measurement into a new regulatory format?

The task is both descriptive and synthetic. As we shall see, the description will suggest that there is little intertwining of quality improvement, quality measurement, and regulation. However, the prescription will indicate that this need not be the case and, in fact, that there have been some impulses in the right direction.

Space does not permit a complete review of all aspects of health care and its regulation. For this reason, I will leave aside certain issues: First, in my review of health care providers, I will omit the topic of long-term care and its regulation. Second, I cannot review all sources of regulation, particularly self-regulation that results from adherence to ethical criteria, a subject that has been addressed in some detail elsewhere (Veatch 1995). As managed care becomes more prominent, the role of ethics will become increasingly complicated (Rodwin 1995). Third, I will not address regulation that is designed to control costs. These issues aside, I turn to an analysis of regulation of quality.

The theoretical basis for regulation in health care

Experts in regulation often avoid defining the term (Breyer 1982). I have referred elsewhere to regulation as any set of influences or rules exterior to the practice or administration of medical care that imposes rules of behavior (Brennan and Berwick 1996, 4). I am particularly interested in rules developed by state legislators and public agencies and in common law rules developed by judicial precedent. To paraphrase another legal theorist, I will address rules that are prescriptive rather than descriptive (Schauer 1991).

Government regulation has a long history. In the 1930s, the New Deal gave tremendous impetus to federal oversight of the economy (Vietor 1994). Another burst of regulatory activity occurred when the redistribution impulses of the Great Society strengthened the earlier New Deal initiatives. Surprisingly, under Presidents Nixon and Ford a host of federal regulatory administrations was added to the bureaucracy in Washington, but the system began to unravel when President Clinton moved toward deregulation (Ayres and Braithwaite 1992).

As Breyer notes, a few common themes run through these regulations, which were designed to achieve certain ends: constrain decentralized, individual decision making in favor of a more coordinated, cohesive approach; control monopolies; provide consumer information; decrease moral hazard and limit insurance arrangements; and balance public welfare against private consumer choice. Regulators accomplish these goals primarily by setting standards through rule making and, secondarily, by using methods of culling.

The problem, to put it bluntly, is that regulation often leads to strife between regulators and the regulated industry, and thus to frustration of the regulatory intent. During the last few years, students of regulation have sought methods to decrease this friction. John Braithwaite, for example, has led the way in advocating a mix of persuasion and punishment to achieve regulatory goals. He would allow extensive use of self-regulation but would impose certain boundaries on industry license. Regulators would retain the ability to sanction the industry in order to ensure that self-regulation occurs, an arrangement he calls "enforced self-regulation." He has developed a full model, entitled "responsive regulation," in collaboration with Ian Ayres (Ayres and Braithwaite 1992).

Don Berwick and I have argued that responsive regulation entails at least five different approaches to improving quality (Brennan and Berwick 1996). The first is repair: identifying quality deficiencies and taking swift action to correct them. The second approach is culling, or removing defects from a system. We have suggested that culling, especially through licensing and disciplinary actions, is the most prevalent method of regulating quality in American health care. A third way is to encourage copying. Japanese industry, for example, provides forums as a way for manufacturers to learn about competitors' innovations. Elementary continuous quality improvement principles give rise to the fourth approach, which can be defined as learning through cycles. First described by Shewart (1937), the Plan-Do-Check-Act cycle summarizes the learning formats used by entities that are engaged in continuous improvement. Fifth, quality improvement emerges through creativity. Some organizations cultivate an atmosphere in which creativity thrives.

Quality-improving regulation in any industry should take advantage of one or more of these five methods to attain its goals. Unfortunately, regulation in every industry, particularly health care, often relies solely on culling. This tendency in turn retards development of other approaches, as culling is often converted to policing and quality improvement is treated as a matter of removing defects rather than as a continuous process of improving standards of health care or, in the case of other industries, manufacturing better products. Thus, traditional regulation can frustrate continuous quality improvement wherever it is applied.

Regulatory formats are changing in health care. A few salutary developments indicate an awareness that traditional culling is corrosive. These developments point the way toward a better mix of continuous quality improvement regulation and modern methods of measurement.

Partial answers to three questions

Returning now to the three questions posed initially, we ask first, "Is there evidence that quality regulation is improving health care delivery?" There is little evidence that regulation has improved the quality of health care. I have noted that empirical strategies could be used to evaluate new quality rules, but there are few standard approaches to quality regulation and few simple outcome measures to evaluate its efficacy. Although measures like mortality rates, readmission, or even patient satisfaction conceivably could be used to compare approaches, research on this possibility has not been done. As a result, we regulate in an empirical void, often addressing anecdotes and hysteria with far-reaching initiatives. The current efforts to regulate managed care are an excellent example of a poorly informed regulatory response.

Second, are regulators cognizant of quality measurement? The answer to this is fortunately "yes." The state data initiatives, the Joint Commission on Accreditation of Healthcare Organization's ORYX program, and the Peer Review Organizations' efforts to redesign the Scope of Work all suggest that quality measurement can be integrated into regulation. Of course, regulators are concerned about the state of quality measurement:

> There is much interest, for instance, in evaluating performance of the individual practitioner. On this front I am skeptical and suggest that we first learn how to crawl. We presently have the about same level of sophistication for measuring health-plan performance. On the bright side, we are rapidly learning about the use of measurement in organized delivery systems such as hospitals. (O'Leary 1995)

The ORYX endorsement of institutional leeway in choice of quality measures and the HEDIS reliance on specific criteria suggest that quality measures will be used more commonly in the future (Radical Statistics Health Group 1995).

Although these are encouraging developments, there is a significant gap between health services research and quality oversight. Consider the relation between quality outcomes and volume of services. Many studies have demonstrated that mortality following coronary artery bypass graft surgery may be related to the volume of procedures performed at specific centers (Grumbach et al. 1995). Mark Chassin has suggested a regulatory strategy that would centralize procedures at high-volume centers or that at least would monitor the number of procedures performed by individual operators.

Like many other hospitals, Brigham and Women's Hospital in Boston has begun to track the outcomes of procedures it carries out. The hospital is also examining the outcomes of individual operators and is recording both the total number of procedures and the outcomes in credentialing files.

To discover whether other institutions were following the same procedures, I conducted a survey of over 100 hospitals, which produced these initial findings: less than 10 percent recorded the number of cases performed in credentialing files; less than 5 percent were recording outcome measures. Thus, although research clearly shows that doctors should perform a threshold number of procedures to maintain proficiency, this finding apparently has not been transmitted to hospital credentialing committees. Nor has any state legislature or hospital association suggested that an individual should reach a threshold of experience before continuing to perform a procedure. Indeed, any such proposals would probably be the subject of significant legal challenges (Brennan and Berwick 1996). The JCAHO stipulates that empirical information should be entered in credentialing files, but there is no information on hospitals' compliance with this requirement. In summary, despite initial steps to integrate quality measurement and improvement into regulatory oversight, there is considerable room for improvement.

Finally, we ask, can regulation promote quality measurement and continuous quality improvement? Astute observers, like Alain Enthoven, worry aloud that any form of regulation would stunt creativity and force slavish compliance with meaningless outcome measurement strategies (Enthoven and Vorhaus 1997). Moreover, any external oversight is prone to mindless policing: the regulator in effect becomes a line boss, investigating the work of physicians or hospitals in order to sanction poor performance. This inspection format, as Don Berwick has argued, frustrates efforts to initiate continuous quality improvement.

However, Berwick and I have argued that this need not be the case. The responsive regulation philosophy, as outlined by Ayres and Braithwaite, encourages self-regulation and innovation, provided that the regulatory agency is able to punish those who do not participate in reasonable programs. The PROs, under the fifth Scope of Work, the Joint Commission, and the NCQA are engaging in just this kind of responsive regulation by allowing organizations to set their own quality agendas, as long as these include measurement of outcomes and reasonable improvement efforts.

I have suggested some ways to reinforce this impulse. First, I recommend that regulators reduce the costs of inspection. The JCAHO and HEDIS surveys require time and attention that are taken away from the energy required for true quality improvement. As the NCQA and the JCAHO continue to minimize the preparation of materials needed for evaluation and to tailor their surveys to fit the internal needs and constraints of the institutions, the survey itself takes on the aspect of a quality consultation.

Second, I believe that regulation should be linked explicitly with shared aims. Regulators should define specific goals and then give hospitals or physicians the opportunity to meet them. We also recommend reducing the competition and duplication among regulators. Very soon, both the NCQA and the JCAHO will be interested in accrediting integrated delivery systems. Competition among accreditors and regulators could improve the accreditation process, but it might also lead to multiple (unnecessary) accreditation surveys.

We also recommend that regulators consider "safe havens" for major innovation. The JCAHO encourages organizations to explore new strategies to improve quality. Regulation can inhibit this kind of creativity. Re-engineering of delivery systems is stymied when regulators dictate the details of their structure.

All these suggestions can be subsumed within one primary goal: to build on existing efforts to integrate continuous quality strategies and quality measurement into regulation. The achievements of the regulators that are accomplishing this goal should be emulated and expanded.

Finally, we must engender public knowledge of quality measurement. Whether they come through voluntary efforts of providers, or are required by the state, any efforts to develop regionally standardized outcome measures and to provide this information to the public must be encouraged. Although some would argue that this is better done under the auspices of voluntary agencies than by state regulators (Wilensky 1997), there is no empirical basis to believe that state initiatives will fail (Derman 1997).

Slavish adherence to traditional principles of regulation, which are devoted to the task of culling "bad apples," will do little to improve the quality of medical care. Regulators, particularly the JCAHO and the NCQA, have realized this. Private and state institutions should be encouraged to continue to identify methods of regulation that permit organizations to measure their own quality, to gauge it against the standards of others, and to adopt strategies for change.

References and further reading

Andrew, G., and H. Sauer. 1996. Do Boards of Medicine Really Matter? The Future of Professional Regulation. *Federation Bulletin* 83:228–36.

Annas, G.J. 1995. Women and Children First. *New England Journal of Medicine* 333:1647–51.

Ayres, I., and J. Braithwaite. 1992. *Responsive Regulation: Transcending the De-Regulation Debate.* New York: Oxford University Press.

Berwick, D.M., and D.L. Walt. 1990. Hospital Leaders' Opinions of HCFA Mortality Data. *Journal of the American Medical Association* 263:247–9.

Brennan, T.A., and D.M. Berwick. 1996. *New Rules: Regulation Markets and the Quality of American Health Care.* San Francisco: Jossey-Bass.

Brennan, T.A., C. Sox, and H.R. Burstin. 1996. Relation between Negligent Adverse Events and the Outcomes of Medical Malpractice Litigation. *New England Journal of Medicine* 335:1963–7.

Breyer, S. 1982. *Regulation as Reform.* Cambridge: Harvard University Press.

Bureau of National Affairs. 1996a. As Action on "Any Willing Provider" Laws Wanes, States Take Up 'Direct Access' Bills. *Health Law Reporter* 5 (March 14):390–1.

—. 1996b. "Without Cause" Terminations Undergoing Scrutiny in Courts, Legislatures. *Health Law Reporter* 5 (December 19):1845.

—. 1997. Lawmakers Move toward Mandating Minimum Stays for Mastectomy Patients. *Health Law Reporter* 6 (January 2):22.

Burstin, H.R., S.R. Lipsitz, and T.A. Brennan. 1992. Socio-Economic Status and Risks for Substandard Medical Care. *Journal of the American Medical Association* 268:2383–7.

—. 1997. *Deterrence in Malpractice Litigation.* (Unpublished manuscript.)

Derbyshire, R.C. 1969. *Medical Licensure and Discipline in the United States.* Baltimore: Johns Hopkins University Press.

Derman, H. 1997. Quality and Liability Issues with the Papanicolaou Smear: Lessons from the Science of Error Prevention. *Archives of Pathology of Laboratory Medicine* 121:287–91.

Enthoven, A., and C.B. Vorhaus. 1997. A Vision of Quality and Health Care Delivery. *Health Affairs* 16:(3):44–58.

Gardner, J. 1996. Bill Bases Payment for ER Care on Symptoms. *Modern Healthcare* (February 15): 68.

Gosfield, A.G. 1997. Who Is Holding Whom Accountable for Quality. *Health Affairs* 16(2):26–41.

Grumbach, K., G.M. Anderson, H.S. Luft, L.L. Roos, and R. Brook. 1995. Regionalization of Cardiac Surgery in the United States and Canada: Geographic Access, Choice, and Outcomes. *Journal of the American Medical Association* 274:1282–8.

Halverson, P.K., G.P. Mays, A.D. Kluzny, and T.B. Richards. 1997. Not-So-Strange Bedfellows: The Models of Interaction Between Managed-Care Plans and Public Health Agencies. *Milbank Quarterly* 75:113–38.

Hannan, E.L., H. Kilbum, M. Racz, E. Shields, and M.R. Chassin. 1994. Improving the Outcomes of Coronary Artery Bypass Surgery in New York State. *Journal of the American Medical Association* 271:761–6.

Hospital Association of New York. 1993. *Recommended Changes in Health Care Regulatory Reform.* New York.

Jenck, S.F. 1997. Can Large Scale Interventions Improve Care? *Journal of the American Medical Association* 277:419–20.

Jost, T.S. 1989. Administrative Law Issues Involving the Medicare Utilization of Quality Control Peer-Review Organization Program: Analysis and Recommendations. *Ohio State Law Journal* 50:1–60.

Leape, L.L., A.G. Lawthers, T.A. Brennan, and W.G. Johnson. 1993. The Preventability of Medical Injury. *Quarterly Review Bulletin* 19:144–51.

Liu, L.L., C.J. Clemens, D.K. Shay, R.L. Davis, and A.H. Novack. 1997. The Safety of Newborn Early Discharge. The Washington State Experience. *Journal of the American Medical Association* 278:293–8.

Mandl, K.D., T.A. Brennan, P.H. Wise, E.Z. Tronick, and C.J. Homer. 1997. Maternal and Infant Health: Effects of Moderate Reductions in Postpartum Length of Stay. *Archives of Pediatrics and Adolescent Medicine* 151:915–21.

Mariner, W.K. 1996. State Regulation of Managed Care and the Employee Retirement Income Security Act. *New England Journal of Medicine* 335:1986–90.

Mellette, R. 1986. The Changing Focus of Peer Review under Medicare. *University of Richmond Law Review* 20:315–25.

Modern Healthcare. 1997. Insurer Strikes Back: Suit Filed Against Texas Law on Right to Sue HMOs. (June 30):78.

National Committee for Quality Assurance. 1994. *Health Plan and Employer Data and Information Set.* Version 2.0. Washington, D.C.

O'Leary, D.S. 1991. Accreditation and Quality Improvement—A Vision for JCAHO Tomorrow. *Quality Review Bulletin* 17:72–7.

—. 1995. Performance Measures: How Are They Developed, Validated and Used? *Medical Care* 33:JS13–JS17.

Pallarito, K. 1995. State Legislatures Enter Debate on Mom, Newborn Hospital Stays. *Modern Healthcare* (June 12):22.

Porter, R.E. 1995. Making the Commitment amid Changes and Challenge. Journal of Medical Licensure Discipline. *Federation Bulletin* 82:67–9.

Prager, L.O. 1997. NCQA Widens Its Scope: Health Plan Accreditor Says Its New Physician Certification Program Will Ease Multiple Audits. *American Medical News* (May 26):3.

Radical Statistics Health Group 1995. NHS Indicators of Success: What Do They Tell Us? 1995. *British Medical Journal* 310:1045–6.

Roberts, J.S., J.G. Coale, and R.R. Redman. 1987. A History of the Joint Commission for Accreditation of Hospitals. *Journal of the American Medical Association* 258:936–40.

Rodwin, M.A. 1995. Strains in the Fiduciary Metaphor: Divided Physician Loyalties and Obligations in a Changing Health Care System. *American Journal of Law and Medicine* 23:241–68.

Rubin, H., W.H. Rogers, K.L. Kahn, L.V. Rubenstein, and R.A. Brook. 1992. Watching the Doctor Watcher: How Well Do Peer-Review Organization Methods Detect Hospital Care-Quality Problems? *Journal of the American Medical Association* 267:2349–54.

Schauer, F. 1991. *Playing by the Rules: A Philosophical Examination of Rule-Based Decision Making in Law and in Life.* New York: Oxford University Press.

Schlesinger, M. 1997. Countervailing Agency: A Strategy of Principled Regulation under Managed Competition. *Milbank Quarterly* 75:35–72.

Schneider, E.C., and A.M. Epstein. 1996. Influence of Cardiac-Surgery Performance Reports on Referral Practices and Access to Care. A Survey of Cardiovascular Specialists. *New England Journal of Medicine* 335:251–6.

Shewart, W. 1937. *Economic Control of Quality of Manufacture of Products.* New York: Van Nostrand Reinhold.

Swartz, K.S., and T.A. Brennan. 1996. Integrated Health Care, Capitated Payment, and Quality: The Role of Regulation. *Annals of Internal Medicine* 124(4):442–8.

Van Tuinen, I., P. McCarthy, S. Wolf, and A. Bame. 1995. *Comparing State Medical Boards.* Washington, D.C.: Public Citizen.

Veatch, R.M. 1995. The Role of Ethics in Quality and Accountability Initiatives. *Medical Care* 33:JS69–JS76.

Vietor, R. 1994. *Contrived Competition: Regulation and Deregulation in America.* Cambridge: Harvard University Press.

Weiler, P., J. Newhouse, H. Hiatt, L. Leape, and T.A. Brennan. 1993. *A Measure of Malpractice.* Cambridge: Harvard University Press.

Wilensky, G.R. 1997. Promoting Quality: A Public Policy View. *Health Affairs* 16(3):24–8.

23

Social regulation of healthcare organizations in the USA: developing a framework for evaluation

Kieran Walshe and Stephen Shortell

Extracts from Walshe K and Shortell SM (2003) Social regulation of healthcare organisations in the United States: developing a framework of evaluation. Health Services Management Research 17: 79–99.

Introduction

Healthcare organizations in the US claim to be among the most regulated institutions in the world (American Hospitals Association, 2001). They are certainly subject to greater regulatory oversight than healthcare organizations in many other countries (Klein, 1987; Scrivens, 1995), an international trend also observed in many other sectors of the economy (Anderson and Kagan, 2000; Kagan and Axelrad, 2000). Healthcare organizations once faced relatively light regulation; however, the rise of managed care and the growing Government role in funding healthcare have seen a gradual but sustained growth in regulatory scrutiny over the past three decades (Altman et al., 1999; Brennan and Berwick, 1996; Levin, 1980). If regulation is ubiquitous in US healthcare, however, it is far from uncontroversial. Some argue that regulation has been an important force for improvement in American healthcare, driving change and raising standards over many years (AHQA, 2000; NCQA, 2000; Schyve and O'Leary, 1998). Other commentators assert that the regulation of healthcare organizations imposes a substantial and unwarranted bureaucratic burden upon them, raises costs, acts as an anticompetitive barrier to entry to the healthcare marketplace, stifles innovation and improvement, and has other negative effects (AHA, 2001; Brennan and Berwick, 1996; Goodman, 1980; Leyerle, 1994). Still others characterize healthcare regulation as captured by providers, and consequently ineffectual, and argue that more aggressive regulatory strategies and greater efforts at enforcement are needed (Dame and Wolfe, 1996; Latimer, 1997).

This debate has not generally been well-informed through empirical evidence from research into the methods, costs and impacts of regulation in healthcare. Despite the substantial and continuing investment by healthcare funders, payors and providers in a wide range of regulatory arrangements, little research has been conducted into how healthcare regulation works in practice (Brennan, 1996). Without such empirical evidence, it has been difficult to develop a consensus among policy makers, healthcare organizations, consumer groups and other stakeholders about when and how regulation should be used.

Of course, the use of regulation in many other settings, both in the US and abroad, has been extensively studied and there is a substantial literature drawing on a range of academic disciplines, particularly economics, law, political science, public policy and sociology (Noll, 1985). There are studies of the regulation of coal mines (Braithwaite, 1985), occupational safety and health in the workplace (Gunningham and Johnstone, 1999), industrial environmental pollution (Gunningham et al., 1998), public or private utilities (Foster, 1992), the financial sector (Chorafas, 2000), government agencies (Hood et al., 1999), social care organizations (Clough, 1994), schools (Wilcox and Gray, 1996), and a host of other types of institutions. There is also a growing body of literature on the theory and practice of regulation, which draws on research from a range of settings to offer some important general theoretical tools and frameworks and generalized, widely relevant insights into the regulatory process (Ayres and Braithwaite, 1992; Baldwin and Cave, 1999; Bardach and Kagan, 1982; Breyer, 1982; Ogus, 1994). It seems, however, that the empirical research, theories and policy experience of regulation in these other settings have had little influence on the development of regulatory policy and practice in healthcare (Brennan and Berwick, 1996).

This paper explores the development of the social regulation of healthcare organizations and its effects on the quality of healthcare in the US, drawing both on the existing literature and on the findings from an exploratory qualitative study of regulators and regulated organizations. It first outlines the nature and need for social and economic regulation, describes the development of social regulation in US healthcare, presents a framework for analysing regulatory arrangements, which is used to compare and contrast two major regulators, and examines what is known about the impact of regulation on performance. The paper also describes a qualitative study undertaken to explore the impact of regulation and the potential characteristics of effective regulation and presents its findings in four main areas: regulatory fragmentation; regulatory methods and processes; the costs of regulation; and the impact of regulation. The paper concludes by drawing on both the wider literature and the qualitative study to outline a tentative evaluative framework for assessing the effectiveness of regulation and to set out some future research needs in this area.

Social and economic regulation

Regulation has been concisely defined as 'sustained and focused control exercised by a public agency over activities that are valued by a community' (Selznick, 1985). It is a collective function, in that a central entity — the regulator — is mandated or empowered to act on behalf of everyone rather than individuals being expected or even entitled to do so for themselves. In a market for goods or services, regulation interposes a third party — the regulator — into the normally bilateral relationship between sellers and buyers. Although Selznick's definition of regulation speaks of a public agency, that is not synonymous with government: non-governmental organizations often play a part in self-regulatory or government-sponsored independent regulatory arrangements.

Regulation is often presented as a consequence of, or a response to, market failure: when conditions such as monopoly or monopsony exist; or where there are major information imbalances between buyers and sellers; or when goods are consumed by one party and paid for by another; or where problems of scarcity or the coordination of provision exist (Ogus, 1994). Regulation is also used to serve social goals, such as the provision of public or collective goods; the implementation of social values such as equity, diversity, social solidarity and compassion; and the holding to account of powerful professional or corporate interests (Noll, 1985).

These different causes tend to produce different regulatory responses. Economic regulation is usually a response to one or more of the conditions of market failure outlined above, and often centres on controlling price, demand or supply (Breyer, 1982). Economic regulation is used widely in US healthcare through, for example, Medicare and Medicaid reimbursement mechanisms, certificate of need controls on hospital and nursing home development, and controls on the health insurance marketplace (Hackey, 1998; Hall, 2000; McClure, 1981). Social regulation may also be a response to some forms of market failure, but it is often an attempt to address wider social goals such as those discussed above. Social regulation is directed at changing the behaviour and performance of organizations, and is also widely used in US healthcare. Examples include the licensing, certification and oversight of healthcare organizations by state and federal agencies, and programmes of accreditation or certification by both governmental and non-governmental agencies (Brennan and Berwick, 1996). Systems for economic and social regulation often exist alongside each other and interact. This paper is primarily focused on the use of social regulation, and its impact on the performance of healthcare organizations, but also draws on the economic regulation literature, particularly in areas where there are important commonalities or contrasts.

A framework for regulatory analysis

Amid such regulatory heterogeneity, it is helpful to have a framework or typology through which different forms of regulatory arrangements can be compared and contrasted. To this end, seven key properties of any system of regulation are outlined in a framework in Table 23.1, drawing on previous work by Hood et al. (1999) and Scrivens (1996), and two contrasting regulatory agencies are described using this framework by way of illustration.

The framework sets out four dimensions concerned with the regulatory environment or context, and three concerned with regulatory processes and systems. The former concern the regulatory organization itself, how it is structured and to whom it is accountable; the goals or objectives of regulation; the scope of regulation, which means what organizations and activities are to be regulated; and the regulatory model underlying the approach to regulation. The latter dimension is particularly important. Regulators can be described as either deterrence- or compliance-oriented (Reiss, 1984). Deterrence regulators see the organizations they regulate as 'amoral calculators', out to get what they can, and only likely to conform with regulation if they are forced to do so. They tend to have distant, formal and rather adversarial relationships with the organizations they regulate, and to make extensive use of formal sanctions and penalties. By contrast, compliance regulators see the organizations they regulate as fundamentally good and well-intentioned, and likely to comply with regulation if they can. They have closer and more friendly relationships with the organizations they regulate, are often involved in support or educational activities, and only use formal sanctions or penalties as a last resort. In practice, regulators often use a mixture of deterrence and compliance strategies. Each has different advantages and disadvantages, and different circumstances may require different approaches.

The three dimensions concerned with regulatory systems and processes are: direction, which means how regulators set and communicate their expectations to those they regulate; detection, which relates to how they measure and monitor performance; and enforcement, which means the methods they use to persuade, influence or make regulated organizations change their behaviour.

It can be seen that the two example regulators described in Table 23.1 using this framework have quite similar regulatory objectives and methods for direction and detection but very different regulatory models and approaches to enforcement. In broad terms, the accreditation programme for hospitals of the Joint Commission on the Accreditation of Healthcare Organizations (JCAHO) is compliance-oriented, educational, and relies primarily on the professionalism of its surveyors and of hospital leaders to achieve change. In contrast, the state and federal regulators of nursing homes are largely deterrence-oriented, use formal and more adversarial survey methods, and have recourse to some serious sanctions and penalties. This may be a reflection of differences in the political power, organizational culture and social context of hospitals and nursing homes, or a consequence of the different status and powers of governmental and non-governmental regulators, or both. There is a lack of research evidence to inform the inevitable debate about which of these two approaches is more effective, or for what situations each is better suited.

Table 23.1 A framework for describing healthcare regulation

Characteristic	Description	Example analysis for JCAHO accreditation of hospitals	Example analysis for state and federal regulation of nursing homes
Regulating organization	The constitution, nature, formal remit or mandate, legal powers and authority, governance and reporting or accountability arrangements of the regulating organization.	Joint Commission on the Accreditation of Healthcare Organizations (JCAHO) is an independent, private sector organization which has no formal legal powers or authority over hospitals. It is governed by a board dominated by representatives of the American Hospitals Association, American Medical Association, American College of Surgeons and similar groups.	CMS and state survey agencies (such as the California Department of Health Services) are jointly responsible for regulating nursing homes. The Federal Nursing Homes Act 1987, state legislation, and extensive federal and state regulations provide these agencies with formal legal powers and authority. The agencies are responsible to state and federal governments and legislatures.
Regulatory goals/objectives	The purpose of regulation, and how clearly or explicitly it is stated.	JCAHO's stated mission is 'to continuously improve the safety and quality of care provided to the public through the provision of health care accreditation and related services that support performance improvement in healthcare organizations'.	The CMS/state agencies aim to 'promote the timely and economic delivery of appropriate quality of care [and] efficiency and quality within the total healthcare delivery system'.
Scope of regulation	The forms or types of organization which are subject to regulation, and the range of functions or activities within those organizations which are regulated.	JCAHO accredits many types of healthcare organization, but this analysis focuses on their accreditation of hospitals. About 4500 hospitals (or 80% of the total) have accreditation. JCAHO's oversight covers almost all areas of hospital performance.	There are about 17,000 nursing homes in the US that are licensed and certified by state agencies on behalf of CMS. The regulators have broad oversight across most areas of nursing home performance.
Regulatory model	The degree to which the regulating organization's philosophy, strategy and methods are oriented towards deterrence or compliance.	Generally compliance-oriented, with enforcement used as a last resort. Major focus on the educational and developmental dimension of the accreditation process. Emphasis placed on quality improvement.	Generally deterrence-oriented, with a strong focus on identifying deficiencies, penalties and sanctions. Surveyors are not allowed to offer nursing homes education, advice or developmental support.

Direction	The methods used to communicate regulatory requirements or directions to regulated organizations.	JCAHO maintains an extensive accreditation manual for hospitals which contains over 500 standards organized around 15 main areas. For each standard there is detailed guidance on its intent, implementation, and assessment.	The CMS state operations manual sets out the conditions of participation for Medicare/Medicaid and outlines in detail the arrangements for surveys and enforcement. In addition, many states have their own, separate legislation and regulations.
Detection	The methods used to measure and monitor the performance of regulated organizations in order to determine whether they comply with regulatory requirements or directions.	Three-yearly accreditation surveys of hospitals, usually involving a four- to five-day visit to the organization by a three-person surveyor team. Visit is preceded by months of preparatory activity, and followed by a report describing compliance with the standards and identifies any recommendations for improvement.	Annual certification surveys of nursing homes, usually involving a three- to four-day visit to the organization by a three- to four-person surveyor team. Surveys are all unannounced and can start at any time. Surveys focus on identifying and categorizing 'deficiencies' (areas where the conditions of participation are not met).
Enforcement	The methods used to persuade, influence or force regulated organizations to make changes to comply with regulatory requirements or directions.	Over 95% of hospitals achieve full accreditation, although many have follow-up reports or visits to check on implementation of recommendations. Denial of accreditation is the only formal sanction, and it is used very rarely (in less than 1% of cases). A limited summary of accreditation report is available to the public on paper and via the JCAHO website.	Only 18% of nursing homes have no deficiencies—on average, each home has about six identified deficiencies. They are graded according to severity. Home can be required to put the problem right, and may face other sanctions including financial penalties, denial of payment, closure to new admissions, imposition of temporary management, and ultimately de-licensing/removal from Medicare/Medicaid.

Discussion and policy implications

The form and structure of regulation is highly dependent on its social, economic and political context, and systems of regulation vary widely from industry to industry and from country to country (Ayres and Braithwaite, 1992; Kagan and Axelrad, 2000). For this reason, it is difficult to prescribe any one particular approach, or to offer any universal templates or models. However, from the extensive literature on regulation in other settings, and the more limited body of work on healthcare regulation, including this exploratory study, some common ground can be established, and some factors which contribute towards effective healthcare regulation can be tentatively proposed. We set out ten such factors below, and summarize them in Box 23.1. This list of the characteristics of effective regulation is a highly provisional one, which may be incomplete and imperfect, and further empirical work is needed to test its utility, but we regard it as a useful first step towards the more rigorous evaluation of regulatory arrangements.

Box 23.1   Some principles for effective regulation

Improvement focus	• Is performance improvement the explicitly stated, primary objective of the regulatory process?
	• Are the regulatory arrangements directed at promoting performance improvement, or are there ways in which they might hinder or slow improvement?
Responsiveness	• Does the regulator have access to and make prompt and timely use of a wide range of different direction, detection and enforcement mechanisms?
	• Does the regulator adapt or tailor its approach to individual regulated organizations, making its use of regulatory mechanisms contingent on the response or behaviour of the organization?
Proportionality and targeting	• Is the level and scope of regulatory intervention appropriately matched to the size and importance of the performance problem or issue?
	• Are regulatory resources focused on or directed towards those organizations or areas where performance problems are known or suspected to exist?
Rigour and robustness	• Are regulations or standards developed through a rigorous process that takes full account of available evidence?

	• Are regulatory methods, especially those for measurement, developed and tested rigorously, and do they achieve adequate validity and reliability in use?
Flexibility and consistency	• Do the regulatory arrangements allow sufficient flexibility for regulatory staff to use appropriate discretion in matching regulatory interventions and actions to individual circumstances or contexts?
	• Is the consistency of regulatory practice maintained, through careful monitoring and comparison of the work of regulatory staff, while taking into account the need for flexibility?
Cost consciousness	• Is the regulator aware of the full costs of regulation, including costs both to the regulatory agency and to regulated organizations?
	• Does the regulatory undertake a proper comparison of the costs and benefits of regulatory interventions, especially when new regulatory interventions are being developed?
	• Does the regulator take steps to minimize the interaction and compliance costs for regulated organizations when it can do so?
Openness and transparency	• Is information about the design regulatory process freely available, so that all stakeholders are informed about how systems for regulation are developed and set up?
	• Is information about the regulatory process itself freely available, so that all stakeholders are informed about the work programme of the regulator, and plans and timescales for its regulatory interventions?
	• Are the results of regulation, including the findings and decisions about individual regulated organizations, freely available to all stakeholders including the public?
Enforceability	• Does the regulator have access to and make prompt and timely use of a wide range of both incentives and sanctions with which it can influence regulated organizations and promote change?
	• Does the regulator use the minimum enforcement action needed in order to secure change?

	• Are improvement and good performance recognised and rewarded by the regulator?
	• When persistent or serious problems of poor performance are identified? Are they dealt with promptly and fully by the regulator? Are top-level sanctions (such as de-licensing) used if they are needed?
Accountability and independence	• Is there a mechanism for holding the regulator accountable for its actions, to those with an interest in the area being regulated (including patients and the public, healthcare funders and payors, healthcare providers, and health policy makers)?
	• Do the governance arrangements for the regulator maintain a balance between different interest groups or stakeholders and avoid any one group being dominant?
	• Does the regulator have sufficient independence of action from stakeholders or interest groups to be able to take, actions that may not be welcomed by some such groups?
Formative evaluation and review	• Does the regulator have systems in place to monitor and formatively evaluate how its systems of regulation work, and to assess their impact on performance?
	• Are the results of evaluation reviewed and used to modify systems of regulation where necessary?

First, it seems that regulation should be primarily directed at *performance improvement*, and its ability to deliver improvement should be the main metric of any evaluation. This might entail preventing poor performance, encouraging and rewarding good performance, and supporting organizations' improvement efforts, but improvement should still be the name of the game. The problem is that the aims of regulation are often unclear, and regulatory means and ends can easily become confused. From our and other studies, it seems the process of regulation can easily become a purpose in itself, at least for regulatory agencies. Too often, it seems that regulatory output is measured in terms of the numbers of standards set, surveys done, deficiencies found, or sanctions imposed. These may at times be useful indicators of regulatory performance, but they are not adequate proxies for real, sustained improvements in the performance of regulated organizations. If the overall aim of improvement is not pursued directly and diligently, it seems that the regulatory process often develops its own momentum, and becomes difficult to change even if it is clearly not working well, or if it creates barriers to improvement rather than promoting it.

Second, it appears that regulation should be *responsive* by design, which means that the regulator should have access to and make full use of a wide range of different methods for direction, detection and enforcement (Ayres and Braithwaite, 1992). The aims of effective regulation are not served well by either of the extremes of deterrence and compliance regulation. Our interviewees spoke eloquently of the frustrations of what might be termed regulatory mismatch — a lack of congruence in aims and ideas between them and the regulators they encountered, because regulatory agencies applied standards and expectations that did not fit the individual healthcare organization very well. Regulators should treat regulated organizations differently, depending on how they behave, and should be able to fit regulatory methods or interventions to the context. What is sometimes called 'one size fits all' or 'cookie cutter' regulation should be avoided, because it does not adequately reward quality care, nor does it do enough to address poor-quality care. Highly prescriptive regulatory designs tend to narrow the scope for this kind of regulatory differentiation, and may therefore make for less effective regulation.

Third, it can be argued that the extent and nature of regulation should be *proportionate* to the perceived quality problems or need for improvement, in the sense that major problems evoke a major regulatory response, but minor issues receive less regulatory attention. The lack of attention to regulatory costs highlighted by our interviews and discussed again below means there is at best an imperfect consideration of whether the costs of a regulatory intervention are merited by its likely benefits. Over-regulation is likely to result in a defensive or adversarial response from regulated organizations, as well as wasting resources; whereas under-regulation is unlikely to provide a sufficient stimulus to bring about necessary improvements. Regulatory attention should also be targeted or focused on those organizations or areas where performance problems are known or suspected to exist, so that the return on investment in regulation (in terms of the scope for improvement identified or realized) is maximized. Regulators have very limited resources in comparison with the organizations they regulate, so every decision to invest regulatory attention in a particular area has important opportunity costs.

Fourth, regulatory methods should be demonstrably *rigorous and robust* in scientific terms — something that many of our interviewees questioned for current regulatory standards and processes. For example, standards should be developed using a formal process of some kind, should take full account of available evidence, and it should be possible to look behind the standards to see the underlying or supporting evidence. When regulators set out to measure things, the tools they use should also be developed and tested properly and should conform to established standards for validity, reliability and general utility. Detection mechanisms such as surveys should also be demonstrably rigorous and robust. This requirement might seem axiomatic, but it is evident that the scientific rigour of some current systems of regulation has, at best, not been demonstrated.

Fifth, systems for regulation need to strike a difficult balance between *flexibility and consistency.* Our study suggests that regulators tend to prioritize consistency, at some cost to their flexibility. For effective regulation, regulatory staff need to have sufficient scope and flexibility to use their discretion and professional judgement in their interactions with regulated organizations, but fairness and equity demand that regulations are applied consistently. Reconciling these two conflicting imperatives may be difficult, but it seems that an overemphasis on consistency is actually the greater threat to effective regulation. In practice, scope for discretion is compatible with consistent treatment, if regulatory staff are well trained and some oversight of their use of discretion is maintained.

Sixth, the regulator should be aware of, and responsive to, the full *costs of regulation,* and use established techniques for assessing costs and benefits in designing systems of regulation. Our interviews suggested that costs are all too frequently discounted or ignored, especially when they fall on other organizations or are hidden because they never appear in any organization's financial accounts labelled as a cost of regulation. There are some well-established technical methods for analysing the cost-effectiveness of regulation (Froud *et al.*, 1998) but this is more a cultural than a technical requirement. There is no point in requiring regulators to measure cost-effectiveness if they treat the task as a hurdle to be overcome and approach regulatory impact assessment determined to show that whatever they do is cost-effective. Rather, the regulator should demonstrate an awareness of and sensitivity to the costs that fall on regulated organizations, and be genuinely committed to minimizing those costs while still pursuing their regulatory mission.

Seventh, the regulatory arrangements should be *open and transparent* so that all stakeholders are able to understand how they work and will know what to expect. Our interview study suggested that privately conducted regulatory processes provoke widespread suspicion about what is going on behind closed doors. The development and implementation of regulation should be undertaken under public scrutiny, and the findings from regulation should also be openly accessible. However, there may be areas of the regulatory process, for example the negotiations between the regulator and a regulated organization over what they must do to achieve regulatory compliance, in which public scrutiny can be counterproductive. Within the general imperative to be open and transparent, there has to be some space for privacy and discretion.

Eighth, the regulator should have a wide range of *enforcement* strategies or mechanisms available to allow it to make change happen when it is needed. Our interviews suggest there is often a gap between the regulator's theoretical powers of enforcement, which sound considerable, and their actual application. Enforcement action is time-consuming and expensive, and some sanctions (such as de-licensing or the removal of accreditation) are impracticable and so are hardly ever used. We suggest the regulatory enforcement mechanisms should include some incentives as well as sanctions and should be used promptly when they are needed, although the regulator should aim to use the minimum enforcement action necessary to secure change. There is a need for a more creative and improvement-oriented approach to enforcement which is less concerned with penalties and more focused on creating and sustaining change.

Ninth, the regulator needs to be both *accountable* and *independent.* A balance needs to be found between ensuring sufficient accountability to the stakeholders in the regulated area, including consumers, providers, funders and the public, and providing the regulator with sufficient space to take actions which may sometimes be unpopular with some groups. The literature tends to focus exclusively on the problems of regulatory capture by providers, but our study suggests that regulators dominated by any one stakeholder group — industry, government, funders, patients or providers — can be damaged by these affiliations, whether real or perceived. Regulators often act as an 'honest broker' in reconciling conflicting stakeholder interests, but to do so they need to be (and be seen to be) relatively independent of any one interest group.

Finally, the regulator should be committed to *evaluation and review* so that the impact of regulation is monitored and evaluated and the results of such reviews are then used to improve the systems of regulation. This might be taken to be self-evident, given the relatively limited literature on the impact of regulation (reviewed earlier), and the mixed messages about the benefits and disadvantages of regulation arising from our study.

If the existing systems of healthcare regulation in the US are measured against the principles for effective regulation set out in Box 23.1, most do not score highly. All too often, US healthcare regulation seems to be adversarial, inflexible, slow, cumbersome and expensive. Performance improvement, though nominally the objective, often appears not to result. Regulatory standards and measures are not usually developed and deployed with the level of scientific rigour and robustness that might be expected. A 'cookie cutter' approach to regulation predominates, in which all organizations are treated the same regardless of their history, perform- ance or response to regulatory intervention. Enforcement mechanisms seem to punish everyone more or less equally, to lack any positive incentives, and yet to be inadequate when dealing with the small number of poorly performing, recalcitrant organizations that need strict enforcement. The costs of regulation are frequently ignored, and regulatory arrangements are rarely properly evaluated. While the wider regulatory literature suggests that these problems are not unique to US healthcare, it seems that much could be learned by examining approaches to regulation in other sectors and countries and incorporating some of the principles set out in Box 23.1 (Gunningham *et al.*, 1998; Hood *et al.*, 1999).

Conclusion

It was noted at the outset of this paper that regulation is a controversial subject, in which different groups (e.g. healthcare providers, consumer groups, regulators, etc.) have divergent views about what regulatory arrangements should be put in place, and that as a consequence regulatory reform is fraught with difficulties.

However, we can suggest a number of sample actions that regulatory agencies and their stakeholders could consider. For example, cooperation among regulatory agencies to coordinate their work and reduce duplication could be improved, especially if it was required by Government or built into their legislative mandate. Regulatory governance could be improved by reforming their board memberships and bringing in all stakeholder groups. To make performance improvement more central to regulation and to encourage partnership, some part of a regulatory agency's income could be linked to improvements in the performance of the organizations it regulates. Better use could be made of regulatory impact analyses, both to test the value of new regulations before they are implemented and to undertake reviews of existing regulations. Limits on the total volume of regulations could be used to make regulators and regulated organizations prioritize, and remove old or outdated regulations.

This study confirms that there is a need for more research into healthcare regulation, aimed at measuring its costs and impact more scientifically, and developing a better understanding of regulatory methods and approaches and how they work. But research alone will not change the way healthcare is regulated in the US. The regulatory community — regulators, regulated organizations, patient or consumer groups, and other stakeholders — needs to escape the current rather polarized and politicized debate and move towards a more considered and empirically founded approach to regulation, in which systems of regulation are carefully developed, then piloted, and formatively evaluated during their implementation, and a greater consensus about their value and their contribution to performance improvement is developed.

References and further reading

Altman, S. H., Reinhardt, U. E. and Shactman, D. (eds.) *Regulating Managed Care: Theory, Practice and Future Options.* San Francisco: Jossey-Bass, 1999

American Health Quality Association (AHQA). *A Measure of Quality: Improving Performance in American Healthcare.* Washington DC: AHQA, 2000

American Hospitals Association. *Patients or Paperwork: the Regulatory Burden Facing America's Hospitals.* Chicago: American Hospitals Association, 2001

Anderson, C. L. and Kagan, R. A. Adversarial legalism and transaction costs: the industrial-flight hypothesis revisited. *International Review of Law and Economics* 2000; **20**: 1–19

Antel, J. J., Ohsfeldt, R. L. and Becker, E. R. State regulation and hospital costs. *Review of Economics and Statistics* 1995; 77(3): 416–22

Ayres, I. and Braithwaite, J. *Responsive Regulation: Transcending the Deregulation Debate.* Oxford: Oxford University Press, 1992

Baldwin, R. and Cave, M. *Understanding Regulation: Theory, Strategy and Practice.* Oxford: Oxford University Press, 1999

Bardach, E. and Kagan, R. *Going by the Book: the Problem of Regulatory Unreasonableness.* Philadelphia: Temple University Press, 1982

Braithwaite, J. *To Punish or Persuade: Enforcement of Coal Mine Safety.* Albany: State University of New York Press, 1985

Brennan, T. A. and Berwick, D. M. *New Rules: Regulation, Markets and the Quality of American Healthcare.* San Francisco: Jossey-Bass, 1996

Brennan, T. A. The role of regulation in quality improvement. *Milbank Quarterly* 1996; **76**(4): 709–31

Breyer, S. G. *Regulation and its Reform.* Cambridge, MA: Harvard University Press, 1982

Chorafas, D. N. *New Regulation of the Financial Industry.* New York: St. Martin's Press, 2000

Clough, R. (ed.) *Insights into Inspection: the Regulation of Social Care.* London: Whiting and Birch, 1994

Conover, C. J. and Sloan, F. A. Does removing certificate of need regulations lead to a surge in health care spending? *Journal of Health Politics, Policy and Law* 1998; **23**(5): 455–81

Dame, L. and Wolfe, S. *The Failure of Private Hospital Regulation: an Analysis of the Joint Commission on Accreditation of Healthcare Organizations' Inadequate Oversight of Hospitals.* Washington, DC: Public Citizen Publications, 1996

Davies, H. T. O., Nutley, S. M., Smith, P. C. (eds.) *What Works? Evidence-Based Policy and Practice in Public Services.* Bristol: Policy Press, 2000

De Ville, K. A. Managed care and the ethics of regulation. *Journal of Medicine and Philosophy* 1999; **24**(5): 492–517

Foster, C. D. *Privatization, Public Ownership and the Regulation of Natural Monopoly.* Oxford: Blackwell, 1992

Froud, J., Boden, R., Ogus, A. and Stubbs, P. *Controlling the Regulators.* London: Macmillan, 1998

Fuchs, B. *Managed Healthcare: Federal and State Regulation.* Washington DC: Congressional Research Service, Library of Congress, 1997

General Accounting Office (GAO). *California Nursing Homes: Care Problems Persist Despite Federal and State Oversight.* GAO/HEHS-98-202. Washington DC, 1998

GAO. *Nursing Homes: Additional Steps Needed to Strengthen Enforcement of Federal Quality Standards.* GAO/HEHS-99-46. Washington DC, 1999a

GAO. *Nursing Homes: Complaint Investigation Processes Often Inadequate to Protect Residents.* GAO/HEHS-99-80. Washington DC, 1999b

GAO. *Nursing Homes: Proposal to Enhance Oversight of Poorly Performing Homes has Merit.* GAO/HEHS-99-157. Washington DC, 1999c

GAO. *Nursing Home Care: Enhanced HCFA Oversight of State Programs Would Better Ensure Quality.* GAO/HEHS-00-6. Washington DC, 1999d

GAO. *Nursing Homes: Sustained Efforts are Essential to Realise Potential of the Quality Initiatives.* GAO/HEHS-00-197. Washington DC, 2000

Goodman, J. C. *The Regulation of Medical Care: is the Price Too High?* San Francisco: Cato Institute, 1980

Gunningham, N., Grabosky, P. and Sinclair, D. *Smart Regulation: Designing Environmental Policy.* Oxford: Clarendon Press, 1998

Gunningham, N. and Johnstone, R. *Regulating Workplace Safety: Systems and Sanctions.* Oxford: Oxford University Press, 1999

Hackey, R. B. *Rethinking Healthcare Policy: the New Politics of State Regulation.* Washington DC: Georgetown University Press, 1998

Hadley, T. R. and McGurrin, M. C. Accreditation, certification and the quality of care in state hospitals. *Hospital and Community Psychiatry* 1988; **39**(7): 739–42

Hall, M. A. The geography of health insurance regulation. *Health Affairs* 2000; **19**(2): 173–84

Harrington, C., Carillo, H., Thollaug, S. C., Summers, P. R. and Wellin, V. *Nursing Facilities, Staffing, Residents and Facility Deficiencies: 1993 Through 1999.* San Francisco: Department of Social and Behavioural Sciences, 2000

Hawes, C. *The History and Impact of Federal Standards in OBRA-87.* New York: Commonwealth Fund, 1996

HCIA Inc./JCAHO. *Comparing Quality and Financial Performance of Accredited Hospitals.* Oakbrook Terrace: JCAHO, 1993

Hood, C., Scott, C., James, O. *et al. Regulation Inside Government.* Oxford: Oxford University Press, 1999

Institute of Medicine. *Improving the Quality of Care in Nursing Homes.* Washington DC: National Academy Press, 1986

Institute of Medicine. *Improving the Quality of Long-Term Care.* Washington DC: National Academy Press, 2001

Jessee, W. F. and Schranz, C. M. Medicare mortality rates and hospital quality: are they related? *Quality Assurance in Health Care* 1990; **2**(2): 137–44

Kagan, R., Axelrad, L. (eds.) *Regulatory Encounters: Multinational Corporations and American Adversarial Legalism.* Berkeley: University of California Press, 2000

Kapp, M. B. Quality of care and quality of life in nursing facilities: what's regulation got to do with it? *McGeorge Law Review* 2000; **31**: 707–31

Klein, R. The regulation of nursing homes: a comparative perspective. *Milbank Quarterly* 1987; **65**(3): 303–47

Latimer, J. The essential role of regulation to assure quality in long term care. *Generations* 1997; **21**(4): 10–14

Levin, A. (ed.) *Regulating Healthcare: the Struggle for Control.* New York: Academy of Political Science, 1980

Leyerle, B. *The Private Regulation of American Healthcare.* New York: ME Sharpe, 1994

Lincoln, Y. S. and Guba, E. G. *Naturalistic Inquiry.* Newbury Park: Sage Publications, 1985

McClure, W. Structure and incentive problems in economic regulation of medical care. *Milbank Memorial Fund Quarterly* 1981; **59**(2): 107–45

Miles, M. B. and Huberman, A. M. *Qualitative Data Analysis: an Expanded Sourcebook.* London: Sage, 1994

Miller, T. E. Managed care regulation in the laboratory of the states. *JAMA* 1997; **278**(13): 1102–9

National Committee for Quality Assurance (NCQA). *The State of Managed Care Quality Report 2000.* Washington DC: NCQA, 2000

Noll, R. G. (ed.) *Regulatory Policy and the Social Sciences.* Berkeley: University of California Press, 1985

Office of Inspector General (OIG). *The External Review of Hospital Quality: the Role of Accreditation.* Washington DC: Department of Health and Human Services, 1999a

OIG. *The External Review of Hospital Quality: the Role of Medicare Certification.* Washington DC: Department of Health and Human Services, 1999b

Ogus, A. *Regulation—Legal Form and Economic Theory.* Oxford: Clarendon Press, 1994

Reiss, A. J. Selecting strategies of social control over organizational life. In: Hawkins, K. and Thomas, J. M. (eds.) *Enforcing Regulation.* Boston: Kluwer-Nijhoff Publishing: 1984: 23–36

Roberts, J. S., Coale, J. G. and Redman, R. R. A short history of the Joint Commission on Accreditation of Hospitals. *JAMA* 1987; **258**(7): 936–40

Rockwell, D. A., Pelletier, L. R. and Donnelly, W. The cost of accreditation: one hospital's experience. *Hospital and Community Psychiatry* 1993; **44**: 151–5

Rosenbloom, D. H. The evolution of the administrative state and transformations of administrative law. In: Rosenbloom, D. H. and Schwartz, R. D. (eds.) *Handbook of Regulation and Administrative Law.* New York: Marcel Dekker Inc., 1994: 3–36

Schyve, P. M. and O'Leary, D. S. The Joint Commission's agenda for change and beyond. In: Caldwell, C. (ed.) *Handbook for Managing Change in Healthcare.* Milwaukee: ASQ Quality Press, 1998: 367–90

Scrivens, E. *Accreditation: Protecting the Professional or the Consumer?* Buckingham: Open University Press, 1995

Scrivens, E. A taxonomy of the dimensions of accreditation systems. *Social Policy and Administration* 1996; **30**(2): 114–24

Selznick, P. Focusing organizational research on regulation. In: Noll, R. (ed.) *Regulatory Policy and the Social Sciences.* Berkeley: University of California Press, 1985: 363–8

Silberman, P. and James, K. Managed care regulations: impact on quality? *Quality Management in Health Care* 2000; **8**(2): 21–39

Vita, M. G. The impact of hospital rate setting programs on hospital and health care expenditures 1975–1985. *Applied Economics* 1995; **27**(10): 917–23

Wiener, C. L. *The Elusive Quest: Accountability in Hospitals.* New York: Aldine de Gruyter, 2000

Wilcox, B. and Gray, J. *Inspecting Schools: Holding Schools to Account and Helping Schools to Improve.* Buckingham: Open University Press, 1996

24

What is measured is what matters: targets and gaming in the English public health care system
Gwyn Bevan and Christopher Hood

Extracts from Bevan G and Hood C (2006) What is measured is what matters: targets and gaming in the English public healthcare system, Public Administration 84(3): 517–38.

Managing public services by targets: and terror?

In the mid-eighteenth century, Voltaire (in *Candide*) famously satirized the British style of naval administration with his quip 'ici on tue de temps en temps un amiral pour encourager les autres'. In the early twentieth century, the USSR's communist czars combined that hanging-the-admirals approach with a system of production targets for all state enterprises. The basic system survived for some 60 years, albeit with various detailed changes over time, before the Soviet system finally collapsed in 1991 (Ericson 1991) – a decline that has been attributed by some to not hanging enough admirals to counter gaming produced by the target system.

In the 2000s, Tony Blair's New Labour government in Britain adopted a watered down version of that system for performance management of public services, especially those in England. Having tagged a new set of government-wide performance targets onto the spending control system in 1998, in 2001 it added a key central monitoring unit working directly to the Prime Minister. From 2001, in England, the Department of Health introduced an annual system of publishing 'star ratings' for public health care organizations. This gave each unit a single summary score from about 50 kinds of targets: a small set of 'key targets' and a wider set of indicators in a 'balanced scorecard' (Secretary of State for Health 2001a, 2002a; Commission for Health Improvement 2003a, b; Healthcare Commission 2004). While the Blair government did not hang the admirals in a literal sense, English health care managers (whose life was perceived to be 'nasty, brutish and short' even before the advent of targets: Cole 2001) were exposed to increased risk of being sacked as a result of poor performance on measured indices (Shifrin 2001) and, through publication of star ratings, also to 'naming and shaming' (Anonymous 2001) (something that had been applied to schools and local government in the previous decade). Although there have been developments in performance assessment of public health care organizations in other UK countries following devolution, the policy context differed from England (Greer 2004): there was no emphasis on a few key targets, nor publication for 'naming and shaming'; nor was performance assessment linked with direct sanctions or rewards (Scottish Executive Health Department 2003; Farrar *et al.* 2004; Auditor General for Wales 2005). Hence these countries offer a natural experiment in assessing the impacts of the system of star ratings.

This paper seeks to explore some of the assumptions underlying the system of governance by targets. To the extent that target systems of this type invite gaming by managers and other actors, are there ways of making targets and performance measures less vulnerable to gaming without scrapping them altogether?

The theory of governance by targets and performance indicators

Governance by targets and measured performance indicators is a form of indirect control necessary for the governance of any complex system (Beer 1966). The form of control that target systems represent is a version of homeostatic control in which: (1) desired results are specified in advance in measurable form; (2) some system of monitoring measures performance against that specification; and (3) feedback mechanisms are linked to measured performance. Ironically perhaps, just as the targets system was collapsing in the USSR, the same basic approach came to be much advocated for public services in the West by those who believed in 'results-driven government' from the 1980s (see Pollitt 1986; Carter *et al.* 1995; Bird *et al.* 2005). It resonated with the ideas put forward by economists about the power of well-chosen *numéraires* linked with well-crafted incentive systems. It often appealed to public managers themselves as well because it could be portrayed as an alternative to the 'double-bind' approach to governing public services, one in which agents must strive to achieve conflicting and often not-fully-stated objectives, such that they fail whatever they do (Dunsire 1978). It also gave managers of complex, pluralistic, professional-heavy public organizations an explicit *rôle* and *raison d'être*.

Targets are sometimes kept secret. The type of regime considered here, however, is one in which targets and measures are published. Performance against those measures is also published (a principle going back at least to Jeremy Bentham's plans for prison management in the 1790s). The rewards and sanctions include: reputational effects (shame or glory accruing to managers on the basis of their reported performance); the award of bonuses and renewed tenure for managers that depend on performance against target; 'best to best' budgetary allocations that reflect measured performance; and the granting of 'earned autonomy' (ascertained from detailed inspection and oversight) to high performers. The last, a principle associated with Ayres and Braithwaite's (1992) idea of 'responsive regulation', was enshrined as a central plank in the New Labour vision of public management in its 1999 *Modernizing Government* White Paper (Cabinet

Office 1999), as well as in a major review of public and private regulation at the end of its second term (Hampton 2004).

Such rewards and sanctions are easy to state baldly, but are often deeply problematic in practice. Summary dismissal of public managers can be difficult (as was the case even in the USSR in its later years). The 'best to best' principle of budgetary allocation will always have to confront rival principles, such as equal shares or even 'best to worst' (implying give the most to the weakest or most disadvantaged units) (Auditor General for Wales 2005). In addition, the earned autonomy principle of proportionate response implies a high degree of discretion accorded to regulators or central agencies that rubs up against rule-of-law ideas of rule-governed administration.

There are also major problems of credibility and commitment in any such system, given the incentives to 'cheat' both by target-setters and target managers (see Nove 1958; Miller 1992; Kornai 1994; Smith 1995; Heinrich 2002; Hood 2002; Propper and Wilson 2003; Bird et al. 2005). One possible way of limiting cheating and establishing commitment is by establishment of independent third parties as regulators or evaluators (Majone 1996; Power 1999). In the English variant of governance by targets and performance indicators in the 2000s – in contrast to the Soviet model – semi-independent bodies of various types, often sector-specific, figured large in the institutional architecture alongside central agencies and government departments. But the commitment and credibility such bodies could add was precarious, given that most of them had only limited independence.

We now consider two linked assumptions that underlie the theory of governance by targets. One is that measurement problems are unimportant, that the part on which performance is measured can adequately represent performance on the whole, and that distribution of performance does not matter. The other is that this method of governance is not vulnerable to gaming by agents.

Assumptions about measurement: synecdoche

As indicated in Figure 24.1, governance by targets implies the ability to set targets relating to some domain (small or large) of total performance which is to be given priority. That domain is here denoted as α, with performance outside that domain (β) assigned lesser importance. So the task is to develop targets measured by indicators, here denoted as $M[\alpha]$, to assess performance on α. The problem, as stated by Carter et al. (1995, p. 49), is that most indicators are 'tin openers rather than dials: by opening up a can of worms they do not give answers but prompt investigation and inquiry, and by themselves provide an incomplete and inaccurate picture'. Hence, typically, there will be a small set of indicators that are 'dials' – good measures ($M[\alpha_g]$) for a subset of α, here denoted as α_g; a larger set of 'tin openers' – imperfect measures ($M[\alpha_i]$) for another subset of α for which there are data available, here denoted as α_i, liable to generate false positives and/or false negatives; and another subset of α, here denoted as α_n, for which there are no usable data available. Accordingly, governance by targets rests on the assumptions

(i) that any omission of β and α_n does not matter; and
(ii) *either* that $M[\alpha_g]$ can be relied on as a basis for the performance regime, *or* that $(M[\alpha_g] + M[\alpha_i])$ will be an adequate basis for that regime.

What underlies these assumptions is the idea of synecdoche (taking a part to stand for a whole). Such assumptions would not be trivial even in a world where no gaming took place, but they become more problematic when gaming enters the picture.

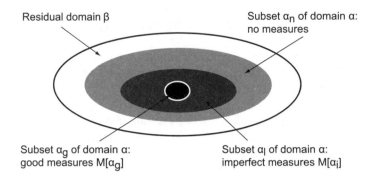

Figure 24.1   Targeting priorities

Assumptions about gaming

Governance by targets rests on the assumption that targets change the behaviour of individuals and organizations, but that 'gaming' can be kept to some acceptably low level. 'Gaming' is here defined as reactive subversion such as 'hitting the target and missing the point' or reducing performance where targets do not apply (β and α_n). For instance, analysis of the failure of the UK government's reliance on money supply targets in the 1980s to control inflation led the economist Charles Goodhart to state his eponymous law: 'Any observed statistical regularity will tend to collapse once pressure is placed on it for control purposes' because actors will change their conduct when they know that the data they produce will be used to control them (Goodhart 1984, p. 94). And the 60-year history of Soviet targets shows that major gaming problems were endemic in that system.

Three well-documented gaming problems of the Soviet system were ratchet effects, threshold effects and output distortions. Ratchet effects refer to the tendency for central controllers to base next year's targets on last year's performance, meaning that managers who expect still to be in place in the next target period have a perverse incentive not to exceed targets even if they could easily do so (Litwack 1993): 'a wise director fulfils the plan 105 per cent, but never

125 per cent' (Nove 1958, p. 4). Such effects may also be linked to gaming around target-setting, to produce relatively undemanding targets, as James (2004, p. 410) claims to have applied to a number of Labour's public spending targets in the UK after 1998. Threshold effects refer to the effects of targets on the distribution of performance among a range of, and within, production units (Bird *et al.* 2005), putting pressure on those performing below the target level to do better, but also providing a perverse incentive for those doing better than the target to allow their performance to deteriorate to the standard (see Figure 24.2), and more generally to crowd performance towards the target. Such effects can unintentionally penalize agents with exceptionally good performance but with a few failures, while rewarding those with mediocre performance crowded near the target range. Attempts to limit the threshold effect by basing future targets on past performance will tend to accentuate ratchet effects and attempts to limit ratchet effects by system-wide targets will tend to accentuate threshold effects. Attempts to achieve targets at the cost of significant but unmeasured aspects of performance (β and α_n) result in output distortions. Various such distortions were well documented for the Soviet regime (Nove 1958, pp. 4–9), including neglect of quality, widely claimed to be an endemic problem from Stalin to Gorbachev (Berliner 1988, pp. 283–4).

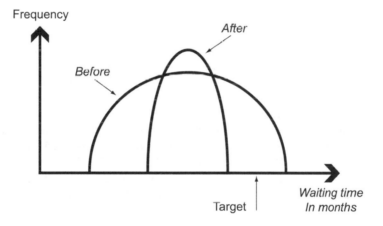

Figure 24.2 Crowding towards the target

The extent of gaming can be expected to depend on a mixture of motive and opportunity. Variations in the motives of producers or service providers can be described in various ways, of which a well-known current one is LeGrand's (2003) dichotomy of 'knights' and 'knaves'. Stretching that dichotomy slightly, we can distinguish the following four types of motivation among producers or service providers:

1. 'Saints' who may not share all of the goals of central controllers, but whose public service ethos is so high that they voluntarily disclose shortcomings to

central authorities. A striking example of such behaviour in the English public health care system was exhibited in 2000 by St George's Healthcare NHS Trust, which twice drew attention to its own failures after two series of bad runs in its heart and lung transplantation programme and suspended its transplant work itself before its status as a designated centre was withdrawn by government (Commission for Health Improvement 2001, pp. 8–10).

2. 'Honest triers' who broadly share the goals of central controllers, do not voluntarily draw attention to their failures, but do not attempt to spin or fiddle data in their favour. Within the English public health care system, a notable example of 'honest trier' behaviour was exhibited in the 1990s by the Bristol Royal Infirmary, which did not attempt to conceal evidence of very high mortality in its paediatric cardiac surgery unit. The problem turned into a major scandal, but the official inquiry report into the issue began by saying that 'The story of paediatric cardiac surgical service in Bristol is not an account of bad people. Nor is it an account of people who did not care, nor of people who wilfully harmed patients' (Secretary of State for Health 2001b, p. 1).

3. 'Reactive gamers' who broadly share the goals of central controllers, but aim to game the target system if they have reasons and opportunities to do so. Such behaviour was highlighted by a question from a voter that apparently non-plussed Prime Minister Tony Blair during the 2005 British general election campaign—that a target for general practitioners in England to see their patients within 48 hours meant that in many cases primary care trusts would not book any appointments more than 48 hours in advance (Timmins 2005).

4. 'Rational maniacs' who do not share the goals of central controllers and aim to manipulate data to conceal their operations. In the English public health care system, a notorious example of a 'rational maniac' is that of the late Dr Harold Shipman who, as a general practitioner, killed at least 215 of his patients between 1975 and 1998 (Secretary of State for Health 2002b, Summary, paras 17–22). Shipman was a 'rational maniac' in that he appeared to be able to stop killing when he had good reason to think he was under suspicion (Secretary of State for Health 2002b, Chapter 13, paras 13.68–13.74). Although Shipman was (we hope) exceptional, Kinnel (2000) claims 'medicine has arguably thrown up more serial killers than all the other professions put together, with nursing a close second'.

Gaming as defined above will not come from service providers in categories (1) and (2) above (though there may be problems about measurement capacity as discussed in the previous sub-section at least for (2)), but will come from those in categories (3) and (4). Accordingly, governance by targets rests on the assumption that

(i) a substantial part of the service provider population comprises types (1) and (2) above, with types (3) and (4) forming a minority;

and

(ii) that the introduction of targets will not produce a significant shift in that population from types (1) and (2) to types (3) and (4)

or

(iii) that $M[\alpha_g]$ (as discussed in the previous sub-section) comprises a sufficiently large proportion of α that the absence of conditions (i) and (ii) above will not produce significant gaming effects.

These assumptions are demanding. LeGrand (2003, p. 103) argues that governance by targets can turn 'knights' into 'knaves' by rewarding those who produce the right numbers for target achievement, even if it means avoidance or evasion and neglect of β and α_n. Berliner (1988, pp. 289–90) observes that 'there have been heroic periods in the USSR when large numbers of people were selfless enough to provide the correct information required by planners to set taut but realistic targets [that is, functioned as actors of types (1) and (2) above]', but argues that such periods were exceptional. Holmstrom and Milgrom (1991) in a classic model of how agents respond to incentives based on targets such as student performance in exams that omit key dimensions of performance (that is, where β and α_n are significant elements of performance), show that neither using a limited set of good signals $(M[\alpha_g])$ nor a larger set of poor signals $(M[\alpha_i])$ will produce results free from significant distortion by gaming. O'Neill (2002, pp. 43–59) argues similarly, albeit in different language, about performance assessment of professionals. So even if a target system begins with assumption (i) above being satisfied, a 'Gresham's law' of reactive gaming may mean that it fails to satisfy assumption (ii). (Gresham's law originally described the inevitability of bad money driving out good, but applied to governance by targets, it means that actors of types (1) and (2) above learn the costs of not gaming the system and shift towards type (3).)

If central controllers do not know how the population of producer units or service providers is distributed among types (1) to (4) above, they cannot distinguish between the following four outcomes if reported performance indicates targets have been met:

1. All is well; performance is exactly what central controllers would wish in all performance domains (α_g, α_i, α_n, β).
2. The organization is performing as central controllers would wish in domains α_g and/or α_i, but this outcome has been at the expense of unacceptably poor performance in the domains where performance is not measured (α_n, β).
3. Although performance as measured appears to be fine ($M[\alpha_g]$, $M[\alpha_i]$) actions are quite at variance with the substantive goals behind those targets (that is, 'hitting the target and missing the point').
4. There has been a failure to meet measured-performance targets ($M[\alpha_g]$, $M[\alpha_i]$), but this outcome has been concealed by strategic manipulation of data (exploiting definitional ambiguity in reporting of data or outright data fabrication).

Discussion

We have argued that the implicit theory of governance by targets requires two sets of heroic assumptions to be satisfied: of robust synecdoche, and game-proof design. And we have shown that there is enough evidence from the relatively short period of its functioning to date to suggest that these assumptions are not justified. The transparency of the system in real time seems to have exacerbated what we earlier described as Gresham's law of reactive gaming.

We see the system of star rating as a process of 'learning by doing' in which government chose to ignore the problems we have identified. A consequence was that although there were indeed dramatic improvements in reported performance, we do not know the extent to which these were genuine or offset by gaming that resulted in reductions in performance that was not captured by targets. Evidence of gaming naturally led many critics of New Labour's targets-and-terror regime to advocate the wholesale abandonment of that system. But the practical alternatives to such a regime (such as specific grants to providers to incentivize particular activities, true 'command and control' from the centre in terms of orders of the day, or governance by a double-bind approach that swings between unacknowledged contradictions) are well-tried and far from problem-free. Nor is health care truly governed by anything approximating a free market in any developed state: regulation and public funding (even in the form of tax expenditures) take centre stage in every case.

We conclude by considering how the theory and practice of governance by targets could be redesigned so that it is less vulnerable to gaming. Although gaming proved to be endemic in the much longer-lived Soviet targets regime, the prospects for a more game-proof design may be better in a mixed-economy system for delivering public services. Accordingly, we make suggestions for making systems of governance by targets more proof against synecdoche and gaming difficulties, by modified ways of specifying targets, measuring performance and monitoring behaviour.

Complete specification of targets and how performance will be measured almost invites reactive gaming by managers of service-providing units. Hence an obvious remedy is to introduce more uncertainty into these specifications (Bevan and Hood 2004) by making them transparent in process and in retrospect but not in real time. Such a design would follow Heald's (2003, p. 730) distinction between 'event' transparency and 'process' transparency, with 'assurance that established procedures have been followed and that relevant documentation is then placed in the public domain' (Heald 2003, p. 71). When targets take the form of general standards (as was proposed for assessment by the Healthcare Commission (2005b) at the time of writing), advance warning of when assessments will be made will be of only limited value to potential gamers. But when targets for performance assessment are defined at a high level of specificity, there needs to be some uncertainty about the monitoring process. In the case of speed cameras, for example, drivers may know the cameras' locations from website or other sources, but do not know whether any particular camera is operating or what precise speed trips the camera into action. It is possible for a lottery to be fully transparent in a real-time process sense if the programming principles behind it can be fully revealed to the players, even if that does not enable them to know the actual numbers it will reveal. Introducing randomness into monitoring and evaluation in order to limit gaming violates only a very extended version of the transparency principle and one that is arguably not appropriate for performance monitoring.

Another way of limiting gaming would be to fill the 'audit hole' referred to earlier. Although British public services in general, and the English health care system in particular, groan under regulation and audit from various inspectors and auditors, audit of the data on which performance assessments are based is both fragmentary and episodic. As the existence of gaming becomes more generally recognized, failure to fill this hole invites the cynical view of the target regime as a 'Nelson's eye' game, in which central government colludes with those who game targets, by seeking improvements in reported performance only, and not providing the organizational clout to ask awkward questions about the robustness of those reported improvements. What is required is a new approach to performance data provision and auditing, similar to that of the 'Office of Performance Data' advocated by Robert Behn (2001).

A second means of monitoring would be by supplementing the arcane and impersonal process of reporting from one bureaucracy to another in a closed professional world by a greater face-to-face element in the overall control system. After all, in democratic theory the ideal of transparency is often seen as face-to-face communication between governors and governed, and even in the Soviet system it has been shown that public criticism of gaming by managers through the media was a salient feature of the overall system that served to limit managerial gaming. Indeed, it could be argued that face-to-face scrutiny of that kind is likely to be far less vulnerable to the gaming strategies that can undermine the target systems described here.

Of course, face-to-face interactions between health care providers and the public are far from problem-free (something graphically brought out by the Shipman case referred to earlier), and it is problems of that kind that has led to the targeting systems monitored by professionals. However, finding a way that an individual like Shipman will stand out from the vast majority (it must be hoped) of medical practitioners who are not serial killers requires, even in retrospect, elaborate statistical analysis. The final report of the Shipman Inquiry (Secretary of State for Health 2004) recommended using a method of statistical monitoring of deaths in general practices which, using historical data, would have identified Shipman in 1988 (Aylin 2003). If such monitoring, using transparent thresholds, had been applied to Shipman when he was in practice, however, then it is likely that he would have managed his murder count and other deaths so that he would have avoided generating a statistical signal. Goodhart's law means that we may be able to use statistical analysis on historical data to generate a reliable signal when the people who generated the data knew that it would not be used for that purpose. But once the individuals concerned know the data they produce will be used for that purpose, their behaviour is likely to alter. Accordingly, if a transparent monitoring system were introduced in response to Shipman, this would probably fail to detect another rational maniac of the Shipman type, but put many other innocent GPs under suspicion of murder (Secretary of State for Health 2003).

Indeed, such a conclusion suggests that even and perhaps especially for the professional monitors, some face-to-face scrutiny mixed with random visitations may serve to limit the problems of synecdoche and gaming, particularly for organizations as complex as acute hospitals, given both ambiguity in definitions and noisy data. Since the 1990s in the US, the Joint Commission on the Accreditation of Health Care Organizations has been seeking to move towards a continuous process of monitoring hospital performance through performance indicators, but the foundation of its accreditation programme continues to be three-yearly inspection (Walshe 2003, p. 63). Evidence of target gaming by the Commission for Health Improvement (2003c and 2004) came also from physical inspections of systems to assure and improve quality of care. Ayres and Braithwaite (1992) observe that it is rare for inspections of nursing homes in the US and Australia to take place without a member of staff giving the inspection team a tip-off of some value. It may be that a visit would have thrown up quality problems such as those in the Bristol heart surgery unit discussed on page 235, lines 8–16, above (where staff were distressed by what was happening), in a way that statistical surveillance on its own could not have done.

However, at the time of writing, if anything, the performance management system has been moving in the direction of widening rather than narrowing the audit hole (Healthcare Commission 2005b). Even though star ratings are due to be abolished, new systems of assessment and inspection emphasize delivery against targets; self-assessment; and surveillance, using readily available data rather than site visits (Healthcare Commission 2005b). These changes, together with the transfer of responsibility for auditing the quality of data in the English NHS from the Audit Commission to the Healthcare Commission (which lacks any physical presence in NHS provider units) suggests less rather than more scope to discover reactive gaming.

None of the measures we propose could be expected to remove gaming completely. But both Soviet history and a broader institutional analysis suggests that they could plausibly be expected to reduce it. And if, as this analysis has shown, there are significant gaming problems in public health care that cannot be prevented by measurement systems that produce a fully robust $M[\alpha_g]$, then corrective action is needed to reduce the risk of the target regime being so undermined by gaming that it degenerates, as happened in the Soviet Union.

References

Anonymous. 2001. 'Behold, a Shining Light', *Health Service Journal*, 20 December, 14–15.

Anonymous. 2005. 'A&E Survey Highlights Dirt and Waiting Times', *Health Service Journal*, 24 February, 7.

Auditor General for Wales. 2005. *NHS Waiting Times in Wales*. Cardiff: The Stationery Office (http://www.agw.wales.gov.uk/publications/2004/agw2004 _9-i.pdf).

Audit Commission. 2003. *Waiting List Accuracy.* London: The Stationery Office (http://www.audit-commission.gov.uk/health/index.asp?catId=english^HEALTH).

Aylin, P. 2003. *Monitoring of Mortality Rates in Primary Care – A Report by Dr Paul Aylin* (http://www.the-shipman-inquiry.org.uk/documentsummary.asp?from =a&id=HP&file=06&page=00001).

Ayres, I. and J. Braithwaite. 1992. *Responsive Regulation.* Cambridge: Cambridge University Press.

Beer, S. 1966. *Decision and Control.* London: Wiley.

Behn, R. 2001. *Rethinking Democratic Accountability.* Washington, DC: Brookings Institution.

Berliner, J.S. 1988. *Soviet Industry from Stalin to Gorbachev.* Aldershot: Edward Elgar.

Bevan, G. and C. Hood. 2004. 'Targets, Inspections and Transparency', *British Medical Journal,* 328, 598.

Bevan, G. and R. Robinson. 2005. 'The Interplay between Economic and Political Logics: Path Dependency in Health Care in England', *Journal of Health Politics, Policy and Law,* 30, 1–2, 53–78.

Bird, S.M., D. Cox, V.T. Farewell, *et al.* 2005. 'Performance Indicators: Good, Bad, and Ugly', *Journal of the Royal Statistical Society,* Series A, 168, 1, 1–27.

British Medical Association. 2005. *BMA Survey of A&E Waiting Times.* London: British Medical Association.

Cabinet Office. 1999. *Modernizing Government* (Cm 4310). London: The Stationery Office (http://www.archive.official-documents.co.uk/document/cm43/4310/ 4310.htm).

Carlisle, C. 2004. 'How the Government Broke its Bristol Inquiry Pledge', *Health Service Journal,* 4 November, 12–13.

Carter, N., R. Klein and P. Day. 1995. *How Organisations Measure Success. The Use of Performance Indicators in Government.* London: Routledge.

Cole, A. 2001. 'Staying Power', *Health Service Journal,* 3 May.

Commission for Health Improvement. 2001. *Report on the Investigation into Heart and Lung Transplantation at St George's Healthcare NHS Trust.* London: The Stationery Office (http://www.chi.nhs.uk/eng/organisations/london/st_georges/ index.shtml).

Commission for Health Improvement. 2002. *Report on the Clinical Governance Review on Surrey and Sussex Healthcare NHS Trust.* London: The Stationery Office (http://www.chi.nhs.uk/eng/organisations/south_east/surrey_sussex/ 2002/surrey.pdf).

Commission for Health Improvement. 2003a. *NHS Performance Ratings. Acute Trusts, Specialist Trusts, Ambulance Trusts 2002/03.* London: The Stationery Office (http://www.chi.nhs.uk/eng/ratings).

Commission for Health Improvement. 2003b. *NHS Performance Ratings. Primary Care Trusts, Mental Health Trusts, Learning Disability Trusts 2002/03.* London: The Stationery Office (http://www.chi.nhs.uk/eng/ratings).

Commission for Health Improvement. 2003c. *What CHI Has Found In: Ambulance Trusts.* London: The Stationery Office (http://www.healthcarecommission.org. uk/NationalFindings/NationalThemedReports/Ambulance/fs/en).

Commission for Health Improvement. 2004. *What CHI Has Found in: Acute Services.* London: The Stationery Office (http://www.healthcarecommission. org.uk/NationalFindings/NationalThemedReports/AcuteAndSpecialist/fs/en).

Department of Health. 2004. *Chief Executive's Report to the NHS – Statistical Supplement,* May 2004. London: Department of Health (http://www.dh.gov.uk/ assetRoot/04/08/26/27/04082627.pdf).

Department of Health. 2005. *Ambulance Services, England.* London: Department of Health (http://www.dh.gov.uk/PublicationsAndStatistics/Statistics/Statistical WorkAreas/StatisticalHealthCare/StatisticalHealthCareArticle/fs/en?CONTENT_ ID=4086490&chk=6NOZfh).

Dunsire, A. 1978. *The Execution Process: Implementation in a Bureaucracy.* Oxford: Martin Robertson.

Ericson, R.E. 1991. 'The Classic Soviet-type Economy: Nature and Implications for Reform', *The Journal of Economic Perspectives,* 5, 4, 11–27.

Farrar, S., F. Harris, T. Scott and L. McKee. 2004. *The Performance Assessment Framework: Experiences and Perceptions of NHS Scotland* (http:// www.scotland.gov.uk/library5/health/pafr.pdf).

Goddard, M., R. Mannion and P.C. Smith. 2000. 'The Performance Framework: Taking Account of Economic Behaviour', in P.C. Smith (ed.), *Reforming Markets in Health Care.* Buckingham: Open University Press, pp. 138–61.

Goodhart, C.A.E. 1984. *Monetary Theory and Practice. The UK Experience.* London: Macmillan.

Greer, S.L. 2004. *Four Way Bet: How Devolution Has Led to Four Different Models for the NHS.* London: The Constitution Unit, School of Public Policy, UCL.

Hampton, P. 2004. *Reducing Administrative Burdens: Effective Inspection and Enforcement.* London: HM Treasury.

Heald, D.A. 2003. 'Fiscal Transparency: Concepts, Measurement and UK Practice', *Public Administration,* 81, 4, 723–59.

Healthcare Commission. 2004. *2004 Performance Rating.* London: The Stationery Office (http://ratings2004.healthcarecommission.org.uk/).

Healthcare Commission. 2005a. *Patient Survey Programme 2004/2005. Emergency Department: Key Findings.* London: Healthcare Commission (http:// www.healthcarecommission.org.uk/NationalFindings/Surveys/PatientSurveys/ fs/en?CONTENT_ID=4011238&chk=0bcNSV).

Healthcare Commission. 2005b. *Assessment for Improvement. The Annual Health Check.* London: Healthcare Commission (http://www.healthcarecommission. org.uk/ContactUs/RespondToAConsultation/CurrentConsultations/fs/ en?CONTENT_ID=4016872&chk=61P6R5).

Heinrich, C.J. 2002. 'Outcomes-based Performance Management in the Public Sector: Implications for Government Accountability and Effectiveness', *Public Administration Review,* 62, 6, 712–25.

Holmstrom, B. and P. Milgrom. 1991. 'Multi-task Principal-agent Analyses: Linear Contracts, Asset Ownership and Job Design', *Journal of Law, Economics and Organisation*, 7, 24–52.

Hood, C. 2002. 'Control, Bargains and Cheating: The Politics of Public-Service Reform', *Journal of Public Administration Research and Theory*, 12, 3, 309–32.

Hoque, K., S. Davis and M. Humphreys. 2004. 'Freedom to Do What You Are Told: Senior Management Team Autonomy in an NHS Acute Trust', *Public Administration*, 82, 2, 355–75.

Howarth, A. 2004. 'Two-hour ambulance delay blamed for teenage boy's death', *The Scotsman*, Monday 18 October.

James, O. 2004. 'The UK Core Executive's Use of Public Service Agreements as a Tool of Governance', *Public Administration*, 82, 2, 397–419.

Kinnel, H.G. 2000. 'Serial Homicide by Doctors: Shipman in Perspective', *British Medical Journal*, 321, 1594–6.

Klein, R.E. 1983. *The Politics of the National Health Service*. London: Longman.

Kornai, J. 1994. *Overcentralisation in Economic Administration*. Oxford: Oxford University Press.

LeGrand, J. 2003 *Motivation, Agency and Public Policy*. Oxford: Oxford University Press.

Litwack, J.M. 1993. 'Coordination, Incentives and the Ratchet Effect', *The Bell Journal of Economics*, 24, 2, 271–85.

Locker, T.E. and S.M. Mason. 2005. 'Analysis of the Distribution of Time that Patients Spend in Emergency Departments', *British Medical Journal*, 10, 1136.

Majone, G. 1996. *Regulating Europe*. London: Routledge.

Marshall, M., P. Shekelle, R. Brook and S. Leatherman. 2000. *Dying to Know: Public Release of Information about Quality of Care*. London: The Nuffield Trust.

Mayor, S. 2003. 'Hospitals Take Short Term Measures to Meet Targets', *British Medical Journal*, 326, 1054.

Miller, G.J. 1992. *Managerial Dilemmas*. Cambridge: Cambridge University Press.

Moran, M. 1999. *Governing the Health Care State*. Manchester: Manchester University Press.

National Audit Office. 2001. *Inappropriate Adjustments to NHS Waiting Lists*. London: The Stationery Office (HC 452) (http://www.nao.gov.uk/publications/nao_reports/01–02/0102452.pdf).

National Audit Office. 2004. *Improving Emergency Care in England*. London: The Stationery Office (HC 1075) (http://www.nao.org.uk/publications/nao_reports/03–04/03041075.pdf).

Nove, A. 1958. 'The Problem of Success Indicators in Soviet Industry', *Economica* (new series), 25, 97, 1–13.

Nove, A. 1961. *The Soviet Economy*. London: George Allen and Unwin.

Office of National Statistics. 2004. *Regional Trends*, No. 38, Table 7.15 'NHS Hospital Waiting Lists: by Patients' Region of Residence, at 31 March 2003'. London: Office of National Statistics (see also Table 7.15 *Regional Trends*, Nos 35, 36 and 37).

O'Neill, O. 2002. *A Question of Trust*. Cambridge: Cambridge University Press.

Pollitt, C. 1986. 'Beyond the Managerial Model: the Case for Broadening Performance Assessment in Government and the Public Services', *Financial Accountability and Management*, 2, 3, 155–86.

Power, M. 1999. *The Audit Society: Rituals of Verification*. Oxford: Oxford University Press.

Propper, C. and D. Wilson. 2003. 'The Use and Usefulness of Performance Measures in the Public Sector', *Oxford Review of Economic Policy*, 19, 250–67.

Public Administration Select Committee. 2003. *Fifth Report. On Target? Government by Measurement (HC 62-I)*. London: The Stationery Office.

Rowan, K., D. Harrison, A. Brady and N. Black. 2004. 'Hospitals' Star Ratings and Clinical Outcomes: Ecological Study', *British Medical Journal*, 328, 924–5.

Rutstein, D.D., W. Berenberg, T.C. Chalmers, *et al.* 1976. 'Measuring the Quality of Medical Care', *New England Journal of Medicine*, 294, 582–8.

Scottish Executive Health Department. 2003. *Performance Assessment Framework 2003/04* (http://www.show.scot.nhs.uk/sehd/mels/hdl2003_53.pdf).

Secretaries of State for Health, Wales, Northern Ireland and Scotland. 1989. *Working for Patients*. CM 555. London: HMSO.

Secretary of State for Health. 2001a. *NHS Performance Ratings Acute Trusts 2000/01*. London: Department of Health (http://www.dh.gov.uk/Publications AndStatistics/Publications/PublicationsPolicyAndGuidance/PublicationsPolicy AndGuidanceArticle/fs/en?CONTENT_n.=4003181&chk=wU4Zop).

Secretary of State for Health. 2001b. *Learning from Bristol – Report of the Public Inquiry into Children's Heart Surgery at the Bristol Royal Infirmary* (the Kennedy Report) (CM 5207(1)). London: The Stationery Office (http://www.bristol-inquiry.org.uk/final_report/).

Secretary of State for Health. 2002a. *NHS Performance Ratings Acute Trusts, Specialist Trusts, Ambulance Trusts, Mental Health Trusts 2001/02*. London: Department of Health (http://www.dh.gov.uk/PublicationsAndStatistics/ Publications/PublicationsPolicyAndGuidance/PublicationsPolicyAndGuidance Article/fs/en?CONTENT_ID=4002706&chk=dBD1wB).

Secretary of State for Health. 2002b. *The Shipman Inquiry, First Report: Death Disguised* (Chair Dame Janet Smith). London: The Stationery Office (http:// www.the-shipman-inquiry.org.uk).

Secretary of State for Health. 2003. *The Shipman Inquiry. Transcript Archive.* Transcript for Day 182 (Tue 14 Oct 2003) (Chair Dame Janet Smith) (http://www.the-shipman-inquiry.org.uk).

Secretary of State for Health. 2004. *The Shipman Inquiry, Fifth Report. Safeguarding Patients: Lessons from the Past – Proposals for the Future*. London: The Stationery Office (Chair Dame Janet Smith) (http://www.the-shipman-inquiry.org.uk).

Shifrin, T. 2001. 'Milburn Puts Managers "on Probation"', *Health Service Journal*, 27 September.

Smith, P. 1995. 'On the Unintended Consequences of Publishing Performance Data in the Public Sector', *International Journal of Public Administration*, 18, 277–310.

Timmins, N. 2005. 'Blair Bemused over GP Waiting Times', *Financial Times*, April 30/May 1, 2.

Tuohy, C.H. 1999. *Accidental Logics. The Dynamics of Change in the Health Care Arena in the United States, Britain and Canada.* New York: Oxford University Press.

Walshe, K. 2003. *Regulating Health Care.* Maidenhead: Open University Press.

PART 6

Quality and safety

Introduction by Kieran Walshe

In 1999, a report titled *To Err is Human* was published by the Institute of Medicine, part of the prestigious National Institutes of Health in the USA (Institute of Medicine, 2000). Publications like these are typically well reported in the professional press (the New England Journal of Medicine, the British Medical Journal, etc.) and, if they are lucky, also get a mention in the broadsheet newspapers like *The New York Times*, *The Washington Post*, *The Times* or *The Guardian*. This was different – the report led the TV news on all channels, and was covered in depth for days across the media, with features in most major newspapers. The reason was straightforward. For the first time, the Institute of Medicine had highlighted the frequency and human cost of medical errors – patients suffering illness or harm because of a failure of the health care system, rather than because of their underlying condition or disease. They estimated that 1 in 20 inpatients suffered an adverse event, and that preventable adverse events were the eighth leading cause of death in the USA, causing more deaths than car accidents, AIDS or breast cancer. Each year between 44,000 and 98,000 US citizens were killed by medical errors. The financial cost was between US$17 billion and US$29 billion a year, half of which was tied up in additional health care costs associated with fixing the health problems resulting from medical errors.

Around the same time, the quality of health care was also making headlines in the UK, because of a scandalous failure in care at a paediatric heart surgery unit in Bristol, which led to the deaths of around 35 babies, and which dragged on for over five years during which the hospital authorities, Royal College of Surgeons, Department of Health and others all knew about the problem but failed to act to resolve it. Three senior and respected doctors were disciplined by the General Medical Council, and two were struck off the medical register. A subsequent public inquiry led by Sir Ian Kennedy was highly critical of the hospital, the Department of Health and the NHS, and its recommendations led to a sea change in clinical attitudes and to substantial legislative reforms (Kennedy, 2001; Smith, 1998).

While some individual health professionals have been interested in the quality of health care for at least 150 years, it has taken a long time in the UK for the health professions collectively to take the problems of poor quality seriously. At times, the professions and health care providers have seemed complacent and self-serving, more inclined to protect their fellow clinicians and their public standing than to reveal or tackle problems of quality and performance. But wider society has begun to realize just how dangerous hospitals and other health care providers can be, and how much can be done to improve the quality and safety of health care by applying approaches and techniques for improvement developed in other industries and sectors. Over the last two decades, the quality and safety agenda has ceased to be the preserve of a small number of pioneers and lone voices in the clinical community, and has increasingly become part of the mainstream of health care provision. Most European countries now have established infrastructures for assuring the quality of health care, with legal requirements for health care organizations to participate in quality assurance, national centres of expertise, and quality management or improvement departments and staff in many or most health care organizations. Increasingly, information about performance is published, and patients have rising expectations of their health care experience and the outcomes of treatment.

At the same time, thinking about the concept of quality, the methods for quality measurement, and the approach to quality improvement has been changing. Once, quality was largely professionally defined, in technical or functional terms, which took little account of the patient's experience or views. Improvement was seen as a matter for the individual clinician or clinical team, to be achieved through education and increased technical or medical expertise. This individualistic and informal approach, typified by the arrangements for 'mortality and morbidity' meetings and medical audit groups, increasingly came to be seen as inadequate both in process and results. Approaches to quality measurement and improvement that had been developed in industry were introduced, which brought both greater rigour to the business of measurement and saw the process of clinical care as just that – an organizational process, to be mapped, planned and evaluated, before changes were introduced to deal with delays, bottlenecks, unnecessary work or waste, rework, and so on.

This part starts with a contribution from Avedis Donabedian (1988), a US public health physician who pioneered research in the field of health care quality, and whose classic textbook on the subject is still in print and relevant to today's health care organizations (Donabedian, 1980). His paper sets out the conceptual territory of quality assessment, and unpacks the portmanteau term 'quality' into some of its separate components – like the technical and the interpersonal dimensions of care. He sets out a typology of structure, process and outcome measurement that is still widely used, and his account of the challenges of measurement using routine sources of data like the medical record is still highly relevant.

Then follow two contributions from Donald Berwick, a paediatrian and founder of the Institute for Healthcare Improvement, who has done more than almost anyone else to bring quality improvement into the mainstream of US health care and to bring industrial methodologies for improvement into widespread use in health care organizations. His 1989 paper from *The New England Journal of Medicine* was, at the time, a huge challenge to the way that the US health care system had been measuring and managing quality for decades, and a call for a complete change of philosophy, towards a system based on the ideas of continuous improvement, which the paper illustrates simply and profoundly. His second paper, from the *British Medical Journal* in 1996, is a concise, elegant and highly readable summary of the principles of continuous improvement. His great skill as a communicator is put to work in showing the congruence between traditional biomedical research and the clinical–scientific paradigm and the methods of industrial quality improvement, particularly the 'Plan Do Study Act' cycle, and the focus on measuring and reducing variation.

This introduction began by mentioning the seminal role of the Institute of Medicine report *To Err is Human* in highlighting the huge human costs of medical errors. The report drew heavily on the work of Lucian Leape, who was one of the leaders of the Harvard Medical Practice Study on which those estimates of harm were based, and which was the first comprehensive epidemiological study of adverse events in acute care. Leape's paper from *The Journal of the American Medical Association* in 1994 predates the IoM report by six years, and its clear and insightful analysis of the causes of medical errors and strategies for their prevention remains one of the best such accounts. He uses examples from the aviation industry to illustrate the challenges for the health care sector, and sets out five practical steps for error prevention.

Finally, the focus shifts to the evaluation of quality improvement programmes – an important concern because of their widespread adoption in health care organizations and systems in many countries. Has the growth of interest and investment in quality and safety brought about worthwhile improvements in patient care? The literature suggests that the implementation of quality improvement systems and programmes is complex and the effectiveness of those programmes is highly variable, which suggests that they need to be used carefully and intelligently. Indeed, the wider quality improvement literature suggests that programme 'failure' is a common and significant problem. In the last paper in this part, John Øvretveit and Dave Gustafson tackle these questions in a paper from *Quality and Safety in Health Care* in 2002, and outline a range of research designs that can be used to test and learn from quality programmes. They set out proposals for future research, and propose an eight-step process for studying a quality improvement programme aimed at producing useful and transferable knowledge about implementation.

Summary

- Poor quality health care costs billions of dollars, and is a leading cause of death. Hospitals are very unsafe places, with complex and vulnerable delivery systems in which mistakes or errors are easily made.
- In the last two decades, growing realization of the costs and effects of poor-quality health care have led governments in many countries to

legislate to require health care organizations to have quality assurance systems in place, and to make it easier for patients and the public to access information on the quality of care.
- Traditionally, systems for assuring or improving quality in health care relied heavily on voluntary participation, professional peer review and educational programmes. But increasingly, modern approaches to quality improvement used widely in other industries have been adopted in health care.
- Quality improvement and assurance programmes can deliver major improvements in the quality of care, but not all of them do, so there is a real need to evaluate their implementation and use the results to improve their design.

References and further reading

Berwick, D.M., Godfrey, A.B. and Roessner, J. (1990) *Curing Healthcare: New Strategies for Quality Improvement.* San Francisco: Jossey-Bass.

Blumenthal, D. and Kilo C M. (1998) A Report card on continuous quality improvement, *Milbank Quarterly,* 76: 625–48.

Donabedian, A. (1980) *Explorations in Quality Assessment and Monitoring* (vols 1–3). Ann Arbor, MI: Health Administration Press.

Halligan, A. and Donaldson, L. (2001) Implementing clinical governance: turning vision into reality. *British Medical Journal,* 322: 1413–17.

Institute of Medicine (2000) *To Err is Human: Building a Safer Health System.* Washington, DC: National Academy Press.

Institute of Medicine (2001) *Crossing the Quality Chasm: A New Health System for the 21st Century.* Washington, DC: National Academy Press.

Kennedy, I. (2001) *Learning from Bristol: The Report of the Public Inquiry into Children's Heart Surgery at the Bristol Royal Infirmary* (1984–1995). London: HMSO.

Scally, G. and Donaldson, L. Clinical governance and the drive for quality improvement in the new NHS in England, *British Medical Journal,* 317: 61–65.

Shojania, K.G. and Grimshaw, J. (2005) Evidence based quality improvement: the state of the science, *Health Affairs,* 24: 138–50.

Shortell, S.M., O'Brien, J.L., Carman, J.M. et al. (1995) Assessing the impact of continuous quality improvement/total quality management: concept versus implementation, *Health Services, Research* 30: 377–401.

Smith, R. (1998) All changed, changed utterly: British medicine will be transformed by the Bristol case, *British Medical Journal,* 316: 1917–18.

Walshe, K. (2007) Understanding what works – and why – in quality improvement: the need for theory-driven evaluation, *International Journal of Quality in Health Care,* 19: 57–59.

The selections

Donabedian, A. (1988) The quality of care: how can it be assessed? *Journal of the American Medical Association*, 260(12): 1743–48.

Berwick, D.M. (1989) Continuous improvement as an ideal in healthcare, *New England Journal of Medicine*, 320(21): 1424–25.

Berwick, D.M. (1996) A primer on leading the improvement of systems, *British Medical Journal*, 312: 619–23.

Leape, L. (1994) Error in medicine, *The Journal of the American Medical Association*, 272: 1851–57.

Øvretveit, J. and Gustafson, D. (2002) Evaluation of quality improvement programmes, *Quality and Safety in Health Care*, 11: 270–75.

25

The quality of care: how can it be assessed?
Avedis Donabedian

Extracts from Donabedian A (1988) The quality of care: how can it be assessed? Journal of the American Medical Association 260(12): 1743–48.

There was a time, not too long age, when this question could not have been asked. The quality of care was considered to be something of a mystery: real, capable of being perceived and appreciated, but not subject to measurement.

The very attempt to define and measure quality seemed, then, to denature and belittle it. Now, we may have moved too far in the opposite direction. Those who have not experienced the intricacies of clinical practice demand measures that are easy, precise, and complete—as if a sack of potatoes was being weighed.

True, some elements in the quality of care are easy to define and measure, but there are also profundities that still elude us. We must not allow anyone to belittle or ignore them; they are the secret and glory of our art. Therefore, we should avoid claiming for our capacity to assess quality either too little or too much. I shall try to steer this middle course.

Specifying what quality is

Level and scope of concern

Before we attempt to assess the quality of care, either in general terms or in any particular site or situation, it is necessary to come to an agreement on what the elements that constitute it are. To proceed to measurement without a firm foundation of prior agreement on what quality consists in is to court disaster.[1]

As we seek to define quality, we soon become aware of the fact that several formulations are both possible and legitimate, depending on where we are located in the system of care and on what the nature and extent of our responsibilities are. These several formulations can be envisaged as a progression, for example, as steps in a ladder or as successive circles surrounding the bull's-eye of a target. Our power, our responsibility, and our vulnerability all flow from the fact that we are the foundation for that ladder, the focal point for that family of concentric circles. We must begin, therefore, with the performance of physicians and other health care practitioners.

As shown in Figure 25.1, there are two elements in the performance of practitioners: one technical and the other interpersonal. Technical performance depends on the knowledge and judgment used in arriving at the appropriate strategies of care and on skill in implementing those strategies. The goodness of technical performance is judged in comparison with the best in practice. The best in practice, in its turn, has earned that distinction because, on the average, it is known or believed to produce the greatest improvement in health. This means that the goodness of technical care is proportional to its expected ability to achieve those improvements in health status that the current science and technology of health care have made possible. If the realized fraction of what is achievable is called *effectiveness*, the quality of technical care becomes proportionate to its effectiveness.

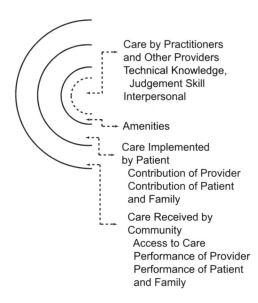

Figure 25.1 Levels at which quality may be assessed

Here, two points deserve emphasis. First, judgments on technical quality are contingent on the best in current knowledge and technology; they cannot go beyond that limit. Second, the judgment is based on future expectations, not on events already transpired. Even if the actual consequences of care in any given instance prove to be disastrous, quality must be judged as good if care, at the time it was given, conformed to the practice that could have been expected to achieve the best results.

The management of the interpersonal relationship is the second component in the practitioner's performance. It is a vitally important element. Through the interpersonal exchange, the patient communicates information necessary for arriving at a diagnosis, as well as preferences necessary for selecting the most appropriate methods of care. Through this exchange, the physician provides information about the nature of the illness and its management and motivates the patient to active collaboration in care. Clearly, the interpersonal process is the vehicle by which technical care is implemented and on which its success depends. Therefore, the management of the interpersonal process is to a large degree tailored to the achievement of success in technical care.

But the conduct of the interpersonal process must also meet individual and social expectations and standards, whether these aid or hamper technical performance. Privacy, confidentiality, informed choice, concern, empathy, honesty, tact, sensitivity—all these and more are virtues that the interpersonal relationship is expected to have.

If the management of the interpersonal process is so important, why is it so often ignored in assessments of the quality of care? There are many reasons. Information about the interpersonal process is not easily available. For example, in the medical record, special effort is needed to obtain it. Second, the criteria and standards that permit precise measurement of the attributes of the interpersonal process are not well developed or have not been sufficiently called upon to undertake the task. Partly, it may be because the management of the interpersonal process must adapt to so many variations in the preferences and expectations of individual patients that general guidelines do not serve us sufficiently well.

Much of what we call the *art of medicine* consists in almost intuitive adaptions to individual requirements in technical care as well as in the management of the interpersonal process. Another element in the art of medicine is the way, still poorly understood, in which practitioners process information to arrive at a correct diagnosis and an appropriate strategy of care.[2] As our understanding of each of these areas of performance improves, we can expect the realm of our art to shrink. Yet I hope that some of the mystery in practice will always remain, since it affirms and celebrates the uniqueness of each individual.

The science and art of health care, as they apply to both technical care and the management of the interpersonal process, are at the heart of the metaphorical family of concentric circles depicted in Figure 25.1. Immediately surrounding the center we can place the amenities of care, these being the desirable attributes of the settings within which care is provided. They include convenience, comfort, quiet, privacy, and so on. In private practice, these are the responsibility of the practitioner to provide. In institutional practice, the responsibility for providing them devolves on the owners and managers of the institution.

By moving to the next circle away from the center of our metaphorical target, we include in assessments of quality the contributions to care of the patients themselves as well as of members of their families. By doing so we cross an important boundary. So far, our concern was primarily with the performance of the providers of care. Now, we are concerned with judging the care as it actually was. The responsibility, now, is shared by provider and consumer. As already described, the management of the interpersonal process by the practitioner influences the implementation of care by and for the patient. Yet, the patient and family must, themselves, also carry some of the responsibility for the success or failure of care. Accordingly, the practitioner may be judged blameless in some situations in which the care, as implemented by the patient, is found to be inferior.

We have one more circle to visit, another watershed to cross. Now, we are concerned with care received by the community as a whole. We must now judge the social distribution of levels of quality in the community.[3] This depends, in turn, on who has greater or lesser access to care and who, after gaining access, receives greater or lesser qualities of care. Obviously, the performance of individual practitioners and health care institutions has much to do with this. But, the quality of care in a community is also influenced by many factors over which the providers have no control, although these are factors they should try to understand and be concerned about.

I have tried, so far, to show that the definition of quality acquires added elements as we move outward from the performance of the practitioners, to the care received by patients, and to the care received by communities. The definition of quality also becomes narrower or more expansive, depending on how narrowly or broadly we define the concept of health and our responsibility for it. It makes a difference in the assessment of our performance whether we see ourselves as responsible for bringing about improvements only in specific aspects of physical or physiological function or whether we include psychological and social function as well.

Before we set out to assess quality, we should have decided (1) how health and our responsibility for it is to be defined, (2) whether the assessment is to be of the performance of practitioners only or also include that of patients and the health care system, and (3) whether the amenities and the management of the interpersonal process are to be included in addition to technical care. In a more practical vein, we need to answer certain questions: Who is being assessed? What are the activities being assessed? How are these activities supposed to be conducted? What are they meant to accomplish? When we agree on the answers to these questions we are ready to look for the measures that will give us the necessary information about quality.

Approaches to assessment

The information from which inferences can be drawn about the quality of care can be classified under three categories: "structure," "process," and "outcome."[1,4]

Structure.—Structure denotes the attributes of the settings in which care occurs. This includes the attributes of material resources (such as facilities, equipment, and money), of human resources (such as the number and qualifications of personnel), and of organizational structure (such as medical staff organization, methods of peer review, and methods of reimbursement).

Process.—Process denotes what is actually done in giving and receiving care. It includes the patient's activities in seeking care and carrying it out as well as the practitioner's activities in making a diagnosis and recommending or implementing treatment.

Outcome.—Outcome denotes the effects of care on the health status of patients and populations. Improvements in the patient's knowledge and salutary changes in the patient's behavior are included under a broad definition of health status, and so is the degree of the patient's satisfaction with care.

This three-part approach to quality assessment is possible only because good structure increases the likelihood of good process, and good process increases the likelihood of a good outcome. It is necessary, therefore, to have established such a relationship before any particular component of structure, process, or outcome can be used to assess quality. The activity of quality assessment is not itself designed to establish the presence of these relationships. There must be preexisting knowledge of the linkage between structure and process, and between process and outcome, before quality assessment can be undertaken.

Knowledge about the relationship between structure and process (or between structure and outcome) proceeds from the organizational sciences. These sciences are still relatively young, so our knowledge of the effects of structure is rather scanty.[5,6] Furthermore, what we do know suggests that the relationship between structural characteristics and the process of care is rather weak. From these characteristics, we can only infer that conditions are either inimical or conducive to good care. We cannot assert that care, in fact, has been good or bad. Structural characteristics should be a major preoccupation in system design; they are a rather blunt instrument in quality assessment.

As I have already mentioned, knowledge about the relationship between attributes of the interpersonal process and the outcome of care should derive from the behavioral sciences. But so far, these sciences have contributed relatively little to quality assessment. I cannot say whether this is because of a deficiency in these sciences or a narrowness in those who assess quality.

Knowledge about the relationship between technical care and outcome derives, of course, from the health care sciences. Some of that knowledge, as we know, is pretty detailed and firm, deriving from well-conducted trials or extensive, controlled observations. Some of it is of dubious validity and open to question. Our assessments of the quality of the technical process of care vary accordingly in their certainty and persuasiveness. If we are confident that a certain strategy of care produces the best outcomes in a given category of patients, we can be equally confident that its practice represents the highest quality of care, barring concern for cost. If we are uncertain of the relationship, then our assessment of quality is correspondingly uncertain. It cannot be emphasized too strongly that our ability to assess the quality of technical care is bounded by the strengths and weaknesses of our clinical science.

There are those who believe that direct assessment of the outcome of care can free us from the limitations imposed by the imperfections of the clinical sciences. I do not believe so. Because a multitude of factors influence outcome, it is not possible to know for certain, even after extensive adjustments for differences in case mix are made, the extent to which an observed outcome is attributable to an antecedent process of care. Confirmation is needed by a direct assessment of the process itself, which brings us to the position we started from.

The assessment of outcomes, under rigorously controlled circumstances, is, of course, the method by which the goodness of alternative strategies of care is established. But, quality assessment is neither clinical research nor technology assessment. It is almost never carried out under the rigorous controls that research requires. It is, primarily, an administrative device used to monitor performance to determine whether it continues to remain within acceptable bounds. Quality assessment can, however, make a contribution to research if, in the course of assessment, associations are noted between process and outcome that seem inexplicable by current knowledge. Such discrepancies would call for elucidation through research.

If I am correct in my analysis, we cannot claim either for the measurement of process or the measurement of outcomes an inherently superior validity compared with the other, since the validity of either flows to an equal degree from the validity of the science that postulates a linkage between the two. But, process and outcome do have, on the whole, some different properties that make them more or less suitable objects of measurement for given purposes. Information about technical care is readily available in the medical record, and it is available in a timely manner, so that prompt action to correct deficiencies can be taken. By contrast, many outcomes, by their nature, are delayed, and if they occur after care is completed, information about them is not easy to obtain. Outcomes do have, however, the advantage of reflecting all contributions to care, including those of the patient. But this advantage is also a handicap, since it is not possible to say precisely what went wrong unless the antecedent process is scrutinized.

This brief exposition of strengths and weaknesses should lead to the conclusion that in selecting an approach to assessment one needs to be guided by the precise characteristics of the elements chosen. Beyond causal validity, which is the essential requirement, one is guided by attributes such as relevance to the objectives of care, sensitivity, specificity, timeliness, and costliness.[1(pp100–118)] As a general rule, it is best to include in any system of assessment, elements of structure, process, and outcome. This allows supplementation of weakness in one approach by strength in another; it helps one interpret the findings; and if the findings do not seem to make sense, it leads to a reassessment of study design and a questioning of the accuracy of the data themselves.

Before we leave the subject of approaches to assessment, it may be useful to say a few words about patient satisfaction as a measure of the quality of care. Patient satisfaction may be considered to be one of the desired outcomes of care, even an element in health status itself. An expression of satisfaction or dissatisfaction is also the patient's judgment on the quality of care in all its aspects, but particularly as concerns the interpersonal process. By questioning patients, one can obtain information about overall satisfaction and also about satisfaction with specific attributes of the interpersonal relationship, specific components of technical care, and the outcomes of care. In doing so, it should be remembered that, unless special precautions are taken, patients may be reluctant to reveal their opinions for fear of alienating their medical attendants. Therefore, to add to the evidence at hand, information can also be sought about behaviors that indirectly suggest dissatisfaction. These include, in addition to complaints registered, premature termination of care, other forms of noncompliance, termination of membership in a health plan, and seeking care outside the plan.

It is futile to argue about the validity of patient satisfaction as a measure of quality. Whatever its strengths and limitations as an indicator of quality, information about patient satisfaction should be as indispensable to assessments of quality as to the design and management of health care systems.

Sampling

If one wishes to obtain a true view of care as it is actually provided, it is necessary to draw a proportionally representative sample of cases, using either simple or stratified random sampling. Because cases are primarily classified by diagnosis, this is the most frequently used attribute for stratification. But, one could use other attributes as well: site of care, specialty, demographic and socioeconomic characteristics of patients, and so on.

There is some argument as to whether patients are to be classified by discharge diagnosis, admission diagnosis, or presenting complaint. Classification by presenting complaint (for example, headache or abdominal pain) offers an opportunity to assess both success and failure in diagnosis. If discharge diagnoses are used, one can tell if the diagnosis is justified by the evidence; the failure to diagnose is revealed only if one has an opportunity to find cases misclassified under other diagnostic headings.

A step below strictly proportionate sampling, one finds methods designed to provide an illustrative rather than a representative view of quality. For example, patients may be first classified according to some scheme that represents important subdivisions of the realm of health care in general, or important components in the activities and responsibilities of a clinical department or program in particular. Then, one purposively selects, within each class, one or more categories of patients, identified by diagnosis or otherwise, whose management can be assumed to typify clinical performance for that class.

This is the "tracer method" proposed by Kessner and coworkers.[7,8] The validity of the assumption that the cases selected for assessment represent all cases in their class has not been established.

Most often, those who assess quality are not interested in obtaining a representative, or even an illustrative picture of care as a whole. Their purposes are more managerial, namely, to identify and correct the most serious failures in care and, by doing so, to create an environment of watchful concern that motivates everyone to perform better. Consequently, diagnostic categories are selected according to importance, perhaps using Williamson's[9] principle of "maximum achievable benefit," meaning that the diagnosis is frequent, deficiencies in care are common and serious, and the deficiencies are correctable.

Still another approach to sampling for managerial or reformist purposes is to begin with cases that have suffered an adverse outcome and study the process of care that has led to it. If the outcome is infrequent and disastrous (a maternal or perinatal death, for example), every case might be reviewed. Otherwise, a sample of adverse outcomes, with or without prior stratification, could be studied.[10-12] There is some evidence that, under certain circumstances, this approach will identify a very high proportion of serious deficiencies in the process of care, but not of deficiencies that are less serious.[13]

Measurement

The progression of steps in quality assessment that I have described so far brings us, at last, to the critical issue of measurement. To measure quality, our concepts of what quality consists in must be translated to more concrete representations that are capable of some degree of quantification—at least on an ordinal scale, but one hopes better. These representations are the criteria and standards of structure, process, and outcome.[14,15]

Ideally, the criteria and standards should derive, as I have already implied, from a sound, scientifically validated fund of knowledge. Failing that, they should represent the best informed, most authoritative opinion available on any particular subject. Criteria and standards can also be inferred from the practice of eminent practitioners in a community. Accordingly, the criteria and standards vary in validity, authoritativeness, and rigor.

The criteria and standards of assessment can also be either implicit or explicit. Implicit, unspoken criteria are used when an expert practitioner is given information about a case and asked to use personal knowledge and experience to judge the goodness of the process of care or of its outcome. By contrast, explicit criteria and standards for each category of cases are developed and specified in advance, often in considerable detail, usually by a panel of experts, before the assessment of individual cases begins. These are the two extremes in specification; there are intermediate variants and combinations as well.

The advantage in using implicit criteria is that they allow assessment of representative samples of cases and are adaptable to the precise characteristics of each case, making possible the highly individualized assessments that the conceptual formulation of quality envisaged. The method is, however, extremely costly and rather imprecise, the imprecision arising from inattentiveness or limitations in knowledge on the part of the reviewer and the lack of precise guidelines for quantification.

By comparison, explicit criteria are costly to develop, but they can be used subsequently to produce precise assessments at low cost, although only cases for which explicit criteria are available can be used in assessment. Moreover, explicit criteria are usually developed for categories of cases and, therefore, cannot be adapted readily to the variability among cases within a category. Still another problem is the difficulty in developing a scoring system that represents the degree to which the deficiencies in care revealed by the criteria influence the outcome of care.

Taking into account the strengths and limitations of implicit and explicit criteria, it may be best to use both in sequence or in combination. One frequently used procedure is to begin with rather abridged explicit criteria to separate cases into those likely to have received good care and those not. All the latter, as well as a sample of the former, are then assessed in greater detail using implicit criteria, perhaps supplemented by more detailed explicit criteria.

At the same time, explicit criteria themselves are being improved. As their use expands, more diagnostic categories have been included. Algorithmic criteria have been developed that are much more adaptable to the clinical characteristics of individual patients than are the more usual criteria lists.[16,17] Methods for weighting the criteria have also been proposed, although we still do not have a method of weighting that is demonstrably related to degree of impact on health status.[18]

When outcomes are used to assess the quality of antecedent care, there is the corresponding problem of specifying the several states of dysfunction and of weighting them in importance relative to each other using some system of preferences. It is possible, of course, to identify specific outcomes, for example, reductions in fatality or blood pressure, and to measure the likelihood of attaining them. It is also possible to construct hierarchical scales of physical function so that any position on the scale tells us what functions can be performed and what functions are lost.[19] The greatest difficulty arises when one attempts to represent as a single quantity various aspects of functional capacity over a life span. Though several methods of valuation and aggregation are available, there is still much controversy about the validity of the values and, in fact, about, their ethical implications.[20,21] Nevertheless, such measures, sometimes called *measures of quality-adjusted life,* are being used to assess technological innovations in health care and, as a consequence, play a role in defining what good technical care is.[22,23]

Information

All the activities of assessment that I have described depend, of course, on the availability of suitable, accurate information.

The key source of information about the process of care and its immediate outcome is, no doubt, the medical record. But we know that the medical record is often incomplete in what it documents, frequently omitting significant elements of technical care and including next to nothing about the interpersonal process. Furthermore, some of the information recorded is inaccurate because of errors in diagnostic testing, in clinical observation, in clinical assessment, in recording, and in coding. Another handicap is that any given set of records usually covers only a limited segment of care, that in the hospital, for example, providing no information about what comes before or after. Appropriate and accurate recording, supplemented by an ability to collate records from various sites, is a fundamental necessity to accurate, complete quality assessment.

The current weakness of the record can be rectified to some extent by independent verification of the accuracy of some of the data it contains, for example, by reexamination of pathological specimens, x-ray films, and electrocardiographic tracings and by recoding diagnostic categorization. The information in the record can also be supplemented by interviews with, or questionnaires to, practitioners and patients, information from patients being indispensable if compliance, satisfaction, and some long-term outcomes are to be assessed. Sometimes, if more precise information on outcomes is needed, patients may have to be called back for reexamination. And for some purposes, especially when medical records are very deficient, videotaping or direct observation by a colleague have been used, even though being observed might itself elicit an improvement in practice.[24,25]

Conclusions

In the preceding account, I have detailed, although rather sketchily, the steps to be taken in endeavoring to assess the quality of medical care. I hope it is clear that there is a way, a path worn rather smooth by many who have gone before us. I trust it is equally clear that we have, as yet, much more to learn. We need to know a great deal more about the course of illness with and without alternative methods of care. To compare the consequences of these methods, we need to have more precise measures of the quantity and quality of life. We need to understand more profoundly the nature of the interpersonal exchange between patient and practitioner, to learn how to identify and quantify its attributes, and to determine in what ways these contribute to the patient's health and welfare. Our information about the process and outcome of care needs to be more complete and more accurate. Our criteria and standards need to be more flexibly adaptable to the finer clinical peculiarities of each case. In particular, we need to learn how to accurately elicit the preferences of patients to arrive at truly individualized assessments of quality. All this has to go on against the background of the most profound analysis of the responsibilities of the health care professions to the individual and to society.

Notes

1   Donabedian A: *The Definition of Quality and Approaches to Its Management*, vol 1: *Explorations in Quality Assessment and Monitoring*. Ann Arbor, Mich, Health Administration Press, 1980.
2   Eraker S, Politser P: How decisions are reached: Physician and patient. *Ann Intern Med* 1982;97:262–268.
3   Donabedian A: Models for organizing the delivery of health services and criteria for evaluating them. *Milbank Q* 1972;50:103–154.
4   Donabedian A: Evaluating the quality of medical care. *Milbank Q* 1966;44:166–203.
5   Palmer RH, Reilly MC: Individual and institutional variables which may serve as indicators of quality of medical care. *Med Care* 1979;17:693–717.
6   Donabedian A: The epidemiology of quality. *Inquiry* 1985;22:282–292.
7   Kessner DM, Kalk CE, James S: Assessing health quality—the case for tracers. *N Engl J Med* 1973;288:189–194.
8   Rhee KJ, Donabedian A, Burney RE: Assessing the quality of care in a hospital emergency unit: A framework and its application. *Quality Rev Bull* 1987;13:4–16.

9 Williamson JW: Formulating priorities for quality assurance activity: Description of a method and its application. *JAMA* 1978;239:631–637.

10 New York Academy of Medicine, Committee on Public Health Relations: *Maternal Mortality in New York City; A Study of All Puerperal Deaths 1930–1932.* New York, Oxford University Press Inc, 1933.

11 Kohl SG: *Perinatal Mortality in New York City: Responsible Factors.* Cambridge, Mass, Harvard University Press, 1955.

12 Rutstein DB, Berenberg W, Chalmers TC, et al: Measuring quality of medical care: A clinical method. *N Engl J Med* 1976;294:582–588.

13 Mushlin AI, Appel FA: Testing an outcome based quality assurance strategy in primary care. *Med Care* 1980;18:1–100.

14 Donabedian A: *The Criteria and Standards of Quality,* vol 2: *Explorations in Quality Assessment and Monitoring.* Ann Arbor, Mich, Health Administration Press, 1982.

15 Donabedian A: Criteria and standards for quality assessment and monitoring. *Quality Rev Bull* 1986;12:99–108.

16 Greenfield S, Lewis CE, Kaplan SH, et al: Peer review by criteria mapping: Criteria for diabetes mellitus: The use of decision-making in chart audit. *Ann Intern Med* 1975;83:761–770.

17 Greenfield S, Cretin S, Worthman L, et al: Comparison of a criteria map to a criteria list in quality-of-care assessment for patients with chest pain: The relation of each to outcome. *Med Care* 1981;19:255–272.

18 Lyons TF, Payne BC: The use of item weights in assessing physician performance with predetermined criteria indices. *Med Care* 1975;13:432–439.

19 Stewart AL, Ware JE Jr, Brook RH: Advances in the measurement of functional states: Construction of aggregate indexes. *Med Care* 1981;19:473–488.

20 Fanshel S, Bush JW: A health status index and its application to health service outcomes. *Operations Res* 1970;18:1021–1060.

21 Patrick DI, Bush JW, Chen MM: Methods for measuring levels of well-being for a health status index. *Health Serv Res* 1973;8:228–245.

22 Weinstein MC, Stason WB: Foundations of cost-effectiveness analysis for health and medical practices. *N Engl J Med* 1977;296:716–721.

23 Willems JS, Sanders CR, Riddiough MA, et al: Cost-effectiveness of vaccination against pneumococcal pneumonia. *N Engl J Med* 1980;303:553–559.

24 Peterson OL, Andrews LP, Spain RA, et al: An analytical study of North Carolina general practice, 1953–1954. *J Med Educ* 1956;31:1–165.

25 *What Sort of Doctor? Assessing Quality of Care in General Practice.* London, Royal College of General Practitioners, 1985.

26

Continuous improvement as an ideal in health care
Donald Berwick

Extracts from Berwick DM (1989) Continuous improvement as an ideal in healthcare, New England Journal of Medicine 320(21): 1424–25.

Imagine two assembly lines, monitored by two foremen.

Foreman 1 walks the line, watching carefully. "I can see you all," he warns. "I have the means to measure your work, and I will do so. I will find those among you who are unprepared or unwilling to do your jobs, and when I do there will be consequences. There are many workers available for these jobs, and you can be replaced."

Foreman 2 walks a different line, and he too watches. "I am here to help you if I can," he says. "We are in this together for the long haul. You and I have a common interest in a job well done. I know that most of you are trying very hard, but sometimes things can go wrong. My job is to notice opportunities for improvement — skills that could be shared, lessons from the past, or experiments to try together — and to give you the means to do your work even better than you do now. I want to help the average ones among you, not just the exceptional few at either end of the spectrum of competence."

Which line works better? Which is more likely to do the job well in the long run? Where would you rather work?

In modern American health care, there are two approaches to the problem of improving quality — two theories of quality that describe the climate in which care is delivered. One will serve us well; the other probably will not.

The theory used by Foreman 1 relies on inspection to improve quality. We may call it the Theory of Bad Apples, because those who subscribe to it believe that quality is best achieved by discovering bad apples and removing them from the lot. The experts call this mode "quality by inspection," and in the thinking of activists for quality in health care it predominates under the guise of "buying right," "recertification," or "deterrence" through litigation. Such an outlook implies or establishes thresholds for acceptability, just as the inspector at the end of an assembly line decides whether to accept or reject finished goods.

Those in health care, who espouse the Theory of Bad Apples are looking hard for better tools of inspection. Such tools must have excellent measuring ability —

high sensitivity and specificity, simultaneously — lest the malefactors escape or the innocent be made victims. They search for outliers — statistics far enough from the average that chance alone is unlikely to provide a good excuse. Bad Apples theorists publish mortality data, invest heavily in systems of case-mix adjustment, and fund vigilant regulators. Some measure their success by counting heads on platters.

The Theory of Bad Apples gives rise readily to what can be called the my-apple-is-just-fine-thank-you response on the part of the workers supervised by Foreman 1. The foreman has defined the rules of a game called "Prove you are acceptable," and that is what the workers play. The game is not fun, of course; the workers are afraid, angry, and sullen, but they play nonetheless. When quality is pursued in the form of a search for deficient people, those being surveyed play defense. They commonly use three tactics: kill the messenger (the foreman is not their friend, and the inspector even less so); distort the data or change the measurements (whenever possible, take control of the mechanisms that may do you harm); and if all else fails, turn somebody else in (and divert the foreman's attention).

Any good foreman knows how clever a frightened work force can be. In fact, practically no system of measurement — at least none that measures people's performance — is robust enough to survive the fear of those who are measured. Most measurement tools eventually come under the control of those studied, and in their fear such people do not ask what measurement can tell them, but rather how they can make it safe. The inspector says, "I will find you out if you are deficient." The subject replies, "I will therefore prove I am not deficient" — and seeks not understanding, but escape.

The signs of this game are everywhere in health care. With determination and enormous technical resourcefulness, the Health Care Financing Administration has published voluminous data for two consecutive years about the mortality profiles of Medicare recipients in almost every hospital in the United States — profiles that are adjusted according to complex multivariate models to show many important characteristics of the patient populations.[1] Such information, though by no means flawless, could be helpful to hospitals seeking to improve their effectiveness. Yet the hundreds of pages of data are dwarfed by the thousands of pages of responses from hospitals, trying to prove whatever hospitals need to prove to build their defenses. What else should we expect?

The same game is being played between aggressive Boards of Registration in Medicine and other regulators that require hospitals and physicians to produce streams of reports on the contents of their closets. In Massachusetts, for example, merely talking with a physician about his or her involvement in a mishap may commit a hospital administrator by law to report that physician to the Board of Registration in Medicine.

The sad game played out in this theory and the predictable response to it imply a particular view of the nature of hazard and deficiency in health care, as it does in any industry playing such a game. The view is that problems of quality are caused by poor intentions. The Bad Apple is to blame. The cause of trouble is people — their venality, incompetence, or insufficient caution. According to this outlook, one can use deterrence to improve quality, because intentions need to be changed; one can use reward or punishment to control people who do not care enough to do what they can or what they know is right. The Theory of Bad Apples implies that people must be made to care; the inevitable response is the attempt to prove that one cares enough.

What a waste! The Theory of Bad Apples let American industry down for decades. It took some visionary theorists, many of them statisticians, in companies with great foresight to learn that relying on inspection to improve quality is at best inefficient, and at worst a formula for failure.[2-6] The Japanese learned first — from American theorists, ironically — that there were far better ways to improve quality, and the result is international economic history.[7] Today, no American companies make videocassette recorders or compact-disc players or single-lens-reflex cameras; we have simply given up. Xerox engineers visiting Japan in 1979 found copiers being produced at half the cost of those manufactured at Xerox's facilities, with only 1/30 the number of defects.[8]

What Japan had discovered was primarily a new, more cogent, and more valid way to focus on quality. Call it the Theory of Continuous Improvement. Its postulates are simple, but they are strangely alien to some basic assumptions of American industry — assumptions fully evident in health care today. These postulates have been codified most forcefully by two American theorists, W. Edwards Deming[5,9] and Joseph M. Juran[4,10] — heroes in Japan today, and among enlightened American companies. Juran and Deming, guided largely by a visionary group of mentors at Western Electric Laboratories (later AT&T Bell Laboratories) in the 1930s, drew on a deepened understanding of the general sources of problems in quality. They discovered that problems, and therefore opportunities to improve quality, had usually been built directly into the complex production processes they studied, and that defects in quality could only rarely be attributed to a lack of will, skill, or benign intention among the people involved with the processes. Even when people were at the root of defects, they learned, the problem was generally not one of motivation or effort, but rather of poor job design, failure of leadership, or unclear purpose. Quality can be improved much more when people are assumed to be trying hard already, and are not accused of sloth. Fear of the kind engendered by the disciplinary approach poisons improvement in quality, since it inevitably leads to disaffection, distortion of information, and the loss of the chance to learn.

Real improvement in quality depends, according to the Theory of Continuous Improvement, on understanding and revising the production processes on the basis of data about the processes themselves. "Every process produces information on the basis of which the process can be improved," say these theorists. The focus is oh continuous improvement throughout the organization through constant effort to reduce waste, rework, and complexity. When one is clear and constant in one's purpose, when fear does not control the atmosphere (and thus the data), when learning is guided by accurate information and sound rules of inference, when suppliers of services remain in dialogue with those who depend on them, and when the hearts and talents of all workers are enlisted in the pursuit of better ways, the potential for improvement in quality is nearly boundless. Translated into cultural norms in production systems and made real through sound statistical techniques, these lessons are at the core of the Japanese industrial revolution.[7] They have proved their worth.

In retrospect, their success is not all that surprising. Modern theories of quality improvement in industry are persuasive largely because they focus on the average producer, not the outlier, and on learning, not defense. Like Foreman 2, the modern quality-improvement expert cares far more about learning and cooperating with the typical worker than about censoring the truly deficient. The Theory of Continuous Improvement works because of the immense, irresistible quantitative power derived from shifting the entire curve of production upward even slightly, as compared with a focus on trimming the tails. The Japanese call it *kaizen* — the continuous search for opportunities for all processes to get better.[11] An epigram captures this spirit: "Every defect is a treasure." In the discovery of imperfection lies the chance for processes to improve.

How far from *kaizen* has health care come! Not that the idea of continuous improvement is alien to medicine; self-development, continuous learning, the pursuit of completeness are all familiar themes in medical instruction and history. Yet today we find ourselves almost devoid of such thinking when we enter the debate over quality. The disciplinarians seek out Bad Apples; the profession, and its institutions by and large, try to justify themselves as satisfactory. It is the rare "customer" and "supplier" of health care today who function as partners in continuous improvement; for the most part, they are playing a different game.

It would be naive to counsel the total abandonment of surveillance and discipline. Even in Japan, there are police. Politically, at least, it is absolutely necessary for regulators to continue to ferret out the truly avaricious and the dangerously incompetent. But what about the rest of us? How can we best be helped to try a little *kaizen* in our medical back yards? What follows are a few small steps.

First, leaders must take the lead in quality improvement. Those who speak for the profession, for health care institutions, and for large-scale purchasers must establish and hold to a shared vision of a health care system undergoing continuous improvement. The volleys of accusation and defense badly need to be replaced by efforts to clarify the goals that producers and payers share, beginning with this assumption: "Health care is very good today; together, we intend to make it even better."

Second, investments in quality improvement must be substantial. In other industries, quality improvement has yielded high dividends in cost reductions[12]; that may occur in health care as well. For the time being, however, improvement requires additional investments in managerial time, capital, and technical expertise. With the high discount rate in health care planning today, such investment calls for steadfast long-term vision. The most important investments of all are in education and study, to understand the complex production processes used in health care; we must understand them before we can improve them.

Third, respect for the health care worker must be reestablished. Physicians, hospital employees, and health care workers, like workers anywhere, must be assumed to be trying hard, acting in good faith, and not willfully failing to do what they know to be correct. When they are caught in complex systems and performing complex tasks, of course clinicians make mistakes; these are unintentional, and the people involved cannot be frightened into doing better. In fact, if they are afraid, they will probably do worse, since they will be wasting their time in self-defense instead of learning.

Fourth, dialogue between customers and suppliers of health care must be open and carefully maintained. As an incentive to improve quality, the threat of taking one's business elsewhere is pale compared with the reminder that one is committed to a long-term relationship. Quality improves as those served (the customers) and those serving (the suppliers) take the time to listen to each other and to work out their inevitable misunderstandings. Just as marriages do not improve under the threat of divorce, neither, in general, will health care.

Fifth, modern technical, theoretically grounded tools for improving processes must be put to use in health care settings. The pioneers of quality improvement — Shewhart,[2,3] Dodge, Juran,[4,10] Deming,[5,9] Taguchi,[13] and others[14] — have left a rich heritage of theory and technique by which to analyze and improve complex production processes, yet until recently these techniques have had little use in our health care systems. The barriers have been cultural in part; physicians, for example, seem to have difficulty seeing themselves as participants in processes, rather than as lone agents of success or failure. The techniques of process flow analysis, control charts, cause-and-effect diagrams, design experimentation, and quality-function deployment, to name a few, are neither arcane nor obvious;[14,15] they require study, but they can be learned. Many will be as useful in health care as they have been in other industries. Processes that can be improved by means of systematic techniques abound in medicine. Those within institutions are obvious, such as the ways in which hospitals dispense medications, transfer information, or equip and schedule operating rooms. But even individual doctors create and use "production processes." In this sense, the way a physician schedules patients constitutes a process, as does the way he or she prescribes medicines, gives a patient instructions, organizes office records, issues bills, or ensures that high-risk patients receive influenza vaccine.

Sixth, health care institutions must "organize for quality." When other types of companies have invested in quality improvement, they have discovered and refined managerial techniques requiring new structures, such as are not currently found in the American hospital or health maintenance organization. Quality engineers occupy a central place in such structures, as quality is brought to center stage in the managerial agenda, on a par with finance. Flexible project teams must be created, trained, and competently led to tackle complex processes that cross customary departmental boundaries. Throughout the organization, a renewed investment must be made in training, since all staff members must become partners in the central mission of quality improvement.

Furthermore, health care regulators must become more sensitive to the cost and ineffectiveness of relying on inspection to improve quality. In some regulatory functions, inspection and discipline must continue, but when such activities dominate, they have an unfavorable effect on the quality of care provided by the average worker. This is not to argue against measuring quality and developing tools to do so; without them, artisans could not improve their craft. The danger lies in a naive and atheoretical belief, rampant today in the orgy of measurement involved in health care regulation, that the assessment and publication of performance data will somehow induce otherwise indolent care givers to improve the level of their care and efficiency. In other industries, reliance on inspection as the agent of change has instead more commonly added cost and slowed progress toward improvement. So it will be in health care. Without doubt, regulators who willingly learn and respect modern principles of quality improvement can have a helpful role. They can do so as the partners of care givers in developing sound measurement tools that represent common values and are for use primarily by the producers themselves; by aggregating data centrally to help care givers learn from each other; by providing technical support and training in methods of quality improvement; and by encouraging and funding studies of the efficacy of technologies and procedures and thus expanding the scientific basis for specifying rational processes of care.

In addition, professionals must take part in specifying preferred methods of care, but must avoid minimalist "standards" of care. Linked closely to the reliance on inspection to improve quality is the search for standards of care, which usually implies minimal thresholds of structure, process, or outcome above which one is safe from being labeled a Bad Apple. Quality-control engineers know that such floors rapidly become ceilings, and that a company that seeks merely to meet standards cannot achieve excellence. Specifications of process (clear, scientifically grounded, continuously reviewed statements of how one intends to behave) are essential to quality improvement, on the other hand, and are widely lacking in medical care. Health care producers who commit themselves to improvement will invest energy in developing specific statements of purpose and algorithms for the clinical processes by which they intend to achieve those purposes. For example, they will specify rules both for routine procedures (e.g., "What is our system for dispensing medications correctly?") and for the content and evaluation of clinical practices (e.g., "What is our best current guess about the proper sequence of tests and therapies for back pain, and how well are they working?"). Ideally, such specifications are guidelines that are appropriate locally and are subject to ongoing assessment and revision.

Finally, individual physicians must join in the effort for continuous improvement. It may seem at first that the Theory of Continuous Improvement, coming as it does from experience in large manufacturing companies, has little relevance to individual physicians, at least those not involved in managed care organizations. But the opposite is true. At the very least, quality improvement has little chance of success in health care organizations without the understanding, the participation, and in many cases the leadership of individual doctors. In hospitals, physicians both rely on and help shape almost every process pertaining to patients' experience, from support services (such as dietary and housekeeping functions) to clinical care services (such as laboratories and nursing). Few can improve without the help of the medical staff.

Furthermore, the theory of quality improvement applies almost as well to small systems (such as a doctor's office) as it does to large ones. Individual physicians caring for individual patients know that defects in the care they provide do not usually stem from inattention or uninformed decisions. Yet hazards and defects do occur. Often they originate in the small but complex sequences on which every doctor depends, even sole practitioners. A test result lost, a specialist who cannot be reached, a missing requisition, a misinterpreted order, duplicate paperwork, a vanished record, a long wait for the CT scan, an unreliable on-call system — these are all-too-familiar examples of waste, rework, complexity, and error in the doctor's daily life. Flawless care requires not just sound decisions but also sound supports for those decisions. For the average doctor, quality fails when systems fail. Without the insights and techniques of quality improvement embedded in their medical practice, physicians are like anyone else who depends on others to get a complicated job done. They can remain trapped by defects they do not create but will nonetheless be held accountable for. The solo doctor who embodies every process needed to ensure highest-quality care is now nearly a myth. All physicians depend on systems, from the local ones in their private offices to the gargantuan ones of national health care.

Physicians who doubt that methods designed to improve quality can help them in daily practice may consider several questions. When quality fails in your own work, why does it fail? Do you ever waste time waiting, when you should not have to? Do you ever redo your work because something failed the first time? Do the procedures you use waste steps, duplicate efforts, or frustrate you through their unpredictability? Is information that you need ever lost? Does communication ever fail? If the answer to any of these is yes, then ask why. How can it be changed? What can be improved, and how? Must you be a mere observer of problems, or can you lead toward their solution? Physicians and health care managers who study and apply the principles of continuous improvement daily will probably come to know better efficiency, greater effectiveness, lower cost, and the gratitude and loyalty of more satisfied patients. They will be able to make better decisions and carry them out more faithfully.

We are wasting our time with the Theory of Bad Apples and our defensive response to it in health care today, and we can best begin by freeing ourselves from the fear, accusation, defensiveness, and naiveté of an empty search for improvement through inspection and discipline. The Theory of Continuous Improvement proved better in Japan; it is proving itself again in American industries willing to embrace it, and it holds some badly needed answers for American health care.

Notes

1   Health Care Financing Administration. Medicare hospital mortality information. Washington, D.C.: Government Printing Office, 1988. (GPO publication no. 1987 O-196860.)

2   Shewhart WA. The application of statistics as an aid in maintaining quality of a manufactured product. I Am Stat Assoc 1925; 20:546–8.

3   *Idem.* Economic control of quality of a manufactured product. New York: D. Van Nostrand, 1931.

4   Juran JM, Gryna FM Jr, Bingham RS Jr, eds. Quality control handbook. New York: McGraw-Hill, 1979.

5   Deming WE. Quality, productivity, and competitive position. Cambridge, Mass.: Massachusetts Institute of Technology, Center for Advanced Engineering Study, 1982.

6   Feigenbaum AV. Total quality control. 3rd ed. New York: McGraw-Hill, 1983.

7   Garvin DA. Managing quality: the strategic and competitive edge. New York: Free Press, 1988.

8   Abelson PH. Competitiveness: a long-enduring problem. Science 1988; 240:865.

9   Deming WE. Out of the crisis. Cambridge, Mass.: Massachusetts Institute of Technology, Center for Advanced Engineering Study, 1986.

10 Juran JM. Managerial breakthrough. New York: McGraw-Hill, 1964.

11 Imai M. Kaizen: the key to Japanese competitive success. New York: Random House, 1986.

12 Crosby PB. Quality is free: the art of making quality certain. New York: McGraw-Hill, 1979.

13 Kackar RN. Off-line quality control, parameter design, and the Taguchi method. J Qual Technol 1985; 17:176–88.

14 Wadsworth HM, Stephens KS, Godfrey AB. Modern methods for quality control and improvement. New York: John Wiley, 1986.

15 Ishikawa K, ed. Guide to quality control. White Plains, N.Y.: Kraus International Publications, 1986.

27

A primer on leading the improvement of systems
Donald Berwick

Extracts from Berwick DM (1996) A primer on leading the improvement of systems, British Medical Journal 312: 619–23.

The nurse called me urgently into the room. The child, she said, was in acute respiratory distress.

I had never met either Jimmy (the 6 year old boy) or his mother (an inner city single teenage parent) before. His asthma attack was severe, his peak expiratory flow rate only 35% of normal. Twenty years ago my next steps would have been to begin bronchodilator treatment, call an ambulance, and send the boy to hospital. That also would have been the story 10 years ago, or five, or two.

But today, when I entered the room, the mother handed me her up to date list of treatments, including nebuliser treatment with β2 agonists, that she had administered with equipment that had been installed in her home. It continued with her graph of Jimmy's slowly improving peak flow levels, which she had measured and charted at home, having been trained by the asthma outreach nurse. She then gave me the nurse's cellular telephone number, along with a specific recommendation on the next medication to try for her son, one that had worked in the past but was not yet available for her to use at home.

My reply was interrupted by a knock on my door. It was the chief of the allergy department in my health maintenance organisation. He worked one floor above me in the health centre and, having been phoned by the outreach nurse, had decided to "pop down" to see if he could help. He also handed me a phial of the same new medication that the mother had just mentioned, suggesting that we try it.

Two hours later Jimmy was not in a hospital bed; he was at home breathing comfortably. Just to be safe the allergy nurse would be paying him a visit later that afternoon.

Improvement and change: a systems view

Any would-be leader of improvement must recognise the indissoluble bond between improvement and change. Not all change is improvement, but all improvement is change.

The central law of improvement

The relation derives from what I will call the central law of improvement: every system is perfectly designed to achieve the results it achieves. This aphorism encodes an understanding of systems that lies at the root of current approaches to making systems function better. The central law reframes performance from a matter of effort to a matter of design.

The central law of improvement implies that better or worse "performance" cannot be obtained from a system of work merely on demand. (A system of work here means any set of activities with a common aim—a doctor's practice, a hospital, or a national health care system.) It implies that the results of health care, such as mortality rates or the speed with which we address a patient's anxiety, are themselves properties of our system of care, just as the length of my maximum long jump is inherent in the nature of my body (which is also a system). Mere effort can, of course, achieve some improvements. But such improvement is not fundamental; it does not often represent a new level of capability.

Learning points

- Not all change is improvement, but all improvement is change
- Real improvement comes from changing systems, not changing within systems
- To make improvements we must be clear about what we are trying to accomplish, how we will know that a change has led to improvement, and what change we can make that will result in an improvement
- The more specific the aim, the more likely the improvement; armies do not take all hills at once
- Concentrate on meeting the needs of patients rather than the needs of organisations
- Measurement is best used for learning rather than for selection, reward, or punishment
- Measurement helps to know whether innovations should be kept, changed, or rejected; to understand causes; and to clarify aims
- Effective leaders challenge the status quo both by insisting that the current system cannot remain and by offering clear ideas about superior alternatives
- Educating people and providing incentives are familiar but not very effective ways of achieving improvement
- Most work systems leave too little time for reflection on work
- You win the Tour de France not by planning for years for the perfect first bicycle ride but by constantly making small improvements

---

Saying that performance is a system characteristic does not imply that performance never varies. Indeed, variation is inevitable. Waiting times go up and down; so do mortality rates. The central law does imply, however, a certain kind of stability—namely, that both average performance and the degree of variation about that average over time are characteristics of the system.

Now along comes a well intended government minister or manager or doctor who wants to improve on the historical performance level of health care. Each, from his or her own platform, tries to cause improvement: the minister publishes league tables; the manager initiates internal audit and links pay to performance; the doctor promises to try harder. According to the central law of improvement, the results everyone wants to change are properties inherent in the system. Only if the league tables cause the creation of new systems can we expect new results. If not, not.

Herein lies the link between improvement and change. If we do not like the current level of performance we must choose between change and frustration.[1] You can see it clearly in the story of Jimmy. He ended up at home and not in hospital because the system of care—of home nebulisation, training for the mother, outreach nurses and home visits, and flexible schedules for consultants and cellular phones—had changed and was capable of sending him home safely and well.

Change of a system, not change in a system

This change in Jimmy's care is change of a system, not change within a system.[2] For Jimmy, change within the system would have meant my trying harder not to admit or waiting longer before doing so; using more of a familiar drug, not turning to a new one; getting the child more quickly to a nebuliser, not moving the nebuliser, the peak flow meter, and the skill to the home.

We must be clear about the distinction between stressing the current system (relying on more of the same) and introducing a truly new system. The former butts without much effect against the walls of historical performance; the latter leaps over them.

The new system of asthma care did not come from me. New systems do not bubble up from below. If we sketch a diagram of "the system of asthma care"—the network of cause and effect that sent Jimmy safely home that day—then the circles will contain the names of people, departments, rules, pieces of equipment, and the matrix of causes will stretch into the channels of nursing command, the purchasing systems, the rules of hiring, the design departments of equipment manufacturers, and the board of the health maintenance organisation where Jimmy and I met. The diagram will show that Jimmy and I are not causes much at all: we are mostly effects. The system could make us helpless; but instead it met our needs. Unified by a common aim, the system let this little boy go home.

To create great health we must create great systems of care for health. Improvement begins in our will, but to achieve improvement we need a method for systemic change, a model for improvement.

A model for improvement

Nolan and colleagues have devised a simple and elegant model for achieving changes that are improvements (Figure 27.1).[3] Nolan's model comprises three basic questions and a fourth element that describes a cycle for testing innovations.

Model for improvement

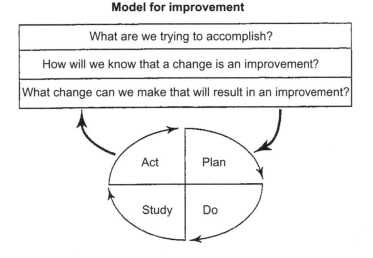

Figure 27.1   A model for improvement from Langley, Nolan, and Nolan.[3] This simple framework can guide specific improvement activities in personal work, teams, or natural work groups

What are we trying to accomplish? Improvement must be intended, and specific aims are crucial. If my daughter tries to learn to ride a bicycle she has a chance of success. If she sets off to "improve transportation" she might not.

How will I know if a change leads to an improvement? Measurement is only a handmaiden to improvement, but improvement cannot act without it. We speak here not of measurement for the purposes of judgment (for deciding whether or not to buy or to accept or reject) but for the purposes of learning (such as from experiment, from others, or from history).

What changes could we make that we think will result in improvement? This question addresses the central law of improvement en face. Since new aims require changes of systems, it is important to be able to identify promising changes and to avoid useless ones. Smart ideas for change can come from many places—from experts, from science, from theory, from experience.

The plan-do-study-act (PDSA) cycle[4] describes, in essence, inductive learning—the growth of knowledge through making changes and then reflecting on the consequences of those changes. Such inductive learning is familiar to scientists, but such formal cycles of action and reflection are unusual in daily work. Nolan's model intends that the enterprise of testing change in informative cycles should be part of normal daily activity throughout an organisation. This is what George Box has called "the democratisation of science," and it amounts to little less than a new view of the nature of work itself.

Lessons from observing the model in action

The simplicity of Nolan's model for improvement belies its sophistication. As we at the Institute for Healthcare Improvement have worked with dozens of organisations trying to achieve specific breakthroughs in performance we have seen how difficult it may be for leaders who intend to induce productive change. These four simple steps—set aims, define measurements, find promising ideas for change, and test those ideas in real work settings—challenge the mettle of the best and push against many deeply held assumptions.

Figure 27.2 "We stack things everywhere in health care—patients in waiting rooms, forms and equipment in bins, laboratory specimens for processing, and phone calls on hold"

Lessons about setting aims

Intending to improve is a necessary first step towards improvement. The more specific the aim the more likely the improvement. Leaders bear the obligation to clarify aims. So many possible agendas are plausible for an organisation that improvement efforts can easily become chaotic unless someone rallies effort around a few specific purposes. Armies do not take all hills at once; someone must say, "Take that hill."

People in health care organisations often rebel against the idea of pulling together around a small set of shared purposes. We are used to suboptimising our local profession or department.[5] Nurses improve nursing; doctors improving doctoring. But part by part improvement will not in general achieve the improvement of systems as a whole. Indeed, collaboration may easily degenerate into the more familiar job of making one's own part better at the expense of the whole.[6]

Figure 27.3 Too many changes rely on stressing the existing system rather than building a new one

Furthermore, without repeated clarification, aims drift. I have seen a team working on reducing costs in an inpatient unit suddenly realise in its tenth hour of meeting that at least half of the group had come to feel that costs ought not to be reduced. No further progress was possible until they had again forged a shared aim. Many teams have found it useful to "recite" aims at each meetings, just to ensure that all members are still on board.

Ambitious aims and external customers

Two specific properties of aims for improvement can be particularly helpful in building momentum for change. Firstly, aims should be ambitious. "Stretch goals" make it immediately obvious that the current system is inadequate and that a new one is required. In our work on reducing caesarean section rates the guidance group chose a reduction of 30% as the breakthrough goal. A less ambitious goal might have led simply to stressing the system to achieve marginal gains. By contrast, a safe reduction of 30% or more required fundamental changes in patient preparation, anaesthesia, labour management, and delivery technique.

Secondly, we have noted how difficult it is to maintain focus on aims that matter to society—that affect the external customers of our work, like patients, families, and communities. It is sometimes easier to focus on internal reorganisation and improve in ways that are unimportant to outsiders. But it is meeting external needs that ultimately determines the success or failure of organisations. Reminding people of this and asking relentlessly, "What external needs are we meeting?" is a mark of effective leadership.

Lessons about measurement

Health care is in the midst of a love affair with measurement. Report cards, league tables, and mandatory reporting about, all in a search for better accountability and an informed consumer. Belief in the wisdom of the market runs deep. But the second question in Nolan's model has little to do with selection, reward, and punishment. It refers to measurement for learning.

All learners need some form of measurement. Firstly, measuring helps one know if a particular innovation should be kept, changed, or rejected. My son, a middle distance runner, found his new shoes to be an improvement because his time in the half mile fell when he wore them. Secondly, measuring can help one understand causes. When the car stops the fuel gauge on "empty" tells us why. Thirdly, and more subtly, developing measurement helps to clarify aims; the answer to Nolan's second question helps refine the answer to the first.

Our institute is working with 12 organisations to improve asthma care. They set out initially to try to reduce severe attacks and chose "visits to emergency rooms" as a measure. This led to a discussion of how emergency room visits are used and refocused the group on effective use of initial emergency visits to institute definitive care. They changed their measurement to "repeat visits to emergency rooms," which better reflected their aims.

This friendliness between measurement and aims comes as a surprise to many health care groups using the Nolan model. They are so used to experiencing measurement as judgment that they have forgotten the role of measurement in improvement.

The best is the enemy of the good

When leaders manage to overcome this fear they often run into a second barrier: the search for perfect measurement. The rooting of health care in scientific research has generated some myopia about the preconditions for inference. When we try to improve a system we do not need perfect inference about a preexisting hypothesis: we do not need randomisation, power calculations, and large samples. We need just enough information to take a next step in learning. Often a small series of patients or a few closely observed events contain more than enough information for a specific process change to be evaluated, refined, or discarded, just as my daughter, in learning to ride her bicycle, sometimes must fall down only once to learn not to try that manoeuvre again. In measurement for improvement the best is often the enemy of the good.

Lessons about finding promising change concepts

Health care is rich in sources of ideas worth testing in the search for improvement: medical journals, professional meetings, colleagues, consulting firms. In fact, good ideas are so abundant that one wonders why systems of medical care change so slowly.[7] Patterns recur in the behaviour of leaders trying to introduce good ideas for change into the system of care. Mostly these are to do with overcoming resistance to change,[8] the immense authority of the status quo in a complex human system.

Effective leaders challenge the status quo both by insisting that the current system cannot remain and by offering clear ideas about superior alternatives. We have noticed that leaders who have a clear-headed view of a promising new approach—what Nolan calls a "change concept"—and who can explain it with confidence are more likely to succeed than those who merely state the new aims and leave it to the workforce to come up with the new ways to achieve those aims.

Leaders cannot get by simply by "empowering" people to discover better ways to work. In practice the workforce rarely comes up with a new concept bolder than one that leaders have already put on the table as the alternative to the status quo.

Two examples of powerful change concepts may show why this is so. One is the concept of "work removal," the idea that work that helps no one should be stopped.[9] Workers rarely do this of their own accord, even if they know the work is waste. The reasons are complicated, involving job security, incentives, and pride, all of which conspire to maintain the status quo. It takes a senior leader, fully confident in the general concept that systems normally contain major chunks of valueless work, to insist that such waste be found and removed. The empowerment comes in giving the workforce the time, authority, and safe harbour to find and remove the waste.

Another change concept, even more powerful but even less likely to be discovered by a workforce, is continuous flow. This is the alternative to batching: making stacks of things to be worked on in due time.[10] We stack things everywhere in health care—patients in waiting rooms, forms and equipment in bins, laboratory specimens for processing, and phone calls on hold. Most industries try to replace batch processing with a more effective and less costly continuous process flow; but this idea challenges basic assumptions in most health care systems. It seems self evident (even though it is not true) that continuous flow systems must be more costly, not less. The concept of continuous flow is at first so foreign that only senior leaders can insist on its use.

In fact, health care leaders have tended to fall back on concepts for change that are familiar but not very powerful—such as educating people and providing different incentives. Both tend to rely on stressing the existing system, rather than building a new one. In particular, teaching people facts so as to change their behaviour is a long, slow road. We have known for years that to reduce the use of an overused laboratory test removing its name from a preprinted laboratory form (requiring a doctor who wants it to write it in) works far better any number of educational sessions about the proper use of the test.[11]

On the other hand, leaders who do want to accelerate improvement by introducing highly leveraged concepts of change, such as continuous flow, need to give people time to assimilate and test those concepts. Most work systems leave too little time for reflection on work. It may be especially helpful to "walk through" actual work systems, especially when searching for waste that can be removed. A team of doctors, nurses, and others in a renal dialysis unit recently took the time, with some facilitation, to walk through their own unit to identify waste in supplies, time, equipment, motion, and other resources. Within an hour they had listed over 60 specific types of waste and could set about stopping many of them.

Groups that do begin to tackle system change sometimes fall victim to one specific and toxic phenomenon that I call "trumping." The telltale phrase that precedes a trump is one like: "Nothing matters unless ... " Or, "We can make no progress at all until ... ." Though not strictly correct, they are true enough to divert group energy entirely, especially when the person throwing the trump has high status. Common trumps in American health care include, for example, malpractice litigation, payment schemes, physician training, and unrealistic patient demands. All are problems, but none need paralyse. Skilful leaders can address the trump and disable it. "That is important, of course," such a leader says, "but surely we are clever enough to find plenty of other routes to improvement, even while we tackle that barrier."

Lessons about using PDSA cycles for learning

The plan-do-study-act cycle is a mnemonic for testing changes in real work settings. It defines activities not normally part of work but which if made part of work can convert a system from at best a merely stable one to one capable of continuous learning.

Effective leaders of improvement insist that the status quo should be challenged continuously through the active testing of promising changes on a small scale. Such testing is totally unfamiliar as part of normal work and most organisations resist the concept. The resistance comes in many disguises, such as the demand for perfect measurement, planning tests so large that they never occur, or extending the time frame ("We'll meet again next month") exactly when it should be shorter ("We'll meet again tomorrow").

In our institute's work we have adopted the question, "What test will you run next Tuesday?" as a way of emphasising that the tests implied in Nolan's model are not large, precisely designed trials that take months or years but small, clever, informative PDSA cycles that can often start within days or hours of their initial motivation. Large scale lessons come as we link small scale cycles cumulatively to each other. My 9 year old daughter may be aiming for the Tour de France, but her route to fame does not involve years of planning the perfect first bicycle ride.

Instead, she takes small, informative steps one by one, using trials to gain knowledge. When such trials, motivated by sound change concepts, do finally occur, the most vulnerable step by far is study. The science in PDSA is in the act of reflection, learning from what one did. Those who want improvement to occur need to reserve specific times to ask, "What did we learn, and how can we build on it?" Reflection on action is so crucial that leaders themselves should probably model it in their personal behaviour.[12]

Conclusions

If we spoke a language different from English perhaps we would have a single word to link together the three facets of our quest: improvement, change, and learning. From the viewpoint of systems they are deeply united. The effective leader must understand that the road to improvement passes through change and that one efficient way to change is to learn from the actions we ourselves take. In trying to escape from the fetters of historical performance the leader of improvement places both popularity and certainty at risk. But this is what it took to send Jimmy home safely in his mothers arms; this is what it will take in the future to improve the lot of those who place themselves in our care.

Notes

1   Batalden PB, Stoltz PK. A framework for the continual improvement of health care. *Joint Commission Journal of Quality Improvement* 1993;19:424–47.
2   Watzlawick P, Weakland I, Fisch R. *Change: principles of problem formulation and problem resolution*. New York: W W Norton, 1974.
3   Langley GJ, Nolan KM, Nolan TW. *The foundation of improvement*. Silver Spring, MD: API Publishing, 1992.
4   Shewhart WA. *Economic control of quality of manufactured product*. New York: Van Nostrand, 1931. (Reprinted Milwaukee, WI: American Society for Quality Control, 1980.)
5   Senge PM. *The fifth discipline: the art and practice of the learning organisation*. New York: Doubleday/Currency, 1980.
6   Axelrod R. *The evolution of cooperation*. New York: Basic Books, 1974.
7   Berwick DM. Eleven worthy aims for clinical leadership of health system reform. *JAMA* 1994;272:797–802. [Abstract]
8   Argyris C. *Overcoming organizational defenses: facilitating organizational learning*. Boston, MA: Allyn and Bacon, 1990.
9   Roberts HV, Zangwill WI. *Quality improvement through waste reduction*. Chicago, IL: University of Chicago Graduate School of Business, 1993.
10 Ohno T. *Toyota production system: beyond large-scale production*. Cambridge, MA: Productivity Press, 1988.
11 Eisenberg JM. *Doctors' decisions and the cost of medical care*. Ann Arbor, MI: Health Administration Press, 1986.

12 Roberts HV, Sergesketter BF. *Quality is personal: a foundation for total quality management*. New York: The Free Press, 1993.

28

Error in medicine
Lucian Leape

Extracts from Leape H (1994) Error in medicine, Journal of the American Medical Association 272: 1851–57.

For years, medical and nursing students have been taught Florence Nightingale's dictum—first, do no harm.[1] Yet evidence from a number of sources, reported over several decades, indicates that a substantial number of patients suffer treatment-caused injuries while in the hospital.[2–6]

In 1964 Schimmel[2] reported that 20% of patients admitted to a university hospital medical service suffered iatrogenic injury and that 20% of those injuries were serious or fatal. Steel et al[3] found that 36% of patients admitted to a university medical service in a teaching hospital suffered an iatrogenic event, of which 25% were serious or life threatening. More than half of the injuries were related to use of medication.[3] In 1991 Bedell et al[4] reported the results of an analysis of cardiac arrests at a teaching hospital. They found that 64% were preventable. Again, inappropriate use of drugs was the leading cause of the cardiac arrests. Also in 1991, the Harvard Medical Practice Study reported the results of a population-based study of iatrogenic injury in patients hospitalized in New York State in 1984.[5,6] Nearly 4% of patients suffered an injury that prolonged their hospital stay or resulted in measurable disability. For New York State, this equaled 98 609 patients in 1984. Nearly 14% of these injuries were fatal. If these rates are typical of the United States, then 180 000 people die each year partly as a result of iatrogenic injury, the equivalent of three jumbo-jet crashes every 2 days.

When the causes are investigated, it is found that most iatrogenic injuries are due to errors and are, therefore, potentially preventable.[4,7,8] For example, in the Harvard Medical Practice Study, 69% of injuries were due to errors (the balance was unavoidable).[8] Error may be defined as an unintended act (either of omission or commission) or one that does not achieve its intended outcome. Indeed, injuries are but the "tip of the iceberg" of the problem of errors, since most errors do not result in patient injury. For example, medication errors occur in 2% to 14% of patients admitted to hospitals,[9–12] but most do not result in injury.[13]

Aside from studies of medication errors, the literature on medical error is sparse, in part because most studies of iatrogenesis have focused on injuries (eg, the Harvard Medical Practice Study). When errors have been specifically looked for, however, the rates reported have been distressingly high. Autopsy studies have shown high rates (35% to 40%) of missed diagnoses causing death.[14-16] One study of errors in a medical intensive care unit revealed an average of 1.7 errors per day per patient, of which 29% had the potential for serious or fatal injury.[17] Operational errors (such as failure to treat promptly or to get a follow-up culture) were found in 52% of patients in a study of children with positive urine cultures.[18]

Given the complex nature of medical practice and the multitude of interventions that each patient receives, a high error rate is perhaps not surprising. The patients in the intensive care unit study, for example, were the recipients of an average of 178 "activities" per day. The 1.7 errors per day thus indicate that hospital personnel were functioning at a 99% level of proficiency. However, a 1% failure rate is substantially higher than is tolerated in industry, particularly in hazardous fields such as aviation and nuclear power. As W. E. Deming points out (written communication, November 1987), even 99.9% may not be good enough: "If we had to live with 99.9%, we would have: 2 unsafe plane landings per day at O'Hare, 16,000 pieces of lost mail every hour, 32,000 bank checks deducted from the wrong bank account every hour."

Why is the error rate in the practice of medicine so high?

Physicians, nurses, and pharmacists are trained to be careful and to function at a high level of proficiency. Indeed, they probably are among the most careful professionals in our society. It is curious, therefore, that high error rates have not stimulated more concern and efforts at error prevention. One reason may be a lack of awareness of the severity of the problem. Hospital-acquired injuries are not reported in the newspapers like jumbo-jet crashes, for the simple reason that they occur one at a time in 5000 different locations across the country. Although error rates are substantial, serious injuries due to errors are not part of the everyday experience of physicians or nurses, but are perceived as isolated and unusual events—"outliers." Second, most errors do no harm. Either they are intercepted or the patient's defenses prevent injury. (Few children die from a single misdiagnosed or mistreated urinary infection, for example.)

But the most important reason physicians and nurses have not developed more effective methods of error prevention is that they have a great deal of difficulty in dealing with human error when it does occur.[19-21] The reasons are to be found in the culture of medical practice.

Physicians are socialized in medical school and residency to strive for error-free practice.[19] There is a powerful emphasis on perfection, both in diagnosis and treatment. In everyday hospital practice, the message is equally clear: mistakes are unacceptable. Physicians are expected to function without error, an expectation that physicians translate into the need to be infallible. One result is that physicians, not unlike test pilots, come to view an error as a failure of character—you weren't careful enough, you didn't try hard enough. This kind of thinking lies behind a common reaction by physicians: "How can there be an error without negligence?"

Cultivating a norm of high standards is, of course, highly desirable. It is the counterpart of another fundamental goal of medical education: developing the physician's sense of responsibility for the patient. If you are responsible for everything that happens to the patient, it follows that you are responsible for any errors that occur. While the logic may be sound, the conclusion is absurd, because physicians do not have the power to control all aspects of patient care.[22] Nonetheless, the sense of duty to perform faultlessly is strongly internalized.

Role models in medical education reinforce the concept of infallibility. The young physician's teachers are largely specialists, experts in their fields, and authorities. Authorities are not supposed to err. It has been suggested that this need to be infallible creates a strong pressure to intellectual dishonesty, to cover up mistakes rather than to admit them.[23] The organization of medical practice, particularly in the hospital, perpetuates these norms. Errors are rarely admitted or discussed among physicians in private practice. Physicians typically feel, not without reason, that admission of error will lead to censure or increased surveillance or, worse, that their colleagues will regard them as incompetent or careless. Far better to conceal a mistake or, if that is impossible, to try to shift the blame to another, even the patient.

Yet physicians are emotionally devastated by serious mistakes that harm or kill patients.[19-21] Almost every physician who cares for patients has had that experience, usually more than once. The emotional impact is often profound, typically a mixture of fear, guilt, anger, embarrassment, and humiliation. However, as Christensen et al[20] note, physicians are typically isolated by their emotional responses; seldom is there a process to evaluate the circumstances of a mistake and to provide support and emotional healing for the fallible physician. Wu et al[21] found that only half of house officers discussed their most significant mistakes with attending physicians.

Thus, although the individual may learn from a mistake and change practice patterns accordingly, the adjustment often takes place in a vacuum. Lessons learned are shared privately, if at all, and external objective evaluation of what went wrong often does not occur. As Hilfiker[19] points out, "We see the horror of our own mistakes, yet we are given no permission to deal with their enormous emotional impact ... The medical profession simply has no place for its mistakes."

Finally, the realities of the malpractice threat provide strong incentives against disclosure or investigation of mistakes. Even a minor error can place the physician's entire career in jeopardy if it results in a serious bad outcome. It is hardly surprising that a physician might hesitate to reveal an error to either the patient or hospital authorities or to expose a colleague to similar devastation for a single mistake.

The paradox is that although the standard of medical practice is perfection—error-free patient care—all physicians recognize that mistakes are inevitable. Most would like to examine their mistakes and learn from them. From an emotional standpoint, they need the support and understanding of their colleagues and patients when they make mistakes. Yet, they are denied both insight and support by misguided concepts of infallibility and by fear: fear of embarrassment by colleagues, fear of patient reaction, and fear of litigation. Although the notion of infallibility fails the reality test, the fears are well grounded.

The medical approach to error prevention

Efforts at error prevention in medicine have characteristically followed what might be called the perfectibility model: if physicians and nurses could be properly trained and motivated, then they would make no mistakes. The methods used to achieve this goal are training and punishment. Training is directed toward teaching people to do the right thing. In nursing, rigid adherence to protocols is emphasized. In medicine, the emphasis is less on rules and more on knowledge.

Punishment is through social opprobrium or peer disapproval. The professional cultures of medicine and nursing typically use blame to encourage proper performance. Errors are regarded as someone's fault, caused by a lack of sufficient attention or, worse, lack of caring enough to make sure you are correct. Punishment for egregious (negligent) errors is primarily (and capriciously) meted out through the malpractice tort litigation system.

Students of error and human performance reject this formulation. While the proximal error leading to an accident is, in fact, usually a "human error," the causes of that error are often well beyond the individual's control. All humans err frequently. Systems that rely on error-free performance are doomed to fail.

The medical approach to error prevention is also reactive. Errors are usually discovered only when there is an incident—an untoward effect or injury to the patient. Corrective measures are then directed toward preventing a recurrence of a similar error, often by attempting to prevent *that* individual from making a repeat error. Seldom are underlying causes explored.

For example, if a nurse gives a medication to the wrong patient, a typical response would be exhortation or training in double-checking the identity of both patient and drug before administration. Although it might be noted that the nurse was distracted because of an unusually large case load, it is unlikely that serious attention would be given to evaluating overall work assignments or to determining if large case loads have contributed to other kinds of errors.

It is even less likely that questions would be raised about the wisdom of a system for dispensing medications in which safety is contingent on inspection by an individual at the end point of use. Reliance on inspection as a mechanism of quality control was discredited long ago in industry.[24,25] A simple procedure, such as the use of bar coding like that used at supermarket checkout counters, would probably be more effective in this situation. More imaginative solutions could easily be found—if it were recognized that both systems and individuals contribute to the problem.

It seems clear, and it is the thesis of this article, that if physicians, nurses, pharmacists, and administrators are to succeed in reducing errors in hospital care, they will need to fundamentally change the way they think about errors and why they occur. Fortunately, a great deal has been learned about error prevention in other disciplines, information that is relevant to the hospital practice of medicine.

Lessons from psychological and human factors research

The subject of human error has long fascinated psychologists and others, but both the development of theory and the pace of empirical research accelerated in response to the dramatic technological advances that occurred during and after World War II.[26] These theory development and research activities followed two parallel and intersecting paths: human factors research and cognitive psychology.

Human factor specialists, mostly engineers, have been largely concerned with the design of the man-machine interface in complex environments such as airplane cockpits and nuclear power plant control rooms. Cognitive psychologists concentrated on developing models of human cognition that they subjected to empirical testing. Lessons from both spheres of observation have greatly deepened our understanding of mental functioning. We now have reasonably coherent theories of why humans err, and a great deal has been learned about how to design work environments to minimize the occurrence of errors and limit their consequences.

A theory of cognition

Most errors result from aberrations in mental functioning. Thus, to understand why errors occur we must first understand normal cognition. Although many theories have been espoused, and experts disagree, a unitary framework has been proposed by Reason[26] that captures the main themes of cognitive theory and is consistent with empirical observation. It goes as follows.

Much of mental functioning is automatic, rapid, and effortless. A person can leave home, enter and start the car, drive to work, park, and enter the office without devoting much conscious thought to any of the hundreds of maneuvers and decisions that this complex set of actions requires. This automatic and unconscious processing is possible because we carry a vast array of mental models, "schemata" in psychological jargon, that are "expert" on some minute recurrent aspect of our world. These schemata operate briefly when required, processing information rapidly, in parallel, and without conscious effort. Schemata are activated by conscious thought or sensory inputs; functioning thereafter is automatic.

In addition to this automatic unconscious processing, called the "schematic control mode," cognitive activities can be conscious and controlled. This "attentional control mode" or conscious thought is used for problem solving as well as to monitor automatic function. The attentional control mode is called into play when we confront a problem, either de novo or as a result of failures of the schematic control mode. In contrast to the rapid parallel processing of the schematic control mode, processing in the attentional control mode is slow, sequential, effortful, and difficult to sustain.

Rasmussen and Jensen[27] describe a model of performance based on this concept of cognition that is particularly well suited for error analysis. They classify human performance into three levels: (1) skill-based, which is patterns of thought and action that are governed by stored patterns of preprogrammed instructions (schemata) and largely unconscious; (2) rule-based, in which solutions to familiar problems are governed by stored rules of the "if X, then Y" variety; and (3) knowledge-based, or synthetic thought, which is used for novel situations requiring conscious analytic processing and stored knowledge.

Any departure from routine, ie, a problem, requires a rule-based or knowledge-based solution. Humans prefer pattern recognition to calculation, so they are strongly biased to search for a prepackaged solution, ie, a "rule," before resorting to more strenuous knowledge-based-functioning.

Although all three levels may be used simultaneously, with increasing expertise the primary focus of control moves from knowledge-based toward skill-based functioning. Experts have a much larger repertoire of schemata and problem-solving rules than novices, and they are formulated at a more abstract level. In one sense, expertise means seldom having to resort to knowledge-based functioning (reasoning).

Mechanisms of cognitive errors

Errors have been classified by Reason and Rasmussen at each level of the skill-, rule-, and knowledge-based model.[26] Skill-based errors are called "slips." These are unconscious glitches in automatic activity. Slips are errors of action. Rule-based and knowledge-based errors, by contrast, are errors of conscious thought and are termed "mistakes." The mechanisms of error vary with the level.

Slips

Skill-based activity is automatic. A slip occurs when there is a break in the routine while attention is diverted. The actor possesses the requisite routines; errors occur because of a lack of a timely attentional check. In brief, slips are monitoring failures. They are unintended acts.

A common mechanism of a slip is *capture*, in which a more frequently used schema takes over from a similar but less familiar one. For example, if the usual action sequence is ABCDE, but on this occasion the planned sequence changes to ABCFG, then conscious attention must be in force after C or the more familiar pattern DE will be executed. An everyday example is departing on a trip in which the first part of the journey is the same as a familiar commuting path and driving to work instead of to the new location.

Another type of slip is a *description error*, in which the right action is performed on the wrong object, such as pouring cream on a pancake. *Associative activation errors* result from mental associations of ideas, such as answering the phone when the doorbell rings. *Loss of activation errors* are temporary memory losses, such as entering a room and no longer remembering why you wanted to go there. Loss of activation errors are frequently caused by interruptions.

A variety of factors can divert attentional control and make slips more likely. Physiological factors include fatigue, sleep loss, alcohol, drugs, and illness.

Psychological factors include other activity ("busyness"), as well as emotional states such as boredom, frustration, fear, anxiety, or anger. All these factors lead to preoccupations that divert attention. Psychological factors, though considered "internal" or endogenous, may also be caused by a host of external factors, such as overwork, interpersonal relations, and many other forms of stress. Environmental factors, such as noise, heat, visual stimuli, motion, and other physical phenomena, also can cause distractions that divert attention and lead to slips.

Mistakes

Rule-based errors usually occur during problem solving when a wrong rule is chosen—either because of a misperception of the situation and, thus, the application of a wrong rule or because of misapplication of a rule, usually one that is strong (frequently used), that seems to fit adequately. Errors result from misapplied expertise.

Knowledge-based errors are much more complex. The problem solver confronts a novel situation for which he or she possesses no, preprogrammed solutions. Errors arise because of lack of knowledge or misinterpretation of the problem. Pattern matching is preferred to calculation, but sometimes we match the wrong patterns. Certain habits of thought have been identified that alter pattern matching or calculation and lead to mistakes. These processes are incompletely understood and are seldom recognized by the actor. One such process is *biased memory*. Decisions are based on what is in our memory, but memory is biased toward overgeneralization and overregularization of the commonplace.[28] Familiar patterns are assumed to have universal applicability because they usually work. We see what we know. Paradoxically, memory is also biased toward overemphasis on the discrepant. A contradictory experience may leave an exaggerated impression far outweighing its statistical importance (eg, the exceptional case or missed diagnosis).

Another mechanism is the *availability heuristic*,[29] the tendency to use the first information that comes to mind. Related are *confirmation bias*, the tendency to look for evidence that supports an early working hypothesis and to ignore data that contradict it, and *overconfidence*, the tendency to believe in the validity of the chosen course of action and to focus on evidence that favors it.[26]

Rule-based and knowledge-based functioning are affected by the same physiological, psychological, and environmental influences that produce slips. A great deal of research has been devoted to the effects of stress on performance. Although it is often difficult to establish causal links between stress and specific accidents, there is little question that errors (both slips and mistakes) are increased under stress. On the other hand, stress is not all bad. It has long been known that "a little anxiety improves performance." In 1908, Yerkes and Dodson[30] showed that performance is best at moderate levels of arousal. Poor performance occurs at both extremes: boredom and panic.[31] *Coning of attention* under stress is the tendency in an emergency to concentrate on one single source of information, the "first come, best preferred" solution.[31] (A classic example is the phenomenon of passengers in a crashed aircraft struggling to open a door while ignoring a large hole in the fuselage a few feet away.) *Reversion under stress* is a phenomenon in which recently learned behavioral patterns are replaced by older, more familiar ones, even if they are inappropriate in the circumstances.[31]

The complex nature of cognition, the vagaries of the physical world, and the inevitable shortages of information and schemata ensure that normal humans make multiple errors every day. Slips are most common, since much of our mental functioning is automatic, but the rate of error in knowledge-based processes is higher.[26]

Latent errors

In 1979, the Three-Mile Island incident caused both psychologists and human factors engineers to reexamine their theories about human error. Although investigations revealed the expected operator errors, it was clear that prevention of many of these errors was beyond the capabilities of the human operators at the time. Many errors were caused by faulty interface design, others by complex interactions and breakdowns that were not discernible by the operators or their instruments. The importance of poor system design as a cause of failures in complex processes became more apparent.[32] Subsequent disasters, notably Bhopal and Chernobyl, made it even clearer that operator errors were only part of the explanation of failures in complex systems. Disasters of this magnitude resulted from major failures of design and organization that occurred long before the accident, failures that both caused operator errors and made them impossible to reverse.[26,32]

Reason[26] has called these *latent errors,* errors that have effects that are delayed, "accidents waiting to happen," in contrast to active errors, which have effects that are felt immediately. While an operator error may be the proximal "cause" of the accident, the root causes were often present within the system for a long time. The operator has, in a real sense, been "set up" to fail by poor design, faulty maintenance, or erroneous management decisions.

Faulty design at Three-Mile Island provided gauges that gave a low pressure reading both when pressure was low and when the gauge was not working and a control panel on which 100 warning lights flashed simultaneously. Faulty maintenance disabled a safety back-up system so the operator could not activate it when needed. Similarly, bad management decisions can result in unrealistic workloads, inadequate training, and demanding production schedules that lead workers to make errors.

Accidents rarely result from a single error, latent or active.[26,32] System defenses and the abilities of frontline operators to identify and correct errors before an accident occurs make single-error accidents highly unlikely. Rather, accidents typically result from a combination of latent and active errors and breach of defenses. The precipitating event can be a relatively trivial malfunction or an external circumstance, such as the weather (eg, the freezing of O-rings that caused the Challenger disaster).

The most important result of latent errors may be the production of psychological precursors, which are pathologic situations that create working conditions that predispose to a variety of errors.[26] Inappropriate work schedules, for example, can result in high workloads and undue time pressures that induce errors. Poor training can lead to inadequate recognition of hazards or inappropriate procedures that lead to accidents. Conversely, a precursor can be the product of more than one management or training failure. For example, excessive time pressure can result from poor scheduling, but it can also be the product of inadequate training or faulty division of responsibilities. Because they can affect all cognitive processes, these precursors can cause an immense variety of errors that result in unsafe acts.

The important point is that successful accident prevention efforts must focus on root causes—system errors in design and implementation. It is futile to concentrate on developing solutions to the unsafe acts themselves. Other errors, unpredictable and infinitely varied, will soon occur if the underlying cause is uncorrected. Although correcting root causes will not eliminate all errors—individuals still bring varying abilities and work habits to the workplace—it can significantly reduce the probability of errors occurring.

Prevention of accidents

The multiplicity of mechanisms and causes of errors (internal and external, individual and systemic) dictates that there cannot be a simple or universal means of reducing errors. Creating a safe process, whether it be flying an airplane, running a hospital, or performing cardiac surgery, requires attention to methods of error reduction at each stage of system development: design, construction, maintenance, allocation of resources, training, and development of operational procedures. This type of attention to error reduction requires responsible individuals at each stage to think through the consequences of their decisions and to reason back from discovered deficiencies to redesign and reorganize the process. Systemic changes are most likely to be successful because they reduce the likelihood of a variety of types of errors at the end-user stage.

The primary objective of system design for safety is to make it difficult for individuals to err. But it is also important to recognize that errors will inevitably occur and plan for their recovery.[26] Ideally, the system will automatically correct errors when they occur. If that is impossible, mechanisms should be in place to at least detect errors in time for corrective action. Therefore, in addition to designing the work environment to minimize psychological precursors, designers should provide feedback through instruments that provide monitoring functions and build in buffers and redundancy. Buffers are design features that automatically correct for human or mechanical errors. Redundancy is duplication (sometimes triplication or quadruplication) of critical mechanisms and instruments, so that a failure does not result in loss of the function.

Another important system design feature is designing tasks to minimize errors. Norman[28] has recommended a set of principles that have general applicability. Tasks should be *simplified* to minimize the load on the weakest aspects of cognition:

short-term memory, planning, and problem solving. The power of *constraints* should be exploited. One way to do this is with "forcing functions," which make it impossible to act without meeting a precondition (such as the inability to release the parking gear of a car unless the brake pedal is depressed). *Standardization* of procedures, displays, and layouts reduces error by reinforcing the pattern recognition that humans do well. Finally, where possible, operations should be easily *reversible* or difficult to perform when they are not reversible.

Training must include, in addition to the usual emphasis on application of knowledge and following procedures, a consideration of safety issues. These issues include understanding the rationale for procedures as well as how errors can occur at various stages, their possible consequences, and instruction in methods for avoidance of errors. Finally, it must be acknowledged that injuries can result from behavioral problems that may be seen in impaired physicians or incompetent physicians despite well-designed systems; methods for identifying and correcting egregious behaviors are also needed.

The aviation model

The practice of hospital medicine has been compared, usually unfavorably, to the aviation industry, also a highly complicated and risky enterprise but one that seems far safer. Indeed, there seem to be many similarities. As Allnutt observed,

> Both pilots and doctors are carefully selected, highly trained professionals who are usually determined to maintain high standards, both externally and internally imposed, whilst performing difficult tasks in life-threatening environments. Both use high technology equipment and function as key members of a team of specialists ... both exercise high level cognitive skills in a most complex domain about which much is known, but where much remains to be discovered.[31]

While the comparison is apt, there are also important differences between aviation and medicine, not the least of which is a substantial measure of uncertainty due to the number and variety of disease states, as well as the unpredictability of the human organism. Nonetheless, there is much physicians and nurses could learn from aviation.

Aviation—airline travel, at least—is indeed generally safe: more than 10 million takeoffs and landings each year with an average of fewer than four crashes a year. But, it was not always so. The first powered flight was in 1903, the first fatality in 1908, and the first midair collision in 1910. By 1910, there were 2000 pilots in the world and 32 had already died.[32] The US Air Mail Service was founded in 1918. As a result of efforts to meet delivery schedules in all kinds of weather, 31 of the first 40 Air Mail Service pilots were killed. This appalling toll led to unionization of the pilots and their insistence that local field controllers could not order pilots to fly against their judgment unless the field controllers went up for a flight around the field themselves. In 1922, there were no Air Mail Service fatalities.[32] Since that time, a complex system of aircraft design, instrumentation, training, regulation, and air traffic control has developed that is highly effective at preventing fatalities.

There are strong incentives for making flying safe. Pilots, of course, are highly motivated. Unlike physicians, their lives are on the line as well as those of their passengers. But, airlines and airplane manufacturers also have strong incentives to provide safe flight. Business decreases after a large crash, and if a certain model of aircraft crashes repeatedly, the manufacturer will be discredited. The lawsuits that inevitably follow a crash can harm both reputation and profitability.

Designing for safety has led to a number of unique characteristics of aviation that could, with suitable modification, prove useful in improving hospital safety.

First, in terms of system design, aircraft designers assume that errors and failures are inevitable and design systems to "absorb" them, building in multiple buffers, automation, and redundancy. As even a glance in an airliner cockpit reveals, extensive feedback is provided by means of monitoring instruments, many in duplicate or triplicate. Indeed, the multiplicity of instruments and automation have generated their own challenges to system design: sensory overload and boredom. Nonetheless, these safeguards have served the cause of aviation safety well.

Second, procedures are standardized to the maximum extent possible. Specific protocols must be followed for trip planning, operations, and maintenance. Pilots go through a checklist before each take-off. Required maintenance is specified in detail and must be performed on a regular (by flight hours) basis. Third, the training, examination, and certification process is highly developed and rigidly, as well as frequently, enforced. Airline pilots take proficiency examinations every 6 months. Much of the content of examinations is directly concerned with procedures to enhance safety.

Pilots function well within this rigorously controlled system, although not flawlessly. For example, one study of cockpit crews observed that human errors or instrument malfunctions occurred on the average of one every 4 minutes during an overseas flight.[32] Each event was promptly recognized and corrected with no untoward effects. Pilots also willingly submit to an external authority, the air traffic controller, when within the constrained air and ground space at a busy airport.

Finally, safety in aviation has been institutionalized. Two independent agencies have government-mandated responsibilities: the Federal Aviation Administration (FAA) regulates all aspects of flying and prescribes safety procedures, and the National Transportation Safety Board investigates every accident. The adherence of airlines and pilots to required safety standards is closely monitored. The FAA recognized long ago that pilots seldom reported an error if it led to disciplinary action. Accordingly, in 1975 the FAA established a confidential reporting system for safety infractions, the Air Safety Reporting System (ASRS). If pilots, controllers, or others promptly report a dangerous situation, such as a near-miss midair collision, they will not be penalized. This program dramatically increased reporting, so that unsafe conditions at airports, communication problems, and traffic control inadequacies are now promptly communicated. Analysis of these reports and subsequent investigations appear as a regular feature in several pilots' magazines. The ASRS receives more than 5000 notifications each year.[32]

The medical model

By contrast, accident prevention has not been a primary focus of the practice of hospital medicine. It is not that errors are ignored. Mortality and morbidity conferences, incident reports, risk management activities, and quality assurance committees abound. But, as noted previously, these activities focus on incidents and individuals. When errors are examined, a problem-solving approach is usually used: the cause of the error is identified and corrected. Root causes, the underlying systems failures, are rarely sought. System designers do not assume that errors and failures are inevitable and design systems to prevent or absorb them. There are, of course, exceptions. Implementation of unit dosing, for example, markedly reduced medication dosing errors by eliminating the need for the nurse to measure out each dose. Monitoring in intensive care units is sophisticated and extensive (although perhaps not sufficiently redundant). Nonetheless, the basic health care system approach is to rely on individuals not to make errors rather than to assume they will.

Second, standardization and task design vary widely. In the operating room, it has been refined to a high art. In patient care units, much more could be done, particularly to minimize reliance on short-term memory, one of the the weakest aspects of cognition. On-time and correct delivery of medications, for example, is often contingent on a busy nurse remembering to do so, a nurse who is responsible for four or five patients at once and is repeatedly interrupted, a classic set up for a "loss-of-activation" error.

On the other hand, education and training in medicine and nursing far exceed that in aviation, both in breadth of content and in duration, and few professions compare with medicine in terms of the extent of continuing education. Although certification is essentially universal, including the recent introduction of periodic recertification, the idea of periodically testing *performance* has never been accepted. Thus, we place great emphasis on education and training, but shy away from demonstrating that it makes a difference.

Finally, unlike aviation, safety in medicine has never been institutionalized, in the sense of being a major focus of hospital medical activities. Investigation of accidents is often superficial, unless a malpractice action is likely; noninjurious error (a "near miss") is rarely examined at all. Incident reports are frequently perceived as punitive instruments. As a result, they are often not filed, and when they are, they almost invariably focus on the individual's misconduct.

One medical model is an exception and has proved quite successful in reducing accidents due to errors: anesthesia. Perhaps in part because the effects of serious anesthetic errors are potentially so dramatic—death or brain damage—and perhaps in part because the errors are frequently transparently clear and knowable to all, anesthesiologists have greatly emphasized safety. The success of these efforts has been dramatic. Whereas mortality from anesthesia was one in 10 000 to 20 000 just a decade or so ago, it is now estimated at less than one in 200 000.[33] Anesthesiologists have led the medical profession in recognizing system factors as causes of errors, in designing fail-safe systems, and in training to avoid errors.[34-36]

Systems changes to reduce hospital injuries

Can the lessons from cognitive psychology and human factors research that have been successful in accident prevention in aviation and other industries be applied to the practice of hospital medicine? There is every reason to think they could be. Hospitals, physicians, nurses, and pharmacists who wish to reduce errors could start by considering how cognition and error mechanisms apply to the practice of hospital medicine. Specifically, they can examine their care delivery systems in terms of the systems' ability to discover, prevent, and absorb errors and for the presence of psychological precursors.

Discovery of errors

The first step in error prevention is to define the problem. Efficient, routine identification of errors needs to be part of hospital practice, as does routine investigation of all errors that cause injuries. The emphasis is on "routine." Only when errors are accepted as an inevitable, although manageable, part of everyday practice will it be possible for hospital personnel to shift from a punitive to a creative frame of mind that seeks out and identifies the underlying system failures.

Data collecting and investigatory activities are expensive, but so are the consequences of errors. Evidence from industry indicates that the savings from reduction of errors and accidents more than make up for the costs of data collection and investigation.[31] (While these calculations apply to "rework" and other operational inefficiencies resulting from errors, additional savings from reduced patient care costs and liability costs for hospitals and physicians could also be substantial.)

Prevention of errors

Many health care delivery systems could be redesigned to significantly reduce the likelihood of error. Some obvious mechanisms that can be used are as follows:

Reduced Reliance on Memory.—Work should be designed to minimize the requirements for human functions that are known to be particularly fallible, such as short-term memory and vigilance (prolonged attention). Clearly, the components of work must be well delineated and understood before system redesign. Checklists, protocols, and computerized decision aids could he used more widely. For example, physicians should not have to rely on their memories to retrieve a laboratory test result, and nurses should not have to remember the time a medication dose is due. These are tasks that computers do much more reliably than humans.

Improved Information Access.—Creative ways need to be developed for making information more readily available: displaying it where it is needed, when it is needed, and in a form that permits easy access. Computerization of the medical record, for example, would greatly facilitate bedside display of patient information, including tests and medications.

Error Proofing.—Where possible, critical tasks should be structured so that errors cannot be made. The use of "forcing functions" is helpful. For example, if a computerized system is used for medication orders, it can be designed so that a physician cannot enter an order for a lethal overdose of a drug or prescribe a medication to which a patient is known to be allergic.

Standardization.—One of the most effective means of reducing error is standardizing processes wherever possible. The advantages, in efficiency as well as in error reduction, of standardizing drug doses and times of administration are obvious. Is it really acceptable to ask nurses to follow six different "K-scales" (directions for how much potassium to give according to patient serum potassium levels) solely to satisfy different physician prescribing patterns? Other candidates for standardization include information displays, methods for common practices (such as surgical dressings), and the geographic location of equipment and supplies in a patient care unit. There is something bizarre, and really quite inexcusable, about "code" situations in hospitals where house staff and other personnel responding to a cardiac arrest waste precious seconds searching for resuscitation equipment simply because it is kept in a different location on each patient care unit.

Training.—Instruction of physicians, nurses, and pharmacists in procedures or problem solving should include greater emphasis on possible errors and how to prevent them. (Well-written surgical atlases do this.) For example, many interns need more rigorous instruction and supervision than is currently provided when they are learning new procedures. Young physicians need to be taught that safe practice is as important as effective practice. Both physicians and nurses need to learn to think of errors primarily as symptoms of systems failures.

Absorption of errors

Because it is impossible to prevent all error, buffers should be built into each system so that errors are absorbed before they can cause harm to patients. At minimum, systems should be designed so that errors can be identified in time to be intercepted. The drug delivery systems in most hospitals do this to some degree already. Nurses and pharmacists often identify errors in physician drug orders and prevent improper administration to the patient. As hospitals move to computerized records and ordering systems, more of these types of interceptions can be incorporated into the computer programs. Critical systems (such as life-support equipment and monitors) should be provided in duplicate in those situations in which a mechanical failure could lead to patient injury.

Psychological precursors

Finally, explicit attention should be given to work schedules, division of responsibilities, task descriptions, and other details of working arrangements where improper managerial decisions can produce psychological precursors such as time pressures and fatigue that create an unsafe environment. While the influence of the stresses of everyday life on human behavior cannot be eliminated, stresses caused by a faulty work environment can be. Elimination of fear and the creation of a supportive working environment are other potent means of preventing errors.

Institutionalization of safety

Although the idea of a national hospital safety board that would investigate every accident is neither practical nor necessary, at the hospital level such activities should occur. Existing hospital risk management activities could be broadened to include all potentially injurious errors and deepened to seek out underlying system failures. Providing immunity, as in the FAA ASRS system, might be a good first step. At the national level, the Joint Commission on Accreditation of Healthcare Organizations should be involved in discussions regarding the institutionalization of safety. Other specialty societies might well follow the lead of the anesthesiologists in developing safety standards and require their instruction to be part of residency training.

Implementing systems changes

Many of the principles described herein fit well within the teachings of total quality management.[24] One of the basic tenants of total quality management, statistical quality control, requires data regarding variation in processes. In a generic sense, errors are but variations in processes. Total quality management also requires a culture in which errors and deviations are regarded not as human failures, but as opportunities to improve the system, "gems," as they are sometimes called. Finally, total quality management calls for grassroots participation to identify and develop system modifications to eliminate the underlying failures.

Like total quality management, systems changes to reduce errors require commitment of the organization's leadership. None of the aforementioned changes will be effective or, for that matter, even possible without support at the highest levels (hospital executives and departmental chiefs) for making safety a major goal of medical practice.

But it is apparent that the most fundamental change that will be needed if hospitals are to make meaningful progress in error reduction is a cultural one. Physicians and nurses need to accept the notion that error is an inevitable accompaniment of the human condition, even among conscientious professionals with high standards. Errors must be accepted as evidence of systems flaws not character flaws. Until and unless that happens, it is unlikely that any substantial progress will be made in reducing medical errors.

Notes

1 Nightingale F. *Notes on Hospitals.* London, England: Longman, Green, Longman, Roberts, and Green; 1863.
2 Schimmel EM. The hazards of hospitalization. *Ann Intern Med.* 1964;60:100–110.
3 Steel K, Gertman PM, Crescenzi C, et al. Iatrogenic illness on a general medical service at a university hospital. *N Engl J Med.* 1981;304:638–642.
4 Bedell SE, Deitz DC, Leeman D, Delbanco TL. Incidence and characteristics of preventable iatrogenic cardiac arrests. *JAMA.* 1991;265:2815–2820.
5 Brennan TA, Leape LL, Laird N, et al. Incidence of adverse events and negligence in hospitalized patients: results of the Harvard Medical Practice Study I. *N Engl J Med.* 1991;324:370–376.
6 Leape LL, Brennan TA, Laird N, et al. The nature of adverse events in hospitalized patients: results of the Harvard Medical Practice Study II. *N Engl J Med.* 1991;324:377–384.
7 Dubois RW, Brook RH. Preventable deaths: who, how often, and why? *Ann Intern Med.* 1988;109:582–589.
8 Leape LL, Lawthers AG, Brennan TA, Johnson WG. Preventing medical injury. *Qual Rev Bull.* 1993;8:144–149.
9 Lesar TS, Briceland LL, Delcoure K, et al. Medication prescribing errors in a teaching hospital. *JAMA.* 1990;263:2329–2334.
10 Raju TN, Thornton JP, Kecskes S, et al. Medication errors in neonatal and paediatric intensive-care units. *Lancet.* 1989;2:374–379.
11 Classen DC, Pestonik SL, Evans RS, Burke JP. Computerized surveillance of adverse drug events in hospital patients. *JAMA.* 1991;266:2847–2851.
12 Folli HL, Poole RL, Benitz WE, Russo JC. Medication error prevention by clinical pharmacists in two childrens' hospitals. *Pediatrics.* 1987;79:718–722.
13 Bates DW, Boyle D, Vander Vliet M, et al. Relationship between medication errors and adverse drug events. *J Gen Intern Med.* In press.
14 Anderson RE, Hill RB, Key CR. The sensitivity and specificity of clinical diagnostics during five decades: toward an understanding of necessary fallibility. *JAMA.* 1989;261:1610–1611.
15 Goldman L, Sayson R, Robbins S, Conn LH, Bettman M, Weissberg M. The value of the autopsy in the three medical eras. *N Engl J Med.* 1983;308:1000–1005.
16 Cameron HM, McGoogan E. A prospective study of 1,152 hospital autopsies, I: inaccuracies in death certification. *J Pathol.* 1981;133:273–283.
17 Gopher D, Olin M, Donchin Y, et al. The nature and causes of human errors in a medical intensive care unit. Presented at the 33rd annual meeting of the Human Factors Society; October 18, 1989; Denver, Colo.

18 Palmer RH, Strain R, Rothrock JK, et al. Evaluation of operational failures in clinical decision making. *Med Decis Making.* 1983;3:299–310.

19 Hilfiker D. Facing our mistakes. *N Engl J Med.* 1984;310:118–122.

20 Christensen JF, Levinson W, Dunn PM. The heart of darkness: the impact of perceived mistakes on physicians. *J Gen Intern Med.* 1992;7:424–431.

21 Wu AW, Folkman S, McPhee SJ, et al. Do house officers learn from their mistakes? *JAMA.* 1991; 265:2089–2094.

22 Berwick DM. E. A. Codman and the rhetoric of battle: a commentary, *Milbank Q.* 1989;67:262–267.

23 McIntyre N, Popper KB. The critical attitude in medicine: the need for a new ethics. *BMJ.* 1989;287:1919–1923.

24 Berwick DM. Continuous improvement as an ideal in health care. *N Engl J Med.* 1989;320:53–56.

25 Deming WE. *Quality, Productivity, and Competitive Position.* Cambridge: Massachusetts Institute of Technology; 1982.

26 Reason J. *Human Error.* Cambridge, Mass: Cambridge University Press; 1992.

27 Rasmussen J, Jensen A. Mental procedures in real-life tasks: a case study of electronic troubleshooting. *Ergonomics.* 1974;17:293–307.

28 Norman DA. *To Err Is Human.* New York, NY: Basic Books Inc Publishers; 1984.

29 Tversky A, Kahneman D. The framing of decisions and the psychology of choice. *Science.* 1981;211:453–458.

30 Yerkes RM, Dodson JD. The relation of strength of stimuli to rapidity of habit formation. *J Comp Neurol Psychol.* 1908;18:459–482.

31 Allnutt MF. Human factors in accidents. *Br J Anaesth.* 1987;59:856–864.

32 Perrow C. *Normal Accidents: Living With High-Risk Technologies.* New York, NY: Basic Books Inc Publishers; 1984.

33 Orkin FK. Patient monitoring during anesthesia as an exercise in technology assessment. In: Saidman LJ, Smith NT, eds. *Monitoring in Anesthesia.* 3rd ed. London, England: Butterworth Publishers Inc; 1993.

34 Gaba DM. Human errors in anesthetic mishaps. *Int Anesthesiol Clin.* 1989;27:137–147.

35 Cooper JB, Newbower RS, Kitz RJ. An analysis of major errors and equipment failures in anesthesia management: considerations for prevention and detection. *Anesthesiology.* 1984;60:34–42.

36 Cullen DJ, Nemeskal RA, Cooper JB, Zaslavsky A, Dwyer MJ. Effect of pulse oximetry, age, and ASA physical status on the frequency of patients admitted unexpectedly to a postoperative care unit. *Anesth Analg.* 1992;74:181.

29

Evaluation of quality improvement programmes

John Øvretveit and David Gustafson

Extracts from Øvretveit J and Gustafson D (2002) Evaluation of quality improvement programmes, Quality and Safety in Health Care 11: 270–75.

In response to increasing concerns about quality, many countries are carrying out large scale programmes which include national quality strategies, hospital programmes, and quality accreditation, assessment and review processes. Increasing amounts of resources are being devoted to these interventions, but do they ensure or improve quality of care? There is little research evidence as to their effectiveness or the conditions for maximum effectiveness. Reasons for the lack of evaluation research include the methodological challenges of measuring outcomes and attributing causality to these complex, changing, long term social interventions to organisations or health systems, which themselves are complex and changing. However, methods are available which can be used to evaluate these programmes and which can provide decision makers with research based guidance on how to plan and implement them. This paper describes the research challenges, the methods which can be used, and gives examples and guidance for future research. It emphasises the important contribution which such research can make to improving the effectiveness of these programmes and to developing the science of qualify improvement.

A quality programme is the planned activities carried out by an organisation or health system to improve quality. It covers a range of interventions which are more complex than a single quality team improvement project or the quality activities in one department. Quality programmes include programmes for a whole organisation (such as a hospital total quality programme), for teams from many organisations (for example, a "collaborative" programme), for external reviews of organisations in an area (for example, a quality accreditation programme), for changing practice in many organisations (for example, a practice guidelines formulation and implementation programme), and for a national or regional quality strategy which itself could include any or all of the above. These programmes create conditions which help or hinder smaller quality improvement projects.

Quality improvement programmes are new "social medical technologies" which are increasingly being applied. One study noted 11 different types of programmes in the UK NHS in a recent 3 year period.[1] They probably consume more resources than any treatment and have potentially greater consequences for patient safety and other clinical outcomes. Yet we know little of their effectiveness or relative cost effectiveness, or how to ensure they are well implemented.

Decision makers and theorists have many questions about these programmes:

- Do they achieve their objectives and, if so, at what cost?
- Why are some more successful than others?
- What are the factors and conditions critical for success?
- What does research tell us about how to improve their effectiveness?

Some anecdotal answers come from the reports of consultants and participants, and there are theories about "critical success factors" for some types of programme. However, until recently there was little independent and systematic research about effectiveness and the conditions for effectiveness. Indeed, there was little descriptive research which documented the activities which people actually undertook when implementing a programme.

Research has made some progress in answering these questions, but perhaps not as much as was hoped, in part because of the methodological challenges. This paper first briefly notes some of the research before describing the challenges and the research designs which can be used. It finishes with suggestions for developing research in this field.

Research into quality improvement programmes

The most studied subcategory of quality programmes is hospital quality programmes, particularly US hospital total quality management programmes (TQM), later called continuous quality improvement programmes (CQI). Several non-systematic reviews have been carried out (Box 29.1).[2-6]

There is evidence from some studies that certain factors appear to be necessary to motivate and sustain implementation and to create conditions likely to produce results. The most commonly reported are senior management commitment, sustained attention and the right type of management roles at different levels, a focus on customer needs, physician involvement, sufficient resources, careful programme management, practical and relevant training which personnel can use immediately, and the right culture.[4-13] These demanding conditions for success raise questions about whether the type of quality programmes which have been tried are feasible for health care. These limited conclusions appear similar across public and private, and across nations. However, there is little research for non-US clinics and hospitals, for public hospitals, or systematic comparative investigation to support this impression.

Box 29.1   Non-systematic reviews of hospital quality programmes

The general conclusions of non-systematic reviews of hospital quality programmes are:

- The label given to a programme (for example, "TQM") is no guide to the activities which are actually carried out: programmes with the same name are implemented very differently at different rates, coverage, and depth in the organisation.
- Few hospitals seem to have achieved significant results and little is known about any long term results.
- Few studies describe or compare different types of hospital quality programmes, especially non-TQM/CQI programmes.
- Most studies have severe limitations (see later).

With regard to research methods, studies have tended to rely on quality specialists or senior managers for information about the programme and its impact, and to survey them once retrospectively. Future studies need to gather data from a wider range of sources and over a longer period of time. Data should also be gathered to assess the degree of implementation of the programme. Implementation should not be assumed; evidence is needed as to exactly which changes have been made and when. Outcomes need to be viewed in relation to how deeply and broadly the programme was implemented and the stage or "maturity" of the programme. To date, for most studies the lack of evidence of impact may simply reflect the fact that the programmes were not implemented, even though some respondents may say they had been. Assessing the degree of implementation could also help to formulate explanations of outcomes. There is a need for studies of organisations which are similar apart from their use of quality methods and ideas, as well the need for more studies to use the same measures—for example, of results, of culture, or of other variables. Many of these points also apply to research into other types of quality programmes.

Other quality improvement programmes

Few other types of quality improvement programmes have been systematically studied or evaluated; there are few studies of national or regional programmes such as guideline implementation or of the effectiveness of quality review or accreditation processes.[14] Managers have reported that organisations which received low scores ("probation") on the US Joint Commission for Accreditation of Healthcare Organisations assessment were given high scores 3 years later but had not made substantive changes.[6] Few studies have described or assessed the validity or value of the many comparative quality assessment systems,[15–18] of external evaluation processes,[19–24] or have studied national or regional quality strategies or programmes in primary health care.[25]

More evaluation research is also being undertaken into quality improvement collaboratives. This is part of a new wave of research which is revealing more about the conditions which organisations and managers need to create in order to foster, sustain and spread effective projects and changes. Collaboratives are similar to hospital quality programmes in that they usually involve project teams, but the teams are from different organisations. The structure of the collaborative and the steps to be taken is more prescribed than most hospital quality programmes.

One study has drawn together the results of evaluations of different collaboratives.[26] This study provides knowledge which can be used to develop collaboratives working on other subjects, helps to understand factors critical to success, and also demonstrates other research methods which can be used to study some types of quality programmes. The study concluded that there was some evidence that quality collaboratives can help some teams to make significant improvements quickly if the collaborative is carefully planned and managed, and if the team has the right conditions. It suggested that a team's success depended on their ability to work as a team, their ability to learn and apply quality methods, the strategic importance of their work to their home organisation, the culture of their home organisation, and the type and degree of support from management. This can help teams and their managers to decide whether they have, or can create, the conditions to be able to benefit from taking part in what can be a costly programme.

There is therefore little research into quality programmes which meets rigorous scientific criteria, but some of the research which has been done does provide guidance for decision makers which is more valid than the reports of consultants or participants. There is clearly a need for more evaluations and other types of studies of quality programmes which answer the questions of decision makers and also build theory about large scale interventions to complex health organisations or health systems. The second part of this paper considers the designs and methods which could be used in future research.

Research challenges

These interventions are difficult to evaluate using experimental methods. Many programmes are evolving, and involve a number of activities which start and finish at different times. These activities may be mutually reinforcing and have a synergistic effect if they are properly implemented: many quality programmes are a "system" of activities. Some quality programmes are implemented over a long period of time; many cannot be standardised and need to be changed to suit the situation in ways which are different from the way in which a treatment is changed to suit a patient.

The targets of the interventions are not patients but whole organisations or social groups which vary more than the physiology of an individual patient: they can be considered as complex adaptive social systems.[27] There are many short and long term outcomes which usually need to be studied from the perspectives of different parties. It is difficult to prove that these outcomes are due to the programme and not to something else, given the changing nature of each type of programme, their target, the environment, and the time scales involved. They are carried out over time in a changing economic, social, and political climate which influences how they are implemented.[28]

One view is that each programme and situation is unique and no generalisations can be made to other programmes elsewhere. This may be true for some programmes, but even then a description of the programme and its context allows others to assess the relevance of the programme and the findings to their local situation. However, at present researchers do not have agreed frameworks to structure their descriptions and allow comparisons, although theories do exist about which factors are critical.

Quasi-experimental designs can be used:[29–30] it may be possible to standardise the intervention, control its implementation, and use comparison programmes within the same environment in order to exclude other possible influences on outcomes. One issue is that many programmes are local interpretations of principles; many are not standardised specific interventions that can be replicated. Indeed, they should not be: flexible implementation for the local situation appears to be important for success.[5] TQM/CQI is more a philosophy and set of principles than a specific set of steps and actions to be implemented by all organisations, although some models do come close to prescribing detailed steps.

Research designs

The difficulties in evaluating these programmes do not mean that they cannot or should not be evaluated. There are a number of designs and methods which can and have been used: these are summarised below and discussed in detail elsewhere.[28–34]

Box 29.2 A qualitative evaluation of external reviews of clinical governance

One example which illustrates the use of qualitative methods is a study of the UK government's programme of external review of clinical governance arrangements in public healthcare provider organisations.[35] Members of the review team as well as senior clinicians and managers were interviewed in 47 organisations before and after the review. A qualitative analysis identified themes and issues and reported common views about how the review process could be improved.

Although most interviewees thought the reviews gave a valid picture of clinical governance, much of the knowledge produced was already known to them but had not been made explicit. It concluded that major changes in policy, strategy, or direction in the organisations had not occurred as a result of the reviews, and suggested that the use of the same process for all organisations was "at best wasteful of resources and perhaps even positively harmful". This study provided the only independent description of the review process and of different stakeholders' assessments as to its value and how the process could be improved. The findings were useful to the reviewers to refine their programme. One of the limitations of the study was that it did not investigate outcomes further than the interviewees' perceptions of impact: "measuring impact reliably is difficult and different stakeholders may have quite different subjective perceptions of impact".[35]

Descriptive case design

This design simply aims to describe the programme as implemented. There is no attempt to gather data about outcomes, but knowledgeable stakeholders' expectations of outcome and perceptions of the strengths and weaknesses of the programme can be gathered. Why is this descriptive design sometimes useful? Some quality programmes are prescribed and standardised—for example, a quality accreditation or external review. In these cases a description of the intervention activities is available which others can use to understand what was done and to replicate the intervention. However, many programmes are implemented in different ways or not described, or may only be described as principles and without a strategy. For the researcher a first description of the programme as implemented saves wasting time looking for impact further down the causal chain (for example, patient outcomes) when few or no activities have actually been implemented.

Audit design

This design takes a written statement about what people should do, such as a protocol or plan, and compares this with what they actually do. This is a quick and low cost evaluation design which is useful when there is evidence that following a programme or protocol will result in certain outcomes. It can be used to describe how far managers and health personnel follow prescriptions for quality programme interventions and why they may diverge from these prescriptions. "Audit" research of quality accreditation or review processes can help managers to develop more cost effective reviews.[35]

Prospective before-after designs: single case or comparative

The single case prospective design gathers specific data about the target of the intervention before and after (or during) the intervention. Outcomes are considered as the differences between the before and after data collected about the target. The immediate target is the organisation and personnel; the ultimate targets are patients.

Box 29.3   Example of a theory testing comparative design

The first comprehensive studies of effectiveness of TQM/CQI programmes in health care also tried to establish which factors were critical for "success".[8-10] The methods used in these studies were to survey 67 hospitals, some with programmes and some without, and later 61 hospitals with TQM programmes, asking questions about the programme and relating certain factors to quality performance improvement. The findings were that, after 3 years, the hospitals could not report clear evidence of results and that few had tackled clinical care processes.

A later study tested hypotheses about associations between organisation and cultural factors and performance.[11] Interviews and surveys were undertaken in 10 selected hospitals. Performance improvements were found in most programmes in satisfaction, market share, and economic efficiency as measured by length of stay, unit costs, and labour productivity. Interestingly, culture was only found to influence the patient satisfaction performance. It was easier for smaller hospitals with fewer complex services to implement CQI. Early physician involvement was also associated with CQI success, a finding reported in other studies.[6-7]

This set of studies has a practical value. The findings give managers a reliable foundation for assessing whether they have the conditions which are likely to result in a successful programme. Another strength of this study was to assess the "depth" of implementation by using Baldridge or EFQM award categories.[19, 21] Limitations of the study were that: precise descriptions of the nature of the different hospital programmes were not given; only one site data gathering visit was undertaken; and less than 2 years was taken for the investigation so that the way the programmes changed and whether they were sustained could not be gauged. Follow up studies would add to our knowledge of the long term evolution of these programmes, any long term results, and explanations about why some hospitals were more successful than others.

Comparative before-after designs produce stronger evidence that any outcomes were due to the programme and not to something else. If the comparable unit has no intervention, this design allows some control for competing explanations of outcomes if the units have similar characteristics and environments. These are quasi-experimental or "theory testing" designs because the researcher predicts changes to the one or more before-after variables, and then gathers the data before and after the intervention (for example, personnel attitudes towards quality) to test the prediction. However, when limited to studying only before-after (or later) differences, these designs do not generate explanations about why any changes occurred (Box 29.2).

Retrospective or concurrent evaluation designs: single case or comparative

In these designs the researcher can use either a quasi-experimental "theory testing" approach or a "theory building" approach. An example of the former is the "prediction testing survey" design. The researcher studies previous theories or empirical research to identify theorised critical success factors—for example, sufficient resources, continuity of management, aspects of culture—and then tests these to find which are associated with successful and unsuccessful programmes (Box 29.3).

Box 29.4 Example of an action evaluation comparative design

A 4 year comparative action evaluation study of six Norwegian hospitals provided evidence about results and critical factors.[4,7,36] It gave the first detailed and long term description about what hospitals in a public system actually did and how the programmes changed over time. The study found consistencies between the six sites in the factors critical for success: management and physician involvement at all levels, good data systems, the right training, and effective project team management. A 9 year follow up is planned.

In contrast, a "theory building" approach involves the researcher in gathering data about the intervention, context, and possible effects during or after the intervention (Box 29.4). To describe the programme as it was implemented, the researcher asks different informants to describe the activities which were actually undertaken.[30] The validity of these subjective perceptions can be increased by interviewing a cross section of informants, by asking informants for any evidence which they can suggest which would prove or disprove their perceptions, and by comparing data from difference sources to identify patterns in the data (Box 29.4).[30,32,33]

The choice of design depends on the type of quality programme (short or long term, prescribed or flexible, stable or changing), for whom the research is being undertaken, and the questions to be addressed (Was it carried out as planned? Did it achieve its objectives? What were the outcomes? What explains outcomes or success or failure?). Descriptive, audit, and single case retrospective designs are quicker to complete and are cheaper but do not give information about outcomes. Comparative outcome designs can introduce some degree of control, thus making possible inferences about critical factors if good descriptions of the programmes and their context are also provided.

Improving future research

Some of the shortcomings of research into quality programmes have been presented earlier. The five most common are:

- Implementation assessment failure: the study does not examine the extent to which the programme was actually carried out. Was the intervention implemented fully, in all areas and to the required "depth", and for how long?
- Outcome assessment failure: the study does not assess any outcomes or a sufficiently wide range of outcomes such as short and long term impact on the organisation, on patients, and on resources consumed.
- Outcome attribution failure: the study does not establish whether the outcomes can unambiguously be attributed to the intervention, or whether something else caused the outcomes.
- Explanation failure: there is no theory or model which explains how the intervention caused the outcomes and which factors and conditions were critical.
- Measurement variability: different researchers use very different data to describe or measure the quality programme process, structure, and outcome. It is therefore difficult to use the results of one study to question or support another or to build up knowledge systematically.

Future evaluations would be improved by attention to the following:

(1) Assessing or measuring the level of implementation of the intervention
(2) Validating "implementation assessment"
(3) Wider outcome assessment
(4) Longitudinal studies
(5) More attention to economics
(6) Explanatory theory
(7) Common definitions and measures
(8) Tools to predict and explain programme effectiveness

Assessing or measuring the level of implementation of the intervention

Studies need to assess how "broadly" the programme penetrated the organisation (did it reach all parts?), how "deeply" it was applied in each part, and for how long it was applied. One of the first rules of evaluation is "assume nothing has been implemented—get evidence of what has been implemented, where and for how long".[30] There is no point looking for outcomes until this has been established. Instruments for assessing "stage of implementation" or "maturation" need to be developed such as the adaptation of the Baldridge criteria used in the study by Shortell et al[5] or other instruments.

Validating "implementation assessment"

Survey responses are one data source for assessing level of implementation and are useful for selecting organisations for further studies. However, these responses need to be gathered from a cross section of personnel, at different times, and supplemented by site visits and other data sources to improve validity.

Wider outcome assessment

With regard to short term impact, data need to be gathered from a wide cross section of organisational personnel and other stakeholders and from other data sources. Most studies also need to gather data about long term outcomes and to assess carefully the extent to which these outcomes can be attributed to the programme. The outcome data to be gathered should be determined by a theory predicting effects, which builds on previous research, or in terms of the specified objectives of the programme, and these links should be made clear in the report.

Longitudinal studies

Retrospective single surveys provide data which is of limited use. We need more prospective studies which follow the dynamics of the programme over long timescales. Many future studies will need to investigate both the intervention and the outcomes over an extended period of time. Very little is known about whether these programmes are continued and how they might change, or about long term outcomes.

More attention to economics

No studies have assessed the resources consumed by a quality improvement programme or the resource consequences of the outcomes. The suspected high initial costs of implementation would look different if more was known about the costs of sustaining the programme and about the possible savings and economic benefits.[37] Long term evaluations may also uncover more outcomes, benefits, or "side effects" which are not discovered in short studies.

Explanatory theory

For hospital programmes there is no shortage of theories about how to implement them and the conditions needed for success, but few are empirically based. For both practical and scientific reasons, future studies need to test these theories or build theories about what helps and hinders implementation at different stages, and about how the intervention produce any discovered outcomes. For other types of quality programmes there is very little theory of any type. Innovation adoption[38] and diffusion theories are one source of ideas for building explanatory theories, for understanding level of implementation, and for understanding why some organisations are able to apply or benefit more from the intervention than others.[38]

Box 29.5 Steps for studying a quality improvement programme

The methods used depend on who the research is for (the research user), the questions to be addressed, and the type of programme. An example of one action evaluation research strategy is presented here.[30,36]

- Conceptualise the intervention. At an early stage, form a simple model of the component parts of the programme and of the activities carried out at different times. This model can be built up from programme documents or any plans or descriptions which already exist, or from previous theories about the intervention.
- Find and review previous research about similar programmes and make predictions. Identify which factors are suggested by theory or evidence to be critical for the success of the programme. Identify which variables have been studied before and how data were collected.
- Identify research questions which arise out of previous research and/or which are of interest to the users of the research.
- Consider whether the intervention can be controlled in its implementation (would people agree to follow a prescribed approach or have they done so if it is a retrospective study?). If not, design part of the study to gather data to describe the programme as implemented and to assess the level of implementation. Consider whether comparisons could be made with similar or non-intervention sites—for example, to help exclude competing explanations for outcomes or to discover assisting and hindering factors.
- Plan methods to use to investigate how the programme was actually carried out, the different activities performed, and to assess the level of implementation. Gather data about the sequence of activities and how the programme changed over time. Use documentary data sources, observation, interviews, or surveys as appropriate describing how informants or other data sources were selected and possible bias. Note differences between the planned programme and the programme in action, and participants' explanations for this as well as other explanations.
- Plan methods to gather data about the effects of the programme on providers and patients if possible. Data may be participants' subjective perceptions, or more objective before and after data (for example, complaints, clinical outcomes), or both. Use data collected by the programme participants to monitor progress and results if these data are valid. Consider how to capture data about unintended side effects—for example, better personnel recruitment and retention.
- Consider other explanations for discovered effects apart from the programme and assess their plausibility.
- To communicate the findings, create a model of the programme which shows the component parts over time, the main outcomes, and factors and conditions which appear to be critical in producing the outcomes.

Specify the limitations of the study, the degree of certainty about the findings, and the answers to the research questions.

Common definitions and measures

Most studies to date have used their own definitions and measures of effects of quality programmes. This is now limiting our ability to compare and contrast results from different evaluation studies and to build a body of knowledge.

Tools to predict and explain programme effectiveness

Future research needs to go beyond measuring effectiveness and to give decision makers tools to predict the effects of their programmes. Decision theory models could be used to create such tools, as could tools which effectively predict the outcomes of particular improvement projects.[39]

In addition there is a need for overviews and theories of quality improvement programmes; we have not described the full range of interventions which fall within this category and have only given a limited discussion of a few. Future research studies need to describe the range of complex large scale quality interventions increasingly being carried out and their characteristics—for example, to describe and compare national or regional quality programmes. More consideration is needed of the similarities and differences between them, of what can be learned from considering the group as a whole, and of how theories from organisation, change management, sociology, and innovation studies can contribute to building theories about these interventions (Box 29.5).

Conclusions

Although there is research evidence that some discrete quality team projects are effective, there is little evidence that any large scale quality programmes bring significant benefits or are worth the cost. However, neither is there strong evidence that there are no benefits or that resources are being wasted. The changing and complex features of quality programmes, their targets, and the contexts make them difficult to evaluate using conventional medical research experimental evaluation methods, but this does not mean that they cannot be evaluated or investigated in other ways. Quasi-experimental evaluation methods and other social science methods can be used. These methods may not produce the degree of certainty that is produced by a triple blind randomised controlled trial of a treatment, but they can give insights into how these processes work to produce their effects.

Conclusive evidence of effectiveness may never be possible. At this stage a more realistic and useful research strategy is to describe a programme and its context and discover factors which are critical for successful implementation as judged by different parties. In a relatively short time this will provide useful data for a more "research informed management" of these programmes.

A science is only as good as its research methods. The science of quality improvement is being developed by research into how changes to organisation and practice improve patient outcomes. However, insufficient attention has been given to methods for evaluating and understanding large scale programmes for improving quality. As these programmes are increasingly used, there is particular need for studies which do not only assess effectiveness, but also examine how best to implement them.

Notes

1   West E. Management matters: the link between hospital organisation and quality of patient care. *Qual Health Care* 2001;**10**:40–8.
2   Bigelow B, Arndt, M. Total quality management: field of dreams. *Health Care Manage Rev* 1995;**20**:15–25.
3   Motwani J, Sower V, Brasier L. Implementing TQM in the health care sector. *Health Care Manage Rev* 1996;**21**:73–82.
4   Øvretveit J, Aslaksen A. *The quality journeys of six Norwegian hospitals*. Oslo: Norwegian Medical Association, 1999.
5   Shortell S, Bennet C, Byck G. Assessing the impact of continuous quality improvement on clinical practice: what will it take to accelerate progress. *Milbank Quarterly* 1998;**76**:593–624.
6   Blumenthal D, Kilo C. A report card on continuous quality improvement. *Milbank Quarterly* 1998;**76**:625–48.
7   Øvretveit J. The Norwegian approach to integrated quality development. *J Manage Med* 2001;**15**:125–41.
8   Shortell S, O'Brien J, Hughes H, *et al.* Assessing the progress of TQM in US hospitals: findings from two studies. *Quality Leader* 1994;**6**:14–17.
9   Shortell M, O'Brien J, Carman J, *et al.* Assessing the impact of continuous quality improvement/total quality management: concept versus implementation. *Health Serv Res* 1995;**30**:377–401.
10 Carman JM, Shortell SM, Foster RW, *et al.* Keys for successful implementation of total qualify management in hospitals. *Health Care Manage Rev* 1996;**21**:48–60.
11 Boerster H, Foster E, O'Connor, *et al.* Implementation of total quality management: conventional wisdom versus reality. *Hospital Health Serv Admin* 1996;**41**:143–59.
12 Gustafson D, Hundt A. Findings of innovation research applied to quality management principles for health care. *Health Care Manage Rev* 1995;**20**:16–24.
13 Gustafson D, Risberg L, Gering D, *et al. Case studies from the quality improvement support system.* ACHPR Research Report 97–0022. Washington: US Department of Health and Human Services, 1997.
14 Shaw C. External assessment of health care. *BMJ* 2001;**322**:851–4.

15 Thompson R, McElroy H, Kazandjian V. Maryland hospital quality indicator project in the UK. *Qual Health Care* 1997;**6**:49–55.
16 Cleveland Health Quality Choice Program (CHQCP). Summary report from the Cleveland Health Quality Choice Program. *Qual Manage Health Care* 1995;**3**:78–90.
17 Rosenthal G, Harper D. Cleveland health quality choice. *Jt Comm J Qual Improve* 1994;**8**:425–42.
18 Pennsylvania Health Care Cost Containment Council (PHCCCC). *Hospital effectiveness report.* Harrisburg: Pennsylvania Health Care Cost Containment Council, 1992.
19 National Institute of Standards and Technology (NIST). *The Malcum Baldridge national quality award 1990 application guidelines.* Gaithersburg, MD: National Institute of Standards and Technology, 1990.
20 Hertz H, Reimann C, Bostwick M. The Malcolm Baldridge National Quality Award concept: could it help stimulate or accelerate healthcare quality improvement? *Qual Manage Health Care* 1994;**2**:63–72.
21 European Foundation for Quality Management (EFQM). *The European Quality Award 1992.* Brussels: European Foundation for Quality Management, 1992.
22 Sweeney J, Heaton C. Interpretations and variations of ISO 9000 in acute health care. *Int J Qual Health Care* 2000;**12**:203–9.
23 Shaw C. External quality mechanisms for health care: summary of the ExPeRT project on visitatie, accreditation, EFQM and ISO assessment in European Union countries. *Int J Qual Health Care* 2000;**12**:169–75.
24 Øvretveit J. Quality assessment and comparative indicators in the Nordic countries. *Int J Health Planning Manage* 2001;**16**:229–41.
25 Wensing M, Grol R. Single and combined strategies for implementing changes in primary care: a literature review. *Int J Qual Health Care* 1994;**6**:115–32.
26 Øvretveit J. How to run an effective improvement collaborative. *Int J Health Care Qual Assur* 2002;**15**:33–44.
27 Plsek P, Wilson T. Complexity science: complexity, leadership, and management in healthcare organisations. *BMJ* 2001;**323**:746–9.
28 Øvretveit J. Evaluating hospital quality programmes. *Evaluation* 1997;**3**:451–68.
29 Cook T, Campbell D. *Quasi-experimentation: design and analysis issues for field settings.* Chicago: Rand McNally, 1979.
30 Øvretveit J. *Action evaluation of health programmes and change: a handbook for a user focused approach.* Oxford: Radcliffe Medical Press, 2002.
31 Øvretveit J. *Evaluating health interventions.* Milton Keynes: Open University Press, 1998.
32 Yin R. *Case study research: design and methods.* Beverly Hills: Sage, 1994.
33 Jick T. Mixing qualitative and quantitative methods: triangulation in action. In: Van Maanen J, ed. *Qualitative methodology.* Beverly Hills: Sage, 1983.

34 Ferlie E, Gabbay J, FitzGerald F, *et al.* Evidence-based medicine and organisational change: an overview of some recent qualitative research. In Mark A, Dopson S, eds. *Organisational behaviour in healthcare: the research agenda.* London: Macmillan, 1999.

35 Walshe K, Wallace L, Freeman T, *et al.* The external review of quality improvement in healthcare organisations: a qualitative study. *Int J Qual Health Care* 2001;**13**:367–74.

36 Øvretveit J. *Integrated quality development for public healthcare.* Oslo: Norwegian Medical Association, 1999.

37 Øvretveit J. The economics of quality: a practical approach. *Int J Health Care Qual Assur* 2000;**13**:200–7.

38 Rogers E. *Diffusion of innovation.* New York: Free Press, 1983.

39 Gustafson D, Cats-Baril W, Alemei F. *Systems to support health policy analysis.* Ann Arbor: Health Administration Press, University of Michigan, 1992.

PART 7

General management and governance

Introduction by Naomi Chambers

In the beginning, there were governors, superintendents and administrators. But against the backcloth of the dawning of the 'new public management' era, the language used to describe the management of health services began to change dramatically in the 1980s. This part focuses on classic texts that have given us some of the new language which we now use, whose ideas endure and whose messages have not dated, and more recent pieces, which are exceptional in helping to make sense of the complexities of health management and governance today.

Herbert Simon (1997) was not concerned with healthcare but he has provided us with an early explication of the limitations of the traditional 'rational economic man' approach to management and administration, which was expanded on later by Mintzberg (1973). In particular, Simon introduced us to the concepts of 'bounded rationality' and 'satisficing'. Very simply, bounded rationality recognizes that in the real world of organizational life, there are limits to the alternative courses of action that can be chosen to solve a problem (because of lack of time, understanding, etc.) and that an administrator (to use the term which was current at the time that Simon wrote) has to make a choice that is 'good enough'; in other words, which satisfices.

As administrators became managers, public management from the 1970s became recognized as both an activity and as a field of study (Hood, 2005). 'New public management' (NPM) then developed out of the identification of the design principles and tools for government reforms that were taking place across a number of countries from the 1980s onwards, and which contrasted with the structures and processes associated with classical government bureaucracies. These included the use of performance management tools, decentralization, outsourcing, privatization and marketization, and the general infiltration of private sector methods into the public sector.

In retrospect, one of the earliest examples of NPM in action was the adoption of the Griffiths report by government. In his letter to the Minister of Health, which constitutes what must rank as the most succinct report ever written about or for the NHS, Sir Roy Griffiths (1983) delivered a courteous but devastating critique of its management. Controversially at the time, Griffiths argued that there are overwhelming similarities rather than deep differences between health management and business management. Griffiths' diagnosis included imprecise management objectives and their monitoring, little measurement of health output, sparse clinical or economic evaluation of particular practices, or sense of how well the service is meeting the needs of the patient and the community. As far as change is concerned, he described the NHS as floating and directionless like a 'mobile', with the labyrinthine processes of consultation resulting in institutionalized stagnation. In bemoaning the absence of identifiable individuals performing the general management role, he eloquently summoned the famous spirit from nineteenth-century nursing in one of the most repeated and memorable descriptions of the challenge for NHS management: '... If Florence Nightingale were carrying her lamp through the corridors of the NHS today she would almost certainly be searching for the people in charge ...' (Griffiths, 1983: 12).

Griffiths' prescription included a new general manager role that would focus on five areas: leadership, cost improvement, motivation of staff, the gearing of professional functions to the overall objectives of the service and consultation for major service reconfiguration. These remain fundamental considerations for health service managers today. Indeed, his report provided the architecture for the management structures still largely in place in the NHS, including resource budgeting (now with the advent of foundation trusts described as service-line economics), the involvement of doctors in management, and the accountability for financial and service quality of the hospital chief executive (Griffiths, 1983). Although geared towards the UK NHS, his diagnosis and prescription has international as well as timeless resonance.

The advent of new roles for the senior managers in the UK NHS also brought new responsibilities for managing strategic change. Andrew Pettigrew, Ewan Ferlie and Lorna McKee's (1992) analysis of the characteristics associated with achieving successful change is simple, compelling and remains pertinent today. They describe eight linked conditions, which are referred to as receptive contexts for change, and which provide high energy around change. The list is familiar and is reproduced from the original text in diagrammatic form in Figure 31.1 but is worth repeating here, almost as a mantra for managers: quality and coherence of policy, positive environmental pressure, supportive organizational culture, fit between change agenda and its locale, simplicity and clarity of goals and priorities, cooperative interorganizational networks, productive managerial–clinical relations and availability of key people leading the change.

Selecting a couple of these conditions, managerial–clinical relations and cooperative interorganisational networks, their continuing relevance can be simply demonstrated. First, we have already alluded to the focus on managerial–clinical relations that has been emphasized by writers from Griffiths and Enthoven onwards, and is also given special mention in the Darzi report (2008). Second, later writers on public leadership have emphasized the importance of building long-term intersectoral relationships and leading across organizations (e.g. Goodwin, 2005; Brookes, 2006). Pettigrew and colleagues also argue that this framework of understanding about change is dynamic: nonreceptivity can move to receptivity, patterns of connections across the eight factors will vary according to local circumstances, and the process will be emergent and iterative. This perspective on strategy presages the emphasis from the late 1990s on understanding and managing health care as a complex adaptive system (e.g. Plsek and Wilson, 2001).

Carrying a central role in relation to strategy, and at the apex of the organization, the work and performance of boards remain problematic. Bob Garratt (1997) has helped significantly in clarifying the responsibilities of directors, the cycle of board activities and balance of board work although his contribution is not always acknowledged in the manuals of best practice. One of his main lines of argument is that there is a clear and iterative cycle of activities in what he calls the 'learning board', which cover policy formulation, strategic thinking, supervision of management and accountability to stakeholders as well as an appropriate balance of attention that should be paid to internal (can you hear your baby cry?) and external issues. As with Higgs (2003), but perhaps going further, he also underlines the need for independence of thought among all directors, not just the non-executive directors. This is a current source of tension in the NHS and one of the paradoxes of the unitary board structure that allows executives to be called to account while they are also full members.

Cornforth (2003) picks up this issue of the paradox at the centre of board working in his typology of public sector boards. He describes broadly six types. At one end, in the compliance model, the board members control and supervise management decisions, and at the other end, in the rubber stamp model, board meetings are largely symbolic and tend to ratify decisions taken by management. In between there is a supporter's club model where the focus is on the improvement of external stakeholder relations, a political model in which a democratic perspective holds sway with different members' interests represented, a co-option model focused on boundary spanning and securing resources from external sources, and finally a partnership model where, as experts, the executives and non-executives share interests and work closely together. Uncreative conflict may occur when individuals hold quite different beliefs about their board and their role on it and it is worth exploring individual perceptions with a degree of honesty to surface these differences. Finally, Cornforth makes a plea for the *reflexive board*, which involves boards consciously trying to develop a greater understanding of their performance, roles and behaviours and making time for board reflection and development.

Garratt and Cornforth both allude to one legitimate role of the board and its meetings, as the performance of an oft-repeated organizational ritual that sends important messages internally and externally about the purpose and values of the organization. Edward Peck, Perri 6, Pauline Gulliver and David Towell and colleagues (2004) elaborate on this further by examining three theories of ritual in relation to boards: as methods of, first, sustaining social solidarity between members of an elite, and second, of institutionalizing codes of speech and, third, of creating consistent patterns of response. They go on to map the different kinds of ritual behaviour that go with the four basic forms of organization drawn from Durkheim's theory of social integration, and indicate some of the consequences of overuse of single forms. In an echo of Cornforth's paradox perspective, they refer also to the principle of requisite variety (Jessop, 2003) in their recommendation about the need for variety and flexibility in the ritual framing of meetings in order to reflect the complexity of the institutional context of health care.

Summary

- There has been a switch from an emphasis on administration to management in health care that mirrors the development of new public management (NPM).
- Private sector models have been influential in recent thinking about strategic and operational management in health care.
- Healthcare boards carry a series of inbuilt tensions as a result of structures, organizational behaviours and rituals.

References and further reading

Brookes, S. (2006) Out with the old, in with the new: why excellent public leadership makes a difference to partnership working, *British Journal of Leadership in Public Services*, 2(1): 52–64.

Darzi, A. (2008) *High Quality Care for All: NHS Next Stage Review Final Report*. London: Department of Health.

Goodwin, N. (2005) *Leadership in Healthcare: A European Perspective*. London: Routledge.

Higgs, D. (2003) *Review of the Role and Effectiveness of Non–executive Directors*. Great Britain Department of Trade and Industry, London: The Stationery Office.

Hood, H. (2005) *Public Management: The Word, The Movement, The Science* in E. Ferlie, L. Lynn and C. Pollitt (eds) *The Oxford Handbook of Public Management*. Oxford: Oxford University Press.

Jessop, B. (2003) *Governance and Meta-governance: On Reflexivity, Requisite Variety and Requisite Irony* in Bang H.P. (ed). *Governance as Social and Political Communication*. Manchester: Manchester: University Press.

Mintzberg, H. (1973) *The Nature of Managerial Work*. New York: Harper Row.

Plsek, P. and Wilson, T. (2001) Complexity, leadership, and management in healthcare organisations, *British Medical Journal*, 323: 746–49.

Simon, H. A. (1997) *Administrative Behaviour: Rationality in Human Behaviour*. New York: The Free Press.

The selections

Griffiths, R. (1983) *Report of the NHS Management Inquiry*. London: HMSO.

Pettigrew, A. Ferlie, E. and McKee, L. (1992) *Shaping Strategic Change*. London: Sage Publications.

Garratt, B. (1997) *The Fish Rots from the Head: This Crisis in our Boardrooms; Developing the Crucial Skills of the Competent Director*. London: HarperCollins.

Cornforth, C. (2003) *The Governance of Public and Non–profit Organisations*. London: Routledge.

Peck, E., Perri 6, Gulliver, P. and Towell, D. (2004) Why do we keep on meeting like this? The board as ritual in health and social care, *Health Services Management Research*, 17: 100–109.

30

Report of the NHS management inquiry
Roy Griffiths

Extracts from Griffiths R (1983) Report of the NHS Management Inquiry, London: HMSO.

General observations

1.   We were brought in not to be instant experts on all aspects of the NHS but, because of our business experience, to advise on the management of the NHS. We have been told that the NHS is different from business in management terms, not least because the NHS is not concerned with the profit motive and must be judged by wider social standards which cannot be measured. These differences can be greatly overstated. The clear similarities between NHS management and business management are much more important. In many organisations in the private sector, profit does not immediately impinge on large numbers of managers below Board level. They are concerned with levels of service, quality of product, meeting budgets, cost improvement, productivity, motivating and rewarding staff, research and development, and the long term viability of the undertaking. All things that Parliament is urging on the NHS. In the private sector the results in all these areas would normally be carefully monitored against pre-determined standards and objectives.

2.   The NHS does not have the profit motive, but it is, of course, enormously concerned with control of expenditure. Surprisingly, however, it still lacks any real continuous evaluation of its performance against criteria such as those set out above. Rarely are precise management objectives set; there is little measurement of health output; clinical evaluation of particular practices is by no means common and economic evaluation of those practices extremely rare. Nor can the NHS display a ready assessment of the effectiveness with which it is meeting the needs and expectations of the people it serves. Businessmen have a keen sense of how well they are looking after their customers. Whether the NHS is meeting the needs of the patient, and the community, and can prove that it is doing so, is open to question.

3.   It therefore cannot be said too often that the National Health Service is about delivering services to people. It is not about organising systems for their own sake. In proposing the NHS in 1944, the Government declared that:

- the real need is to bring the country's full resources to bear upon reducing ill health and promoting good health in all its citizens; and,
- there is a danger of over-organisation, of letting the machine designed to ensure a better service itself stifle the chances of getting one.

Our advice on management action is not directly about the nature of the services provided to patients. But the driving force behind our advice is the concern to secure the best deal for patients and the community within available resources; the best value for the taxpayer; and the best motivation for staff. As a caring, quality service, the NHS has to balance the interests of the patient, the community, the taxpayer and the employees.

4.   One of our most immediate observations from a business background is the lack of a clearly-defined general management function throughout the NHS. By general management we mean the responsibility drawn together in one person, at different levels of the organisation, for planning, implementation and control of performance. The NHS is one of the largest undertakings in Western Europe. It requires enormous resources; its role is very politically sensitive; it demands top class management.

5.   Management in this sense is currently provided only:

a.   by the Secretary of State and the Minister of State (Health), but they have to attend to their many other demanding responsibilities within DHSS, Government and Parliament and to the electorate;
b.   by the Permanent Secretary, but he has also to meet the demands of the other main businesses within the DHSS and the requirement for him to support Ministers in their other responsibilities;
c.   at Regional and District level, by Chairmen appointed on a non-executive, part-time basis (notionally two to three days a week, but in practice often demanding more time).

This position is understandable but the problem arises in that the required management support is given at the centre within the DHSS by senior officials and groups, none of which is concerned full time with the totality of NHS management; and at Regional and District level by professional officers required to work in consensus management teams where each officer has the power of veto.

The position is complicated by the fact that Unit managers (administrator, nurse and clinician) are still being appointed following the 1982 reorganisation. At no level is the general management role clearly being performed by an identifiable individual. In short if Florence Nightingale were carrying her lamp through the corridors of the NHS today she would almost certainly be searching for the people in charge.

6. Absence of this general management support means that there is no driving force seeking and accepting direct and personal responsibility for developing management plans, securing their implementation and monitoring actual achievement. It means that the process of devolution of responsibility, including discharg-

ing responsibility to the Units, is far too slow. The centre is still too much involved in too many of the wrong things and too little involved in some that really matter. For example, local management must be allowed to determine its own needs for information, with higher management drawing on that information for its own purposes. The Units and the Authorities are being swamped with directives without being given direction. Lack of the general management responsibility also means that certain major initiatives are difficult to implement.

7. The accountability review process is a good, recent development which provides a powerful management tool. But the management task is so demanding and continuous that, without moving in the direction we are recommending, it is difficult to see how this process can be sustained effectively given the other pressures on Ministers and senior officials. The Review process needs to be extended beyond Districts to Units of Management, particularly the major hospitals, and it should start with a Unit performance review based on management budgets which involve the clinicians at hospital level. Real output measurement, against clearly stated management objectives and budgets, should become a major concern of management at all levels.

8. Above all, of course, lack of a general management process means that it is extremely difficult to achieve change. To the outsider, it appears that when change of any kind is required, the NHS is so structured as to resemble a "mobile": designed to move with any breath of air, but which, in fact never changes its position and gives no clear indication of direction. There are good reasons as to how this has arisen and, indeed, some argument as to why in fact it is desirable. But, over the rest of the decade when there is likely to be very considerable pressure on resources, at least as compared with likely demand, the NHS needs the ability to move much more quickly. Equally if the emphasis is on devolution, then it needs a strong management process to enable this to be achieved, simply holding at the centre sufficient control to ensure that appropriate standards and services are maintained.

9. On the other hand, the presence of a general management process would be enormously important in:

a) providing the necessary leadership to capitalise on the existing high levels of dedication and expertise among NHS staff of all disciplines, and to stimulate initiative, urgency and vitality;

b) bringing about a constant search for major change and cost improvement. It can be argued that the NHS delivers an effective, low cost, medical service to the individual patient. But, given an effective management process, the same level of care could be delivered more efficiently at lower cost, or a superior service given at the same cost. We were not asked to look for detailed ways of increasing efficiency or making savings, or to highlight specific inefficiencies we may have observed. Line management should be free to determine how to achieve this, drawing on established management techniques and recent developments in audit or "Rayner scrutinies". Major cost improvement programmes can and should be initiated within the NHS, aiming at much higher levels of efficiency to be sustained over much longer periods than at present.

These should carry with them the inbuilt incentive that a significant proportion of the savings made can be used locally to bring about further change and improvement. It is almost a denial of the management process to argue that the modest levels of cost improvement at present required of the NHS are unachievable without impacting seriously on the level of services;

c) securing proper motivation of staff. Those charged with the general management responsibility would regard it as vital to review incentives, rewards and sanctions. Merit awards would be considered. Redeploying the non-efficient performer would also be important, with dismissal as a last resort;

d) ensuring that the professional functions are effectively geared into the overall objectives and responsibilities of the general management process. The primary reporting relationship of the functional managers should be to the general manager, who should set, by agreement with the functional managers, the priorities and programmes for their work. The relationship with the professions at other levels should simply be one of seeking guidance or monitoring of the professional aspects of their work. The present position leads to unnecessary duplication of staff; too many purely professional meetings, from the centre to the Unit; and the tackling of overall tasks in a fragmented and divisive manner. Any apparent advantages of the functional specialisms are nowadays more than offset by the need to establish the general management process effectively;

e) making sense of the process of consultation. The NHS is a matter of considerable importance to all members of the community and is political in the best sense. A very great deal of importance is attached to ensuring that the views of the community at all levels are taken into account in any decision. The reality is, however, that by any business standards the process of consultation is so labyrinthine and the rights of veto so considerable, that the result in many cases is institutionalised stagnation – a result particularly enhanced by the fact that the machinery of implementation is generally weak and, as such, cannot ensure that the processes of consultation are effectively implemented and quickly brought to a conclusion.

16. The Chairman of each Authority should be responsible for initiating this change according to local requirements and possibilities. The main criterion should be the identification of general management skills and experience: the further away from direct patient care the more important it becomes to look for such skills not necessarily professional disciplines. There can be no "single-bullet" solution for the whole of the NHS and the timescale will vary according to the task to be tackled.

The Unit

17. Units of management (particularly the major hospitals) provide the bedrock for the whole NHS management process. It is there where most of the hospital patients are seen, most of the money is spent and most of the staff are employed.

Surprisingly, given the welter of reports on almost every aspect of the NHS over the past 30 years, there has been no major review of the internal management of the hospitals since the Bradbeer Report of 1954 (when most hospitals had an individual manager in the shape of the hospital secretary, house governor or medical superintendent). We have therefore commissioned some small-scale studies, with the support of the clinicians at six hospitals, looking, from the perspective of the patient and the clinician, at the management of the Unit as reflected in the treatment and administrative handling of the patient.

18. The 1982 NHS reorganisation has not yet resulted in the devolution of real decision taking to Unit and hospital level. Many hospitals do not yet have budgets. Most hospitals and Units are big enough in management terms to take all their own day-to-day management decisions. The onus should be on higher management to argue away from this position, if they think there is clear and accepted justification for taking particular decisions at an identified higher level of management.

19. We believe that urgent management action is required, if Units are to fulfil their role and provide the most effective management of their resources. This particularly affects the doctors. Their decisions largely dictate the use of all resources and they must accept the management responsibility which goes with clinical freedom. This implies active involvement in securing the most effective use and management of all resources. The nearer that the management process gets to the patient, the more important it becomes for the doctors to be looked upon as the natural managers. This should be more explicitly recognised:

- in the doctors' training – undergraduate, postgraduate, in-service, and in preparation for particular clinical management posts; and
- in constructing the system of management budgets in a way which supports this work and meets the medical requirement and interest.

20. We have not recommended that all consultants' contracts should be held at District level – even though many strong representations were made to us that that should be the position; we believe that if there is a coherent management process, it should not matter where the contract of employment is held. If our recommendations are implemented, we believe the management problems related to the holding of contracts at present felt to exist would disappear.

21. In identifying a Unit general manager we believe that the District Chairman should go for the best person for the job, regardless of discipline. The main criterion for appointment should be the ability to undertake the general management function at Unit level and manage the total Unit budget.

Other aspects of management

Personnel

22. In the personnel field, as in all other aspects of our recommendations, the essential changes required will need to be led from the top by an energetic, new

style of management. We have accordingly proposed the appointment (initially from outside the NHS and the Civil Service) of a Personnel Director whose main responsibility would be to ensure that personnel relations support the new style of management we are recommending. The opportunities to influence pay, career, appointment and retention of staff are all important aspects of line management's responsibility to ensure real motivation of all staff, characterised by the more thrusting and committed style of management which is implicit in all our recommendations. In particular the Personnel Director would ensure that formal structures of communication and informal means of consultation were established to secure the full commitment and involvement of staff.

31

Shaping strategic change
Andrew Pettigrew, Ewan Ferlie and Lorna McKee

Extracts from Pettigrew A, Ferlie E and McKee L (1992) Shaping Strategic Change. London: Sage Publications.

Receptivity and change in the NHS: the eight factors

The rather scattered and eclectic literature review has established there is not a strong social science tradition of theorizing about receptive context for change. Neither is there a great welter of empirical studies in organizational settings seeking to describe and explain differences in the rate, pace and depth of change in contrasting contexts. Before going on to synthesize our own findings about why Districts facing similar environmental and policy pressures behave at times similarly and at times differently in achieving outcomes, there are some final intellectual caveats to be made about the structure of our argument.

First, the eight factors outlined in Figure 31.1, which are derived inductively from our studies of strategic service change in the NHS, should be seen as providing a linked set of conditions which provide high energy around change. This energy and the capabilities which underpin it cannot be conjured up over a short period of time through the pulling of a single lever. The past weighs a heavy hand in determining local perceptions, and layers of competence emerge only slowly to enable and protect champions of change. The factors represent a pattern of association rather than a simple line of causation, and should be seen as a series of loops rather than a causal path between independent and dependent variables (Pettigrew, 1990).

Secondly, notions of receptivity and non-receptivity are dynamic not static concepts. Receptive contexts for change can be constructed through processes of cumulative development but such processes are reversible, either by the removal of key individuals or ill considered or precipitous action. But movement from non-receptivity to receptivity is equally possible (the Preston acute sector case study perhaps illustrated the beginnings of such a process), encouraged either by the environment or 'policy' changes at higher tiers and by managerial and professional action at local level.

Thirdly, in the way that continued processes are reversible so they are also indeterminate in their outcomes and implications. We are presenting a view of

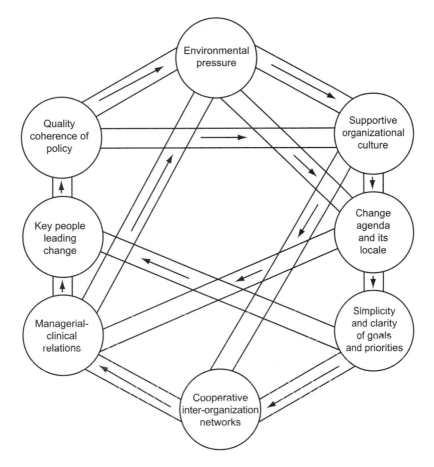

Figure 31.1 Receptive contexts for change: the eight factors

change processes which recognizes emergence, possibility, precariousness and iteration. Although it is possible to identify patterns in such processes (and our eight factors organize such patterns), those factors have to be constructed, maintained, elaborated and fashioned idiosyncratically in particular localities.

Finally, our observations may be limited as our sample has been drawn from Districts selected as carrying a high strategic service change load as defined in the terms current in the mid 1980s. Our Districts may not be typical, and we need to test the robustness of our findings against successor managerial change agendas (see, for example, Pettigrew et al., 1991).

Factor 1: The quality and coherence of 'policy' – analytical and process components

The quality of 'policy' generated at local level was found to be important, both from an analytic and a process perspective. It was not always enough to take perhaps dated central policy 'off the shelf', and the policy as well as the managerial process was important. Analytically, data played a major role in substantiating a solid case, especially in relation to convincing scientific publics, and we would not generally support the argument of 'paralysis by analysis' (Peters and Waterman, 1982). The ordering of such data within clear conceptual thinking helped frame strategic issues, especially where they were initially characterized by complexity and uncertainty, and gave direction. Strong testing of initial thoughts was also important in ensuring that a strategic framework considered questions of coherence between goals, was feasible (a strategy should not create unsolvable problems) and complemented the service strategy with parallel functional strategies (such as finance, human resources, communications).

Perhaps analytical considerations represent necessary conditions, while sufficient conditions relate to attention to processes of negotiation and change. Here the starting point was critical: a broad vision seemed more likely to generate movement than a blueprint. Such broad visions were found to have significant process and implementation benefits in terms of commitment-building and allowing interest groups to buy into the change process, and allowing top-down pressure to be married with bottom-up concern as the field gets scripted in rather than scripted out.

The role of broad, rather imprecise visions in stimulating change processes has also been reported by Pettigrew (1985a), Baier, March and Saetren (1986) and Pettigrew and Whipp (1991). Baier et al. note that policy support may increase with the ambiguity of proposed policies, but at the cost of administrative complications. There may be a threshold effect in operation here. Our own studies of attempts to close psychiatric hospitals demonstrate that the absence of a shared world view at the front end of the policy process can cause inertia.

It was also important to marry strategic and operational change by breaking a strategy down into actionable pieces. Policy had also to be matched to a realistic and achievable financial framework, and wobbling regional capital budgets in particular could destabilize strategic change exercises. Finally, long-term issues (such as psychiatry) needed to be kept on change agendas, which could be difficult in the NHS where there is a tendency for every issue to be famous for 15 minutes.

Factor 2: Availability of key people leading change

An important factor which makes change highly contextually sensitive is the availability of key people in critical posts leading change. We do not here refer to heroic and individualistic 'macho managers', but rather leadership exercised in a much more subtle and pluralist fashion. The small group – as well as one individual – could be an effective vehicle, so conscious team-building could be important, with selectors (such as District Chairs) pulling together officers from diverse constituencies and providing complementary assets or skills. There was a critical role for continuity: paradoxically there is a requirement for a substantial degree of stability in the effective management of strategic change and the case studies do not support the argument that posts should rotate every two years, at least where there is a strategic change exercise underway.

The link between the unplanned movement of key personnel and the draining of energy, purpose, commitment and action from major change processes has now been established from a whole series of research studies (Klein, 1976; Goodman and Dean, 1982; Kanter, 1985; Pettigrew, 1985a). What is rarely mentioned as a corollary of the problem is that the change process or programme then goes into a period of regression leaving the newcomer manager to start again but now possibly in a soured and non-receptive context for change.

The diversity of leadership was also apparent both in terms of its occupational base (clinicians as well as managers) and hierarchical level. Many frontline workers (for instance in HIV/AIDS) demonstrated great commitment and skill in the development of services. Often it was personalities not posts that were important: personal skills were more important in managing change than formal status or rank within the organization. Recent research (Pettigrew and Whipp, 1991) and writing (Nadler and Tushman, 1990) in private sector strategic change processes also points to the need to broaden and deepen the leadership cadre if long-term results are to be achieved in change processes.

Pettigrew and Whipp (1991) specifically use the term 'leading change' rather than 'leadership' to denote the collective, complementary and multi-faceted aspect of leading change. Leadership, they suggest, has too many connotations of individualism, and too often, one-dimensional heroism. The tasks of leading change are about the resolution of a pattern of interwoven problems, not the tackling of single great issues. The problems of maintaining simultaneous action over a long-term process are at their sharpest in leading change. The need appears to be for not boldness nor decisiveness, as much as for a combination of planning, opportunism and the adroit timing of interventions. The task of leading change is as difficult if not more difficult in the NHS, and we saw a similar pattern of diversity and complementarity being fashioned and used in our receptive contexts.

Factor 3: Long-term environmental pressure – intensity and scale

Studies of strategic change outside the NHS (Pettigrew, 1985a; Tushman and Romanelli, 1985) have highlighted the significant role of intense and large-scale environmental pressure in triggering periods of radical change. The picture in the NHS is more complex, as in some instances excessive pressure can deflect or drain energy out of the system. Goodman and Dean (1982) have noted the same phenomenon in private sector change. They note that inadequate environmental buffering is a key factor in helping to drain energy out of major change processes. In other cases environmental pressure can produce movement, especially if the pressure is skilfully orchestrated. Perhaps the use to which financial pressure is put depends on the prevailing distribution of power, history and assumptions of each District. In some of our Districts, financial crises produced a wide range of pathological organizational reactions such as delay and denial, collapse of morale and energy and the scapegoating and defeat of managers (Dutton, 1987).

Financial crisis was here seen as a threat to the organization, rather than as an opportunity for radical reconfiguration. In others (such as Paddington in the late 1970s) financial crisis was even played up and skilfully orchestrated by management in order to accelerate the process of rationalization.

Factor 4: A supportive organizational culture

'Organizational culture' is a currently fashionable term and remains a fascinating but difficult topic to study. 'Culture' refers to deep-seated assumptions and values far below surface manifestations (who gets to park in front of the hospital?), officially espoused ideologies, or even patterns of behaviour. The past weighs a heavy hand in shaping these values, setting expectations about what is and what is not possible. This may be both a strength (as in Parkside's experience in the acute sector) or a weakness, as difficult experiences in the past are projected forward.

Lorsch (1986) has discussed the invisible barrier of culture causing strategic myopia and therefore inertia in organizations. For him, a supportive organizational culture is about challenging and changing beliefs about success and how to achieve it. This factor and requirements to encourage flexibility were illustrated in our case data.

Broadly our studies in both the public and the private sector conclude that tremendous energy is required to effect cultural change. Programmatic change strategies contain important weaknesses (Beer et al., 1990), but there are some other clues about how culture change management is being attempted. One avenue is through the use of leaders as role models for a wider diffusion process. Another feature is the attempt to create a general managerial cadre as opposed to a small number of general managers. There may be a role for action as a demonstration effect as behavioural change may precede attitudinal change. We know that rewards – broadly defined – may be important, and that there is an extremely important role for Human Resource Management policies and practices, somewhat neglected perhaps in the NHS in the past.

It is not possible in the NHS to talk of a single culture, but rather of a collection of different subcultures which may inhabit the same District. If we concentrate on the managerial subculture, we can select out some features of a District culture associated with a high rate of change:

- Flexible working across boundaries with purpose-designed structures rather than formal hierarchies; non-representational mode of working; focus on skill rather than rank or status.
- An open, risk-taking approach. Some innovations may fail, but it is important that the innovators are not punished.
- Openness to research and evaluation.
- A strong value base which helps give focus to what otherwise might be a loose network.
- Strong positive self-image and sense of achievement.

Such features of local culture do not, of course, develop by accident. They develop characteristically from the values and change experiences of key leaders in the District, interlinked with environmental pressure and effective managerial–clinician relations.

Factor 5: Effective managerial–clinical relations

The managerial–clinical interface was obviously critical. The pattern found was one of wide variation in the quality of such relations, and when clinicians had gone into opposition, they could exert a powerful block on change. Perhaps more surprisingly managers varied in the extent to which they saw relationship-building and trading with clinicians as a core part of their brief.

The importance of effective managerial–clinical relations in stimulating strategic change has also been reported in studies of the US health care system. Shortell, Morrison and Friedman (1990) present this as a dominant theme in their work, emphasizing the significance of looking for common ground, involving selected physicians early on in planning, carefully identifying the needs and interests of key physicians, and working on a daily basis to build a climate of trust, honesty and effective communications (1990, p. 237). Hocking (1991) has identified a similar pattern in the university sector, where relationships between professionals and administrators can be a stimulant or block to major change.

Manager–clinician relations were easier where negative stereotypes had broken down, perhaps as a result of the emergence of mixed roles or perspectives. For managers, it was important to understand what clinicians valued (medical records may be not so important to managers, but are of great importance to clinicians), and hence what they had to do to engage in effective trading relations. Those managers who were best were those semi-immersed in the world of clinicians, which was a great advantage enjoyed by those general managers who had been previously NHS Administrators. It is helpful to understand the implications of medical workflow for the design of a hospital, and perhaps even help clinicians to do their own planning (such as Approvals in Principle) as a way of earning trust.

From a clinical perspective, there is an important group of clinicians – who have often come up through the MEC – who think managerially and strategically. Clinical directors may increasingly form a second such hybrid group, and they will be directly linked to their business managers. These are clinicians who think across the patch, and may even be able to speak for the medical community as a whole. Such strategic clinicians are critical people for management to identify, foster and encourage and under no circumstances should they be driven into opposition by trivia. Considerable managerial acumen was needed to foster positive alliances and managers sometimes had to enter into deals, offering incentives while holding on to the core objective, and enforcing penalties where this was seen as politically possible.

Upward and downward spirals in the pattern of managerial clinician relations were evident in some of the case studies: relationships could quickly sour but were slow to build up.

The formation of lines of communication – to teams, to the MEC, to newly appointed clinicians – itself takes a long period of time.

Factor 6: Cooperative inter-organizational networks

Many changes in the priority group sector in particular were underscored by the development and management of inter-organizational networks with such agencies as Social Services Departments and voluntary organizations. DHAs had little power in such settings, but rather had to win influence. A number of features could enrich these networks, such as the existence of boundary spanners who crossed agency divides (e.g. DHA members who also served on SSD Committee) and clear referral and communication points.

The most effective networks were both informal and purposeful (rather than self-absorbed and narcissistic), but – as a consequence of the personalities not posts argument – also fragile and vulnerable to turnover. One Director of Social Services might be interested in mental handicap, the next in the elderly. But at their best such networks provided opportunities for trading and education, for commitment and energy-raising and for marrying top-down and bottom-up concerns. The significance of purposeful networks and their role as arenas for trust-building, bargaining and deal making is a key part of Rosabeth Kanter's (1985) perspective and data on how substantial change occurs.

Factor 7: Simplicity and clarity of goals and priorities

This focusing issue arises from the conclusion that managers varied greatly in their ability to narrow the change agenda down into a set of key priorities, and to insulate this core from the constantly shifting short-term pressures apparent in the NHS. The danger was that the number of 'priorities' would escalate until they became meaningless. Rather, persistence and patience in pursuit of objectives over a long period seemed to be associated with achieving strategic change. So managers may be wise to ignore or minimize some of the ever-changing sources of pressure, while using others to amplify their pre-existing change objectives. Skills in complexity and conflict reduction could also be important here, in trying to contain complex problems in simpler organizational frameworks.

The question of simplicity and clarity of goals and priorities is one aspect of a much more general analytical and practical problem of how the nature of the context of change influences the rate and pace of change. Dufour (1991) cites Van Meter and Van Horn (1976) and Grindle (1980) as important contributors to the debate about how implementation gaps are linkable to variability in the content of change. Thus Van Meter and Van Horn (1976) argue the implementation process is likely to be influenced by the amount of change involved and the extent of goal consensus among the participants. Grindle (1980) indicates that changes with long-range objectives, requiring considerable behavioural adaptation, and depending on networks of widely dispersed units (characteristics present in our cases of psychiatric hospital closure) will be far more difficult and onerous to implement. Dufour's own research (1991) on factors influencing the rate and pace of closure of general practitioner maternity units also contributes to the debate about how content may influence pace of change. He is able to show in some of his cases how the shrinking and de-escalation of the change content brought sudden movement in previously contentious and deadlocked processes. Thus one way to simplify and clarify is to shrink the problem at the outset, or alternatively to break the problem into more manageable and actionable pieces once the change process is underway.

Factor 8: The fit between the district's change agenda and its locale

Private sector research on, for example, human resource change has indicated that various features of the locale where change is to occur may inhibit or accelerate change. Thus Hardy's studies (1985) of organizational closures demonstrate how and why climate building for such changes is linkable to high levels of unemployment and consequential changes in the power balance between managers and trade unionists. There is also evidence (for example, Bassett, 1986; Marchington, 1989) that the incidence and timing of joint consultative arrangements is often linked to the enhanced opportunities afforded by 'green field sites'.

In the NHS the nature of the locale also had an impact on how easy it was to achieve change:

- The degree of coterminosity with SSDs.
- Whether there is one large centre of population or two or more major towns.
- Whether there is a teaching hospital presence.
- The strength and nature of the local political culture.
- The nature of the local NHS workforce.

While many of these factors may appear beyond management control, awareness of their influence could nevertheless be important in anticipation of potential obstacles to change. Some of them may also be reshaped in the long term by higher tiers (boundary changes, removal of local authority and trade union representatives from the DHA) or locally through Human Resource Management activities.

Some implications of the findings

We repeat that the eight features of receptivity should not be seen as a shopping list or as discrete factors but, as Figure 31.1 indicates, they represent a highly intercorrelated combination which taken together may raise energy levels around change in ways which are highly District-specific. Thus, in, for example, Paddington the timing and rate and pace of change was influenced by the combined and additive effect of seven of the eight features in our model. Environmental pressure over a long period of time was a constant stimulus for change to rationalize acute service provision. For this pressure to be recognized and effectively orchestrated, a team of change leaders had to be built and an evolving sense of focus, direction and purpose created. The team over time learned progressively how to evolve and negotiate a pattern of agreement with key clinicians, and work with key actors in and outside the Districts in ways which additively constructed stepping stones for change. The small movements forward further enhanced the receptivity for change and allowed further action to occur, sometimes occasioned by chance, and other times as a result of planned activity. The fact that, compared with Bloomsbury, there was a simpler political and structural context for change (there being only one teaching hospital in Paddington, compared with two in Bloomsbury) also eased the on-going process of change and learning. But even in this relatively receptive setting for change, the process was full of complexity, indeterminism and simultaneity. Dead ends and blocks emerged. Sudden opportunities for movement had to be exploited on a constantly moving stage. Energy once orchestrated had to be sustained. We repeat there is no simple recipe, no quick fix in managing complex change.

32

The fish rots from the head
Bob Garratt

Extracts from Garratt B (1997) The Fish Rots from the Head: The Crisis in our Boardrooms: Developing the Crucial Skills of the Competent Director. London: Harper Collins.

The board's role in the learning organization

There is a simple three-level hierarchy in organizations which the Chinese have used for some 5,000 years, and the Greeks (whose words we still use in English) evolved some 3,500 years ago:

Policy

Strategy

Tactics/Operations

Policy and strategy are the worlds of the board and directors. The remaining ninety-nine percent of the people in the organization will spend their lives in the operations loops of learning, dealing tactically with the immediate problems of crises and deviations from plans. This is both necessary and sufficient for work groups, but it should not preclude them from having an input on policy and strategy. They too are living in the changing outside world and may well have good information or ideas for the board on how to help redirect the business to keep it alive within its energy niches.

Taking the three-level hierarchy of policy, strategy, and operations, one can overlay a figure-of-eight, or double-loop, of learning over the hierarchy which puts the board at the *centre* of the learning cycles, not at the top of the organization. The *Learning Board* should be the central processor for the two cycles of organizational learning – operational (day-to-day) and policy/strategic (long-term).

In the operations loop of learning the customer-facing staff, supervisors, managers and support staff are charged with listening carefully to the external and internal customers and then creating and improving systems of product or service delivery which are effective from the customer's point of view. Once the customer is convinced of your promises about 'good value for money', then you can set *effectiveness levels* of performance for your staff to aspire to before you begin to focus on organizational efficiency – whilst ensuring you always keep that public perception of effectiveness firmly in the customer's sight. 'Bottom-line' fixation to the exclusion of customers' concerns looks wonderful to the accountants in the short term, but tends quickly to create a non-learning organization. It is a very good way of losing everyone's job in the long term.

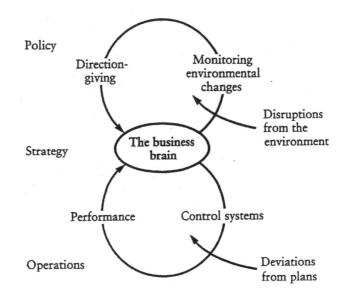

Figure 32.1 The double loop of learning, part i

In the policy loop of learning, the directors are both listening to what operations tell them is going on, and simultaneously monitoring the complexity and chaos of the continual changes in those external environments which create their ecological niches for their enterprise – the levels outside of which the organization will die. These levels must be monitored in the following environments: political, physical environmental, economic, social, technological and trade. The dynamic balances struck here by the board are crucial to the effectiveness of the organization in relation to the outside world.

It is the board's role to ensure that the dynamic balance is kept between organizational effectiveness and organizational efficiency. When the chips are down, it is usually better to maintain customer-perceived organizational effectiveness at all costs, provided the cash keeps flowing, rather than internally-perceived organizational efficiency, since concentration on efficiency alone usually leads to corporate collapse in the medium term.

The Learning Board is the centre of the Learning Organization's 'business brain'. This model allows for a clearer understanding of the tasks of the board, who should take the leading roles, and when.

External
environment
(towards
organizational
effectiveness)

Reframing
loop

Policy

The business
brain

Strategy/
integration

Internal
environment
(towards
organizational
efficiency)

Operations
loop

Operations

Figure 32.2   The double loop of learning, part ii

There are two sides to a Learning Board: *Conformance* and *Performance*. 'Conformance' involves two aspects: Accountability (conformance to legislation, regulation, shareholder and stakeholder wishes and audits) and Supervision of Management (conformance to key performance indicators, cashflow, budgets and projects). 'Performance' involves Policy Formulation and Strategic Thinking, which drive the whole enterprise forward allowing it to survive and grow by maintaining and developing its position in its energy niches.

So the detailed model of the Learning Board is shown in Figure 32.3 (opposite).

Directors' roles

One can immediately sense whether a board is a conformance-orientated or performance-orientated type. A deeper question is whether they do this con- sciously or unconsciously. Do the directors position themselves and budget their time so that they can learn continuously from actions and feedback? What roles should the executive and independent directors take to ensure such continuous learning? There are many ways of dividing up the combinations of short- and long-term thinking and internal and external orientations amongst directors; none is right for all occasions. It is up to the chairman to ensure that such division of labour is effective.

One way is for the independent directors to be focused on the policy role with the executive directors focusing on the conformance aspects of accountability and supervision of management. Strategy is agreed by both types of director.

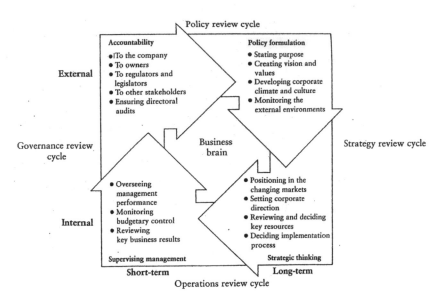

Figure 32.3 The full learning board model

Other boards will say this is not correct and focus their independent directors on the external aspects of policy and accountability, leaving the executive directors to deal with the internal aspects of strategy and supervision of management. I think that this is also a very useful working definition for the basic definition of responsibilities of the chairman (policy and accountability) and the chief executive (strategy and supervision of management).

But it is not the only possibility. Given the growing diversity of many boards it is not wise to be too prescriptive here as the best split of the roles and responsibilities depends on the combination of personalities and capabilities at the time. What is important is that a board fully addresses the issues of 'who does what': where scarce resources are best deployed at board level, and whether the chairman and chief executive's roles are explicit to both the board and the stakeholders.

I have noted in my work that the biggest problems seem to arise if the dividing line between independent and executive directors is drawn diagonally from top left to bottom right of the Learning model. Here the chairman is definitely responsible for policy and the chief executive for supervision of management, but there is every possibility for confusion and argument about strategy and accountability unless there is a highly robust process by which the directors debate and reach consensus. Such a process is rarely well-developed and so turf wars break out between the two types of director.

Similarly, a line drawn top right to bottom left often leaves the chairman clearly responsible for accountability (which is the law in many countries), and the CEO for strategic thinking. But it also means that policy and supervision of management are likely to be contentious. In theory, sharing these two between all directors leads to solutions of the highest common factor. My observation is that they more often fall into the lowest common denominator trap.

A better approach is for the board as a whole to design the main focus of their responsibilities collectively as simply *directors*, to allocate leadership appropriately, based on the individuals available, and to review the outcomes of these decisions at least annually as part of the corporate governance audit process.

The key point is that *independence of thought* is demanded of *all* directors when on a board. This requires that they use their 'naive intelligence' to advantage, pursue discriminating questions until they get a satisfactory answer that they and other board members understand, are not put off by the technobabble from other disciplines, and pursue the company's interests above all else. It is the chairman's role to ensure that this happens.

The role of the board and its directors in the twenty-first century will be more and more concerned with balancing internal and external issues in a rapidly changing world. Directoral competence – independence of imagination and thought, plus the nous to run an effective enterprise – will determine an organization's success. Directing is becoming a proper job in itself. It is each director's duty to ensure that he or she is trained for it.

33

The governance of public and non-profit organisations
Chris Cornforth

Extracts from Cornforth C (2003) The Governance of Public and Non-Profit Organizations: What do boards do? London: Routledge.

The reflexive board: maintaining a dynamic balance

A theme throughout has been the inadequacy of current academic theories of boards as a way of understanding boards or as a guide to action. Each of the different theories tends to give pre-eminence to one particular role of boards [see Table 33.1]. They ignore the multiple and sometimes conflicting roles that boards play and the way these may shift over time in response to changing circumstances. Contextual factors need to be explicitly built into our theories of organisational governance.

Equally, much of the prescriptive or 'how to do it' literature on boards is flawed. In the desire to improve board performance there is a tendency to portray an idealised or heroic model of the board (Herman, 1989). The board is simultaneously strategic – driving forward organisational performance; a careful steward of the organisation's resources; accountable to the organisation's stakeholders; a critical friend to management – able to offer support but also monitor and challenge poor performance; a vital source of information and contacts on external threats and opportunities, etc. The danger with this idealised view of boards is that if the gap with practice is too large, it can become demotivating and provide a poor guide to action (Herman, 1989; Cornforth, 1995).

The boards of non-profit organisations and quangos also face new challenges. There are increased pressures for improved performance and accountability. Public and non-profit organisations are increasingly subjected to scrutiny by the media, and their failings are quickly pointed out. At the same time public and political concern over the performance of many types of organisations has grown. Regulatory regimes have been tightened. Many funders are requiring organisations to specify performance targets and put in place systems to monitor and report on their performance. As the demands on boards are increasing, there are growing problems of recruitment, and many board members report lack of time as the main constraint on their involvement.

How can boards deal in a realistic way with these new challenges and the difficult and often ambiguous roles they have to carry out? Relying on how things have been done previously or simple prescriptions by themselves is unlikely to be adequate. Boards need to become more *reflexive*. This involves boards consciously trying to develop a greater understanding of their behaviour, roles and impact. As part of this process boards need to develop a capacity to regularly review their composition, the roles they play, board performance and how they work together and with management. As a result, the reflexive board will need to give a high priority to its own maintenance and development. Unfortunately, under pressure of time, this is a function that often is neglected.

This raises the question, who should be responsible for board development and relations with management? While formally it is usually regarded as the board chair's responsibility to carry out this function, they often do not have time to carry out this role. Noting this problem, Drucker (1990: 13) suggests the only answer is to assign this responsibility to the chief executive. However, this runs the danger of the board becoming the creature of the chief executive. Again it is unlikely that there is one best way to resolve this tension. What is most important is that boards and senior management find a way to ensure board review and development stay on the board's agenda.

Boards also need new conceptual tools to help them reflect on and understand the complex challenges they face. Hopefully, the paradox perspective presented in this book will provide one useful framework for enabling boards to think about their different roles and the difficult tensions and ambiguities they face. Rather than search for the right board model or approach, boards need to try to find the right balance between the different 'pulls' created by the paradoxes given the circumstances they face. Board dysfunctions or problems usually occur when boards become attracted to one 'pole' and are no longer able to maintain a 'balance', for example, when boards trust and support management so much that they forget to scrutinise their proposals and ask the hard questions, or become so involved in operational detail that they forget the big picture and neglect the organisation's strategy.

Table 33.1   A comparison of theoretical perspectives on organisational governance

Theory	Interests	Board members	Board role	Model
Agency theory	Owners and managers have different interests	Owners' representatives	Compliance/ conformance: safeguard owners' interests oversee management check compliance	Compliance model

Stewardship theory	Owners and managers share interests	Experts	Improve performance: add value to top decisions/strategy partner/support management	Partnership model
Democratic perspective	Members/the public contain different interests	Lay representatives	Political: represent constituents/ members reconcile conflicts make policy control executive	Democratic model
Stakeholder theory	Stakeholders have different interests	Stakeholder representa- tives: elected or appointed by stakeholder groups	Balancing stakeholder needs: balance stakeholder needs make policy/strategy control management	Stakeholder model
Resource dependency theory	Stakeholders and organisation have different interests	Chosen for influence with key stakeholders	Boundary spanning: secure resources maintain stakeholder relations being external perspective	Co-option model
Managerial hegemony theory	Owners and managers have different interests	Owners' representatives	Largely symbolic: ratify decisions give legitimacy managers have real power	'Rubber- stamp' model

References and further reading

Charity Commission (2000) *Annual Report 1999–2000*, London: The Stationery Office.

Cornforth, C. (1995) 'Governing Non-profit Organizations: Heroic Myths and Human Tales', in *Researching the UK Voluntary Sector: Conference Proceedings*, London: National Council of Voluntary Organisations.

Cornforth, C. and Edwards, C. (1998) *Good Governance: Developing Effective Board –Management Relations in Public and Voluntary Organisations*, London: CIMA Publishing.

Drucker, P. (1990) *Managing the Non-Profit Organization*, Oxford: Butterworth-Heinemann.

Garratt, B. (1996) *The Fish Rots from the Head: the Crisis in our Boardrooms: Developing the Crucial Skills of the Competent Director*, London: HarperCollins.

Harris, M. (1993) 'Exploring the Role of Boards Using Total Activities Analysis', *Nonprofit Management and Leadership*, 3, 3, 269–281.

Harris, M. (2001) 'Boards: Just Subsidiaries of the State?', in M. Harris and C. Rochester (eds) *Voluntary Organisations and Social Policy in Britain: Perspectives on Change and Choice*, London: Palgrave.

Herman, R. D. (1989) 'Concluding Thoughts on Closing the Board Gap', in R. Herman and J. Van Til (eds) *Nonprofit Boards of Directors: Analyses and Applications*, New Brunswick, NJ: Transaction.

John, G. (2001) 'In Praise of Context', *Journal of Organizational Behavior*, 22, 31–42.

Kramer, R. (1985) 'Towards a Contingency Model of Board–Executive Relations', *Administration in Social Work*, 9, 3, 15–33.

Lorsch, J. W. and MacIver, E. (1989) *Pawns or Potentates: The Reality of America's Corporate Boards*, Boston: Harvard Business School Press.

Middleton, M. (1987) 'Nonprofit Boards of Directors: Beyond the Governance Function', in W. Powell (ed.) *The Nonprofit Sector: A Research Handbook*, New Haven, CT: Yale University Press.

Mowday, R. T. and Sutton, R. I. (1993) 'Organizational Behavior: Linking Individuals and Groups to Organizational Contexts', *Annual Review of Psychology*, 44, 195–229.

Nolan (1996) *Second Report of the Committee on Standards in Public Life: Local Spending Bodies*, 1, London: HMSO.

Ostrower, F. and Stone, M. M. (2001) 'Governance Research: Trends, Gaps and Prospects for the Future', paper presented at the Association for Research on Nonprofit Organizations and Voluntary Action (ARNOVA) Annual Conference, Miami, Florida, 27 November–1 December.

Rousseau, D. M. and Fried, Y. (2001) 'Location, Location, Location: Contextualizing Organizational Research', *Journal of Organizational Behavior*, 22, 1–13.

34

Why do we keep on meeting like this? The board as ritual in health and social care
Edward Peck, Perri 6, Pauline Gulliver and David Towell

Extracts from Peck E, Perri 6, Gulliver P and Towell D (2004) Why do we keep on meeting like this? The board as ritual in health and social care. Health Services Management Research 17: 100–109.

Introduction

The formal meeting is one of the fundamental bases of organizational life, as much in public services as in the private sector. In England, organizations in the National Health Service (NHS) are overseen by boards of executive and non-executive directors. These formal meetings are typically ascribed roles that involve the setting and monitoring of policy and strategy. However, researchers have two opposed views of meetings. One view is that the work of meetings is *instrumental, palpable and explicit*: they are there to make decisions, to engage in deliberation, to conciliate about content in conflicts. They are to be measured, on this view, by how far they decide efficiently and effectively what they are officially supposed to decide (Simon, 1997).

The other view is that meetings are for doing something organizationally important but which is unspoken, does not appear on the agenda, and which gets done successfully or otherwise, in the course of participants being in the same place and speaking or remaining silent according to certain conventions. Meetings are places where participants tell narratives about who they are collectively, sustain culture, organize shared emotions, and conciliate over social relations in conflicts. This second view is that the work of meetings is *social, symbolic* and *implicit*: they are held to maintain organizational cohesion above all (Weick, 1995).

In this paper, we explore the relationship between these two views. Our conclusions reflect on the place of the formal meeting in organizational life and the implications of extending the membership of these boards to include groups that have previously been excluded.

The formal meeting as organizational ritual

There is an extensive literature on ritual. For the purposes of this paper, the characteristics of ritual-like activities can be limited to those set out by Bell (1997) in her synthesis of the anthropological research. She identifies six characteristics: formalism; traditionalism; invariance; rule-governance; symbolism; and performance. Each of these is briefly introduced in the following paragraphs, with connections made back to the review of the research literature on boards.

Bell notes that 'formality is one of the most frequently cited characteristics of ritual' (p.139). The limitations on how something can be expressed, she argues, also restricts what can be expressed. She points to the nature of formal speech as an example, which 'tends to be more conventional and less idiosyncratic or personally expressive' (p.139) than common speech. 'Formalistic' is itself one of the terms that Winkler (1975) uses to describe the activity of the boards that he observed, and Brannen et al. (1976) comment on the formal way in which presentations were made to the BSC divisional boards.

'Most rituals appeal to tradition or custom in some way' (p.145), Bell claims, although she also recognizes that 'it is hard to make any clear distinction between traditionalism and many other complex modes of ritualization' (p.149). The apparent points of continuity between the boards observed by Brannen et al. (1976) and those described by van Vree (1999) suggests that tradition plays a strong part in the life of formal meetings.

Bell sees invariance as 'one of the most common characteristics of ritual-like behaviour ... a disciplined set of actions marked by precise repetition' (p.150). The consistency of behaviour described in the study by Peck (1995) suggests such discipline.

Observance of rules within ritual, according to Bell, 'hold individuals to communally approved patterns of behaviour, they testify to the legitimacy and power of that form of communication and perhaps they also encourage human interaction by constraining the possible outcomes' (p.155). Pettigrew (1992) draws attention to the 'norms' of board conduct and Bell herself sees the 'complex negotiations that attend formal bargaining between company management and labour unions' (p.155) as an example of a rule-governed ritual.

Bell suggests that two sorts of activities using symbols make them characteristic of rituals. The first is their use to differentiate some places from others by means of distinctive acts or responses. Whilst acknowledging the importance of the differentiation of place, some anthropologists (e.g. Turner, 1995; 1982) put more emphasis on the importance of ritual and its symbols in the structuring of time. The second, for Bell, is 'the way they evoke experiences of a greater, higher or more universalized reality—the group, the nation, humankind ...' (p.159). The importance attached to minutes of formal meetings as symbols of continuity and difference in the life of organizations is central to the research of Le Rocker and Howard (1960).

In respect of performance, it is 'the deliberate, self-conscious "doing" of highly symbolic actions in public' (Bell, 1997; p.160) that makes rituals what they are.

The description of Starkweather of board behaviour as a 'fiction' stresses the performative aspects of the meetings that he has experienced.

This identification of formal meetings as organizational ritual starts to explain both their longevity and their continued influence in the context of research evidence which typically reports that these meetings do not do what they are supposed to do (e.g. set and monitor policy and strategy). It also opens up the potential for examining formal meetings in health and social care organizations as settings where central processes in the organizational life take place; processes, that is, other than organizational decision-making.

Schwartzman (1989) identifies two such functions for formal meetings. First, she argues that 'meetings are an important sense-making for organizations and communities because they define, represent, and also reproduce social entities and relationships' (p.39). Second, she contends that 'meetings may be a major form for the creation of community or organizational identity ... the event becomes a vehicle for the reading as well as validation of social relations within a cultural system' (p.41).

The paper will focus upon three theories of meeting ritual from this literature: as a method of sustaining social solidarity between members of any community (e.g. Durkheim, 1995); as a way of institutionalizing codes of speech that both reflect and reify power relationships (e.g. Bernstein, 1971); and as a process of creating consistent patterns of response within which issues of importance are selected and addressed (Goffman, 1967).

The case study of the JCB as ritual

One influential way of thinking about the variety of basic ways of organizing, and the relationships between them, involves four basic forms: individualism; hierarchy; enclave; and isolates (Thompson *et al.*, 1990; Douglas, 1970; 1982a; 1982b). On this account, meetings dominated by any one of each of these styles will tend to adopt distinct ritual forms. These styles will reflect—but more importantly reinforce—their institutional form of solidarity. The nature of these ritual forms follows from the principle of organization, and, indeed, they arise because of the institutional imperative to *enact* that principle of organization in order to bind people into it.

Consider first the hierarchical form. Here, the ritual order must display both the importance of the collective character of the organization (in this case, the joint board) to its members and to any observers, and subtly remind people of the boundary between insiders and outsiders; but it must also mark differences of status and role within the group of insiders. As this paper has illustrated, when such rituals are effective in their own institutional terms, they generate very particular emotions that serve to bind people into the structure of the hierarchy. A deferential respect for seniors is combined with a controlled sense of one's own role. Over time, being part of the ritual reinforces both the emotional commitment and loyalty that the member feels, and also the sense of security that one's contributions and role are valued. However, when they fail in their own terms, such rituals can produce demoralization and bemusement and a sense of banality and sham among the 'lowerarchy'.

Each of the four basic ways of organizing can be shown to produce distinctive emotions when they are successful and when they fail in their own terms. Figure 34.1 summarizes the main characteristics of each; it shows the four basic forms as being derived from a cross-tabulation, first introduced by Douglas (1970) of Durkheim's (1951) two basic dimensions of social organization, and it also draws on Handelman (1982).

Isolate	Hierarchy
Exemplars of ritual style: satirical stand-up comedy	Exemplars of ritual style: processions
Emotions elicited in ritual, when successful in its own institutional terms: irony, ridicule, stoic will to endure	Emotions elicited in ritual, when successful in its own institutional terms: respectful deference for status, amour-propre for own role, commitment, sense of security
Emotions elicited when less successful: bitterness, sense of arbitrariness, opacity and banality	Emotions elicited when less successful: demoralization, confusion and bemusement at opacity and complexity of institutions
	Sense of banality
Individualism	Exclave
Exemplars of ritual style: trade fair, street market	Exemplars of ritual style: religious revivalist meeting, militant picketing strikers meeting
Emotions elicited in ritual, when successful in its own institutional terms: aspiration, exictement, controlled envy for competetive rivalry	Emotions elicited in ritual, when successful in its own institutional terms: passionate commitment, collective effervescence, passionate rejction of outsiders and those seen as insiders who have betrayed the institution
Emotions elicited when less successful: insecurity, dejection at own defeat, frustration at what seems futile and self-defeating rivalry	Emotions elicited when less successful: schism

Figure 34.1 How different styles of organization produce different kinds of ritual, with different consequences

Conclusion

This paper argues that researchers should be wary of putting too much emphasis on the instrumental purposes of formal meetings. Such a focus creates expectations amongst researchers undertaking observational research, especially those unfamiliar with the meeting-as-ritual, that can only be disappointed and where their papers will repeatedly report on the apparent failure of meetings. However, this requires that studies of formal meetings in organizations develop a different focus, and one that moves beyond descriptions of whether or not they fulfilled their constitutional role.

Rather, the emphasis should be on formal meetings as rituals, exploring the ways in which they create and recreate social solidarity. One such theory-driven approach to this research has been presented and applied in this paper. It has argued that the task of researchers is to see local systems as settlements between all four of the potential forms identified in Figure 34.1, where potential instabilities of each of the single forms and each of the two- and three-way hybrids may be contained or exhibited. The principle of requisite variety in the ritual order of meetings may be the only viable way to allow articulation of all the institutional forms that make up the health and social care system, and further studies should examine the extent to which these are used. Amongst the options available include the following:

- separation: distinct rituals for different occasions;
- exchange: distinct forms of ritual for different parts of one meeting;
- tolerated spaces: where all four forms can be articulated without disturbing any too much (e.g. special away-day sessions with specific ritual order where all stakeholders are given space to operate according to their own code).

Each of these is fragile. Separation can limit conflict, but it can also result in the distinct meetings suffering all the problems of single-ritual forms. Exchange is sometimes hard to structure well. Tolerated spaces often work best in provisional settings rather than over the long term. Often, it will be necessary for organizations to use each of these in turn. However, we have a lot still to learn about the *social, symbolic* and *implicit* roles of formal meetings, and the theoretical frameworks that can enable us to understand them.

Finally, the presence of users and carers at formal meetings is often described as being 'tokenistic'. The discussion in this paper suggests that this description both distinguishes unhelpfully between them and other categories of attendees, as the contribution of all the members is largely symbolic, and also fails to give sufficient weight to the impact upon the enactment of the ritual of users and carers being present.

References and further reading

Bavly, D. What is the board of directors good for? *Long Range Planning*, 1986; 19(3): 20–5

Bell, C. *Ritual: Perspectives and Dimensions*. New York: Oxford University Press, 1997

Bernstein, B. *Class, Codes and Control, vol 1: Theoretical Studies Towards a Sociology of Language*. London: Routledge and Kegan Paul, 1971

Brannen, P., Batstone, E., Fatchett, D. and White, P. *The Worker Directors*. London: Hutchinson, 1976

Douglas, M. *Natural Symbols: Explorations in Cosmology*. London: Routledge, 1970

Douglas, M. Cultural bias. In: Douglas, M. (ed.) *In the Active Voice*. London: Routledge and Kegan Paul, 1982a; 183–254

Douglas, M. (ed.) *Essays in the Sociology of Perception*. London: Routledge and Kegan Paul, 1982b

Durkheim, É. *Suicide: a Study in Sociology*. Spaulding, J. R. and Simpson, S. London: Routledge, 1951

Durkheim, É. *Elementary Forms of Religious Life*. Fields, K. New York: Free Press, 1995

Ferlie, E., Ashburner, L., Fitzgerald, L. and Pettigrew, A. *The New Public Management in Action*. Oxford: Oxford University Press, 1996

Goffman, E. *Interaction Ritual: Essays on Face-to-Face Behaviour*. New York: Pantheon Press, 1967

Hacking, I. World making by kind making: child abuse for example. In: Douglas, M. and Hull, D. (eds.) *How Classification Works: Nelson Goodman Among the Social Sciences*. Edinburgh: Edinburgh University Press, 1992; 180–238

Handelman, D. Reflexivity in festival and other cultural events. In: Douglas, M. (ed.) *Essays in the Sociology of Perception*. London: Routledge and Kegan Paul, 1982; 162–190

Le Rocker, F. and Howard, K. What decisions do hospital trustees actually make? *The Modern Hospital* 1960; **94**(4): 83–7

Mace, M. *Directors: Myth and Reality*. Cambridge, MA: Harvard University Press, 1971

Mauss, M. *The Gift: the Form and Reason for Exchange in Archaic Societies*. New York: W. W. Norton. *Année sociologique*, 2e série 1990; **1**: 30–186

Peck, E. The Performance of an NHS Trust Board: actor's accounts, minutes and observation. *British Journal of Management* 1995; **6**(2): 135–55

Peck, E., Gulliver, P. and Towell, D. *Modernising Partnerships: an Evaluation of Somerset's Innovations in the Commissioning and Organization of Mental Health Services* (Final report). London: Institute for Applied Health and Social Policy, King's College, 2002

Pettigrew, A. On studying managerial elites. *Strategic Management Journal* 1992; **13**:163–82

Schwartzman, H. B. *The Meeting: Gatherings in Organizations and Communities*. New York: Plenum, 1989

Secretaries of State for Health, Wales, Northern Ireland and Scotland. *Working for Patients. The Health Services: Caring for the 1990s*, Cm 555. London: HMSO, 1989

Secretary of State for Health. *Valuing People: a New Strategy for Learning Disability for the 21st century*, Cm 5086. London: HMSO, 2001

Simon, H. A. *Administrative Behaviour: A Study of Decision-Making Processes in Administrative Organizations*, 4th edn. New York: Free Press, 1997

Somerset Health Authority/Somerset County Council (1998). Constitution of the Somerset Joint Commissioning Board, Taunton, Somerset HA and Somerset CC

Starkweather, D. Hospital board power. *Health Services Management Research* 1988; 1(2): 74–86

Thompson, M., Ellis, R. J. and Wildavsky, A. *Cultural Theory*. Boulder, Colorado: Westview Press, 1990

Turner, V. W. *The Ritual Process: Structure and Antistructure*. New York: Aldine de Gruyter, 1995

Turner, V. W. *From Ritual to Theatre: the Human Seriousness of Play*. New York: PAJ Publications, 1982

van Vree, W. *Meetings, Manners and Civilization: the Development of Modern Meeting Behaviour*. London University Press, 1999

Waldo, C. N. *Boards of Directors*. Westport: Connecticut: Quorum, 1985

Weick, K. E. *Sense Making in Organizations*. London: Sage, 1995

Westrup, C. The play of information systems development: drama and ritual in the development of a nursing information system. *Information Technology and People* 1996; 9(2): 24–42

Winkler, J. The two faces of capitalism. *The Director* 1974; 26(10): 91–4

Winkler, J. Company directors ... or corporate knights. *The Director* 1975; 27(1): 85–7

Winkler, J. The fly on the wall of the inner sanctum: observing company directors at work. In: Moyser, G. and Wagstaffe, M. (eds.) *Research Methods for Elite Studies*. London: Allen and Unwin, 1987; 120–32

PART 8

Evidence-based policy and management

Introduced by Kieran Walshe

The idea that evidence, from well-conducted research studies, should inform the decision making of professionals like doctors, nurses, teachers, social workers, managers and even policy makers is far from new, and might also seem relatively uncontroversial. After all, who would argue that medical practice or school education should be based on precedent, tradition or professional myths and nostrums rather than a scientifically rigorous assessment of what worked? Yet, in practice, for many decades, that is more or less what has happened. Decisions about teaching literacy, sentencing policy, residential care, health system design, medical practice, and so on have been shaped as much – or more – by the countervailing forces of tradition ('we've always done it this way') and fashion ('this is the next new idea about how to do it').

In the 1990s, a remarkable movement that started among clinical epidemiologists at McMaster University in Canada and medical researchers in the UK and elsewhere began to make a persuasive argument for change – and, remarkably, to secure increasing support among the medical establishment. The rise of 'evidence-based medicine' was founded on three key factors. First, there was growing evidence of the gap between optimal and actual medical practice, and the harm that could result from failing to apply the best research evidence to the care and treatment of patients. As Table P8.1 shows, it was not difficult to find stark examples of overuse (operations and treatments in common use that were known to be ineffective), underuse (procedures of proven efficacy that were not being used routinely) and misuse (procedures where the evidence for their use was inadequate, and there was much variation in clinical practice). Second, there was much effort invested in organizing and presenting the vast body of medical research literature in order to synthesize and systematize it and make it accessible to clinicians. The Cochrane Collaboration was founded with the ambitious long-term aim of developing and maintaining systematic reviews of the literature oriented around the questions about accurate diagnosis and effective treatment, which clinicians needed to be able to answer. Third, there was a paradigmatic shift in thinking about how to train and develop clinicians, away from fact-based medical education and towards the scientific, clinical–epidemiological method and a focus on problem-based learning and lifelong continuing professional development.

There was, of course, a reactionary response from some segments of the health care professions – arguing, with some justification, that evidence-based medicine seemed to want to reduce the complex science and art of clinical practice to a 'cook-book' of guidelines, protocols and procedures, which left no space for legitimate professional judgement. At times, the enthusiastic adherents of evidence-based medicine seemed to overclaim the extent to which research evidence could really be used to tackle real-life clinical questions, and it was clear that in many areas of medicine, and in other areas of professional practice like physiotherapy and nursing, there was a woeful lack of relevant and rigorous research evidence.

Table P8.1 Examples of the research practice gap in clinical and management practice

	Clinical	Managerial
Overuse	Dilatation and curettage (D&C) surgery for menorrhagia – widely used but shown to have no therapeutic benefit	Mergers and reorganizations as a response to organizational performance problems
Underuse	Thrombolytic therapy given to people who have had a heart attack, to make a subsequent heart attack less likely	Skill-mix changes to replace expensive health care professionals with lower-cost staff
Misuse	Stroke care in acute hospitals – huge variations in service design and configuration	Total quality management and other forms of quality improvement programmes

The evidence-based medicine movement made great strides in shifting the thinking, not just of clinicians but also of health care managers and policy makers about how health services should be provided. Internationally, the adoption of new technologies – particularly expensive pharmaceuticals – became a much more systematic and planned process driven less by the marketing endeavours of pharmaceutical companies and more by health technology assessments, taking a cold, hard look at the cost-effectiveness of new drugs and comparing them with existing treatments before authorizing their use.

But the ideas of evidence-based practice also began to take hold in other areas of the public domain – like education, criminal justice, social care, housing and welfare reform. Moreover, clinicians in health care organizations, subject to the new disciplines of evidence-based medicine and the concomitant restrictions on their 'clinical freedom' to prescribe and treat as they liked, began to ask the difficult question – why shouldn't managers be expected to show that their actions and initiatives were backed by good, scientific evidence? It was not difficult to come up with examples of overuse, underuse and misuse in the managerial domain (see Table P8.1). Managers and policy makers intent on reconfiguring hospital services, merging healthcare organizations or introducing new organizational initiatives were rightly asked for the evidence that these changes would 'work'. Just as some clinicians found the new discipline of evidence-based medicine and the constraints it imposed on their clinical practice somewhat irksome, so plenty of managers and policy makers argued that it was inappropriate, impractical or unwise to try to bring the rationalist, empirical and scientific paradigm of evidence-based medicine to bear on the messy world of policy making and organizational leadership.

The rise of evidence-based policy and management is still a work in progress, and a debate that has yet to play out to the end. The readings that follow aim to illustrate and explore a range of perspectives; first, by examining the inexorable rise of evidence-based medicine and then by reviewing its spread from medicine to other domains and sectors.

If there is a founding father of the evidence-based medicine movement, it is Archie Cochrane, whose monograph on effectiveness and efficiency in health services published in 1972 was the product of a lifetime in public health and epidemiology research. Many people see this work as the manifesto for evidence-based medicine, and his importance is reflected in the naming of the eponymous Cochrane Collaboration. The book is a reflective, personal and sometimes idiosyncratic account of his efforts to understand why we know so little about the effectiveness of health services. The chapter from his book that is included here focuses on the nature of and need for evidence.

The rise of the evidence-based medicine movement is neatly and clearly explained in the next reading by William Rosenberg and Anna Donald. Writing in 1995, when the ideas were still relatively new to most medical practitioners, they set out the case for making better use of evidence in clinical decision making, and argue strongly that it is practical and feasible to use research evidence in everyday clinical problem solving. Their paper is an intensely practical guide, which cuts through the hubris and makes it clear that ordinary practitioners can and should do much to practise evidence-based medicine. This paper is nicely matched by the third contribution, from David Naylor, who writes reflectively and sensitively about the difficulties that clinicians encounter in trying to bring the new ideology of evidence-based medicine to bear in the real world. He explores the 'grey zone' of clinical practice, where evidence either does not exist or cannot answer important questions, and argues for a careful reconciliation of the new evaluative sciences and the traditional skills of clinical reasoning and professional judgement – what might be called the science and art of medicine. This is not a reactionary rejection of evidence-based medicine, but a thoughtful exploration of its limits.

The fourth and fifth papers in this part turn their attention to the ideas, concepts and debates of evidence-based management. First, Kieran Walshe and Tom Rundall discuss the parallels and difference between the clinical and managerial worlds, and the extent to which the ideas of evidence-based medicine, rooted in a positivist, empirically led view of the scientific method can be transferred to the world of organizations and social interventions, usually the preserve of social scientists. They argue that while there are important differences between the two worlds (which help to explain why clinicians and managers find it hard to communicate sometimes, and why people who cross the divide like clinical directors often find it hard to reconcile the two), the basic principles of using evidence to inform decision making are eminently transferable. It is a point that is amply demonstrated by the final paper from Denise Rousseau. Extracted from her presidential address to the Academy of Management in the USA, it is a practical, rational call for the wider management community – both in academia and in practice – to embrace the case for evidence-based management. She makes important links to the school of scientific management and the idea of the natural science of organizations and sets out ways in which the ideas of evidence-based management can be realized through better management education, more relevant and applied research, and efforts to create 'linkage and exchange' between academics and practitioners in the field of management.

Summary

- It may sound obvious that important decisions should be based on sound evidence about what works, but in many fields like healthcare, education and public policy this has often been far from the case. Examples of practices and behaviours that fly in the face of the evidence abound.

- The 'evidence-based medicine' movement has done much to change the thinking of clinicians (especially doctors) about how they use evidence in diagnosis and treatment decisions, and what can be done to improve the effectiveness of medical care. It has led to a much more rigorous, empirically based, scientific approach to evaluating new drugs and therapies, for example.

- The ideas of evidence-based medicine have begun to be taken up in many other domains, where the same gap between research and practice is found. While the nature of evidence and knowledge may be different, the underlying philosophy has broad appeal, arguing as it does for rigour and empiricism to be brought to bear in making decisions, and for precedent, tradition, supposition and opinion to have rather less influence.

- Applying the ideas of evidence-based medicine to policy and management decisions is a useful and important discipline, and there is much that could be done to develop a stronger foundation for evidence-based practice in the management community.

References and further reading

Davies, H.T.O., Nutley, S.M. and Smith, P.C. (eds) (2000) *What Works? Evidence-Based Policy and Practice in Public Services.* Bristol: The Policy Press.

Kovner, A.R., Elton, J.J. and Billings, J (2000) Evidence-based management, *Frontiers of Health Services Management,* 16(4): 3–46.

Lavis, J., Gruen, R., Davies, H. and Walshe, K. (2006) Working within and beyond the Cochrane Collaboration to make systematic reviews more useful to healthcare managers and policymakers, *Healthcare Policy,* 1(2): 21–33.

Lemieux-Charles, L. and Champagne, F (2004) *Using Knowledge and Evidence in Healthcare: Multidisciplinary Perspectives.* Toronto: University of Toronto Press.

Lomas, J. (2000) Using linkage and exchange to move research into policy at a Canadian foundation, *Health Affairs,* 19(3): 236–40.

National Audit Office (2003) *Getting the Evidence: Using Research in Policy Making.* London: NAO.

Nutley, S.M., Walter, I. and Davies, H.T.O. (2007) *Using Evidence: How Research can Inform Public Services.* Bristol: The Policy Press.

Pfeffer, J. and Sutton, R.I. (2006) *Hard Facts, Dangerous Half-truths and Total Nonsense: Profiting from Evidence Based Management.* Harvard: Harvard Business School Press.

Sackett, D.L. and Rosenberg, W.M. (1995) The need for evidence-based medicine, *Journal of the Royal Society of Medicine,* 88(11): 620–24.

Tranfield, D., Denyer, D. and Smart, P. (2003) Towards a methodology for developing evidence informed management knowledge by means of systematic review, *British Journal of Management,* 14: 207–22.

The readings

Cochrane, A. (1972) *Effectiveness and Efficiency: Random Reflections on Health Services.* Nuffield Provincial Hospitals Trust [chapter 4: pp 20–25].

Rosenberg, W. and Donald, A. (1995) Evidence based medicine: an approach to clinical problem-solving, *British Medical Journal,* 310: 1122–26.

Naylor, C.D. (1995) Grey zones of clinical practice: some limits to evidence based medicine, *Lancet,* 345: 840–42.

Walshe, K. and Rundall, T. (2001) Evidence based management: from theory to practice in healthcare, *Milbank Quarterly,* 79(3): 429–57. (extract.)

Rousseau, D. (2006) Is there such a thing as evidence based management? *Academy of Management Review,* 31(2): 256–69. (extract.)

35

Effectiveness and efficiency: random reflections on health services
Archie Cochrane

Extracts from Cochrane A (1972) Effectiveness and efficiency: Random Reflections on Health Services. London, Nuffield Provincial Hospitals Trust.

Evaluation of evidence

Two of the most striking changes in word usage in the last twenty years are the upgrading of 'opinion' in comparison with other types of evidence, and the downgrading of the word 'experiment'. The upgrading of 'opinion' has doubtless many causes, but one of the most potent is, I am sure, the television interviewer and producer. They want everything to be brief, dramatic, black and white. Any discussion of evidence is written off as lengthy, dull, and grey. I have seldom heard a television interviewer ask anyone what his evidence was for some particular statement. Fortunately it does not usually matter; the interviewers only want to amuse (hence the interest in pop singers' views on theology), but when they deal with medical matters it can be important.

The fate of 'experiment' is very different. Its current meaning, according to the *OED* and normal scientific use, is 'to test a hypothesis'. It has been taken over by journalists and debased from its usual meaning and is now being used in its archaic sense of 'action of trying anything', hence the endless references to 'experimental' theatres, art, architecture, and schools. (Someone once told me of a notice pinned to a church door referring to 'experimental' baptism. I spent a happy half-hour designing trials to measure the relative baptismal effectiveness of waters from the Jordan, the Tweed, and the Taff.) This misuse of 'experiment' has, I think, altered people's attitudes to observational and experimental evidence.

The general scientific problem with which we are primarily concerned is that of testing a hypothesis that a certain treatment alters the natural history of a disease for the better. The particular problem is the value of various types of evidence in testing the hypothesis. The oldest, and probably still the commonest form of evidence proffered, is clinical opinion. This varies in value with the ability of the clinician and the width of his experience, but its value must be rated low, because there is no quantitative measurement, no attempt to discover what would have happened if the patients had had no treatment, and every possibility of bias affecting the assessment of the result. It could be described as the simplest (and worst) type of observational evidence.

Moving up the scale at the observational level, the main changes introducing improvement are the appearance of 'comparison' groups, the introduction of measurement and the exclusion of possible bias from the measurements. Comparison groups as they appear in the literature are a very mixed lot. Some are positively grotesque, such as that old favourite 'those who refused treatment'. They are usually very different from the theoretical 'control' group, which should be the same in all respects, which might influence the course of the disease, as the treated group. This, of course, puts a limit on the possible accuracy of this sort of investigation as we seldom if ever know all the characteristics that might influence the course of the disease.

The best index in these sort of comparisons is the fact of death, where there is little possibility of bias due to observer difference, but whenever other measurements are made steps have to be taken to be sure the measurements have been made without knowledge of which person has been treated. But even with all these sophistications observational evidence is never very satisfactory. An example comes from Palmer's work in my own unit investigating a rather different form of therapy (4). He took very detailed smoking histories from all the boys in a secondary modern school on two occasions, one year apart. He then obtained a list of all the boys who had been caned for smoking during that period. He was thus able to compare 'change in smoking habit' in caned and uncaned boys (Table 35.1). The results appear at first very striking. Those caned increased their cigarette consumption significantly more than those who were not caned, but when one thinks about it the results do not tell us anything at all. They are equally compatible with caning increasing, decreasing, or having no effect on cigarette consumption.

Observational evidence is clearly better than opinion, but it is thoroughly unsatisfactory. All research on the effectiveness of therapy was in this unfortunate state until the early 1950s. The only exceptions were the drugs whose effect on immediate mortality were so obvious that no trials were necessary, such as insulin, sulphonamide, and penicillin.

Table 35.1 Change brought about in smoking habits of schoolboys by caning, 1961–2

	Change in smoking habit				
	Increase	Same	Decrease	Total	X^2 (2df)
Caned	8 (35%)	10 (43%)	5 (22%)	23 (100%)	All caned v. All uncaned
Uncaned	10 (8%)	82 (67%)	31 (25%)	123 (100%)	12.9 ($P<0.01$)

Source: Modified from J. W. Palmer's Table IV (4).

The critical step forward which brought an experimental approach into clinical medicine can be variously dated. As previously mentioned I personally like to associate it with the publication in 1952 by Daniels and Hill (2). At any rate there is no doubt that the credit belongs to Sir Austin Bradford Hill. He has been much honoured but I doubt if we honour him enough. His ideas have only penetrated a small way into medicine, and they still have to revolutionize sociology, education, and penology. Each generation will, I hope, respect him more. (My pet idea is that there should be a 'Bradford' awarded to the best medical statistical paper of the year!)

The basic idea, like most good things, is very simple. The RCT approaches the problem of the comparability of the two groups the other way round. The idea is not to worry about the characteristics of the patients, but to be sure that the division of the patients into two groups is done by some method independent of human choice, i.e. by allocating according to some simple numerical device such as the order in which the patients come under treatment, or, more safely, by the use of random numbers. In this way the characteristics of the patients are randomized between the two groups, and it is possible to test the hypothesis that one treatment is better than another and express the results in the form of the probability of the differences found being due to chance or not.

The RCT is a very beautiful technique, of wide applicability, but as with everything else there are snags. When humans have to make observations there is always a possibility of bias. To reduce this possibility a modification has been introduced: the 'double-blind' randomized trial. In this neither the doctor nor the patients know which of the two treatments is being given. This eliminates the possibility of a great deal of bias, but one still has to be on one's guard.

There are other snags: first a purely statistical one. Many research units carry out hundreds of these so-called tests of significance in a year and it is often difficult to remember that, according to the level of significance chosen, 1 in 20 or 1 in 100 will be misleading. Another snag has been introduced by the current tendency to put too much emphasis on tests of significance. The results of such tests are very dependent on the number in the groups. With small numbers it is very easy to give the impression that a treatment is no more effective than a placebo, whereas in reality it is very difficult indeed to exclude the possibility of a small effect. Alternatively, with large numbers it is often possible to achieve a result that is statistically significant but may be clinically unimportant. All results must be examined very critically to avoid all the snags.

Another snag is that the technique is not always applicable for ethical reasons. There is, of course, no absolute medical ethic but the examples I quote here represent the majority of medical opinion at present, though I do not necessarily agree with them myself. They are: surgery for carcinoma of the lung, cytological tests for the prevention of cervical carcinoma, and dietetic therapy for phenylketonuria. No RCTs have ever been carried out to test the value of these standard therapies and tests. In the first two cases the RCT technique was not available when the surgical and medical innovations were made for carcinoma of the lung and cervix. By the time such RCTs were considered by medical scientists the one-time 'innovations' were embedded in clinical practice. Such trials would necessarily involve denying the routine procedure to half a group of patients and at this stage are nearly always termed unethical. It can be argued that it is ethically questionable to use on patients a procedure whose value is unknown, but the answer is that it is unethical not to do so if the patient will otherwise die or suffer severe disability and there is no alternative therapy. Such trials, it must be accepted, cannot be done in areas where the consensus of medical opinion is against them. This means, on the one hand, that patients' interests are very well protected and on the other that there are sections of medicine whose effectiveness cannot at present be measured and which, *in toto*, probably reduce the over-all efficiency of the NHS.

There are other limitations on the general applicability of the RCT. One important area is the group of diseases where improvement or deterioration has to be measured subjectively. It was hoped that the double-blind modification would avoid this trouble, but it has not been very successful in, say, psychiatry. Similarly the assessment of the 'quality of life' in such trials has proved very difficult. A good example is the various forms of treatment attempted for recurrences after operation for carcinoma of the breast. We have so far failed to develop any satisfactory way of measuring quality. Another area is relatively unimportant but worth mentioning: the rare diseases. Here the problem is the scarcity. For instance, in one case of porphyria variegata, in one acute attack renal dialysis appeared to be life-saving. In the next two it had no effect. It would need co-operation from most countries in Europe to complete a trial of this condition in a reasonable time.

Another very different reason for the relatively slow use of the RCT in measuring effectiveness is illustrated by its geographical distribution. If some such index as the number of RCTs per 1,000 doctors per year for all countries were worked out and a map of the world shaded according to the level of the index (black being the highest), one would see the UK in black, and scattered black patches in Scandinavia, the USA, and a few other countries; the rest would be nearly white. It appears in general it is Catholicism, Communism, and underdevelopment that appear to be against RCTs. In underdeveloped countries this can be understood, but what have Communism and Catholicism against RCTs? Is authoritarianism the common link, or is Communism a Catholic heresy? Whatever the cause this limitation to small areas of the world has certainly slowed down progress in two ways. There are too few doctors doing the work and the load on the few is becoming too great. An RCT is great fun for the co-ordinator but can be very boring for the scattered physicians filling in the forms.

In writing this section in praise of the RCT I do not want to give the impression that it is the only technique of any value in medical research. This would, of course, be entirely untrue. I believe, however, that the problem of evaluation is the first priority of the NHS and that for this purpose the RCT is much the most satisfactory in spite of its snags. The main job of medical administrators is to make choices between alternatives. To enable them to make the correct choices they must have accurate comparable data about the benefit and cost of the alternatives. These can really only be obtained by an adequately costed

RCT. (For a much better account of RCTs the reader is referred to P. D. Oldham's book *Measurement in Medicine*, published by English Universities Press, London, 1968.)

References

1. McKeown T, Lowe CR (1966). An introduction to social medicine, pp 3–18. Oxford: Blackwell Scientific Publications.
2. Daniels M, Hill AB (1952). Chemotherapy of pulmonary tuberculosis in young adults. An analysis of the combined results of three Medical Research Council trials. British Medical Journal 1: 1162.
3. Office of Health Economics (1971). Off Sick. OHE Publications no 36.
4. Palmer JW (1965). Smoking, caning and deliquency in a secondary modern school. British Journal of Preventive Social Medicine 19: 18.

36

Evidence-based medicine: an approach to clinical problem-solving
William Rosenberg and Anna Donald

Extracts from Rosenberg W and Donald A (1995) Evidence based medicine: an approach to clinical problem-solving. British Medical Journal 310: 1122–26.

Doctors within the NHS are confronting major changes at work. While we endeavour to improve the quality of health care, junior doctors' hours have been reduced and the emphasis on continuing medical education has increased. We are confronted by a growing body of information, much of it invalid or irrelevant to clinical practice. This article discusses evidence-based medicine, a process of turning clinical problems into questions and then systematically locating, appraising, and using contemporaneous research findings as the basis for clinical decisions. The computerisation of bibliographies and the development of software that permits the rapid location of relevant evidence have made it easier for busy clinicians to make best use of the published literature. Critical appraisal can be used to determine the validity and applicability of the evidence, which is then used to inform clinical decisions. Evidence-based medicine can be taught to, and practised by, clinicians at all levels of seniority and can be used to close the gulf between good clinical research and clinical practice. In addition it can help to promote self directed learning and teamwork and produce faster and better doctors.

Doctors must cope with a rapidly changing body of relevant evidence and maximise the quality of medical care despite the reduction in junior doctors' working hours and scarce resources. We are deluged with information, and although much of it is either invalid or irrelevant to clinical practice, an increasing amount comes from powerful investigations such as randomised controlled trials. Yet we continue to base our clinical decisions on increasingly out of date primary training or the overinterpretation of experiences with individual patients,[1] and even dramatically positive results from rigorous clinical studies remain largely unapplied.[2] Doctors need new skills to track down the new types of strong and useful evidence, distinguish it from weak and irrelevant evidence, and put it into practice. In this paper we discuss evidence-based medicine, a new framework for clinical problem solving which may help clinicians to meet these challenges.

What is evidence-based medicine?

Evidence-based medicine is the process of systematically finding, appraising, and using contemporaneous research findings as the basis for clinical decisions. For decades people have been aware of the gaps between research evidence and clinical practice, and the consequences in terms of expensive, ineffective, or even harmful decision making.[3] [4] Inexpensive electronic databases and widespread computer literacy now give doctors access to enormous amounts of data. Evidence-based medicine is about asking questions, finding and appraising the relevant data, and harnessing that information for everyday clinical practice.

Most readers will recognise that the ideas underlying evidence-based medicine are not new. Clinicians identify the questions raised in caring for their patients and consult the literature at least occasionally, if not routinely. The difference with using an explicit, evidence-based medicine framework is twofold: it can make consulting and evaluating the literature a relatively simple, routine procedure, and it can make this process workable for clinical teams, as well as for individual clinicians. The term "evidence-based medicine" was coined at McMaster Medical School in Canada in the 1980s to label this clinical learning strategy, which people at the school had been developing for over a decade.[5]

Evidence-based medicine in practice

Evidence-based medicine can be practised in any situation where there is doubt about an aspect of clinical diagnosis, prognosis, or management.

Four steps in evidence-based medicine

- Formulate a clear clinical question from a patient's problem

- Search the literature for relevant clinical articles

- Evaluate (critically appraise) the evidence for its validity and usefulness

- Implement useful findings in clinical practice

Setting the question

A 77 year old woman living alone is admitted with non-rheumatic atrial fibrillation and her first bout of mild left ventricular failure, and she responds to digoxin and diuretics. She has a history of well controlled hypertension. An echocardiogram shows moderately impaired left ventricular function. She is an active person and anxious to maintain her independence. During the ward round on the following day a debate ensues about the risks and benefits of offering her long term anticoagulation with warfarin, and rather than defer to seniority or abdicate responsibility to consensus by committee, team members convert the debate into a question: "How does her risk of embolic stroke, if we don't give her anticoagulant drugs, compare with her risk of serious haemorrhage and stroke if we do?"

The questions that initiate evidence-based medicine can relate to diagnosis, prognosis, treatment, iatrogenic harm, quality of care, or health economics. In any event, they should be as specific as possible, including the type of patient, the clinical intervention, and the clinical outcome of interest. In this example two questions are prepared for a literature search. One question relates to prognosis and her susceptibility: "How great is the annual risk of embolic stroke in a 77 year old woman with non-rheumatic atrial fibrillation, hypertension, and moderate left ventricular enlargement if she is not given anticoagulants?" The other question concerns treatment and asks, "What is the risk reduction for stroke from warfarin therapy in such a patient, and what is the risk of harming her with this therapy?"

Finding the evidence

The second step is a search for the best available evidence. To conduct searches on a regular basis, clinicians need effective searching skills and easy access to bibliographic databases. Increasingly the access can be proved by ward or surgery based computers, complemented by assistance in obtaining hard copies of articles, and enabled by librarians who teach searching skills and guide the unwary through the 25000 biomedical journals now in print.[6] [7]

Two sorts of electronic databases are available. The first sort is bibliographic and permits users to identify relevant citations in the clinical literature, using variations of Medline. The second sort of database takes the user directly to primary or secondary publications of the relevant clinical evidence–the rapidly growing numbers include the Cochrane Database of Systematic Reviews, Scientific American Medicine on CD-ROM, and the ACP Journal Club (a bimonthly supplement to the Annals of Internal Medicine which abstracts the relevant and rigorous articles on diagnosis, prognosis, treatment, quality of care, and medical economics from over 30 general medical journals). All these databases are, or soon will be, available on line from local, national, and international networks such as the internet.

While clinicians may make greater use of meta-analyses in the future, the ability to appraise critically publications of all types will remain an invaluable skill. Searches may fail to uncover well conducted and relevant meta-analyses and often it will be impractical for a busy clinician to conduct an independent systematic review of the literature each time a clinical question is generated. On these occasions the most effective strategy will be to seek out the best of the available literature and to appraise critically the evidence by using skills that can readily be learnt.

Appraising the evidence

The third step is to evaluate, or appraise, the evidence for its validity and clinical usefulness. This step is crucial because it lets the clinician decide whether an article can be relied on to give useful guidance. Unfortunately, a large proportion of published medical research lacks either relevance or sufficient methodological rigour to be reliable enough for answering clinical questions.[8] To overcome this, a structured but simple method, named "critical appraisal," developed by several teams working in North America and the United Kingdom, enables individuals without research expertise to evaluate clinical articles. Mastering critical appraisal entails learning how to ask a few key questions about the validity of the evidence and its relevance to a particular patient or group of patients. Its fundamentals can be learnt within a few hours in small tutorials, workshops, interactive lectures, and at the bedside by a wide range of users, including those without a biomedical background. This strategy has been developed for many different types of articles, and can be used to evaluate original articles about diagnosis, treatment, prognosis, quality of care, and economics as well as to evaluate reviews, overviews, and meta-analyses for their validity and applicability.

The table shows a typical set of critical appraisal questions for evaluating articles about treatment. Although they reflect common sense, the questions are not entirely self explanatory; some instruction is needed to help clinicians apply them to specific articles and individual patients. Self directed learning materials have been developed to help users apply different critical appraisal questions to the different sorts of clinical research articles on diagnosis, prognosis, therapy, quality of care, economic analysis, and screening. These materials include the JAMA series of user's guides and the text Clinical Epidemiology: A Basic Science for Clinical Medicine.[9] Week long training workshops in evidence-based medicine are held in various venues, but we have found that even people with limited experience can readily learn how to practise evidence-based medicine in the context of their own clinical practice. As with any other skill, expertise and speed come with practice, and experienced practitioners can learn to appraise critically most articles in under 10 minutes, transforming themselves from passive, opinion based spectators to active, evidence-based clinicians.

Critical appraisal questions used to evaluate a therapy article[10] [11]			
	Yes	Can't tell	No
Are the results valid?			
Was the assignment of patients to treatments randomised?			
Were all patients who entered the trial properly accounted for and attributed at its conclusion?			

Was follow up complete?

Were patients analysed in the groups to
which they were randomised?

Were patients, health workers, and study
personnel blinded to treatment?

Were the groups similar at the start of the trial?

Aside from the experimental intervention,
were the groups treated equally?

What are the results?
   How large was the treatment effect?
   How precise was the treatment effect?

Will the results help me care for my patients?
   Can the results be applied to my patient care?
   Were all clinically important outcomes considered?
   Are the likely benefits worth the potential
   harms and costs?

Acting on the evidence

Having identified evidence that is both valid and relevant, clinicians can either
implement it directly in a patient's care or use it to develop team protocols or even
hospital guidelines. They can also use evidence to revolutionise continuing medical
education programmes or audit. In our experience, implementing the evidence is
best learned through group discussions, either on ward rounds or in other
meetings of the clinical team in which members explore ways of incorporating the
evidence into a patient's clinical management.

Other requirements for practising evidence-based medicine

The ability to present published evidence quickly and clearly is crucial for clinical
teams with little time and much information to absorb.[12] Medical journals have led
the way here with structured abstracts to help readers quickly retrieve key
information. Such clarity and quickness are equally important for clinicians when
they present evidence to their team. A preset, one page, user friendly summary
such as the one developed by doctors in training at McMaster University in
Ontario (unpublished data) can help this process and was the model for the
critically appraised topic that appears in the table.

Added advantages in practising evidence-based medicine

For individuals

- Enables clinicians to upgrade their knowledge base routinely

- Improves clinicians' understanding of research methods and makes them more critical in using data

- Improves confidence in management decisions

- Improves computer literacy and data searching techniques

- Improves reading habits

For clinical teams

- Gives team a framework for group problem solving and for teaching

- Enables juniors to contribute usefully to team

For patients

- More effective use of resources

- Better communication with patients about the rationale behind management decisions

Support from senior clinicians is critical to the success of introducing evidence-based medicine.[13] Seniors who practice evidence-based medicine are excellent role models for training newcomers and allocating questions according to the skills and time commitments of individual team members. Even when senior staff are themselves unfamiliar with evidence-based medicine, their willingness to admit uncertainty, to encourage scepticism, and to be flexible can help the team to accommodate new evidence which may contradict previous assumptions and practice.

Does it work?

An evidence-based approach to clinical care has been practised in many countries under various guises. In the structured form described above it attracts both support and criticism, often within the same hospital. The problem, ironically, is that the approach is difficult to evaluate.[14] It is a process for solving problems, and it will have different outcomes depending on the problem being solved. Trying to monitor all the possible outcomes would be impossible, especially since many are difficult to quantify. For example, a medical student who learns the importance of good research methodology through practising critical appraisal may later on carry out better research, but it would be hard either to quantify this or to link it directly to evidence-based medicine.

None the less, evidence of the effectiveness of evidence-based medicine is growing as it spreads to new settings. Short term trials have shown better and more informed clinical decisions following even brief training in critical appraisal,[15] and although graduates from traditional medical curriculums progressively decline in their knowledge of appropriate clinical practice, graduates of a medical school that teaches lifelong, self directed, evidence-based medicine are still up to date as long as 15 years after graduation.[16] The review of the benefits and drawbacks of evidence-based medicine that follows draws on our experience of teaching and practising evidence-based medicine with clinicians and purchasers in Oxford.

Advantages

An immediate attraction of evidence-based medicine is that it integrates medical education with clinical practice. We have observed that students and doctors who begin to learn evidence-based medicine become adept at generating their own questions and following them through with efficient literature searches. For example, learners quickly learn to pick out good review articles and to use resources such as the ACP Journal Club when they are appropriate to the question being asked.[17]

Another advantage of evidence-based medicine is that it can be learnt by people from different backgrounds and at any stage in their careers. Medical students carrying out critical appraisals not only learn evidence-based medicine for themselves but contribute their appraisals to their teams and update their colleagues. At the other extreme, seasoned clinicians can master evidence-based medicine and transform a journal club from a passive summary of assigned journals into an active inquiry in which problems arising from patient care are used to direct searches and appraisals of relevant evidence to keep their practice up to date.

The evidence-based approach is being taken up by non-clinicians as well. Consumer groups concerned with obtaining optimal care during pregnancy and childbirth are evolving evidence-based patient choice. The critical appraisal skills for purchasers project in the former Oxford region involves teaching evidence-based medicine to purchasers who have no medical training so that it can inform their decisions on purchasing.[18]

A third attraction of evidence-based medicine is its potential for improving continuity and uniformity of care through the common approaches and guidelines developed by its practitioners. Shift work and cross cover make communication between health workers both more important and more difficult. Although evidence-based medicine cannot alter work relationships, in our experience it does provide a structure for effective team work and the open communication of team generated (rather than externally imposed) guidelines for optimal patient care. It also provides a common framework for problem solving and improving communication and understanding between people from different backgrounds, such as clinicians and patients or non-medical purchasers and clinicians.

Evidence-based medicine can help providers make better use of limited resources by enabling them to evaluate clinical effectiveness of treatments and services. Remaining ignorant of valid research findings has serious consequences. For example, it is now clear that giving steroids to women at risk of premature labour greatly reduces infant respiratory distress and consequent morbidity, mortality, and costs of care,[19] and it is equally clear that aspirin and streptokinase deserve to be among the mainstays of care for victims of heart attack.

Disadvantages

Evidence-based medicine has several drawbacks. Firstly, it takes time both to learn and to practise. For example, it takes about two hours to properly set the question, find the evidence, appraise the evidence, and act on the evidence, and for teams to benefit all members should be present for the first and last steps. Senior staff must therefore be good at time management. They can help to make searches less onerous by setting achievable contracts with the team members doing the searches and by ensuring that the question has direct clinical usefulness. These responsibilities of the team leader are time consuming.

Establishing the infrastructure for practising evidence-based medicine costs money. Hospitals and general practices may need to buy and maintain the necessary computer hardware and software. CD-ROM subscriptions can vary from £250 to £2000 a year, depending on the database and specifications. But a shortage of resources need not stifle the adoption of evidence-based medicine. The BMA provides Medline free of charge to members with modems, and Medline is also available for a small fee on the internet. Compared with the costs of many medical interventions (to say nothing of journal subscriptions and out of date texts), these costs are small and may recover costs many times their amount by reducing ineffective practice.

Inevitably, evidence-based medicine exposes gaps in the evidence.[4] This can be frustrating, particularly for inexperienced doctors. Senior staff can help to overcome this problem by setting questions for which there is likely to be good evidence. The identification of such gaps can be helpful in generating local and national research projects, such as those being commissioned by the York Centre for Reviews and Dissemination.[20]

Another problem is that Medline and the other electronic databases used for finding relevant evidence are not comprehensive and are not always well indexed. At times even a lengthy literature search is fruitless. For some older doctors the computer skills needed for using databases regularly may also seem daunting. Although the evidence-based approach requires a minimum of computer literacy and keyboard skills, and while these are now almost universal among medical students and junior doctors, many older doctors are still unfamiliar with computers and databases. On the other hand, creative and systematic searching techniques are increasingly available,[21,22] and high quality review articles are becoming abundant. In the absence of suitable review articles, clinicians who have acquired critical appraisal skills will be able to evaluate the primary literature for themselves.

Finally, authoritarian clinicians may see evidence-based medicine as a threat. It may cause them to lose face by sometimes exposing their current practice as obsolete or occasionally even dangerous. At times it will alter the dynamics of the team, removing hierarchical distinctions that are based on seniority; some will rue the day when a junior member of the team, by conducting a search and critical appraisal, has as much authority and respect as the team's most senior member.[23]

Notes

1   Smith R. Filling the lacuna between research and practice: an interview with Michael Peckham. BMJ 1993;307:1403–7.
2   Faber RG. Information overload. BMJ 1993;307:383.
3   Haines A, Jones R. Implementing findings of research. BMJ 1994;308:1488–92.
4   Chalmers I, Dickersin K, Chalmers TC. Getting to grips with Archie Cochrane's agenda. BMJ 1992;305:786–7.
5   Evidence Based Medicine Working Group. Evidence-based medicine. JAMA 1992;268:2420–5.
6   Wyatt J. Uses and sources of medical knowledge. Lancet 1991;338:1368–73.
7   Marshall JG. The impact of the hospital library on clinical decision making: the Rochester study. Bulletin of the Medical Library Association 1992;80:169–78.
8   Altman DG. The scandal of poor medical research. BMJ 1994;308:283–4.
9   Sackett DL, Haynes RB, Guyatt GH, Tugwell P. Clinical epidemiology: a basic science for clinical medicine. 2nd ed. Boston: Little Brown, 1991.
10 Users' guides to the medical literature: how to use an article about therapy or prevention. I. JAMA 1993;270:2598–601.
11 Users' guides to the medical literature: how to use an article about therapy or prevention. II. JAMA 1994;271:59–63.
12 Lock S. Structured abstracts. BMJ 1988;297:156.
13 Guyatt G, Nishikawa J. A proposal for enhancing the quality of clinical teaching: results of a department of medicine's educational retreat. Medical Teacher 1993;15:147–61.
14 Audet N, Gagnon R, Marcil M. L'enseignement de l'analyse critique des publications scientifiques medicales, est-il efficace? Revision des etudes et de leur qualite methodologique. Can Med Assoc J 1993;148:945–52.
15 Bennet KJ, Sackett DL, Haynes RB, Neufeld VR. A controlled trial of teaching critical appraisal of the clinical literature to medical students. JAMA 1987;257:2451–4.

16 Shin JH, Haynes RB, Johnston ME. The effect of problem-based, self-directed undergraduate education on life-long learning. Can Med Assoc J 1993;148:969–76.
17 Milne R, Chambers L. Assessing the scientific quality of review articles. J Epidemiol Community Health 1993;47:169–70.
18 Dunning M, McQuay H, Milne R. Getting a GRiP. Health Service Journal 1994;104:24–6.
19 Crowley P, Chalmers I, Keirse MJ. The effects of corticosteroid administration before pre-term delivery: an overview of the evidence from controlled trials. Br J Obstet Gynaecol 1990;97:11–25.
20 Sheldon T, Chalmers I. The UK Cochrane Centre and the NHS Centre for Reviews and Dissemination: respective roles within the information systems strategy of the NHS R&D programme, co-ordination and principles underlying collaboration. Health Economics 1994;3:201–3.
21 Farbey R. Searching the literature: be creative with Medline. BMJ 1993;307:66.
22 Jadad AR, McQuay H. Searching the literature: be systematic in your searching. BMJ 1993;307:66.
23 West R. Assessment of evidence versus consensus or prejudice. J Epidemiol Community Health 1993;47:321–2.

37

Grey zones of clinical practice: some limits to evidence-based medicine

David Naylor

Extracts from Naylor CD (1995) Grey zones of clinical practice: some limits to evidence based medicine, Lancet, 345: 840–42.

In a recent attack on evidence-based medicine, a philosopher[1] urged doctors to defend clinical reasoning based on experience and pathophysiological mechanisms and criticised the effects of clinical epidemiology and health services research on practice. As head of a publicly funded institute concerned with abetting the translation of evidence into practice in Canada, I wish those effects were even more pervasive. But a backlash is not surprising in view of the inflated expectations of outcomes-oriented and evidence-based medicine and the fears of some clinicians that these concepts threaten the art of patient care.

Evidence-based medicine offers little help in the many grey zones of practice where the evidence about risk-benefit ratios of competing clinical options is incomplete or contradictory. Almost by definition, this intellectual terrain is poorly charted, but research by RAND illustrates its potential dimensions. To develop criteria for assessing the appropriateness of clinical procedures, RAND convenes panels of clinical experts who rate hundreds of hypothetical cases on a risk-benefit scale.[2,3] Inevitably ratings for some scenarios cluster in the uncertain middle of the scale, while for some others disagreement among expert panelists precludes categorisation. When ratings of a given nation's experts are applied to charts audited in the same country, there is a surprising proportion of grey-zone procedures (Table 37.1). Table 37.2 illustrates how cross-national panelists ratings yield different results when applied to the same data. In the face of uncertainty, US experts are more action-oriented than their counterparts in England; Canadians, as usual, sit somewhere in the middle. Other RAND work shows that surgeons view surgery with much less uncertainty than physicians, and generalists are more conservative than specialists.[4-7]

All these ratings reflect not only evidence but also inference and experience. Consequently, panelists may be "pooling ignorance as much as distilling wisdom";[8] and the decision-rules for what is equivocal versus inappropriate are themselves arbitrary.[9] If one demanded evidence from randomised controlled trials in support of each indication, the grey zone would be wider.[10] Furthermore, these data are from post hoc audits of discrete procedures studied partly because of their resource implications. The evidence for those procedures, as well as the clinical rationale for their use in any given patient, is (one hopes) better developed than for many smaller-ticket items in routine practice. Thus the boundaries of the grey zones are themselves uncertain, varying with the evidence and its interpretation. Clinical medicine seems to consist of a few things we know, a few things we think we know (but probably don't), and lots of things we don't know at all.

Why is the grey zone so large?

Ours is an era of chronic and expensive diseases. There are no vaccines yet for atherosclerosis, cancer, arthritis, or AIDS. Until the ongoing revolution in molecular biology pays more concrete dividends we shall be muddling along with what Lewis Thomas characterised as "halfway technologies".[11] However, medical mudding is a profitable business, and the proliferation of new tests, devices, and drugs continues at an unprecedented pace.

Although life would be simpler if these new technologies were always appraised in rigorous studies with clinically relevant endpoints, current data are often insufficient to guide practice. Another difficulty arises from the Malthusian growth of uncertainty when multiple technologies are combined into clinical strategies. Take two technologies and they can be used in two different sequences; take five, and the number of possible sequences is one hundred and twenty. Furthermore, the elements in a clinical strategy are usually tested in separate studies, leaving few data on the chains of conditional probabilities that link sequences of tests, treatments, and outcomes. The play of uncertainty can be shown quantitatively when formal decision analysis is used as a tool to compare clinical strategies. The outcome is often either a "toss-up" that rests squarely in the grey zones, or highly dependent on assumptions about one or more poorly defined variables in the model.[12]

When evidence alone cannot guide clinical actions, some will espouse minimalism whereas others will favour intervention based on inference and experience. This conflict in philosophies is nothing new. A hundred years ago, Osler's *The Principles and Practice of Medicine* was praised by many but panned by some because of the author's unrelenting scepticism about unproven treatments. Of course, those treatments endorsed by Osler were generally supported only by findings from uncontrolled and unblinded case-series. The revolution in standards of evidence required before clinical practices are accepted as legitimately beneficial came about during the past 30 years. The cornerstone method remains the randomised trial, abetted now by the widespread application of meta-analysis to synthesise results from multiple trials. It is sobering to look back and recognise how expert panels and guideline-setting bodies misguided the profession by failing to aggregate the totality of information available from randomised trials;[13] it is more disturbing to look ahead and ask how practitioners can synthesise information from the scores of trials published every month.

Table 37.1 Proportions of procedures done for uncertain indications, based on expert panel criteria

Procedure	Location/sample	Year	n	% uncertain (95% CI)
Carotid endarterectomy	USA, Medicare beneficiaries in 3 states[4,16]	1981	1302	32 (30–34)
	USA, 5 Veterans' Administration teaching hospitals in California[17]	1981	107	32 (23–42)
Upper gastrointestinal endoscopy	USA, Medicare beneficiaries in 3 states[16]	1981	1585	11 (9–13)
Hysterectomy	USA, 7 health maintenance organisations, cases without cancer or emergency surgery[18]	1989–90	642	25 (22–29)
Percutaneous transluminal coronary angioplasty	USA, 15 hospitals in New York State[19]	1990	1306	38 (35–41)

Confidence intervals were calculated if not reported.

Table 37.2 Appropriateness of indications for cardiovascular procedures and cross-national differences in expert panel assessments

Procedure	Location/sample	Year	n	Panel nationality	Appropriate	Uncertain	Inappropriate
Coronary artery bypass graft	USA, 4 hospitals in Washington State[7]	1979–80	386	American	62	25	13
		1982		British	41	24	35
	UK, 3 hospitals in Trent region[20]	1987–88	319	American	67	26	7
				British	57	27	16
	Canada, 13 hospitals in Ontario and British Columbia[21]	1980–90	556	American	88	9	3
				Canadian	85	11	4
	USA, 15 hospitals in New York State[21]	1990	1336	American	91	7	2
				Canadian	85	10	6
Coronary angiography	USA, 4 hospitals in Washington State[7]	1979–80	376	American	50	23	27
		1982		British	11	29	60
	USA, Medicare beneficiaries in 3 states[8]	1981	1677	American	74	9	17
				British	39	19	42

UK, 3 hospitals in Trent region[20]	1987–88	320	American	71	12	17
			British	49	30	21
Canada, 20 hospitals in Ontario and British Columbia[21]			American	77	18	5
			Canadian	58	33	9
USA, 15 hospitals in New York State[21]	1990	1333	American	76	20	4
			Canadian	51	39	10

Against this backdrop, one better appreciates the importance of *Effective Care in Pregnancy and Childbirth*.[14] This compendium of meta-analyses has shaken obstetrics world wide, not only for what it shows to be true but also for the innumerable clinical strategies that it puts in question. As an outgrowth of the maternity care compendium, the International Cochrane Collaboration is developing meta-analyses of all randomised trials in all areas of medicine, along with plans to disseminate the findings widely. The Cochrane Collaboration is an enterprise that rivals the Human Genome Project in its potential implications for modern medicine. Nevertheless, we should be under no illusions about what its work will yield. There will be surprises as we learn that some treatments were prematurely discarded on the basis of trials too small to detect a meaningful treatment effect; there will be validation for many strategies adopted on the basis of high quality modern trials; but a huge amount of the output will be inconclusive and will augment the grey zones of practice until a new generation of research is completed.

Reconciling the new evaluative sciences and old arts

In view of the limits of clinical research evidence one might expect paralytic indecisiveness to be more common in practice. However, the human psyche is malleable, and practice forgiving enough that clinicians rapidly become comfortable making decisions under conditions of uncertainty. Many treatments are genuinely effective, some diseases remit irrespective of treatment, and a "dose of doctor" is often salutary for patients in ambulatory care who present with unexplained fatigue, undiagnosable odd spells, vague fleeting pains, and gut motility disorders. We become confident in our educated guesswork to the point where it is easy to confuse personal opinion with evidence, or personal ignorance with genuine scientific uncertainty.

It does not help matters when clinical-guideline-writers fall into the same trap, marshalling an expert consensus that fails to distinguish fact from fervour. If clinical guidelines and other trappings of evidence-based medicine are to be credible, they must distil the best evidence about what ought to be done in practice in ways that honestly acknowledge what we do and do not know about a topic. Read the recent compendium from the Canadian Task Force on the Periodic Health Examination, a group of physicians trained in clinical epidemiology, and, happily, that is exactly what occurs. There are no less than seventy-six preventive manoeuvres characterised by inconclusive evidence and labelled as "grade C recommendations", where "decision-making must be guided by factors other than medical scientific evidence".[15]

More generally, the prudent application of evaluative sciences will affirm rather than obviate the need for the art of medicine. Clinical reasoning, with its reliance on experience, analogy, and extrapolation, must be applied to traverse the many grey zones of practice. Eliciting and respecting patients' preferences is especially important when there is reasonable doubt about the best course of action. There will also be a place for the art of communicating in ways that help patients live with what we don't know, or what they think we know and won't tell them. And even good evidence can lead to bad practice if applied in an unthinking or unfeeling way.

In sum, the limits to medical evidence continue to limit the ambit of evidence-based medicine. The craft of caring for patients can flourish not merely in the grey zones where scientific evidence is incomplete or conflicting but also in the recognition that what is black and white in the abstract may rapidly become grey in practice, as clinicians seek to meet their individual patients' needs. To paraphrase Osler, let us agree that good clinical medicine will always blend the art of uncertainty with the science of probability. But let us also hope that the blend can be weighted heavily towards science, whenever and wherever sound evidence is brought to light.

Notes

1 Tanenbaum SJ. What physicians know. *N Engl J Med* 1993; **329**: 1268–71.
2 Brook RH, Chassin MR, Fink A, Solomon DH, Kosecoff JB, Park RE. A method for the detailed assessment of the appropriateness of medical technologies. *Int J Tech Asses Health Care* 1986; **2**: 53–64.
3 Park RE, Fink A, Brook RH, et al. Physician ratings of appropriate indications for three procedures: theoretical indications vs indications used in practice. *Am J Publ Health* 1989; **79**: 445–47.
4 Leape LL, Park RE, Kahan JP, Brook RH. Group judgments of appropriateness: the effect of panel composition. *Qual Assur Health Care* 1992; **4**: 151–59.
5 Kahn KL, Park RE, Brook RH, et al. The effect of comorbidity on appropriateness ratings for two gastrointestinal procedures. *J Clin Epidemiol* 1988; **41**: 115–22.
6 Fraser GM, Pilpel D, Hollis S, Kosecoff JB, Brook RH. Indications for cholecystectomy; the results of a consensus panel approach. *Qual Assur Health Care* 1993; **5**: 75–80.
7 Brook RH, Kosecoff JB, Park RE, Chassin MR, Winslow CM, Hampton JR. Diagnosis and treatment of coronary artery disease: comparison of doctors' attitudes in the USA and the UK. *Lancet* 1988; i: 750–53.
8 Scott E, Black N. When does consensus exist in expert panels? *J Publ Health Med* 1991; **13**: 344.

9   Phelps CE. The methodologic foundations of studies of the appropriateness of medical care. *N Engl J Med* 1993; **329**: 1241–45.

10 Lomas J, Anderson GM, Enkin M, Vayda E, Roberts R, MacKinnon B. The role of evidence in the consensus process. *JAMA* 1988; **259**: 3001–08.

11 Thomas L. On the science and technology of medicine. In: Knowles JH, ed. Doing better and feeling worse. New York: W W Norton and Co, 1977: 35–46.

12 Kassirer JP, Moskowitz AJ, Lau J, Pauker SG. Clinical decision analysis: a progress report. *Ann Intern Med* 1987; **106**: 275–91.

13 Antman EM, Lau J, Kupelnick B, Mosteller F, Chalmers TC. A comparison of results of meta-analyses of randomized control trials and recommendations of clinical experts: treatments for myocardial infarction. *JAMA* 1992; **268**: 240–48.

14 Chalmers I, Enkin M, Kierse MJNC. Effective care in pregnancy and childbirth. New York: Oxford University Press, 1991.

15 The Canadian Task Force on the Periodic Health Examination. The Canadian guide to clinical preventive health care. Ottawa: Ministry of Supply and Services, 1994.

16 Chassin MR, Kosecoff JB, Park RE, et al. Does inappropriate use explain geographic variations in the use of health care services? A study of three procedures. *JAMA* 1987; **258**: 2533–37.

17 Merrick NJ, Brook RH, Fink A, Solomon DH. Use of carotid endarterectomy in five California Veterans Administration medical centers. *JAMA* 1986; **256**: 2531–35.

18 Bernstein SJ, McGlynn EA, Siu AL, et al. The appropriateness of hysterectomy: a comparison of care in seven health plans. *JAMA* 1993; **269**: 2398–402.

19 Hilborne LH, Leape LL, Bernstein SJ, et al. The appropriateness of use of percutaneous transluminal coronary angioplasty in New York State. *JAMA* 1993; **269**: 761–65.

20 Bernstein SJ, Kosecoff JB, Gray D, Hampton JR, Brook RH. The appropriateness of the use of cardiovascular procedures. *Inr J Tech Asses Health Care* 1993; **9**: 3–10.

21 McGlynn EA, Naylor CD, Anderson GM, et al. Comparison of the appropriateness of coronary angiography and coronary artery bypass graft surgery between Canada and New York State. *JAMA* 1994; **272**: 934–40.

38

Evidence-based management: from theory to practice in health care
Kieran Walshe and Thomas Rundall

Extracted from Walshe K and Rundell TG (2001) Evidence based management: from theory to practice in healthcare, Milbank Quarterly, 79(3): 429–57.

Over the last decade, there has been a significant shift in the way that health care professionals use evidence from scientific research in their clinical practice. The concept of evidence-based health care (Sackett and Rosenberg 1995) has become part of the language of clinicians, managers, policymakers, and researchers in health services throughout the world. Though the notion of evidence-based health care is far from new (Cochrane 1972) and the extent of its uptake in clinical practice is uneven, the diffusion and adoption of the ideas associated with evidence-based health care during the 1990s provide a remarkable testament to their power and their relevance to the current problems and challenges of health care systems in many countries (Davies and Nutley 1999). Moreover, the concept has begun to spread to fields outside health care, with the establishment of initiatives for evidence-based practice in social care, criminal justice, and education (Davies, Nutley, and Smith 1999; Boruch, Petrosino, and Chalmers 1999), and interest in its methodologies in many other scientific fields (Petticrew 2001).

However, the leaders and managers of health care organizations, while often doing much to encourage clinicians to adopt an evidence-based approach to clinical practice, have been slow to apply the ideas to their own managerial practice (Hewison 1997). The rise of evidence-based clinical practice was prompted in part by the existence of unexplained wide variations in clinical practice patterns, by the poor uptake of therapies of known effectiveness, and by the persistent use of technologies that were known to be ineffective. These problems are found equally in managerial practice in health care organizations, and in the way that decisions about how to organize, structure, deliver, or finance health services are made, yet what might be called evidence-based management has made slow progress (Kovner, Elton, and Billings 2000).

This article describes the main principles of evidence-based health care, documents its increasing acceptance, and explores the reasons for its popularity. It discusses the applicability of the ideas of evidence-based practice to health care management, and presents a comparison of the culture, research base, and decision-making processes in the two domains, which helps to explain the slow progress of evidence-based management to date. The work of the Center for Health Management Research is described and used to explore the practicalities of evidence-based managerial practice. The article concludes by outlining an agenda for action to promote the development of evidence-based management in health care. While the article focuses on clinical and managerial decision making, we believe much of its content is equally relevant to policymakers and the way that health policy decisions are made.

Evidence-based management: a slow start

There is plenty of evidence that a research practice gap exists in health care policy and management (Lomas 1997), and that the problems of overuse, underuse, and misuse that were described earlier in the clinical context can also be seen in the way that health care organizations are managed and health services are delivered. These instances have received far less attention and been less well documented than some of their clinical equivalents, however (see Table 38.1). Though quantitative data are hard to come by, there is little doubt that these problems represent very significant costs to health care organizations, or that they have a real impact on the quality of care and on patient outcomes.

At first sight, overuse seems to be the predominant problem in health care management. Managerial practice has often been criticized for being influenced by fads and fashions that are adopted overenthusiastically, implemented inadequately, then discarded prematurely in favor of the latest trend (Abrahamson 1996; Walston and Bogue 1999; Staw and Epstein 2000). However, it is also true that some promising managerial innovations are very slow to spread, and underuse can be observed (Christensen, Bohmer, and Kenagy 2000). More significantly, in almost every area of managerial practice, we find massive variations between individual health care managers and health care organizations that cannot easily be explained, which probably indicate that substantial misuse exists.

Nevertheless, evidence-based management seems to have made little or no progress in health care so far, at least in comparison with its clinical cousin. While a few academics and practicing managers have written about it in largely positive terms (Hewison 1997; Stewart 1998; Homa 1998; Axelsson 1998; Kovner, Elton, and Billings 2000), governments, policymakers, and managers themselves have shown a conspicuous lack of interest. Although there are some encouraging developments—such as the Cochrane Collaboration's effective practice and organization of care groups (Halladay and Bero 2000), the U.K. government's new health service delivery and organizational research program (Fulop, Allen, Clarke, et al. 2001), the recently established Canadian Health Services Research Foundation (Lomas 2000), and a new initiative to promote evidence-based management by the Association for University Programs in Health Administration—we are still a long way from seeing managers make proper use of evidence in their decision making.

Table 38.1   Examples of the research-practice gap in health care management

Overuse	• The usage of organizational mergers as a response to problems of service quality, capacity or financial viability in health care organizations (Blumenthal and Edwards 2000; Arndt, Bigelow, and Dorman 1999) • The measurement of patient satisfaction using poorly conceptualized, poorly designed instruments, which produce data that often are not used (Sitzia and Wood 1997; van Campen, Sixma, Friele, et al. 1995)
Underuse	• The replacement of physicians with other health professionals in providing many routine health services, especially in primary care and accident and emergency department settings (Richardson, Maynard, Cullum, et al. 1998; Richards, Carley, Jenkins-Clarke, et al. 2000) • The concentration of workload for particular procedures at institutions that handle substantial volumes of those procedures and have better patient outcomes (Dudley, Johansen, Brand, et al. 2000; Luft, Bunker, and Enthoven 1979)
Misuse/ variation	• The use of community-based treatment ("hospital at home" schemes and the like) as an alternative to hospital inpatient care (Shepperd and Iliffe 1998) • The involvement of clinicians in the management of health care provider organizations, and the structuring of clinical management arrangements (Succi and Alexander 1999; Guthrie 1999) • The adoption and implementation of total quality management or continuous quality improvement initiatives (Shortell, Bennett, and Byck 1998; Blumenthal and Kilo 1998)

Comparing the use of evidence in health care management and in clinical practice

The culture, research base, and decision-making processes of clinical practice and of health care management are different in many ways (see, e.g., Mintzberg 1973; Freidson 1980; 1986; 1994; Bazerman 1998; Drucker 1998; and Schein 1988). This section highlights some of the differences, mainly by comparing the worlds of doctors and health care managers, which may help explain why evidence-based practice has been slow to progress in health care management. Of course, there are also many similarities between the clinical and managerial worlds, and neither is as homogeneous or as straightforward as this kind of comparative analysis may suggest. However, this simplified and generalized comparison may be useful in understanding whether and how the ideas of evidence-based practice might be transferred from the clinical domain to the managerial domain (See Table 38.2).

Culture

The clinical culture is highly professionalized, with a formal body of knowledge that is shared by all members of the profession and acts as a frame of reference for intraprofessional dialogue and debate. Entry to the profession is controlled—limited to people who share that formal knowledge and have undergone specific training. This helps produce a disciplinary coherence in knowledge, attitudes, and beliefs, which fits well with the structured and directed approach to knowledge that is found in evidence-based practice. In contrast, health care managers are a highly diverse group drawn from different professional and disciplinary backgrounds, and they often lack even a shared language or terminology with which to describe and discuss what they do. Many (though not all) have some qualification in management or health care administration, but there is no specified formal body of knowledge, training, or registration *required* to become a health care manager, and many clinicians take on health care management roles with little or no formal management training at all. Personal experience and self-generated knowledge play a much larger part in determining how managers approach their jobs, and there is much less reliance on a shared body of formal knowledge in decision making. It is not surprising, therefore, that managers may be less willing and less able to understand, accept, and use research findings in their practice, both as a group and as individuals.

The clinical culture values scientific knowledge and research. Through their training, clinical professionals are imbued with the primacy of the scientific method as a way of knowing, and with a profound respect for the research process and its outputs. Many clinicians receive some research-methods training as part of their professional development, and have some ongoing involvement in research. The structure of the profession bestows high status on those who engage in research or pursue an academic career. Clinicians often have a twin career track in research and clinical practice, and the structure of clinical academic departments and academic health care facilities is predicated on the idea that individuals will practice, teach, and research. In contrast, the managerial culture is intensely pragmatic, and values the application of ideas in practice more than it does the search for knowledge about those ideas. Managers lack an adequate understanding of the research process, often have no research training, rarely have any ongoing involvement in research, and are sometimes actively suspicious of the motives and values of research and researchers. Health care managers and researchers in health care management are not one community but two. Very few successful managers are also successful researchers, and it is rare for individual careers to span both worlds. We know of no posts in health care organizations in which senior managers practice, teach, and do research in the way that is routine for many senior clinicians. In general, practicing managers are much better rewarded than management researchers, at least in financial terms. As a result, there is a research-practice gap, not just in managerial practice, but between managers and researchers themselves.

Table 38.2 A comparison of clinical practice and health care management

	Clinical practice	Health care management
Culture	• Highly professionalized, with a strong formal body of knowledge and control of entry to the profession, resulting in coherence of knowledge, attitudes, and beliefs	• Much less professionalized, with much less formal body of knowledge, no control of entry, and great diversity among practitioners
	• High value placed on scientific knowledge and research, with many researchers who are also practitioners (and vice versa)	• Personal experience and self-generated knowledge highly valued; intensely pragmatic
		• Less understanding of research; some suspicion of value and of motives of researchers
		• Divide between researchers and practitioners, with little interchange between the two worlds
Research and evidence	• Strong biomedical, empirical paradigm, with focus on experimental methods and quantitative data	• Weak social sciences paradigm, with more use of qualitative methods and less empiricism
	• Belief in generalizability and objectivity of research findings	• Tendency to see research findings as more subjective, contingent, and less generalizable
	• Well-organized and indexed literature, concentrated in certain journals with clear boundaries; amenable to systematic review and synthesis	• Poorly organized and indexed research literature, spread across journals and other literature sources (including gray literature), with unclear boundaries; heterogeneous and not easy to review systematically or synthesize
Decision making	• Many clinical decisions taken every day, mostly by individual clinicians with few constraints on their decision	• Fewer, larger decisions taken, usually by or in groups, often requiring negotiation or compromise, with many organizational constraints
	• Decisions often homogeneous, involving the application of a general body of knowledge to specific circumstances	• Decisions are heterogeneous, and less based on applying a general body of knowledge to specific circumstances
	• Long tradition of using decision support systems (handbooks, guidelines, etc.)	• No tradition of using any form of decision support
	• Results of decisions often relatively clear, and some immediate feedback	• Results of decision and causal relationship between decision and subsequent events often difficult to determine

The clinical and managerial cultures are profoundly different in many respects, and while some aspects of the clinical culture seem inherently supportive of the ideas of evidence-based practice, some traits of the managerial culture are neutral, at best, and positively antagonistic to such ideas, at worst. Gaining greater acceptance of the need for evidence-based managerial practice requires either some substantial changes in the managerial culture or the adaptation of the ideas of evidence-based practice so that they are more congruent with the existing values and beliefs of managers.

Research and evidence

Not only do clinicians generally have a greater respect for research and the scientific method than managers do, they also have a different understanding of what research is. Clinicians and managers come from very different research traditions that might be very broadly characterized as the biomedical sciences versus the social sciences, and this affects the way they engage with and use research.

The clinicians' biomedical background emphasizes the use of experimental methods (with the randomized controlled trial seen as the "gold standard" of research methodologies), quantitative data, and empiricism. These research methods—and the processes of meta-analysis and systematic review that are then used to synthesize research findings—are well suited to the explicit, empirical paradigm of evidence-based health care. In contrast, managers may come from an academic discipline in which observational methods are used, qualitative research is more accepted and may even be the norm, and there is perhaps a greater focus on theoretical development than on empirical theory testing. Synthesizing, generalizing, and transferring research findings from one setting to another are contested concepts, and the methodological challenges are much greater (Popay, Rogers, and Williams 1998).

This difference may make clinicians more positivist in their outlook, ready to believe that there is an objectively determinable "right answer" to research questions, and so more willing to adhere to the findings from research. In comparison, managers may, quite rightly, view the results of research as more subjective, and contingent on the context for the research and on the characteristics of the researchers themselves. Faced with research findings, especially those that contradict their own experience or ways of doing things, managers may be less willing to change their own views.

The evidence base for most clinical professions is both well-defined and relatively well organized. Because clear professional boundaries have been established, there will generally be a readily identifiable set of journals and other media through which research findings are disseminated. Those dissemination channels are almost all within the health care research and practice community, and are often controlled by the professions themselves. Good bibliographic services (e.g., Medline) index the research literature and make searching for relevant research relatively easy. While the volume of research evidence and the rate at which it is published may present problems, the clinical literature is well organized and indexed. The boundaries of research relevant to health care management, on the other hand, are much more difficult to set. There are some journals specific to this area, but much relevant research is published in clinical or general management journals, or in a wide range of books, reports, and other outputs. While some specialist bibliographic services exist (e.g., Healthstar), their coverage is less comprehensive, so searching for relevant research can be laborious. The so-called gray literature (e.g., unpublished research reports) is much more important, but is often not indexed anywhere. This means that the processes of secondary research synthesis and meta-analysis, which have been so fundamental to the growth of evidence-based clinical practice, are much more difficult to apply to the managerial literature. Overall, managers may be acting quite rationally when, faced with such a limited and disjointed research literature, they place more faith in their personal experience and beliefs.

Clinical and managerial ideas about the generalizability or transferability of research findings from one setting to another are also often different. In biomedical research there is often, rightly or wrongly, a presumption of high generalizability, based on belief in the universality of the scientific method. Research on a particular clinical topic may have taken place in different countries, with different populations and health care systems, but the results can often still be combined or used together. In contrast, the actual or perceived transferability of managerial research findings is rather lower. The research methods used, the importance of local organizational context and culture, and the structural differences between health organizations and health systems all make research transfer more problematic. For example, whereas research undertaken in a Californian hospital on the clinical management of endstage kidney disease may easily be used by British clinicians, it is much less straightforward to take the findings of a U.S. study of the leadership styles of hospital chief executives and to make them relevant to chief executives in British hospitals.

Overall, the tightly defined, well-organized, highly quantitative, and relatively generalizable research base for many clinical professions provides a strong and secure foundation for evidence-based practice and lends itself to a systematic process of review and synthesis and to the production of guidelines and protocols. In contrast, the loosely defined, methodologically heterogeneous, widely distributed, and hard-to-generalize research base for health care management is much more difficult to use in the same way. There are real methodological and conceptual problems involved in framing research questions, searching the literature, appraising studies, and synthesizing or combining their results, which make the development of evidence-based management more challenging.

How decisions are made

Managers and clinicians make very different sorts of decisions, and make them in different ways, so it is not surprising that the way they use (or could use) evidence in their decision making differs, too.

Clinicians make many decisions each day about the treatment of individual patients, and it is these decisions that have been the focus of the evidence-based practice movement. The time scale for each decision may be very short—a matter of minutes or less—and they therefore need systems to help them collect and assimilate the relevant clinical information and reach the right diagnostic or therapeutic decision quickly. They often use decision support systems of one sort or another, whether they are handbooks, reference guides, textbooks, clinical guidelines, or more sophisticated computer-based tools. These systems are useful because many clinical decisions are basically similar (involving the application of the same body of knowledge to different patients with the same condition). The nature of clinical decision making both promotes and limits the development of evidence-based practice. On the one hand, clinicians need and are used to working with decision support aids (even if they don't call them that), so it should be possible to promote evidence-based practice by improving or replacing some of those existing systems. On the other hand, because of the short time scale of decision making and the sheer volume of decisions, evidence has to be delivered as close to the point of care as possible, and be very easy to access, understand, and use. The practical and logistical challenges of evidence-based clinical practice are considerable.

In comparison, managers make rather fewer but larger decisions, and the time scale for those decisions is usually longer. Major managerial decisions may take weeks, months, or even years to be made and implemented, and it can be difficult even to discern or describe the decision-making process or to pin down when a decision is actually made. Managerial decisions are more heterogeneous, in the sense that they do not usually involve the application of the same body of knowledge to a series of similar but different circumstances, so guidelines or decision support aids are seldom used in decision making. In any case, intuition often plays a part in decisions that would defy any rule-based, procedural analysis. In some ways, the different time scale and size of managerial decisions should make it easier to find and use research evidence in decision making, but the lack of what might be termed an explicit decision process and decision support infrastructure can make promoting evidence-based management practice more difficult.

Although their decisions may be constrained by resource availability, or by other restrictions imposed by health care organizations, clinicians generally have considerable clinical freedom and they make most of their decisions individually. They may seek the advice of colleagues, and some decisions may be made in group settings, such as medical rounds, nursing team meetings, or case conferences. However, the great majority of decisions are made by clinicians as individuals, in a relatively unconstrained context. For managers, decision making is much more of a team or group activity. Managers make most of their decisions in concert with others—through formal committees or informal groups—and securing the support of others for a decision is often a key part of the process, involving negotiation and consensus building both before and after the decision is made. Managerial decisions are also often significantly constrained by organizational or wider system requirements, such as resource availability, pressures in the health care marketplace, organizational policies and procedures, and stakeholders' views and interests. These factors may act as limitations, or may even directly conflict with research findings. Because of the constrained, contested, and political nature of many managerial decisions, it may be difficult for managers to apply research evidence even when it is available.

Finally, the results of clinical decision making are often—though far from always—apparent in the subsequent progress of the patient concerned, so there is an immediate feedback to the decision-making clinician about the effects of the decision. In contrast, the results of many managerial decisions are more difficult to discern, both because the time scale for their effects is longer and because there are many potential sources of confounding or bias that make connecting the decision and its effects more difficult. In this sense, the results of clinical decisions may be much more visible (both to the decision maker and to others) than the results of managerial decisions.

Overall, the clinical and managerial decision-making processes are very different. The technical challenges of delivering relevant evidence to clinicians to support their decision making may be great, but the ideas of evidence-based practice fit well with the nature of those decisions and the way they are made. For managers, the technical challenges of delivering the evidence are probably rather less, but the way that decisions are made means that there are few existing traditions, systems, or processes that can be used to bring evidence to bear.

The future development of evidence-based management in health care

There is certainly considerable scope for making better use of research evidence when deciding how to organize, structure, deliver, or finance health services. Managers and policymakers are on shaky ground if they argue that the principles of evidence-based health care—which they have advocated so enthusiastically for clinical practice—do not apply to them. However, managerial and clinical practice are very different, and so the implementation of evidence-based practice in health care management is unlikely simply to follow the established clinical model, which in any case is not as straightforward to apply as it might first appear (Nutley and Davies 2000). Government agencies, health care organizations, research funders, academic centers involved in teaching and researching health policy and management, and the professional associations for health care managers all have some part to play in this transition toward more evidence-based managerial practice.

If evidence is to play a greater part in managers' decision making, it will be necessary to change managers' attitudes toward research evidence and the research process. We need to make managers more aware of research, more interested in undertaking or participating in research, and better equipped to understand and act on the results of research. This kind of cultural and attitudinal change is unlikely to happen quickly, but it is not difficult to identify a number of actions that would help to promote it, some of which are already under way in some places (Lomas 2000). For example, health care organizations could provide training for managers in research methods, critical appraisal, and accessing the research literature. They could provide resources and support to enable managers to undertake or participate in research within their own organizations. They could also offer more opportunities for managers to obtain postgraduate degrees, and promote such study through their personnel policies and career structures. Academic centers could provide more health management and policy programs, and could increase the focus on research and evidence-based practice in existing programs. Together, academic centers and health care organizations could use joint or visiting appointments, temporary transfers, fellowships, and other mechanisms to build greater long-term managerial involvement in research, and to bring health management researchers into more direct involvement in health care management. They could collaborate in setting up organizations like CHMR to promote the development of evidence-based practice. These measures would all start to reduce the unhealthy divide that currently exists between the research and practitioner communities in health care management, and to create a culture that would be more supportive of evidence-based practice.

However, the implementation of evidence-based management practice is also likely to need government-led or systemwide changes to—and increased investment in—the research and dissemination infrastructure. These steps can help ensure that a coherent needs-related program of health care management research is undertaken and that the results are then managed and disseminated in ways that maximize their uptake. For example, research funding organizations could develop more rigorous practitioner-focused approaches to assessing research need, and could collaborate more closely in planning the research they commission. They could move funding toward more secondary research projects, aimed at synthesizing existing research knowledge, and invest more in disseminating their findings. Whether through the existing dissemination infrastructure (such as journals and new entities like the Cochrane Collaboration) or through new channels of communication, the results of all this research need to be presented in simple, clear, accessible, and widely available evidence reports. Academic and practitioner health management journals could collaborate to present research findings in a format that managers find accessible and through journals that managers actually read. Health care organizations could invest more in their local knowledge management systems for managers, with better library access, more information resources, and more professional support for managerial decision making.

These changes would not only create a cadre of health care managers who are more able and willing to use evidence in their own decision making, and so contribute to an improvement in the quality of health care management. They would also enable managers to be better equipped to deal with the complexities of clinical practice, and support the wider development of evidence-based health care. In the long term, it is surely in the interests of all stakeholders in the health care system to have better, more evidence-based processes for making managerial decisions and developing health care policy.

References and further reading

Abrahamson, E. 1996. Management Fashion. *Academy of Management Review* 21(1):254–85.

Adelman, N., L. Chester, and K. Slack. 2000. The HSR Proj Database: Update on Health Services Research in Progress. *Health Affairs* 19(4):257–8.

Antman, E., J. Lau, B. Kupelnick, F. Mosteller, and I. Chalmers. 1992. A Comparison of the Result of Meta-analysis of Randomized Controlled Trials and Recommendations of Clinical Experts. *Journal of the American Medical Association* 268:240–8.

Arndt, M., B. Bigelow, and H. Dorman. 1999. In Their Own Words: How Hospitals Present Corporate Restructuring in Their Annual Reports. *Journal of Health Care Management* 44(2):117–31.

Axelsson, R. 1998. Towards an Evidence-based Health Care Management. *International Journal of Health Planning and Management* 13:307–17.

Bazerman, M. 1998. *Judgment in Managerial Decision Making,* 4th ed. New York: John Wiley.

Black, N. 1997. A National Strategy for Research and Development: Lessons from England. *Annual Review of Public Health* 18:485–505.

Blackler, F. 1995. Knowledge, Knowledge Work and Organizations: An Overview and Interpretation. *Organization Studies* 16(6):1021–46.

Blumenthal, D., and N. Edwards. 2000. A Tale of Two Systems: The Changing Academic Health Center. *Health Affairs* 19(3):86–101.

Blumenthal, D., and C.M. Kilo. 1998. A Report Card on Continuous Quality Improvement. *Milbank Quarterly* 76(4):625–48.

Boruch, R., A. Petrosino, and I. Chalmers. 1999. *The Campbell Collaboration: A Proposal for Systematic, Multinational and Continuous Reviews of Evidence.* London: School of Public Policy, University College London.

Chalmers, I., and D. Altman. 1995. *Systematic Reviews.* London: BMJ Publishing.

Chalmers, I., D. Sackett, and C. Silagy. 1997. The Cochrane Collaboration. In *Nonrandom Reflections on Health Services Research,* eds. A. Maynard and I. Chalmers. London: BMJ Books.

Christensen, C. M., R. Bohmer, and J. Kenagy. 2000. Will Disruptive Innovations Cure Health Care? *Harvard Business Review* 78(5):102–12.

Cochrane, A.L. 1972. *Effectiveness and Efficiency: Random Reflections on Health Services.* London: Nuffield Provincial Hospitals Trust.

Davidoff, F., B. Haynes, D. Sackett, and R. Smith. 1995. Evidence-based Medicine. *British Medical Journal* 310(6987): 1085–6.

Davies, H.T.O., and S. M. Nutley. 1999. The Rise and Rise of Evidence in Healthcare. *Public Money and Management* 19(1):9–16.

Davies, H.T.O., S.M. Nutley, and PC. Smith. 1999. What Works? The Role of Evidence in Public Sector Policy and Practice. *Public Money and Management* 19(1):3–5.

De Long, D.W., and L. Fahey. 2000. Diagnosing Cultural Barriers to Knowledge Management. *Academy of Management Executive* 14(4):113–27.

Department of Health. 1997. *The New NHS: Modern, Dependable.* London: Stationery Office.

Department of Health. 1998. *A First Class Service: Quality in the New NHS.* London: Department of Health.

Dopson, S., L. Locock, D. Chambers, and J. Gabbay. 2001. Implementation of Evidence-based Medicine: Evaluation of the PACE Programme. *Journal of Health Services Research and Policy* 6(1):23–31.

Drucker, P. 1998. *The Profession of Management.* Boston: Harvard Business Review.

Dudley, R.A., K.L. Johansen, R. Brand, D.J. Rennie, and A. Milstein. 2000. Selective Referral to High-volume Hospitals: Estimating Potentially Avoidable Deaths. *Journal of the American Medical Association* 283(9):1159–66.

Ferlie, E., M. Wood, and L. Fitzgerald. 1999. Some Limits to Evidence-based Medicine: A Case Study from Elective Orthopaedics. *Quality in Health Care* 8(2):99–107.

Florin, D. 1996. Barriers to Evidence-based Policy. *British Medical Journal* 313:894–5.

Freidson, E. 1980. *Doctoring Together: A Study of Professional Social Control.* Chicago: University of Chicago Press.

Freidson, E. 1986. *Professional Powers: A Study of the Institutionalization of Formal Knowledge.* Chicago: University of Chicago Press.

Freidson, E. 1994. *Professionalism Reborn: Theory, Prophecy and Policy.* Cambridge: Polity Press.

Fulop, N., P. Allen, A. Clarke, and N. Black. 2001. From Health Technology Assessment to Research on the Organisation and Delivery of Health Services: Addressing the Balance. *Health Policy* (in press).

Gladwell, M. 2000. *The Tipping Point.* Boston: Little, Brown.

Graham, J. 1998. Perspectives. AHCPR's Evidence-based Centers: Will Their Findings Guide Clinical Practice? *Medicine and Health* 52(32):suppl. 1–4.

Guthrie, M.B. 1999. Challenges in Developing Physician Leadership and Management. *Frontiers of Health Services Management* 15(4):3–26.

Halladay, M., and L. Bero. 2000. Implementing Evidence-based Healthcare. *Public Money and Management* 20(4):43–50.

Harrison, S. 1998. The Politics of Evidence-based Medicine in the United Kingdom. *Policy and Politics* 26(1):15¡31.

Hewison, A. 1997. Evidence-based Medicine: What about Evidence-based Management? *Journal of Nursing Management* 5:195–8.

Homa, P. 1998. What's Your Evidence? *Health Management* 2(6):18–21.

Institute of Medicine. 1999. *The National Round-table on Health Care Quality: Measuring the Quality of Care.* Washington: Institute of Medicine.

Isham, G. 1999. Prospects for Radical Improvement: The National Guidelines Clearinghouse Project Debuts on the Internet. *Healthplan* 40(1):13–15.

Ketley, D., and K.L. Woods. 1993. Impact of Clinical Trials on Clinical Practice: Example of Thrombolysis for Acute Myocardial Infarction. *Lancet* 342(8876):891–4.

Klein, R. 2000. From Evidence-based Medicine to Evidence-based Policy? *Journal of Health Services Research and Policy* 5(2):65–6.

Kovner, A.R., J.J. Elton, and J. Billings. 2000. Evidence-based Management. *Frontiers of Health Services Management* 16(4):3–46.

Lohr, K.N., K. Eleazer, and J. Mauskopf. 1998. Health Policy Issues and Applications for Evidence-based Medicine and Clinical Practice Guidelines. *Health Policy* 46:1–19.

Lomas, J. 1997. *Improving Research Dissemination and Uptake in the Health Sector: Beyond the Sound of One Hand Clapping.* Hamilton, Ontario: CHEPA, McMaster University.

Shortell, S.M., J.A. Alexander, P.P. Budetti, L.R. Burns, R.R. Gillies, T.M. Waters, and H.S. Zuckerman. 2001. Physician-System Integration: Introductory Overview. *Medical Care* (in press).

Shortell, S.M., C.L. Bennett, and G.R. Byck. 1998. Assessing the Impact of Continuous Quality Improvement on Clinical Practice: What It Will Take to Accelerate Progress. *Milbank Quarterly* 76(4):593–624.

Sitzia, J., and N. Wood. 1997. Patient Satisfaction: A Review of Issues and Concepts. *Social Science and Medicine* 45(12):1829–43.

Staw, B., and L. Epstein. 2000. What Bandwagons Bring: Effects of Popular Management Techniques on Corporate Performance, Reputation, and CEO Pay. *Administrative Science Quarterly* 45(3):523–56.

Stewart, R. 1998. More Art than Science? *Health Service Journal* (26 March):28–9.

Succi, M.J., and J.A. Alexander. 1999. Physician Involvement in Management and Governance: The Moderating Effects of Staff Structure and Composition. *Health Care Management Review* 24(l):33–44.

Swales, J. 1998. Research and Development in the NHS. *Journal of the Royal Society of Medicine* 91(36):Suppl. 18–20.

Taylor, R., B. Reeves, P. Ewings, S. Binns, J. Keast, and R. Mears. 2000. A Systematic Review of the Effectiveness of Critical Appraisal Skills Training for Clinicians. *Medical Education* 34(2):120–5.

Tonelli, M.R. 1998. The Philosophical Limits of Evidence-based Medicine. *Academic Medicine* 73(12):1234–40.

van Campen, C, H. Sixma, R.D. Friele, J.J. Kerssens, and L. Peters. 1995. Quality of Care and Patient Satisfaction: A Review of Measuring Instruments. *Medical Care Research and Review* 52(1):109–33.

Walshe, K., and C. Ham. 1997. *Acting on the Evidence: Progress in the NHS.* Birmingham: NHS Confederation.

Walston, S.L., and R.J. Bogue. 1999. The Effects of Reengineering: Fad or Competitive Factor? *Journal of Healthcare Management* 44(6):456–74.

39

Is there such a thing as evidence-based management?
Denise Rousseau

Extracts from Rousseau DM (2006) Is there such a thing as evidence-based management? Academy of Management Review, 31(2): 256–69.

Introduction

I explore the promise organization research offers for improved management practice and how, at present, it falls short. Using evidence-based medicine as an exemplar, I identify ways of closing the prevailing "research-practice gap"—the failure of organizations and managers to base practices on best available evidence. I close with guidance for researchers, educators, and managers for translating the principles governing human behavior and organizational processes into more effective management practice.

Evidence-based management means translating principles based on best evidence into organizational practices. Through evidence-based management, practicing managers develop into experts who make organizational decisions informed by social science and organizational research—part of the zeitgeist moving professional decisions away from personal preference and unsystematic experience toward those based on the best available scientific evidence (e.g., Barlow, 2004; DeAngelis, 2005; Lemieux-Charles & Champagne, 2004; Rousseau, 2005; Walshe & Rundall, 2001). This links how managers make decisions to the continually expanding research base on cause-effect principles underlying human behavior and organizational actions.

Evidence-based management, as in the example above, derives principles from research evidence and translates them into practices that solve organizational problems. This isn't always easy. Principles are credible only where the evidence is clear, and research findings can be tough for both researchers and practitioners to interpret. Moreover, practices that capitalize on a principle's insights must suit the setting (e.g., who is to say that the particular performance indicators the executive director uses are pertinent to all units?). Evidence-based management, despite these challenges, promises more consistent attainment of organizational goals, including those affecting employees, stockholders, and the public in general. This is the promise that attracted me to organizational research at the beginning of my career—but it remains unfulfilled.

My great disappointment, has been that research findings don't appear to have transferred well to the workplace. Instead of a scientific understanding of human behavior and organizations, managers, including those with MBAs, continue to rely largely on personal experience, to the exclusion of more systematic knowledge. Alternatively, managers follow bad advice from business books or consultants based on weak evidence. Because Jack Welch or McKinsey says it, that doesn't make it true. (Several decades of research on attribution bias indicate that people have a difficult time drawing unbiased conclusions regarding why they are successful, often giving more credit to themselves than the facts warrant. Management gurus are in no way immune.)

Sadly, there is poor uptake of management practices of known effectiveness (e.g., goal setting and performance feedback [Locke & Latham, 1984]). Even in businesses populated by MBAs from top-ranked universities, there is unexplained wide variation in managerial practice patterns (e.g., how [or if] goals are set, selection decisions made, rewards allocated, or training investments determined) and, worse, persistent use of practices known to be largely ineffective (e.g., downsizing [Cascio, Young, & Morris, 1997]; high ratios of executive to rank-and-file employee compensation [Cowherd & Levine, 1992]). The result is a research-practice gap, indicating that the answer to this article's title question is no—at least not yet. What it means to close this gap and how evidence-based management might become a reality are the matters I turn to next.

Why evidence-based management is important and timely

Evidence-based management is not a new idea. Chester Barnard (1938) promoted the development of a natural science of organization to better understand the unanticipated problems associated with authority and consent. Since Barnard's time, however, we have struggled to connect science and practice without a vision or model to do so. Evidence-based management, in my opinion, provides the needed model to guide the closing of the research-practice gap. In this section I address why evidence-based management is timely and practical.

Calling attention to facts: "Big E Evidence" and "little e evidence"

An evidence orientation shows that decision quality is a direct function of available facts, creating a demand for reliable and valid information when making managerial and organizational decisions. Improving information continues a trend begun in the quality movement over thirty years ago, giving systematic attention to discrete facts, indicative of quality (e.g., machine performance, customer interactions, employee attitudes and behavior [Evans & Dean, 2000]). This trend continues in recent developments regarding open-book management (Case, 1995; Ferrante & Rousseau, 2001) and the use of organizational fact finding and experimentation to improve decision quality (Pfeffer & Sutton, in press).

In all the attention we now give to evidence, it helps to differentiate what might be called "Big E Evidence" from "little e evidence." Big E Evidence refers to generalizable knowledge regarding cause-effect connections (e.g., specific goals promote higher attainment than general or vague goals) derived from scientific methods—the focus of this article. Little e evidence is local or organization specific, as exemplified by root cause analysis and other fact-based approaches the total quality movement introduced for organizational decision making (Deming, 1993; Evans & Dean, 2000). It refers to data systematically gathered in a particular setting to inform local decisions. As the saying goes, "facts are our friends," when local efforts to accumulate information relevant to a particular problem lead to more effective solutions.

Although decision makers who rely on scientific principles are more likely to gather facts systematically in order to choose an appropriate course of action (e.g., Sackett et al., 2000), fact gathering ("evidence") doesn't necessarily lead decision makers to use social science knowledge ("Evidence") in interpretating these facts. In my introductory example of the health care system, the executive director might have concluded that the performance differences across the twenty clinics were due to something about the clinics or their managers. It was his knowledge of a basic principle in psychology that gave him an alternative and, ultimately, more effective interpretation. However, systematic attention to local facts can prompt managers to look for principles that account for their observations. The opening example illustrates how scientific principles and local facts go together to solve problems and make decisions.

Opportunity to better implement managerial decisions

In highly competitive environments, good execution may be as important as the strategic choices managers make. Implementation is a strong suit of evidence-based management through the wealth of research available to guide effective execution (e.g., goal setting and feedback [Locke & Latham, 1984]; feedback and redesign [Goodman, 2001]). Indeed, with greater orientation toward scientific evidence, health care management's guidelines frequently reference social and organizational research on implementation (e.g., Lemieux-Charles & Champayne, 2004; Lomas, Culyer, McCutcheon, McAuley, & Law, 2005). The continued wide variation we observe in how organizations execute decisions (e.g., in goal clarity, stakeholder participation, feedback processes, and allowance for redesign) is remarkable, given the advanced knowledge we possess about effective implementation and what is at stake should implementation fail.

Better managers, better learning

Given the powerful impact managers' decisions have on the fate of their firms, managerial competence is a critical and often scarce resource. Improved managerial competence is a direct outgrowth of a greater focus on evidence-based management. Managers need real learning, not fads or false conclusions. When managers acquire a systematic understanding of the principles governing organizations and human behavior, what they learn is *valid*—that is to say, it is repeatable over time and generalizable across situations. It is less likely that what managers learn will be wrong.

Today, the poor information commonly available to managers regarding the organizational consequences of their decisions means that experiences are likely to be misinterpreted—subject to perceptual gaps and misunderstandings. Consider the case of a supervisor who overuses threats and punishment as behavioral tools. A punisher who keys on the fact that punishing suppresses behavior can completely miss its other consequence—its inability to encourage positive behavior. Status differences and organizational politics make it unlikely that the punisher will learn the true consequences of that style, by limiting and distorting feedback.

The reality is that managers tend to work in settings that make valid learning difficult. This difficulty is compounded by the widespread uptake of organizational fads and fashions, "adopted overenthusiastically, implemented inadequately, then discarded prematurely in favor of the latest trend" (Walshe & Rundall, 2001; 437; see also Staw & Epstein, 2000). In such settings managers cannot even learn why their decisions were wrong, let alone what alternatives would have been right. Evidence-based management leads to valid learning and continuous improvement, rather than a checkered career based on false assumptions.

Organizational legitimacy is another product of evidence-based management. Where decisions are based on systematic causal knowledge, conditioned by expertise leading to successful implementation, firms find it easier to deliver on promises made to stockholders, employees, customers, and others (e.g., Goodman & Rousseau, 2004; Rucci, Kirn, & Quinn, 1998). Legitimacy is a result of making decisions in a systematic and informed fashion, thus making a firm's actions more readily justifiable in the eyes of stakeholders. Yet, given evidence-based management's numerous advantages, why then is the research-practice gap so large? I next turn to the array of factors that align to perpetuate this evidence-deprived status quo.

Why managers don't practice evidence-based management

The research-practice gap among managers results from several factors. First and foremost, managers typically do not know the evidence. Less than 1 percent of HR managers read the academic literature regularly (Rynes, Brown, & Colbert, 2002), and the consultants who advise them are unlikely to do so either. Despite the explosion of research on decision making, individual and group performance, business strategy, and other domains directly tied to organizational practices, few practicing managers access this work. (I note, however, that of the four periodicals the Academy publishes, it is the empirical *Academy of Management Journal* to which company libraries most widely subscribe. So there is some recognition that this research exists!)

Evidence-based management can threaten managers' personal freedom to run their organizations as they see fit. A similar resistance characterized supervisory responses to scientific management nearly 100 years ago, when Frederick Taylor's structured methods for improving efficiency were discarded because they were believed to interfere with management's prerogatives in supervising employees. Part of this pushback stems from the belief that good management is an art—the "romance of leadership" school of thought (e.g., Meindl, Erlich, & Dukerich, 1985), where a shift to evidence and analysis connotes loss of creativity and autonomy. Such concerns are not unique: physicians have wrestled with similar dilemmas, expressed in the aptly titled article "False Dichotomies: EBM, Clinical Freedom and the Art of Medicine" (Parker, 2005).

Managerial work itself differs from clinical work and other fields engaged in evidence-based practice in important ways. First, managerial decisions often involve long time lags and little feedback, as in the case of a recruiter hiring someone to eventually take over a senior position in the firm. Years may pass before the true quality of that decision can be discerned, and, by then, the recruiter and others involved are likely to have moved on (Jaques, 1976). Managerial decisions often are influenced by other stakeholders who impose constraints (Miller, 1992). Obtaining stakeholder support can involve politicking and compromise, altering the decision made, or even whether it is made at all. Incentives tied to managerial decisions are subject to contradictory pressures from senior executives, stockholders, customers, and employees. Last, it's not always obvious that a decision is being made, given the array of interactions that compose managerial work (Walshe & Randall, 2001). A manager who declines to train a subordinate, for example, may not realize that particular act ultimately may lead the employee to quit.

Evidence-based management can be a tough sell to many managers, because management, in contrast to medicine or nursing, is not a profession. Given the diverse backgrounds and education of managers, there is limited understanding of scientific method. With no formally mandated education or credentials (and even an MBA is no guarantee), practicing managers have no body of shared knowledge. Lacking shared scientific knowledge to add weight to an evidence-based decision, managers commonly rely on other bases (e.g., experience, formal power, incentives, and threats) when making decisions acceptable to their superiors and constituents.

Firms themselves—particularly those in the private sector—contribute to the limited value placed on science-based management practice. Although pharmaceutical firms advertise their investment in biotechnology and basic research, the typical business does not have the advancement of managerial knowledge in its mission.

Historically leading corporations such as Cadbury, IBM, and General Motors were actively engaged in research on company selection and training practices, employee motivation, and supervisory behavior. Their efforts contributed substantially to the early managerial practice evidence base. But few organizations today do their own managerial research or regularly collaborate with those who do, despite the considerable benefits from industry university collaborations (Cycrt & Goodman, 1997); the globally experienced time crunch in managerial work and the press for short-term results have reduced such collaborations to dispensable frills. Nonetheless, hospitals participate in clinical research and school systems evaluate policy interventions.

In contrast to more evidence-oriented domains, such as policing and education, management is most often a private sector activity. It is less influenced by public policy pressures promoting similar practices while creating comparative advantage via distinctiveness. Businesses are characterized by the belief that the particulars of the organization, its practices, and its problems are special and unique—a widespread phenomenon termed the *uniqueness paradox* (Martin, Feldman, Hatch, & Sitkin, 1983). Observed among clinical care givers and law enforcement practitioners too, the uniqueness paradox can interfere with transfer of research findings across settings—unless dispelled by better education and experience with evidence-based practice (e.g., Sackett et al., 2000).

Yet, despite all these factors, the most important reason evidence-based management is still a hope and not a reality is not due to managers themselves or their organizations. Rather, professors like me and the programs in which we teach must accept a large measure of blame. *We typically do not educate managers to know or use scientific evidence.* Research evidence is not the central focus of study for undergraduate business students, MBAs, or executives in continuing education programs (Trank & Rynes, 2003), where case examples and popular concepts from nonresearch-oriented magazines such as the *Harvard Business Review* take center stage. Consistent with the diminution of research in behavioral course work, business students and practicing managers have no ready access to research. No communities of experts vet research regarding effective management practice (in contrast to the collaboratives that vet health care, criminal justice, and educational research [e.g., Campbell Collaboration, 2005; Cochrane Collaboration, 2005]). Few MBAs encounter a peer-reviewed journal during their student days, let alone later. Consequently, it's time to look critically at the role we educators play in limiting managers' knowledge and use of research evidence.

Evidence-based management and our role as educators

How professors contribute to the research-practice gap

Management education is itself often not evidence-based, something Trank and Rynes implicitly recognize (2003) as the "dumbing down" of management education. They also persuasively demonstrated that, in place of evidence, behavioral courses in business schools focus on general skills (e.g., team building, conflict management) and current case examples. Through these stimulating, ostensibly relevant activities, we capture student interest, helping to deflect the criticism "How is this going to help me get my first job?" Business schools reinforce this by relying heavily on student ratings instead of assessing real learning (Rynes, Trank, Lawson, & Ilies, 2003).

Stimulating courses and active learning must be core features of training in evidence-based management, because these educational features are good pedagogy. The manner and content of our approaches to behavioral courses perpetuate the research-practice gap.

Weak research-education connection

Pick up any popular management textbook and you will find that Frederick Herzberg's work lives, but not Max Weber's. Herzberg's long-discredited two-factor theory is typically included in the motivation section of management textbooks, despite the fact that it was discredited as an artifact of method bias over thirty years ago (House & Wigdor, 1967). I asked a famous author of many best-selling textbooks why this was so. "Because professors like to teach Herzberg!" he answered. "Students want updated business examples but can't really tell if the research claims are valid."

This conversation suggests that professors are likely to teach what they learned in graduate school and not necessarily what current research supports. (Since many management professors are adjuncts valued for their practical experience but are from diverse backgrounds, even educators of comparable professional age may not share scientific knowledge.) I suspect that the persistence of Herzberg will continue until all the professors who learned the two-factor theory in graduate school (c. 1960–1970) retire.

Failure to manage student expectations

Student expectations do drive course content, and current evidence indicates that there is a strong preference for turnkey, ready-to-use solutions to problems these students will face in their first jobs (Trank & Rynes, 2003). What efforts do we make to manage these expectations? Unless students are persuaded to value science-based principles and their own role in turning these principles into sound organizational practice, it will be nigh impossible for faculty to resist the pressure to teach only today's solutions.

We might start by asking students who they think updates more effectively—practitioners trained in solutions or in principles. Effective practices in 2006 need not be the same as those in 2016, let alone 2036, when the majority of today's business students will still be working. If we teach solutions to problems, such as how to obtain accurate information on a worker's performance, students will acquire a tool—perhaps, for example, 360-degree feedback. Yet they won't understand the underlying cognitive processes (whether feedback is task related or self-focused), social factors (the relationships between ratees and raters), and organizational mechanisms (used for developmental purposes or compensation decisions), which explain how, when, and why 360-degree feedback might work (or not).

Lack of models for evidence-based management

Case methods are de rigueur in business schools, helping to develop students' analytic skills and familiarity with conditions they will face as practicing managers. The cases that I find most effective are those that have an individual manager as a protagonist (as opposed to those that describe an organization without developing one or two central personalities). A central character creates tension and evokes student identification with the events taking place. That character is typically a manager, who can be the change agent responsible for solving the problem or a catalyst for the dysfunctional behavior on which the cases focus.

Either way, students have a model—a positive or negative referent—from which they can learn how to behave (or not) in the future. As with most complex behaviors, from parenting to managing, people learn better when they have competent models (Bandura, 1971). Nonetheless, in twenty-five years of using cases in class, I cannot recall a single time in which a protagonist reflected on research evidence in the course of his or her decision making.

No expectation for updating evidence-based knowledge throughout the manager's career

Upon graduation, few business students recognize that the knowledge they may have acquired can be surpassed over time by new findings. Although social science knowledge continues to expand, business school training does not prepare graduates to tap into it. Neither students nor managers have clear ideas of how to update their knowledge as new evidence emerges.

There are few models of what an "expert" manager knows that a novice does not (see Hill, 1992, for an exception). In contrast, expert nurses are known to behave in very different ways from novices or less-than-expert midcareer nurses (Benner, 2001). They more rapidly size up a situation accurately and deal simultaneously with more co-occurring factors. In the professions, extensive postgraduate development exists to deepen expertise to produce a higher quality of practice. In contrast, business schools often imply that MBAs know all they need to know when they graduate.

Our own zeitgeist promoting evidence-based practice of management

Forty years elapsed between Semmelweis's discoveries and the formulation of germ theory. One hundred years later, even basic infection reducing practices such as hand washing still are not consistently performed in hospitals (Johns Hopkins Medicine, 2004). Considering the personal growth and social and organizational changes evidence-based practice requires, our own evidence-based management zeitgeist still has plenty of time to run.

The first challenge is consciousness raising regarding the rich array of evidence that can improve effectiveness of managerial decisions. Educating opinion leaders, including prominent executives and educators, in the nature and value of evidence-based approaches builds champions who can get the word out. Updating management education with the latest research must be ongoing, demanding that educators and textbook writers apprise themselves of new research findings. The onus is on researchers to make generalizability clearer by providing better information in their reports regarding the context in which their findings were observed. All parties need to put greater emphasis on learning how to translate research findings into solutions. In the case of researchers, too much information that might affect the translations of findings to practice remains tacit, in the apparent minutiae research reports omit, known only to the researcher. Educators need to help students acquire the metaskills for designing solutions around the research principles they teach. Managers must learn how to experiment with possible evidence-based solutions and to adapt them to particular settings. We need knowledgesharing networks composed of educators, researchers, and manager/ practitioners to help create and disseminate management-oriented research summaries and practices that best evidence supports.

Building a culture in which managers learn to learn from evidence is a critical aspect of effective evidence use (Pfeffer & Sutton, in press). Developing managerial competence historically has been viewed as a training issue, underestimating the investment in collective capabilities that is needed (Mohrman, Gibson, & Mohrman, 2001).

The promises of evidence-based management are manifold. It affords higher-quality managerial decisions that are better implemented, and it yields outcomes more in line with organizational goals. Those who use evidence (E and e) and learn to use it well have comparative advantage over their less competent counterparts. Managers, educators, and researchers can learn more systematically throughout their careers regarding principles that govern human behavior and organizational actions and the solutions that enhance contemporary organizational performance and member experience. A focus on evidence use may also ultimately help to blur the boundaries between researchers, educators, and managers, creating a lively community with many feedback loops where information is systematically gathered, evaluated, disseminated, implemented, reevaluated, and shared.

The promise of evidence-based management contrasts with the staying power or stickiness of the status quo. Like the QWERTY keyboard created for manual typewriters, but inefficient in the age of word processing, management-as-usual survives, despite being out of step with contemporary needs. Failure to evolve toward evidence-based management, however, is costlier than mere inefficiency. It deprives organizations, their members, our students, and the general public of greater success and better managers. Please join with me in working to make evidence-based management a reality.

References and further reading

Anderson, J. R., Fincham, J. M., & Douglass, S. 1997. The role of examples and rules in the acquisition of a cognitive skill. *Journal of Experimental Psychology: Learning, Memory, and Cognition*, 23: 932–945.

Bandura, A. 1971. *Social learning theory.* New York: General Learning Press.

Barlow, D. H. 2004. Psychological treatments. *American Psychologist,* 59: 869–878.

Barnard, C. I. 1938. *Functions of the executive.* Cambridge, MA: Harvard University Press.

Benner, P. 2001. *From novice to expert: Excellence and power in clinical nursing practice* (commemorative ed.). Menlo Park, CA: Addison-Wesley.

Bennis, W. G., & O'Toole, J. 2004. How business schools lost their way. *Harvard Business Review,* 82(3): 96–104.

Campbell Collaboration. 2005. *hffp://www.campbellcollaboration.org/,* accessed December 5.

Cascio, W. F., Young, C. E., & Morris, J. K. 1997. Financial consequences of employment-change decisions in major U.S. corporations. *Academy of Management Journal,* 40: 1175–1189.

Case, J. 1995. *Open-book management: The coming business revolution.* New York: Harper Business.

Cochrane Collaboration. 2005. *http://www.cochrane.org/index0.htm,* accessed December 5.

Cowherd, D., & Levine, D. I. 1992. Product quality and pay equity between lower-level employees and top management: An investigation of distributive justice theory. *Administrative Science Quarterly,* 37: 302–320.

Cyert, R. M., & Goodman, P. S. 1997. Creating effective university-industry alliances: An organizational learning perspective. *Organizational Dynamics,* 25(4): 45–57.

DeAngelis, T. 2005. Shaping evidence-based practice. *APA Monitor,* 35(3): 26–31.

Deming, W. E. 1993. *The new economics for industry, government, and education.* Cambridge, MA: Massachusetts Institute of Technology.

Desvarieux, M., Demmer, R. T., Rundek, T., Boden-Abala, B., Jacobs, D. R., Jr., Sacco, R. L., & Papapanou, P. N. 2005. Periodontal microbiota and carotid intima-media thickness: The oral infections and vascular disease epidemiology study (INVEST). *Circulation,* 111: 576–582.

Evans, J. R., & Dean, J. W., Jr. 2000. *Total quality: Management, organization, and strategy* (2nd ed.). Cincinnati: South-Western Publishing.

Eysenbach, G., & Kummervold, P. E. 2005. Is cybermedicine killing you? The story of a Cochrane disaster. *Journal of Medical Internet Research,* 7(2): article e21.

Ferrante, C. J., & Rousseau, D. M. 2001. Bringing open book management into the academic line of sight. In C. L. Cooper & D. M. Rousseau (Eds.), *Employee versus owner issues* (Trends in Organizational Behavior Series), vol. 8: 97–116. Chichester, UK: Wiley.

Franklin, D. 2005. Antibiotics aren't always the answer. *New York Times,* August 30: D5.

Frieze, I. H. 1976. Causal attributions and information seeking to explain success and failure. *Journal of Research in Personality,* 10: 293–305.

Gladwell, M. 2002. *The tipping point: How little things can make a big difference.* New York: Back Bay Books.

Goodman, P. S. 2001. *Missing organizational linkages.* Newbury Park, CA: Sage.

Goodman, P. S. 2005. *The organizational learning contract.* Working paper, Tepper School of Business, Carnegie Mellon University, Pittsburgh.

Goodman, P. S., & Rousseau, D. M. 2004. Organizational change that produces results. *Academy of Management Executive,* 18(3): 7–19.

Hill, L. A. 1992. *Becoming a manager: How new managers master the challenges of leadership.* Boston: Harvard Business School Press.

House, R. J., & Wigdor, L. A., 1967. Herzberg's dual-factor theory of job satisfaction and motivation. *Personnel Psychology,* 23: 369–389.

Jadad, A. R., Haynes, R. B., Hunt, D., & Browman, G. P. 2000. The internet and evidence-based decision-making: A needed synergy for efficient knowledge management in health care. *Canadian Medical Association Journal,* 162: 362–365.

Jaques, E. 1976. (Reprinted in 1993.) *A general theory of bureaucracy.* London: Gregg Revivals.

Jimerson, S. R., Anderson, G., & Whipple, A. 2002. Winning the battle and losing the war: Examining the relation between grade retention and dropping out of high school. *Psychology in the Schools,* 39:441–457.

Johns Hopkins Medicine. 2004. Expert on hospital infections talks about hand washing. *http://www.hopkinsmedicine.org/Press_releases/2004/10_28_04.html,* October 28.

Kerr, S., & Jermier, J. M. 1978. Substitutes for leadership: Their meaning and measurement. *Organizational Behavior and Human Performance,* 22: 375–403.

Kersting, K. 2005. Integrating research into teaching. *APA Monitor,* 35(1): 19.

Kinicki, A., & Kreitner, R. 2003. *Organizational behavior: Key concepts, skills and best practices.* New York: McGraw-Hill.

Kolata, G. 2004. Program coaxes hospitals to see treatments under their noses. *New York Times,* December 2: A1, C8.

Kovner, A. R., Elton, J. J., & Billings, J. D. 2005. Evidence-based management. *Frontiers of Health Services Management,* 16(4): 3–24.

Lemieux-Charles, L., & Champagne, F. 2004. *Using knowledge and evidence in healthcare: Multidisciplinary perspectives.* Toronto: University of Toronto Press.

Locke, E. A., & Latham, G. P. 1984. *Goal setting: A motivational technique that works.* Englewood Cliffs, NJ: Prentice-Hall.

Lomas, J., Culyer, T., McCutcheon, C., McAuley, L., & Law, S. 2005. *Conceptualizing evidence for health system guidance.* Final report to Canadian Health Services Research Foundation, Ottawa, Ontario.

Martin, J., Feldman, M., Hatch, M., & Sitkin, S. B. 1983. The uniqueness paradox in organizational stories. *Administrative Science Quarterly,* 28: 438–453.

Meindl, J. R., Erlich, S. B., & Dukerich, J. M. 1985. The romance of leadership. *Administrative Science Quarterly,* 30: 78–101.

Miller, G. J. 1992. *Managerial dilemmas: The political economy of hierarchy.* Cambridge: Cambridge University Press.

Mohrman, S. A., Gibson, C. B., & Mohrman, A. M. 2001. Doing research that is useful to practice: A model and empirical exploration. *Academy of Management Journal*, 44: 357–375.

Mohrman, S. A., & Mohrman, A. M., Jr. 1997. *Designing and leading team-based organizations: A workbook for organizational self-design*. San Francisco: Jossey-Bass.

National Association of School Psychologists (NASP). 2005. Position statement on grade retention and social promotion. *www.nasponline.org/information/pospaper_graderetent.html*, accessed November 24.

Parker, M. 2005. False dichotomies, EBM, clinical freedom and the art of medicine. *Medical Humanities*, 31: 23–30.

Pfeffer, J., & Sutton, R. I. In press. *Hard facts, dangerous half-truths, and total nonsense: Profiting from evidence-based management*. Boston: Harvard Business School Press.

Rousseau, D. M. 2005. Evidence-based management in health care. In C. Korunka & P. Hoffmann (Eds.), *Change and quality in human service work*: 33–46. Munich: Hampp.

Rucci, A. J., Kirn, S. P., & Quinn, R. T. 1998. The employee-customer-profit chain at Sears. *Harvard Business Review*, 76(1): 82–97.

Rynes, S. L., Brown, K. G., Colbert, A. E. 2002. Seven common misconceptions about human resource practices: Research findings versus practitioner beliefs. *Academy of Management Executive*, 18(3): 92–103.

Rynes, S. L., Trank, C. Q., Lawson, A. M., & Ilies, R. 2003. Behavioral coursework in business education: Growing evidence of a legitimacy crisis. *Academy of Management Learning & Education*, 2: 269–283.

Sackett, D. L., Straus, S. E., Richardson, W. S., Rosenberg, W., & Haynes, R. B. 2000. *Evidence-based medicine: How to practice and teach EBM*. New York: Churchill Livingstone.

Schank, R. C. 2003. *Every curriculum tells a story*. Unpublished manuscript, Carnegie Mellon University, Pittsburgh.

Schön, D. 1983. *The reflective practioner: How professionals think in action*. London: Temple Smith.

Sherman, L. W. 2002. Evidence-based policing: Social organization of information for social control. In E. Waring & D. Weisburd (Eds.), *Crime and social organization*: 217–248. New Brunswick, NJ: Transaction.

Staw, B., & Epstein, L. 2000. What bandwagons bring: Effects of popular management techniques on corporate performance, reputation, and CEO pay. *Administrative Science Quarterly*, 43: 523–556.

Thompson, L., Gentner, D., & Lowenstein, J. 2003. Avoiding missed opportunities in managerial life: Analogical training more powerful than individual case training. In L. L. Thompson (Ed.), *The social psychology of organizational life*: 163–173. New York: Psychology Press.

Trank, C. Q., & Rynes, S. L. 2003. Who moved our cheese? Reclaiming professionalism in business education. *Academy of Management Learning & Education*, 2: 189–205.

Tyler, T. 1990. *Why people obey the law.* New Haven, CT: Yale University Press.

Walshe, K., & Rundall, T. G. 2001. Evidence-based management: From theory to practice in health care. *Milbank Quarterly,* 79: 429–457.

Whyte, W. F. 1948. *Human relations in the restaurant industry.* New York: McGraw-Hill.

PART 9

The social context of health
Introduction by Ann Mahon

Attempts to define health may be narrow and negative (health as the absence of illness or disease) or broad and positive (health as a complete state of well-being). This is not simply of academic interest because the lens employed in looking at health has important implications. Rob Baggott points out that the distinctions between positive and negative definitions of health have a bearing on the *boundaries* of health policy:

> Adopting the negative approach marks out a much smaller territory for analysis. Here policy analysis focuses on the provision of health services. However if a positive approach is taken health policy analysis becomes a much wider field of study, incorporating a huge range of social, economic, environmental and political processes affecting individual and community health and well–being.
>
> (Baggott, 2007: 1–2)

Individuals, families, communities and societies experience and define health, illness and disease in the context of where they live and work, so that political, economic, social and cultural factors determine what is considered to be health, illness and disease but also what is considered to be the appropriate domains of State, market and individual responsibility. Some of the vast amount of research exploring how people define, experience and explain health and well-being was recently synthesized by Hughner and Klein (2004). They found that, for example, for some people health is about their functional ability – to play a sport, to walk a short distance to the local shop, to carry out the skills needed for their work, to look after their children and other family members. A loss of function leaving someone unable to play a sport, carry out day-to-day activities, work in paid or unpaid employment is thus defined as a decline in health status. For others health might be about maintaining equilibrium and the connectedness between mind, body and spirit, while health for others might be about freedom and choice – to live their life in the way they wish to, to make choices about when to get up and go to bed, and when and what to eat. Similarly, explanations for how and why people remain healthy are also socially derived so for some it is the healing power of meditation; for others it is attitude and a positive outlook on life; for others it is accounted for in the 'bad habits' adopted by themselves or by others – not looking after yourself, smoking, drinking too much alcohol and eating the wrong food. Lay people also comment on other external factors so that socio-economic factors, government policy and the impact of government institutions, stress associated with living in contemporary society and genetic predispositions are also seen as influencing or determining health. What this synthesis reveals is a clear emphasis by laypeople on what is now referred to as the social determinants of health – that is the factors outside of health care that impact upon the health of the population.

Wilkinson and Marmot, two of the most enduring and influential writers in the field of inequalities in health, distilled some of the key themes and policy options in the relationship between population health and factors outside of health care systems (Marmot and Wilkinson, 2003). While they recognize health care as an important determinant of health (see Part 10 for a fuller discussion of this debate), they identify 10 other broad factors as being more important. These include health inequalities within and between different countries, caused by inequalities in socio-economic conditions and played out in many different ways through poor housing, overcrowding, poor sanitation and reduced life chances in relation to education and employment. Early life experiences, in terms of attachment, nutrition and health and social welfare have also been identified as having a significant impact on health in later life. Both work and unemployment are identified as factors determining health. For those in work hazards may be direct such as an industrial accident or contamination but there is also increasing awareness of how psychological factors relating to autonomy, for example, impact on working life and subsequent physical and mental health. While work may cause ill health, Wilkinson and Marmot suggest it is better to have a job than not. Unemployment, uncertainty associated with job loss and the decline in material circumstances all contribute to a decline in health affecting poorer individuals and their families disproportionately. Other social factors explored in Marmot and Wilkinson's review include transport, food, addiction, social support, social exclusion and stress.

Lay people, academics like Michael Marmot and Richard Wilkinson and reformers and philanthropists, like Edwin Chadwick (who is the author of one of the readings selected in this part) have a long tradition of recognizing the social factors that influence health. However, in the field of health policy and management, the emphasis has tended to be on the provision of formal health care with policy makers and managers concerned with allocating resources and managing and delivering health services to the sick, topics that are explored in some detail in this reader. The balance is slowly but undoubtedly changing and many governments and health care systems now recognize the impact that social, economic and environmental factors have on health and policies are being developed that encourage intersectoral and collaborative working between organizations and government agencies and between countries at European and international levels. It is against this contemporary background that the six readings selected for this part of the reader are introduced. Most of the readings represent ideas that have become (almost) commonplace concepts driving health policy today but which at the time of publication (or presentation) were seen as ground-breaking, politically unpalatable, threatening, weak in evidence and politically motivated.

The first two selections provide two different but not unconnected contributions connecting primary care with socio-economic conditions. The World Health Organization's Alma Ata declaration is reproduced in full and it is almost breathtaking to realize how such a concise document presented at the WHO conference in 1978 in Alma Ata (now known as Almaty in Kazakhstan) has subsequently been recognized as 'the defining moment in contemporary history of primary healthcare' (Smith, 2006: 117). In its 10 sections, the declaration begins by restating the WHO's broad and positive definition of health as encompassing 'a state of complete physical, mental and social well-being, and not merely the absence of disease or infirmity' – but also as a human right. It then sets out the role of governments, the 'common concern' that countries must share in relation to health inequalities within countries and in particular between developed and developing countries, and it defines primary care, both as an integral part of a country's health system but also as the overall social and economic development of the community. The declaration has been a major influence in the development of a broad and holistic definition of primary care in many countries and its declaration remains as relevant today as in 1978.

A few years earlier, while working as a GP in the Welsh valleys, Julian Tudor Hart wrote one of his most influential and enduring contributions to health care. The inverse care law was and remains a damning description of a law that drives access to healthcare – that 'the availability of good medical care tends to vary inversely with the need for it in the population served'. This law plays out not just in primary care but in hospital care and community care and health promotion so that those in greatest need of prevention are least likely to access it with the consequence of increasing rather reducing inequalities.

Edwin Chadwick's 'General Report on the Sanitary Conditions of the Labouring Population of Great Britain' is the oldest of the selections in this reader and is one of a number of historical documents that vividly described the appalling social conditions that characterized industrial towns growing prolifically as a consequence of the industrial revolution. Friedrich Engels, Charles Booth and Seebohm Rowntree, among others, made similar historical contributions that offer vivid descriptions of the social conditions that people were living in and how these conditions were directly related to health and well-being. An excellent historical account of the relationship between poverty, inequality and health is offered by Davey Smith, Dorling and Shaw (2001).

More contemporaneously two readings have had an impact on health policy on a global level. During the 1970s public health authorities in Canada, the UK and the USA were increasingly aware that 'their traditional duties had been superseded by new challenges' and that 'a new approach was needed' (MacDougall, 2007). Although the political context in each of these counties was not receptive to such radical proposals, they have in due course gone on to stimulate debate and reframe how problems are defined and addressed. Marc Lalonde, a Canadian Minister of Health, made the case for a broader conceptualization of health setting out two broad objectives and five strategies, including a health promotion strategy.

Following on from the Lalonde report came the publication of the 'Black Report'. Commissioned by a Labour Health Minister in 1977 and reporting to a Conservative Government in 1981, the report on Inequalities in Health was Chaired by Sir Douglas Black. Hugely political, dismissed by government as unaffordable and subsequently critiqued on the basis of its political bias and weak or absent economic costings (e.g. Oliver and Nutbeam (2003)), the Black Report went on to underpin public health policy in England, combining, as it did, the masses of descriptive data on inequalities in health with the political enthusiasm of the (New) Labour government in the late 1990s. Sally McIntyre offers an excellent and detailed overview of the Black Report and the rationale for the choice of explanatory framework (MacIntyre, 1997).

Finally, extracts from the second Wanless Report, commissioned to consider the wider determinants of health in England and the cost-effectiveness of action (Wanless, 2004), make up the final reading. Readers are encouraged to read the full original document but the extracts selected provide some background in terms of history, but also in terms of the thorny issue of 'public health – whose responsibility?', particularly in the context of the different scenarios of public engagement set out by Wanless in his earlier report (Wanless, 2002). At one level it appears that the readings end where they began – emphasizing the importance of involving individuals and communities in different aspects of health and healthcare. The Alma Ata declaration stated in section IV that people have both 'the right and duty to participate individually and collectively in the planning and implementation of their healthcare' and the subsequent development of user and patient involvement in healthcare is described more fully by McIver (2006). Wanless states that 'Individuals are ultimately responsible for their own and their children's health and it is the aggregate actions of individuals which will be responsible for whether or not such an optimistic scenario as "fully engaged" unfolds'. For Wanless, individuals must take responsibility for their own health behaviours. The other readings selected here provide a strong argument and evidence base for ensuring that individual responsibilities are encouraged and developed *alongside* policies that integrate individual responsibilities with actions by other organizations and government bodies that address the social determinants of health, many of which are simply outside of the scope of individuals' influence and ultimately are political in nature. Crawford (1977) warns, in another classic paper that is relevant here, that a victim blaming ideology inhibits our understanding and recognition of the social determinants of health and instead substitutes an unrealistic determinist behavioural model. The debate continues.

Summary

- Adopting a positive and broad definition of health has a bearing on what is considered to be within or outside of the realms of health policy and management.
- Lay people and academics have a strong tradition of describing and explaining health and illness behaviours with reference to the social context where they are constructed, experienced and managed.
- Since the 1970s governments have increasingly recognized the limits of narrow definitions of health and the need to look and respond to the social determinants of health, which include, in addition to healthcare, factors such as inequalities in health, work, employment, social exclusion, addiction and food.
- Most of the readings selected in this part provide an historical and political background to the relationship between contemporary health policy and the social determinants of health.
- The increasing attention to the role and responsibilities of individuals in maintaining a healthy lifestyle should be balanced with actions by governments and others to address those factors outside of the influence of individuals and their families.

References and further reading

Baggott, R. (2007) *Understanding Health Policy*. Bristol: Polity Press and Social Policy.

Crawford, R. (1977) You are dangerous to your health: the health and politics of victim blaming, *International Journal of Health Services*, 7(4): 364–678.

Davey Smith, G., Dorling, D. and Shaw, M. (2001) *Poverty, Inequality and Health in Britain*. London: The Policy Press.

Engels, F. (1999) *The Condition of the Working Class in England*. Oxford: Oxford Classics.

Hughner, R.S. and Klein, S.S. (2004) Views of health in the lay sector: a compilation and review of how individuals think about health, *Health*, 8(4): 395–422.

MacDougall, H. (2007) Reinventing public health: a new perspective on the health of Canadians and its international impact, *Journal of Epidemiology and Community Health*, 61(11): 958.

MacIntyre, S. (1997) The Black Report and beyond: what are the issues? *Social Science and Medicine*, 44(6): 72–745.

Marmot, M. and Wilkinson, R. (eds) (2003) *Social Determinants of Health: The Solid Facts*. Geneva: World Health Organization.

McIver, S. (2006) User perspectives and user involvement, in K. Walshe and J. Smith (eds) *Healthcare Management*. Maidenhead: Open University Press.

Oliver, A. and Nutbeam, D. (2003) Addressing health inequalities in the United Kingdom: a case study, *Journal of Public Health Medicine,* 25(4): 281–87.

Wanless, D. (2002) *Securing Our Future: Taking a Long-term View.* London: HM Treasury.

The readings

Declaration of Alma Ata (1978) *International Conference on Primary Health Care,* Alma Ata, USSR, 6–12 September.

Tudor Hart, J. (1971) The Inverse Care Law, *The Lancet,* 27 February, 406–12.

Chadwick, E. (1842) *Report from the Poor Law Commissioners on an Inquiry into Sanitary Conditions of the Labouring Population of Great Britain.* London: Poor Law Commission.

Black, D. (Chair) (1982) Report of a Research Working Group *Inequalities in Health.* London: Department of Health and Social Services.

Lalonde, M. (1974) *A New Perspective on the Health of Canadians.* Ottawa: Health Canada.

Wanless, D. (2004) *Securing Good Health for the Whole Population.* London: HM Treasury.

40

Declaration of Alma-Ata
World Health Organization

Extracts from Declaration of Alma Ata (1978) International Conference on Primary Health Care, Alma Ata, USSR, 6–12 September.

The International Conference on Primary Health Care, meeting in Alma-Ata this twelfth day of September in the year Nineteen hundred and seventy-eight, expressing the need for urgent action by all governments, all health and development workers, and the world community to protect and promote the health of all the people of the world, hereby makes the following

Declaration:

I

The Conference strongly reaffirms that health, which is a state of complete physical, mental and social wellbeing, and not merely the absence of disease or infirmity, is a fundamental human right and that the attainment of the highest possible level of health is a most important world-wide social goal whose realization requires the action of many other social and economic sectors in addition to the health sector.

II

The existing gross inequality in the health status of the people particularly between developed and developing countries as well as within countries is politically, socially and economically unacceptable and is, therefore, of common concern to all countries.

III

Economic and social development, based on a New International Economic Order, is of basic importance to the fullest attainment of health for all and to the reduction of the gap between the health status of the developing and developed countries. The promotion and protection of the health of the people is essential to sustained economic and social development and contributes to a better quality of life and to world peace.

IV

The people have the right and duty to participate individually and collectively in the planning and implementation of their health care.

V

Governments have a responsibility for the health of their people which can be fulfilled only by the provision of adequate health and social measures. A main social target of governments, international organizations and the whole world community in the coming decades should be the attainment by all peoples of the world by the year 2000 of a level of health that will permit them to lead a socially and economically productive life. Primary health care is the key to attaining this target as part of development in the spirit of social justice.

VI

Primary health care is essential health care based on practical, scientifically sound and socially acceptable methods and technology made universally accessible to individuals and families in the community through their full participation and at a cost that the community and country can afford to maintain at every stage of their development in the spirit of self-reliance and self-determination. It forms an integral part both of the country's health system, of which it is the central function and main focus, and of the overall social and economic development of the community. It is the first level of contact of individuals, the family and community with the national health system bringing health care as close as possible to where people live and work, and constitutes the first element of a continuing health care process.

VII

Primary health care:

1. reflects and evolves from the economic conditions and sociocultural and political characteristics of the country and its communities and is based on the application of the relevant results of social, biomedical and health services research and public health experience;
2. addresses the main health problems in the community, providing promotive, preventive, curative and rehabilitative services accordingly;
3. includes at least: education concerning prevailing health problems and the methods of preventing and controlling them; promotion of food supply and proper nutrition; an adequate supply of safe water and basic sanitation;

maternal and child health care, including family planning; immunization against the major infectious diseases; prevention and control of locally endemic diseases; appropriate treatment of common diseases and injuries; and provision of essential drugs;

4. involves, in addition to the health sector, all related sectors and aspects of national and community development, in particular agriculture, animal husbandry, food, industry, education, housing, public works, communications and other sectors; and demands the coordinated efforts of all those sectors;

5. requires and promotes maximum community and individual self-reliance and participation in the planning, organization, operation and control of primary health care, making fullest use of local, national and other available resources; and to this end develops through appropriate education the ability of communities to participate;

6. should be sustained by integrated, functional and mutually supportive referral systems, leading to the progressive improvement of comprehensive health care for all, and giving priority to those most in need;

7. relies, at local and referral levels, on health workers, including physicians, nurses, midwives, auxiliaries and community workers as applicable, as well as traditional practitioners as needed, suitably trained socially and technically to work as a health team and to respond to the expressed health needs of the community.

VIII

All governments should formulate national policies, strategies and plans of action to launch and sustain primary health care as part of a comprehensive national health system and in coordination with other sectors. To this end, it will be necessary to exercise political will, to mobilize the country's resources and to use available external resources rationally.

IX

All countries should cooperate in a spirit of partnership and service to ensure primary health care for all people since the attainment of health by people in any one country directly concerns and benefits every other country. In this context the joint WHO/UNICEF report on primary health care constitutes a solid basis for the further development and operation of primary health care throughout the world.

X

An acceptable level of health for all the people of the world by the year 2000 can be attained through a fuller and better use of the world's resources, a considerable part of which is now spent on armaments and military conflicts. A genuine policy of independence, peace, détente and disarmament could and should release additional resources that could well be devoted to peaceful aims and in particular to the acceleration of social and economic development of which primary health care, as an essential part, should be allotted its proper share.

The International Conference on Primary Health Care calls for urgent and effective national and international action to develop and implement primary health care throughout the world and particularly in developing countries in a spirit of technical cooperation and in keeping with a New International Economic Order. It urges governments, WHO and UNICEF, and other international organizations, as well as multilateral and bilateral agencies, non-governmental organizations, funding agencies, all health workers and the whole world community to support national and international commitment to primary health care and to channel increased technical and financial support to it, particularly in developing countries. The Conference calls on all the aforementioned to collaborate in introducing, developing and maintaining primary health care in accordance with the spirit and content of this Declaration.

41

The Inverse Care Law
Julian Tudor Hart

Extracts from Tudor Hart J (1971) The Inverse Care Law, The Lancet, 27th February, 406–12.

Summary

The availability of good medical care tends to vary inversely with the need for it in the population served. This inverse care law operates more completely where medical care is most exposed to market forces, and less so where such exposure is reduced. The market distribution of medical care is a primitive and historically outdated social form, and any return to it would further exaggerate the maldistribution of medical resources.

Interpreting the evidence

The existence of large social and geographical inequalities in mortality and morbidity in Britain is known, and not all of them are diminishing. Between 1934 and 1968, weighted mean standardised mortality from all causes in the Glamorgan and Monmouthshire valleys rose from 128% of England and Wales rates to 131%. Their weighted mean infant mortality rose from 115% of England and Wales rates to 124% between 1921 and 1968.[1] The Registrar General's last Decennial Supplement on Occupational Mortality for 1949–53 still showed combined social classes I and II (wholly non-manual) with a standardised mortality from all causes 18% below the mean, and combined social classes IV and V (wholly manual) 5% above it. Infant mortality was 37% below the mean for social class I (professional) and 38% above it for social class V (unskilled manual).

A just and rational distribution of the resources of medical care should show parallel social and geographical differences, or at least a uniform distribution. The common experience was described by Titmuss in 1968:

> "We have learnt from 15 years' experience of the Health Service that the higher income groups know how to make better use of the service; they tend to receive more specialist attention; occupy more of the beds in better equipped

and staffed hospitals; receive more elective surgery; have better maternal care, and are more likely to get psychiatric help and psychotherapy than low-income groups—particularly the unskilled."[2]

Non-statistical evidence

There is massive but mostly non-statistical evidence in favour of Titmuss's generalisations. First of all there is the evidence of social history. James[3] described the origins of the general practitioner service in industrial and coalmining areas, from which the present has grown:

> The general practitioner in working-class areas discovered the well-tried business principle of small profits with a big turnover where the population was large and growing rapidly; it paid to treat a great many people for a small fee. A waiting-room crammed with patients, each representing 2s. 6d. for a consultation ... not only gave a satisfactory income but also reduced the inclination to practise clinical medicine with skilful care, to attend clinical meetings, or to seek refreshment from the scientific literature. Particularly in coalmining areas, workers formed themselves into clubs to which they contributed a few pence a week, and thus secured free treatment from the club doctor for illness or accident. The club system was the forerunner of health insurance and was a humane and desirable social development. But, like the "cash surgery", it encouraged the doctor to undertake the treatment of more patients than he could deal with efficiently. It also created a difference between the club patients and those who could afford to pay for medical attention ... in these circumstances it is a tribute to the profession that its standards in industrial practices were as high as they were. If criticism is necessary, it should not be of the doctors who developed large industrial practices but of the leaders of all branches of the profession, who did not see the trend of general practice, or, having seen it, did nothing to influence it. It is particularly regrettable that the revolutionary conception of a National Health Service, which has transformed the hospitals of the United Kingdom to the great benefit of the community, should not have brought about an equally radical change in general practice. Instead, because of the shortsightedness of the profession, the N.H.S. has preserved and intensified the worst features of general practice ...

This preservation and intensification was described by Collings[4] in his study of the work of 104 general practitioners in 55 English practices outside London, including 9 completely and 7 partly industrial practices, six months after the start of the N.H.S. Though not randomly sampled, the selection of practices was structured in a reasonably representative manner. The very bad situation he described was the one I found when I entered a slum practice in Notting Hill in 1953, rediscovered in all but one of five industrial practices where I acted as locum tenens in 1961, and found again when I resumed practice in the South Wales valleys. Collings said:

the working environment of general practitioners in industrial areas was so limiting that their individual capacity as doctors counted very little. In the circumstances prevailing, the most essential qualification for the industrial G.P ... is ability as a snap diagnostician—an ability to reach an accurate diagnosis on a minimum of evidence ... the worst elements of general practice are to be found in those places where there is the greatest and most urgent demand for good medical service ... Some conditions of general practice are bad enough to change a good doctor into a bad doctor in a very short time. These very bad conditions are to be found chiefly in industrial areas.

In a counter-report promoted by the British Medical Association, Hadfield[5] contested all of Collings' conclusions, but, though his sampling was much better designed, his criticism was guarded to the point of complacency, and most vaguely defined. One of Collings' main criticisms—that purpose-built premises and ancillary staff were essential for any serious upgrading of general practice—is only now being taken seriously; and even the present wave of health-centre construction shows signs of finishing almost as soon as it has begun, because of the present climate of political and economic opinion at the level of effective decision. Certainly in industrial and mining areas health centres exist as yet only on a token basis, and the number of new projects is declining. Aneurin Bevan described health centres as the cornerstone of the general practitioner service under the N.H.S., before the long retreat began from the conceptions of the service born in the 1930s and apparently victorious in 1945. Health centre construction was scrapped by ministerial circular in January, 1948, in the last months of gestation of the new service; we have had to do without them for 22 years, during which a generation of primary care was stunted.

Despite this unpromising beginning, the N.H.S. brought about a massive improvement in the delivery of medical care to previously deprived sections of the people and areas of the country. Former Poor Law hospitals were upgraded and many acquired fully trained specialist and ancillary staff and supporting diagnostic departments for the first time. The backlog of untreated disease dealt with in the first years of the service was immense, particularly in surgery and gynæcology. A study of 734 randomly sampled families in London and Northampton in 1961[6] showed that in 99% of the families someone had attended hospital as an outpatient, and in 82% someone had been admitted to hospital. The study concluded:

When thinking of the Health Service mothers are mainly conscious of the extent to which services have become available in recent years. They were more aware of recent changes in health services than of changes in any other service. Nearly one third thought that more money should be spent on health services, not because they thought them bad but because "they are so important", because "doctors and nurses should be paid more" or because "there shouldn't be charges for treatment". Doctors came second to relatives and friends in the list of those who had been helpful in times of trouble.

Among those with experience of pre-war services, appreciation for the N.H.S., often uncritical appreciation, is almost universal—so much so that, although most London teaching-hospital consultants made their opposition to the new service crudely evident to their students in 1948 and the early years, and only a courageous few openly supported it, few of them appear to recall this today. The moral defeat of the very part-time, multi-hospital consultant, nipping in here and there between private consultations to see how his registrar was coping with his public work, was total and permanent; lip-service to the N.H.S. is now mandatory. At primary-care level, private practice ceased to be relevant to the immense majority of general practitioners, and has failed to produce evidence of the special functions of leadership and quality claimed for it, in the form of serious research material. On the other hand, despite the massive economic disincentives to good work, equipment, and staffing in the N.H.S. until a few years ago, an important expansion of well-organised, community-oriented, and self-critical primary care has taken place, mainly through the efforts of the Royal College of General Practitioners; the main source of this vigour is the democratic nature of the service—the fact that it is comprehensive and accessible to all, and that clinical decisions are therefore made more freely than ever before. The service at least permits, if it does not yet really encourage, general practitioners to think and act in terms of the care of a whole defined community, as well as of whole persons rather than diseases. Collings seems very greatly to have underestimated the importance of these changes, and the extent to which they were to overshadow the serious faults of the service—and these were faults of too little change, rather than too much. There have in fact been very big improvements in the quality and accessibility of care both at hospital and primary-care level, for all classes and in all areas.

What should be done?

Medical services are not the main determinant of mortality or morbidity; these depend most upon standards of nutrition, housing, working environment, and education, and the presence or absence of war. The high mortality and morbidity of the South Wales valleys arise mainly from lower standards in most of these variables now and in the recent past, rather than from lower standards of medical care. But that is no excuse for failure to match the greatest need with the highest standards of care. The bleak future now facing mining communities, and others that may suffer similar social dislocation as technical change blunders on without agreed social objectives, cannot be altered by doctors alone; but we do have a duty to draw attention to the need for global costing when it comes to policy decisions on redevelopment or decay of established industrial communities. Such costing would take into account the full social costs and not only those elements of profit and loss traditionally recognized in industry.

The improved access to medical care for previously deprived sections under the N.H.S. arose chiefly from the decision to remove primary-care services from exposure to market forces. The consequences of distribution of care by the operation of the market were unjust and irrational, despite all sorts of charitable modifications. The improved possibilities for constructive planning and rational distribution of resources because of this decision are immense, and even now are scarcely realised in practice. The losses predicted by opponents of this change have not in fact occurred; consultants who no longer depend on private practice have shown at least as much initiative and responsibility as before, and the standards attained in the best N.H.S. primary care are at least as good as those in private practice. It has been proved that a national health service can run quite well without the profit motive, and that the motivation of the work itself can be more powerful in a decommercialised setting. The gains of the service derive very largely from the simple and clear principles on which it was conceived: a comprehensive national service, available to all, free at the time of use, non-contributory, and financed from taxation. Departures from these principles, both when the service began (the tripartite division and omission of family-planning and chiropody services) and subsequently (dental and prescription charges, rising direct contributions, and relative reductions in financing from taxation), have not strengthened it. The principles themselves seem to me to be worth defending, despite the risk of indulging in unfashionable value-judgments. The accelerating forward movement of general practice today, impressively reviewed in a symposium on group practice held by the Royal College of General Practitioners,[9] is a movement (not always conscious) toward these principles and the ideas that prevailed generally among the minority of doctors who supported them in 1948, including their material corollary, group practice from health centres. The doctor/patient relationship, which was held by opponents of the Act to depend above all on a cash transaction between patient and doctor, has been transformed and improved by abolishing that transaction. A general practitioner can now think in terms of service to a defined community, and plan his work according to rational priorities.

Return to the market?

The past ten years have seen a spate of papers urging that the N.H.S. be returned wholly or partly to the operation of the market. Jewkes,[10] Lees,[11] Seale,[12] and the advisory planning panel on health services financing of the British Medical Association[13] have all elaborated on this theme. Their arguments consist in a frontal attack on the policy of removing health care from the market, together with criticism of faults in the service that do not necessarily or even probably depend on that policy at all, but on the failure of Governments to devote a sufficient part of the national product to medical care. These faults include the stagnation in hospital building and senior staffing throughout the 1950s, the low wages throughout the service up to consultant level, over-centralised control, and failure to realise the objective of social and geographical equality in access to the best medical care. None of these failings is intrinsic to the original principles of the N.H.S.; all have been deplored by its supporters, and with more vigour than by these critics. The critics depend heavily on a climate of television and editorial opinion favouring the view that all but a minority of people are rich enough and willing to pay for all they need in medical care (but not through taxation), and that public services are a historically transient social form, appropriate to indigent populations, to be discarded as soon as may be in favour of distribution of health care as a bought commodity, provided by competing entrepreneurs. They depend also on the almost universal abdication of principled opposition to these views, on the part of its official opponents. The former Secretary of State for Social Services, Mr. Richard Crossman, has agreed that the upper limit of direct taxation has been reached, and that "we should not be afraid to look for alternative sources of revenue less dependent on the Chancellor's whims ... I should not rule out obtaining a higher proportion of the cost of the service from the Health Service contribution."[14] This is simply a suggestion that rising health costs should be met by flat-rate contributions unrelated to income—an acceptance of the view that the better-off are taxed to the limit, but also that the poor can afford to pay more in proportion. With such opposition, it is not surprising that more extravagant proposals for substantial payments at the time of illness, for consultations, home visits, and hospital care, are more widely discussed and advocated than ever before.

The Inverse Care Law

In areas with most sickness and death, general practitioners have more work, larger lists, less hospital support, and inherit more clinically ineffective traditions of consultation, than in the healthiest areas; and hospital doctors shoulder heavier case-loads with less staff and equipment, more obsolete buildings, and suffer recurrent crises in the availability of beds and replacement staff. These trends can be summed up as the inverse care law: that the availability of good medical care tends to vary inversely with the need of the population served.

If the N.H.S. had continued to adhere to its original principles, with construction of health centres a first priority in industrial areas, all financed from taxation rather than direct flat-rate contribution, free at the time of use, and fully inclusive of all personal health services, including family planning, the operation of the inverse care law would have been modified much more than it has been; but even the service as it is has been effective in redistributing care, considering the powerful social forces operating against this. If our health services had evolved as a free market, or even on a fee-for-item-of-service basis prepaid by private insurance, the law would have operated much more completely than it does; our situation might approximate to that in the United States,[15] with the added disadvantage of smaller national wealth. The force that creates and maintains the inverse care law is the operation of the market, and its cultural and ideological superstructure which has permeated the thought and directed the ambitions of our profession during all of its modern history. The more health services are removed from the force of the market, the more successful we can be in redistributing care away from its "natural" distribution in a market economy; but this will be a redistribution, an intervention to correct a fault natural to our form of society, and therefore incompletely successful and politically unstable, in the absence of more fundamental social change.

Notes

1   Hart, J. T. *J. R. Coll. gen. Practnrs* (in the press).
2   Titmuss, R. M. Commitment to Welfare. London, 1968.
3   James, E. F. *Lancet*, 1961, i, 1361.
4   Collings, J. S. *ibid.* 1950, i, 555.
5   Hadfield, S. J. *Br. med. J.* 1953, ii, 683.
6   Family Needs and Social Services. Political and Economic Planning, London, 1961.
7   Department of Health and Social Security, Annual Report for 1969. London, 1970.
8   General Practice Today. Office of Health Economics, paper no. 28, London, 1970.
9   *J. R. Coll. gen. Practnrs*, 1970, 20, suppl. 2.
10 Jewkes, J., Jewkes, S. The Genesis of the British National Health Service. Oxford, 1961.
11 Lees, D. S. Health through Choice. An Economic Study of the British National Health Service. Hobart paper no. 14, Institute of Economic Affairs, London, 1961.
12 Seale, J. *Br. med. J.* 1962, ii, 598.
13 Report of the Advisory Panel of the British Medical Association on Health Services Financing. B.M.A., London, 1970.
14 Crossman, R. H. S. Paying for the Social Services. Fabian Society, London, 1969.
15 Williams, R. The Long Revolution. London, 1961.

42

Report from the Poor Law Commissioners on an inquiry into Sanitary Conditions of the Labouring Population of Great Britain
Edwin Chadwick

Extracts from Chadwick E (1842) Report from the Poor Law Commissioners on an inquiry into Sanitary Conditions of the Labouring Population of Great Britain. London: Poor Law Commission.

Recapitulation of conclusions

The last cited instance of the practical operation of measures for the abatement of the nuisances attendant on common lodging-houses may also be submitted as an instance of the advantages derivable from the extension of such fields of inquiries as the present. On each of the chief points included in it there would have been a loss of what I hope will be deemed valuable corroborative information, had the inquiry been confined either to England or to Scotland. The observation of the important productive use of the refuse of the city of Edinburgh would have been of comparatively little value as evidence leading to practical applications, apart from the observation of what is accomplished by the practical application of science to sewerage and drainage for the immediate and cheapest removal of all the refuse of towns by water through closed drains afforded by the operation in the Holborn and Finsbury division of the metropolis. It may be stated confidently that, if the inquiry could conveniently have had still further extension as to time and place, the information would have been strengthened and rendered more complete. From incidental facts I have met with, I am led to believe that the whole of the effects which are the subject of the present report would have been still more strikingly displayed in many parts of Ireland.

After as careful an examination of the evidence collected as I have been enabled to make, I beg leave to recapitulate the chief conclusions which that evidence appears to me to establish.

First, as to the extent and operation of the evils which are the subject of the inquiry:—
That the various forms of epidemic, endemic, and other disease caused, or aggravated, or propagated chiefly amongst the labouring classes by atmospheric

impurities produced by decomposing animal and vegetable substances, by damp and filth, and close and overcrowded dwellings prevail amongst the population in every part of the kingdom, whether dwelling in separate houses, in rural villages, in small towns, in the larger towns—as they have been found to prevail in the lowest districts of the metropolis.

That such disease, wherever its attacks are frequent, is always found in connexion with the physical circumstances above specified, and that where those circumstances are removed by drainage, proper cleansing, better ventilation, and other means of diminishing atmospheric impurity, the frequency and intensity of such disease is abated; and where the removal of the noxious agencies appears to be complete, such disease almost entirely disappears.

That high prosperity in respect to employment and wages, and various and abundant food, have afforded to the labouring classes no exemptions from attacks of epidemic disease, which have been as frequent and as fatal in periods of commercial and manufacturing prosperity as in any others.

That the formation of all habits of cleanliness is obstructed by defective supplies of water.

That the annual loss of life from filth and bad ventilation are greater than the loss from death or wounds in any wars in which the country has been engaged in modern times.

That of the 43,000 cases of widowhood, and 112,000 cases of destitute orphans relieved from the poor's rates in England and Wales alone, it appears that the greatest proportion of deaths of the heads of families occurred from the above specified and other removable causes; that their ages were under 45 years; that is to say, 13 years below the natural probabilities of life as shown by the experience of the whole population of Sweden.

That the public loss from the premature deaths of the heads of families is greater than can be represented by any enumeration of the pecuniary burdens consequent upon their sickness and death.

That, measuring the loss of working ability amongst large classes by the instances of gain, even from incomplete arrangements for the removal of noxious influences from places of work or from abodes, that this loss cannot be less than eight or ten years.

That the ravages of epidemics and other diseases do not diminish but tend to increase the pressure of population.

That in the districts where the mortality is the greatest the births are not only sufficient to replace the numbers removed by death, but to add to the population.

That the younger population, bred up under noxious physical agencies, is inferior in physical organization and general health to a population preserved from the presence of such agencies.

That the population so exposed is less susceptible of moral influences, and the effects of education are more transient than with a healthy population.

That these adverse circumstances tend to produce an adult population short-lived, improvident, reckless, and intemperate, and with habitual avidity for sensual gratifications.

That these habits lead to the abandonment of all the conveniences and decencies of life, and especially lead to the overcrowding of their homes, which is destructive to the morality as well as the health of large classes of both sexes.

That defective town cleansing fosters habits of the most abject degradation and tends to the demoralization of large numbers of human beings, who subsist by means of what they find amidst the noxious filth accumulated in neglected streets and bye-places.

That the expenses of local public works are in general unequally and unfairly assessed, oppressively and uneconomically collected, by separate collections, wastefully expended in separate and inefficient operations by unskilled and practically irresponsible officers.

That the existing law for the protection of the public health and the constitutional machinery for reclaiming its execution, such as the Courts Leet, have fallen into desuetude, and are in the state indicated by the prevalence of the evils they were intended to prevent.

Secondly. As to the means by which the present sanitary condition of the labouring classes may be improved:—

The primary and most important measures, and at the same time the most practicable, and within the recognized province of public administration, are drainage, the removal of all refuse of habitations, streets, and roads, and the improvement of the supplies of water.

That the chief obstacles to the immediate removal of decomposing refuse of towns and habitations have been the expense and annoyance of the hand labour and cartage requisite for the purpose.

That this expense may be reduced to one-twentieth or to one-thirtieth, or rendered inconsiderable, by the use of water and self-acting means of removal by improved and cheaper sewers and drains.

That refuse when thus held in suspension in water may be most cheaply and innoxiously conveyed to any distance out of towns, and also in the best form for productive use, and that the loss and injury by the pollution of natural streams may be avoided.

That for all these purposes, as well as for domestic use, better supplies of water are absolutely necessary.

That for successful and economical drainage the adoption of geological areas as the basis of operations is requisite.

That appropriate scientific arrangements for public drainage would afford important facilities for private land-drainage, which is important for the health as well as sustenance of the labouring classes.

That the expense of public drainage, of supplies of water laid on in houses, and of means of improved cleansing would be a pecuniary gain, by diminishing the existing charges attendant on sickness and premature mortality.

That for the protection of the labouring classes and of the ratepayers against inefficiency and waste in all new structural arrangements for the protection of the public health, and to ensure public confidence that the expenditure will be beneficial, securities should be taken that all new local public works are devised and conducted by responsible officers qualified by the possession of the science and skill of civil engineers.

That the oppressiveness and injustice of levies for the whole immediate outlay on such works upon persons who have only short interests in the benefits may be avoided by care in spreading the expense over periods coincident with the benefits.

That by appropriate arrangements, 10 or 15 per cent, on the ordinary outlay for drainage might be saved, which on an estimate of the expense of the necessary structural alterations of one-third only of the existing tenements would be a saving of one million and a half sterling, besides the reduction of the future expenses of management.

That for the prevention of the disease occasioned by defective ventilation, and other causes of impurity in places of work and other places where large numbers are assembled, and for the general promotion of the means necessary to prevent disease, that it would be good economy to appoint a district medical officer independent of private practice, and with the securities of special qualifications and responsibilities to initiate sanitary measures and reclaim the execution of the law.

That by the combinations of all these arrangements it is probable that the full ensurable period of life indicated by the Swedish tables; that is, an increase of 13 years at least, may be extended to the whole of the labouring classes.

That the attainment of these and the other collateral advantages of reducing existing charges and expenditure are within the power of the legislature, and are dependent mainly on the securities taken for the application of practical science, skill, and economy in the direction of local public works.

And that the removal of noxious physical circumstances, and the promotion of civic, household, and personal cleanliness, are necessary to the improvement of the moral condition of the population; for that sound morality and refinement in manners and health are not long found co-existant with filthy habits amongst any class of the community.

I beg leave further to suggest, that the principles of amendment deduced from the inquiry will be found as applicable to Scotland as to England; and if so, it may be submitted for attention whether it might not be represented that the structural arrangements for drainage would be most conveniently carried out in the same form as in England, that is by commissions, of the nature of commissions of sewers adapted, as regards jurisdiction to natural or geological areas, and including in them the chief elected officers of municipalities, and other authorities now charged with the care of the streets and roads or connected with local public works.

The advantages of uniformity in legislation and in the executive machinery, and of doing the same things in the same way (choosing the best), and calling the same officers, proceedings, and things by the same names, will only be appreciated by those who have observed the extensive public loss occasioned by the legislation for towns which makes them independent of beneficent, as of what perhaps might have been deemed formerly aggressive legislation. There are various sanitary regulations, and especially those for cleansing, directed to be observed in 'every town except Berwick and Carlisle;' a course of legislation which, had it been efficient for England, would have left Berwick and Carlisle distinguished by the oppression of common evils intended to be remedied. It was the subject of public complaint, at Glasgow and in other parts of Scotland, that independence and separation in the form of general legislation separated the people from their share of the greatest amount of legislative attention, or excluded them from common interest and from the common advantages of protective measures. It was, for example, the subject of particular complaint, that whilst the labouring population of England and Ireland had received the advantages of public legislative provision for a general vaccination, the labouring classes in Scotland were still left exposed to the ravages of the small-pox. It was also complained by Dr. Cowan and other members of the medical profession, that Scotland had not been included in the provisions for the registration of the causes of death which they considered might, with improvements, be made highly conducive to the advancement of medical science and the means of protecting the public health.

I have the honour to be,
Gentlemen,
Your obedient servant,
EDWIN CHADWICK

43

Report of a research working group: inequalities in health
Douglas Black

Extracts from Black D (1982) Report of a Research Working Group, Inequalities in Health. London: Department of Health and Social Services.

Concepts of health and inequality

Throughout history different meanings have been given to the idea of 'health'. One is freedom from clinically ascertainable disease, which has been central to the development of medicine. In ancient Greece the followers of Asclepius believed that the chief role of the physician was to 'treat disease, to restore health by correcting any imperfections caused by the accidents of birth or life' (Dubos, 1960, p. 109). Beginning with primitive surgical intervention and herbal treatment, a tradition was established which was to prove, extraordinarily powerful, accelerating in the eighteenth century with the rise of science and again in the twentieth century as a consequence of the massive resources provided for research and innovation in medical technologies. The Cartesian philosophy of the body conceived as a machine and the body controlled as a machine provided an impetus for scientific experiment and a stream of practical outcomes which for an increasing proportion of the population seemed to validate a mechanistic perspective.

There can be no doubt about the success with which such an 'engineering' approach in medicine has been applied. Medical education became concerned with the structure and functions of the body and with disease processes, and medical science became represented predominantly by the acute hospital with its concentration of technological resources (Abel-Smith, 1964). The relatively restricted and familiar use of the word 'health' is therefore associated with the belief systems and the practice of a medicine from which its origins can be traced. Health, which derives from a word meaning whole, is the object of the healing process. To heal is literally to make whole or to restore health. The structure of medicine and of the health services helps to sustain this meaning. Some (for example, McKeown, 1976) have argued however that this development in medicine has distorted our understanding of the problems of human health and well-being and that there are alternative or complementary approaches which it is increasingly important to clarify and properly finance.

Much wider meanings have been given to the word 'health', which hold major implications for the organization of society and the pattern upon which personal life may be modelled. To the followers of the ideas symbolized in ancient Greece by the goddess Hygeia, rational social organization and rational individual behaviour were all-important to the promotion of human health. It was an attribute to which men were entitled if they governed their lives wisely and is echoed in today's 'life-style' approaches to good health. According to them, 'the most important function of medicine is to discover and teach the natural laws which will ensure a man a healthy mind in a healthy body' (Dubos, 1960, p. 109). Implicit also are ideas of the good life: not just freedom from pain, discomfort, stress and boredom, which themselves extend beyond the competence of clinicians to diagnose or treat, but positive expression of vigour, well-being and engagement with one's environment or community. In some respects this more comprehensive approach reached its apogee in the definition of health adopted at the foundation of the World Health Organization at the end of the Second World War as a 'state of complete physical, mental and social well-being and not merely the absence of disease or infirmity'. Adherents of this more comprehensive approach, which is usually called 'social', have worked both within and outside medicine. In most countries there are movements for physical fitness and good diet. Immunization is a standard public health practice. And through direct and indirect 'health education' and counselling, higher standards of health are encouraged. In the case of children this wider conception of health directs concern not only to the presence or absence of disease, but to growth and development, physical, cognitive and emotional. (There is, anyway, abundant evidence for the interaction of disease and development in infants. Low-birth-weight babies show a higher mortality and also incidence of neurological and physical disorder (Birch and Gussow, 1970, p. 52) and, later in life, there is evidence for the aetiological significance of even mild under-nutrition in inhibiting growth (Marshall, 1977, p. 118).) It becomes relevant to look at evidence relating to acuity of hearing and vision in children, and at heights, weights and age at the onset of puberty, even though none of these things is in any sense an aspect of 'disease'. Given the significance of this kind of thinking, we consider that the different meanings of 'health' and hence of national objectives in maintaining and promoting health are often not given as much attention as they might be, a point we shall return to. Plainly for our purposes the 'social model' of health is more relevant than the 'medical' and we have therefore in the main followed it.

The two models are not, of course, either exclusive or exhaustive. (Discussions based essentially on the 'medical model' are given by Black (1979) and by Dollery (1978)). Conceptions of health and illness vary among different groups within a single society and between societies, as well as in any single society over time (Morris, 1975). It is in part for this reason that 'illness behaviour' – the response to symptoms and the tendency or reluctance to define any symptom as a health problem and to seek medical care – varies between cultural and social groups (Mechanic, 1968). Conceptions are moreover in constant process of adaptation or revision. Changes occur by virtue of scientific discovery and innovation, and developments in professional judgements of needs and the status of different diseases and treatments. They also occur in response to the pressure of established interests, and the extent of public anxiety about illness or safety, as well as the current level of demand for health, environmental and social services. Thus one result of research on the elderly and disabled, and the heightening of public interest and concern about their problems, has been that pain, discomfort, debility and different forms of incapacity have come to play a more prominent part in social and medical conceptions. If we consider mental illness or mental handicap, or the history of 'fringe' medicine, to take very diverse examples, we can see how conceptions of health and illness have changed. And just as conceptions themselves may gradually change, elements within them are accorded different weight or priority. We make this point for two reasons. The first is that our understanding of 'health' will always be evolving, and we must be prepared to absorb new knowledge about changes in health and social conditions. The second is to make better judgements about the strengths and weaknesses of the present health care services.

Concepts of inequality

The distribution of health or ill-health among and between populations has for many years been expressed most forcefully in terms of ideas on 'inequality'. These ideas are not just 'differences'. There may be differences between species, races, the sexes and people of different age, but the focus of interest is not so much natural physiological constitution or process as outcomes which have been socially or economically determined. This may seem to be straightforward, but the lengthy literature, and widespread public interest in the subject of inequality, show that factors which are recognizably or discernibly man-made are not so easy to disentangle from the complex physical and social structure in which man finds himself. Differences between people are accepted all too readily as eternal and unalterable. The institutions of society are very complex and exert their influence indirectly and subtly as well as directly and self-evidently. For some the concept of inequality also carries a moral reinforcement, as a fact which is undesirable or avoidable. For others the moral issue is relatively inconsequential. For them differences in riches or work conditions are an inevitable and hence 'natural' outcome of the history of attempts by man to build society, and they conclude that the scope for modification is small and, besides other matters, of little importance.

Central to the development of work on inequality has been the development of concepts of 'social class': that is *segments of the population sharing broadly similar types and levels of resources, with broadly similar styles of living and* (for some sociologists) *some shared perception of their collective condition*. This too has been controversial and there remains considerable controversy within sociology about the origins and relative importance of class in relation to social inequalities and social change.

Throughout this report we shall employ occupation as a basis of class because of its convenience. In particular we shall use the Registrar General's categories as follows:

I. Professional (for example accountant, doctor, lawyer) (5 per cent)*
II. Intermediate (for example manager, nurse, schoolteacher) (18 per cent)
III N. Skilled non-manual (for example clerical worker, secretary, shop assistant) (12 per cent)
III M. Skilled manual (for example bus driver, butcher, carpenter, coal face worker) (38 per cent)
IV. Partly skilled (for example agricultural worker, bus conductor, postman) (18 per cent)
V. Unskilled (for example cleaner, dock worker, labourer) (9 per cent).

Summary

In examining the state of health of a population it is necessary to remember there are different meanings of 'health' which have different implications for action to improve health. On the one hand 'health' can be conceived as the outcome of freeing man from disease or disorder, as identified throughout history by medicine. On the other hand, it can be conceived as man's vigorous, creative and even joyous involvement in environment and community, of which presence or absence of disease is only a part. While there are many indicators of health and ill-health, including mortality rates, morbidity rates, sickness-absence rates and restricted activity rates, we concentrate most attention in this report, mainly for practical reasons, on mortality rates.

Different meanings are also given to the term 'inequality'. Interest tends to be concentrated on those (substantial) differences in condition or experience among populations which have been brought about by social or industrial organization and which tend to be regarded as undesirable or of doubtful validity by groups in society. Inequality is difficult to measure and trends in inequalities in the distribution of income and wealth, for example, cannot yet be related to indicators of health, except indirectly. Partly for reasons of convenience, therefore, occupational status or class (which is correlated closely with various other measures of inequality) is used as the principal indicator of social inequality in this report.

The pattern of present health inequalities

Inequalities in health take a number of distinctive forms in Britain today. This chapter examines the pattern of inequalities according to a number of criteria: the relationships between gender and mortality, race and mortality, regional background and mortality, plus a range of measures of ill-health. But undoubtedly the clearest and most unequivocal is the relationship between occupational class and mortality.

Occupational class and mortality

Every death in Britain is a registered and certified event in which both the cause and the occupation of the deceased or his or her next of kin are recorded. By taking the actual incidence of death among members of the Registrar General's occupational classes and dividing this by the total in each occupational class it is possible to derive an estimate of class differences in mortality. This shows that on the basis of figures drawn from the early 1970s, when the most recent decennial survey was conducted, men and women in occupational class V had a two-and-a-half times greater chance of dying before reaching retirement age than their professional counterparts in occupational class I. Even when allowance is made for the fact that there are more older people in unskilled than professional work, the probability of death before retirement is still double.

What lies behind this gross statistic? Where do we begin to look for an explanation? If we break it down by age we find that class differences in mortality are a constant feature of the entire human life-span (see Figure 43.1). They are found at birth, during the first year of life, in childhood, adolescence and adult life. At *any* age people in occupational class V have a higher rate of death than their better-off counterparts. This is not to say that the differences are uniform; in general they are more marked at the start of life and, less obviously, in early adulthood.

At birth and during the first month of life the risk of death in families of unskilled workers is double that of professional families. Children of skilled manual fathers (occupational class IIIM) run a 1.5 times greater risk.

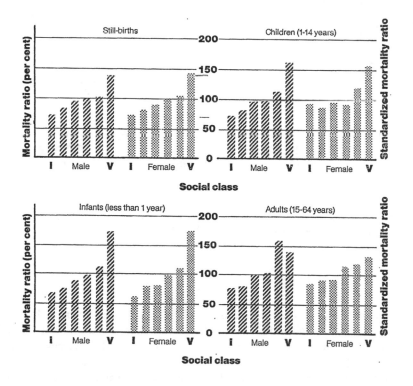

Figure 43.1   Mortality by occupational class and age. Relative mortality (%) is the ratio of rates for the occupational class to the rate for all males (or females). (*Source:* Occupational Mortality 1970–72, HMSO, 1978, p. 196.)

For the next eleven months of a child's life this ratio widens still further. For the death of every one male infant of professional parents, we can expect almost two among children of skilled manual workers and three among children of unskilled manual workers. Among females the ratios are even greater.

If we measure this against different causes of death – Figure 43.2 – we find that the most marked class gradients are for deaths from accidents and respiratory disease, two causes closely related to the socio-economic environment. Other causes, associated with birth itself and with congenital disabilities, have significantly less steep class gradients.

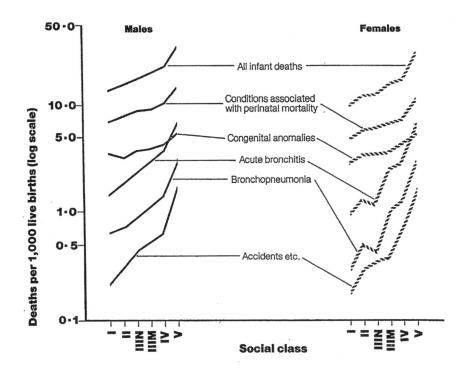

Figure 43.2 Infant mortality by sex, occupational class and cause of death. (*Source:* Occupational Mortality 1970–72, *HMSO, 1978, p. 158.*)

Between the ages of 1 and 14 relative class death rates narrow, but are still clearly visible. Among boys the ratio of mortality in occupational class V as compared with I is of the order of 2 to 1, while among girls it varies between 1.5 and 1.9 to 1.

Once again the causes of these differences can be traced largely to environmental factors. Accidents, which are by far the biggest single cause of childhood deaths (30 per cent of the total), continue to show the sharpest class gradient. Boys in class V have a ten times greater chance of dying from fire, falls or drowning than those in class I. The corresponding ratio of deaths caused to youthful pedestrians by motor vehicles is more than 7 to 1. Trailing somewhere behind this, but also with a marked class gradient, are infectious and parasitic diseases, responsible for 5 per cent of all childhood deaths, and pneumonia, responsible for 8 per cent of the total. Most other causes of death show less clear evidence of class disadvantage (Figure 43.3).

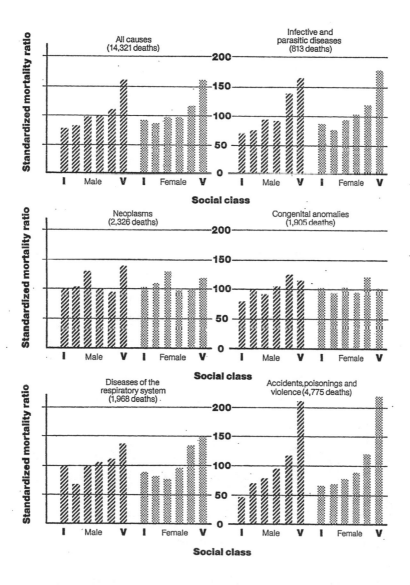

Figure 43.3 Class and morality in childhood (males and females 0–14). (*Source:* Occupational Mortality 1970–72, *HMSO, 1978, p. 160.*)

Among adults, taken in this context to be people aged between 15 and 64, class differences appear to narrow further, but the overall statistic conceals a large difference for those in their twenties and thirties and a relatively small one for adults nearer pension age.

As in childhood the rates of death from accidents and infectious disease show steep class gradients, but equally an extraordinary variety of non-infectious diseases like cancer, heart and respiratory disease also show marked class differences (Figure 43.4).

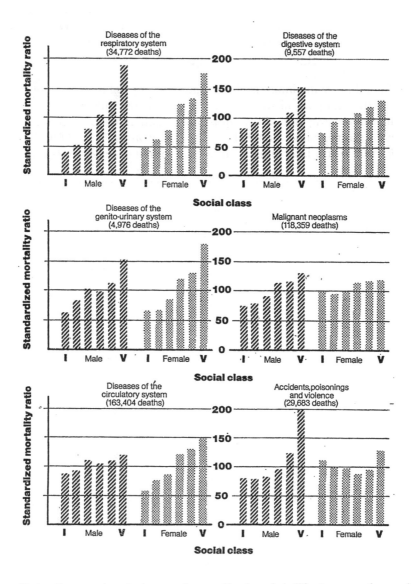

Figure 43.4 Occupational class and morality in adult life (men and married women 15–64), by husband's occupation. (*Source:* Occupational Mortality 1970–72, *HMSO, 1978.*)

Finally, as pension age is reached, class differences in mortality diminish still further, but by this age classification by occupational class becomes less meaningful. Information about occupation and cause of death recorded on death certificates for people over 75 is sometimes imprecise or inaccurate, particularly in the case of widows who, dying in their seventies or later, may still be classified according to the last occupation of husbands who may have died many years earlier. Again, there is some movement late in working life from skilled to unskilled occupations which is not reflected in the occupation reported at death. A minority of men, dying in their sixties, are recorded with the skilled occupation held for most of their working life rather than the unskilled occupation they may have had in the last five or ten years of that life.

Occupational class may therefore be a weak indicator of life-style and life chances over lengthy periods. Bearing this in mind, data about the mortality of men aged 65 to 74 in 1970/72 showed that there were very large differences between some groups of manual and non-manual workers. For example, the mortality ratio for former miners and quarrymen was 149, gas, coke and chemical makers 150, and furnace, forge, foundry and rolling mill workers 162, compared with administrators and managers with a ratio of 88 and professional, technical workers and artists with a ratio of 89 (OPCS, 1978, p. 107).

Conclusions

Several conclusions can be drawn. First, while cultural and genetic explanations have some relevance – the latter is particularly important in early childhood – more of the evidence is explained by what we call 'materialist' or 'structural' explanations than by any other.

Secondly, some of the evidence on class inequalities in health can be understood in terms of specific features of the socio-economic environment: features such as accidents at work, overcrowding and smoking, which are strongly class-related in Britain. Since such features are recognized objectives of various areas of social policy we feel it sensible to offer them as contributory factors, to be dealt with in their own right, and not to discuss their incidence further in social-structural terms. The same is true of other aspects of the evidence which we feel show the importance of health services themselves. Ante-natal care, for example, is important in preventing perinatal death, and international evidence suggests that much can be done through improvement of ante-natal care and of its uptake. The international evidence also suggests the importance of preventive health within health policy, despite studies, which suggest that few of the differences in mortality either between nations, or between British regions, can be explained in terms of health care provision. But beyond this there is undoubtedly much which cannot be understood in terms of the impact of such specific factors. Much, we feel, can only be understood in terms of the more diffuse consequences of the class structure: poverty, work conditions (and what we termed the social division of labour) and deprivation in its various forms in the home and immediate environment, at work, in education and the upbringing of children and more generally in family and social life.

It is this acknowledgement of the complex nature of the explanation of health inequalities – involving access to and use of the health services; specific issues in other areas of social policy; and more general features of class, material inequality and deprivation – which informs and structures the recommendations we make.

Notes
*The percentages are of the total number of economically active and retired males.

References and further reading
Abel-Smith, B., *The Hospitals 1800–1948*, Heinemann, 1964.

Birch, H. G., and Gussow, J. D., *Disadvantaged Children: Health, Nutrition and School Failure*, New York, Harcourt, Brace and World, 1970.

Black, D., 'The Paradox of Medical Care', *Journal of the Royal College of Physicians*, 13, 57, 1979.

Dollery, C., *The End of an Age of Optimism*, Nuffield Provincial Hospitals Trust, 1978.

Dubos, R., *Mirage and Health*, Allen & Unwin, 1960.

Help for the Disabled, Louis Harris International, 1974.

McKeown, T., *The Role of Medicine: Dream, Mirage or Nemesis?*, Nuffield Provincial Hospitals Trust, 1976.

Marshall, W. A., *Human Growth and Its Disorders*, Academic Press, 1977.

Mechanic, D., *Medical Sociology: A Selective View*, New York, Free Press, 1968.

Morris, J. N., *Uses of Epidemiology*, 3rd edn, Churchill Livingstone, 1975.

OPCS, *Occupational Mortality 1970–72, Decennial Supplement*, HMSO, 1978.

44

A new perspective on the health of Canadians
Marc Lalonde

Extracts from Lalonde M (1974) A New Perspective on the Health of Canadians. Ottawa: Health Canada.

The ideas proposed in this paper provide a universal framework for examining health problems and for suggesting courses of action needed for their solution. Because they are comprehensive, they have a unifying effect on all the participants in decisions which affect health, bringing together into one common front:

1. the health professions,
2. the health institutions,
3. the scientific community,
4. the educational system,
5. municipal governments,
6. provincial governments,
7. the federal government,
8. the business sector and trade unions,
9. the voluntary associations, and
10. the Canadian people as individuals.

The Health Field Concept disregards questions of jurisdiction which may be important to governments but are not of primary concern to the people of Canada when their health is at stake. It identifies requirements for health without regard to the niceties of professional or sectoral boundaries, and it focuses attention on the broad and important factors underlying the health of the population.

   In putting the Heath Field Concept to work, that is, in using it for analysing federal health policy, it was found that HUMAN BIOLOGY, ENVIRONMENT and LIFESTYLE were national in character and that problems in these areas tended to pervade Canada's population with little regard for provincial boundaries, always excepting purely local environmental matters. Protecting the food supply from contamination and drugs from being abused, as well as recognizing alcohol abuse, smoking, obesity, lack of physical fitness, chronic illness, mental illness, venereal disease and traffic deaths as national health problems, opens up corridors in which federal leadership can function with considerable jurisdictional freedom as long as it leads, reinforces and supplements, without duplication or conflict, the goals and services of the provinces, and respects the provincial ascendancy in health care services. In short, the first three elements of the Health Field Concept are open to federal initiatives in addition to those which are already under way.

Turning to the expressed and latent needs and wants of the Canadian people, this paper responds strongly to the recent trends and attitudes of Canadian society. The preservation and enhancement of the environment are the goals of a very strongly felt need and constitute a powerful current of popular opinion. In the lifestyle area, nutrition and weight control, as well as mass physical recreation, are subjects of growing interest, indicating an increased desire by many Canadians to break out of an unhealthy pattern of living. These and similar national lifestyle concerns can be eased by measures growing out of the Health Field Concept, assuming such measures are wisely chosen and respond to Canadian needs.

For a more particular community, that of the research scientists, this paper not only gives due recognition to the need for research in basic human biology, but also points out the necessity of linking up the purposes and uses of health research to problems in the environment, in lifestyle and in the delivery of care.

For the health professions, who often despair of getting patients to act on their advice to reduce self-imposed risks, and of governments to attack the underlying causes of sickness and death, this paper offers them the opportunity to recruit powerful forces to their cause.

Voluntary associations, dedicated to increasing the awareness of Canadians of the factors influencing health and to the gravity of specific diseases, will more easily be able to identify and marshal the assistance of those who share their goals.

Neglected segments of the Canadian population, in terms of health, can look forward to getting more of the attention they deserve. The chronically ill, the aged, the mentally ill, the economically-deprived, the troubled parents, and others who either are at high risk or are receiving insufficient health care, can expect that programs for populations will increasingly recognize and respond to their needs.

The federal role suggested by this paper constitutes a promising new departure. In the past the Federal Government has limited its activities in the health field to its traditional responsibilities such as quarantine medicine and the protection of the food supply, to product safety, to ensuring accessibility to personal health care through substantial financial assistance to provincial health insurance plans, and to financing research. The basis for concentrating its interests in these areas has been the belief that the improvement of personal health care was the principal means of raising the level of health of the Canadians. In 1973, for example, the federal contribution to provincial health insurance plans was 2,300 millions of dollars, and financial barriers to medical and hospital care have largely been eliminated.

The evidence uncovered by the analysis of underlying causes of sickness and death now indicates that improvement in the environment and an abatement in the level of risks imposed upon themselves by individuals, taken together, constitute the most promising ways by which further advances can be made.

Accordingly, it is the intention of the Government of Canada, first, to maintain at a high level the services and support provided through its present activities in health protection, research and the financing of personal health care. To these will be added measures directed at specific national health problems, chosen in consultation with provinces, consumers, professions and associations according to their gravity and incidence, and aimed at removing or reducing the factors underlying sickness and death.

Some of these measures in time will no doubt be directed at environmental factors, others will be directed at lifestyle risks, still others will expand the horizons of health research, and yet others will encourage more personal care services to neglected parts of the Canadian population. In every case the measures will be based upon the expressed interest and concern of all those who contribute to the health of Canadians, including in particular the people themselves.

Since direct health care is already consuming some 7% of the wealth that Canadians produce annually, it is evident that the rate at which the Government of Canada can expand its activities in the field of health is severely limited by financial considerations. It is also true that measures directed at the prevention of illness will take some time before they are translated into savings in the costs of providing curative health services.

These two factors make it imperative that the measures developed in consultation with provinces, professions and associations be chosen with great care, and with due regard for the costs and benefits that can be anticipated. In choosing the measures, consideration will be given to a number of factors, among which will be:

1. the gravity of the health problem,
2. the priorities of those who share in decision-making,
3. the availability of effective solutions, results of which are measurable,
4. the costs involved, and
5. the multiplier effect of federal initiatives in marshalling and accelerating support from all those who make vital contributions to raising the level of health or who have a key role in controlling the cost of health services.

With the foregoing considerations in mind, and with the recognition that the good health of Canadians is an objective that shines brightly above the thicket of jurisdictions and special interest groups, the Government of Canada proposes to take steps that will start the nation on the road to levels of health even higher than those that Canada now enjoys.

In taking these steps, the Government of Canada, in cooperation with others, will pursue *two broad objectives*:

1. *To reduce mental and physical health hazards* for those parts of the Canadian population whose risks are high, and
2. *To improve the accessibility* of good mental and physical health care for those whose present access is unsatisfactory.

In pursuit of these two objectives, *five strategies* are proposed:

1. A *Health Promotion Strategy* aimed at informing, influencing and assisting both individuals and organizations so that they will accept more responsibility and be more active in matters affecting mental and physical health.
2. A *Regulatory Strategy* aimed at using federal regulatory powers to reduce hazards to mental and physical health, and at encouraging and assisting provinces to use their regulatory powers to the same end.
3. A *Research Strategy* designed to help discover and apply knowledge needed to solve mental and physical health problems.
4. A *Health Care Efficiency Strategy* the objective of which shall be to help the provinces reorganize the system for delivering mental and physical health care so that the three elements of cost, accessibility and effectiveness are balanced in the interests of Canadians.
5. A *Goal-Setting Strategy* the purpose of which will be to set, in cooperation with others, goals for raising the level of the mental and physical health of Canadians and improving the efficiency of the health care system.

45

Securing good health for the whole population
Derek Wanless

Extracts from Wanless D (2004) Securing Good Health for the Whole Population. London: HM Treasury.

Background to the review

The 2002 report "Securing Our Future Health: Taking A Long-Term View" set out an assessment of the resources required to provide high-quality health services in the future. It was based on first catching up, and then keeping up with other developed countries, which had moved ahead of us over recent decades.

That report illustrated the considerable difference in expected cost depending upon how well our health services became more productive and how well people became fully engaged with their own health. Resources were needed not only to satisfy short-term objectives, particularly access to service, but also to invest in improving supply, by building the capacity of the workforce, improving information technology support and renewing premises, and to invest in reducing demand by enhancing the promotion of good health and disease prevention.

Many of the benefits of engaging people in living healthier lives occur in the long term but there are also immediate and short-term benefits when demand for health services can be reduced, especially in those areas such as acute services where capacity is seriously constrained.

This further review has been focused particularly on prevention and the wider determinants of health in England and on the cost-effectiveness of action that can be taken to improve the health of the whole population and to reduce health inequalities. It was asked to consider consistency of current policy with the public health aspects of the "fully engaged" scenario outlined in the 2002 report. The definition of public health for this review has been drawn very widely; essentially it considers public health to be "the science and art of preventing disease, prolonging life and promoting health through the organised efforts and informed choices of society, organisations, public and private, communities and individuals."

The recent history of public health

This review commissioned a study looking at examples of approaches to public health in other countries. By and large, the key barriers to success overseas are similar to those identified in this report. What is striking is that there has been so much written often covering similar ground and apparently sound, setting out the well-known major determinants of health, but rigorous implementation of identified solutions has often been sadly lacking.

There has also been limited assessment of the long-term impact on population health, and inequalities, of key policies such as agriculture or the built environment and this has led to situations difficult to resolve even in the longer term.

That said there have been considerable successes too. Protection against infectious diseases, often major killers in the past, has generally been very effective and remains a vital and successful part of public health. The initial HIV/AIDS campaign was a powerful and positive case study and changes in behaviour such as seatbelt wearing have been effectively introduced and gained widespread acceptance.

The growing public concern about issues such as obesity, children's diet and smoking in public places seems to signal a change in the current climate for public health. This is a welcome and necessary first step towards public engagement. The announcement of the forthcoming consultation period and of a White Paper on Public Health suggests that the conclusions and recommendations of this Review will be addressed by Government. It is vital that they are and the Review therefore concentrates on the frameworks and processes, which are likely to encourage sustained action. If they are not, yet another opportunity to act will have been missed and the health care services will continue to run faster and faster to stand still.

Who is responsible and what support is needed?

Individuals are ultimately responsible for their own and their children's health and it is the aggregate actions of individuals, which will ultimately be responsible for whether or not such an optimistic scenario as "fully engaged" unfolds. People need to be supported more actively to make better decisions about their own health and welfare because there are widespread, systematic failures that influence the decisions individuals currently make.

These failures include a lack of full information, the difficulty individuals have in considering fully the wider social costs of particular behaviours, engrained social attitudes not conducive to individuals pursuing healthy lifestyles and addictions. There are also significant inequalities related to individuals' poor lifestyles and they tend to be related to socio-economic and sometimes ethnic differences.

These failures need to be recognised. They can be tackled not only by individuals but by wide ranging action by health and care services, government – national and local, media, businesses, society at large, families and the voluntary and community sector. Collective action must however respect the individual's right to choose whether or not to be "fully engaged".

Shifting social norms is a legitimate activity for Government where it has set for the nation objectives for behaviour change. This may take time to achieve, may require careful judgement and it may at some stage be appropriately underpinned by regulation, for example the wearing of seatbelts. The main levers for Government action: taxes, subsidies, service provision, regulation and information are considered.

Actions should be based on sound principles and good practices. A framework for assessing priorities is vital and it should help identify which economic instrument seems the most appropriate in each case. Interventions should tackle failures as directly as possible and should ensure total costs are kept to a minimum and are less than the expected discounted benefits. The overall distribution of the impacts of all interventions to address a particular failure should be considered. Individual programmes might worsen inequalities but still be very beneficial at the whole population level; they should be accompanied by campaigns adequately addressing the resulting inequalities. Individuals should balance their right to choose their own lifestyle against any adverse impacts their choices have on others.

To assist the full engagement of the population, advice should be available freely and in formats all find accessible, including the development of internet and telephone services. The developing NHS Direct brand should be considered for expanded use in this way.

Annual communication about the state of the population's health and of the main determinants of health should be made available at national and local authority levels to encourage understanding. As would be standard practice in marketing any product or service to the public, part of the regular management process should be to obtain feedback from the population and important subgroups about whether the messages being communicated about public health were being received and understood. Information should also be routinely collected about the acceptability to them of possibly controversial state interventions.

Information and research

The very poor information base has been a major disappointment as it was when writing the 2002 report. There is a need for significant and continuous improvement if evidence is going to be used to drive decisions. The lack of conclusive evidence for action should not, where there is serious risk to the nation's health, block action proportionate to that risk and, for example for infectious diseases and terrorist threats, a good deal of subjective and experienced judgement is needed.

But generally evidence-based principles still need to be established for public health expenditure decisions. Although there is often evidence on the scientific justification for action and for some specific interventions, there is generally little evidence about the cost-effectiveness of public health and preventative policies or their practical implementation. Research in this area can be technically difficult and there is a lack of depth and expertise in the core disciplines. This, coupled with a lack of funding of public health intervention research and slower acceptance of economic perspectives within public health, all contribute to the dearth of evidence of cost-effectiveness. This has led to the introduction of a very wide range of initiatives, often with unclear objectives and little quantification of outcomes and it has meant it is difficult to sustain support for initiatives, even those which are successful. It is evident that a great deal more discipline is needed to ensure problems are clearly identified and tackled, that the multiple solutions frequently needed are sensibly co-ordinated and that lessons are learnt which feed back directly into policy.

Targets and their achievement

In recent years, governments have set targets for many determinants of health where behaviour change has been considered desirable and of benefit as well as for the reduction of health inequalities. But those targets do not have comprehensive coverage and have not always met the requirements of stretching ambition and realism. The philosophies behind them have been inconsistent. So, the smoking targets set in 1998 could be considered unambitious while the obesity targets (1992) and the physical activity target (2002) seem highly aspirational. In none of these cases does the target setting process encourage a belief that resource management to achieve improvement will be optimal.

In spite of numerous policy initiatives being directed towards public health they have not succeeded in rebalancing health policy away from the short-term imperatives of health care. So it is not surprising to hear the view regularly expressed that we have a "National Sickness Service", dealing, as a priority, indeed almost an exclusive focus, with an urgent need to improve short-term access and quality. As a result, public health practitioners generally seem to feel undervalued.

Objective setting in future

The setting of quantified national objectives for changing the prevalence of all the important determinants of health status for the medium and long term would help inform future resource planning projections and immediate decisions. A great deal of research, analytic thinking and consensus building is required to ensure these objectives are carefully defined and the responsibilities for delivery are understood. They would also be a major input into local decisions. And it is locally that much of the activity needs to be planned and implemented by networks of local authorities, health organisations and community and voluntary groups.

It is recommended that the Government should seek advice about what the objectives for all major determinants of health should be and that these should be subdivided where appropriate to cover important groups within the population, for example by age, ethnicity or social class, particularly those key to achieving the inequality objectives. It is suggested that, for these determinants, it may be appropriate to set three year and seven year objectives and that they should be reassessed regularly, say a year before the three year period is up, in the light of their importance for future health care demands, performance being achieved at home and abroad, evidence of what is working and its cost-effectiveness. It is to be expected that some objectives would be reassessed upwards and others down but that all should be kept close to a trend which represents the best that we can do.

Delivery

While recent policy and activity has been directed at strengthening the public health role of the NHS and local government and facilitating partnership working to improve population health, difficulties remain in some areas due to capacity problems, the impact of recent organisational changes and the lack of alignment of performance management mechanisms between partners.

One of the most important components of the "fully engaged" scenario was the assumption of increasing productivity gains. High productivity must also be a feature of public health activity and measures of productivity will be required in public health, as they are in health care services. Adequate workforce capacity will need to be created with appropriately broad skill mixes. Because more of the activity will be concerned with monitoring, interpreting data, identifying risk, educating people and motivating them to change behaviour, the required mix of skills will change. The role of self-care, the development of "the expert patient", possibly playing a much greater role in assisting other patients, and the role of community pharmacists will also need to be developed to expand overall capacity in the increasingly important management of chronic conditions and take pressure off traditionally skilled people.

In the future, knowledge of genetics and of individual risk factors could have an increasing influence in successfully creating a "fully engaged" population through individualised health promotion and disease prevention. It is assumed that much of this development will take place in primary care, which will change greatly over the next decade if the health services are to move away from dealing predominantly with the sick. Information Management and Technology (IM&T) will be a massive driver of change and the big commitment which is being made to improved technology in the NHS will have, as part of its justification, the possibility of helping the identification of personalised risks from the information stored about the individual. In order to discover how quickly these changes might happen and to help find the evidence about the effectiveness of enhanced risk management, it is recommended that an experiment should be established across a range of primary care units to assess the benefits of additional resource in information systems, in monitoring risk, in varying degrees of attention and in advisory services. The experiment should be directed towards areas of inequality, given that access to services there is a crucial issue, which must be resolved.

Primary care will not be the only support for individuals. Many organisations will play a part in engaging individuals in thinking about their future health. Employers may for example be able to create business cases for encouraging their employees to consider the mental and physical health risks they face. Some interesting examples were drawn to our attention. None were in the public sector. The NHS clearly should be thinking more about the health of its employees and should pilot exercises to see what benefits it can obtain from taking action to improve their health. Reduced absenteeism and better productivity and staff morale would all be valuable for an organisation under continuing pressure.

Our health services must evolve from dealing with acute problems through more effective control of chronic conditions to promoting the maintenance of good health. This will need to be fully taken into account when resource allocation formulae are revised. The implications for total government spending of these significant shifts in emphasis, which will be reinforced by this Review, cannot be estimated at this stage.

I have concluded that all the activity underway could well put us on course for the solid progress scenario but the efficiency of the spending being incurred needs to be kept under close review. A step change will be required to move us on to a fully engaged path. In practice, full engagement will mean achieving the best outcomes that individuals in aggregate are willing to achieve with strong leadership and sound organisation of all the many efforts being made to help them.

PART 10

Cultural critiques of formalized health care systems

Introduction by Ann Mahon

Several parts of this reader have pointed to a loss of trust in medicine and health care (Part 5), medical errors and accidents (Part 6), the relatively recent introduction of evidence-based practice in preference to custom and fashion (Part 8) and a recognition of the need to widen the domain of health policy to include the social determinants of health (Part 9). The readings selected in this final part of the reader introduce some broader and critical perspectives about the impact of formalized health care systems on individuals and their families, on communities and on society at large. They also trace, chronologically, the origins of the shift from institutionalization towards community care – Goffman – our contemporary concerns about medicalization and hospital-acquired infections and the growth of 'self-help' movements – Illich and Kennedy – and more recently the response from medicine addressing the balance for those who believe that radical critiques, uncritically taken on board, have the effect of 'throwing the baby out with the bathwater' – Bunker and Tallis.

In the aftermath of the Second World War there was enormous optimism about the role of health care in contributing to a decline in infectious diseases, an increase in life expectancy and a reduction in inequalities in health. However, during the 1960s and particularly the 1970s some damning reappraisals about the role of health care emerged and the contributions from Illich, Kennedy and Goffman have been selected to give a flavour of the emerging critiques at that time. Polemic in tone and literary in style made Illich's and in particular Goffman's writings both accessible and open to criticism. Bunker and more recently Tallis, are examples of readings that have attempted to respond to these 'cultural critiques' of medicine. Bunker's plea for a scientific and logical assessment of the contribution of medicine makes an interesting companion to Tallis' personal defence of medicine grounded in his career as Consultant Geriatrician (and philosopher).

Ivan Illich's work has what Levin refers to as 'shock appeal' (Levin, 2003). Illich identified three levels of pathogenic medicine that created physician-induced disease or 'iatrogenesis'. First, clinical iatrogenesis – damage inflicted by doctors on individuals, second, social iatrogenesis where society is encouraged to consume medicine at all stages in the lifecycle leading to overmedicalization and ultimately 'the expropriation of health'. Third, he talks about cultural iatrogenesis. At this level health professions have a deeper, culturally health-denying effect insofar as they destroy the potential of people to deal with their human weakness and vulnerability in a unique and autonomous way. Medicine exerts a self-reinforcing loop of negative institutional feedback – medical nemesis – the inevitable punishment for attempts to be heroic rather than human. Illich believes that the reversal of nemesis can only come from within man. Medical nemesis is resistant to medical intervention. In contemporary terms, concerns with cultural iatrogenesis might be termed 'social capital and positive psychology'. However, given the increasing attention to social determinants of health and the role of lifestyle, alongside debates about the role of medicine, Illich's concerns about iatrogenesis perhaps are less credible now than they might have been? The publication of Medical nemesis followed the challenge set by Archie Cochrane (see Part 8: Evidence-based policy and management) to improve efficacy. Even where medical care is successful and adds to longevity for Illich, this simply presents more opportunities to accumulate chronic disease; a view challenged by Tallis among others. However, as Smith points out in the editorial to a special edition of the British Medical Journal devoted to medicalization, 'What was a radical polemic in 1974 is in some sense mainstream in 2002' (Smith, 2002).

Ian Kennedy, Professor of Law (1983), offers a view on the practise of medicine – what it is and what it claims to be; hence, the title of his book (based on the 1980 Reith lectures) 'The Unmasking of Medicine'. By Kennedy's own admission, his writings are aggressive in style and designed to stimulate debate and he acknowledges Illich among others as a key influence. For Kennedy the nature of modern medicine is deleterious to the health and well-being of the population. Kennedy makes a number of key points where he believes medicine has taken the 'wrong path', points that are perhaps more familiar to us now than then. Medicine is self-consciously scientific, curative, problem-solving, disease-focused, interventionist and hospital-oriented, seduced by technology and elitist. Like Illich he refers critically to the notion of medicalization and the social control function performed by medicine, particularly in the diagnosis and treatment of the mentally ill, studied some decades earlier by Erving Goffman.

Erving Goffman considers the mental patient using the notion of the career. The main concern is with the moral aspects of career – the sequence of changes that career entails in the person's self and in his framework of image for judging himself and others. He identifies three phases in the career of the mental patient. Pre-patient, inpatient and ex-patient. He emphasizes the social beginning of the patient career as distinct from the symptoms experienced or interpreted outside of the mental institution. He makes the association between the career of the mental patient and hospitalization and the fate of those in jails, monasteries and concentration camps. He is subjected to mortifying experiences. As a patient one's past mistakes and present progress are under constant moral review.

Goffman, like Illich, offers a dark and pessimistic account of the impact of formalized health care or more specifically of psychiatric institutions on mental patients. 'Asylums' concentrates on the individual self – the patient – and the distinct phases that a patient passes through. Using the concept of the career, Goffman's work is concerned with the moral aspects and as such his work makes a principled, passionate and enduring critique of mental institutions from the perspective of the 'underdog' and with what Manning describes as a 'tone of moral outrage'. Elliot Freidson, reflecting on Goffman's contribution to sociology, refers to him as 'the ethnographer of the self' and argues that 'What gives Goffman's work a value that will endure far longer than most sociology is its intense individual humanity and its style' (Freidson, 1983: 359).

Bunker (1995) assembled an inventory of the benefits of medical care extrapolating from the results of clinical trials and meta-analyses. He estimated that medical care could be credited with five of the thirty years of increased life expectancy during the last century and with three of the seven years' increase in life expectancy since 1950. These estimates may appear conservative in the context of a paper defending the role of health care but in comparison to earlier works (perhaps most notably Thomas McKeown's assessment of the relative role of health care in the rise of life expectancy), they present a strong defence for health care in general and medical care in particular. Bunker recognizes the importance of social factors in determining health but argues that we know little about how they might act to influence the health of individuals. In writing this paper he is responding not just to the view that medicine has had little impact but also to the view that it is impossible to quantify. To do this he selected conditions for which strong evidence of efficacy was available and admitted that the current knowledge about the impact of medicine is more speculative than precise, but nevertheless informs the debate in a context where the scientific basis of medicine is increasing. Thus, practical implications for increasing access to timely and effective health care emerge from Bunker's analysis and contrast with his view that government inaction regarding the association between socio-economic status and health may be due to the absence of practical solutions. Bunker's paper raises some important issues relating to how scarce resources should be invested in order to improve the health of the population. Should our focus be on encouraging people to live healthy lifestyles? Should the wider determinants of health be addressed so that employment, addiction and nutrition become the focus of investment rather than specific health care interventions? Bunker, not surprisingly, favours investment in health care. But Bunker's analysis has its flaws. He is perhaps unduly optimistic about the role of health care (McKee, 2001). However, others are less convinced that attempts to quantify the relative contributions of medical and other interventions are useful, meaningful or possible (Tudor Hart, 2001). Nevertheless, as Frankel points out, Bunker makes an important contribution to the debate in two ways. First, he was a pioneer of critical, quantitative analysis of the benefits of medical care and, second, he offered a formal response to Thomas McKeown (Frankel, 2001). Curiously, what he does not explore (but which he addresses in subsequent publications; for example, Bunker, 2001) is the concept of iatrogenesis.

Ray Tallis offers a very personal account. He argues that scientific medicine has never been in better shape and there have been significant improvements in recent decades. Yet, despite this, there is pessimism, a pessimism that concerns him because he believes that medicine is in danger of being corrupted from the outside and is struggling to survive. He challenges some stereotypes associated with the power of doctors and the powerlessness of patients and looks at the accusations of medicalization from the perspective of the doctor or as he refers to it 'medicalization from the inside'. He argues that accusations made at medicine are often societal rather than medical in origin. Tallis ends with a comment that the notion of the 'expert patient' is not entirely new and consultation is a meeting between experts. This is a salutary note to policy makers and professionals introducing innovations in health care that, like the expert patient, often have a history and endurance that precedes them.

All the readings selected here could and probably should be considered essential reading for health managers and policy makers. The polemic nature of some contributions has probably enhanced their influence because of the debate or dismay they have generated and in that vein the last word here goes to Frankel:

> It is a dull fact that where polarised positions exist either there is no single truth, or the truth lies somewhere between the fortified positions of the key protagonists.
>
> (Frankel, 2001)

Summary

- There was enormous optimism about the role of health care and its potential to improve the health of populations and reduce inequalities in health. During the 1970s such optimism was tempered by the emergence of writings that reappraised the role of health care, collectively referred to as cultural critiques of medicine in particular, but also health care in general.
- Illich identified three levels of pathogenic medicine that created physician-induced disease 'iatrogenesis'. Continuing in the Illichian tradition, Kennedy argued that the nature of modern medicine is deleterious to the health and well-being of the population and medicine has taken the 'wrong path'. Like Illich, he refers critically to the notion of medicalization and the social control function performed by medicine, particularly in the diagnosis and treatment of the mentally ill, studied some decades earlier by Erving Goffman.
- Polemics stimulate debate but the reality is likely to lie in between polarized positions.

References and further reading

Bunker, J. (2001) *The Role of Medical Care in Contributing to Health Improvements Within Societies, International Journal of Epidemiology*, 30: 1260–63.

Frankel, S. (2001) Commentary: medical care and the wider influences upon population health: a false dichotomy, *International Journal of Epidemiology*, 30: 1260–63.

Freidson, E. (1983) Celebrating Erving Goffman. Paper presented at a memorial sessions for Erving Goffman at the Eastern Sociological Society Meeting in Baltimore, 4 March.

Levin, L. (2003) Ivan Illich, *Journal of Epidemiology and Community Health*, 57: 935.

Smith, R. (2003) Limits to medicine. *Medical Nemesis: The Expropriation of Health*. London: Marion Boyars.

Tudor Hart, J. (2001) Commentary: can health outputs of routine practice approach those of clinical trials? *International Journal of Epidemiology*, 30: 1263–67.

The readings

Illich, I. (1977) Limits to medicine. *Medical Nemesis: The Expropriation of Health*. London: Marion Boyars.

Kennedy, I. (1983) *The Unmasking of Medicine*. London: Granada Publishing.

Goffman, E. (1961) *Asylums: Essays on the Social Situation of Mental Patients and Other Inmates*. London: Penguin.

Bunker, J. (1995) Medicine matters after all, *Journal of the Royal College of Physicians of London*, 29(2): 105–12.

Tallis, R. (2004) *Hippocratic Oaths*. Atlantic Books.

46

Limits to medicine
Ivan Illich

Extracts from Illich I (1977) Limits to Medicine, Medical Nemesis: The Expropriation of Health. London: Marion Boyars.

Defenseless patients

The undesirable side-effects of approved, mistaken, callous, or contraindicated technical contacts with the medical system represent just the first level of pathogenic medicine. Such *clinical iatrogenesis* includes not only the damage that doctors inflict with the intent of curing or of exploiting the patient, but also those other torts that result from the doctor's attempt to protect himself against the possibility of a suit for malpractice. Such attempts to avoid litigation and prosecution may now do more damage than any other iatrogenic stimulus.

On a second level,[1] medical practice sponsors sickness by reinforcing a morbid society that encourages people to become consumers of curative, preventive, industrial, and environmental medicine. On the one hand defectives survive in increasing numbers and are fit only for life under institutional care, while on the other hand, medically certified symptoms exempt people from industrial work and thereby remove them from the scene of political struggle to reshape the society that has made them sick. Second-level iatrogenesis finds its expression in various symptoms of social overmedicalization that amount to what I shall call the expropriation of health. This second-level impact of medicine I designate as *social iatrogenesis*.

On a third level, the so-called health professions have an even deeper, culturally health-denying effect insofar as they destroy the potential of people to deal with their human weakness, vulnerability, and uniqueness in a personal and autonomous way. The patient in the grip of contemporary medicine is but one instance of mankind in the grip of its pernicious techniques.[2] This *cultural iatrogenesis* is the ultimate backlash of hygienic progress and consists in the paralysis of healthy responses to suffering, impairment, and death. It occurs when people accept health management designed on the engineering model, when they conspire in an attempt to produce, as if it were a commodity, something called "better health." This inevitably results in the managed maintenance of life on high levels of sublethal illness. This ultimate evil of medical "progress" must be clearly distinguished from both clinical and social iatrogenesis.

I hope to show that on each of its three levels iatrogenesis has become medically irreversible: a feature built right into the medical endeavor. The unwanted physiological, social, and psychological by-products of diagnostic and therapeutic progress have become resistant to medical remedies. New devices, approaches, and organizational arrangements, which are conceived as remedies for clinical and social iatrogenesis, themselves tend to become pathogens contributing to the new epidemic. Technical and managerial measures taken on any level to avoid damaging the patient by his treatment tend to engender a self-reinforcing iatrogenic loop analogous to the escalating destruction generated by the polluting procedures used as antipollution devices.[3]

I will designate this self-reinforcing loop of negative institutional feedback by its classical Greek equivalent and call it *medical nemesis*. The Greeks saw gods in the forces of nature. For them, nemesis represented divine vengeance visited upon mortals who infringe on those prerogatives the gods enviously guard for themselves. Nemesis was the inevitable punishment for attempts to be a hero rather than a human being. Like most abstract Greek nouns, Nemesis took the shape of a divinity. She represented nature's response to *hubris*: to the individual's presumption in seeking to acquire the attributes of a god. Our contemporary hygienic hubris has led to the new syndrome of medical nemesis.[4]

By using the Greek term I want to emphasize that the corresponding phenomenon does not fit within the explanatory paradigm now offered by bureaucrats, therapists, and ideologues for the snowballing diseconomies and disutilities that, lacking all intuition, they have engineered and that they tend to call the "counterintuitive behavior of large systems." By invoking myths and ancestral gods I should make it clear that my framework for analysis of the current breakdown of medicine is foreign to the industrially determined logic and ethos. I believe that the *reversal of nemesis* can come only from within man and not from yet another managed (heteronomous) source depending once again on presumptious expertise and subsequent mystification.

Medical nemesis is resistant to medical remedies. It can be reversed only through a recovery of the will to self-care among the laity, and through the legal, political, and institutional recognition of the right to care, which imposes limits upon the professional monopoly of physicians. My final chapter proposes guidelines for stemming medical nemesis and provides criteria by which the medical enterprise can be kept within healthy bounds. I do not suggest any specific forms of health care or sick-care, and I do not advocate any new medical philosophy any more than I recommend remedies for medical technique, doctrine, or organization. However, I do propose an alternative approach to the use of medical organization and technology together with the allied bureaucracies and illusions.

Notes

1   The distinction of several levels of iatrogenesis was made by Ralph Audy, "Man-made Maladies and Medicine," *California Medicine*, November 1970, pp. 48–53. He recognizes that iatrogenic "diseases" are only one type of

man-made malady. According to their etiology, they fall into several categories: those resulting from diagnosis and treatment, those relating to social and psychological attitudes and situations, and those resulting from man-made programs for the control and eradication of disease. Besides iatrogenic clinical entities, he recognizes other maladies that have a medical etiology.

2 "Das Schicksal des Kranken verkörpert als Symbol das Schicksal der Menschheit im Stadium einer technischen Weltentwicklung": Wolfgang Jacob, *Der kranke Mensch in der technischen Welt*, IX. Internationaler Fortbildungskurs für praktische und wissenschaftliche Pharmazie der Bundesapothekerkammer in Meran (Frankfurt am Main: Werbe- und Vertriebsgesellschaft Deutscher Apotheker, 1971).

3 James B. Quinn, "Next Big Industry: Environmental Improvement," *Harvard Business Review* 49 (September–October 1971): 120–30. He believes that environmental improvement is becoming a dynamic and profitable series of markets for industry that pay for themselves and in the end will represent an important addition to income and GNP. Implicitly the same argument is being made for the health-care field by the proponents of no-fault malpractice insurance.

4 The term was used by Honoré Daumier (1810–79). See reproduction of his drawing "Némésis médicale" in Werner Block, *Der Artzt und der Tod in Bildern aus sechs Jahrhunderten* (Stuttgart: Enke, 1966).

47

The unmasking of medicine
Ian Kennedy

Extracts from Kennedy I (1983) The Unmasking of Medicine. London: Granada Publishing.

The new magicians

My view can be stated briefly. Modern medicine has taken the wrong path. An inappropriate form of medicine has been created, in large part by doctors and medical scientists, and eagerly accepted by a willing populace. I will go further. The nature of modern medicine makes it positively deleterious to the health and well-being of the population. We have all been willing participants in allowing the creation of a myth, because it seems to serve our interests to believe that health can be achieved, illness can be vanquished and death postponed until further notice, while it serves the interests of doctors to see themselves and be seen as, if not miracle workers (and of course they would be the first to deny this), then at least possible miracle workers.

Science has destroyed our faith in religion. Reason has challenged our trust in magic. What more appropriate result could there be than the appearance of new magicians and priests wrapped in the cloak of science and reason? Please understand that it is we, all of us, who have hitched our wagon to the wrong star, scientific medicine. The unhappy consequence is that medicine is perceived and pursued in ways which do not best serve the needs of society. We do not put to best use the skills and abilities of those who have become its practitioners.

At the outset, it is crucial for understanding that certain ground be cleared before the enquiry can proceed. Medicine has perhaps two primary goals. One is the maintenance and promotion of health. The other is the care and treatment of the sick. In the achievement of the first goal, that of health, medicine can play only a relatively minor role. We have seen already that health, properly understood, is the product of the complex interaction of political, economic and social forces, well beyond the power of those who work in the name of medicine to control. They include such diverse factors as the level of affluence we have, the food we eat, the home we live in and the job (if any) we have. For the most part, however, health is not perceived in these terms. The medical model of health, which has it that health is the product of medical care and the intervention of doctors, dominates the thinking of doctors. And we, of course, have also come to be persuaded to accept this view. This is not only unfortunate and misleading, it is calculated to produce attitudes and policies positively antithetical to producing and maintaining health. The social model of health, quite simply, is successfully elbowed out. It barely gets a look-in. As a consequence, we have been persuaded to look to medicine to provide us with health, rather than to ourselves, to Government and to our social and political institutions. This is the first sense in which medicine has taken the wrong path, and I make this point here because it is so important in establishing the background against which any discussion of medicine must take place. I will return to it again and again, here and subsequently.

There is also, here, a second sense in which we can talk of a wrong turn. For, even in those circumstances in which medicine can have any real effect on our health, the way in which it is conceived of, taught and practised takes it in directions which are not such as to achieve the results it is capable of, nor necessarily productive of health. If we turn to the second goal of medicine, caring for those whose health is impaired, here again, on balance, medicine has taken the wrong path. This is what, in particular, I want to suggest in the points which follow.

First, as now taught and practised, medicine is avowedly and self-consciously scientific. Far be it from me to stand against the tide of history and suggest there is more to understanding and caring than contained within the four corners of science. But an education which demands high skills in scientific subjects before going to medical school, and involves years of breathing the heady air of one field after another of scientific endeavour once there, produces what it is intended to produce: a doctor who sees himself as a scientist. It may not produce what is so often needed: someone who can care. I am not suggesting that medical education should not be scientific. Of course it must. But room must be found for other disciplines, particularly the humanities.

My next point is that modern medicine has come to be thought of as dispensing cures. The image created of medicine has increasingly become that of a curative discipline in which the model of the doctor is that of the engineer/mechanic applying the techniques of medical science to cure a sick engine. This reaches its high point in what I see as an attitude to death in which dying has come to be regarded as an illness. Call it an illness and you hold out hope of treatment, control and even cure. Doctor, patient and family become locked in an unholy *danse macabre*. Medicine provides another variation on the theme of the pursuit of immortality, with the respirator symbolizing some kind of Promethean eternity. But the engineer/mechanic model is an unfortunate one. Quite simply, the problems that beset us now do not seem readily amenable to cure. And I speak now of the generality of ills: those that kill us before our time, such as cancer, heart disease, respiratory problems, and accidents; or those that chip away at our daily pursuit of tranquillity – colds and coughs, aches and pains and simple unhappiness. I do not seek, indeed it would be quite wrong, to belittle the contribution scientific medicine has made and continues to make, both in curing infections, at least in their short-term effects, and in controlling and soothing numerous otherwise intolerable conditions – in reducing sickness, even if it has had little effect on mortality.

The idea of the doctor as an engineer, applying scientific principles directed towards cures, produces a further consequence, which I shall make my third point. It is that doctors are encouraged to adopt the mentality of problem-solvers. Problems exist out there in the world which it is their job to solve. What is wrong with that? Well, it is wrong in several respects. It is a mentality which creates problems. Indeed, the more efficiently doctors look for problems, the more they find and the more problem-solvers we need. It is a mentality which converts modern medical care into crisis care. We wait for a crisis, a problem, then we take it to the doctor and expect him to solve it. It is a mentality which fosters the impression that the problem can be solved, an impression all of us readily adopt. Finally, it is a mentality which ignores the notion that problems can be avoided, that waiting for them to arise and then responding to them is a less than adequate way of providing health care.

Fourth, another consequence of perceiving medicine as a scientific exercise has meant that it is conceptualized and practised largely in terms of specific diseases. Medicine is thus committed to a process of reductionism. The totality of a complex human being, the product of innumerable forces, involving subtle balances and interrelationships, is broken down. He becomes no more than a collection of parts, one or more of which is diseased. Each disease then has its particular name, *locus* and nature. It is this entity called the disease which then receives attention, not the person. I am not suggesting that we should abandon the notion of disease. It serves a purpose and anyway it is too much a part of our vocabulary to exorcize it now. But, if illness is seen only in terms of specific diseases, this induces a form of tunnel vision. The very skill of the doctor with detail may cause him to lose sight of the whole. Miss A becomes an X-ray projected on a screen, Baby B becomes a bad case of meningitis, Mr C becomes the pain in the neck at four o'clock.

Of course, I readily concede that there are doctors who would regard this as an unwarranted criticism, who seek to practise a type of medicine which looks to all the circumstances of the patient. They are, I would suggest, adopting such an approach despite their formal training rather than as a consequence of it. They are responding to the reality of the problems they confront. Theirs are not as yet, however, the views and values which direct the future shape of medicine.

My fifth point is that modern medicine teaches that the appropriate response of the doctor to our complaint is to do something, and something aimed at a particular disease entity. If he has been educated to think of himself as an applied scientist and problem-solver and if there is a disease lurking somewhere, then it is his job to seek it out and remedy it. This has meant that medical responses have more and more taken the form of action against a disease entity, whether surgical excision, or irradiation, or chemical destruction or, if these are not possible, symptomatic relief. Whatever is decided upon, some form of bodily intervention which is disease-specific is usually sought. Something must be done to satisfy both the expectations of the patient and the professional pride of the doctor, and it has to be done to the disease, which is portrayed in terms redolent of morality or religion, as something bad, or wrong, which is possessing the body. The process has become one of applying taxonomical skills so as to identify the disease and then deciding upon the appropriate disease-specific response.

Indeed the process may be even less complicated. A study conducted by members of the Institute of Medical Sociology of the University of Aberdeen showed that the consultant, knowing the limited range of treatments he has available, is typically concerned from the outset of his contact with the patient with the simple question: 'Which treatment is most suitable?' The choice is then validated by appeal to the diagnosis.

What is wrong with this mentality of doing something? It is medicine by reflex: wait for the problem and do something. It causes larger and more important questions to be ignored, such as how the state of affairs came about, or what the long- or short-term effects of the chosen response will be. It is particularly unlikely that the question 'Should anything be done at all?' will be raised. These questions will tend to be lost in the display of pseudo-scientific wizardry.

The sixth point concerning the inappropriate form medicine has taken is that medicine is increasingly thought of in terms of hospitals. Indeed, the number of hospitals is often cited as a measure of the quality of health care. For example, as Michael Ryan points out in his book *The Organization of Soviet Medical Care*, the Soviet Union was able to claim in the mid-1970s that, except for Sweden and Norway, it had overtaken all other industrialized nations in the ratio of hospital beds to population size. The implication was that its system of health care had equally advanced, despite the long-standing inadequacy of its primary care services, particularly in the countryside. The nonsense of this approach is obvious. Indeed, apart from units concerned with accidents and, perhaps to a limited extent, obstetrics, the fact that an ever-increasing proportion of our Health Service budget, now around 65 per cent, goes to hospitals could be said to be evidence of the failures of health care and how we perceive it.

If ever there was a case of putting the cart before the horse, this is it. If preventive medicine, school health care, community health care and general primary care meant anything, hospitals would be far less needed. Hospitals are the epitome of the problem-solving, disease-oriented, applied science, engineering approach.

The reasons why medicine is increasingly equated with hospitals are many. Medical students are trained in hospitals. Hospitals are where they learn to see themselves as applied scientists, problem-solvers and curers. Hospitals, particularly teaching hospitals, are where all the interesting problems are. As Professor Miller argues, 'there is an excessive concentration on the hospital as opposed to the community, and on the relatively small amount of serious illness that is treated in institutions, at the expense of attention to common causes of disablement'.

In fact, it is general practitioners who deal with between 90 and 95 per cent of all complaints taken to doctors. Furthermore, a 1973 study, *Present State and Future Needs of General Practice*, published by the Royal College of General

Practitioners, showed that the illnesses GPs were consulted about were not the stuff of dramatic documentaries. They were, instead, predominantly minor ones, such as coughs, stomach upsets, tonsillitis and earache. These outnumbered tenfold complaints of major illnesses such as bronchitis and pneumonia. An average GP sees only one or two cases of cancer a year. A congenital abnormality could be expected only once in every five years.

Hospital doctors see themselves, and encourage others to see them, as an elite. Those in the teaching hospitals are, of course, a kind of super-elite, leaders of the medical world, shapers of medical education. These teachers become the role models for the future.

Let me now come to my seventh point. With the increasing emphasis on hospitals as the hub of medical care has come another unfortunate feature of modern medicine: that medicine is and should be an enterprise calling for the use of ever more advanced and complex technology. Christian Barnard filled the massive football stadium in Rio twice when he talked of how he performed the world's first heart transplant, yet the majority of his audience could not afford the simple medicine to rid themselves of their intestinal worms.

My eighth, and final, point concerning the inappropriateness of the way medicine is perceived concerns the notion of illness. I have already spent some time considering this notion and here will confine myself to two matters.

The first is the extent to which the notion of illness has been expanded. We have seen that at base illness is a socially determined and evaluative term susceptible of being put to different uses, so as to confer or deny the status of 'ill' on suitable candidates. The growing categorization of perceptions and circumstances as illnesses has been a feature of the past decades. Much of this expansion has come through the notion of labelling, through the application of taxonomical skills.

Nowhere is this more true than in the area of mental illness. Indeed, an argument can be made for the proposition that the categories of mental illness came first, the product of theorizing, and only later did there emerge a growing army of people to fill these categories. But the process is not limited to mental illness. The response to many of the problems of old age – which are, in fact, problems of, for example, relative poverty, lack of adequate heating, and social isolation – has been to treat them as separate, quite unrelated illnesses, and thereby to medicalize them. The elderly are seen as ill. The consequence is that resources are directed to the provision of doctors, nurses and hospital beds, rather than to redressing the social ills the elderly encounter. In the process, not only is it probable that more money is ultimately spent than would otherwise be necessary, but also the elderly are denied the opportunity to retain the dignity that illness so easily robs them of.

The expansion of the notion of illness also meets a social need. It allows us to sweep under the social rug whole groups of people who are otherwise a nuisance. They may not seek to be categorized as ill. Indeed they may resist or resent it. But, if doctors are prepared to say that particular forms of behaviour, or merely the incidents of growing old, are indeed illnesses, who are we to protest? The twinge of guilt we may feel about neglecting our fellow men, or even locking them away, is salved by the reassuring knowledge that they are ill and are now in the best possible hands in the circumstances. And, provided we keep our hospitals for the mentally ill and long-stay patients out in the backwoods, and their hostels in the decaying urban centres – indeed, anywhere but in our own particular neighbourhood – we can keep up this fiction. In fact, we have in this way created a separate society for the dispossessed and disadvantaged. Forgotten or underprivileged patients are looked after in these institutions by doctors and nurses from overseas, while the menial work is also done by immigrants – 'The underprivileged caring for each other in mutual understanding', as Michael Wilson puts it in his book *Health is for People*. Or is it mutual resentment? You may be intrigued to learn, by the way, that the domestic running costs, just food, laundry, cleaning and so on, of an average mental hospital are about one-third of those of a London teaching hospital. That many are there in the first place is bad enough; that they should be so shabbily dealt with demonstrates the extent of the neglect.

Let me now turn to my second point concerning the notion of illness. It has, with disease, become the central concern of modern medicine. If we were to start all over again to design a model for modern medicine, most of us, I am sure, would opt for a design which concerned itself far, far more with the pursuit and preservation of health, of well-being. What we have instead is the very opposite: a system of medicine which reacts, which responds, which waits to pick up the broken pieces – a form of medicine, in short, concerned with illness, not health. A moment's thought demonstrates the folly of this. But the interests which combine to produce this state of affairs are too well entrenched for any redirection to be accomplished easily. Nonetheless, the significance of the present state of medicine should not be underestimated.

These are some of the ways in which medicine has taken the wrong path. They are, of course, painted with the broad brush. It is important to realize that I am not denying that every day up and down the country wonderful things are being done. Despite this, could the nation's health be better, or if not better then no worse, at some gain, financial and social, to the citizenry if medicine took a different form? But the present state of medicine will take some changing. It is cultivated by the medical profession. It flatters the self-esteem of the doctor to see himself as the applied scientist and problem-solver spreading health. The present state of medicine has readily been adopted by a lay public, persuaded naively that herein lies the path to health, and with expectations which may be unwarranted but which are, of course, a product of the claims made by medicine.

48

Asylums: essays on the social situation of mental patients and other inmates
Erving Goffman

Extracts from Goffman E (1961) Asylums: Essays on the Social Situation of Mental Patients and Other Inmates. London: Penguin.

Persons who become mental hospital patients vary widely in the kind and degree of illness that a psychiatrist would impute to them, and in the attributes by which laymen would describe them. But once started on the way, they are confronted by some importantly similar circumstances and respond to these in some importantly similar ways. Since these similarities do not come from mental illness, they would seem to occur in spite of it. It is thus a tribute to the power of social forces that the uniform status of mental patient cannot only assure an aggregate of persons a common fate and eventually, because of this, a common character, but that this social reworking can be done upon what is perhaps the most obstinate diversity of human materials that can be brought together by society. Here there lacks only the frequent forming of a protective group life by ex-patients to illustrate in full the classic cycle of response by which deviant subgroupings are psychodynamically formed in society.

This general sociological perspective is heavily reinforced by one key finding of sociologically oriented students in mental-hospital research. As has been repeatedly shown in the study of non-literate societies, the awesomeness, distastefulness, and barbarity of a foreign culture can decrease to the degree that the student becomes familiar with the point of view to life that is taken by his subjects. Similarly, the student of mental hospitals can discover that the craziness or 'sick behaviour' claimed for the mental patient is by and large a product of the claimant's social distance from the situation that the patient is in, and is not primarily a product of mental illness. Whatever the refinements of the various patients' psychiatric diagnoses, and whatever the special ways in which social life on the 'inside' is unique, the researcher can find that he is participating in a community not significantly different from any other he has studied. Of course, while restricting himself to the off-ward grounds community of paroled patients, he may feel, as some patients do, that life in the locked wards is bizarre; and while on a locked admissions or convalescent ward, he may feel that chronic 'back' wards are socially crazy places. But he need only move his sphere of sympathetic participation to the 'worst' ward in the hospital, and this, too, can come into social focus as a place with a livable and continuously meaningful social world. This in no way denies that he will find a minority in any ward or patient group that continues to seem quite beyond the capacity to follow rules of social organization, or that the orderly fulfilment of normative expectations in patient society is partly made possible by strategic measures that have somehow come to be institutionalized in mental hospitals.

The career of the mental patient falls popularly and naturalistically into three main phases: the period prior to entering the hospital, which I shall call the prepatient phase; the period in the hospital, the inpatient phase; the period after discharge from the hospital, should this occur, namely, the ex-patient phase.[1] This paper will deal only with the first two phases.

The prepatient phase

A relatively small group of prepatients come into the mental hospital willingly, because of their own idea of what will be good for them, or because of wholehearted agreement with the relevant members of their family. Presumably these recruits have found themselves acting in a way which is evidence to them that they are losing their minds or losing control of themselves. This view of oneself would seem to be one of the most pervasively threatening things that can happen to the self in our society, especially since it is likely to occur at a time when the person is in any case sufficiently troubled to exhibit the kind of symptom which he himself can see. As Sullivan described it,

> What we discover in the self-system of a person undergoing schizophrenic change or schizophrenic processes, is then, in its simplest form, an extremely fear-marked puzzlement, consisting of the use of rather generalized and anything but exquisitely refined referential processes in an attempt to cope with what is essentially a failure at being human – a failure at being anything that one could respect as worth being.[2]

Coupled with the person's disintegrative re-evaluation of himself will be the new, almost equally pervasive circumstance of attempting to conceal from others what he takes to be the new fundamental facts about himself, and attempting to discover whether others, too, have discovered them.[3] Here I want to stress that perception of losing one's mind is based on culturally derived and socially engrained stereotypes as to the significance of symptoms such as hearing voices, losing temporal and spatial orientation, and sensing that one is being followed, and that many of the most spectacular and convincing of these symptoms in some instances psychiatrically signify merely a temporary emotional upset in a stressful situation, however terrifying to the person at the time. Similarly, the anxiety consequent upon this perception of oneself, and the strategies devised to reduce this anxiety, are not a product of abnormal psychology, but would be exhibited by any person socialized into our culture who came to conceive of himself as someone losing his mind. Interestingly, subcultures in American society apparently differ in the amount of ready imagery and encouragement they supply for such self-views, leading to differential rates of *self*-referral; the capacity to take this disintegrative view of oneself without psychiatric prompting seems to be one of the questionable cultural privileges of the upper classes.[4]

For the person who has come to see himself – with whatever justification – as mentally unbalanced, entrance to the mental hospital can sometimes bring relief, perhaps in part because of the sudden transformation in the structure of his basic social situation; instead of being to himself a questionable person trying to maintain a role as a full one, he can become an officially questioned person known to himself to be not so questionable as that. In other cases, hospitalization can make matters worse for the willing patient, confirming by the objective situation what has theretofore been a matter of the private experience of self.

Once the willing prepatient enters the hospital, he may go through the same routine of experiences as do those who enter unwillingly. In any case, it is the latter that I mainly want to consider, since in America at present these are by far the more numerous kind.[5] Their approach to the institution takes one of three classic forms: they come because they have been implored by their family or threatened with the abrogation of family ties unless they go 'willingly'; they come by force under police escort; they come under misapprehension purposely induced by others, this last restricted mainly to youthful prepatients.

The prepatient's career may be seen in terms of an extrusory model; he starts out with relationships and rights, and ends up, at the beginning of his hospital stay, with hardly any of either. The moral aspects of this career, then, typically begin with the experience of abandonment, disloyalty, and embitterment. This is the case even though to others it may be obvious that he was in need of treatment, and even though in the hospital he may soon come to agree.

The case histories of most mental patients document offences against some arrangement for face-to-face living – a domestic establishment, a work place, a semi-public organization such as a church or store, a public region such as a street or park. Often there is also a record of some *complainant*, some figure who takes that action against the offender which eventually leads to his hospitalization. This may not be the person who makes the first move, but it is the person who makes what turns out to be the first effective move. Here is the *social* beginning of the patient's career, regardless of where one might locate the psychological beginning of his mental illness.

The final point I want to consider about the prepatient's moral career is its peculiarly retroactive character. Until a person actually arrives at the hospital there usually seems no way of knowing for sure that he is destined to do so, given the determinative role of career contingencies. And until the point of hospitalization is reached, he or others may not conceive of him as a person who is becoming a mental patient. However, since he will be held against his will in the hospital, his next-of-relation and the hospital staff will be in great need of a rationale for the hardships they are sponsoring. The medical elements of the staff will also need evidence that they are still in the trade they were trained for. These problems are eased, no doubt unintentionally, by the case-history construction that is placed on the patient's past life, this having the effect of demonstrating that all along he had been becoming sick, that he finally became very sick, and that if he had not been hospitalized much worse things would have happened to him – all of which, of course, may be true. Incidentally, if the patient wants to make sense out of his stay in the hospital, and, as already suggested, keep alive the possibility of once again conceiving of his next-of-relation as a decent, well-meaning person, then he, too, will have reason to believe some of this psychiatric work-up of his past.

Here is a very ticklish point for the sociology of careers. An important aspect of every career is the view the person constructs when he looks backward over his progress; in a sense, however, the whole of the prepatient career derives from this reconstruction. The fact of having had a prepatient career, starting with an effective complaint, becomes an important part of the mental patient's orientation, but this part can begin to be played only after hospitalization proves that what he had been having, but no longer has, is a career as a prepatient.

The inpatient phase

The last step in the prepatient's career can involve his realization – justified or not – that he has been deserted by society and turned out of relationships by those closest to him. Interestingly enough, the patient, especially a first admission, may manage to keep himself from coming to the end of this trail, even though in fact he is now in a locked mental-hospital ward. On entering the hospital, he may very strongly feel the desire not to be known to anyone as a person who could possibly be reduced to these present circumstances, or as a person who conducted himself in the way he did prior to commitment. Consequently, he may avoid talking to anyone, may stay by himself when possible, and may even be 'out of contact' or 'manic' so as to avoid ratifying any interaction that presses a politely reciprocal role upon him and opens him up to what he has become in the eyes of others. When the next-of-relation makes an effort to visit, he may be rejected by mutism, or by the patient's refusal to enter the visiting room, these strategies sometimes suggesting that the patient still clings to a remnant of relatedness to those who made up his past, and is protecting this remnant from the final destructiveness of dealing with the new people that they have become.[6]

Usually the patient comes to give up this taxing effort at anonymity, at not-hereness, and begins to present himself for conventional social interaction to the hospital community. Thereafter he withdraws only in special ways – by always using his nickname, by signing his contribution to the patient weekly with his initial only, or by using the innocuous 'cover' address tactfully provided by some hospitals; or he withdraws only at special times, when, say, a flock of nursing students makes a passing tour of the ward, or when, paroled to the hospital grounds, he suddenly sees he is about to cross the path of a civilian he happens to know from home. Sometimes this making of oneself available is called 'settling down' by the attendants. It marks a new stand openly taken and supported by the patient, and resembles the 'coming-out' process that occurs in other groupings.[7]

Once the prepatient begins to settle down, the main outlines of his fate tend to follow those of a whole class of segregated establishments – jails, concentration camps, monasteries, work camps, and so on – in which the inmate spends the whole round of life on the grounds, and marches through his regimented day in the immediate company of a group of persons of his own institutional status.

Like the neophyte in many of these total institutions, the new inpatient finds himself cleanly stripped of many of his accustomed affirmations, satisfactions, and defences, and is subjected to a rather full set of mortifying experiences: restriction of free movement, communal living, diffuse authority of a whole echelon of people, and so on. Here one begins to learn about the limited extent to which a conception of oneself can be sustained when the usual setting of supports for it are suddenly removed.

While undergoing these humbling moral experiences, the inpatient learns to orient himself in terms of the 'ward system'.[8] In public mental hospitals this usually consists of a series of graded living arrangements built around wards, administrative units called services, and parole statuses. The 'worst' level often involves nothing but wooden benches to sit on, some quite indifferent food, and a small piece of room to sleep in. The 'best' level may involve a room of one's own, ground and town privileges, contacts with staff that are relatively undamaging, and what is seen as good food and ample recreational facilities. For disobeying the pervasive house rules, the inmate will receive stringent punishments expressed in terms of loss of privileges; for obedience he will eventually be allowed to reacquire some of the minor satisfactions he took for granted on the outside.

The institutionalization of these radically different levels of living throws light on the implications for self of social settings. And this in turn affirms that the self arises not merely out of its possessor's interactions with significant others, but also out of the arrangements that are evolved in an organization for its members.

Learning to live under conditions of imminent exposure and wide fluctuation in regard, with little control over the granting or withholding of this regard, is an important step in the socialization of the patient, a step that tells something important about what it is like to be an inmate in a mental hospital. Having one's past mistakes and present progress under constant moral review seems to make for a special adaptation consisting of a less than moral attitude to ego ideals. One's shortcomings and successes become too central and fluctuating an issue in life to allow the usual commitment of concern for other persons' views of them. It is not very practicable to try to sustain solid claims about oneself. The inmate tends to learn that degradations and reconstructions of the self need not be given too much weight, at the same time learning that staff and inmates are ready to view an inflation or deflation of a self with some indifference. He learns that a defensible picture of self can be seen as something outside oneself that can be constructed, lost, and rebuilt, all with great speed and some equanimity. He learns about the viability of taking up a standpoint – and hence a self – that is outside the one which the hospital can give and take away from him.

The setting, then, seems to engender a kind of cosmopolitan sophistication, a kind of civic apathy. In this unserious yet oddly exaggerated moral context, building up a self or having it destroyed becomes something of a shameless game, and learning to view this process as a game seems to make for some demoralization, the game being such a fundamental one. In the hospital, then, the inmate can learn that the self is not a fortress, but rather a small open city; he can become weary of having to show pleasure when held by troops of his own, and weary of having to show displeasure when held by the enemy. Once he learns what it is like to be defined by society as not having a viable self, this threatening definition – the threat that helps attach people to the self society accords them – is weakened. The patient seems to gain a new plateau when he learns that he can survive while acting in a way that society sees as destructive of him.

The moral career of a person of a given social category involves a standard sequence of changes in his way of conceiving of selves, including, importantly, his own. These half-buried lines of development can be followed by studying his moral experiences – that is, happenings which mark a turning point in the way in which the person views the world – although the particularities of this view may be difficult to establish. And note can be taken of overt tacks or strategies – that is, stands that he effectively takes before specifiable others, whatever the hidden and variable nature of his inward attachment to these presentations. By taking note of moral experiences and overt personal stands, one can obtain a relatively objective tracing of relatively subjective matters.

Each moral career, and behind this, each self, occurs within the confines of an institutional system, whether a social establishment such as a mental hospital or a complex of personal and professional relationships. The self, then, can be seen as something that resides in the arrangements prevailing in a social system for its members. The self in this sense is not a property of the person to whom it is attributed, but dwells rather in the pattern of social control that is exerted in connexion with the person by himself and those around him. This special kind of institutional arrangement does not so much support the self as constitute it.

In this paper, two of these institutional arrangements have been considered, by pointing to what happens to the person when these rulings are weakened. The first concerns the felt loyalty of his next-of-relation. The prepatient's self is described as a function of the way in which three roles are related, arising and declining in the kinds of affiliation that occur between the next-of-relation and the mediators. The second concerns the protection required by the person for the version of himself which he presents to others, and the way in which the withdrawal of this protection can form a systematic, if unintended, aspect of the working of an establishment. I want to stress that these are only two kinds of institutional rulings from which a self emerges for the participant; others, not considered in this paper, are equally important.

In the usual cycle of adult socialization one expects to find alienation and mortification followed by a new set of beliefs about the world and a new way of conceiving of selves. In the case of the mental-hospital patient, this rebirth does sometimes occur, taking the form of a strong belief in the psychiatric perspective, or, briefly at least, a devotion to the social cause of better treatment for mental patients. The moral career of the mental patient has unique interest, however; it can illustrate the possibility that in casting off the raiments of the old self – or in having this cover torn away – the person need not seek a new robe and a new audience before which to cower. Instead he can learn, at least for a time, to practise before all groups the amoral arts of shamelessness.

Notes

1   This simple picture is complicated by the somewhat special experience of roughly a third of ex-patients – namely, readmission to the hospital, this being the recidivist or 'repatient' phase.

2   Harry Stack Sullivan, *Clinical Studies in Psychiatry*, edited by Helen Swick Perry, Mary Ladd Gawel, and Martha Gibbon (New York: Norton, 1956), pp. 184–5.

3   This moral experience can be contrasted with that of a person learning to become a marihuana addict, whose discovery that he can be 'high' and still 'op' effectively without being detected apparently leads to a new level of use. See Howard S. Becker, 'Marihuana Use and Social Control', *Social Problems*, III (1955), pp. 35–44; see especially pp. 40–41.

4   See Hollingshead and Redlich, op. cit., p. 187, Table 6, where relative frequency is given of self-referral by social-class grouping.

5   The distinction employed here between willing and unwilling patients cuts across the legal one of voluntary and committed, since some persons who are glad to come to the mental hospital may be legally committed, and of those who come only because of strong familial pressure, some may sign themselves in as voluntary patients.

6   The inmate's initial strategy of holding himself aloof from ratifying contact may partly account for the relative lack of group formation among inmates in public mental hospitals, a connexion that has been suggested to me by William R. Smith. The desire to avoid personal bonds that would give licence to the asking of biographical questions could also be a factor. In mental hospitals, of course, as in prisoner camps, the staff may consciously break up incipient group formation in order to avoid collective rebellious action and other ward disturbances.

7   A comparable coming out occurs in the homosexual world, when a person finally comes frankly to present himself to a 'gay' gathering not as a tourist but as someone who is 'available'. See Evelyn Hooker, 'A Preliminary Analysis of Group Behavior of Homosexuals', *Journal of Psychology*, XLII (1956), pp. 217–25; see especially p. 221. A good fictionalized treatment may be found in James Baldwin's *Giovanni's Room* (New York: Dial, 1956), pp. 41–57. A familiar instance of the coming-out process is no doubt to be found among prepubertal children at the moment one of these actors sidles *back* into a room that had been left in an angered huff and injured *amour propre*. The phrase itself presumably derives from a *rite-de-passage* ceremony once arranged by

upper-class mothers for their daughters. Interestingly enough, in large mental hospitals the patient sometimes symbolizes a complete coming out by his first active participation in the hospital-wide patient dance.

8   A good description of the ward system may be found in Ivan Belknap, *Human Problems of a State Mental Hospital* (New York: McGraw-Hill, 1956), Ch. ix, especially p. 164.

49

Medicine matters after all
John Bunker

Extracts from Bunker J (1995) Medicine matters after all, Journal of the Royal College of Physicians of London, 29(2): 105–12.

There is a widely held view that medical care contributes little to health. 'Most doctors now understand', Morrison and Smith state in a recent issue of the *British Medical Journal* (*BMJ*), that 'health results from a combination of social, economic, and psychological as well as purely biological phenomena';[1] they suggest that politicians are reluctant 'to invest heavily in health services when they have only a small effect on health', and Smith later asks 'if health care has only a limited impact on the health of the population should doctors encourage the shift of resources from health care to education, housing, and employment, which might have a greater impact?'.[2] The premise and its political consequences could hardly be more clearly stated.

My colleagues and I, challenging the premise, have assembled an inventory of the benefits of medical care. Extrapolating from the results of clinical trials and meta-analyses we estimate that medical care can be credited with five of the 30 years of increased life-expectancy during this century and with three of the seven years of increase in life-expectancy since 1950.[3] By comparison, whatever individual contribution social, economic, or psychological phenomena have made to life-expectancy is purely speculative, for there are no data by which to measure their specific effects.

The contribution of medical care to improvement in the quality of life has been largely ignored in the debate; while its importance is clear enough, there has been no easy way to measure it. But it is possible, again extrapolating from clinical trials, to estimate the number of years of poor quality of life that individuals today can be spared. I estimate that medical care has the potential to provide partial or complete relief from an average of five years of the poor quality of life associated with severe chronic disease.[4]

The view that medicine contributes little to health harks back 20 years to the publication of Thomas McKeown's *The role of medicine*.[5] McKeown attributed the dramatic increase in life-expectancy of the previous 100 years primarily to nutritional, environmental, and behavioural factors, but he conceded that the evidence was no more than circumstantial. He believed that he had shown that medical care was not responsible and concluded that social and environmental factors must have been the cause.

In a second edition[6] McKeown acknowledged that 'it is not possible to estimate with any precision the contribution which therapeutic and other advances have made to the decline of the multiple non-infective causes of death which together were associated with about a quarter of the reduction of mortality in this century'. He thus acknowledged the possibility that medical care had made a larger contribution, but as late as 1993 a *BMJ* review of citations of *The role of medicine* concluded that the problem of a 'relatively small impact of clinical medicine on health outcomes [is] still with us'.[7] Recent publications addressing the determinants of health barely mention the contribution of medical care,[8,9] some arguing that there is too much.[10,11]

It is not that McKeown's conclusions have gone unchallenged: distinguished leaders in medicine including Walsh McDermott, Paul Beeson, and Sol Levine have argued that medicine does, indeed, do good, but that 'what the doctor does is something that is extraordinarily difficult to analyze and measure';[12] that 'although most clinicians do not doubt that there has been substantial improvement in the treatment of disease during the past few decades, it is difficult to assess the dimensions';[13] and that 'the use of easily available data such as mortality statistics ... which were not collected to test the proposition at issue ...' may not be the most appropriate way to address the question.[14]

McKeown drew his conclusions from an epidemiological analysis of public health data from years prior to 1971. The quarter century that followed has seen an explosion of new medical treatments, many of which have been shown in clinical trials and meta-analyses to result in considerable improvements in health; and at the same time evidence crediting medical care with the extension of life began to appear. The American economist Jack Hadley compared expenditures by the government's Medicare program with regional death rates and calculated that for every 10% increase in expenditure there was a 1–2% fall in mortality.[15] But conflicting data also appeared, in which national age-specific death rates were found to be greater in countries with greater numbers of doctors, and presumably more medical care.[16] Efforts to separate the effects of medical care from those of other determinants using aggregate data have been fraught with similar difficulties. Examination of the effect of individual medical interventions, one at a time, has offered a more appropriate approach, and this is the approach we have taken.

For both life-expectancy and quality of life analyses we selected conditions for which strong evidence of efficacy, usually in clinical trials, was available, and whose prevalence is sufficient to create a notable impact when their effect is spread across the entire population. Many less common or rare, but important, conditions were therefore not included.

Outcomes of medical care

Life expectancy

Estimation of months or years of increased life-expectancy attributable to the treatment of a particular condition involved a two-step procedure: estimation of increases in life-expectancy from the decline in diagnosis-specific death rates, and estimation of how much of an improvement could be attributed to medical care specifically. Documentation of the decline in disease-specific death rates was based on annual reports from the National Center for Health Statistics (NCHS) in Hyattsville, Maryland.[17] The proportion of improvement attributable to medical treatment was based, whenever possible, on clinical trials and meta-analyses.

Comprehensive annual reports of death rates have been published by NCHS since 1950. The age-adjusted death rate for the American population fell from 840 per 100,000 in 1950 to 523 per 100,000 in 1989, with a rise in life-expectancy of 7.1 years. (Life-expectancy in England and Wales rose by almost exactly the same amount during the same period, and I assume that the break-down by diagnosis was roughly similar in our two countries.) 'Diseases of the heart' were by far the largest contributors to the improvement, their age-adjusted death rate falling from 307 to 156 per 100,000 during the 39 year period, constituting just under half of the fall in death rate from all causes (151/317 = 0.48). As a first approximation, we estimated that the fall in death rate from heart disease contributed 0.48 × 7.1, ie 3.38 years of improved life-expectancy.

Death rates for diseases of the heart, as well as for cerebrovascular diseases and one or two other diagnoses, are also reported by the National Center for Health Statistics by ten year age intervals, from which it was possible to construct an adjusted life-table and hence more precise estimates of the change in life-expectancy attributable to these diseases. The change in life-expectancy, based on the life-table adjusted for the age-specific fall in heart disease deaths, was almost identical to the approximation based on age-adjusted death rates,[3] allowing us to rely on the approximate method for other diagnoses.

For an estimation of how much of the fall in death rates from heart disease and improved life expectancy to attribute to medical care, we relied heavily on Goldman and Cook's 1984 analysis.[18] They reviewed evidence of the efficacy of medical intervention in heart disease and estimated that 40% of the decline in cardiac death rates for the years between 1968 and 1976 could be attributed to coronary care units, treatment of hypertension, and medical and surgical treatment of ischaemic heart disease. Accepting their analysis, we credited medical care with 40% of the 3.38 years of increased life-expectancy associated with the fall in cardiac deaths for the entire 39 year period. Medical treatment at the beginning of the period, we assume, contributed somewhat less than 40%, but treatment at the end has clearly contributed a good deal more.

Tables 49.1 and 49.2 present our estimates of the gains in life-expectancy credited to clinical preventive and clinical curative services, respectively. We credit curative services with three and a half to four years of increased life-expectancy, with the potential of adding an additional year and a half if efficacious care were made more widely available. We credit clinical preventive services with a current gain in life-expectancy of a year and a half and the potential for an additional seven or eight months.

All told, we estimated that together, clinical preventive and curative services can be credited with about five of the 30 years increased life-expectancy gained in the United States and in Great Britain during this century, ie 17 or 18%. This is certainly a good deal more than McKeown was able to identify 24 years ago, but still a relatively small contribution. To place a five year change in life-expectancy in perspective, however, it may be useful to consider that a gain of five years in life-expectancy is equivalent to a halving of death rate at every age. And for comparison, the gain of five years in life-expectancy is roughly equivalent to the loss in life-expectancy that an individual suffers by smoking a pack a day starting at age 20; and it is roughly equivalent to the difference in life-expectancy between the top grade and unskilled workers in the Whitehall study of British civil servants.[19]

Quality of life

Much of the debate over the contribution of medical services to health has been based on death rates and life-expectancy, since they are relatively easy to measure. The majority of medical care is, of course, devoted to improving the quality of life, or, more accurately, to relief from the poor quality of life associated with many chronic diseases. The need to measure quality of life and to assess its response to therapy has been recognised for a good many years. Sophisticated measurement instruments are now in widespread use in clinical research, but only fragmentary data are yet available by which to determine the impact of medical care on the quality of life at the population level.

Table 49.1 Clinical preventive services: estimated numbers at risk and gains in life expectancy for those receiving selected successful services, with gain in life expectancy for the US population and potential gain not yet achieved. (Reprinted with permission from *The Milbank Quarterly*[3])

Clinical preventive service	Relevant population	Individuals affected by condition in the absence of preventive service	Gain per individual receiving preventive service	Proportion of those at risk receiving preventive service	Gain in life expectancy distributed across US population	
					Current	Potential
Screening for hypertension	All over age[3]	58 million[a] (10 million moderate or severe)	3 months	50%	1.5–2 months	1.5–2 months
Screening for cancer of cervix	Adult women	13,000[b]	96 days	60%–90%	2 weeks[c]	1 week[c]
Screening for colorectal cancer	All 50–80 years of age	155,000[b]	2 weeks	Unknown	Unknown	1 week
Counselling to stop smoking	Smokers	Smokers (approximately one-third of population)[a]	3 months	Unknown	Unknown	1 month
Immunisation for diphtheria	All children	40 deaths per 100,000[b]	10 months	73%–85% preschool; 97%–98% entering school	10 months	0
Immunisation for poliomyelitis	All	2,500 deaths[b]	3 weeks	73%–85% preschool; 97%–98% entering school	3 weeks	0
Immunisation for tetanus	All	2,500 deaths[b]				
Immunisation for smallpox	All	NA[d]	3–6 months[e]	Almost all before immunisations; almost nobody today	3–6 months	0
Immunisation for influenza	All over 65	10,000–40,000 deaths[b]	3 weeks	30%	1 week	3 weeks
Pneumococcal immunisation	All over 65	400,000 cases[b]	6 weeks	14%	1 week	6 weeks
Hepatitis-B immunisation	All	21,000 cases[b]	1.5–2 weeks	10%	1–2 days	1.5–2 weeks
Hormone replacement	Postmenopausal women	8,000 deaths[b]	3 months	50%	3 weeks[c]	3 weeks[c]
Aspirin prophylaxis for heart attack	Men over 40	Approximately 30% of men	Unknown	Unknown	Unknown	Unknown

[a] Prevalence (all cases); [b] Incidence (new cases per annum); [c] Double for single sex;
[d] Not applicable following worldwide eradication; [e] Limited to this century only.

Table 49.2 Clinical curative services: for selected diagnoses, estimated numbers at risk and gains in life expectancy for those receiving successful treatment, with gain in life expectancy for the US population and potential gain not yet achieved. (Reprinted with permission from *The Milbank Quarterly*[3])

Condition treated	Relevant population	Number at risk	Gain per individual receiving successful treatment (years)	Gain in life expectancy distributed across US population	
				Current	Potential
Cancer of cervix	Adult women	13,000[b]	21[d]	2 weeks[c]	1 week[c]
Colorectal cancer	All	155,000[b]	12[d]	2 weeks	1 week
Peptic ulcer	All	250,000[b]	10[e]	2 weeks	Unknown
Ischaemic heart disease[f]	All	6 million[a]	14[e]	1.2 year	6–8 months
Hypertension	All	58 million[a]	10[e]	3.5–4 months[g]	3.5–4 months[g]
Kidney failure	All	41,000[b]	11[e]	2–3 months	Unknown
Infant respiratory failure	Premature infants	75,000–100,000[b]	20–30[d]	3–4 months	Unknown
Appendicitis	All	273,000[b]	50[d]	4 months	0
Diabetes	All	6 million[a]	25	6 months	Unknown
Pregnancy	Women 15–44	4 million[b]	45	2 weeks[c]	0
Pneumonia and influenza	All	400,000–1 million[b]	9[e]	3 months	0
Tuberculosis	All	27,000 cases[b]	15[e]	3 months[h]	Uncertain[h]
Trauma	All	50–65 million[b]	24–38	1.5–2 months	3–4 months

[a] Prevalence (all cases).
[b] Incidence (new cases per annum).
[c] Double for women.
[d] For cancer of the cervix, colon cancer, infant respiratory distress syndrome, and appendicitis, we have made rough approximations based on mean age at death and life expectancy at that age.
[e] 'Gain in expectation of life at birth due to eliminating specified cause of death by race and sex, for those who would have died, United States, 1979–81' (National Center for Health Statistics, Curtin and Armstrong 1988, Table E).[39]
[f] Includes coronary-artery surgery, coronary-care units, and medical management of heart disease.
[g] Impact of treatment of hypertension on stroke and heart mortality.
[h] Increased likelihood of poor compliance with treatment regimens and increased frequency of infection with drug-resistant strains of tuberculosis make these estimates speculative and subject to change.

Ideally, one would like a single index of quality of life to pair with that for life-expectancy. One candidate for this purpose that has gained some currency, particularly among medical economists, is the quality-adjusted life year, or QALY.

The QALY may be useful as a semi-quantitative basis for resource allocation; it incorporates information on both life-expectancy and quality of life, and by providing a single number may give an impression of precision. The quality of life component is a subjective one, however, and may be a poor reflection of what patients actually value.[20]

Whatever its merits in setting priorities for the purchase of services, the QALY is of little use to doctors or patients in making clinical decisions. It does not help to answer the patient's question, 'doctor, will the cataract operation allow me to read again?', nor will it help the doctor in his efforts to instruct a patient in balancing the risks of stroke or heart attack against the unpleasant side effects of antihypertensive therapy. If we want to measure these and similar questions more precisely, there are more sophisticated 'multidimensional' measures of quality of life, such as the Nottingham Health Profile and the SF-36, a 36 question 'short-form' instrument that measures functional status, mental health, and perceived well-being.

But what of the need for a global index of quality of life that could be used to estimate this important component of medicine's contribution to the public's health? It would be of some interest to see this expressed in QALYs, and perhaps such a summary statistic will be forthcoming. There are also global measures, such as disability-free years and health-adjusted life years. Global indices of disability such as these have the same problem as do 'vital statistics', including population life-expectancy: unless disaggregated, there is no way of identifying the individual determinants, let alone how much each contributes. If disaggregation allowed us to make sense of life-expectancy, perhaps the same route would be successful in estimating the impact of medical care on quality of life at the population level.

When medical care is successful in improving the quality of life, or in relief from poor quality of life, it does so in many ways: by relieving pain, dyspnoea, or depression; by restoring function, by improving vision; by preventing stroke, by preventing osteoporosis. If we want to summarise such disparate conditions, we are immediately faced with the well-known apples and oranges problem. There is, however, a common denominator: severe chronic disease manifests itself in ways that profoundly depress quality of life; these manifestations can be readily measured and, added up, present an impressive inventory of the burden of chronic disease. Their prevention or response to treatment can also be measured and provide an equally impressive index of medicine's contribution to health.

As a first approximation I have developed such an inventory, again from secondary sources, of the months and years that an individual, or cohort of individuals, has been spared the lessened quality of life associated with common severe illnesses, mostly chronic, a few acute.[4] Based on the inventory presented in Table 49.3, I estimate that, on average, an individual has been relieved as a result of medical care from about five years of poor quality. Estimates of increases in the quality of life that I attributed to the treatment of hypertension illustrate how the estimates were made.

Table 49.3 Effects of treatments for selected conditions, estimated numbers at risk, and symptomatic and functional relief for those receiving treatment. (Adapted with permission from *The Milbank Quarterly*[3]).

Condition/ symptoms	Number at risk	Lifetime risk	Treatment	Relief of symptoms in treated patients	Proportion treated	Potential years of relief per 100 population
Unipolar depression	10.5 million[a]	8–12% men 20–26% women	Drugs, ECT psychotherapy	70–80%	50%	11
Ischaemic heart disease and angina	150,000–200,000[b]	10–15% men 3–5% women	Coronary artery revascularisation; drugs	50–66% for 5 yrs.	?	20
Osteoarthritis pain, joint dysfunction	86,000[b] hip 41,000[b] knee 16 million[a]	3–4% hip 1.5–2% knee	Joint replacement	85–90% pain relief 70–80% functional improvement	?	20
Rheumatoid arthritis	2.1 million[a]	0.7% men 1.6% women	Drugs, physiotherapy	Partial symptomatic & functional improvement	Nearly all	20
Cancer, terminal; severe pain	450,000–475,000[a]	30%	Analgesic drugs	Nearly complete relief	40–50%	15–30
Peptic ulcer severe pain	250,000[b]	10–15% men 4–15% women	H2 receptor blocking drugs	80–90% healed in 4–8 wks	?	65–70
Gallstones with biliary colic	0.5–1 million[b]	27% women 9% men	Cholecystectomy	2/3 pain relief at 2 years	?	
Migraine, severe	18 million women, 5.6 million men[a]	10–15%	Medication	50–75% relief	?	12–13
Post-operative pain	22 million operations[b]	90%	Epidural anesthesia, self-medication	Nearly complete relief	25%	15
Benign prostatic hypertrophy	125,000[b]	20–45%	Prostatic resection	79–93% relief of symptoms	?	25
Osteoporosis & fracture	1 million[b] (women)	10–12% by age 65, over 20% aged 80	Hormone replacement therapy; calcium	20% reduction in fractures in 1st 2 years, then 60% reduction	50%	17.5

Condition/ symptoms	Number at risk	Lifetime risk	Treatment	Relief of symptoms in treated patients	Proportion treated	Potential years of relief per 100 population
Poliomyelitis with paralysis	All	0.5 to 1% prior to 1950	Vaccine	Nearly complete protection	74% preschool 98% entering school	15–20
Rubella syndrome	All	0.5 to 1% prior to 1969	Maternal vaccine	Nearly complete protection	98%	18
Non-fatal stroke	1.9 million[a]	5% by age 70	Treatment of hypertension	50% reduction in incidence	50%	10–20
Asthma	10 million[a]	5–10%	Medication	Relief of dyspnoea cough & wheezing	50%	65–70
Myopia and presbyopia	All but blind	nearly 100%	Lenses	Visual acuity adequate for most activities	Nearly all at some time	
Cataract:	6 million[a]	5–10%	Lens removal; intraocular implant	75–95% improvement in visual acuity	?	20–40
Impaired hearing	18 million[a] elderly	35–50%	Hearing aid	Improved social function, communica-tion	?	50
Trauma	50–65[b] million	Nearly all	Surgical correction rehabilitation	Restoration of function, pain relief improved appearance	?	20–30

? = not known; [a] = prevalence; [b] = incidence.

The treatment of hypertension contributes to the quality of life by lessening the probability of non-fatal myocardial infarction and non-fatal stroke. Goldman and Cook[18] attributed 8.7% of the fall in fatal ischaemic heart disease that occurred between 1968 and 1976 to the treatment of hypertension. Deaths attributed to diseases of the heart fell, as discussed in the foregoing sections on life-expectancy, from 307 to 156 per 100,000 between 1950 and 1989, about two-thirds of which were attributed to ischaemic heart disease.[17] If it is assumed that for every 100 ischaemic heart deaths there were 200 non-fatal ischaemic heart attacks, and if we assume that patients survive on average ten years after a non-fatal ischaemic heart attack, we estimate that there have been approximately 150 fewer years of post-myocardial disability per 100 population in the lifetime of individuals today than there would have been had deaths from ischaemic heart disease remained unchanged from those of 1950. We credited 8.7% of this improvement, 13 years, to the treatment of hypertension. An increase in the medical control of hypertension above the 50% reported in 1986 by Drizd and associates[21] could further increase this benefit, perhaps to as high as 20 years per 100 population.

The age-adjusted death rate from cerebrovascular disease in the United States declined from 88.6 per 100,000 in 1950 to 28.0 in 1989.[17] The reported death rate for strokes varies between 20% and 33%. We estimated, therefore, that between 120 and 240 fewer non-fatal strokes per 100,000 occurred in 1989 than occurred in 1950. Assuming a five year average survival for patients suffering non-fatal stroke, and therefore 600 to 1,200 fewer years per 100,000 of survival with stroke, I estimate that there has been a decline in years with stroke of between 45 and 90 per 100 population. Marked increase in medical control of hypertension during this period from less than 10% to approximately 50%,[21] and the 45% reduction in stroke observed in randomised trials of anti-hypertensive drugs[22,23] could explain as much as 15–20% of the reduction in stroke morbidity. Accordingly, I credit the treatment of hypertension with a reduction of ten to 20 years of stroke-related poor quality of life per 100 population.

The doctor-patient relationship

What happens between the doctor and patient during the medical encounter has a profound impact on outcome. Its importance is unquestioned, but it has generally been assumed that it could not be measured. On close examination, however, one can find considerable quantitative evidence of benefits.

To begin with, there are some clear-cut effects for which quantification is straightforward. The general practitioner, as primary care doctor, is, by definition, a gate keeper, in that he or she must decide whether or not to treat and whether or not to refer. The assessment and recommendation for or against therapeutic intervention have a profound impact on outcome, the magnitude of which is reflected in two and three-fold variations in rates of medical and surgical intervention. How the clinician's evaluation (with or without an explicit diagnosis) and recommendation are communicated to the patient will also have a large impact on outcome. Poor communication about drugs is considered to be largely responsible for the failure of 30–55% of patients in America to adhere to prescribed drug regimens.[24]

The decision to perform discretionary surgery is similarly affected by information and advice given to the patient. Variations in what Wennberg calls surgeons' 'practice styles',[25] their preferences for one or another therapeutic approach, account for large variations in outcome. The patient's participation when adequately informed, as in the increasingly popular 'shared decision making' mode, has already resulted in large changes in operation rates for benign prostatic hypertrophy and for early breast cancer.[26,27]

Knowledge and belief are also key determinants of a patient's peace of mind. The provision of information can enhance patients' sense of control or 'self-efficacy', and perhaps optimism, each of which is strongly associated with improved health status. Individuals who believe that their health is good live longer than others who manifest similar risk factors, but who assess their health as poorer.[28] Men recovering from myocardial infarction who 'comply' with prescribed medicine, whether active or placebo, and who can be assumed to have a more optimistic view of their prospects, die at half the rate of those who fail to take the randomly prescribed medication.[29,30]

Optimism, a sense of hope, perhaps, a sense of control over one's medical destiny (or, at least, that one's destiny is in the hands of a trusted doctor) may be the common features that lead to better outcomes. If optimism and sense of control promote health, can they be enhanced by doctors in their capacity as information givers and carers? Surgical patients randomised to preoperative instruction on how much pain to expect after the operation required less postoperative medication and were discharged earlier by the medical staff (who were uninformed as to the randomised status of each patient).[31,32] Patients suffering from rheumatoid or osteoarthritis randomised to instruction in self-management reported less pain and required fewer subsequent medical visits than control patients.[33] Surprisingly, the better outcomes were independent of subsequent memory of the instructions or whether the recommended practices were adopted, leading the investigators to conclude that the positive effects were mediated by enhancing a sense of control.

The mechanism by which the positive effects of counselling, encouragement, and reassurance are mediated may not be known, but the effect is a large one. The placebo effect that accompanies a wide spectrum of medical and surgical interventions is estimated to be responsible for about a third of their therapeutic effects.[34,35] The effect is equally large in 'natural experiments' such as the Whitehall study of British civil servants, in which mortality rates vary two-fold across employment levels, even after adjustment for all relevant risk factors, an effect that has been attributed to control over one's professional and personal life in higher employment grades.[19]

Finally, the transfer of information alone is a product of the doctor-patient encounter and has an important value independent of its use in any medical decision. Asch and his colleagues, in an article entitled 'Knowing for the sake of knowing: the value of prognostic information', developed a data-based model in which the practice of performing tests that cannot alter management plans is justified by the prognostic information it provides to patients.[36] Berwick has demonstrated that such information has monetary value to patients,[37] and Sox has reported an earlier return to full activity of men with clinically unimportant chest pain when randomised to receive an electrocardiogram and measurement of serum creatine phosphokinase.[38]

Conclusions

In a time of political ferment when hard choices must be made as to where and how to spend public and private funds, it is important that decisions be made on the basis of the best available information. Our estimates of medicine's contribution to health are more than speculative and less than precise; they are approximations extrapolated from secondary sources. We have urged that better data, analysed with more sophisticated methods, be developed as the basis for a continually updated inventory of life-expectancy and quality of life as improved by medical care.[3]

These, or similar data, do not tell decision-makers what choices to make, but they do help to inform the decision process. The public and its representatives in Parliament or in Congress must choose among a large spectrum of competing social programmes, only some of which are designed to improve health; and among programmes to improve health, medical care is only one of several. Education, housing, and employment, as the *British Medical Journal* has reminded us,[2] also affect health. But if we have been slow to document the effects of medical care, and if our data are less precise than we would like, they are considerably firmer than any that can be presented for the non-medical determinants of health.[9]

It is true that education, income, and occupation are strongly associated with health, but, except for occupation, they are not independent determinants; they may, indeed, be proxies for other determinants yet to be identified, and we have only the vaguest idea of the mechanism by which they may affect health. Education, housing, and employment are all highly important goods in their own right, of course, with urgent and valid needs. Let us not, however, imagine that enough is known about their effect on health to divert resources to them for that reason alone.

The association of socioeconomic status with health has been known for a great many years, but governments have been reluctant to take compensatory action. Governmental inaction might reasonably be attributed to the absence of a practical solution; indeed it is still unclear how to correct the disparities in health that have been documented across all income and occupational levels, not merely between the well-to-do and the poor and unemployed.[39] By contrast, the scientific basis of medicine is increasingly well understood, the outcomes of medical care are being widely documented, and the cumulative benefits to the population can now be tabulated as the basis for political action.

References

1   Morrison I, Smith R. The future of medicine. *Br Med J* 1994;**309**:1099–100.
2   Smith R. Medicine's core values. *Br Med J* 1994;**309**:1247–8.
3   Bunker JP, Frazier HS, Mosteller F. Improving health: measuring effects of medical care. *Milbank Quarterly* 1994;**72**:225–58.
4   Bunker JP. The role of medical care in improving the quality of life: an inventory from secondary sources. In: *Proceedings of an international symposium on quality of life and health.* Oxford: Blackwell Scientific Publishing, 1995; (in press).
5   McKeown T. *The role of medicine: dream, mirage, or nemesis?* London: Nuffield Provincial Trust, 1976.
6   McKeown T. *The role of medicine: dream, mirage, or nemesis?* (2nd ed). Princeton: Princeton University Press, 1979.

7 Alvarez-Dardet C, Ruiz MT. Thomas McKeown and Archibald Cochrane: a journey through the diffusion of their ideas. *Br Med J* 1993;**306**:1252–4.

8 Evans RG, Barer ML, Marmor TR (eds). *Why are some people healthy and others not? The determinants of health of populations.* New York: Aldine de Gruyter, 1994.

9 Frank JW, Mustard JF. The determinants of health from a historical perspective. *Daedalus* 1994;**123**:1–19.

10 Evans RG. Health care as a threat to health: defence, opulence, and the social environment. *Daedalus* 1994;**123**:21–42.

11 Lavis JN, Stoddart GL. Can we have too much health care? *Daedalus* 1994;**123**:43–60.

12 McDermott W. Medicine: the public good and one's own. *Perspect Biol Med* 1978;**21**:167–87.

13 Beeson PB. Changes in medical therapy during the past half century. *Medicine* 1980;**59**:79–99.

14 Levine S, Feldman JJ, Elinson J. Does medical care do any good? In Mechanic D (ed). *Handbook of health, health care, and the health professions.* New York: Free Press, 1983,394–404.

15 Hadley J. *More medical care, better health?* Washington: Urban Institute Press, 1982.

16 Cochrane AL, St Leger AS, Moore F. Health service "input" and mortality "output" in developed countries. *J Epidem Comm Health* 1978;**32**:200–5.

17 National Center for Health Statistics. *Health, United States 1991.* Hyattsville, Maryland, 1992.

18 Goldman L, Cook EF. The decline in ischemic heart disease mortality rates: an analysis of the comparative effects of medical interventions and changes in lifestyle. *Ann Int Med* 1984;**101**:825–36.

19 Marmot MG, Davey Smith G, Stansfeld S, Patel C, *et al.* Health inequalities among British civil servants: the Whitehall II study. *Lancet* 1991;**337**:1387–93.

20 Fallowfield L. Discussion. In: Hopkins A (ed). *Measures of the quality of life and the uses to which such measures may be put.* London: Royal College of Physicians of London, 1992, 61–62, 104–5, 119.

21 Drizd T, Dannenberg AL, Engle A. Blood pressure levels in persons 18–74 years of age in 1976–80, and trends in blood pressure from 1960 to 1980 in the United States. In: *Vital and health statistics*, (Series 11, No. 234. DHHS pub. no. (PHS) 86–1684). Washington: National Center for Health Statistics, 1986.

22 MacMahon S, Peto R, Cutler J, Collins R, *et al.* Blood pressure, stroke, and coronary heart disease: Part 1, prolonged differences in blood pressure: prospective observational studies corrected for the regression dilution bias. *Lancet* 1990;**335**:765–74.

23 Collins R, Peto R, MacMahon S, Hebert P, *et al.* Blood pressure, stroke, and coronary heart disease: Part 2, short-term reductions in blood pressure: overview of randomised drug trials in their epidemiological context. *Lancet* 1990;**335**:827–38.

24 Kessler DA. Communicating with patients about their medications. *N Engl J Med* 1991;**325**:1650–2.

25 Wennberg JE. Small area analysis and the medical care outcome problem. In: Sechrest L, Perrin E, Bunker J (eds). *Research methodology: strengthening causal interpretations of nonexperimental data.* Washington DC: US Government Printing Office, 1990, 177–206.

26 Barry MJ, Fowler FJ. Patient reactions to a program designed to facilitate patient participation in treatment decisions for BPH. *Med Care* 1995; (in press).

27 Baum M. Personal communication.

28 Idler EL, Kasl S. Health perceptions and survival: do global evaluations of health status really predict mortality? *J Gerontology* 1991;**46**:S55–65.

29 The Coronary Drug Project Research Group. Influence of adherence to treatment and response of cholesterol on mortality in the coronary drug project. *N Engl J Med* 1980;**303**:1038–41.

30 Horwitz RI, Viscoli CM, Berkman L, Donaldson RM, *et al.* Treatment adherence and risk of death after a myocardial infarction. *Lancet* 1990;**336**:542–5.

31 Egbert LD, Battit GE, Welch CE, Bartlett MK. Reduction in post-operative pain by encouragement and instruction of patients. *N Engl J Med* 1964;**270**:825–8.

32 Mumford E, Schlesinger HJ, Glass GV. The effects of psychological intervention on recovery from surgery and heart attacks. *Am J Public Health* 1982;**72**:141–51.

33 Holman H, Mazonson P, Lorig K. Health education for self-management has significant early and sustained benefits in chronic arthritis. *Trans Assoc Am Phys* 1989;**102**:204–8.

34 Beecher HK. The powerful placebo: a quantitative study of bias. *JAMA* 1955;**159**:1602–6.

35 Beecher HK. Surgery as placebo. *JAMA* 1961;**176**:1102–7.

36 Asch DA, Patton JP, Hershey JC. Knowing for the sake of knowing: the value of prognostic information. *Med Decis Making* 1990;**10**:47–57.

37 Berwick DM, Weinstein MC. What do patients value? Willingness to pay for ultrasound in normal pregnancy. *Med Care* 1985;**23**:881–93.

38 Sox HC, Margulies I, Sox CH. Psychologically mediated effects of diagnostic tests. *Ann Int Med* 1981;**95**:680–5.

39 National Center for Health Statistics, Curlin LR, Armstrong RJ. *United States life tables eliminating certain causes of death. US decennial life tables for 1979–81.* (Vol 1, no 2). Hyattsville, Maryland, DHSS pub No (PHS) 88–1150–2, 1988.

50

Hippocratic oaths
Ray Tallis

Extracts from Tallis R (2004) Hippocratic Oaths. Atlantic Books.

A (very) personal introduction

Nothing could be more serious than the care of ill people, nor more deserving of intelligent discussion. Few topics attract such media coverage; the National Health Service is never far from the top of the political agenda; and most people regard good health – and access to first-class care when they fall ill – as supremely important. It is, therefore, regrettable that discussion of medicine – of medical science, of clinical practice, of the profession itself – is frequently ill-informed. Comment is often shallow, even when it is not riddled with errors of fact, interpretation or emphasis. Reactive, piecemeal and disconnected from the big picture, much analysis lacks historical perspective and ignores the complex reality of medical care.

Notwithstanding all the books, column inches, air-time and screen-time devoted to it, therefore, the practice of medicine remains virtually invisible. *Hippocratic Oaths,* which contemplates the art of medicine from a broad perspective while not losing sight of the details, aims at making medicine more visible. This is worthwhile not only because scientific medicine is one of the greatest triumphs of humankind; but also because illness is potentially a mirror, albeit a dark one, in which we may see something of what we are, at the deepest level. Making medicine truly visible may cast some light on the greater mystery of what it is to be a human being. That mystery is the starting point of this book.

Medicine, objectively, has never been in better shape. Its scientific basis, the application of this science in clinical practice, the processes by which health care is delivered; the outcomes for patients, the accountability of professionals, and the way doctors and their patients interact with each other – all have improved enormously even during my thirty years as a practitioner. Yet the talk is all of doom and gloom: short memories have hidden the extraordinary advances of the last century. The danger is that endless predictions of crisis may become self-fulfilling by making the key roles of doctor and nurse deeply unattractive. This would be a disaster, given that further progress will require more, not less, medical and nursing time.

The curious dissociation between what medicine has achieved and the way in which it is perceived originates outside of medicine itself. While medical practice is continuously improving, it has not kept up with patients' rising expectations. Many things are much better than they were, but few things are as good as people have been led to expect. Changes in patients' expectations reflect changes in the world at large. What is more, there is a tension between the consumerist values of society and the values that have hitherto informed medicine at its best; values that have driven its gradual transformation from a system beleaguered by fraud, venality and abuse of power[1] to a genuinely caring profession whose practices are informed by biological science and underpinned by clinical evidence.

I believe that medicine is in danger of being irreversibly corrupted. This threat comes not from within (where its values are struggling to survive) but from society at large. The most serious dangers emanate from those for whom the moral high ground is a platform for self-advancement, many of whom have never borne, or have been willing to bear, the responsibilities that weigh on the daily life of practitioners. The unthinking voices of those who have a shallow understanding of the real challenges of medicine (and an even shallower appreciation of its achievements) will make patient care worse not better. Their influence already threatens to bring about a disastrous revolution in the values and attitudes of health-care professionals: if we are not careful, the patient-as-client will receive service-with-a-smile from a 'customer-aware' self-protecting doctor delivering strictly on contract. If the current debased public perception is not challenged, medicine may become the first blue-collar profession, delivered by supine, sessional functionaries. This will not serve the longer term interests of people who fall ill.

Everyone agrees that we need to rethink medicine; in particular its relationship to society at large. This book offers an introduction to that rethink. We need to take a long view and to unpeel the layers of second-order discussion that takes so much for granted and has hidden the reality of a deeply human, and humane, profession. Only on the basis of an appreciation of what has been achieved, and a better understanding of the ends, aims and ultimate limitations of medical care, shall we be able to begin an intelligent examination of the present discontents and the future path; and arrive at a clearer understanding of what might be expected of medicine and of those who deliver medical care.

The empowered consumer

Exaggerating the power of doctors goes hand in hand with exaggerating the powerlessness of the patient. The demonized doctor-perpetrator is linked with the canonization of the patient-victim as if decline in physicianly goodness must be compensated by an increase in patient saintliness.

The very suspicion which has sustained the attacks on the standing of doctors is that people are not trustworthy: that is why we are invited to believe medical power to be intrinsically malign and that, without ever-closer regulation of activities, doctors will behave badly. Left to themselves, they will be negligent, blundering, idle, uncaring, ignorant, fraudulent scoundrels who will damage patients by acts of commission or omission. But patients are people, too, and will share the faults of their all-too-human doctors. The emphasis on patients as 'consumers' is an inadvertent reminder that they are essentially self-interested.

For a physician to talk of the (necessary, understandable) selfishness of patients may be rather shocking. Despite all the cynical talk, it is still assumed that the patient – doctor relationship is one in which the doctors cares and the patient is cared for, the doctor is trustworthy and the patient trusts, the doctor respects and the patient is respected. In other words, the doctor is expected to have human qualities that consumerism cannot accommodate. And so we have a lopsided idealism: the patient is an empowered consumer while the doctor must altruistically treat the patient as an end in himself or herself. Most importantly, she will not pass judgement on the patient, whatever demands for treatment, time and attention he makes. She will certainly not judge the patient as harshly as would another patient, a fellow consumer, waiting in the same queue. Indeed, she will welcome the extra challenge presented by the patient-as-consumer because it is evidence of the empowerment of the hitherto powerless.

The implication that 'the empowered patient' is a new species created by politicians and other advocates implies that medicine overall is not patient-empowering. This is a grotesque, indeed curious libel. The doctor who gets you back on your feet, relieves you of pain, helps you recover your independence, assists you in dealing with incontinence, or postpones your death, is empowering in a direct, fundamental and radical way that can be matched by few other professionals. Indeed, empowerment is what medicine is largely about. In some cases, of course, the treatment doesn't work; in a minority of cases, the treatment is worse than the disease. This will be disempowering but only incidentally so: the adverse effects of unsuccessful treatments are rarely the result of a direct intention to kill or maim. Even a doctor who cannot cure your condition, but at least shares with you his understanding of what is going on, is empowering. In some cases the attempt to communicate that understanding will fail and in other cases the understanding will be wrong: doctors make mistakes like other human beings.

For some critics of the medical profession, this will be beside the point: those who are preoccupied with the medical profession's power to disempower are often concerned more with the *process* – humiliating, undignified, inconvenient – than with the *outcome*. And there will indeed be cases where the experience of the treatment will be more disabling, humiliating, dependency-creating, than the illness. But this is not routine and certainly not intrinsic to the patient–doctor relationship.

Others who are preoccupied with the power of both individual doctors and of the medical profession will focus on 'medicalization': the translation of human unhappiness, foibles and faults – all the various ways in which humans may deviate from the stipulated norm – into medical problems. The profession has been criticized for medicalizing sexual diversity, grief following bereavement, hyperactivity in children, and childbirth, in pursuit of their ambition to be agents of social control. However, there have been equally vocal critics of profession's failure to acknowledge the same conditions as medical problems: doctors have been pilloried for freeing sexual deviants, who subsequently turn out to be dangerous repeat offenders, from institutions; for not diagnosing pathological grieving and withholding antidepressants; for failing to diagnose badly behaved children as having Attention Deficiency Hyperactivity Syndrome and not offering medical treatment; and for failing to intervene in childbirth.

'Medicalization' is often forced on doctors by the families of patients, as the following examples demonstrate.[2]

> An old man has attempted suicide with digoxin. The psychiatrist finds nothing wrong with his psyche but writes that the patient's intentions to commit suicide were serious. The family, the social worker, and the legal adviser of the hospital concur that the patient should be restrained in bed. The physician is the one to write the order. On the day the patient is extubated [has the nasogastric tube removed] he tells his story. He is lonely, sick and in pain. His wife died and he is disappointed with his daughters. He wants to die. Because the physician fears litigation, he renews his order of constraint. He knows that he has done wrong.

> The family of a sixty-year-old man with terminal metastatic cancer refuses to take him back home. His pains are well controlled, and they know that nothing more can be done for him. But we cannot conceive that he will die at home, they say. The task to comfort and cope with the dying man is left to the doctor who has known him less than a week.

Another aspect of medicalization is described by Roy Porter:

> Thanks to diagnostic creep or leap, ever more disorders are revealed. Extensive and expensive treatments are then urged, and the physician who chooses not to treat may expose himself to malpractice accusations. Anxieties and interventions spiral upwards like a space-shot off course ... Doctors and 'consumers' are becoming locked within a fantasy that *everyone* has *something* wrong with them, everyone and everything can be cured.[3]

As the authors of the paper from which these examples are taken, say:

> These aspects of medicalization make doctors miserable. The bad things of life: old age, death, pain, and handicap are thrust on doctors to keep families and society from facing them. Some of them are an integral part of medicine, and accepted as such. But there is a boundary beyond which medicine has only a small role. When doctors are forced to go beyond that role they do not gain power or control: they suffer.

This is how 'medicalization' looks from the inside. It is more often imposed on doctors by societal expectations than imposed on patients by a power-hungry profession wanting to expropriate every human woe or variation for itself.[4] It is illustrated by the treatment of homosexuality as a sickness. An issue of the *British Medical Journal* on the thirtieth anniversary of the official declassification of homosexuality as a mental illness speaks of its medicalization as part of 'medicine's shameful past' and 'one of its many mistakes'.[5] This is unfair. From the standpoint of the twenty-first century, this does look barbaric; but from the standpoint of the 1950s and 1960s, this was comparatively enlightened and more liberal than the views in the population as a whole. After all, until 1967 in the UK and much later in other parts of the world, homosexuality was a criminal offence with jail as the standard management plan. What is more, it was the medical profession, against much internal and external resistance, that accepted that homosexuality was a personal choice rather than a crime or a sickness. In this respect the profession has been doubly enlightened: first decriminalizing and then demedicalizing what many – notably in the Catholic and Anglican churches and in Islam – still condemn as a mortal sin. The 'shameful past' is the past of society as a whole, not medicine in particular, which remains ahead of much disempowering public opinion.

The idealization of the patient as the marginalized, put-upon, disempowered victim of medicine, or of a system of care (the NHS) that 'seems to work for its own convenience not the patient's',[6] ignores the fact that the patient is primarily self-interested and how his or her self-interest is potentially in conflict with that of other patients. An anger that is not exactly selfless may none the less be moralized: in asserting their rights, in expropriating power for themselves, patients often believe they act on behalf of others; as victims they are striking blows for victims everywhere. Time and again one hears it said by a complainant that his only motive for suing for compensation is to protect others from the injustice/the wrong/the blunder in future.

The emphasis on the 'disempowering doctor' when clinicians have never been more able and willing to liberate patients from the intimate disempowerments of illness, reflects how technology and technological skill – in short, expertise – are taken most for granted when they are most effective: the hard-won, uncertain and limited benefits of the past were more appreciated than the massive advances upon which medicine presently stands.[7] Routine success ceases to be success.

Because illness is intrinsically disempowering, those who try to deal with its impact tend to be experienced as agents of disempowerment, even in those cases where treatment is entirely successful. The very processes of cure and care seem to compound the loss of volition resulting from illness. Clinicians, although they aim to restore the health and freedom of the patient, may seem to be part of the problem – a consequence of illness, rather than the solution. Anger at the disempowerment of illness is especially likely to be transferred to those who try to alleviate it where the process is complex, inconvenient and painful, and the treatments, notwithstanding their net benefits, have adverse effects.

The General Medical Council's list of the doctor's duties includes the command to 'listen to patients and respect their views'. This is more than giving the patient air-time to describe her symptoms: it includes acknowledging her expertise. A good consultation is a meeting between experts: while doctors are experts on medical problems in general, patients are experts on how they themselves experience these problems. Only the patient can determine whether she is finding a treatment of net benefit.

In my own clinic, I often leave it to the patient who has had only rare minor epileptic fits, to decide whether she wants to continue her anti-epileptic medication, with its side effects, or try doing without, knowing that this carries an increased risk of recurrence of fits, with implications for driving and other potential undesirable consequences. The same applies to the preference for medication: if the patient says tablet A is preferable to tablet B, then it would be absurd for me to contradict this, assuming that both tablets have the same general efficacy and range of indications. I can bring the recent pharmaceutical literature to the discussion and the patient brings her direct experience: we have the basis for a dialogue in which each of us respects the other's expertise. None of this is in the slightest bit revolutionary or even exceptionally progressive.

Patients with chronic diseases will certainly be experts. Providing that they have reflected responsibly on their experiences and acknowledge the limitations of generalization from a single case to others, they have much to give other patients with the same condition. If after fifteen years of living with diabetes I wasn't some kind of expert on it, there must be something wrong with me and/or my clinical advisers.

Expert patients are often employed to instruct, encourage and support others. What this brings to medical care is not as novel, or as subversive of the medical establishment or challenging to the hegemony of doctors, as is sometimes suggested. Doctors have for a long time encouraged patients to consult other patients, particularly when they are contemplating medical procedures about which they may be uncertain, such as amputations and colostomies. And support groups run by patients have long been welcomed by physicians. Moreover, it is routine in the research into the comparative benefits of treatments to include patient preferences, and quality of life measures, in a systematic way. The 'expert patient', in other words, is not new, except as a term of ideology: and here problems may arise.

A patient who is expert on his or her own condition is not always an expert on other patients, even those who have the same condition. This follows from the very fact emphasized by those who stress the expertise of the patient: that every patient is different. Extrapolating from one's own experience to that of others is rarely straightforward and this makes some expert patients a liability. A patient who, on the basis of her own bad experiences with medication, advises others that they should give up theirs may be well-intentioned but is dangerously irresponsible. She is setting her own experience of a single case against the experience of many thousands of other patients. Clinical advice is best rooted in rigorously conducted trials which tap into the experiences of patients in a way that minimizes bias and the play of chance. However, the use of expert patients as a new 'epistemic community', a special caste whose views have to be deferred to, should be evaluated as carefully as any other therapeutic ploy.

Notes

1 The history of tribal or traditional medicine and, until relatively recently, of Western professionalized medicine.

2 Leonard Leibovici and Michel Lievre, 'Medicalization: peering from inside medicine', *British Medical Journal*, 2002, 324: 866.

3 Roy Porter, *The Greatest Benefit to Mankind: A Medical History of Humanity from Antiquity to the Present* (London: HarperCollins, 1997), p. 718.

4 Some have suggested that the very use of the term 'patient' is disempowering, recommending alternative terms such as 'user' and 'client'. This has been debated by J. Neuberger and R. Tallis, 'Do we need a new word for patients?', *British Medical Journal*, 1999, 318: 1756–8.

5 Rhona MacDonald, 'Lessons from medicine's shameful past', *British Medical Journal*, 2004, 328: 411.

6 Alan Milburn, 'Redefining the National Health Service', speech to the New Health Network, 4 February 2002. Tell this to the surgeon who has got out of his bed night after night, or the physician who works 59 hours a week on a 37.5-hour contract, or a nurse who again and again is late picking up her children because there is too much to do on the ward, to the GP who will have seen a total of 250,000 patients in his forty-year career, or a manager who comes in Sunday after Sunday to implement the latest government initiative. In the most recent survey of NHS staff (reported in *Hospital Doctor*, 8 April 2004), 75 per cent of staff said they routinely worked more than their contracted hours. Twelve per cent worked more than ten hours of unpaid overtime in an average week. Finally, in a recent survey of 1,001 doctors, 77 per cent of respondents reported that their job prevented them from spending adequate time with their family (*Hospital Doctor*, 8 April 2004, pp. 10–11).

7 This in part explains why, as Theodore Dalrymple has pointed out in *Mass Listeria. The Meaning of Health Scares* (London: André Deutsch, 1998), p. 61, that 'trust in the medical profession seems to be inversely proportional to the scientific basis of its practice: it was accorded the most authority when it least deserved it.'

Index

HEALTHCARE MANAGEMENT

Kieran Walshe and Judith Smith (eds)

"... this is an excellent text. It is well constructed and appropriately pitched and, because the editors seek feedback on its style and content, it is likely to retain its relevance in future editions."

Nursing Management

This comprehensive text covers all of the major aspects of healthcare management and is written by experts in the field. The book is structured into three main sections, bracketed by an introductory chapter setting the policy context and offering an overview/map of what follows; a concluding chapter draws together the key themes and offers a view about the future development and trends in healthcare management.

The main sections of the book examine:

- The health policy and practice context for healthcare management
- The specific challenges of managing healthcare organizations
- Key managerial techniques and methods that managers need to be able to use effectively in their practice

Chapters include self-test exercises, summary boxes, further reading and a list of web-based resources.

This book is key reading for researchers, managers and healthcare policy makers with a genuine interest in the links between the theory and practice of healthcare management and how best practice might be achieved within healthcare systems.

Contributors: Lawrence Benson, Carol Brooks, Ruth Boaden, Naomi Chambers, Deborah Davidson, Jennifer Dixon, Jenny Douglas, Tim Freeman, Jon Glasby, Neil Goodwin, Andrew Hine, Paula Hyde, Kim Jelphs, Justin Keen, Helen Lester, Ann Mahon, Anne McBride, Ruth McDonald, Shirley McIver, Steve Onyett, Helen Parker, Edward Peck, Suzanne Robinson, Ann Shacklady-Smith, Judith Smith, Anne Tofts, Tom Walley, Kieran Walshe, Juliet Woodin.

Contents: *List of figures – List of tables – List of boxes – List of contributors – Preface – Introduction: The current and future challenges of healthcare management – Part I Setting the context – The politics of healthcare and the health policy process: Implications for healthcare management – Financing healthcare: Funding systems and healthcare costs – Healthcare systems: An overview of health service provision and service delivery – Managing healthcare technologies and innovation – Health and well-being: The wider context for healthcare management – Part II Managing healthcare organisations – Managing in primary care – Managing in acute care – Managing in mental health – Service and capital development – Healthcare system strategy and planning – Healthcare commissioning and contracting – Information technology and information systems: So beguiling, so difficult – Human resource management in healthcare – Working with healthcare professionals – Governance and the work of health service boards – Managing in partnership with other agencies – Performance measurement and improvement – Part III Management theories, models and techniques – Leadership and its development in healthcare – Organisational development and organisational design – Personal effectiveness – Appreciating the challenge of change – Managing resources – Managing people: The dynamics of teamwork – User perspectives and user involvement – Quality improvement in healthcare – Research, evaluation and evidence-based management – Conclusions: Complexity, change and creativity in healthcare management – Index.*

2006 552pp

978-0-335-22119-6 (Paperback) 978-0-335-22120-2 (Hardback)

LEADERSHIP FOR NURSING AND ALLIED HEALTH CARE PROFESSIONALS

Veronica Bishop (ed)

The aim of this book is to empower would be leaders of nursing and allied health professions to be effective. Leadership in nursing and those health care professions allied to medicine has rarely been a highly visible clear cut business, and certainly many consider that, particularly in the UK, within the past decade a severe erosion of power bases within the professions has occurred. There is no single reason for this – ownership of health care is now very diverse. No patient wants a powerless professional taking care of them, yet we tend not to own any significant level of power in policy making terms. Our professions have been caught in a web of strong threads which stem from such sources as gender stereotyping, medical dominance and inadequate professional leadership which conspire to keep us in the place where others would have us. To strengthen leadership within the professions allied to medicine (PAMs) it is necessary to understand policy and professional contexts, and to review activities across the Atlantic and across Europe, now a growing entity with major implications for healthcare and nursing.

The text examines differences between leadership and management, inspirational education to support would be leaders, and a major UK programme to promote politically aware leaders. The importance of collaboration in achieving standards and quality without loss of identity of one's discipline, or of the core values that make working in healthcare a challenge well worth accepting are examined. It is time for us to take stock, to promote and support our articulate and strategic thinkers, and to let them shine. Experts from a wide breadth of countries and knowledge have come together to help to achieve this.

Contents: *What is leadership? – Leadership and management: is there a difference? – Leadership challenges: professional power and dominance in healthcare – Leadership for the allied health professions – Developing political leaders in nursing – Education for leadership: transformatory approaches – Clinical leadership and the theory of cogruent leadership – Pulling the threads together: grasping the nettle.*

2009 224pp

978-0-335-22533-0 (Paperback) 978-0-335-22532-3 (Hardback)